Freshfields on Corporate Pensions Law 2014

Freshfields on Corporate Pensions Law 2014

General Editors

David Pollard, Partner, Freshfields Bruckhaus Deringer LLP
Charles Magoffin, Partner, Freshfields Bruckhaus Deringer LLP
Dawn Heath, Partner, Freshfields Bruckhaus Deringer LLP

Editors and Contributors:

Kathleen Healy
Richard Ballard
Sarah Falk
Andrew Murphy
Sarah Thomas
Susan Doris-Obando
Lara Zellick
Leanne Turner
Vanessa Jakovich
Holly Insley
Suhasini Gunasena
Laura Harrington
Julia Chirnside
Alex Fricke
Sara Chambers
Lindsay McLeod
Jenna Poon

Kate Bland
Martin MacLeod
Robbie Li
Alison Chung
David Mendel
Harriet Sayer
Miranda Lewin
Hannah Machin
Catherine Roylance
Nicola Squire
Alison Wald
Bethan Harris
Jim Arnold
Stephanie Heskett
Cheryl Gayer
Alan Tindal

www.freshfields.com

 FRESHFIELDS BRUCKHAUS DERINGER

Bloomsbury Professional

Bloomsbury Professional Ltd, Maxwelton House, 41–43 Boltro Road, Haywards Heath, West Sussex, RH16 1BJ

© Freshfields Bruckhaus Deringer LLP 2014

Bloomsbury Professional is an imprint of Bloomsbury Publishing plc

A CIP Catalogue record for this book is available from the British Library.

ISBN: 978 1 78043 451 3

Typeset by Columns Design XML Ltd, Reading
Printed and bound in Great Britain by CPI Group (UK) Ltd, Croydon, CR0 4YY

Preface

The law on occupational pensions is complex and keeps changing.

Occupational pensions are important in the UK.

- Members (and their dependants) depend on occupational pensions to provide pensions over and above the state pension and any direct personal savings.

- Employers are under statutory and contractual obligations to fund them. Deficits appear on corporate balance sheets. For employers with large schemes (by comparison with the employer) business profitability can depend on the performance of the trustees on investment or on changes in interest rates or longevity.

- Trustees are under fiduciary and statutory duties.

- The Pensions Regulator is established to monitor and regulate. It has significant powers, particularly on 'moral hazard' issues.

- A support fund, the Pension Protection Fund, is available as a longstop (and funded by levies)

Because it is so important:

- Parliament and the government are always producing legislation.

- The EU intervenes sporadically.

- The Pensions Regulator issues statements, guidance and takes action to use its powers.

- There are UK court decisions and Ombudsman determinations.

- The European Court issues delphic 'judgments' from time to time.

The Freshfields pensions team constantly takes account of this, including:

- changes in legislation;

- a stream of court decisions – some on fundamental issues; and

- changes in Regulator practices and attitudes.

This book is intended to give an insight for those involved with pension schemes, but in particular employers, on various legal topics. The chapters are not on the technical end of legal advice, but intended instead to be overviews. Each scheme and situation may well be affected by individual facts or documents. So this is not a substitute for legal advice, but hopefully a starting point.

For this edition we have reviewed and revised the existing material. There are also 17 new sections for this edition:

Money Purchase Pension Schemes: Comparison of Trust Based (OPS) with Contract Based (PP)	Section 1.3
The end of contracting-out in April 2016	Section 1.4
European proposals to reform the regulation of pension schemes	Section 1.5
Pensions Bill 2014: A new statutory objective for the Pensions Regulator	Section 2.7
Reservoir Trusts and Charged Accounts	Section 2.8
Asset backed funding structures	Section 2.9
Section 75: grace periods	Section 3.7
Section 75 and relevant transfer deductions	Section 3.8
Moral hazard powers are a provable debt: *Nortel/Lehman*	Section 4.12
The Kodak restructuring	Section 4.17
Tupe and pensions: Issues remaining after *Beckmann*, *Martin* and *Procter & Gamble*	Section 6.7
Pensions issues on paying dividends	Section 6.9
Olympic Airlines: Problems with PPF entry for companies in insolvency outside the UK	Section 9.5
Things you may not know about trustee liability	Section 11.6
Trustee directors: liabilities, indemnities and exonerations	Section 11.7
Commutation and member options: trustee duties and the role of the actuary	Section 14.12
Maternity and paternity rights: overview	Section 14.13

The law is stated as at 30 January 2014. This will gradually get out of date as new legislation is passed and new cases decided. We aim to issue periodic updates on the most important issues from time to time. We intend to update this book in due course. Please contact us if you have any comments or points. Let us know if you spot any mistakes.

David Pollard
Charles Magoffin
Dawn Heath

Freshfields Bruckhaus Deringer LLP
65 Fleet Street
London
EC4Y 1HS

david.pollard@freshfields.com
charles.magoffin@freshfields.com
dawn.heath@freshfields.com

This material is for general information only and is not intended to provide legal advice.

© Freshfields Bruckhaus Deringer LLP 2014

www.freshfields.com

Contents

Contents

Contents

General editors

David Pollard is a solicitor and partner of Freshfields Bruckhaus Deringer, based in London in the Employment, Pensions and Benefits department. He specialises in all aspects of pensions advice, including acquisitions and disposals, joint ventures, terminations, pension scheme reconstructions, the implications of insolvency for employees and pensions, winding up pension schemes and pensions litigation.

David is the author of the leading books *Corporate Insolvency: Employment and Pension Rights* (Bloomsbury Professional, 2013) and *The Law of Pension Trusts* (OUP, 2013). He is a contributor to three looseleaf books: *Tolley's Pensions Law*; *Tolley's Employment Law* and *Tolley's Insolvency Law*, and was the co-editor of the book *Guide to the Pensions Act 1995* (Tolley, 1995). He is also the co-editor of the journal *Trust Law International*.

In 1998, David was awarded the Wallace Medal by the Association of Pension Lawyers (APL) for excellence in communicating pensions issues. He was Chairman of the Association of Pension Lawyers from 2001 to 2003 and has been a vice chair of the Industrial Law Society.

David has a mathematics and law degree from St John's College, Cambridge.

Charles Magoffin is a solicitor and partner of Freshfields Bruckhaus Deringer. Based in London in the Employment, Pensions and Benefits department, he specialises in advice on pensions issues in relation to mergers and acquisitions, funding, security, investments, benefit design, member disputes, distress and insolvency and buyouts.

Charles is a member of the Association of Pension Lawyers' International Committee and the Society of Pension Consultants' European Committee.

Charles is also qualified as a solicitor in Australia. Charles has a BA and an LLB in law from the University of Sydney.

Dawn Heath is a solicitor and partner of Freshfields Bruckhaus Deringer. Based in London in the Employment, Pensions and Benefits department, she advises employers, trustees and financial institutions on all aspects of pensions law, with a particular focus on UK defined benefit pension schemes and their associated challenges.

Dawn is heavily involved in industry forums seeking to shape the future of pensions law, including being a member of the Legislative and Parliamentary Committee of the Association of Pension Lawyers (having previously served on the Investment Committee from 2010 to 2012).

Dawn has a degree in Law with European law from Nottingham University.

Abbreviations

Pensions

AA	annual allowance (*Finance Act 2004*)
AVC	additional voluntary contribution
AWA	approved withdrawal arrangement (*Employer Debt Regulations*)
CARE	career average revalued earnings
CETV	cash equivalent transfer value
CIS	collective investment scheme (eg a unit trust)
CN	contribution notice
CPI	consumer price index
DB	defined benefit
DC	defined contribution (money purchase)
DRA	default retirement age
ECE	employment-cessation event (*Employer Debt Regulations*)
ERI	employer related investment (*PA 1995, s 40*)
FAA	flexible apportionment arrangement (*Employer Debt Regulations*)
FSD	financial support direction
GMP	guaranteed minimum pension
GN	guidance note (actuarial)
GPP	group personal pension
IMA	investment management agreement
LEL	lower earnings limit
LPI	limited price indexation
LTA	lifetime allowance (*Finance Act 2004*)
MND	member-nominated director
MNT	member-nominated trustee
NEST	national employee savings trust
NIC	national insurance contribution
NPA	normal pension age (preservation legislation)
NRD	normal retirement date
OPS	occupational pension scheme
PIP	pension input period (*Finance Act 2004*)
PP	personal pension
QPSIP	qualifying pension scheme indemnity provision (*Companies Act 2006*)
RAA	regulated apportionment arrangement (*Employer Debt Regulations*)

RPI	retail prices index
SAA	scheme apportionment arrangement (*Employer Debt Regulations*)
SERPS	state earnings related pension scheme
SIP	statement of investment principles
SPA	state pension age
S2P	state second pension
WA	withdrawal arrangement (*Employer Debt Regulations*)

Legislation

ARD	Acquired Rights Directive
CA	Companies Act
CTA	Corporation Tax Act
ERA	Employment Rights Act
FA	Finance Act
FSMA	Financial Services and Markets Act
IA	Insolvency Act
ICTA	Income and Corporation Taxes Act
Iorp	Directive on Institutions for Occupational Retirement Provision (2003/41/EC)
ITEPA	Income Tax (Earnings and Pensions) Act
ITTOIA	Income Tax (Trading and Other Income) Act
MFR	Minimum Funding Requirement
PA	Pensions Act
PSA	Pension Schemes Act
SI	Statutory Instrument
SSF	Scheme Specific Funding (PA 2004, Part 3)
SSPA	Social Security Pensions Act
TULRCA	Trade Union and Labour Relations (Consolidation) Act
Tupe	Transfer of Undertakings (Protection of Employment) Regulations

Age Regulations	The Employment Equality (Age) Regulations 2006
Age Exceptions Order	The Equality Act (Age Exceptions for Pension Schemes) Order 2010
Consultation Regulations	The Occupational and Personal Pension Schemes (Consultation by Employers and Miscellaneous Amendment) Regulations 2006
Employer Debt Regulations	The Occupational Pension Schemes (Employer Debt) Regulations 2005
Investment Regulations	The Occupational Pension Schemes (Investment) Regulations 2005

Abbreviations

MFR Regulations	The Occupational Pension Schemes (Minimum Funding Requirement and Actuarial Valuations) Regulations 1996
PPF Entry Rules Regulations	The Pension Protection Fund (Entry Rules) Regulations 2005
Scheme Funding Regulations	The Occupational Pension Schemes (Scheme Funding) Regulations 2005

Courts

CA	Court of Appeal
EAT	Employment Appeal Tribunal
ECJ	European Court of Justice (now part of the Court of Justice of the European Union)
ET	Employment Tribunal
HL	House of Lords (Supreme Court from October 2009)
PC	Privy Council
SC	Supreme Court
UT	Upper Tribunal

Judges

C	Chancellor (replaced the Vice-Chancellor from October 2005)
CJ	Chief Justice (High Court)
J	Justice (High Court)
LJ	Lord Justice (Court of Appeal)
MR	Master of the Rolls
V-C	Vice-Chancellor

Other bodies

APL	Association of Pension Lawyers
BAS	Board of Actuarial Standards
BERR	Department for Business, Enterprise & Regulatory Reform (became BIS in June 2009)
BIS	Department for Business, Innovation and Skills (created in June 2009 by a merger of BERR and the Department for Innovation, Universities and Skills)
DP	Determinations Panel (of TPR)
DSS	Department of Social Security (became the DWP in June 2001)
DTI	Department of Trade and Industry (became BERR in June 2007)
DWP	Department for Work and Pensions
FMLC	Financial Markets Law Committee
HMRC	Her Majesty's Revenue and Customs
IT	Independent Trustee

Opra	Occupational Pensions Regulatory Authority (replaced by the Pensions Regulator in April 2005)
PPF	Pension Protection Fund
TPR	the Pensions Regulator

Insolvency processes

CVA	Company voluntary arrangement
CVL	Creditors' voluntary liquidation
MVL	Members' voluntary liquidation

Useful websites

Websites

Organisation and website	Details
APL: www.apl.org.uk	Association of Pension Lawyers: The APL has a website and most of the papers given at its conferences find their way on to it. But you now have to be a member to access them.
Australia: Austlii www.austlii.edu.au	Australasian Legal Information Institute: Australian cases (including state courts) and materials.
BAILII: www.bailii.org	The newer British Isles equivalent of Austlii. It contains British and Irish case law and legislation, EU case law, Law Commission reports, and other law-related British and Irish material.
Canada: CANLII www.canlii.org/en/index.php	Canadian Legal Information Institute: Canadian cases, including the provinces.
Employment Appeal Tribunal www.employmentappeals.gov.uk	Hears appeals from the Employment Tribunal. The ET has jurisdiction in most employment matters and for discrimination cases.
European Courts http://curia.europa.eu/en/content/ jurisp/cgi-bin/form.pl?lang=en	Judgments of the European Union Courts (CJEU) from 1997 (earlier caselaw is also available).
Financial Markets Law Committee www.fmlc.org	Some papers on insolvency issues.
Freshfields Bruckhaus Deringer LLP www.freshfields.com	Publications page includes copies of various briefings. Includes many on employment and pensions issues.
House of Lords www.publications.parliament.uk/ pa/ld/ldjudgmt.htm	This page lists html versions of all House of Lords judgments delivered since 14 November 1996. Not searchable (but try BAILII). From October 2009, see the Supreme Court website.

Organisation and website	Details
Legislation: Office of Public Sector Information www.legislation.gov.uk	This site provides links to the full text of all UK Parliament Public General Acts (from 1988 onwards) and all statutory instruments (from 1987 onwards) as they were originally enacted. For more recent legislation, the explanatory memorandum is also available.
Pensions Ombudsman www.pensions-ombudsman.org.uk	Includes determinations of the Ombudsman in a searchable form.
The Pensions Regulator www.thepensionsregulator.gov.uk	Includes various codes of practice and guidance. Also a few decisions of the determinations panel.
Privy Council www.jcpc.gov.uk (from 2009) www.privy-council.org.uk (1999 to 2009)	Privy Council judgments since 1999 (yes, there are still some appeals, notably from the Isle of Man, the various Channel Isles, Jamaica, Mauritius, the Cayman Islands, Bermuda, Gibraltar and Brunei).
Supreme Court www.supremecourt.gov.uk	The Supreme Court took over from the House of Lords in relation to legal appeals from October 2009. Supreme Court decisions are on this website.

Subscription needed

Justis – UK official law reports (a subscription service).
Lexis Nexis – All England Law Reports etc. A subscription service.
Perspective/Pendragon – a commercial site dedicated to pensions. Includes a 'time travel' option to see what was in force on earlier dates.

Table of Cases

Table of Cases

Table of Cases

Table of Cases

Table of Statutes

Table of Statutory Instruments

Table of Statutory Instruments

Chapter 1

Retirement benefit arrangements in the UK

1.1 Retirement benefit arrangements in the UK: an overview

Summary

This chapter gives an overview of the retirement benefit system in the UK, looking at:

- types of retirement benefit provision in the UK; and
- occupational pension schemes in more detail.

Many of the points raised are discussed in more detail in later chapters.

Types of retirement benefit provision

1.1.1   Retirement benefits in the UK are provided through a combination of state (social security) benefits and supplementary arrangements.

Supplementary arrangements are those providing benefits over and above those provided by the state. As UK social security benefits are comparatively low, supplementary provision is common.

Social security

1.1.2   Employers and employees are required to make contributions to the state social security system. Among the benefits this provides are two principal retirement benefits:

1.1.2 *Retirement benefit arrangements in the UK*

- the state basic pension, a flat-rate pension to which all individuals who have made sufficient National Insurance Contributions (NICs) are entitled; and

- the State Second Pension (S2P), an additional earnings-related element. This was previously the State Earnings-Related Pension Scheme (SERPS).

The state pension age was 60 for women and 65 for men, but from 2010 it has been 65 for everyone except women born before 6 April 1955, for whom there is a sliding scale of state pension ages. *The Pensions Act 2011* will raise the state pension age further, so that from October 2020 the state pension age will rise to 66.

Instead of simply supplementing state benefits, an occupational (i.e. employer-sponsored) or personal pension scheme may also provide benefits which replace those provided by S2P. This is known as contracting out (of S2P) and was popular in the UK when generous rebates applied. Where a scheme is contracted out, employers and employees pay reduced rate NICs (see *Contracting out of state benefits,* **1.1.31** below).

Supplementary provision

1.1.3   Retirement benefits to supplement the state benefits may be provided via occupational pension schemes or personal pension plans. (Note that in the UK the words 'scheme' and 'plan' are used interchangeably). Since October 2001, new stakeholder pension schemes (usually personal pensions) have also been available.

Occupational pension schemes

1.1.4   Occupational pension schemes are retirement benefit arrangements sponsored and administered by or on behalf of an employer. There are two main types.

Defined benefit (DB): benefits are determined by reference to a pension of a target amount at normal retirement age, which is normally related to the amount of the member's annual pay and length of service with the employer. There are two common types known as 'final salary' and 'career average'.

Defined contribution (DC): only the level of the contributions required from the employer/employee is specified. The benefits ultimately paid out will depend on what those contributions will buy (hence the other common name for these schemes, 'money purchase').

DB schemes are described further below.

In a DC scheme, the contributions are invested. When the member retires, the value of the accumulated fund is used to provide the member with an income for life (usually by buying an annuity from an insurance company).

DC schemes present less risk for employers, as contributions are stable (typically, a fixed percentage of the employee's salary). As a result they have become much more popular in recent times and most new pension schemes will be DC. Many employers have closed their DB schemes to new members and now offer DC arrangements.

Such an arrangement may be an occupational pension scheme, or could take the form of a group personal pension plan (GPP) – discussed below.

It is possible to have a hybrid occupational pension scheme, providing both salary-related and money purchase benefits. There are various types of hybrid scheme: some offer different types of benefit structure to different categories of employees or have a single DB or DC structure coupled with an underlying guarantee of the other type. Some even start off as DC plans, but switch to DB benefits when the employee reaches a certain age.

Some employers offer a separate scheme (or a separate section in the main scheme) for highly remunerated employees, providing a higher level of benefits than the level received by other employees (often known as an executive scheme or section).

The regime applying to occupational pension schemes is considered in more detail later in this chapter.

Personal pension schemes

1.1.5   The alternative to an occupational pension scheme is a personal pension scheme. This is a contract between an individual and a personal pension scheme provider – typically an insurance company or bank. It is always a money purchase arrangement.

An active member of an occupational pension scheme used (before the tax rules changed in 2006) only to be able to contribute to a personal pension scheme in very limited circumstances. Historically, personal pension plans were taken out by individuals acting alone, particularly those who were self-employed or who had opted out of their employer's occupational pension scheme. However, it is becoming more common for employers to offer group personal pensions (GPPs). Under this arrangement the employer agrees to pay contributions to a personal pension scheme if it is taken out with a particular provider which offers special terms to the employees of that employer. The plan remains personal to the individual.

Stakeholder schemes

1.1.6   As a result of UK government concerns that many workers in the UK did not have any supplementary pension provision, a new type of scheme was introduced in 2001, aimed especially at lower paid employees and those who change employers frequently.

A stakeholder scheme is a type of DC pension arrangement similar to a personal pension. It is usually administered by a third party such as an insurance company, and its administration charges are capped by law at 1 per cent of the fund value per annum.

Before October 2012, each employer in the UK with five or more qualifying employees needed to provide access to a stakeholder scheme for its employees. However, the employer does not have to contribute to the stakeholder scheme. An employer may be exempt even from these requirements if it already provides an occupational scheme or GPP which satisfies certain criteria (eg it offers membership to any employee over age 18 with at least three months' service who has earnings above a certain level and, in the case of a GPP, the employer contributes at least 3 per cent of pay).

Employees do not have to join the stakeholder scheme nominated by their employer, but are free to choose any stakeholder scheme available on the market.

The stakeholder pension regime will terminate as auto-enrolment obligations (see below) are bought in.

Auto enrolment

1.1.7   Phased in from 2012, there is to be a general requirement for all employers to auto-enrol employees in a qualifying pension arrangement. Employees and the state (by tax relief) will also contribute. Employees will be able to opt out of this requirement. See **19** (Auto enrolment) below.

Occupational pension schemes

Legislation

1.1.8   The principal statutes governing occupational pension schemes are the *Pension Schemes Act 1993*, the *Pensions Act 1995* and the *Pensions Act 2004*.

There is also a wealth of regulations. Because private sector occupational pension schemes are normally set up under trust (see *Trusts and trustees* **1.1.14** below), trust law is also relevant.

Tax: registered schemes

1.1.9   Favourable tax treatment is available for occupational pension schemes if they are registered with (before 5 April 2006, approved by) the UK tax authority, Her Majesty's Revenue and Customs (HMRC), previously called the Inland Revenue. To qualify, the scheme must comply with requirements which are set out in the *Finance Act 2004* and monitored by HMRC.

With a registered occupational pension scheme an employer can claim relief against corporation tax for its contributions and employees are not (subject to not exceeding the annual allowance) taxed on those contributions.

Members (and, following the member's death, spouses etc) pay income tax on their pension when they receive it (but lump sums are tax-free up to certain limits).

A new pensions tax regime came into force on 6 April 2006. The key elements of this are:

- There is a single lifetime allowance on tax-advantaged pension saving; for the tax year 2010/2011 this was £1.8 million (the lifetime allowance) but it reduced to £1.5 million for tax year 2012/13. The *Finance Act 2013* provides that it will further reduce to £1.25m for 2014/15.

- If contributions exceed the lifetime allowance, tax is charged on the excess at 25 per cent (55 per cent if the excess benefits are paid as a lump sum).

- Tax relief is given on a member's contributions up to 100 per cent of UK earnings up to a limit which in 2010/11 was £255,000 (the annual allowance). This has reduced for the tax year 2011/12 to £50,000 (detailed provisions are in the *Finance Act 2011*). The *Finance Act 2013* provides that it will further reduce to £40,000 for 2014/15.

- The member is liable to pay income tax on the value of any benefit accrual in a relevant year exceeding the annual allowance (before 2011/12, this did not apply in the year that the benefits are taken in full).

The Chancellor, George Osborne, in his Autumn Statement on 5 December 2012 outlined the government's intentions on various issues, including:

1.1.9 *Retirement benefit arrangements in the UK*

Pensions tax relief – 2014/15

The Chancellor said that the government intends to reduce the pension tax allowances from 2014/15, by cutting the annual allowance from £50,000 to £40,000 and reducing the lifetime allowance from £1.5m to £1.25m. This change was made by the *Finance Act 2013*.

Extra statutory objective for TPR?

The Department for Work and Pensions (DWP) is to consult on giving The Pensions Regulator (TPR) a statutory objective to consider the effect of recovery plans on sponsoring employers. In the statement it was revealed that 'the DWP will consult on providing the Pensions Regulator with a new statutory objective to consider the long-term affordability of deficit recovery plans to sponsoring employers'. It said this reflected the Government's determination to 'ensure that defined benefit pensions regulation does not act as a brake on investment and growth'. The *Pensions Bill 2014* includes a change – see *Pensions Bill 2014: a new statutory obligation for the Pensions Regulator*, **2.7** below.

Discount rate consultation

The DWP will launch a consultation into smoothing the discount rates used to calculate scheme liabilities, seeking views on whether companies undergoing valuations in 2013 or later should be able to take a longer-term view of projected returns. The Chancellor stated that the 'government recognises that volatility in measures of pension scheme deficits can make it hard for companies to manage their investment plans and attract external funding'.

Commenting at the same time, TPR has said that it will continue to regulate according to the legislative framework as set by Government and Parliament, and it is for them to decide if the balance of that framework should change. They also stated that they 'welcome the wider debate that a transparent consultation will bring to these fundamental issues'.

Regulators

The Pensions Regulator

1.1.10 Occupational pension schemes are overseen by the Pensions Regulator (TPR), which was established on 6 April 2005 by the *Pensions Act 2004*.

TPR enforces compliance with pensions legislation. It has powers to investigate schemes suspected of not fulfilling their legal obligations, to disqualify individuals from being trustees of pension schemes and to impose fines.

TPR replaced the previous regulator, the Occupational Pensions Regulatory Authority (OPRA). TPR's aims include protecting members' benefits and taking steps to reduce the likelihood of claims being made against the Pension Protection Fund (see below). It has much wider, more proactive powers than OPRA had, including powers to impose contribution rates where these cannot be agreed between trustees and employers (see *Key players,* **1.1.13** below); power to investigate schemes and to freeze schemes under investigation; and power to direct employers, trustees and others to take certain steps.

In some circumstances TPR can require third parties who are 'connected or associated' with an employer in relation to an underfunded DB scheme to make contributions to it (known as TPR's 'moral hazard' powers – see **4.1** below).

There are also requirements under the *Pensions Act 2004* for certain parties to make reports to TPR to help it in carrying out its functions (see **13.1** and **13.2** below).

Pension Protection Fund

1.1.11 The Pension Protection Fund (PPF) was established from 6 April 2005 to compensate members of DB pension schemes where the sponsoring employer is insolvent and leaves unfunded liabilities in a pension fund that commences winding up after 5 April 2005.

Certain existing pensions in payment will receive full compensation, but with reduced future increases, while other benefits will be subject to a compensation cap. The PPF is financed by a levy on DB schemes by reference to the number of members they have. The levy includes a flat-rate levy and a risk-based levy, which will be determined by reference to, among other things, the funding level of the scheme, the investments and the financial strength of the employer.

See *Pension Protection Fund*, Chapter **5** below.

Pensions Ombudsman

1.1.12 The Pensions Ombudsman is an independent public official who can investigate and decide complaints of maladministration against trustees or employers and disputes about the way that pension schemes are run. A complaint to the Pensions Ombudsman is normally based on written submissions rather than oral hearings.

7

Unlike court proceedings, a complaint to the Pensions Ombudsman does not put the member at risk of having costs awarded against him if his complaint fails.

Key players

1.1.13   An occupational pension scheme is a three-sided relationship between the employer, the trustees of the scheme (see below) and the member.

Trusts and trustees

1.1.14   An occupational pension scheme is usually set up under trust in order to qualify as a registered scheme with the tax-privileged status described above. A trust is a legal arrangement under which cash and assets are given to trustees (administrators with fiduciary duties ie duties of good faith) to hold and manage for the benefit of third parties, known as beneficiaries (broadly, the employers, the members of the scheme and those entitled to benefits after a member's death). The assets of the trust are usually entirely separate from those of the employer, so that the trust's assets are protected from the employer's creditors.

Where a plan is established under trust, it is the trust that is responsible for providing benefits. The employer does not have direct liability for benefits, but only an obligation to fund the trust to provide the benefits (see *Funding*, **1.1.29** below). The plan and the trust are effectively the same thing.

A pension scheme's trustees may be individuals or a company (a corporate trustee). Although the trustees, or directors of the trustee company, may be employees of the sponsoring employer, their duties as trustees are owed to the beneficiaries. The principal duty on trustees is to exercise their powers for a proper purpose, which usually means in the best interests of the beneficiaries. Failure to comply with trustee duties may lead to a personal claim against the trustee. This may force the trustees into conflict with the employer. Employee trustees have some protections against dismissal on the grounds of their trustee activities.

The administrative procedures of the trust, the duties and powers of the trustees and employers, and the benefits to be provided are set out in detail in a trust deed and rules. In addition to the duties and powers conferred by the trust deed, trustees have duties and powers under general trust law and specific pensions legislation, in particular the *Pensions Act 1995* and the *Pensions Act 2004*, which may override the trust deed.

By law, certain powers and responsibilities under the pension scheme may belong exclusively to the trustees. Where the law does not specify who should have certain powers and responsibilities, the trust deed should make this clear. Some powers and responsibilities may belong exclusively to the trustees, whereas others may belong exclusively to the principal employer (see *Employers*, **1.1.16** below) or may need to be exercised jointly by both parties.

Member-nominated trustees

1.1.15 To encourage member representation, the *Pensions Act 2004* requires most schemes to include persons nominated by the scheme members as trustees. In the case of a corporate trustee, this requirement applies instead to the directors of the trustee company. (See **11.1** below)

Employers

1.1.16 A scheme may be set up for the employees of a single employer or as a centralised or group scheme for the employees of more than one employer. Most registered UK occupational pension schemes must have a designated principal employer. This is normally the main employer participating in the pension scheme. The principal employer usually holds key decision-making powers in connection with the scheme.

Other employers that participate in the scheme are known as participating employers. To participate, an employer must usually be in the same corporate group as the principal employer. Participating employers may have certain powers in relation to their own employees.

In the UK there are also industry-wide pension schemes – large occupational schemes for non-associated employers. These primarily occur in the former nationalised industries. These schemes differ in some respects from conventional occupational schemes and specific advice should be taken if dealing with such schemes.

DB schemes

1.1.17 DB schemes provide a pension based on certain fixed factors (eg a formula related to the employee's salary and period of service). Salary for pension purposes (pensionable salary) is commonly restricted to basic pay, or basic pay plus specified fluctuating amounts (eg certain bonuses).

There are currently three main types of DB arrangement (the DWP consulted in November 2012 on more variants including 'defined ambition').

1.1.18 *Retirement benefit arrangements in the UK*

Final salary schemes

1.1.18   These provide a pension based on a stated fraction or percentage of the employee's final pensionable salary (eg 1/80th or 1/60th) for each year of pensionable service. Often the final pensionable salary will be, say, an average of pensionable pay over the last three years before leaving service. Pensionable service normally means the most recent period of service (employment) from the date of joining the pension scheme.

Career average revalued earnings schemes (CARE schemes)

1.1.19   These provide a pension based on an average of the employee's pay over his working life. In the current economic climate, an increasing number of employers are considering changing to this basis for new employees.

Cash balance schemes

1.1.20   In these schemes the benefit is defined as a lump sum (calculated as a percentage of pay and service) which is then converted to a pension at retirement (often by purchase of an annuity from an insurance company). Contributions are typically credited to an interest-bearing account as a percentage of the employee's pay.

Membership and benefits

1.1.21   Pension scheme members are issued with a members' booklet which summarises the benefit provisions of the scheme. Generally, if something in the booklet conflicts with something in the trust deed and rules, it is what the trust deed and rules say that counts legally, but there are circumstances in which booklets or announcements can confer rights on, or bind, members.

The typical benefits payable on retirement are a pension and a cash lump sum (which is tax free up to certain limits). The lump sum may be provided in addition to the pension or in exchange for part of the amount of pension ('commutation') or a combination of both – this will depend on the rules of the relevant pension scheme.

Under current UK law, membership of an occupational pension scheme cannot be made compulsory.

Retirement at normal retirement date

1.1.22   The scheme rules will usually specify a normal retirement date (NRD) for members.

Early retirement

1.1.23   Benefits may be taken before NRD where permitted by the scheme rules. However, the early retirement pension is often reduced by an actuarial factor to reflect the cost of having to pay the benefits over a longer period. The *Finance Act 2004* lays down restrictions on the early payment of benefits: broadly, benefits may not be taken before age 55 except in circumstances of serious ill-health (for some scheme members transitional provisions can mean that a reduced age can still apply). Where early retirement is due to ill-health, many schemes waive the actuarial reduction, although this can be expensive.

Late retirement

1.1.24   Scheme rules may allow a member to defer taking his pension beyond his NRD, though many provide that this must be not later than the day before the member's 75th birthday (the tax laws used to apply special provisions from age 75, although these have been changed by the *Finance Act 2011*).

The benefits payable on late retirement will be greater than if the member had retired at NRD, either because an actuarial increase is applied to take account of late payment or because his employment after NRD continues to count for accrual of pension benefits.

Leaving service

1.1.25   Under the *Pension Schemes Act 1993*, if an individual leaves employment after at least two years' pensionable service in an occupational pension scheme, his or her accrued benefits (the benefits built up in the scheme) are vested, meaning that the employee has an entitlement to those benefits (starting at normal pension age), even if they are not payable immediately. Some schemes allow earlier vesting.

A member with at least three months' but less than two years' pensionable service has the right to request either a transfer payment from the scheme to another registered pension scheme or a refund of the contributions he or she has paid into the scheme (but not to any contributions paid by the employer).

A member who leaves the service of the employer and whose pension has vested may leave his or her benefits in the scheme until he or she reaches retirement age, becoming a deferred pensioner. At NRD benefits will be based on the pensionable salary at the time of leaving pensionable service, revalued on a statutory basis – see *Indexation* at **14.8** below. Alternatively, he or she may choose to require a transfer value to be paid (representing the value of their accrued benefits) from the previous employer's scheme to a personal pension scheme or to the new employer's scheme, provided it is a suitable pension arrangement and is willing to accept the transfer.

Scheme amendments

1.1.26   UK law (*Pensions Act 1995, s 67* as amended by the *Pensions Act 2004*) protects the accrued benefits of occupational pension scheme members. Schemes are permitted to make a rule change that could have a detrimental effect on the rights a member has acquired in the scheme, but only provided certain steps are taken and requirements are met. The two routes to amendment under *s 67* (though a combination can be used) are:

- obtaining written consent from each affected member (which has to be done in the case of certain specified amendments); or

- meeting the 'actuarial equivalence' requirements: certain conditions must be met when calculating the actuarial value of subsisting rights, and the scheme actuary must give an appropriate certificate.

See *section 67*, **14.7** below.

Death benefits

1.1.27   Typically, schemes also provide benefits on the death of a member, usually dependants' pensions, and on death in service, a lump sum. Some or all of these benefits are often funded by relevant insurance.

Lump sum death benefits are often paid under discretionary trusts. This means that the trustees of the scheme have a discretion to decide to whom the benefits are payable and in what proportions, and as a result no tax is payable.

Funding and contributions

Contributions

1.1.28   Occupational pension schemes may be contributory (meaning that the employees pay contributions as well as the employer) or non-contributory (only the employer contributes), though non-contributory schemes are rare today. The employee contribution rate, if any, will be set out in the rules of the scheme, and will usually be a fixed percentage of pensionable salary from time to time.

Usually DB schemes will be balance of cost schemes, where the employer pays the remaining contributions necessary to meet the balance of the costs of the scheme. In DC schemes, employer contributions are usually at a flat rate, but may vary, for example according to the level of employee contributions (there may be an element of employer matching of the employee's contributions) or the member's age (in which case employer contributions are said to be age-related).

Funding

1.1.29 The amount that an employer is required to contribute to a DB scheme is determined by a combination of the rules of the scheme and overriding statutory requirements. Scheme rules will give the trustees and/or the company the power to determine contribution rates. The amount required will vary with the scheme's funding position and the economic climate. Many UK pension funds which enjoyed funding surpluses in the 1990s and suspended employer contributions are now experiencing significant deficits.

In addition, a change in the statutory calculation basis of the liabilities of pension schemes has meant that schemes which were in surplus on the old statutory basis could now be underfunded on the new, higher, buyout basis. The buyout basis tests whether there would be sufficient assets to secure liabilities if the scheme was wound up and all benefits bought out with insurance policies.

A trustee-appointed actuary is required to assess the funding position of the scheme regularly. The actuary, in assessing the funding position, uses a variety of assumptions to value the assets and liabilities of the scheme at different points in time. The assumptions used are of two types: demographic (eg mortality rates) and economic (such as inflation, pay rises and interest rates).

The statutory funding regime (*Part 3* of the *Pensions Act 2004*) envisages that funding valuations and ongoing contributions will be agreed between the trustees and the employers. If not agreed TPR has the power to specify what should apply.

The trustees are required periodically to prepare a schedule of contributions, which must be certified by an actuary, showing separately the rates and due dates for all contributions payable by the employers and any compulsory contributions payable by members. There are strict rules on when the contributions must be paid into the scheme and penalties for failure to comply.

If there is a funding surplus (currently very unlikely), a contribution holiday (suspension or reduction of contributions) may be possible. In effect all or part of the surplus is used to defray the employer's contributions. An excessive surplus in a scheme (calculated on a very conservative basis) used (before April 2006) to prejudice the tax treatment of the scheme unless promptly reduced, though it is fairly unusual to find such surpluses. However, repayments of surplus to the employer from registered schemes are permitted only in very restricted circumstances and are subject to high tax rates.

DC schemes are not subject to these requirements, though a payment schedule is required showing when contributions are due, and again, penalties apply for late payment.

Investments

1.1.30 A pension fund is typically invested in a mixture of investments: equities, fixed-term securities, real estate and cash to meet the scheme's liability profile. There is a good degree of investment freedom in the UK, though the *Pensions Act 2004* has implemented the investment requirements of the *EU Occupational Pension Schemes Directive* (Iorp) by, for example, prohibiting most trustees from borrowing money (save for temporary liquidity) and requiring trustees and fund managers to exercise their powers of investment or discretions in a manner calculated to ensure the 'security, quality, liquidity and profitability' of the portfolio.

The pension scheme's trustees are required to produce a statement of investment principles (or SIP) setting out their investment policies and their attitude to risk, and must also appoint an investment manager to manage the investments (the employer may not dictate investment strategy). The 2001 Myners Review of Institutional Investment proposed a code of best practice for dealing with investments.

Generally speaking, tax registered pension schemes enjoy tax-free growth on all investment returns, except for dividends on UK equities, where the fund may not reclaim corporation tax already deducted by the issuer.

Contracting out of state benefits

1.1.31 Employees may opt out of S2P (the earnings-related portion of the state scheme) by joining a pension scheme that is contracted out. The pension scheme then provides additional benefits known as contracted-out benefits in place of the state benefits.

For service before April 1997, guaranteed minimum pensions (GMPs) applied to members of schemes contracted out on a salary related basis. GMPs are minimum benefits to which the member is entitled from the scheme in lieu of the state pension. Legislation provides for minimum annual increases to GMPs.

Since April 1997, pension schemes contracted out on a salary-related basis must comply with a statutory reference scheme test. The benefits provided by the pension scheme must be assessed by the actuary as likely to be broadly equivalent to, or better than, a hypothetical reference scheme. These benefits are called 'Section 9(2B) benefits'. It is a more flexible test than the old GMP system.

DC schemes (including personal pensions) used to be able to contract out by providing 'protected rights': pension rights derived from minimum payments made to the member's individual account and certain other payments including age-related rebates paid by the UK government. The amount of benefit payable is not guaranteed.

It was also possible to have a contracted out mixed-benefit scheme, where one section of the scheme was contracted out on the (salary related) reference scheme test basis and another on the (money purchase) protected rights basis.

Contracting out on a DC basis was abolished from April 2012.

In 2013, the government announced that it is proposing, as part of its move to a single tier state pension, that contracting-out on a salary related basis will also be abolished. This will take effect from April 2016. The *Pensions Bill 2014* will, if enacted, provide for this – see *The end of contracting-out in 2016*, **1.4** below.

1.2   Company directors – potential liability for pension benefits?

Summary

Where a company has established an occupational pension scheme, it is the employer who has the primary responsibility for funding the scheme.

But it is conceivable that in some circumstances individual directors of the company could also incur a potential liability in relation to a UK occupational pension scheme. This briefing looks at the potential for such a personal liability.

In practice such personal liabilities on directors is rare (at least absent fraud). But directors may need to consider the potential for personal liability (and whether any liability is covered by their relevant D&O insurance).

Funding of occupational pension schemes

1.2.1   Generally occupational pension schemes are established by an employer, or by a group of employers. The obligation on the employer company to fund the scheme (to enable it to provide the relevant benefits) will arise:

- under the trust deed and rules governing the scheme, providing for:

    – on-going funding (although such rules usually, but not always, include an ability for the company to terminate its liability); and

    – (commonly, but not universally) an indemnity in favour of the trustees;

- under pensions legislation – in particular the scheme specific funding obligations in the *Pensions Act 2004* and the debt on the employer provisions in *section 75* of the *Pensions Act 1995*;[1] or

- conceivably under the contract of employment with the individual employees (although in a defined benefit context, such a contractual obligation is unusual).

1.2.2   The relevant funding liabilities primarily rest with the employer company. As such they do not impose a direct liability on another group entity

---

1   See *Scheme specific funding requirements*, **2.1** and *Debt on the employer – an overview of section 75 of the Pensions Act 1995*, **3.1**.

(eg a holding company for a director), absent an express assumption responsibility (eg a guarantee).

1.2.3   The pension scheme itself and the relevant legislation also impose duties and liabilities on the trustees. These include:

- obligations to pay the right benefits;

- obligations to comply with the various statutory duties (eg in relation to valuations, investments etc).

1.2.4   Duties on trustees under the scheme's trust deed and rules are commonly limited by:

- exoneration provisions applicable if the trustee acts in good faith etc (some of these cannot apply to investment matters); and

- limits on the benefits to be provided by reference to the available funds in the scheme.

Statutory liabilities (and penalties) may not be so limited but usually (under the pensions legislation) have an exception where there is a reasonable excuse.

1.2.5   Trustees are also protected by reimbursement for liabilities incurred in good faith etc by indemnities out of the assets of the scheme (although this cannot cover criminal or civil penalties etc). In some but not all cases there is also an indemnity from the employer.

1.2.6   Other group companies can also be made liable to fund (or give a guarantee to) a pension scheme if the Pensions Regulator exercises its 'moral hazard powers' to issue a contribution notice (CN) or financial support Direction (FSD).[2]

Director liability

1.2.7   Given the primary liabilities to fund and provide benefits under an occupational scheme mentioned above, what are the circumstances in which an individual who is a director of an employer (or director of a holding company) can incur a personal liability to the trustee or to scheme members?

Such a personal liability could arise under a variety of provisions:

---

2   See '*TPR moral hazard powers: Extracting pension scheme funding from third parties: overview*', **4.1** below.

1   **Breach of statutory duty:** if the employer company becomes liable to a civil penalty or a criminal offence, liability can extend personally to a director.

2   **Moral hazard liability:** if the director is 'connected' or 'associated' with an employer company then potentially a contribution notice (CN) could be made against him or her.[3]

3   **Knowing help in discrimination:** directors can be personally liable if they knowingly help unlawful discrimination by the company or the pension scheme.

4   **Assist in a breach of trust:** directors can be personally liable if they knowingly assist in a breach of trust by the trustee of the pension scheme.

5   **Maladministration:**   directors   may   perhaps   be   liable   for maladministration causing injustice in relation to the pension scheme (under the jurisdiction given to the Pensions Ombudsman).

6   **Tort – eg negligence:** It is also possible that directors could incur a personal liability in tort, for example by participating in fraud or deceit or making a negligent misstatement (on which a scheme member or employee may rely) or (less likely) by incurring a direct duty of care in negligence.[4]

1.2.8   A director may also incur a liability *to the company* if he or she breaches a relevant duty owed to the company (in relation to the pension scheme) or if some other statutory responsibility owed to the company applies (eg wrongful trading).

In practice such personal liabilities of directors to the trustee or to members is rare (at least absent fraud). But directors may need to consider the potential for personal liability (and whether any liability is covered by their relevant D&O insurance).

We will look at these in turn.

Breach of statutory duty

1.2.9   The pensions legislation contains numerous examples of penalties for breach of duties imposed on an employer company. In many cases breach of duty can give rise to a civil penalty (sought by the Pensions Regulator) or in extreme cases be a criminal offence.

---

3   If the employer is a company, a financial support direction (FSD) cannot be made against an individual.

4   See *Chandler v Cape plc* [2012] EWCA Civ 525 – although this was a case involving personal injury and a claim against the holding company rather than an individual director.

Examples of potential civil penalties on an employer are:

- failing to pay across deducted employee contributions within the required time without a reasonable excuse (*PA 1995, s 49*);

- failure to notify the Pensions Regulator of a 'notifiable event' or to report a breach of law (*PA 2004, ss 69* and *70*);

- failure without reasonable excuse to pay contributions under the schedule of contributions (*PA 2004, s 228*).

Examples of criminal sanctions on employers include:

- failing to provide information required by the Pensions Regulator by a formal notice under *section 72* (*PA 2004, s 77*);

- knowingly or recklessly providing misleading information to the Regulator (*PA 2004, s 80*);

- wilful failure to comply with the auto-enrolment duty (*PA 2008, s 45*).

Consent/connivance/neglect needed

1.2.10   In most cases where a civil penalty or criminal offence is applicable to a company, the statute goes on to envisage that a director (or other officer) can also be liable[5] if the penalty or offence was incurred or committed by the company (broadly):

- due to the consent or connivance of the director; or

- was attributable to the neglect of the director.

Amount?

Civil penalties are generally limited to £5,000 for individuals – *PA 1995, s 10(2)(a)*. Criminal penalties can include fines or imprisonment.

Risk?

In practice such direct sanction against a company is comparatively rare, let alone a 'look through' against a relevant director or officer. However the potential is there (and criminal sanctions have been used in other circumstances eg health and safety legislation).

---

5   Civil penalties: *PA 1995, s 10(5)*. Criminal offences: *PA 1995, s 115*; *PA 2004, s 309*; and *PA 2008, s 46*.

Contribution Notices (CNs)

1.2.11 A director of an employer company is an 'associate' of an employer and so potentially someone against whom a contribution notice (CN) could be made. A director of a holding company is not connected with or associated with a subsidiary (absent some other connection) so is not potentially within this net.

A financial support direction (FSD) cannot be made by the Pensions Regulator in relation to an individual in circumstances where the employer is a company – *PA 2004, s 43(6)*.

In order for a contribution notice to be made the normal tests would need to be complied with, in particular that:

- a relevant act or omission had occurred; and

- the Pensions Regulator considers it reasonable to issue the notice – *PA 2004, s 38*.

Generally for contribution notice purposes, the relevant act or omission must be one by an employer which has effect to prevent or reduce recovery under *section 75* or to materially adversely affect support for the scheme.

Must be 'party to' or 'knowingly assist'

However:

- a CN can also be made on persons who were a 'party to a relevant act or deliberate failure to act' – *PA 2004, s 38(3)(a)*.

- For this purpose, persons are a party to the relevant act for deliberate failure if they 'knowingly assist in the act or failure' – *PA 2004, s 38(6)(a)*.

1.2.12 To date, only six cases have been publically determined by the Determinations Panel of the Pensions Regulator relating to moral hazard powers. Only two of these, *Bonas* and *Desmonds* have involved contribution notices (the other four were for FSDs).

In both claims were made directly against individual directors.

Bonas

In *Bonas*[6] the Determinations Panel decided not to issue a contribution notice against the director of the subsidiary who had been involved in the pre-tax sale. There seems to have been no appeal from that decision (and the overall claim has been settled).

Desmonds

In *Desmonds*,[7] the Determinations Panel determined to issue CNs against two shareholder directors (one for £900k, the other for £100k), but refused against others.

It seems that these directors owned a substantial shareholding in the employer company.

Risk?

1.2.13   Overall then, the prospect of a contribution notice against the individual director may be relatively small, but it should be something taken into account by the individual directors.

This applies in particular to when a board is agreeing to arrangements which could be deemed to be within the CN regime (perhaps a payment of dividend or grant of security by employer?).

Given that the relevant employer company may, in those circumstances already have the pension liability and it may be too late to reverse the transaction, the Pensions Regulator may be inclined to look more at individual directors involved.

What involvement is needed?

1.2.14   The precise requirement for the individual to 'knowingly assist' in an act or failure is untested. It may be that there is more than a requirement to know that the act is being carried out – instead a requirement to know the relevant act is one which could lead to a contribution notice.

---

6   See *The Bonas case – judicial guidance on CNs*, **4.8**.
7   See *CNs against directors: Desmond & Sons*, **4.15**.

It is also not clear what is required for 'assistance' in this context – would (for example) participating in a board meeting that resolves a particular action (eg payment of a dividend?) be enough, or is some more direct assistance needed?

Defences

1.2.15   The CN regime was extended by the *Pensions Act 2008* to cover acts or omissions that have the effect of reducing employer support (in addition to those with a main purpose of reducing a potential *section 75* debt). The new test is more objective, so potentially, it is now easier for a CN to be made.[8]

However, for the new post-2008 objective test, there is a defence available if the target (here the director) can show that the position of the pension scheme was considered and reasonable mitigation put in place – *PA 2004, s 38A*.

Amount?

1.2.16   The amount of a CN is generally limited to the amount of the buy-out deficit in the scheme (ie the amount of the debt potentially due for the employer under *s 75*). Otherwise it is limited by the need for the Regulator to consider it reasonable.

Overall risk?

1.2.17   Difficult to quantify (and will be very fact specific).

- Liability is not automatic. The Regulator has to show the conditions are met and that the issue of a CN would be reasonable.

- The Regulator would need to decide to act. This is a costly exercise for the Regulator (which will be concerned at the drain on its resources). Currently only six public cases have arisen since the powers were granted in 2005, and all have been after an employer insolvency. But the Regulator may be more often using the potential threat of use of its powers to seek contributions (this would not usually be public – but see Great Lakes[9]).

- A lack of personal gain will be a reason for no order (or reduced) – see *Bonas* – but the amounts concerned can potentially be very large.

---

8   See *Contribution notices,* **4.7.**
9   *See TPR builds a track record,* **4.11** and TPR's statement: http://www.thepensionsregulator. gov.uk/press/pn11–16.aspx

Knowingly helping illegal discrimination

1.2.18   The *Equality Act 2010* consolidated the obligations on both employers and trustees of occupational pension schemes not to discriminate on a prohibited ground (sex, race, age, disability, religion, sexual orientation etc).

This duty (and liability for any discrimination) applies to an employer or a trustee of an occupational pension scheme. However, liabilities are also imposed on a person who 'knowingly helps' another do anything which contravenes the relevant duties – *Equality Act 2010, s 112*.[10]

1.2.19   There is not a vast amount of case law in this area, but there has been some recently. It seems that a third party (such as director) can be liable under this 'knowingly helps' provision in the *Equality Act* if:

- the third party is aware of the intended acts (that are discriminatory);

- but the third party does not have to know that they are illegal under the discrimination legislation.[11]

1.2.20   In practice, claims against individuals (eg directors or insolvency practitioners) have only tended to be brought where there has been some financial problem with the underlying employer company. But again the potential for claims needs to be kept in mind.

Amount

1.2.21   Discrimination claims are for the amount of loss suffered.

There is no monetary cap.

Awards can be joint and several on all those involved (including the company).

Assisting in a breach of trust

1.2.22   In the 1870s, the House of Lords in *Barnes v Addy*[12] made it clear that a third party can be directly liable to beneficiaries of a trust in some circumstances where the third party has been involved in a breach of trust by the trustee, ie has procured or assisted the breach of trust. This accessory liability

---

10   The *Equality Act 2010* re-enacted previous provisions to the same effect in the previous Acts and regulations. It uses the terms 'knowingly help' instead of 'knowingly aids', but there is probably no distinction.
11   See Hale LJ in *Hallam v Avery* [2000] 1 WLR 966 at para [44].
12   (1874) LR 9 Ch App 244.

does not require the third party to have benefited personally nor to have received any trust property.

It is perhaps conceivable that a director could incur personal liability under this rule if he or she was involved in a breach of trust by the pension scheme trustees.

Maladministration

1.2.23 A director of an employer could be someone involved in the administration of a scheme and so potentially within the jurisdiction of the Pensions Ombudsman (*PSA 1993*). This could perhaps mean that a claim could be brought by a member against such a director for 'maladministration causing injustice'.

Such cases do not leap to mind and may be met by the argument that the true defendant here should be the company (as employer) and not a director.[13]

Direct tort liability?

1.2.24 It is also conceivable that an individual director could owe a direct duty of tort to an individual employee (or trustee of the pension scheme). This could, for example, be for fraud, deceit etc. It is also potentially possible that a director could incur a personal liability by reason of negligent misstatement.

In relation to such 'non wilful' torts, generally a director acting in good faith should not incur a personal responsibility or liability. This is, however, a developing area of the law.[14]

It seems unlikely that a director could be liable for negligence (or negligent mistake) to an employee or trustee in relation to pensions matters. Any such relevant liability would be in relation to financial matters (where a duty of care of negligence is more difficult to prove).[15]

---

13 See for example the House of Lords in *Re Paycheck Services 3 Ltd; Revenue and Customs Commissioners v Holland* [2010] UKSC 51; [2011] 1 BCLC 141 holding that any liability on a corporate director for payment of an unlawful dividend did not extend to a director of that corporate director.

14 See *MCA Records v Charly Records* [2003] 1 BCLC 93 (Court of Appeal).

15 There is an analogy here to cases holding no liability on directors of a trustee company – eg *HR v JAPT* [1997] OPLR 123. But note the recent decision of the Court of Appeal imposing a liability on a holding company for breach of a duty of care owed to employees of a subsidiary in relation to health and safety issues in *Chandler v Cape PLC* [2012] EWCA Civ 525.

Breach of duty owed to the company

1.2.25   A director of course owes the usual statutory and fiduciary duties to the relevant company of which he is a director.

It is conceivable that such duties could give rise to a personal liability to the company if there is a breach that is connected with the pension scheme. For example a failure to carry out his duties with appropriate skill or care (*CA 2006, s 174*) or where a statutory obligation is incurred (eg for wrongful trading).

Directors and officers insurance

1.2.26   Directors should consider whether any D&O (directors and officers) insurance that they hold in relation to them as a director extends to cover the potential duties and liabilities mentioned above.

1.3 Money Purchase Pension Schemes: comparison of trust based (OPS) with contract based (PP)

Summary

Employers are increasingly looking at contributing to a defined contribution (DC) or money purchase pension arrangement for employees. This can be a way of complying with the auto-enrolment duties being phased in under the *Pensions Act 2008*. In the private sector, employers have the choice as to whether such arrangements will be 'trust based' or 'contract based':

- Trust based:
  established under trust as an occupational pension scheme (OPS); or

- Contract based:
  an arrangement established as a personal pension (PP) under a contract with an external provider. The external provider is regulated under the financial services legislation and typically uses an insurance policy or a unit trust as the funding mechanism. This can be a self-invested personal pension (SIPP).

This section looks at the advantages and disadvantages from a legal perspective for an employer using one of the above two structures.

Differences between trust based and contract based DC arrangements

1.3.1 Trust based and contract based DC arrangements provide a similar end product – a savings pot for the employee to use to fund his or her own pension provision. Despite this similarity, these arrangements are regulated differently in many ways, although the differences are gradually becoming less significant. For example:

- the 2006 tax rules removed many differences in the tax treatment; and

- the government has said that it is looking at removing the two year vesting period allowed for OPS but not PPs.

1.3.2 The differences are summarised in the table below. The main differences are:

1.3.3   Tax: The tax rules are now the same for both a PP and a DC OPS. There can be some difference on tax relief at source.

1.3.4   Early leavers: An OPS may be better for an employer because members' benefits only vest after two years pensionable service unless the scheme's rules provide otherwise. Previously, early leavers were only entitled to a return of their own contributions if they left employment before two years of pensionable service (or such earlier date as provided for in the rules). As a result, the portion of their benefits attributable to employer contributions became available to be used for other purposes (eg to be used to meet expenses or contributions for other employees). Members in a PP are immediately vested in their benefits.

However, the pensions legislation changed in April 2006 so that leavers with less than two years' pensionable service (but more than three months pensionable service) must be given the right to request a transfer of all their benefits (including employer contributions) to another plan. The potential savings for an employer in respect of early leavers is probably much reduced.

In addition, the government said (in September 2011) that it is looking at removing the two year vesting period currently allowed for OPS (but not currently allowed for PPs). The *Pensions Bill 2014* envisages making this change (for pure money purchase benefits) for those who join the scheme after the change comes into force.

1.3.5   Trapped surplus offsets: The risk of trapped surplus in a defined benefit (DB) scheme can be reduced by attaching a DC section to the DB section of the scheme. If the rules are structured properly, any surplus in the DB section can be used to offset employer obligations to contribute to the DC section – *Barclays Bank v Holmes* (2000). This is not possible for a PP (or freestanding OPS). See *Surplus and overfunding in pension schemes*, **2.5** below.

1.3.6   Trustees needed for an OPS: An OPS requires trustees to administer the scheme. The trustees will have a number of legal duties which may attract claims if it is alleged that they have not acted appropriately. An OPS will also need to comply with the member-nominated trustee (MNT) obligations. There are no trustees needed for a PP.

1.3.7   Investment monitoring: One of the duties trustees of an OPS have is to monitor the investments in the fund (either the investments selected by the employer or the investment menu offered to members) and, in particular, the default fund used for members who fail to make a choice (although the extent of any legal duty in this area is unclear). Trustees could potentially face claims in relation to their role in monitoring investments. The trustees carry out a useful monitoring role in an OPS – where no such role exists for a PP.

1.3.8 **More employer involvement in OPS:** An OPS requires more employer involvement – eg appointing trustees. This can be desirable because, for example, there can be better branding and more oversight of investment/ operations. However, this involvement could also cause some issues. These issues include the trustees looking for indemnities from the employer and the employer having statutory payment obligations under the 2005 Employer Debt Regulations (eg to pay the PPF levy amount (although this is small for DC benefits) or if a 'criminal deficit' (ie resulting from an offence involving dishonesty or an intent to defraud) arises).

1.3.9 **Costs and charges:** The costs and charges of a PP will either be debited from member accounts or (if agreed by the employer) paid by the employer. Costs and charges of running an OPS are more likely to be paid directly by the employer. The actual amount of the charges will depend on factors such as the size of the scheme and the arrangement made with the provider.

1.3.10 **Political risk:** There is probably more risk for an OPS of future legislation imposing further obligations on trustees or employers. For example, the Pensions Regulator issued a Code of Practice in November 2013 on *'Governance and administration of occupational defined contribution trust-based pension schemes'*.[16] This consultation envisages, amongst other things, a code of practice for DC trustees.

1.3.11 **Financial services regulation:** A PP is a financial services product that needs to be promoted and marketed in accordance with the rules of the Financial Services Authority (FSA) (eg any promotional literature needs to be approved by an authorised person). An OPS is not governed by the FSA. In practice we would expect the PP provider to be on top of this.

1.3.12 **Employer-related investment:** An OPS needs to comply with the limits on employer-related investment (eg no loans to the employer and no more than 5% of the fund invested in shares of the employer). A PP does not have such limits.

1.3.13 **Legislation:** There are still some (marginal) differences in the legislation (eg on stakeholders and *Tupe* transfers).

1.3.14 **Age discrimination:** There are more express exemptions for an OPS than a PP under age discrimination legislation. Age-related contribution rates and length of service exemptions apply to both an OPS and a PP. The exemption relating to closing a scheme (or section) to new entrants does not apply to a PP.

---

16   Code of Practice 13 on the TPR website: http://www.thepensionsregulator.gov.uk

1.3.15   Risk benefits: It is easier to incorporate risk benefits (eg a death in service lump sum or payments on incapacity) under an OPS than a PP. For example, if an employer wants to provide a lump sum benefit on death that is intended to top-up a member's pot to a target amount, it is easier to have such an arrangement under an OPS.

1.3.16   Branding: An OPS is easier to 'brand' as a benefit from the employer – but this may well be possible in a SIPP as well.

1.3.17   Member bankruptcy: A member pension under an OPS may be less at risk from a claim by a trustee in bankruptcy than for a PP.

1.3.18   Lien over funds: An OPS can include a lien in favour of the employer for any liability of the member to the employer arising out of a criminal, negligent or fraudulent act or omission by the member (*Pensions Act 1995, s 91*). A PP cannot include such a charge or lien.

Conclusion

1.3.19   There continue to be some differences between a PP and an OPS for DC provision, although the gap is narrowing. The choice between providing DC benefits by using an OPS or a PP will depend on the employer's individual circumstances (and risk appetite).

1.3.20

Overview table

Issue	OPS better for employer?	PP better for employer?
Tax /contributions	Equal	Equal
Early leaver vesting/member refunds	✓✓✓	
Trapped surplus offset possible?	✓✓	
Trustee needed for an OPS		✓
Potential liabilities		✓
Monitoring of scheme	✓	
More employer involvement in OPS		✓✓
Employer pays levy/criminal deficit		✓

1.3.20 *Retirement benefit arrangements in the UK*

Issue	OPS better for employer?	PP better for employer?
Costs and charges	Depends	Depends
Political risk		✓
Financial services regulation	✓	
Employer-related investment		✓
Legislation (eg TUPE)		✓
Age discrimination exemptions	✓	
Risk benefits integration possible	✓	
Branding	marginal	
Member bankruptcy	✓	
Lien to employer possible	✓	

1.4   The end of contracting-out from 2016

Summary

The Government has announced that it will legislate so that, from April 2016, a single-tier state pension will replace the current two-tier system of: (1) basic state pension; and (2) additional state pension.

The consequence of this is that from April 2016, occupational pension schemes, including defined benefit (DB) pension schemes, will no longer be able to contract-out of the state second pension (S2P). This will mean that employers and employees who are currently 'contracted-out', will pay increased National Insurance Contributions (NICs).

These changes will be introduced by the *Pensions Bill 2014 (PB 2014)* if enacted. Employers will want to review their pension schemes alongside the *PB 2014* provisions in order to understand the potential impact of the new legislation.

This section sets out the key changes introduced by the *PB 2014* and the main consequences for employers.

1.4.1

Overview of issues to consider

Issues arising on abolition of contracting-out	Points to consider
1. Benefits	• NICs will go up (for employer and employee) • Should future service benefits go down to reflect this? • Statutory amendment power may help

1.4.1 *Retirement benefit arrangements in the UK*

Issues arising on abolition of contracting-out	Points to consider
2. Integration	• If existing benefits are integrated with the state pension (eg a basic pension or LEL offset from benefits or contributions), should this continue? • How will the state pension changes impact? • What if the scheme has become contracted-in but introduced offsets to member contributions and benefits – will these still work?
3. Amendments	If changes are wanted: • consider existing amendment power • note statutory power (for 5 years) • need to consult
4. GMPs	• The rate of revaluation may change if scheme rules provide for it to be fixed on leaving contracted-out service • Anti-franking will apply to members with a GMP who remain in pensionable service
5. Protection rule	• Express 'protection rule' will (under current legislation) need to be inserted
6. Consultation	• Statutory obligation to consult about changes in contracted-out status will not apply • Usual obligation to consult about 'listed changes' will apply if benefit changes are envisaged
7. Auto-enrolment checks	• If existing DB scheme is used for auto-enrolment, new checks needed when scheme ceases to be contracted-out

Contracting-out

1.4.2   Contracting-out is the process where employees cease to accrue the additional State Pension, (now the S2P, previously known as the State Earnings Related Pension Scheme (SERPS)) and instead join a contracted-out occupational pension scheme. The employer and the employees pay lower

NICs. The employees receive a pension from the contracted-out scheme rather than the additional State Pension. Contracting-out on a money purchase basis (eg by reference to a personal pension) ended in April 2012.

1.4.3   From 1997, DB contracted-out schemes have had to meet a scheme quality test which aims that a certain level of benefit will be provided to members of the contracted-out scheme. The scheme's actuary has to certify that (in his or her opinion) the scheme envisages benefits (in at least 90% of cases) which are as good as the set of benefits provided by a 'reference scheme' (laid down in regulations).

1.4.4   While in the short term the state receives a lower immediate NICs income, the state no longer has to pay an additional state pension (out of future tax or NICs) to contracted-out employees. To reflect this, sponsoring employers of contracted-out schemes and the participating employees, receive a rebate in NICs.

1.4.5   This ability to contract-out and its corresponding NICs rebate, is attractive to sponsoring employers and so is common in DB occupational pension schemes. From April 2016 however, this benefit associated with DB occupational schemes will be removed.

Key changes

1.4.6   Abolition of contracting-out:

(a)   The introduction of a single flat rate pension means that from April 2016 it will no longer be possible to contract-out of the S2P. Active members under DB occupational schemes and the sponsoring employers will have to pay full rate NICs after this date.

(b)   The NICs rebate for active members (1.4% of relevant earnings) and for employers (in respect of the employees who are active members) – 3.4% of relevant earnings), will end. Relevant earnings are earnings between the Lower Earnings Limit (LEL) and the Upper Accrual Point (UAP).

1.4.7   Move to single-tier state pension – impact on integration with basic state pension:

(a)   Many pension schemes have benefit structures which integrate the benefits under the basic state pension. Examples of this include bridging pensions (paid between retirement and state pension age) and deductions from pensionable salary of a multiple of the basic state pension.

(b)   The new single-tier pension structure will impact on scheme rules and so employers should review pension schemes to identify any rules which use terminology which relates to the previous two-tier system or basic state pension provision.

1.4.8 Move to single-tier state pension – if no change is made to the contracted-out scheme:

(a) From April 2016 with the move to the single-tier state pension, if no changes are made to a contracted-out scheme:

> (i) the current scheme benefit accrual will continue;

> (ii) member and employer contributions to the scheme will remain unchanged;

> (iii) members will qualify for S2P for future service; and

> (iv) both member and employer NICs will rise.

GMPs and contracting-out legislation

1.4.9 Schemes are required to revalue GMPs (in line with orders under *PSA 1993, s 148*) while an active member with a GMP is in contracted-out service. Schemes also need to provide for GMPs to be revalued after the member leaves contracted-out service (even if the member remains in pensionable service). This revaluation can be on a *s 148* order basis or on a fixed rate basis (the rate is fixed by order – currently it is 4.75%pa compound). The ending of contracting-out may require current administrative practice to change.

1.4.10 The complex anti-franking legislation currently applies to deferred members with a GMP. The rules aim to ensure that revaluation on the GMP element of a member's pension is paid in addition to the pension at leaving and not offset against it. When contracting-out is abolished, the rules will also apply to members with a GMP who remain in pensionable service.

1.4.11 Current legislation[17] requires a scheme that ceases to be contracted-out to include an express 'protection rule' which provides that the total amount of benefits under the scheme for each member at normal pension age will not be less that the aggregate of:

● the member's *section 9(2B)* rights and GMPs;

● any other benefits attributable to pre-6 April 1997 contracted-out pensionable service; and

● any benefits attributable to non-contracted-out pensionable service.

---

17 The *Occupational Pension Schemes (Contracting-out) Regulations 1996*, reg 45.

Statutory amendment power

1.4.12 In recognition of the immediate financial and administrative implications of the abolition of contracting-out, the *PB 2014, clause 24*(2) will provide sponsoring employers with a method of recovering some or all of the additional cost of increased employer NICs.

1.4.13 The *PB 2014* will allow employers to amend contracted-out schemes to increase employees' contributions and/or reduce future accrual rates, in order to offset the increase in employer NICs.

1.4.14 This new statutory power is limited to private sector employers. The power will not apply to public service pension schemes.

1.4.15 The sponsoring employer of a contracted-out scheme, looking to amend employee contributions, will not have to seek the consent of the pension scheme trustees before using the statutory power under the *PB 2014*. Nevertheless employers should still ensure that they comply with the implied 'Imperial' duty of mutual trust and confidence.[18]

1.4.16 The exercise of the power will also be subject to certain restrictions. These restrictions include:

- limiting amendments to future benefits[19] – the power may not be used in a way that would or might adversely affect the subsisting rights of a member of the scheme or a survivor of a member of the scheme. *Schedule 14* of the *PB 2014* intends to ensure that all contracted-out rights accrued by employees, through salary related contracted-out schemes prior to the abolition of contracting-out, remain unaffected;

- obtaining actuarial certification that the modifications comply with statutory requirements (ie that the conditions set out below at **1.4.17** have been met);[20] and

- limiting the statutory modification power so that it must be exercised within a period of five years from 6 April 2016.[21]

1.4.17 The new statutory amendment power will also be subject to the following conditions:[22]

---

18 *Imperial Group Pension Trust Ltd v Imperial Tobacco Ltd* [1991] 2 All ER 597.
19 *PB 2014, para 3(1), Schedule 14.*
20 *PB 2014, para 6(1), Schedule 14.*
21 *PB 2014, clause 24(6).*
22 *PB 2014, para 2(2), Schedule 14.*

- employee's annual contributions cannot be increased beyond the annual increase in the employer's NICs in respect of them;

- employee's annual future benefits cannot be reduced by more than the annual increase in the employer's NICs in respect of them; and

- the sum of any annual increase in contributions and reduction in members' benefits could not be more than the annual increase in the employer's NICs in respect of them.

1.4.18   Regulations are to define what is meant by: total annual employee contributions of the relevant members; the annual increase in an employer's NICs in respect of the relevant members; and a scheme's liabilities in respect of the relevant members.[23]

Impact of statutory amendment power

1.4.19   These conditions aim to ensure that any amendments to employee contributions and/or future accrual rates purely act to offset the increased costs of employer NICs.

1.4.20   It is expected that the majority of employers with DB arrangements will make amendments to employee contributions and future accrual rates, putting themselves into a broadly cost neutral position. Employers will want to ensure that all of the amendments to the previously contracted-out schemes are measured and well communicated to employees.

1.4.21   In practice it is unclear how amendments to employee contributions to reflect increased employer NICs will work. While NICs are payable only in respect of earnings between the LEL and UAP, member contributions are generally based on pensionable earnings which may be in excess of the UAP. Therefore the mechanism for introducing amendments to employees' contributions, may not be as straight forward as increasing all contributions by 3.4%.

1.4.22   The power will not be available for employers of contracted-in schemes which have integrated offsets that may be affected by the abolition of contracting-out. Employers may need to reach agreement with trustees in order to effect necessary changes.

---

23   *PB 2014, para 2(3), Schedule 14.*

Pensions consultations

1.4.23   Currently under the *Pension Schemes Act 1993* an employer must, where it terminates its pension scheme's contracted-out status, inform affected employees and consult with any trade unions. Under the *PB 2013*, the Government has confirmed that there will be no requirement to consult on ending contracting-out in April 2016, as this will arise automatically on the implementation of the legislation and so be outside the employer's control.

1.4.24   Regardless of the change to the contracting-out provisions, a consultation requirement will arise under the *Pensions Act 2004*, where an employer proposes to make a 'listed change' that affects the scheme. In this case the employer must still carry out a consultation (of at least 60 days) in accordance with the *2006 Consultation Regulations*.[24] This consultation requirement will be triggered whether the employer is using the new statutory modification power or not, with no new impact on the timetable for implementing changes to scheme rules.

1.4.25   The following changes to a DB pensions scheme are 'listed changes':

- to make any increase in member contributions by or on behalf of members or members of a particular description;[25] and

- modifying the rate of future accruals.[26]

Protected persons

1.4.26   Some former nationalised industries (now in the private sector) are protected from any changes to their pension scheme rules by legislation made at the time of privatisation in the early 1990s. This body of legislation, collectively referred to as the Protected Persons Regulations (the PPRs), require new private sector employers to continue to provide pensions benefits to employees who were employed at the time of privatisation, which are as good as those they were receiving in the public sector. The PPRs prevent an employer from making changes which reduce future pension accruals or increase employee contributions.[27]

---

24 *The Occupational and Personal Pension Schemes (Consultation by Employers and Miscellaneous Amendment) Regulations 2006.* See '*Pensions Act 2004: employers' consultation obligations*', **15.1** below.
25 *Consultation Regulations 2006, reg 8(1)(f).*
26 *Consultation Regulations 2006, reg 8(3)(c) and (d).*
27 DWP Paper – Abolition of Contracting out: Consultation on a statutory override for Protected Persons Regulations (January 2013).

1.4.27   The relevant nationalised industries are coal, electricity, rail and London Transport. As an overview, in coal and electricity, pension scheme changes can be made in limited circumstances if approved by the majority of members. In the case of rail, any amendment of the pension scheme which is less favourable to the members is prohibited. Finally for London Transport, amendments to the pension scheme are usually only effective with the consent of each affected member.

1.4.28   Due to the PPRs, relevant private sector employers of former nationalised industry employees, will not be able to use the new statutory power under the *PB 2014* to amend pension scheme rules to adjust employee contributions. It could only be used if the PPRs are overridden or amended by new legislation. If the PPRs are not overridden, then these employers will face the additional costs of full rate employer NICs without being able to make a corresponding change to reduce pension scheme liabilities.

1.4.29   The Government carried out a consultation, which closed on the 14 March 2013, on the question of whether the PPRs should be relaxed to allow employers to amend their contributions to offset the lost NICs rebate. Although the response to the consultation has not been formerly published, affected employers said in discussions that they would not implement amendments to schemes so as to introduce differential treatment for protected and non-protected persons. Employers were of the opinion that such division of a scheme would be unfair, detrimental to industrial relations and overall very difficult to communicate to members. The Government understands that it is necessary to examine this point further in recognition of the need to balance the expectations of both employers and employees.

Auto-enrolment

1.4.30   Before April 2016 contracted-out DB schemes automatically satisfy the quality test for schemes to be qualifying schemes for auto-enrolment purposes. From April 2016 when contracting-out is abolished, this automatic qualification will no longer be available. DB schemes will from April 2016 need to meet the 'test scheme standard' (under the auto-enrolment legislation[28]) in order to be a qualifying scheme. The 'test standard' is a quality requirement for DB schemes with members in employment that are not contracted out of S2P. It provides a bench-mark for retirement provisions. This will potentially result in greater complexity for sponsoring employers.

---

28   *Pensions Act 2011, s 11.*

1.5   European proposals to reform the regulation of pension schemes

Summary

This section looks at the proposals for a new European risk-based supervisory regime for institutions for occupational retirement provisions (IORPs), or funded pension schemes.

The European Commission intends to publish a proposal for a new Directive to improve governance and disclosure standards of pension funds. This proposal was originally due in December 2012, but has been subject to several delays.

Plans to address the solvency of pension funds have been postponed indefinitely (following widespread criticism from across the pensions industry, and opposition from the UK, Netherlands, Germany and Ireland).

However, both employers and trustees should remain alert to the increased costs and compliance burden which could result from the remaining proposals.

The review

1.5.1   The European Commission is carrying out a review of the 2003 IORP Directive (Directive 2003/41/EC on the activities and supervision of institutions for occupational retirement provision). The review follows the publication of the Commission's White Paper on 'adequate, safe and sustainable pensions' in February 2012.[29]

1.5.2   Following detailed advice from the European Insurance and Occupational Pensions Authority (EIOPA) in February 2012, a revised draft of the directive (IORP II) is now expected in autumn 2013 (twice delayed from earlier due dates of December 2012 and summer 2013).

1.5.3   The current IORP Directive provides a European framework for pension scheme funding and, in particular, underpins how employers fund defined benefit (DB) occupational pension schemes. It was implemented in the UK by the *Pensions Act 2004*.

---

29   European Commission, 'White paper: An agenda for adequate, safe and sustainable pensions' (16 February 2012).

1.5.4   *Retirement benefit arrangements in the UK*

1.5.4   The initial aims of the review were to:

(i)   complete the Single Market for occupational retirement provision, by harmonising the solvency and valuation rules of defined benefit pension funds in European member states;

(ii)   strengthen protection for scheme members;

(iii)   facilitate cross-border activity; and

(iv)   ensure a level playing field between institutions for occupational retirement provision (IORPs), or funded pension schemes, and insurers (in light of Solvency II insurance regime).

EIOPA Advice (*February 2012*)

1.5.5   The Commission proposes to establish a Europe-wide risk-based supervisory regime for institutions for IORPs.

1.5.6   EIOPA's advice proposed that this could be achieved by adopting a three pillar approach for IORP II, which is drawn from the approach to banking regulation set out in the Basel II and III accords and from the forthcoming requirements for insurance companies set out in Solvency II Directive (2009/138/EC):[30]

Pillar I: quantitative requirements. Including the valuation of assets and liabilities, technical provisions, and the treatment of security mechanisms and investment rules. Central to the Pillar I proposals is a 'holistic balance sheet' approach.[31]

Pillar II: qualitative requirements. Including the supervision of IORPs, requirements for key individuals and outsourced functions, risk management, internal controls and internal audit and actuarial functions.

Pillar III: disclosure requirements. Including the provision of information from IORPs to supervisors, members and beneficiaries.

1.5.7   Following the May 2013 announcement, the proposal for IORP II will now focus on Pillars II and III, following concerns that the solvency standards under review would inflate pension deficits and restrict the availability of long term investment finance (eg through altering incentives to hold long term assets). Commissioner Barnier has made assurances that he has:

---

30   EIOPA advice to European Commission on the review of the IORP Directive 2003/41/EC (15 February 2012).
31   See below.

'no desire to penalise national systems which work well. And especially [does] not want, in the current fragile economic situation, to harm the ability of pension funds to play their role as long-term investors.'

1.5.8 However, given the extensive interaction between the governance standards and solvency requirements outlined in EIOPA's advice, the European reforms could still have an impact on the deficits reported by pension funds.

Governance requirements

1.5.9 The governance requirements of Solvency II provided the starting point for EIOPA's advice. Solvency II includes a two stage process by which insurance firms will be: (i) required to show compliance with funding requirements; and (ii) monitored by supervisors.

Governance Requirements under Solvency II

Stage 1 – the Own Risk and Solvency Assessment (ORSA): The firm undertakes an internal assessment, known as the ORSA, in which it evaluates its solvency needs and its compliance with technical provisions. Firms are required to perform and ORSA 'regularly and without any delay following any significant change in their risk profile'.[32] EIOPA has suggested that this would be a useful way for pension funds to assess their risk profile, given that pension funds operate on a long term cycle and the ORSA provides a forward looking approach.

Stage 2 – the Supervisory Review Process (SRP): Supervisors review the firm's ORSA as part of its SRP. This process is a means by which supervisors review the firms' procedures for complying with the Solvency II regime and is a means for them to identify any deteriorating financial circumstances. As a result of this SRP, the supervisor may point out material weaknesses and deficiencies in that undertaking (eg in its governance requirements or in the amount of capital held). Solvency II provides for the SRP to be conducted 'regularly', but gives supervisors discretion to establish the minimum frequency and scope of these reviews having regard to the nature, scale and complexity of the activities of the undertaking concerned.[33]

---

32 *Article 45(5), Solvency II Directive.*
33 *Article 36(6), Solvency II Directive.*

1.5.9 *Retirement benefit arrangements in the UK*

As with the ORSA, EIOPA have indicated that they think that the SRP is a useful starting point for a new supervisory regime for pension funds. Although EIOPA suggests that supervisors will also need to take account of the security mechanisms open to pension funds (such as the employer covenant).

1.5.10 This approach indicates how the Commission could continue to pursue its aim of maintaining a level playing field between insurance companies and pension funds. However, the current proposals fail to appreciate how IORPs differ from the regulated insurance community. In the UK, the differences are stark: there are more than ten times as many DB pension schemes than insurers, they are regulated by different entities, have different relationships with investors, and perform different social functions.

1.5.11 The insurance regulatory regime (including the forthcoming Solvency II requirements) assumes intensive regulator involvement and oversight. The relatively small number of UK insurers (fewer than 600) makes it feasible for the UK's Prudential Regulatory Authority to do this. But it is difficult to see how the Pensions Regulator (TPR) could take a similar approach with the much greater number of DB occupational pension schemes.

1.5.12 This approach to governance also demonstrates how the IORP II proposals could still have an impact on scheme funding – even if the new Directive does not prescribe new solvency standards. Under Solvency II the supervisor can address deficiencies in an insurer's financial position by requiring it to hold extra capital, known as a capital add-on. Member states also have discretion to require the amount of the add-on to be published – that is, to disclose to the market that it does not approve of the firm's risk management and/or governance. The new governance regime under IORP II could therefore strengthen TPR's powers to intervene in pension scheme funding, if TPR has identified weaknesses.

Other governance requirements

EIOPA has set out further recommendations for the governance systems of pension funds, particularly in relation to how they manage risk:

Risk management: Pension funds could be required to put in place a more rigorous system for identifying and responding to risks.

Internal control systems: These could include obligations to undertake regular assessments of compliance and meet whistle-blowing requirements.

Fit and proper persons: fit and proper criteria (eg for adequate qualifications and good reputation) will apply to personnel who run, or have key functions in pension funds.

Further proposals

– Internal audit

– Actuarial function

– Appointment of depositories and safekeeping of assets

– Outsourcing

Outsourcing

1.5.13 EIOPA made three recommendations concerning the outsourcing of key functions of pension funds:

1 Service providers should face greater obligations to co-operate with supervisors, and provide information and access to their premises, particularly in the case of cross border schemes.

2 Pension funds should be required to monitor the provision of outsourced functions, to ensure that service to members is maintained and that this did not lead to an increase in operational risk.

3 Any outsourcing of key functions should be formally documented in a legally enforceable written document.

Disclosure requirements

1.5.14 The third pillar of EIOPA's advice considered the disclosure requirements of pension funds to: (i) supervisors, and (ii) members and beneficiaries.

Disclosure to supervisors

1.5.15 Supervisory authorities already have substantial powers to require information from pension funds, supervise their relationships with service providers and carry out on-site inspections.

For this reason, EIOPA suggested that there may not be any need to grant greater powers to supervisors. If any reforms were to be made, these would aim to harmonise the form and type of information which pension funds are required to provide.

Disclosure to members

1.5.16   EIOPA's advice on disclosure to members has received more positive response than most of their proposals – perhaps because it addressed concerns particular to DB and DC pension funds, rather than insurance firms. EIOPA emphasised that their main objective was to help members understand issues which are both important and difficult for members and to equip them to make the decisions needed to plan for their retirement.

'People generally find retirement planning a difficult issue. At the same time, saving for retirement is one of the most important elements of lifetime financial planning. Information requirements are an essential element of the protection of IORP members, especially when they bear the investment risk. Current and potential members/beneficiaries need information to "understand" and make judgments about on the one hand the functioning of an IORP and its scheme, and if applicable to make informed decisions (concerning the provider, different investment options, opting-in or out). On the other hand, people need information to make choices about their broader retirement planning, the IORP scheme being only one element of it. Finally, information requirements contribute to trust in the pension sector, in this case specifically in IORPs.'

Source: EIOPA's advice to European Commission

1.5.17   EIOPA proposed introducing six principles for reforming the disclosure regime:

1   Information should be provided in all phases of members' participation in the scheme, proportionally to the choices to be made.

2   Information should be: (i) correct, (ii) understandable and (iii) not misleading.

3   Information overload should be avoided.

4   Information has to make clear the risks to which they are exposed.

5   In the case of DB schemes, it should be made clear that any benefit adjustment mechanism (ie any possibility to reduce pension rights) should be part of the description of the risk-sharing mechanisms in place (ie which of the main stakeholders, such as members, beneficiaries, employers, bears the risk of a funding deficit). This will be less relevant in

the United Kingdom, where there are statutory restrictions on changing or reducing accrued rights.

6   The potential of digital devices in delivering and making available information efficiently and effectively should be taken into account.

Solvency standards (Pillar I): postponed but not forgotten

1.5.18   There was widespread criticism from across the pensions industry and public opposition from the UK, Netherlands, Germany and Ireland to the original proposals for solvency standards. Despite this, Commissioner Barnier has confirmed that solvency rules for pension funds remain an 'open issue', declaring that 'we must face up to the weaknesses in some occupational pension funds'.

1.5.19   In February 2013, Pensions Europe, a representative of national associations of pension funds, advised the Commission to shift the focus of its proposals towards governance and disclosure requirements.[34] The European Parliament's Committee on economic and monetary affairs similarly stated that it is not convinced that Europe-wide requirements concerning own capital or balance-sheet valuation would be appropriate.[35] Criticisms of Pillar I include:

- It is unworkable, as security and adjustment mechanisms cannot be valued on a consistent basis with balance sheet items with a current value, and are particularly sensitive to the assumptions based on current economic conditions.

- It does not appreciate the difficulty of valuing a sponsor covenant.

- Implementing the holistic balance sheet would be a complex and costly exercise, and could lead to increased labour costs.

- The introduction of explicit valuations could increase the level of the deficits reported by IORPs and the onus on employers to make up the shortfall in funding, which would divert capital and encourage the closure of further DB schemes in favour of defined contribution schemes.

- Insurers are not an appropriate comparator for pension funds.

- The introduction of assumption-driven capital requirements might affect the strategic asset allocation of IORPs and discourage investment in long-term financing.

---

34   PensionsEurope, 'Position Paper on the Quantitative Impact Study (QIS) on IORPs' (11 February 2013).

35   European Parliament, 'Opinion of the Committee on Economic and Monetary Affairs for the Committee on Employment and Social Affairs on an Agenda for Adequate, Safe and Sustainable Pensions' (27 February 2013), para 34.

1.5.19 *Retirement benefit arrangements in the UK*

• The possible requirement to use a risk-free discount rate (such as gilts flat) is inconsistent with UK governmental policy.

1.5.20 These concerns were reinforced in April 2013 when EIOPA published the preliminary results of its quantitative impact study (QIS) on the effects of applying the 'holistic balance sheet' approach to pension funds (see below).[36] The QIS was conducted in autumn 2012 in eight European countries: Belgium, Germany, Ireland, Netherlands, Norway, Portugal, Sweden and the United Kingdom. The results estimated that pension funds in the United Kingdom would have a deficit of 527 billion Euros under the new solvency regime (an increase from what has been estimated to be 350 billion Euros under the current regime).

Holistic balance sheet

The holistic balance sheet would require IORPs to produce valuations that, in addition to stating actual assets and liabilities, would take into account various adjustment mechanisms (such as conditional indexation and benefit reductions) and, in a major departure from current UK practice, count as assets security mechanisms, sponsor support and pension guarantee schemes. It would also be used to assess whether IORPs have met two new sets of minimum and solvency capital requirements, and to set further restrictions on the discount rate to be used when calculating a best estimate of an IORP's liabilities.

---

36 EIOPA, 'QIS on IORPs: Preliminary Results for the European Commission' (9 April 2013)

Chapter 2

Scheme Funding

2.1 Scheme-specific funding requirements – *Pensions Act 2004, Part 3*

Summary

The Pensions Act 2004 includes the UK's scheme specific funding (SSF) regime. This sets out the framework for deciding how employers must fund their defined benefit occupational pension schemes.

The deficit shown in the employer's accounts calculated using accounting standards can differ significantly from that calculated under the SSF regime.

This section outlines the regime's requirements and pitfalls.

Introduction

2.1.1   *Part 3* of the *Pensions Act 2004* and the *Occupational Pension Schemes (Scheme Funding) Regulations 2005* (the Scheme Funding Regulations) set out a framework for deciding how employers must fund their defined-benefit (DB) occupational pension schemes on an ongoing basis – this is the scheme specific funding regime (SSF). There is also a code of practice and guidance provided by the Pensions Regulator.

SSF contrasted with company accounts

2.1.2   It is important for companies and pension scheme trustees to be familiar with the SSF regime if they are to understand a company's ongoing cash obligation to fund its pension scheme. The pension liability in the company accounts may not be a good guide. Depending on the spread between the SSF discount rate and the accounting discount rate (based on gilts and AA corporate bonds), the pension scheme deficit that is disclosed in the corporate accounts (ie measured on an FRS17/IAS19 accounting basis) may differ (sometimes significantly) from the deficit measured on an SSF basis.

Other factors may also cause the FRS17 or IAS19 calculation to show a different deficit from that measured on a SSF basis. For example, companies' financial accounts and the SSF regime may use different standards when predicting a pension scheme member's life expectancy – pension scheme trustees are required to make 'prudent' assumptions for SSF but the accounting standard looks for a 'best estimate'.

Which schemes are excluded from the SSF regime?

2.1.3   Certain occupational schemes are excluded from the SSF regime, including those that provide only money purchase benefits (and insured death benefits), non-tax registered schemes with fewer than 100 members, schemes with fewer than two members and schemes (or a section of a scheme) being wound up.

Key features of the SSF regime – Part 3, Pensions Act 2004

Statutory funding objective – s 222

2.1.4   Every DB scheme is subject to a statutory funding objective (SFO): it must have sufficient and appropriate assets to cover its 'technical provisions'. This is the term used in the EU IORP Directive to mean, broadly, the amount of assets a scheme needs to hold now, on the basis of the actuarial methods and assumptions used, to pay its accrued benefits as they fall due in the future.

The Scheme Funding Regulations give more detail on how a scheme's technical provisions are to be calculated. Trustees must determine the actuarial methods and assumptions to be used and usually agree these with the employers (see below) after obtaining advice from the scheme actuary. The Scheme Funding Regulations provide that:

- an accrued benefits funding method must be used (described in TPR's code of practice – see later);

- in calculating the technical provisions the trustees must take into account the actuary's estimate of the scheme's solvency on a buy-out basis and act in accordance with a set of defined principles; and

- the principles require a large degree of 'prudence' to be used in, for example, choosing the actuarial and mortality assumptions and the discount rates.

Prudence

Unhelpfully, the legislation does not define 'prudence'.

However, the Pensions Regulator (TPR), has commented that it:

'interpret[s] prudence as taking a margin on the cautious side of a best estimate (or expected value) ... However, whilst each assumption must be chosen prudently, [TPR] take[s] the view that an appropriate overall level of prudence in the technical provisions should be the paramount objective. Consequently we accept that the degree of prudence adopted could differ between assumptions in order to achieve a target level of prudence in the technical provisions as a whole. Indeed, in the extreme, for some less key assumptions it might be appropriate to assume best estimate, as long as overall technical provisions are adequately prudent.'

Source: TPR's guidance on mortality assumptions (September 2008, as subsequently updated).

The trustees must usually agree the actuarial methods and assumptions with the employers. The assumptions that are used can significantly affect the valuation of the scheme's assets and liabilities and, therefore, the employer's ongoing obligation to fund the scheme. In particular, assumptions about future returns on equities and bonds can be subjective and there may be scope for discussion between the employer and trustees. Similarly, employers with large schemes may consider investigating the mortality experience within their own scheme (rather than a more generic table) if they are concerned about the longevity assumptions that the trustees may adopt.

In addition to the SFO, some pension scheme trustees adopt a separate (and often more demanding) subsidiary funding objective. For example, the trustees' subsidiary objective may be for the scheme to be funded to a level that allows them to pay out benefits under the scheme rules without further support from the employer. How close the employer is to meeting this subsidiary funding objective may also influence the decisions that the trustees make under the SSF regime.

Statement of funding principles – s 223

2.1.5   Within 15 months of each valuation date under the SSF regime, the trustees should aim to prepare (and usually agree with the employers) a statement of funding principles (SFP). This is the written statement of their policy for ensuring that the SFO is met. It also defines the period within which any failure to meet it is to be remedied.

The statement must record the methods and assumptions used in calculating the scheme's technical provisions.

TPR 'believe[s] that, in order to comply with the spirit of the legislation and best practice as far as the regulator is concerned, the statement should include an explanation of the trustees' reasoning behind the assumptions chosen' (Scheme funding Q&As, March 2010).

Actuarial valuations and reports – s 224

2.1.6   Actuarial valuations must be prepared at least every three years. They must be based on a funding approach consistent with the strategy set out in the scheme's SFP and annual reports.

The Scheme Funding Regulations provide that actuarial valuations must contain the actuary's certification of the calculation of the technical provisions and his or her estimate of the scheme's solvency.

In addition to triennial valuations, the trustees must provide annual actuarial reports giving an update in each of the intervening years between valuations. Following each actuarial valuation or report, members and beneficiaries must be sent a summary funding statement.

Actuarial valuations should generally be in place within 15 months of their effective date and reports must be in place within 12 months of their effective date. The effective dates are the dates at which the information in the valuation and reports are referenced (ie the date given on the report, which is the date at which the figures are correct).

Recovery plan – s 226

2.1.7   If the valuation shows that the SFO is not met, the trustees must put in place (usually in agreement with the employers) a recovery plan, setting out the period over which the deficit is to be remedied. A copy of each recovery plan must be sent to TPR. These should be in place within 15 months of the actuarial valuation's effective date.

The employer needs to be aware that the trustees will often be looking to clear the deficit as quickly as the employer can reasonably afford. This is because TPR wants trustees to consider carefully the periods over which deficits are paid off. However, the trustees may be willing to accept a longer period or negotiate on the pattern of contributions in certain circumstances.

TPR's code of practice ('Funding Defined Benefits') includes some useful points for the trustees to take into account when considering the structure of a recovery plan (eg a shorter recovery period is likely to be appropriate if most of the members are already receiving a pension or if there may be difficulty in pursuing an overseas employer).

Trustees and employers can renegotiate a recovery plan if there is a change in circumstances. If, for example, the employer's financial circumstances worsen the trustees may agree to revise and restructure an existing recovery plan (see TPR's statements from February 2009 and February 2008 on its website for more information).

The opposite is also true; if the employer's financial circumstances improve (eg because it carries out a successful rights issue) the trustees may ask to revise the recovery plan on the basis that the employer can now reasonably afford to pay more to the scheme.

Schedules of contributions – s 227

2.1.8   Schedules of contributions for five-year periods (or the length of the recovery plan, if longer) should be in place within 15 months of the actuarial valuation's effective date. The code of practice makes recommendations on how to structure the schedule in the interests of clarity and on certain items that need not be included, provided an explanatory note appears (eg professional fees met directly by the employer). It specifically recommends that the Pension Protection Fund (PPF) levy should be treated as an annual expense item – and if it forms part of the employer's overall contribution rate a note to this effect should be included, indicating the assumed annual amount of the levy.

What happens if the funding documentation is not in place within the 15-month deadline?

2.1.9   Notice must be given to the Pensions Regulator, which then has power to decide on the relevant documents – see *TPR and regulation of scheme funding,* **2.2** below. The trustees may be liable to a civil penalty if they have not taken all reasonable steps to comply with this time limit – eg *Pensions Act 2004, s 227(8)* – see *Penalties,* **2.3.5** below. In practice TPR usually stands back if it looks as if the parties are moving towards being able to agree the documents.

Is employer agreement or consultation needed?

2.1.10 The *Pensions Act 2004* and the Scheme Funding Regulations provide that the trustees must generally agree with the employer the SFO, the SFP, the recovery plan and the schedule of contributions – *s 229*.

But this requirement for employer consent does not apply if the scheme trust deed gives the trustees unilateral power to determine the employer contribution rate (but see **2.1.13** below) and does not give the employer power to suspend contributions. In those cases, the trustees must instead consult the employer about each of these matters. The requirement for agreement with the employer still applies if, for example, it is currently the scheme actuary who fixes the employer contribution rate or if employers have the power to suspend their contribution obligation under the deed.

Where the SSF regime requires trustees to agree the funding rate with the employer, but they fail to reach agreement, the matter must be referred to TPR, which has the power to give directions, including imposing a schedule of contributions for the scheme – *s 231* and **2.2** below.

To determine how the SSF regime will affect the balance of power, employers and trustees should look at the funding rules in their governing trust documentation. A summary of the position is set out in TPR's code of practice: see the table.

Employer agreement and consultation	
Scheme rules	*Effect of legislation*
Trustees have, unrestrained by conditions, the power to determine the contribution rate and no other person has the power to reduce or suspend contributions.	Trustees are required to consult the employer but the employer's agreement is not required (*paras 9(1)–(3) of Sch 2*). The code of practice recommends, however, that the trustees should seek to obtain the employer's agreement.
Trustees have, subject to conditions, the power to determine the contribution rate and no other person has the power to reduce or suspend contributions.	If the conditions are satisfied, trustees are required to consult the employer but the employer's agreement is not required (*paras 9(1)* to *9 (4) of Sch 2*). The code of practice recommends, however, that the trustees should seek to obtain the employer's agreement.

Employer agreement and consultation	
Scheme rules	*Effect of legislation*
The contribution rate is determined by, or on the advice of, a person other than the trustees or the employer (usually the actuary).	Trustees must obtain the employer's agreement. They must take into account the other person's recommendations on the method and assumptions for calculating the technical provisions and on the preparation of any recovery plan (*regs 5(3)(b)* and *8(2)(e)*); TPR must also take into account this other person's recommendations when exercising any of its *Part 3* powers: see *s 231(2)* and *reg 14(1)*.

Source: TPR code of practice 03.

Code of practice

2.1.11   TPR's code of practice 03 summarises the requirements of the Scheme Funding Regulations and cross-refers to other codes of practice (eg on notifiable events) where appropriate. It introduces a system of symbols, or flags, to indicate where the principle being set out is varied in certain cases (eg for cross-border schemes or schemes with fewer than 100 members).

The code of practice recommends that the trustees put in place an action plan for the valuation process, taking into account all the steps that will need to be taken and the dates for completing each step. It also emphasises the importance of record keeping, especially in relation to decisions made, and of employers and trustees providing each other with information and keeping an open dialogue.

The legislation contains numerous references to steps being taken within 'a reasonable period'. The code gives guidance on what constitutes a reasonable period (eg a recovery plan should be sent to TPR within ten working days, as should a report to TPR that the trustees and the employer have failed to reach agreement where required).

2.1.12 *Scheme Funding*

Using the employer's assets to plug the deficit

2.1.12 Many employers continue to seek alternatives to the traditional method of using cash to fund the pension scheme. As a result, contingent assets – for example, giving the trustees security over the employer's property or a guarantee from a group company, or paying contributions into an escrow arrangement (rather than directly into the scheme) – are becoming more prevalent. Such a solution can help reassure the trustees that members' benefits are secure without diverting cash from the business operations or trapping surplus cash within the scheme (see *Avoiding a blocked surplus?* **2.5.12** below). TPR and the PPF also recognise that contingent assets can improve the security of members' benefits, and certain types of contingent assets (eg guarantees) will have the further benefit of reducing the PPF levy for the scheme.

Does the SSF framework set out the maximum funding that the trustees can demand?

2.1.13 In two cases, *British Vita*[1] (2007) and *Marine Pilots*[2] (2010), Mr Justice Warren held that the SSF regime operates alongside the scheme rules rather than replacing them. The effect of these judgments appears to be that the SSF regime sets a minimum standard for funding requirements. To the extent the rules allow for provision less than this minimum standard, they are overridden by the SSF regime. However, the SSF regime does not set a maximum cap that the trustees can recover from the employer. So, for example, the trustees may be able to seek additional contributions under the scheme rules even if the trustees and employer have already agreed and put in place a schedule of contributions under the SSF legislative regime.

Warren J in *Marine Pilots* suggested that the scheme rules would also continue to be relevant even if TPR used its SSF powers to impose the schedule of contributions. However, there has been no formal ruling on this point.

The SSF and corporate transactions

2.1.14 Depending on the balance of power between trustees and employers, scheme funding negotiations can complicate or, at worst, scupper a transaction. For example, in a bid situation the trustees may be concerned about the bidder's commitment to funding the pension scheme deficit. To mitigate against this,

---

1   *British Vita Unlimited v British Vita Pension Fund Trustees Ltd* [2007] EWHC 953 (Ch), [2008] 1 All ER 37 (Warren J).
2   *PNPF Trust Co Ltd v Taylor* [2010] EWHC 1573 (Ch) (Warren J).

trustees may, depending on their powers under the rules, demand that the deficit be paid in full immediately or seek to increase the employer's contributions to the scheme. This may act as a 'poison pill' during a proposed takeover.

Informing the trustees early on about a proposed transaction, and its effects on the pension scheme deficit, may help keep trustees 'onside' in future funding negotiations and avoid action that threatens a transaction.

Furthermore, employers have a legal duty to inform trustees of material events in some circumstances. For more information see *When should employers disclose a proposed transaction to trustees or to the Pensions Regulator,* **13.4**.

When sharing information with the trustees, it can be helpful to put a confidentiality agreement in place.

Equally it may be helpful for a company that is taking over the employer to discuss, with the trustees, how it intends to deal with the scheme. Before Kraft's takeover of Cadbury in 2010, the Cadbury pension scheme trustees were reported as stating that they were seeking 'further discussions with Kraft, so they and their advisers can assess how the long-term covenant will be affected, the effect on the deficit and therefore what remedies trustees will be seeking from Kraft'.

Conflicts of interest

2.1.15   If an employer's director or employee is also a trustee then potential conflicts of interest can arise during funding discussions. Failure to address conflicts can lead to conflicted trustees breaching the fiduciary duties they owe to both the employer and the scheme. TPR may also use its powers if conflicts are not dealt with – for example, it may replace the trustees with independent trustees. In the case of *DP Dental Laboratory Retirement Benefit Scheme* (2009), TPR cited the failure to deal with conflicts in funding negotiations as a reason for appointing independent trustees. Clearly, if TPR replaces the trustees this may disrupt a transaction because parties may have to wait for TPR's regulatory process to finish and the employer may need to start fresh negotiations once the new trustees are in place.

There are a number of strategies that can be used to manage conflicts. For example, a trustee can exclude himself from the trustee board's decision-making process. For more information see:

- *Conflicts of interest: the Pensions Regulator's guidance,* **12.1**; and

- *Should the finance director also be a pension trustee?,* **12.2**.

Dealing with conflicts early on can also avoid negative publicity. For example, in the BA-Iberia merger, some publicity surrounded the perceived conflict that

2.1.15 *Scheme Funding*

arose because of Roger Maynard's position as trustee chairman and his other appointments in BA and Iberia. Roger Maynard was reported as having resigned as trustee chairman in December 2009.

Practical steps for SSF

2.1.16 Employers and trustees should examine their trust deed and rules to check the current balance of power.

They should also be aware of key dates – for example, the next triennial valuation – and plan how to manage the process.

Multi-employer schemes

2.1.17 Multi-employer schemes should consider putting in place arrangements to nominate one employer to act for the others (eg on consultation and agreement) – see *Multi-employer pension schemes: giving authority to the principal company,* **10.3**.

Section 75 and moral hazard

2.1.18 Although understanding the SSF regime is important, this only sets out a company's ongoing pensions liability.

On the occurrence of certain events, in particular if only one employer ceases to employ active members in a multi-employer pension scheme, a debt is triggered under *Pensions Act 1995, s 75*. Broadly, if this debt is triggered, the employer (or former employer) is required to pay its share of the debt as a lump sum rather than according to the schedule of contributions or recovery plan. Furthermore, the scheme deficit that the employer is liable for will be measured on a buy-out basis. The buy-out basis often reveals a much larger deficit than that measured on an SSF or IAS 19/FRS 17 accounting basis. For more information see *Multi-employer pension schemes and section 75 debts,* **3.2.**

TPR can also use its 'moral hazard' powers to make an employer (or connected or associated third party) make a contribution to, or put financial support in place for, the scheme even if this is over and above what has been agreed in the schedule of contributions or recovery plan. For more information see *TPR: Moral Hazard Powers: Extracting pension scheme funding from third parties,* **4.1**

2.1.19 In October 2013, the Pensions Regulator issued a statement about 'Double Counting'. In this statement TPR expressed concerns about what it considers to be attempts by some trustees and employers to 'double count' payments made under the schedule of contributions as also satisfying *section 75* debt obligations. TPR stated that it considered that in some circumstances such arrangements could unduly fetter the discretion of trustees on funding and risk causing the scheme to be ineligible to enter the Pension Protection Fund (as being an agreement to reduce the *s 75* debt and so triggering *reg 2(2) of the PPF Entry Rules Regulations* – see **5.1.2** below).

The TPR statement expressly states that it does not provide a definitive interpretation of the law and that trustees should seek their own legal advice.

The TPR statement does not deal with a situation where (say) the schedule of contributions expressly provides that future contributions by the remaining employers are to be reduced to reflect a *s 75* payment that has been made by a departing employer.

Such an arrangement seems clearly not to fall foul of the concerns expressed by TPR in its statement (it does not restrict the ability of the trustees to review the schedule of contributions in the light of the exit, nor does it cancel or waive the *s 75* debt). In practice trustees and employers may still include such a provision in the schedule of contributions and recover plan in suitable cases eg where it deals with the potential exit of a small employer in circumstances where a large employer (which is the primary support for the scheme) would remain (indeed the covenant supporting the scheme may improve). TPR may well make comments about such a provision when it reviews the funding arrangements, but it seems clear that in suitable cases such a provision can be supported.

Revision of existing funding plans etc

2.1.20   Once a schedule of contributions (and recovery plan) has been agreed and put in place it is binding on the employer. Amounts stated on the schedule as payable are treated as if a debt (see *Employer failure to pay pension contributions,* **2.3** below).

The schedule of contributions will be expressed to last for the longer of:

●   five years; or

●   the period shown in the recovery plan to become fully funded if longer.

(*Scheme Funding Regulations, reg 10(2)*)

The *Scheme Funding Regulations* also envisage that an existing recovery plan and schedule of contributions will be 'reviewed, and if necessary revised' within 15 months of the effective date of each later actuarial valuation (which must be at least every three years) – *regs 8(1) and 9(2)* of the *Scheme Funding Regulations.*

2.1.20 *Scheme Funding*

The trustees are also given a discretion to review and if necessary revise a recovery plan if they consider that there are reasons which may justify a variation to it. The Regulator's Code of Practice 03 ('Funding defined benefits') advises trustees (at para 137) that:

> 'Where trustees are advised that the impact of events on the funding level of the scheme is likely to be material, it will usually be appropriate to commission an early valuation and then review and if necessary revise any funding documents.'

In practice the trustees may be inclined to consider such a review if there has been (or there is the prospect of being) an event with the potential for a material adverse effect on the scheme (or the strength of an employer). This could apply if there is a corporate transaction – see *Pensions: when should employers disclose a proposed transaction to trustees or the Pensions Regulator,* **13.4**.

Any revision to the funding documents will be governed by the same principles as outlined above – ie usually requiring agreement between the trustees and the employers (or in default of agreement fixed by TPR – see **2.2**). The existing funding plans will remain in effect while new ones are being negotiated.

The legislation is not very clear on the process to be followed here on a subsequent set of funding documents. If, for example, the position of the fund has improved ahead of what was envisaged in the earlier valuation (eg investment returns have been greater than expected), then the employer may well look for a downward variation in the recovery plan and schedule of contributions. But there is no express requirement for the trustees to agree to this (although in practice it is to be expected that most would).

2.2 TPR and regulation of scheme funding

2.2.1

Summary

The Pensions Regulator has a general review role in relation to scheme funding. Broadly it has a specific ability to impose scheme funding provision where the trustees and the employer are unable to agree on scheme funding, however, in practice it is uncommon for the Pensions Regulator to impose its own provisions on the parties. The Pensions Regulator prefers instead to facilitate agreement between the trustees and the employer, ie to act as a 'referee and not a player'.

Even where trustees and employers reach agreement on ongoing valuations and funding, the Pensions Regulator will still review the position. It sits behind the trustees and considers what has been agreed.

TPR issued a statement in 2006 as to how it proposed to exercise its powers to regulate the funding of defined benefits. This was updated in September 2008.

This section looks at the approach outlined in the 2008 statement and notes how it differed from the consultation draft statement published in October 2005. It also looks at later TPR statements on funding, including those published in April 2012 and May 2013.

In 2006 the Pensions Regulator (TPR) finalised and published its statement 'How the Pensions Regulator will regulate the funding of defined benefits' (the TPR Statement). It was updated in September 2008 (the 2008 Statement).

This is available on its website at: http://www.thepensionsregulator.gov.uk/docs/funding-statement.pdf

It gives details on how TPR intends to monitor and investigate funding arrangements under the statutory funding regime for defined benefit occupational pension schemes. It is a revised version of the consultation draft statement which TPR issued on 31 October 2005, taking account of comments from respondents to the consultation.

The Statement adds another layer of guidance on top of TPR's Code of Practice No 3, *Funding Defined Benefits*, which came into force 15 February 2006. For background information on the *Pensions Act 2004* funding regime, which came

2.2.1 *Scheme Funding*

into force on 30 December 2005, see *Scheme funding requirements – Part 3, Pensions Act 2004,* **2.1** above.

TPR's general approach to scheme funding

2.2.2 TPR's statutory objectives include protecting the benefits of members of occupational schemes and reducing the risk of calls on the Pension Protection Fund (PPF) – *Pensions Act 2004, s 5*. It may intervene in schemes where the trustees have failed to comply with their duties and if the funding of their scheme poses a risk to those statutory objectives.[3]

However, TPR's aim is that trustees and employers should work together without TPR's involvement. If TPR does become involved, it will use its statutory powers of intervention only if it considers it cannot achieve an equally good outcome by informal means (eg requesting more information and allowing a reasonable time for recommended steps to be taken). However, 'Trustees should not assume that the absence of any immediate regulatory intervention means that they satisfy the requirements of *Part 3* of the *Pensions Act 2004* or have set sufficiently robust provisions to adequately protect their members' (2008 Statement, para 4.1.2).

The 2008 Statement made the point that TPR's long-term objective is to strengthen scheme funding through effective implementation of the new regime. Defined benefit (DB) schemes were required to implement the new regime for valuations with effective dates falling on or after 22 September 2005. TPR hoped that by the end of 2009 all DB schemes subject to *Part 3* would have completed valuations and that those with a shortfall will have agreed a recovery plan which takes into account:

- prudent assumptions for the technical provisions; and

- appropriate recognition of risks to members taking account of what is reasonably affordable for employers:

  'Our position is that the best means of delivering the members' benefits is usually for the scheme to have the continued support of a viable employer' (2008 Statement, para 3.18).

TPR's general approach is therefore based on the following guiding principles (2008 Statement, para 2.5):

---

3 The *Pensions Bill 2013* (introduced to Parliament on 9 May 2013 and published on 10 May 2013) includes a further statutory objective for TPR in relation to its scheme funding role to 'minimise any adverse impact on the sustainable growth of an employer.' See *Pensions Bill 2014: A new statutory objective for the Pensions Regulator,* **2.7** below.

- Protecting members.

- Scheme-specific approach, looking especially at:

  - the strength of the employer and its ability to eliminate shortfall; and

  - the scheme's maturity (eg a new scheme with a strong employer could look risky on paper but not be so in reality).

- Risk-based intervention: focusing on the schemes that pose the greatest risk to members' benefits and to the PPF.

- Proportionate: striking a balance between elimination of the shortfall and how quickly the employer can reasonably afford to eliminate it.

- Preventative: taking action where possible before risks materialise.

- Practicable given resources and information available to TPR.

- TPR will act 'as a referee, not a player'.

How TPR will identify schemes presenting the greatest risk

2.2.3   TPR notes that most DB schemes are likely to be underfunded, so it needs to prioritise those schemes that pose the greatest risk to its statutory objectives. It will identify these by means of triggers for intervention:

- technical provisions are not prudent;

- recovery plans are inappropriate; and

- non-agreement between trustees and employers.

TPR made it clear that the triggers are not targets; they are 'only component parts in our regulatory toolkit and not the standards against which we will measure DB pension schemes'. (The only reference in TPR's 2008 Statement to funding targets is that trustees of schemes still subject to the minimum funding requirement (MFR) should aim for funding targets higher than the MFR in the run-up to the first valuation under new regime.) The triggers will be kept under regular review.

How will TPR find out about schemes' funding levels?

2.2.4

- Reports under *Part 3* of the *Pensions Act 2004*, eg;

  - by trustees under *s 229* – failure to reach agreement on scheme funding; and

2.2.4 *Scheme Funding*

–   by actuaries unable to certify calculations of technical provisions or schedules of contributions.

●   Recovery plans submitted to TPR.

●   Notifiable event reports (*Pensions Act 2004, s 69*).

●   Scheme returns.

●   Requests for clearance.

●   Trustee requests for guidance on funding plan proposals.

●   Market intelligence.

Technical provisions trigger

2.2.5   A scheme's 'technical provisions' (the term taken from the EU Occupational Pensions Directive, Iorp) means, broadly, the amount of assets a scheme needs to hold now, on the basis of the actuarial methods and assumptions used, to pay its accrued benefits as they fall due.

TPR's primary focus will be to ensure that the scheme's technical provisions have been calculated using methods and assumptions which are prudent given the scheme's circumstances.

TPR will make an initial assessment by comparing the *s 179* (PPF risk-based levy valuation) and FRS17/IAS19 liabilities (IAS19 if available), regardless of which is higher.

It will then look at the strength of the employer covenant (including information from credit rating agencies) to assess if the trigger has come into operation.

The introduction of the technical provisions trigger represented a significant departure from the October 2005 consultation document, which instead referred to a funding target trigger and stated that TPR was likely to intervene if the funding level fell within 70 to 80% of full buyout (which it said was the *s 179* range). This was dropped. The later technical provisions trigger is less restrictive, and TPR is at pains to emphasise that neither *s 179* nor FRS17/IAS19 is a funding target. The revised approach involves looking at all the circumstances.

Recovery plan trigger

2.2.6   Under the *Pensions Act 2004* the recovery plan must set out the period over which the shortfall is to be met; this must be appropriate having regard to the nature and circumstances of the scheme. The code of practice states that 'trustees should aim for shortfall to be eliminated as quickly as employer can reasonably afford' – the future viability of the employer is important.

TPR's 2008 Statement notes that triggers include recovery plans with:

- a recovery period longer than ten years;

- a recovery plan that is significantly 'back-end loaded' (higher contributions towards the end of the period); and

- underlying assumptions, especially investment assumptions which, appear inappropriate/unrealistic/over-optimistic.

The period in the 'longer than ten years' trigger is not set in stone: TPR may also look at schemes where it believes that the employer can reasonably afford to pay off the shortfall more quickly, but in such cases it will focus its resources on schemes with weak or weakening employers. Furthermore, as noted in the code of practice, in some circumstances a shorter recovery period is likely to be appropriate (eg if most members are pensioners). Conversely longer periods may also be appropriate in some cases (see the 2012 Statements below).

Trustees and employers must show that they have taken:

- appropriate advice; and

- all available steps to minimise the risk of the funding position deteriorating further, that is to say:

    - the investment policy 'strikes an appropriate balance between any upside potential of riskier asset classes whilst containing any downside risk'; and

    - there is an appropriate balance between the cost of employer contributions going towards eliminating a shortfall and those going towards providing continued accrual of benefits.

If the employer is unable to pay contributions at the required level, TPR may require trustees and employers to consider modifying future accrual of benefits if they have not properly considered this option (see *PA 2004, s 229*).

It is important to note that the technical provisions and recovery plan triggers are not to be used in isolation: TPR will look at the interaction between them.

2.2.7 *Scheme Funding*

TPR's Annual Funding Statement 2012

2.2.7   In April 2012, TPR published its first annual funding statement[4] for trustees and employers of DB pension schemes (the 2012 Statement).

The 2012 Statement confirms that there are to be no changes to the current scheme-specific regime (contained in Pensions Act 2004). However, TPR rejected calls for allowances to reflect the unparalleled low yield on UK government gilts, instead advising trustees and employers that they should not assume current low gilt yields will return to 'normal' levels when reaching funding agreements.

While recognising the complicated nature of the current economic environment, TPR stated that it believed that the majority of schemes should be able to deal with ongoing deficits without making changes to existing recovery plans, or by 'modest' contribution increases or extensions to recovery periods. The key actions are summarised below:

●   Employers must ensure the pension scheme is treated in an equitable manner with other demands on available cash and explore any available flexibilities in the recovery plan where appropriate;

●   Trustees must ensure that scheme funding processes are completed on time and accurately, undertaking the employer covenant evaluation early in the process;

●   Trustees should also consider whether deficit reduction assumptions should rely on any strongly held views about future financial conditions and, if so, what contingency plans should be in place in case these expectations are not borne out in practice; and

●   Finally, pensions managers should ensure that all scheme data and documentation is in good order to facilitate the timely completion of valuation processes.

2.2.8   In an accompanying statement, 'Scenarios for scheme funding plans in the current economic conditions' (April 2012), TPR outlined various options for employers and trustees to consider where the pension scheme is faced with:

   (i)   a slight increase in deficit;

  (ii)   a greater increase in deficit; and

 (iii)   a low security scheme (ie with a struggling employer).

---

4   http://www.thepensionsregulator.gov.uk/docs/pension-scheme-funding-in-the-current-environment-statement-april-2012.pdf

Scenario	TPR statement	Options
1. A slight increase in deficit	*'Schemes faced with these circumstances will only need minor changes to their funding strategy from the last valuation.'*	• **Contribution increases**: – to maintain end date of previously agreed recovery plan – in line with the increase in dividends since the last valuation. • **Contingent assets** or making payments into an escrow arrangement. • **Additional action** – eg contribution increase if the employer covenant weakens.
2. A greater increase in deficit	*'Schemes in this position will require employer support (in the form of increased contributions or security) to be made tangible, in order to agree a reasonable recovery plan.'*	• **Maintaining the existing recovery plan length**: through contribution increases. OR • **Extension to the recovery plan**: underwritten by the property assets, as contingency in the event of employer insolvency. • **Further mitigation**: contingent contribution increases, or contingent assets.

Scenario	TPR statement	Options
3. A low security scheme	*'These types of schemes may have to consider increased risk in the scheme in the short term by factoring into their recovery plan assumptions about increases in the "return relative to gilts" (or by lengthening the recovery plan). We expect trustees to monitor their ongoing risks closely, and here in particular, the experience of these assumptions.'*	• Equitable treatment of interest payments and deficit repair contributions. • Interest on debt and pension scheme contributions reduced proportionately for a period to fund investment in the business. • Dividends not to be taken unless the next valuation shows an improved position. • Extension of the recovery plan. • Taking some account of gilt yield reversion, that is not matched in a fall in equity markets, in the recovery plan assumptions.

October 2012 Speech by TPR chairman

2.2.9   The chair of TPR, Michael O'Higgins, gave a speech[5] in October 2012 on funding issues. this includes various comments on the funding regime, including pointing out the flexibility of the provisions (in particular on the length of recovery plans). He commented on the need to avoid 'reckless prudence':

> 'The best support for a DB pension is a properly funded scheme supported by a strong employer. While we believe contributions should be made where they are affordable, we do not want trustees to be "recklessly prudent" in the valuation assumptions they make and in their negotiations with employers. There will be occasions when the right thing to do for the employer and the scheme will be to invest in

---

5   On TPR's website at: http://www.thepensionsregulator.gov.uk/press/michael-ohiggins-professional-pension-show-2012.aspx

the growth of the sponsoring company rather than making higher pension contributions.

Trustees can welcome this where it improves the employers' ability to fund the scheme over the longer term.'

2.2.10   On 5 December 2012, the UK Government announced that the Department for Work and Pensions (DWP) would consult on whether to permit smoothing asset values and the discount rates used to calculate scheme liabilities in valuations from 2013. The DWP also consulted on whether TPR should have a new statutory objective to consider the long-term affordability of deficit recovery plans to sponsoring employers.[6]

The Chancellor confirmed in the 2013 Budget that the government will not introduce any smoothing element for asset values, but that a new TPR statutory objective would be created. The new objective is contained in the Pensions Bill 2013 and currently states that TPR's new, additional objective is to 'to minimise any adverse impact on the sustainable growth of an employer' in relation to its scheme funding-related powers.

TPR's Annual Funding Statement 2013

2.2.11   In May 2013 TPR published its 2013 annual funding statement (2013 Statement) for trustees and employers of DB pension schemes.[7] The 2013 Statement builds on the key messages of the 2012 Statement.

In the press release accompanying the 2013 Statement, the Chair of TPR, Michael O'Higgins commented as follows:

'I want to see pension trustees agree long-term strategies with employers that protect the interests of retirement savers, whilst also enabling viable businesses to thrive and grow. We expect them to mitigate the risks to their scheme, but this does not require them to be overly prudent.'[8]

The following key themes can be drawn from the 2013 Statement:

• Trustees can use the flexibility available in setting discount rates, investment assumptions and recovery plans to adopt an approach that best suits the individual characteristics of their scheme and employer.

---

6   HM Treasury, Autumn Statement (December 2012) paragraph 1.137.
7   http://www.thepensionsregulator.gov.uk/docs/DB-annual-funding-statement-2013.pdf
8   http://www.thepensionsregulator.gov.uk/press/pn13–17.aspx

2.2.11 *Scheme Funding*

- The treatment of a pension scheme should be compared to that of other stakeholders, taking into account priority ranking, and continue to reflect the scheme's status as a credit to the employer.

- TPR encourages trustees to take an integrated approach to addressing covenant, investment and funding risks.

- TPR is moving away from setting triggers focused on individual items in assessing the funding risk of individual schemes, but is taking a broader approach in looking at a suite of risk indicators, including the following:

    - whether the recovery plan contributions and amount of investment risk appropriately reflects the relative strength of the employer and also the affordability of contributions;

    - any specific issues and concerns relating to deterioration in sponsor covenant strength or possible avoidance;

    - the shape of recovery plans including initial low levels of contributions;

    - the investment performance assumed over the life of the recovery plan; and

    - any significant issues that TPR had with previous valuation submissions.

TPR procedure

2.2.12 TPR will make a further assessment of the scheme's circumstances, to decide whether to intervene (informally or using statutory powers if necessary), including considering whether intervention is likely to protect the interests of the members and of the PPF.

Information likely to be requested is (among other things):

- management accounts;
    - employer's latest audited accounts, plus updated information, for example, budgets and forecasts, including projected cash flow;
    - latest statement of investment principles;
    - latest statement of funding principles;
    - latest actuarial valuation and any actuarial report; trustee minutes;
    - scheme rules; and
    - where available, any independent reports or advice to trustees on matters such as scheme investments, financial strength of employer and use of contingent assets.

Factors TPR is likely to consider include:

- whether the trustees have taken appropriate advice;

- whether the trustees have considered all appropriate factors, including the code of practice;

- the assumptions used;

- the circumstances of the scheme and the employer, especially the employer covenant;

- the steps taken by the employer/trustees to mitigate the funding risk (eg modification of future accrual); and

- any contingent assets accepted by the trustees.

TPR published in November 2010 guidance on the approach trustees are expected to take when considering the use of contingent assets in a scheme's funding strategy. This is part of their guidance on monitoring employers support.

See www. http://www.thepensionsregulator.gov.uk/guidance/monitoring-employer-support.aspx.

Special circumstances: additional considerations

2.2.13   Specific additional issues arise regarding certain types of scheme:

- employers subject to economic regulation (generally privatised industries):

  - effect of any periodic price review on the employer's ability to eliminate shortfall; and

  - franchise agreements (eg rail industry) – the outgoing franchisee will not necessarily be required to eliminate the shortfall before the end of the franchise term;

- multi-employer schemes:

  - whether industry-wide or for associated employers; and

  - whether investments are pooled or segregated;

- cross-border schemes:

  - requirement for full funding within two years means the recovery plan trigger cannot be used.

Non-agreement between trustees and employer

2.2.14 The PA 2004 funding regime requires trustees and employers to try to reach agreement within 15 months after the effective date of the actuarial valuation on a number of issues, including: method and assumptions for the calculation of:

- the technical provisions;
- the content of the statement of funding principles;
- content of any recovery plan; and
- content of the schedule of contributions.

If trustees and employer are unable to reach agreement on these funding issues within the statutory timeframe, trustees should show TPR that they have 'explored all reasonable avenues' (eg alternative dispute resolution (ADR), mediation) (see paragraph 8.2, 2008 Statement), and provide details of negotiations with the employer and of the reasons for non-agreement.

TPR may give limited additional time to:

- reach agreement on certain issues;
- explore additional actuarial calculations; and
- explore ADR.

If this still does not lead to agreement, TPR may decide to (2008 Statement, para 8.5):

- require a skilled person's report, eg from the actuary regarding the calculations of the technical provisions using any methods and assumptions TPR specifies;
- modify future accrual of benefits;
- issue a direction as to the calculation of the technical provisions, indicating the method and assumptions to be used;
- direct how a recovery plan is to be drawn up, including its length;
- impose a schedule of contributions;
- issue a freezing order (stopping future accrual) while considering whether to order a scheme wind-up; and
- order a scheme wind-up.

Contribution failure report

2.2.15   Trustees must report to TPR and to the scheme members where a contribution failure is likely to be materially significant to TPR in the exercise of its functions. The code of practice gives guidance on what is likely to be materially significant to TPR (para 163):

- the employer appears to be involved in fraudulent evasion of its obligation to pay members' pension deductions;

- there is reasonable cause to believe other dishonesty is involved;

- there is an immediate risk to members' benefits, for example, pensions in payment normally met by the employer contribution;

- contributions remain unpaid 90 days after the due date (unless a one-off or infrequent administrative error then discovered and corrected);

- the employer appears not to have adequate procedures or systems in place for the payment of contributions and not to be taking adequate steps to rectify this; or

- the trustees conclude, after discussions with the employer, that there is for any reason no early prospect of contribution underpayments being corrected.

TPR explains in its 2008 Statement (section 9) that it is likely to ask for an explanation from the employer. If it is not satisfied and intervenes, TPR may:

- issue an improvement notice regarding the unresolved procedural or system problems;

- impose a financial penalty on the employer if the improvement notice is ineffective or if the contribution failure appears to have been deliberate;

- recover unpaid contributions on behalf of the trustees if trustees are unable or unwilling to do it themselves;

- modify future accrual if the employer is unwilling or unable to pay contributions at the level required and the trustees and the employer are unable to agree themselves to such modification;

- issue a financial support direction if appropriate;

- impose a freezing order if the employer appears unable or unwilling to continue to pay contributions at the level required; or

- in extreme circumstances, order a scheme wind-up where the employer is unwilling or unable to pay adequate contributions.

TPR states that it can impose a financial penalty (ie a civil penalty) on the employer if the contribution failure appears to have been deliberate. This power

2.2.15 *Scheme Funding*

is set out in *s 228(4)(b)* of the *Pensions Act 2004* where the contribution failure is without reasonable excuse.

See *Employer failure to pay pension contributions*, **2.3** below.

2.3 Employer failure to pay DB pension contributions

2.3.1

Summary

This section looks at the consequences of employers not paying contributions to pension schemes due under a schedule of contributions or paying them late.

In particular it looks at the notification obligations that may arise and the sanctions that could be imposed on employers.

Schedule of contributions

2.3.2   Under the scheme specific funding regime contained in *Part 3* of the *Pensions Act 2004*, most defined benefit occupational pension schemes must maintain a schedule of contributions (see *Scheme specific funding requirements* **2.1**).

If an amount specified in the schedule of contributions (and recovery plan) is not paid on the due date, it is enforceable by the trustees as a debt. The trustees will have the usual remedies of an unsecured creditor (eg bring court proceedings or seek to wind up the employer). There may also be increased rights if the employer has granted security or there is a guarantee or other contingent asset in place.

The trustees will want to be able to demonstrate that they have taken reasonable steps to protect the scheme. Usually this will be to seek to enforce the debt unless there is a good reason not to (eg if they can be persuaded that recovery is likely to be greater out of a restructuring than it would be out of a normal enforcement).

Trustees are obliged to keep records of any action taken by them to recover any unpaid contributions (or any *s 75* debt) under *reg 11(2)* of the *2005 Scheme Funding Regulations*.

Scheme winding-up

2.3.3   The trustees may also have powers under the scheme trust deed and rules. For example, they may have a power to wind-up the scheme (and so trigger a *s 75* buy-out debt on the employer – see **3.1** below) if the employer

2.3.3   *Scheme Funding*

defaults in any of its obligations. The precise wording of the relevant rules will need to be considered.

It is quite common to find a provision allowing the trustees to wind up a scheme if the employer serves a notice saying that it will cease to contribute. Mere failure to pay seems unlikely to trigger this right. However, if there is a more general provision allowing the trustees to act if there is a deficit, this could be triggered if the employer fails to take action to secure the solvency of the scheme following a demand by the trustees to do so.

The scheme rules would need to be checked to see if they contain any partial winding-up provisions. These can be complex to operate.

Notifications

2.3.4   There are special notification rules applicable to a failure to pay under the statutory schedule of contributions.

If the trustees 'have reasonable cause to believe that the failure is likely to be of material significance in the exercise by the Pensions Regulator (TPR) of any of its functions', they are obliged to give notice of the failure:

- to TPR; and

- to all the members of the pension scheme;

within a reasonable period – *Pensions Act 2004, s 228(2)*.

TPR's Code of Practice 03 ('Funding defined benefits') includes some guidance on what is likely to be material (paragraphs 163 and 164). Leaving aside fraud, dishonesty or mistaken failure to pay, the guidance indicates that failure to pay is likely to be material if:

- there is an immediate risk to members' benefits;

- contributions remain unpaid for more than 90 days; or

- the trustees 'conclude, after discussions with the employer, that there is no early prospect of contribution underpayments being corrected, for example because of the financial circumstances of the employer or for any other reason'.

If the trustees decide that the failure is material and a report is necessary, the report must be made within a 'reasonable period'. The Regulator's Code of Practice suggests that:

74

- ten working days is reasonable for a report to the Regulator; and

- one month is reasonable in the case of reports to members.

Note that the obligation is for the trustees to make a report to all members. This will include active members (current employees), deferred members and pensioners.

If employee contributions under a schedule of contributions are not paid on time and this is of 'material significance', this gives TPR power to decide on the funding arrangements – *Pensions Act 2004, s 231(1)(g)*.

If there is in fact a failure to pay contributions the employer may feel it also wants to notify members (at least its current active employees) explaining the position.

The reporting obligation is on the trustees not on the employer. However, it may be argued that a failure by an employer to pay contributions due under the schedule of contributions, is also a breach of a duty arising under an enactment and so requires a report by the employer to TPR under *s 70* of the *Pensions Act 2004* – see, *Reporting breaches of the law*, **13.2**.

Penalties

2.3.5   The trustees can be subject to a civil penalty of up to £50,000 under *s 10* of the *Pensions Act 1995* if they fail to report to TPR and members in accordance with *s 228* of the *Pensions Act 2004*. If the trustee is a company then liability may also extend to directors of the trustee company (up to £5,000 maximum in respect of any one individual).

A civil penalty can also be levied by TPR on the employer if it fails 'without reasonable excuse' to make a payment due under the schedule of contributions. One circumstance that might justify non-payment is in a restructuring where there is a general standstill.

TPR actions following notification

2.3.6   TPR explains in section 9 (Contribution failure) of its Statement on Funding (see **2.1** above) that it is likely to ask for an explanation from the employer. If it is not satisfied and intervenes, TPR may:

- issue an improvement notice regarding the unresolved procedural or system problems;

- impose a financial penalty on the employer if the improvement notice is ineffective or if the contribution failure appears to have been deliberate;

- recover unpaid contributions on behalf of the trustees if trustees are unable or unwilling to do it themselves;

- modify future accrual if the employer is unwilling or unable to pay contributions at the level required and the trustees and the employer are unable to agree themselves to such modification;

- issue a financial support direction if appropriate (see *TPR Moral hazard powers*, **4.1**);

- impose a freezing order if the employer appears unable or unwilling to continue to pay contributions at the level required; or

- in extreme circumstances, order a scheme wind-up where the employer is unwilling or unable to pay adequate contributions.

Notifiable events

2.3.7   Separately from the notification requirements set out above, there is an obligation on an employer to notify TPR 'as soon as reasonably practicable' following a notifiable event in relation to the employer (*Pensions Act 2004, s 69* – see *Notifiable events*, **13.1**). The notifiable events include a decision that is intended to result in a debt (including a contingent debt) that is or may become due to the scheme not being paid in full. In some circumstances this could apply to a failure to pay contributions.

Failure to notify TPR could render the employer liable for a civil penalty (unless it has a reasonable excuse) – see **2.3.5** above.

Defined contribution schemes

2.3.8   An occupational pension scheme providing only money purchase benefits (or money purchase benefits plus defined benefits only on death) will not be subject to the scheme specific funding regime and so will not maintain a schedule of contributions – *s 221(1)(a)* of the *Pensions Act 2004*; and *reg 17* of the *Scheme Funding Regulations*.

However, most money purchase schemes must still prepare, maintain (and if necessary revise) a 'payment schedule'. Although a payment schedule must contain similar information to a schedule of contributions, unlike a schedule of contributions it does not need to be certified by the scheme actuary (*Pensions Act 1995, s 87*).

Personal pensions/stakeholder pensions: direct payment arrangements

2.3.9 Where there is a direct payment arrangement by employers to a personal pension or stakeholder pension scheme the provider must monitor the payment of contributions by or on behalf of the employer under the direct payment arrangements (*Pension Schemes Act 1993, s 111A*).

Similar notification requirements to those that apply to a failure to pay under a schedule of contributions apply to a failure to pay under a payment schedule or under direct payment arrangements.

TPR's Code of Practice 05 ('Reporting late payment of contributions to occupational money purchase schemes') and Code of Practice 06 ('Reporting late payment of contributions to personal pensions') state that late payments are likely to be considered as material where contributions remain unpaid 90 days after their due date (see paras 14 and 21 respectively).

Member contributions

2.3.10 An employer must pay to an occupational or personal pension scheme any contributions deducted from members' pay within 19 days of the end of the month in which the contributions are deducted (this is commonly referred to as the '19-day rule'). Contracted-out minimum payments (to arrangements contracted-out on a money purchase basis) need to be paid by the employer to the trustees within 14 days of the end of the tax month in which the liability arose (*Pensions Act 1995, s 49*; and *reg 32* of the *Contracting-out Regulations 1996*).

It is an offence under *s 49* of the *Pensions Act 1995* and *s 111A* of the *Pension Schemes Act 1993* for a person knowingly to be concerned in the fraudulent evasion of this duty by an employer.

An employer that fails to pay member contributions within the prescribed time may be subject to a civil penalty under *s 10* of the *Pensions Act 1995*.

Other contributions

2.3.11 The position on any other amounts payable (ie not covered by the schedule of contributions) depends on whether or not there is a legal obligation on the employer to pay (eg under the terms of the governing trust deed).

If there is a legal obligation, failure to pay on the due date is treated, effectively, as a loan by the trustees to the employer. Loans to an employer (or an associated employer) are usually illegal under *s 40* of the *Pensions Act 1995* (restriction on employer-related investments) – see *Employer-related investment limits*, **17.5**. The *s 40* prohibition does not apply if the amounts owing are due under the schedule of contributions or payment schedule (*reg 13(6)* of the *Investment Regulations 2005*).

Money purchase benefits

2.3.12   If contributions are being credited towards money purchase benefits, the member may lose out if they are paid or invested late.

The Pensions Ombudsman has held in at least three cases that late payment may be maladministration (even if the statutory time limits have been met). He found that there was maladministration (and so a case for compensation):

- in the case of Mr Hall [L00363], where there was an eight-day delay (from the date of receipt of cleared funds) in investing funds; and

- in the cases of Mr Lavender [J00119] and Mr Nuthall [G00543], where there was a delay in investing additional voluntary contributions.

2.4 Who is the employer?

Summary

It can be important to know which company (often within a group) is the 'employer' in relation to an occupational pension scheme. This is because:

- The rules of the scheme will usually limit accrual of benefits to employees of a participating employer. The rules will often impose obligations on participating employers.

- The pensions legislation applies to those entities which fall within the statutory definition of 'employer' – ie a person 'employing persons in the description of employment to which the scheme relates'.

Unfortunately, identifying an employer can be difficult, both:

- as a factual matter; and

- because interpreting the legislation can be difficult (there are three mutually inconsistent High Court decisions on this).

This section looks to identify the legal issues.

Scheme rules

2.4.1   The rules of a pension scheme usually require a participating employer to have executed a deed of participation (or adherence) agreeing to participate in the scheme and to comply with the scheme rules.[9]

2.4.2   They may also deal with what happens after a company ceases to be an employer or serves a notice withdrawing from the scheme. It is important to note that most of the cases mentioned below deal with industry-wide schemes involving many (non-associated) employers and involved schemes where there was no express power allowing an employer to withdraw.

---

9   A formal adherence was (broadly) required by the pre-2006 tax rules.

2.4.3 *Scheme Funding*

Scheme rules and former employers

2.4.3   Scheme rules can also impose liabilities on former employers. There have been a series of cases involving industry-wide pension schemes where the courts have confirmed that trustees can amend the scheme to impose continued funding liabilities on entities who adhered to the scheme in the past, even though they are no longer employers of any active members in the scheme.

2.4.4   These cases have generally involved multi-employer industry-wide pension schemes – those for marine pilots (PNPF) or merchant navy officers (MNOPF) or merchant navy ratings (MNRPF). These schemes are rather different from most other schemes in that they give a unilateral power of amendment to the trustee and have no express provision allowing an employer (or other participating entity) to withdraw.

The terms of the amendment power under the scheme is crucial here (as probably is the absence in the relevant schemes of a withdrawal provision).

2.4.5   In the *Pilots* case,[10] Warren J held that the terms of a scheme were wide enough to allow amendments to make various entities liable for a share of a deficit in scheme. In the *Stena* case[11] in 2011, the Court of Appeal followed *Pilots* and held that an amendment power was wide enough to allow an amendment to make a former employer liable to contribute further to the scheme.

2.4.6   In a 2005 case, *MNOPF Trustees Ltd v F T Everard & Sons Ltd*,[12] Patten J found that former employers who signed deeds of participation remained liable for contribution payments that were brought in by deed of amendment to deal with deficits that arose long after they ceased employing active members in the scheme. A similar result was reached with a former employer in a more recent Scottish case (also involving the MNOPF) in December 2010 – *Re Burton*.[13]

Implications of being a statutory employer[14]

2.4.7   The pensions legislation operates by applying to both:

---

10 *PNPF Trust Co Ltd v Taylor* [2010] EWHC 1573 (Ch), Warren J.
11 *Stena Line Ltd v Merchant Navy Ratings Pension Fund Trustees Ltd* [2011] EWCA Civ 543.
12 *MNOPF Trustees Ltd v F T Everard & Sons Ltd* [2005] EWHC 446 (Ch), Patten J.
13 *Re Burton* [2010] CSOH 174, Lord Drummond Young.
14 The July 2011 TPR statement uses the term 'statutory employer' to refer to any entity which could have a liability under the legislation – ie including former employers (where the legislation provides). We use the term 'statutory employer' just to cover those with in the definition in *Pensions Act 2004, s 318* and *Pensions Act 1995, s 124*.

- 'employers' (as defined in the legislation); and

- in many cases, 'former employers'.

The statutory definition of 'employer' in the pensions legislation can be quite difficult to apply. Generally it is defined as a person 'employing persons in the description[15] of employment to which the scheme relates'.[16]

2.4.8   Note that this does not expressly require the relevant entity to have entered into a deed of participation with the scheme (see 'Identifying the Employers' **2.4.18** below). A group entity that has employment relationships with scheme members may, for example, have failed to enter a deed of participation, but in some cases the scheme history and the employment relationship may mean that it could still be considered a statutory employer. Equally, not all entities that have formally signed a deed of participation will necessarily be statutory employers.

The cases so far provide that the definition does not limit a statutory employer to someone that currently employs one or more persons who is an 'active member' (ie accruing benefits) under the scheme.

2.4.9   For most purposes, the statutory employer is an employer (or former employer) of persons in employment related to the scheme. The statutory employer(s) will be the employer(s) legally responsible for:

- Paying contribution under scheme specific funding and meeting the scheme funding objective under *Part 3* of the *Pensions Act 2004*;

- paying the statutory *'section 75'* debt – triggered when an employer leaves a multi-employer scheme, on scheme wind up or an employer entering an insolvency process;

- triggering entry to a Pension Protection Fund assessment period (on employer insolvency).

For example understanding who are the statutory employers can be relevant in deciding whether or not a scheme is a multi-employer scheme for *section 75* purposes.

---

15 Some legislation used to say 'description *or category*' of employment, but the deletion of 'or category' seems not to make any difference in practice – see Warren J in *Pilots* at para [462].

16 *Section 318(1)(a)* of the *Pensions Act 2004, Pensions Act 1995, s 124* as extended by *regulation 9* of the *Occupational Pension Scheme (Employer Debt) Regulations 2005*, *regulation 2* and *paragraph 3* of *Schedule 2* to the *Occupational Pension Scheme (Scheme Funding) Regulations 2005*, and *regulation 1* of the *Pension Protection Fund (Entry Rules) Regulations 2005* (as amended, or under previous legislation applicable at the relevant time).

2.4.10   *Scheme Funding*

2.4.10   The identity of a statutory employer is also important for other reasons, including the ambit of TPR's moral hazard powers (*Pensions Act 2004*) and identifying the entities in which investment is caught by the limits on employer-related investment (*Pensions Act 1995, s 40* – see *Employer-related investment*, **17.5**).

TPR statement: Identifying the statutory employer

2.4.11   In a bid to promote safeguards to pension schemes, the Pensions Regulator (TPR) published a statement in July 2011: 'Identifying your statutory employer', setting out the importance of and way of doing so.[17]

2.4.12   In the statement, TPR sets out the legal responsibility of a statutory employer (or former employer) for meeting the scheme specific funding requirements of a defined benefit (DB) scheme and meeting a *section 75* debt, amongst others. If a scheme is unable to identify its statutory employer, it may not ultimately be eligible for PPF protection (as this depends on the statutory employer entering an insolvency process – see *the Pension Protection Fund*, **5.1**). This may result in the members being seriously disadvantaged.

2.4.13   TPR has advised trustees that they should act immediately in determining the statutory employer. From November 2011 onwards, trustees have been required to identify the statutory employers in the scheme return form sent to TPR.

TPR has also set-out the basic steps for how to identify the statutory employer in its statement, but emphasises that if the trustees:

> 'are not 100% sure of the position ... [they] need to take action by requesting information from employers such as employment records and historic documents which note any employer departures from the scheme'.

Failing this, TPR suggests that trustees should seek legal advice.

Identifying the employers

2.4.14   Broadly, there are two major issues here:

Factual: Identifying the actual employers (this can be difficult in a group with many employers).

---

17   This is on TPR's website athttp://www.thepensionsregulator.gov.uk/docs/identifying-your-statutory-employer-statement-july-2011.pdf

Legal: Interpreting the legal definitions of 'employer' and 'former employer' to see how this applies. For example:

- Do companies with eligible employees who could join the scheme, but not have no actual active members on the scheme, count as employers?

- If members have benefits that continue to be linked to continued service (eg salary linkage for past benefits?), are they treated as 'active members' for statutory purposes?

- Do any companies that have ceased to participate count still as an 'employer'?

Identifying the employers: factual issues

2.4.15   The broad definition of statutory employer could also catch any other entities that have a legal employment relationship with either active members of the scheme or other employees who are eligible to join the scheme – even if these entities have not entered into a formal deed of participation.

2.4.16   The employment contracts of active members of the scheme should therefore be reviewed in order to establish who their employer is and therefore whether there are any other statutory employers in respect of the scheme.

2.4.17   In some cases it may be difficult to identify which entity is the legal employer (eg an employee may have an employment contract with an entity that is a 'division' or a 'business' but which is not a legal entity, or records may be lost). If there is doubt as to the identity of the employer, the following information required in order to identify a statutory employer of a member of the scheme may include:

- employment records (including contract details, National Insurance records, payroll information);

- historic documents regarding employer participation and departures from the scheme;

- HMRC information, for example a list of employers which have been allocated ECON numbers in relation to a scheme; and

- past scheme accounts to indicate the likely scheme funding position at the time of historical departures, and whether payments of *section 75* debts were made to the scheme.[18]

---

18   Paragraph 16, TPR, 'Identifying your Statutory Employer'.

2.4.18   *Scheme Funding*

Identifying the employers: pensions legal issues

2.4.18   Once the factual issue (of who is actually the employer) has been resolved, the question arises as to whether or not a particular employer counts as a statutory employer (and whether any entity that was at one stage a statutory employer has now ceased to be one). To repeat, the statutory definition in the pensions legislation is generally is whether the entity is someone who is

> 'employing persons in the description of employment to which the scheme relates'.

2.4.19   This definition has been considered in three High Court cases over the past few years: *Hearn*,[19] *Cemex*[20] and *Pilots*.[21] Unfortunately the judges did not agree. The analysis below represents a view on the legislation in the light of these cases:

- An entity employing active members (who are currently accruing benefits under the scheme) will be an employer. Retaining death benefits probably does not make an employee an active member. An employee retaining benefits with salary linkage to current salary (but no extra service) probably does make the employee an active member (but this is untested).

- There is a consistent approach in these cases that a company can be (and remain) a statutory employer even after it has ceased to employ any active members in the scheme provided that it continues to employ persons who could become active members (*Cemex* and *Pilots*).

  - Such potential members can include persons who could join the scheme only if the trustees or employer consents (*Cemex* and *Pilots*). The limits of this approach are not clear.

- A company probably needs to employ one or more active members in order to be a statutory employer under the provisions for on-going funding in *Part 3* of the *Pensions Act 2004* (*Hearn,* but some doubts thrown on this in *Pilots*).

- If the company has ceased to employ anyone, it will have ceased to be a statutory employer (*Pilots* and *Hearn*) (although it can still remain liable as a 'former employer' – see below).

- Employees who are pensioners or deferred members of a scheme probably should be ignored for this purpose (*Pilots*, not following *Cemex*).

---

19   *Hearn v Dobson* [2008] EWHC 160 (Ch), Morgan J.
20   *Cemex UK Marine Ltd v MNOPF Trustees Ltd* [20091 EWHC 3258 (Ch), Peter Smith J.
21   *PNPF Trust Co Ltd v Taylor* [2010] EWHC 1573 (Ch), Warren J.

- The rules change for 'former employers' if a scheme becomes frozen (ie ceases to have any active members at all).

- In some areas – including in relation to the PPF and *section 75*, there are special rules potentially deeming former employers to remain 'employers'.

- The *section 75* rules changed from 6 April 2008, so that an employment-cessation event (ECE) occurs on or after that date only if an entity ceases to employ active members in the scheme. But there are transitional provisions[22] that can catch entities that remained statutory employers before that date (while ceasing to employ any active members).

Former employers

2.4.20 Some pensions legislation (in particular the debt on the employer in *section 75* and the Pensions Regulator's moral hazard powers) applies to former statutory employers as well as current statutory employers.

2.4.21 Generally an entity which is a statutory employer is often treated as remaining an employer for statutory purposes if:

- **The scheme becomes frozen** (ie no longer has any active members):

  In this case the last employers of active members before the scheme became frozen are treated as remaining employers for statutory purposes – eg scheme specific funding, debt on the employer (*section 75*), employer-related investment, PPF, Pensions Regulator powers.

- **The leaving employer fails to pay any relevant *section 75* debt**:

  In this case some of the regulations deem a company to remain an employer for statutory purposes until the *section 75* debt is actually paid (or a scheme apportionment arrangement agreed etc). this applies for *section 75* purposes and also PPF scheme entry purposes.

Scheme rules and former employers

2.4.22 Scheme rules can also apply to former employers. There have been a series of cases involving industry-wide pension schemes where the courts have confirmed that trustees can amend the scheme to impose continued funding liabilities on entities who adhered to the scheme in the past, even though they are no longer employers of any active members in the scheme – see above.

---

22 *Regs 2(3) and (4), the Occupational Pension Schemes (Employer Debt and Miscellaneous Amendment) Regulations 2008* (SI 2008/731).

Ceasing to be a statutory employer

2.4.23   An entity will only cease to be a statutory employer where:

(a)   it ceases to employ at least one or more persons who are active members in the scheme; and

(b)   it does not employ one or more persons who could become active members of the scheme (potentially even if consent from the trustee or employer to join is needed).[23]

2.4.24   It seems that an entity which ceases to have any employees who are active members of a scheme will cease to be a statutory employer if:

- it ceases to have any employees at all; or

- (in our view) it retains employees but expressly terminates its participation under the scheme (eg serves a notice of cessation)[24] ; or

- it retains employees but none are eligible to join the scheme – eg because there are pensioners or deferred members in the scheme[25] or (in our view) because the scheme is closed to new entrants (both DB and DC).

2.4.25   If a scheme is closed to new entrants,[26] the second limb of the test in the paragraph above should not (in our view) be an issue.

2.4.26   An entity which has ceased to be a statutory employer in relation to a scheme can still remain liable as a 'former employer' if there is an express provision in the relevant regulations. This applies for *section 75* and PPF purposes, but not (in our view) scheme specific funding purposes (*Hearn*).

A former employer could also retain liability (outside statute) under the terms of the specific scheme (depending on the relevant provisions) (see below).

Former employers and section 75

2.4.27   A former employer remains deemed to have liability as if an employer if it has not met one of:

---

23 *Cemex* and *Pilots*. These cases refer to the meaning of an 'employment-cessation event' for *section 75* purposes as it applied before 6 April 2008. The precise limits of this 'eligible to join with consent' expansion is difficult to see (it is not amplified in either decision) and in our view, is wrong. An entity ceasing to employ any active members may perhaps remain a statutory employer, but probably ceases to fall within the scheme specific funding provisions (*Hearn*).

24 This has not been tested in court but seems logical.

25 *Pilots*, not following *Cemex*.

26 If a section stayed open for DC entrants, the scheme would not count as a frozen scheme unless the DC section was completely separated from the DB sections.

- Conditions A to I in *regulation 9* of the *Employer Debt Regulations – s 75* purposes; or

- one of Conditions A to E in *regulation 1(5)* of the *PPF Entry Rules Regulations* – PPF entry purposes.

2.4.28 It is therefore necessary to identify whether former statutory employers have fully withdrawn from the scheme or owe any outstanding *section 75* debts. If no debt arose when the relevant entity ceased to be a statutory employer (ie before 2008 it ceased to employ active and potential members or after 2008 it ceased to employ active members), this would satisfy Conditions A or B of the *Employer Debt Regulations* and Condition D of the *PPF Entry Rules Regulations*.

2.4.29 The level of debt payable under *section 75* will depend upon when the ECE occurred – ie (before 6 April 2008) when the participating employer ceased to be a statutory employer in relation to the scheme:

(a) If this occurred before 2 September 2005,[27] the exit debt would have been calculated on a 'minimum funding requirement' (or MFR) basis.

(b) If this occurred on or after 2 September 2005 it must be calculated as a share of any deficit in the scheme calculating benefit liabilities on the buyout basis (ie the estimated cost of securing benefits by purchasing matching annuities with an insurer), which will be considerably greater.

2.4.30 In the case of employers exiting before 2 September 2005 it is more likely that a scheme was not have been in deficit on the MFR basis at the time that the relevant entities ceased to participate in the scheme (because the MFR test was easier to meet than the buy-out test). If that is right, no debt would have been triggered and so these entities would not now continue to be an employer for statutory purposes under the 'former employer' provisions. However, to prove this, it will be necessary to look at the funding position *on the relevant cessation date*, which may not be easy (eg absent scheme accounts).

2.4.31 This may be primarily a question of fact. If the records show that the relevant scheme was (say) substantially over the MFR level of funding at each relevant year end, can an estimate of the net assets and MFR level be made so that there is little doubt that this would still apply as at a cessation date?

2.4.32 Alternatively:

- Condition H of the Employer Debt Regulations would apply where the

---

27 See the *Occupational Pension Schemes (Employer Debt etc) (Amendment) Regulations 2005* (SI 2005/2224).

debt is not paid solely because the employer was not notified of it (and the amount of it) sufficiently in advance of the applicable time for it to be paid before that time; and

- Condition I of the Employer Debt Regulations and Condition D of the PPF Entry Rules Regulations would apply if the debt 'is unlikely to be recovered without disproportionate cost or within a reasonable time'.

Whether a 'reasonable time' has elapsed will depend upon when the debt is taken to arise – ie whether upon the date of the employee cessation event, or at the time of formal cessation as confirmed by an actuary's certificate.

2.4.33   We think it likely that because a debt arising over six years ago cannot now be enforced (under the *Limitation Act 1980*), absent fraud or concealment, Condition I (and Condition D) will therefore often apply for cessation over six years ago (ie before January 2006). But this is untested.

Allocation between employers of liability for employees

Section 75

2.4.34   In relation to *section 75* debts, the liabilities attributable to employment with any employer should be determined by the trustees or managers, after consulting the actuary and the relevant employer.

Employees should be attributed to an employer where liabilities to or in respect of that member arose as a result of pensionable service with that employer.

Where the trustees are unable to determine the liabilities attributable to an employer, the liabilities will be attributable to either the most recent employer, or attributable 'in a reasonable manner' to one or more employers (*Regulation 6(4)* of the *Employer Debt Regulations*).

PPF

2.4.35   Similarly, the PPF FAQs set out that for PPF purposes, as 'reasonable estimates' may be used 'where necessary'.[28] In particular, the guidance suggests that orphan members 'should be allocated between the remaining participating employers of the scheme in proportion to the number of non-orphan scheme members belonging to each participating employer.'

---

28   http://www.pensionprotectionfund.org.uk/FAQs/Pages/details.aspx?itemid=119&search=t& subjectid=14 (published Tuesday, 16 June 2009).

Defined contribution employers

2.4.36   Special statutory rules can apply if an entity has only ever participated in relation to defined contribution members of a scheme. See for example the Employer Debt Regulations.

Such an entity may not count as a statutory employer (but it may still do if it has previously employed members who were entitled to defined benefits).

2.4.37   Absent such an express statutory provision an employer participating for DC members only may still be incurring a funding liability for the DB section. For an example of this (before the legislation changed), see *Pitmans Trustees Ltd v Telecommunications Group plc*.[29]

---

29   [2004] EWHC 181 (Ch), Sir Andrew Morritt V-C.

2.5   **Surpluses and overfunding in pension schemes**

Summary

This section looks at the issues for an employer where its tax-registered occupational pension scheme becomes overfunded (or may become overfunded).

Once money has been paid into an occupational pension scheme, it's relatively difficult for there to be a refund back to the relevant employers. There is also a free-standing tax charge at 35%.

An employer's ability to make use of a surplus within an ongoing scheme (without any payment back) is limited. This will become more pressing as an issue if it become likely that the scheme could become overfunded.

Trustees also need to be aware of the potential issues as it could impact on an employer's willingness to fund at a particular rate.

Employers should consider the risk of overfunding and if mitigation measures should be taken to reduce the risk (eg pay less into the scheme, instead giving security outside the scheme) or to give more chance of being able to take advantage of a surplus (eg by reducing future contributions to a defined contribution section of the scheme).

Overfunding or surpluses

2.5.1   Occupational defined benefit pension schemes effectively envisage a particular level of benefits being paid in the future. The amount of funding in a scheme (the scheme's assets, ignoring any funding obligation on the employer) at any particular time and its ratio to the estimated ongoing value of the liabilities is obviously crucially dependent on the actuarial assumptions used in valuing the benefit liabilities. Asset values are commonly now an open market value. Crucial estimates or assumptions on liabilities include:

- rate of return on investments (or the discount rate);

- anticipated life expectancy;

- rate of salary increases or inflation; and

- proportion of members married or with children, etc.

All actuarial valuations are effectively estimates or projections of the capital value of anticipated future benefit liabilities. The only exception to this is when a scheme is wound-up and bought-out so that all the benefits are being secured with another provider (another pension scheme or insurance annuity policy).

2.5.2 A critical component in any actuarial valuation is the discount rate used – how are the anticipated future benefit payments discounted to a net current value? The larger the discount rate (or rate of return on investments), the smaller the net present value capital amount of the benefit liabilities and so more likely for there to be an actuarial 'surplus'.

This is a crucial issue when looking at actuarial valuations. Looking at the common valuation methods (see also **2.2** above), the following should be noted:

Valuation method	Discount rate
Company accounts (FRS 17/IAS 19)	AA corporate bonds
Scheme-specific funding	As agreed with trustees (usually) (NB: TPR says it is generally looking for more than FRS17)
PPF valuation (*section 179* – ongoing)	Buyout (see below) approximation – but only valuing PPF protected benefits
Buyout (*section 75*)	Insurance company discount rates (usually government gilts less a margin)

Therefore if a surplus is estimated, it may well only be transient. It could be affected by (say) a change in asset values or an increase in benefit liabilities (eg longevity or change in interest rates).

Surplus in company accounts

2.5.3 In recent years, the combination of:

- a reduction in yield on government bonds (gilts) (used commonly in assessing buyout rates, and, more commonly, recently, in relation to scheme-specific funding); and

- rising AA corporate bond yields,

have meant that in many cases a surplus can be shown in a sponsoring company's accounts (under the relevant accounting standards, FRS 17 or IAS 19) but that the valuation used by trustees when agreeing scheme-specific funding for an ongoing valuation (and also any *section 75* buyout valuation) still shows a significant deficit.

2.5.4 *Scheme Funding*

2.5.4   In these circumstances, a surplus on an accounting basis could still mean a deficit on the scheme-funding basis, so that there needs to be a recovery plan with deficit contributions and that the trustees are not likely to allow contribution holidays, etc.

2.5.5   A surplus on the accounting measure can still result in an increase in the company's net assets as shown in its accounts. Whether or not such a surplus is shown as an asset in the company's accounts can depend on the operation of an accounting interpretation, IFRIC 14.[30] This interpretation is difficult to analyse as a legal matter, (accounting advice is needed) but broadly IFRIC 14 states that the employer needs to have an unconditional right to use the surplus at some point during the life of the plan or on its wind-up for a surplus to be recognised in the employer's accounts.

Even if a surplus appears, it seems not to be a realised profit when calculating distributable reserves (a deficit is probably a realised loss).[31]

Surplus on the PPF basis

2.5.6   Surplus on the PPF basis can be helpful in that:

- it can reduce the risk-based PPF levy;

- it can mean that various events are no longer notifiable to the Pensions Regulator under the notifiable events regime (see **13.1** below);

- it can make it easier to agree corporate transactions with the Pensions Regulator or the trustees; and

- there are some (complicated) provisions allowing settlement or discharge of a *section 75* debt without prejudicing the scheme's ultimate eligibility to enter the PPF if needed. Notification to the PPF is required – see *reg 2(3)* of the *Pension Protection Fund* (*Entry Rules*) *Regulations 2005*.

Surplus on scheme-specific funding basis

2.5.7   Surplus on the scheme-specific funding basis (under *Part 3* of the *Pensions Act 2004*) may well be useful in that:

---

30 International Financial Reporting Interpretations Committee (IFRIC) issued an Interpretation, IFRIC 14, in July 2007 on 'IAS 19 – the limit on a defined benefit asset, minimum funding requirements and their interaction'.
31 See the ICAEW Technical Release: TECH50/04 (Guidance on the effect of FRS 17 'Retirement benefits' and IAS 19 'Employee benefits' on realised profits and losses) issued in November 2004 – see www.icaew.com

- there will be no need for a recovery plan (under scheme-specific funding);

- if there is no recovery plan, the other funding documents do not have to be provided to the Pensions Regulator under *s 226(6)* of the *Pensions Act 2004*, although they well be requested by TPR anyway – for example, as part of its annual return mechanics;

- it may mean that there is not a 'relevant deficit'. Various employer-related events (eg change of structure, return of capital) could (without a surplus) otherwise be potentially 'Type A' events (and so may involve considering whether clearance from the Pensions Regulator would be desirable). A surplus may mean that there is less need for clearance – see TPR's clearance guidance (June 2009) at para 49; and

- it may well be possible to agree with the trustees that any surplus can be used to offset ongoing contributions – for example, for future service benefits or, potentially, even to fund money purchase sections (see the *Barclays Bank* case discussed below).

Contribution reductions

2.5.8   The easiest way for employers to take advantage of a surplus in an occupational pension scheme was, in the past, to reduce future contributions (in particular, the cost of future service benefits). Such a course has been approved by the courts. For example, this has been held not to be contrary to:

- the main purpose of a scheme;

- a provision in a scheme prohibiting refunds to an employer; or

- any implied good faith duty.

On this, see the House of Lords in *National Grid v Mayes*,[32] where Lord Hoffmann held:

- 'There are only two ways of dealing with an actuarial surplus. You can pay more money out of the scheme or you can reduce the amount of money coming in.'

- A surplus in a scheme may also help in agreeing investment choices with trustees and may also encourage the employer towards funding towards a buyout target.

---

32   [2001] UKHL 20, [2001] 2 All ER 417, HL.

2.5.9   *Scheme Funding*

2.5.9   However, the increasing closing of schemes both to new members and future accrual of defined benefits can often mean that the ability of employers to use surpluses by meeting other contributions is getting more limited.

Such an offset would still usually be possible if the employer had included a defined contribution (DC or money purchase) arrangement within the same scheme as the defined benefit (DB) arrangement. Unless the rules of the scheme prohibit, then the contributions would otherwise be payable by the employer to the scheme for the DC members could be met by a reduction of surplus (in effect a transfer from the DB section to the DC section). It is preferable if such a cost transfer provision is allowed under the scheme's rules. Such a provision was upheld by Neuberger J in *Barclays Bank v Holmes*.[33] See also the determination of the Pensions Ombudsman (22 October 2004) in the *IBM case* (*K00516*).

Contribution rule

2.5.10   The terms of the scheme's contribution rule will be of importance. The trustees may look to strengthen the actuarial assumptions (with the result that any surplus is removed or reduced) to give greater security for members.

2.5.11   If contributions (and actuarial assumptions) are fixed at the discretion of the trustees (or perhaps the actuary), such an approach may be difficult for an employer to challenge legally. But, conversely, if the contributions and actuarial assumptions need to be agreed by the employer, then a contribution reduction approach may well be something the employer is able to insist on. Ultimately, *Part 3* of the *Pensions Act 2004* gives the Pensions Regulator power to break a funding deadlock (see **2.1** and **2.2** above).

Avoiding a blocked surplus?

2.5.12   In the absence of an ongoing funding obligation (DB or DC), then the primary method for an employer to obtain immediate value out of a surplus in an occupational pension scheme would be by a cash refund out of the scheme. However, the terms of the scheme may not allow this and pensions (and tax) legislation is not helpful here (see below).

2.5.13   In practice, it will often be better for employers (who look as though they may be getting towards a surplus) to consider reducing contributions to reduce the risk of 'overshooting': in effect trying to reduce deficit contributions

---

33   [2001] OPLR 37. See further discussion in *Surpluses and overfunding in pension schemes*, **2.5** below.

paid into the scheme (until they are needed) rather than ending up with a surplus that cannot be refunded (or can only be refunded with a tax charge).

Trustees may well be concerned about the impact on security for benefits under the scheme if such course is followed. One option can be for an employer to seek to negotiate with the trustees:

- the removal or cancellation of unhelpful protective provisions – for example, a provision in the scheme that provides for the trustee to be required (or have a discretion) to use a surplus on winding-up to augment benefits instead of repaying to the employers; or

- to agree that instead of contributions being made in to the scheme (where they would run the risk of being 'trapped'), security is instead given by the company – for example a contribution is paid into a separate account or fund over which a mortgage or charge is given to the trustees. TPR has recently suggested that this route should be considered where schemes are at or close to their funding targets and the trustees and employer consider that market changes and contributions may lead to surplus funding (para 15, TPR statement on *Pension scheme funding in the current environment*, April 2012 – see **2.2** above).

This would then help with any security concerns of the trustees. This practice is sometimes called an escrow account route, but the precise legal status of an escrow account can be unclear and using a trust can give rise to difficult tax consequences. A mortgage or charge is a more tax transparent and easier solution in many cases.

One issue for employers would be that payments into a mortgaged account or fund will generally not attract tax relief until such time as they are in fact paid in to the underlying registered pension scheme.

Surplus refunds

2.5.14   Once money has been paid into a tax-registered occupational pension scheme, it's relatively difficult for there to be a refund back to the relevant employers. There is also a free-standing tax charge at 35%.

The legal issues are considered further in **2.6** below.

2.6 Surplus refunds out of a pension scheme

Summary

This section looks at the issues for an employer where it is looking for a refund out of a tax-registered occupational pension scheme that has become overfunded (or may become overfunded).

Once money has been paid into an occupational pension scheme, it is relatively difficult for there to be a refund back to the relevant employers. The scheme will need to be overfunded on a buyout basis and trustee consent will be needed (if the scheme is not winding-up). There is also a free-standing tax charge at 35%.

Overfunding or surpluses

2.6.1   Section **2.5** above on *Surpluses and overfunding in pension schemes* looks at why surpluses can arise in defined benefit occupational pension schemes and ways in which employers can deal with the issue (for example, by contribution reductions or funding outside the scheme instead of into the scheme).

This section goes on to look at the issues if a surplus refund payment out of the scheme to the employer is envisaged.

Surplus refunds

2.6.2   The three main legal issues that need to be considered in relation to any potential for there to be a refund out of a pension scheme and back to an employer because of surplus in that scheme (ie by the actual payment of cash or assets rather than an offsetting against future contributions) are set out below.

- **The scheme deed and rules** – is such a refund allowed under the scheme deed and rules? If not can they be amended to permit a refund?

- **Pensions legislation** – pensions legislation imposes restrictions on refunds of surplus. In particular:

  - *section 37* of the *Pensions Act 1995* (as amended) deals with refunds of surplus from ongoing schemes; and

  - *section 76* of the *Pensions Act 1995* deals with refunds of surplus out of schemes in winding-up.

Generally the two sections impose notification obligations to the members and to the Pensions Regulator before any payment is made and (in the case of an ongoing scheme) only allow refunds where there is a surplus over the *section 75* buyout liability[34] (so that a surplus on scheme-specific funding or PPF alone would not qualify).

- **The tax position** – surplus refund payments out of a tax-authorised occupational pension scheme to an employer can be authorised payments under the *Finance Act 2004*. But various conditions have to be met (see below).

  In addition, there is a free-standing tax at 35% (this was reduced from 40% in May 2001) that has to be deducted at source by the pension trustees. This tax charge cannot be offset against other losses. If any payment to the employer doesn't qualify as an 'authorised surplus payment' then there can be further tax charges, including an authorised payments charge and an authorised payment surcharge (see below).

Trust deed and rules

2.6.3   Many occupational pension schemes include an express restriction on amendments to the scheme that would allow payments back to the employer. These were included historically to reinforce applications for tax-approved status for occupational pension schemes on the basis that the relevant scheme needed to be established under a 'irrevocable trust' and so that payments could not been seen as later reverting to the employer.

The attitude of the Inland Revenue to tax refunds changed over the years, particularly following the *Finance Act 1986*, which provided for a specific tax charge on schemes in surplus and on employer refunds.

2.6.4   However, case law is fairly clear that existing specific prohibitions in a scheme on refunds to an employer did not cease to apply merely because the tax practice changed (assuming that the specific wording did not itself refer to the tax rule) – see for example *Harwood–Smart v Caws*.[35] Removing a prohibition on refunds would often not be possible.

2.6.5   The Occupational Pensions Board (OPB) used (before its abolition) to have a power to amend schemes to override refund prohibitions, but this power was removed by the *Pensions Act 1995*.

---

34 The *Occupational Pension Schemes* (*Payments to Employer*) *Regulations 2005* (SI 2005/802), *reg 5(4)*.
35 [2000] OPLR 227.

2.6.6   *Scheme Funding*

2.6.6   Care needs to be taken even in relation to an existing refund provision where a prohibition on refunds is contained in the scheme's amendment power. The courts have tended to read restrictions in the amendment power across into general powers – see the House of Lords in *National Grid v Mayes*[36] and the Court of Appeal in the British Airways pensions case, *Stephens v Bell*.[37] Making a transfer to another scheme (without a restriction) may be for an improper purpose – see the decision of Knox J in *Hillsdown Holdings v Pensions Ombudsman*.[38]

2.6.7   Scheme rules would need to be examined closely to see whether (say) a provision envisaging a refund to employers on a winding-up of the scheme had actually properly been included over the years. If the prohibition on refunds had been in the original deeds, but the power to repay on winding-up had only been included later, then it may well be invalid.

2.6.8   Complex issues can arise in relation to obtaining member consent to changes or looking to a resulting trust where (say) a scheme is wound up, but no power is given to the trustees to increase benefits (*Air Jamaica v Charlton*).[39]

2.6.9   If a scheme is wound up, the terms of the winding-up would need to be considered carefully. Some schemes provide for any remaining surplus (after all benefits have been secured) to be repaid to the employers. But others give a discretion to the trustees to use any remaining surplus to increase benefits, with a refund to the employers only to the extent that the monies are not so used.

Discretion with trustees?

2.6.10   This can cause difficult issues for the trustees in deciding how to exercise their discretion in such cases. There is judicial guidance in *Thrells (1974) Pension Scheme v Lomas*[40] and *Alexander Forbes Trustee Services v Halliwell*.[41] It is clear that there is not an automatic presumption that trustees should use all surplus to give benefit improvements to members. Conversely there is no automatic presumption of repayment of surplus to employers.

2.6.11   Some schemes envisage that the employer needs to consent to any use of surplus for the benefit of members. This should be seen as giving a veto to the employer, but some recent cases have (somewhat oddly and in special

---

36   [2001] UKHL 20, [2001] 2 All ER 417.
37   [2002] EWCA Civ 672; [2002] OPLR 207.
38   [1997] 1 All ER 862.
39   [1999] 1 WLR 1399.
40   [1992] OPLR 22.
41   [2003] OPLR 355.

circumstances) overridden this requirement – *Bridge Trustees v Noel Penny (Turbines)*[42] and *Scully v Coley*.[43]

Modify the power?

2.6.12   It may be possible (depending on the scheme's amendment power) to agree with trustees (as part of funding arrangements) to modify the winding-up surplus provision to provide more clarity as to what would happen to any resulting surplus. The trustees would need to act for a proper purpose in agreeing a relevant change, but may think this is the right thing to do given that not doing it may otherwise mean that the employer is more reluctant to fund the scheme (because it's more worried about overshooting).

Tax rules

2.6.13   A surplus refund to an employer from a tax-registered pension scheme can be an authorised payment for tax purposes (under the *Finance Act 2004, s 177*). The payment needs to fall within the *Registered Pension Schemes (Authorised Surplus Payments) Regulations 2006*. These broadly state that the payment must satisfy the requirements in sections *37* or *76* of the *Pensions Act 1995* (see below). Certain other payments (eg on the death of a member or from schemes exempt from *ss 37* or *76*) are also allowed.

2.6.14   There is a free-standing tax at 35%,[44] which has to be deducted at source by the scheme administrator for tax purposes (usually the trustees) – *Finance Act 2004, s 207*. As stated above, this tax charge cannot be offset against other losses.

If any payment to the employer doesn't qualify as an 'authorised surplus payment' then there can be further tax charges, including an authorised payments charge and an authorised payment surcharge.

Pensions legislation

Section 37 – refunds from ongoing schemes

2.6.15   *Section 37* of the *Pensions Act 1995* (substituted from 6 April 2006 by the *Pensions Act 2004*) deals with when surplus refunds can be made out of an ongoing scheme.

---

42   [2008] EWHC 2054 (Ch).
43   [2009] UKPC 29.
44   This was reduced from 40% in May 2001.

2.6.15   *Scheme Funding*

The section overrides scheme rules to the effect that any surplus refund can only be made with the agreement on the trustees (even if the rules provide a unilateral power for the employer to pay surplus refunds). The section states:

- any surplus refund cannot exceed the amount of the surplus on a buyout basis;

- that actuarial advice and certificates must be given;

- the trustees must be satisfied that it's in the interest of the members that the proposal is exercised; and

- notices have been given to the members in advance.

2.6.16   The relevant regulations are the *Occupational Pension Schemes (Payment to Employers) Regulations 2006.*[45] They set out the relevant notification requirements both to members and to the Pensions Regulator. The regulations also deal with assessing how a refundable surplus can be calculated – they require the *section 75* insurance buyout methodology to be used.

2.6.17   If a refund is to be made under *section 37* (this is now pretty rare), a relevant resolution may need to be passed under the transitional provisions in *section 251* of the *Pensions Act 2004* (as amended by the *Pensions Act 2011*).

2.6.18   Where a scheme is winding-up, *s 37* of the *Pensions Act 1995* does not apply, but instead *s 76* of the *Pensions Act 1995* governs the position.

Some schemes are exempt from the requirements of both *s 37* and *s 76* (eg schemes that are small self-administered schemes or are not tax registered).

Limited price indexation repealed

2.6.19   The requirement (under the previous *section 37*) for pensions in payment to receive limited price indexation was in effect repealed with effect on and from 6 April 2006 by the *Pensions Act 2004* (substituting a new *section 37*). Accordingly there is no longer a requirement that limited price indexation be given to pensions before any surplus refund can be made.

Negotiation with trustees

2.6.20   In practice, given the need to obtain the consent of the trustees to any surplus payment, and the express requirement that any surplus refund must be in the members' interest, it was common for there to be a fair degree of

---

45   SI 2006/802.

negotiation with the trustees over a package. In effect agreement would be reached between the trustees and the employer for benefit improvements in exchange for the surplus refund payment.[46]

Section 76 – winding-up

2.6.21   *Section 76* (and the relevant regulations) deals with when payment can be made out of a scheme to the employer.

Unlike *section 37*, there is no requirement for trustee consent if this is not required under the terms of the scheme.

There remains an obligation to notify the Pensions Regulator and the members in advance of any payment.

It would seem that the reference to members here includes previous members who have been bought out as part of the winding-up (see the *Thrells* case, mentioned above).

---

46 For more on this see the article by David Pollard: *Pensions law and surpluses: a fair balance between employer and members?* (2003) 17 *Trust Law International* 2 and David Pollard *The Law of Pension Trusts* (2013, OUP), chapter 20.

2.7 Pensions Bill 2014: a new statutory objective for the Pensions Regulator

Summary

This section looks at the proposals for a new statutory objective for the Pensions Regulator (the Regulator), announced by the Chancellor of the Exchequer in the 2013 Budget.

It looks at:

– what the new objective involves;

– how it compares with the Regulator's existing objectives;

– the impact of the new objective on the Regulator, scheme members and scheme sponsors

– when the new objective will be enacted; and

– background information on the Regulator's powers.

What is the proposed new statutory objective?

2.7.1 The *Pensions Bill 2014* includes a proposed amendment to the objectives of the Pensions Regulator as set out in *section 5* of the *Pensions Act 2004*. The proposed change is to insert a new objective:

'in relation to the exercise of its functions under Part 3 only, to minimise any adverse impact on the sustainable growth of an employer'.

Part 3 of the *Pensions Act 2004* contains the provisions relating to the statutory scheme specific funding regime.

2.7.2 This change derives from the Budget statement on 20 March 2013, when the Chancellor of the Exchequer, George Osborne, announced that the government will propose legislation to give the Pensions Regulator a new additional statutory objective. The new objective was to be:

'to support scheme funding arrangements that are "compatible with sustainable growth for a sponsoring employer and fully consistent with the 2004 funding legislation".'

The Chancellor's statement read:

'The Government will provide the Pensions Regulator (TPR) with a new objective to support scheme funding arrangements that are compatible with sustainable growth for the sponsoring employer and fully consistent with the 2004 funding legislation. The precise wording of this new objective will be set out in legislation that the Department for Work and Pensions (DWP) will publish later in spring 2013. Implementation of the new objective will be subject to review after 6 months and TPR will revise its Code of Practice to reflect their forthcoming new objective as soon as possible in 2013.'

2.7.3   The Budget announcement followed the Department of Work and Pensions (DWP) call for evidence on this issue in January 2013.

The Minister for Pensions, Steve Webb said:

'The best guarantee of a pension scheme keeping its promises is to make sure that the sponsoring employer prospers. This new objective for the Pensions Regulator will help ensure that trustees and employers have the flexibility to come up with plans which deal with pension scheme deficits and benefit both scheme members and firms.'

The Regulator's existing objectives

2.7.4   The Regulator's current statutory objectives (in the *Pensions Act 2004*) focus on the protection of benefits under pension schemes and the protection of the Pension Protection Fund (PPF) against the risk of increased liabilities. This has generated comments that the regime does not allow for other critical economic issues to be balanced against these objectives.

The current objectives (*Pensions Act 2004, s 5*) are:

---

5 Regulator's objectives

(1)   The main objectives of the Regulator in exercising its functions are—

    (a)   to protect the benefits under occupational pension schemes of, or in respect of, members of such schemes,

    (b)   to protect the benefits under personal pension schemes of, or in respect of, members of such schemes within subsection (2),

    (c)   to reduce the risk of situations arising which may lead to compensation being payable from the Pension Protection Fund (see Part 2),

---

> (ca)   to maximise compliance with the duties under Chapter 1 of Part 1 (and the safeguards in sections 50 and 54) of the Pensions Act 2008 [*these are the auto-enrolment duties*], and
>
> (d)   to promote, and to improve understanding of, the good administration of work-based pension schemes.

The significance of the new objective

2.7.5   The aim of the new objective looks to be to encourage the Regulator to take a more balanced policy view of the costs of funding a pension scheme, weighing the interests of scheme members looking for security against the cost to the employer of achieving security. This may lead to an easing of funding pressure on defined benefit (DB) scheme sponsors, freeing up funds to channel into their businesses rather than into their pension deficits.

On the other hand, this new objective may cause a shift in the balance of power from scheme members to scheme sponsors. Indeed, DB scheme sponsors with large sums of money at stake may be more ready to attack or challenge the Regulator's decisions.

2.7.6   The Regulator may also need to take a different approach towards proposals towards which it has previously been hostile, such as pre-pack sales out of administrations. Moreover, it may lead to funds increasingly being diverted away from financing pension deficits. Larger deficits would potentially reduce some security for members and potentially increase the likelihood of schemes having to cut benefits and requiring assistance from the PPF.

Previous consultation

2.7.7   In the January 2013 call for evidence, the DWP stated:

In considering whether changes to the funding regime are appropriate, the Government needs to weigh up impacts on:

- Members – defined-benefit pension rights are obligations which cannot be altered once rights have accrued. The Government is committed to ensuring that members' interests are protected.

- Sponsoring employers – the best security for a defined-benefit pension scheme and its members is a properly-funded scheme backed by a solvent, profitable sponsor. The Government recognises that for each scheme a balance needs to be struck between these two elements.

- The Pension Protection Fund, which provides a safety net for members of pension schemes and is funded by a levy. The Government wants to ensure that it understands the potential impacts on the levy of any smoothing of assets and liabilities.

- The wider economy – the Government wants to ensure that the protections in place for members within the defined-benefit pensions regulation system do not act as a brake on investment and growth.

2.7.8   The DWP then referred to the Regulator's existing objectives, and went on to comment:

The argument for a new statutory objective is that the current objectives focus explicitly on protecting members and the Pension Protection Fund but do not explicitly require the Pensions Regulator to consider the long term affordability of deficit repair contributions to sponsoring employers of the pension schemes.

Representations have been made to the Department for Work and Pensions that an explicit statutory objective or duty which focussed on the sponsoring employers would have the effect of redressing the perceived imbalance.

On the other hand, there is an argument that implicitly in the Pensions Regulator's Funding Defined Benefits Code of Practice 16 (which states that trustees should consider the affordability for the employer) and through operational practice, the Pensions Regulator already gives regard to the effect of deficit repair contributions on sponsoring employers. There is recognition that the best way for members' benefits and the Pension Protection Fund to be protected in the longer term is a properly funded scheme backed by an ongoing sponsoring employer.

When considering whether to exercise its regulatory powers, legislation requires the Pensions Regulator to take into account those parties who are directly affected by the exercise of those powers. Where the regulatory power being considered relates to how a scheme is funded the sponsoring employer would very likely be considered to be a directly affected party.

The call for evidence focused on a slightly different change to that now being proposed:

What would be the advantages of a new statutory objective for the Pensions Regulator to consider the long term affordability of deficit recovery plans to sponsoring employers?

The Regulator's reaction

2.7.9   The Regulator's chairman, Michael O'Higgins, commented in a press release on budget day:

2.7.9 Scheme Funding

'We regulate according to the legislative framework set by Government and Parliament.

'In light of the Government's proposal for a new objective to take account of the sustainable growth plans of the sponsoring employer, we will make the changes required, building on the 2004 funding regime, as part of a review of the Code of Practice for defined benefit (DB) funding that we will launch as soon as possible this year.

'In addition, we will shortly publish an annual funding statement which will set out our guidance to trustees in the context of current economic circumstances, including the flexibilities available to trustees and company sponsors in the current regime, particularly the freedom to choose the basis on which contribution levels and valuations are calculated.

'We will engage fully with stakeholders and the industry on both the revision of the Code of Practice and the next annual funding statement.'

Background

2.7.10 The current economic crisis is providing a crunch test for the new regulatory structure for occupational pensions put in place from April 2005. The key crunch issue for funded occupational pension schemes is how much they are going to cost, and how much advanced funding should be provided.

In the UK, having developed a system with no statutory funding requirements up to 1997, and then tried out a modified system based on a minimum funding requirement (the MFR, fixed at the same prescribed level for every relevant scheme) from 1997 to 2005, the Government (and Parliament) changed direction in the Pensions Act 2004 to set up a new system.

2.7.11 The old MFR basis was criticised as too inflexible ('one size fits all'). And the Government had not been able to resist, in a previous downturn, reducing the level required. So instead a new regulatory regime was enacted. Ironically this was at the same time that the EU was producing a directive for the funding of occupational pension schemes which pointed more towards a minimum funding requirement basis.

2.7.12 The post 2004 regime has two limbs.

First, political pressure required that a support fund be set up – this is the Pension Protection Fund (PPF). Ultimately in employer insolvency situations, an underfunded defined benefit pension scheme can enter this fund and a

106

minimum, protected level of benefits should be provided to members. The PPF is funded by the assets received from the schemes entering it and by levies on all other defined benefit pension schemes, which increase the costs to employers of funding those schemes.

Second, a new statutory funding regime was put in place. This recognises that individual situations are different. It does not set out a funding test applicable to every scheme (unlike the MFR). Instead the funding obligations are 'scheme specific', with the employer and trustee usually needing to agree. This is backed up with a new proactive and dynamic Pensions Regulator set up with new powers.

2.7.13   The aim of the Pensions Regulator is to be 'risk based' and generally to monitor pension schemes. Unlike the previous regulator (Opra), the new Regulator was given increased powers and the 'mission statement' (see above) of protecting occupational pension benefits and minimising claims on the PPF. Arguably the Regulator was envisaged as being the 'military wing' of the PPF.

2.7.14   The existence of the PPF means that, for the first time, it is important for every pension scheme and its sponsoring employer to have some comfort on the funding position of every other pension scheme. Otherwise there could be an increasing number of underfunded schemes entering the PPF and so hitting all other schemes by increases in levies.

Parliament boots this one off to the Regulator

2.7.15   But, in practice, Parliament and the Government realised that setting funding levels for each scheme centrally had its own problems. As a result, in true time honoured political fashion, instead of giving any guidance on this fairly fundamental issue, it booted the ball off to another player. The Pensions Regulator would be the one who would police levels of funding within occupational pensions schemes.

The legislative framework gives fairly wide powers to the Regulator, which in turn back up increased powers given to trustees on funding. The legislation (and TPR guidance), but tends to use words like 'prudent' when looking at funding levels.

2.7.16   This vagueness is deliberate, as the framework envisages a 'scheme specific' funding basis – in effect agreement must be reached between employers and trustees as to future funding rates, and a recovery plan if there is a deficit. If the trustees have a unilateral right to fix funding under the trust deed, then this seemingly remains unilateral (though there can be difficulties in interpreting precisely how the statutory wording interacts with the wording in the underlying scheme – another problem caused by the legislation).

2.7.17 *Scheme Funding*

2.7.17 If agreement cannot be reached between the employer and the trustees, then the Regulator is given power to fix the funding rates itself. The Pensions Act 2008 also gave further powers to Regulator to intervene even if the funding rates have been agreed between the trustees and the employer. This would apply if the Regulator felt the amounts agreed were not 'prudent'.

Business needs vs funding – how to resolve?

2.7.18 These points mean that the Regulator, and to a degree trustees, are faced with quandary. Should they seek to protect benefits in occupational pension schemes (which the legislation says is the primary role for the Regulator)? Or do they have to take into account the ability of the employer to pay? Should funding of the pension scheme take priority over (say) business needs? To put it in context, should (for example) an airline be forced to pay money into the pension scheme rather then buy new aircraft?

2.7.19 All of this was readily foreseeable at the time the legislation was put in place, but these questions have now been brought into stark relief by the current economic circumstances. In effect there has been a 'double whammy' applied to pension schemes. Employers have become weaker, and often there has been a reduction of funding levels in the pension scheme through a combination of sharp falls in asset values (particularly equities) and a seemingly inexorable rise in liabilities (eg with increased longevity projections).

How should trustees and the Regulator deal with this situation?

2.7.20 Should they ask for more funding, to be paid more quickly, on the basis that the weakening of the employer covenant means that it is more likely that there could be insolvency leaving the scheme underfunded?

Conversely, does the fact that the employer is weaker mean that the trustee should not be pushing for more money, on the grounds that the company cannot reasonably afford to pay?

2.7.21 Trustees in these situations will, of course, look to the views of the Regulator. After all, the Regulator has been given the new powers and can, in effect, can override a funding decision in any event. So, the Regulator is faced with a need to give some guidance to trustees and to employers as to how it will assess funding plans in the future. But it is not staffed at a level that would allow it to do this on an individual basis for every scheme. And how will it decide what is appropriate in any specific case, given the Regulator's current main statutory objectives are to protect pension benefits, rather than (noticeably) to protect jobs, enable businesses to continue, or even to encourage the future provision of pensions by employers?

2.7.22   Thrust by the legislation into this position, the Regulator stands to be criticised whatever it does. If it pushes for the increased funding into schemes then it runs the risk of deepening the severity of the recession for employers and increasing insolvencies and unemployment as a result. Conversely if it allows trustees to reduce their demands for contributions, then it runs the risk of increased future levels of claims on the PPF, and hence sharply increased levy payments by other schemes and ultimately by the sponsoring employers, which could find the increased cost burden unsustainable.

What does the Regulator do?

2.7.23   Understandably, faced with this dilemma and its current main objectives, the Regulator has acted cautiously.

On the one hand, it has restated its previous position that trustees should not be aiming to drive employers into insolvency (this is the last resort). The best position for a pension scheme is a strong supporting employer.

So far, so easy.

2.7.24   But short of a potential insolvency, how does the Regulator expect trustees to deal with requests by employers to reschedule contribution plans or deal with increased deficits? Statements from the Regulator point to a need for trustees to consider the position carefully. It would not expect employers to renegotiate extended recovery periods if, at the same time, they were still paying dividends. Otherwise, it has said that it may look favourably on proposals in which recovery plans were extended or back-end loaded in appropriate circumstances.

This demonstrates the difficulty of reconciling the merits of:

- clear general guidance or prescriptive legislation, which runs the risk of being inappropriate to a particular scheme; and

- the flexibility of a structure where individual circumstances play a large part, which gives rise to lack of certainty and of which it could be said that policy all depends on how the Regulator feels on the day.

2.7.25   Tabloid newspapers characterise such situations by the headlines 'Post code lottery' (where there are regional variations) compared to 'One size fits all' (where there are not). Another example of 'heads you win, tails I lose'.

2.7.26   *Scheme Funding*

2.7.26   In practice trustees and employers (and pension lawyers) have been looking to see how well the Regulator copes with dealing with this conundrum. Given the size of pension schemes and their importance to members, it is vital for the Regulator to get the balance right. Too far one way or the other, and it runs the risk of either driving many employers out of business or destroying the pension system through the under provision of benefits and excessive claims on the PPF.

2.7.27   At the end of the day the Regulator needs to keep its main objectives in mind. Currently these direct it to consider benefit security as its main objective. True there is already a duty on the Regulator to consider the impact of its actions on those directly affected (*Pensions Act 2004, s 100*). But to a lawyer, this falls far short of weighing against the main objectives stated earlier in the Act. If more balance is to be required from the Regulator, a new objective is needed.

Parliament has given the Regulator a lot of powers, but precious little guidance on how it thinks they should be used.

2.7.28   The proposal for a new objective based on growth may go some way towards giving that guidance to the Regulator.

The question ultimately remains is whether the Regulator is properly structured and resourced to take account of all these risks. An important social policy issue has been delegated by Parliament (and the Government) to the Regulator.

A new growth duty?

2.7.29   The Government is also consulting on a new growth duty for non-economic regulators, aimed at ensuring that regulators uphold the highest standards of public protection without holding business back. The Treasury 'is attracted' to applying this new duty to the Pensions Regulator.

The 2013 Budget report stated:

> 'Across the entire regulatory system, the Government is taking action to shift the balance of regulation in favour of private sector investment and growth. This is particularly important for the regulation of defined benefit (DB) pensions as recent economic conditions have put companies sponsoring DB schemes under significant financial pressure ...'

2.7.30   The Government is also consulting on a new growth duty for non-economic regulators and is attracted, subject to the results of that consultation, to applying such a new duty to TPR.

The Department for Business, Innovation and Skills (BIS) had already started consultation on the potential for a new growth duty for regulators generally. The BIS consultation opened on 8 March 2013 and closed on 19 April 2013: The consultation paper is at: http://www.bis.gov.uk/assets/brdo/docs/publications-2013/13–684-growth-consultation.pdf.

One of the questions in the BIS consultation is: 'Question 8: Should the Pensions Regulator be included in the scope of the growth duty?'

Smoothing of assets and liabilities in scheme funding valuations

2.7.31 Following consultation, the Government has confirmed that will not be pursuing a change in legislation to permit the 'smoothing' of asset values and liabilities in funding valuations. This would have involved the averaging of asset prices and discount rates over a longer period of time, instead of using current market spot rates.

The 2013 Budget Report stated that the DWP consultation 'did not reveal a strong case' for amending existing legislation. Industry bodies such as ACA and NAPF have welcomed this decision.

2.8   Reservoir trusts and charged accounts

Summary

Funding defined benefit liabilities remains a challenge for many companies with defined benefit pension schemes. Recent improvements in gilt yields have significantly improved the funding position for many and have caused some to become concerned about the risk of trapping surplus assets in their pension scheme.

This section and the next section provide an overview of three of the main structures being used (namely, asset backed contributions, reservoir trusts and charged accounts), the benefits of using them and the associated risks.

This section looks at two structures – reservoir trusts and charged accounts – which are increasingly being used as a way of mitigating the risk of trapped surplus. In both cases assets are contributed (or charged) by the employer, but are held outside the pension scheme trust. Instead they are held in a separate trust (reservoir trust) or are mortgaged or charged to the pension trustee.

This section explains how they work and outlines the key advantages and disadvantages of both structures.

What is a reservoir trust?

2.8.1   In broad outline, a reservoir trust is a funding trust set up in connection with a pension scheme in order to receive and hold payments from the pension scheme's sponsoring company. Both the pension scheme and the employer are beneficiaries of the trust. The trustee is directed to make payments out of the trust in specified circumstances. The reservoir trusts assets provide (in effect) additional funding security for the pension scheme, but have the key advantage for the company that there is a reduced risk of creating a trapped surplus in the pension scheme. For an overview of trapped surplus issues, see *Surplus and overfunding in pension schemes*, **2.5** above.

A reservoir trust will often have the same trustee as the pension scheme in connection with which it has been set up. However, it is administered separately from the main scheme under its own trust deed.

Advantages and disadvantages

2.8.2   In addition to mitigating the risk of creating a surplus in the pension scheme, a reservoir trust has the following potential advantages from a company point of view:

(a)   improved employer covenant rating; and

(b)   the assets held in the reservoir trust may potentially (with the right structuring) qualify (under accounting standards FRS17 or IAS19) as plan assets in the employer's accounts (with beneficial balance sheet implications).

2.8.3   But the disadvantages are that:

(a)   there is no tax deduction available for the company on its funding payments;

(b)   the tax position is complex (see below);

(c)   the payment triggers need to be carefully specified; and

(d)   the trustee needs to decide whether or not the reservoir trust is really a form of security and so needs to be registered at the Companies Registry (as being equivalent to a charge over the assets of the company).

2.8.4   Additional benefits from a pension scheme trustee point of view are that:

(a)   the trust fund within the reservoir trust constitutes (in effect) extra security for funding;

(b)   if so structured, any income from the trust can be used to reduce the deficit and pay trustee expenses;

(c)   assets in the reservoir trust are not subject to the same investment restrictions as apply to registered pension schemes under the *Pensions Act 1995*, therefore the trustee may (if the company agrees) take advantage of the greater investment freedom to try eg a riskier investment strategy for the reservoir trust. Alternatively the trustee may prefer to apply the same investment strategy to both the reservoir trust and the pension scheme; and

(d)   assets held in the reservoir trust should be protected from company creditors in the case of company insolvency under UK law. However, it is questionable how easily the trustee access those assets and transfer them to the pension scheme in an insolvency situation, particularly in other jurisdictions, such as the USA (see *Insolvency*, **2.8.14** below).

113

2.8.4   *Scheme Funding*

One main disadvantage of the reservoir trust is the more complex tax treatment. (See '*Tax treatment*' below for further details.)

How does a reservoir trust work?

2.8.5   An agreed sum or assets are transferred by the company into an account in the name of the trustee of the reservoir trust (the RT Trustee). The RT Trustee holds:

(a)   the fund on trust for the company and the pension scheme trustee (and pension scheme); and

(b)   (often) any income on the fund on trust for the company.

Payment events (eg company insolvency or failure to pay contributions or the company giving notice) define when the RT Trustee is required to pay all or part of the fund to the pension scheme trustee (for the pension scheme). The RT trust deed usually provides that any money/assets remaining in the account/fund after specific events (eg when all pension scheme liabilities have been bought out or discharged) are paid to the company.

2.8.6   For tax reasons (see **2.8.9** below), the RT trust is sometimes structured so that any income earned on the assets in the reservoir trust is first paid out to the company, perhaps into a company escrow account. The company then can pay the RT Trustee's expenses from the escrow account before paying the remaining income to the pension scheme as a tax deductible contribution to the pension scheme.

2.8.7   In addition to any income payments, capital funds can be released regularly (eg annually) from the reservoir trust to either the scheme or the company. Who receives those release payments is likely to depend on the funding level of the scheme. If overfunded (eg by an agreed percentage on an agreed basis), the company may receive payments from the reservoir trust. If underfunded (by an agreed percentage on an agreed basis), the scheme may receive payments. The funding level is determined by regular (eg annual) actuarial valuations of the pension scheme.

2.8.8   Further release payments may be made, eg:

(a)   following an enforcement event (such as company insolvency),[47] to the pension scheme; or

---

47   This runs the risk that the trigger runs foul of the 'anti-deprivation' rule applicable in insolvencies. But in practice this risk may be small where there is a commercially legitimate transaction, entered into by the parties in good faith – *Belmont Park Investments Pty Ltd v BNY Corporate Trustee Services Ltd* [2011] UKSC 38.

(b)   if directed by the Company, to the pension scheme; or

(c)   following a buy-out of the pension scheme, to the company.

Tax treatment of a reservoir trust

2.8.9   The tax position is complex and it is safest to get formal clearance from HMRC. The analysis below reflects our understanding based on previous clearances:

(a)   **Corporation tax deduction.** Contributions to the reservoir trust by the company are not deductible for corporation tax purposes.

A deduction should however be available for the company as and when an amount is paid from the reservoir trust to the pension scheme, so long as this is done to satisfy a contribution due from the company to the pension scheme (under the scheme's schedule of contributions[48] or otherwise under the funding legislation).

A corporation tax deduction should also be available if any income is paid from the trust to the company and an equivalent amount is paid from the company to the pension scheme.

(b)   **Income tax.** Where income on the reservoir trust assets is mandated to the company (ie it is paid directly to the company without passing through the hands of the RT trustee), the company will prima facie be liable to corporation tax on that income (and not the reservoir trustee). However, provided an equivalent amount is paid by the company into the pension scheme a matching corporation tax deduction should be available for the company.

Such an income trust means that income tax should not be payable by the reservoir trust, but the inheritance tax position should be considered (the payments could be seen as the use of surplus and so a periodic charge may be payable)

(c)   **Capital gains tax.** CGT will be payable by the RT trustee on chargeable capital gains (currently at a rate of 28%).

(d)   **Inheritance tax.** An inheritance tax periodic charge of up to 6% (0.15% per quarter) may apply. These may be limited to any surplus assets in the reservoir trust when these exit the reservoir trust to be distributed to the company (rather than the pension scheme) or on the tenth anniversary of the trust.

---

48 It is helpful to amend the schedule of contributions to allow for payments out of the Reservoir Trust.

(e)   **Disguised remuneration.** No disguised remuneration charges should arise in relation to reservoir trusts. The position is not clearcut, but HMRC have been willing to date to give clearance to this effect.

Charged accounts

How does a charged account work?

2.8.10   The company establishes a segregated fund (eg a bank account or investment account) with a bank or fund manager. Investments in the account or fund are assets of the company.

The company grants formal security (eg a mortgage or fixed charge) over the fund in favour of the pension trustee as security for the company's obligations to the pension scheme. The charge is then registered at Companies House and notice of the charge is given to the bank or fund manager.

Issues which commonly arise in relation to the notice of charge are:

(a)   whether in future joint (company/trustee) or single instructions are required in relation to the funds in the account;

(b)   what happens on an event of default, ie are joint instructions still required or can the trustee give sole instructions after a default? Does the account-holding bank have to police whether a default has occurred or can it rely on the trustee certifying that a default has occurred? and

(c)   should the bank have a set-off right? The trustee will be concerned that the bank should not be able to set off (or combine) any part of the credit in the charged account against any other liabilities (eg of the company to the bank on another account). The general principle is that a bank cannot set off a credit balance in one company account against a debit balance in another account of the same company if it has actual or constructive notice that either account is a trust account (ie the company is not the beneficial owner). Once notice has been given, the account-holding bank will therefore not be able to exercise a right of set off in relation to the charged account (save for any debit balances in place before notice is received), unless there is an agreement to the contrary (which is sometimes found in the bank account terms and conditions). The trustee may look for an agreement from the bank not to exercise any set off rights or (if this proves difficult) look for the account to be with a new bank (not otherwise used by the company) or for the account to be in the name of the trustee.

The fund is invested in accordance with an investment strategy agreed between the company and trustee. Income and gains could either be credited to the fund or paid out (say to the company).

Advantages and disadvantages

2.8.11   A charged account, like a reservoir trust, can mitigate the risk of creating a surplus in the pension scheme and can potentially improve how the pension trustee sees the employer covenant rating. It has the following additional advantages over a reservoir trust:

(a)   the tax treatment is much more straightforward (income and gains on the charged assets are treated as belonging to the company until a relevant enforcement event, no IHT charges should apply);

(b)   if it meets PPF conditions (in particular, the charged account deed must be based on the PPF's standard form document), it can be recognised by the PPF for its levy calculation; and

(c)   the relevant fund more easily appears as a company asset in its accounts.

2.8.12   The disadvantages of a charged account compared to a reservoir trust structure are that:

(a)   it usually requires registration as a charge at the Companies Registry;

(b)   it is more likely to impact on relevant covenants (eg negative pledges) under the company's borrowing arrangements (reservoir trust may not be covered); and

(c)   the pension scheme trustee may be subject to more delay if trying to enforce the charge in an insolvency situation.

Investment

2.8.13   Both a reservoir trust and a charged account can (depending on size and likely length of existence) require the company and the trustee to agree how the relevant fund is to be invested.

In practice it is common for the relevant agreement to provide for the company and the trustee to need to agree a statement of funding principles (with a default to a cash fund in a bank account). Issues include:

(a)   the restrictions on investments by a registered pension scheme (*Pensions Act 1995* and regulations) should not apply;

(b)   the tax impact of various different types of investment (for the company and the scheme); and

(c)   is a match with the pension scheme's investment strategy wanted?

2.8.14   *Scheme Funding*

Insolvency

2.8.14   Under UK law, in a company insolvency:

- assets held on trust are assets of the trustee and are treated as falling outside the company's property (even if the company is the trustee); and

- the holder of a charge over company assets has a priority claim in the company's insolvency.

In either case, provided the trust or charge

- was validly constituted;

- was duly registered at the Companies Registry (if a charge);[49] and

- cannot be set aside on the basis of the specific preference or transaction at an undervalue provisions under insolvency legislation,

the assets which are subject to the trust or charge should be safe from the company's creditors if that company goes insolvent.

Reservoir trust

2.8.15   The reservoir trust deed is likely to provide that on a company insolvency or default the trust assets are transferred to the pension scheme. The case law suggests that such a clause may not be contrary to the anti-deprivation rules under insolvency law (although this is a difficult legal area and there is some legal uncertainty on the point). A further risk is that the reservoir trust is held to be in effect a charge which, if not registered at the Companies Registry, would be void as against an administrator or liquidator of the company.

Assuming that: (i) the clause transferring ownership of the reservoir trust assets from the company to the pension scheme on insolvency works; and (ii) the reservoir trust is not registrable as a charge, under UK law the reservoir trust assets are likely to be bankruptcy remote and immediately accessible for the pension scheme.

2.8.16   Other laws may be relevant and may need to be considered. For example, under US law, if assets are held by a third party pursuant to an escrow or trust agreement, they may be outside the jurisdiction of the US Bankruptcy Court and not subject to a stay (see below).

---

49   Special rules apply if the charge falls within the *Financial Collateral Arrangements (No 2) Regulations 2003 (SI 2003/3226)*.

Charged account

2.8.17   Although a valid fixed charge would (if duly registered) protect the charged assets for the pension scheme in an insolvency situation, like any charge[50] the pension scheme trustee could encounter some delay when trying to enforce the charge.

Under the *Insolvency Act 1986*, on a company administration a moratorium on legal process applies. This means that the trustee could not enforce its charge without leave of the court or the administrator. However, in practice if the charged asset is not used for the company's business (and provided the charge is a fixed rather than floating charge),[51] the court or administrator are likely to consent to enforcement of the charge.

2.8.18   Other laws may be relevant and may need to be considered. For example, under US law similarly there is a stay on enforcement of security where a company enters Chapter 11 proceedings. However, it is more difficult in the USA to gain the court's consent to lift the stay and enforce a charge (although it is technically possible where the charged assets are not needed for an effective reorganisation of the chargor). The presumption in the USA is that the court will not give its consent to enforcement of the charge.

2.8.19

Comparison: reservoir trusts and charged accounts

Criterion	Reservoir Trust	Charged Account
Can fund be shown as an asset in pension scheme accounts or valuation?	NO	NO

---

50   Special rules apply if the charge falls within the *Financial Collateral Arrangements (No 2) Regulations 2003 (SI 2003/3226)*.
51   Where the account which is charged in favour of the pension scheme trustee is a variable fund rather than (say) a fixed fund or cash account, there may be an argument that the trustee has a floating rather than a fixed charge, because the assets in the fund are likely to change. This is likely to depend on the degree of control held by the pension trustee. Unlike fixed charges, floating charges rank behind preferential debts and insolvency expenses and are more vulnerable to dealings by an administrator (*Insolvency Act 1986, para 69, Sch B1*).

2.8.19   *Scheme Funding*

Criterion	Reservoir Trust	Charged Account
Reduction in PPF levy?	NO	(usually) NO[52]
Is there an upfront tax deduction?	NO	NO
Is the tax treatment otherwise difficult?	YES	NO
Does it require registration as a charge?	(probably) NO	(usually) YES
Can it impact on negative pledges?	(usually) NO	(usually) YES
Are the assets protected from company creditors on a company insolvency (in the same way as a straight contribution)?	YES (provided not a charge)	YES (subject to floating charge issues)
Enforceable on company entering administration?	Should be (provided not a charge)	Should be (but will need court or administrator consent)

---

52 Cash in a charged bank account can be recognised by the PPF for its levy calculation provided it meets the relevant PPF conditions, including use of the PPF's standard form document.

2.9   Asset backed funding structures

Summary

Employers and trustees are becoming increasingly innovative in the measures they are adopting to support their pension schemes. Asset backed funding arrangements – such as asset backed contributions, reservoir trusts and charged accounts – are proving attractive alternatives to cash contributions. They offer sponsoring employers an opportunity to retain assets in their businesses whilst increasing the security available for members' benefits.

However, they also raise certain additional risks for both employers and trustees and are subject to increasing scrutiny from the Pensions Regulator (TPR), which released updated guidance on asset-backed contributions in November 2013.

This section and the previous section provide an overview of three of the main structures being used (namely, asset backed contributions, reservoir trusts and charged accounts), the benefits of using them and the associated risks.

This section focuses on asset backed contributions. It explains the benefits and risks which employers should consider when negotiating these arrangements, the key terms which can be used to protect the interests of both parties, and TPR's main concerns about these structures.

Introduction

2.9.1   Asset backed contributions (ABCs) are arrangements under which the sponsoring employer of a pension scheme transfers group assets into a special purpose vehicle (SPV), which uses those assets to generate an income stream for the pension scheme.

This type of structure usually involves the following steps (as shown in the diagram below):

- The sponsoring employer pays a cash contribution into its pension scheme. This is invested by the scheme in an SPV (usually a Scottish Limited Partnership, for reasons set out below).

- The trustees of the pension scheme use that contribution to invest in the SPV.

2.9.1 Scheme Funding

- The SPV uses these investment proceeds to acquire an asset (eg trade receivables, intellectual property or real estate) from the employer (or another entity in the corporate group).

- The asset is then leased or licensed back to entities in the employer's group in return for regular payments to the SPV (eg in the form of royalties or rents).

- The Trustees take account of the SPV asset (and income) when looking at on-going funding.

- SPV uses the income it receives to pay pre-agreed distributions to the trustees throughout the term of their investment. Any surplus value in the SPV can be returned to the sponsoring employer and other investing partners over the term of their investment (eg where the pension scheme's deficit has been reduced substantially).

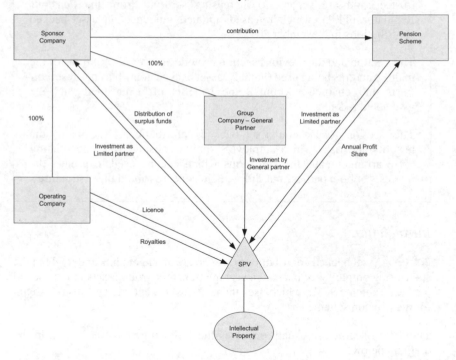

2.9.2 The trustees may also hold further rights to the capital they have invested in the SPV. This could take the form of regular repayments of this capital over the term of their investment, or the right to a lump sum (or 'bullet') payment at the end of the term. As with the repayment of any surplus cash to the employer, such lump sum payments would usually be linked to the funding level of the pension scheme.

Benefits and risks

2.9.3   The following benefits afforded by ABCs have encouraged a steady flow of this type of structure in recent years.

Benefits for company	Benefits for trustee
• Reduction in the actuarial funding deficit and levies payable to the Pension Protection Fund (PPF) • Reduction of demands on the employer for cash payments (which can instead be invested in the business) • Realisation of the value of company assets • Assets can still be used in the employer's business • Upfront tax deduction, if certain conditions are met (see 'Tax Treatment' below) • Ability to return surplus cash to the sponsoring employer, reducing the risk of overfunding the pension scheme • Recovery payments to the pension scheme may be reduced or spread over a longer period • Structure can be tailored to the needs of the employer's business and / or the pension scheme	• Reduction in the actuarial funding deficit and PPF levies • Employers are able to invest more in the business, which can strengthen the employer covenant over the long term • Maturing assets may be a good match for the pension scheme liabilities • Increased security for members' benefits (these structures are bankruptcy remote) • Trustees gain control over key business asset upon occurrence of trigger events (which can increase their negotiating power with sponsoring employer)

2.9.4   There are, however, certain risks that both pension scheme trustees and companies will need to take into account, especially when comparing ABCs with alternative funding arrangements.

Risks for company	Risks for trustee
• Change in law (eg on employer related investments, tax treatment, Scottish independence)	• Change in law (eg on employer related investments, tax treatment, Scottish independence)
• Loss of flexibility and control of key business asset	• Weakened employer covenant due to loss of control of key assets
• Partially reduced ability to enter into de-risking arrangements eg if those require liquid assets (eg buy-ins, buy-outs and longevity swaps)	• Partially reduced ability to enter into de-risking arrangements eg if those require liquid assets (eg buy-ins, buy-outs and longevity swaps)
	• Complexity (especially when valuing investments and collateral, and setting up structure)
	• Scrutiny from TPR
	• Potential for increased credit risk due to
	– longer recovery period
	– inflexible schedule of payments
	– correlation between risks affecting value of the employer covenant and risks affecting value of assets backing the ABC

Key terms

2.9.5   ABC arrangements tend to be bespoke structures, tailored to the needs and assets of the parties involved. However, we would expect a deal of this type to address the following issues:

- **Duration**: unlike a recovery plan (which TPR advise should be limited to the period the company can reasonably afford), ABCs tend to have a longer lifecycle of up to 25 years (see *Tax treatment*, **2.9.12** below).

- **Type of underlying asset**: employers should consider what type of assets they use in their business which could be invested in this type of arrangement (eg intellectual property, stock, real estate etc). Importantly, they should assess the impact that any rights granted to the trustee over such asset (or restrictions required by the trustee on the use of the asset) will have on their business.

- **Valuation of underlying asset**: how will the parties value this underlying asset: (i) upon the initial transfer, and (ii) on an ongoing basis?

- **Trigger points for the security**: the trustee would usually seek the right to enforce greater rights over the SPV where certain events occur (eg failure to pay, breach of lease/licence or insolvency of employer).

- **Value of interest in SLP**: How will the arrangement be reflected in the company's accounts or in the pension scheme's accounts? This is usually done by calculating a net present value for the income stream payable under the ABC structure. The Pension Regulator has emphasised that this should be calculated using an appropriate discount rate which reflects the risk of non-receipt of distant payments.

- **Protections for trustees**: there are various ways in which a trustee could seek to ensure that the value of this arrangement is maintained (eg regular valuations of the SPV assets, with requirements for the employer to add further assets or make a cash top up if the asset value falls, or restrictions on how the underlying asset can be used).

- **Income Stream**: the payments made to the trustee through this arrangement will need to be structured so as to benefit from appropriate tax reliefs (see *Tax treatment*, **2.9.12** below).

- **Impact on funding arrangements**: How will the on-going pension scheme funding arrangements be affected by the SPV investment and the income stream? TPR has warned trustees that ABCs can sometimes leave trustees unable to agree higher payments under a recovery plan even where they are affordable and appropriate.

- **Protections against overfunding**: eg allowing payments to stop, or be paid to the employer, if the pension scheme reaches a pre-determined funding level.

- **Exit mechanism**: parties may wish to give themselves the flexibility to end this arrangement before the full term expires – eg through a put option (allowing the trustees to sell the SPV to the company for pre-agreed price) or a call option (giving the company the right to buy the asset for a pre-agreed price).

- **Change of law**: the documents should address what will happen if there is a change in law which affects the cost or legality of the structure (see *Employer related investment risks* and *Tax treatment*, below). For instance, they could agree a period for paying off a scheme deficit through contributions direct from the employer.

- **Compliance with SIP and investment laws**: the trustees will need to ensure that the structure complies with the scheme's statement of investment principles (SIP) and the other investment laws (eg written advice, scheme assets predominantly in listed securities).

2.9.6 *Scheme Funding*

Employer related investment risks

2.9.6   Trustees would breach the employer related investment (ERI) legislation[53] if the scheme's assets exceed the 5% cap on owning:

- assets used in the employer's business,

- shares in a group 'company' of the employer (eg which held the underlying assets), or

- an interest in a transparent entity (such as a partnership constituted under English law), the assets of which are used by the employer.

2.9.7   The penalties for breaching these rules can be severe. They include civil penalties of up to £5,000 and criminal sanctions. Any resources of a pension scheme which are invested in breach of ERI restrictions are excluded from calculation of scheme's assets for purposes of the statutory funding regime. Furthermore, such an investment could be deemed to be unauthorised, which would mean that the trustees could be personally liable for any resulting losses.

2.9.8   On its face, an ABC structure looks to run the risk of breaching the ERI restrictions – after all the aim is that the employer asset is used to fund the scheme. However, trustees are permitted to own an interest in a Scottish Limited Partnership (SLP), which holds assets used in the employer's business, without breaching the ERI rules. There are two reasons for this:

- Scottish partnerships (unlike English partnerships have "corporate personality". This means that the interest held by the trustees is the partnership interest, not an interest in the underlying asset; and

- the interest in the partnership is not a share or security.

2.9.9   This is a due to the way that 'company' is defined for the purposes of the ERI legislation.

A company is defined as: (i) a body corporate, or (ii) an unincorporated body constituted under the law of a country or territory outside the UK. An SLP is an unincorporated body constituted in a territory within the UK. It therefore falls outside the definition of 'company', and accordingly an interest in an SLP does not constitute a 'share' in an employer (or associate) under the ERI legislation. Furthermore, unlike English partnerships, it is not transparent from a tax perspective, so the pension scheme would record its interest in the SLP on its balance sheet, rather than the underlying assets.

---

53 See *Employer-related investment limits: PA 1995*, **17.5** below.

2.9.10   Care also needs to be taken that:

- the SLP does not constitute a collective investment scheme or an alternative investment fund for the purposes of UK and European financial services regulation (this is usually met by ensuring that the trustee and the SLP partners are all in the same group of companies); and

- no part of the transaction is at an undervalue for the scheme.

2.9.11   The trustees and employer will need to consider three issues on this SLP exception:

- **Incompatibility with EU law?** The European Directive on Institutions for Occupational Retirement Provision (IORP) differs from the UK legislation, in that it refers to 'undertakings' rather than 'companies'.

- **Future changes in legislation:** what happens if the ERI legislation changes in the future?

- **Scottish independence:** This would mean that SLPs would cease to be constituted within the UK, and would therefore fall within the definition of company. Accordingly, holding shares in an SLP in the employer's group would constitute an employer related investment.

Parties can mitigate this risk by including an underpin which provides for what will happen if the law changes and this type of structure is disallowed.

Tax treatment

2.9.12   The *Finance Act 2012* introduced new rules on the tax treatment of ABCs. These allow employers to benefit from an up front tax deduction on non-cash contributions made using an ABC where they are able to satisfy certain criteria. The rules set requirements for payments made under 'structured finance arrangements', which include:

- payments to a pension scheme must be made annually and may not increase by more than 5% p.a. or increase in the retail prices index;

- the term of the ABC cannot exceed 25 years; and

- a prohibition on back-end loaded bullet payments.

HMRC published updated guidance on this type of tax relief in August 2013, which sets out examples of how the conditions will apply to different forms of ABC (eg that involve new or existing partnerships).

Given the value of this relief, the parties may wish to seek clearance from HMRC that it will apply to their ABC arrangement.

2.9.13 *Scheme Funding*

Accounting treatment

2.9.13 Both employers and trustees will need advice on how these arrangements should be reflected in the employer's consolidated accounts and the accounts of the pension scheme. In particular, the employer should consider whether the assets subject to the arrangements should be recognised as a scheme asset, or continue to be shown in the employer's accounts, and the impact of the arrangement on any pension scheme deficit reported under IAS 19 or FRS17.

The Pensions Regulator's view

2.9.14 TPR has recognised that allowing employers to retain cash within their business can improve their covenant to the pension scheme and that ABCs can 'improve a scheme's security by providing access to valuable assets which were previously out of reach'.[54]

However, TPR also emphasises that although a scheme's deficit can appear substantially reduced on 'day one' of an ABC arrangements, trustees should remain alert to the ongoing risk of payment default by the sponsoring employer and/or the SPV. Trustees should consider this ongoing credit risk when evaluating the funding position of the scheme and comparing ABCs to funding through 'less risky alternatives' (eg direct cash contributions).

'The use of complex vehicles and structures to deliver asset-backed contributions to schemes has also increased. This can lead to increases in risk where advisers to schemes have not anticipated all the implications of using this structure. It is vital that trustees understand the risks they are taking and consider carefully whether a more complex approach to supporting the scheme, which may involve additional risk taking by the scheme, is preferable to a straightforward one.'

Source: The Pensions Regulator, Corporate Plan 2013–2016 (May 2013)

2.9.15 Although it is not necessary to seek clearance from TPR when implementing an ABC structure, trustees are required to notify TPR after they have executed this type of arrangement when providing details of the scheme's recovery plan and annual scheme return. TPR also notes in their guidance on

---

54 The Pensions Regulator, Asset-backed contributions (November 2013).

128

employer related investments that, when considering whether the ERI restrictions have been breached, they will consider whether the structure:

(a)   provides 'demonstrably better protection' for members' benefit than the alternatives;

(b)   complements, or is underpinned by, alternative arrangements; and

(c)   replaces, or adds to, direct cash payments from employers.[55]

2.9.16   TPR's guidance on ABCs highlights the following further issues and responsibilities which trustees should consider:

(a)   **Funding negotiations**: trustees and sponsoring employers should continue to seek to reduce any funding shortfall in the scheme as quickly as the employer can reasonably afford, even where an ABC arrangement is used. Trustees should assess how the recovery period and payments due under an ABC structure compare to the terms which might be available under a standard recovery plan, and whether entering into such an arrangement would fetter their discretion in future funding negotiations;

(b)   **Value of underlying asset**: trustees should evaluate whether the assets used in ABC structures provide adequate support for the payments promised (especially where these are back-end loaded), and should ensure they are valued independently rather than relying solely on the audit valuation;

(c)   **Legal claims to underlying asset**: trustees should ensure they have sufficient legal claims to the asset. In particular, TPR has urged trustees to consider whether they would be able to access the value of the underlying asset quickly (eg through 'step in' rights) or whether they are reliant on another party (eg the general partner of the SLP) to enforce their obligations;

(d)   **Risk of illegality/change in law**: trustees should take specialist legal advice on whether restrictions on employer related investments apply. Trustees should recognise risk of the law changing and include an "underpin" in their funding arrangements in case this occurs; and

(e)   **Communication to members**: members should be informed in a 'clear and transparent manner' (eg in a summary funding statement).

---

55   The Pensions Regulator, Employer related investments (November 2010).

2.9.17 *Scheme Funding*

2.9.17

TPR on the role of advisors

In order to evaluate a proposal, trustees will generally need to obtain extensive legal, actuarial, asset valuation and covenant advice ... Before entering into an ABC, trustees will also need to take investment advice and consider whether the decision to make the investment needs to be delegated to a fund manager.

Source: The Pensions Regulator, *Asset-backed contributions* (November 2013).

Chapter 3

Debt on the employer – *section 75* issues

3.1 Debt on the employer – an overview of *s 75* of the *Pensions Act 1995*

Summary

Section 75 of the *Pensions Act 1995* is a key piece in the statutory funding regime. It imposes a debt obligation on an employer (or former employer) in relation to a relevant occupational pension scheme if a relevant trigger event occurs. The debt is based on the funding shortfall, looking at the cost of securing benefits on a buy-out basis (ie the cost of securing benefits based on purchasing matching annuity policies with an insurer).

A debt under *s 75* of the *Pensions Act 1995* can be triggered in a wide range of circumstances (eg on a reorganisation, business sale, share sale or if reducing pension costs). Once triggered, an employer that participates in a defined benefit pension scheme may be required to make a large lump sum payment to the pension scheme trustees.

This section provides an overview of the *s 75* legislation and the underlying *Employer Debt Regulations 2005*.

What is a s 75 debt?

3.1.1   Under *ss 75* and *75A* of the *Pensions Act 1995* and the *Occupational Pension Schemes (Employer Debt) Regulations 2005 (SI 2005/678* as amended), an employer that participates in a defined benefit (DB) occupational pension scheme can, in specified circumstances, become liable for some or all of the shortfall in the scheme's funding.

3.1.1 *Debt on the employer – section 75 issues*

The benefit liabilities in the scheme are measured on a buy-out basis. This tests whether there would be sufficient assets to secure benefit liabilities with matching insurance policies and can result in a significant debt. The buy-out measurement usually leads to the employer owing a much larger debt than had appeared in the company's accounts using the FRS17/IAS19 accounting measure.

If a *s 75* debt is triggered, the obligation is for the employer to pay it in a lump sum to the pension scheme trustees. This can be contrasted with employers' obligations to fund the scheme on an on-going basis according to a schedule of contributions (before a *s 75* debt is triggered – see *Scheme specific funding*, **2.1**).

Section 75 of the *1995 Act* does not apply to the following schemes:

- money purchase schemes;
- unfunded public sector schemes;
- public sector schemes providing pensions to local government employees;
- UK parliamentary schemes;
- Scottish parliamentary schemes;
- schemes to which a minister of the Crown etc has given a guarantee;
- schemes that are not registered with HM Revenue and Customs (under the *Finance Act 2004*);
- scheme for overseas employee falling within *ICTA 1988, s 615* (unless approved as an EU cross-border scheme – see **8.1**);
- schemes with fewer than two members;
- schemes that are relevant lump sum retirement benefit schemes;
- schemes with fewer than 12 members where all members are trustees of the scheme;
- Chatsworth Estate Settlement Pension Scheme;

Who calculates the debt?

3.1.2   The trustees are responsible for determining, calculating and verifying the value of assets. They must use the value attributed to the assets in the latest scheme accounts. In an employment cessation event case, the trustees can decide, having consulted the employer, to carry out an updated assessment.

The trustees also determine the amount and value of the benefit liabilities that are to be taken into account. But the capital buy out value of the benefit amount must be calculated and verified by the scheme actuary.

The calculations are as at the trigger date (eg using an estimate of annuity rates as at that date) – *Singer & Friedlander case*.[1]

When is a s 75 debt triggered?

3.1.3   An employer's *s 75* debt arises immediately before any of the following occur:

- the scheme begins to wind up;
- the employer suffers an insolvency event in the UK (eg appointment of a liquidator, an administrative receiver, an administrator etc) (*PA 2004, s 121*);
- the trustees apply to enter the Pension Protection Fund (PPF) under a *s 129*[2] notice because they become aware that the employer is unlikely to continue as a going concern (alternatively, the trustees can receive the notice from the PPF);
- the employer starts a members' voluntary liquidation (MVL); or
- an 'employment-cessation event' occurs in relation to an employer who participates in a multi-employer scheme.

An employment-cessation event occurs if:

> '(i)   an employer has ceased to employ at least one person who is an active member of the scheme; and
>
> (ii)   at least one other employer who is not a defined contribution employer continues to employ at least one active member of the scheme.'

Employment-cessation events can occur (and therefore, trigger a *s 75* debt) in several circumstances; for example, sale of an employer (or employer's

---

1   *BEST Trustees plc (as Trustee of the Singer & Friedlander Ltd Pension & Assurance Scheme) v Kaupthing Singer & Friedlander Ltd (in admin)* [2012] EWHC 629 (Ch), [2012] 3 All ER 874 (Sales J).

2   *Section 129* of the *Pensions Act 2004* applies in relation to some employers who cannot enter an insolvency process (eg charities or trade unions). It provides for the trustees and Pensions Regulator to be able to trigger the PPF process by a notice to the Pension Protection Fund if the scheme's employer is unlikely to continue as a going concern.

3.1.3 *Debt on the employer – section 75 issues*

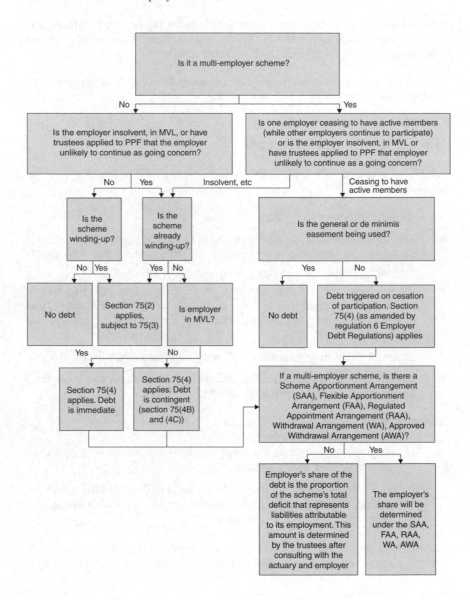

business) out of the corporate group or during an internal reorganisation or where the last remaining active member employed by a particular company dies or retires – these are discussed at *Multi-employer pension schemes and s 75 debts – the elephant trap,* **3.2** below.

Note that if all employers in the same scheme cease to have active members at the same time (ie the scheme becomes 'frozen'), there is no employment-cessation event and so no debt is immediately triggered at that point – but the former employer is deemed to remain an employer for *s 75* purposes. This means a *s 75* debt may be triggered on the later winding-up of the scheme or an employer insolvency. However, former employers can, in these circumstances, choose an earlier time for the employment-cessation event to be treated as occurring in relation to it and then pay the *s 75* debt at that time (and so no longer have the burden of the residual liability).

The employer does this by giving a notice to the trustees, specifying the date on which it wants the employment-cessation event to be treated as taking effect, which must be within three months before or three months after the date of the notice.

When is the debt payable?

3.1.4   The employer will not be required immediately to pay the *s 75* debt if it is triggered because of an employer insolvency event or *s 129* notice to the PPF. Instead, this debt is contingent on the scheme beginning to wind up or an insolvency practitioner issuing a scheme failure notice (ie notice that the employer cannot be rescued as a going concern and that another company is not willing to assume responsibility for the employer's pension scheme).

However, if the debt is triggered because of an employment-cessation event or member's voluntary liquidation, the debt becomes payable as at that date (but may take some time to be calculated).

If the debt is triggered by the scheme winding-up (with no employer insolvency), the trustees have to choose the time for fixing the debt calculation. This can be any date in the period starting on the date of scheme winding-up and ending on the date of employer insolvency.

The actual amount of the debt is usually fixed by a certificate provided by the scheme actuary. Some case law[3] indicates that (absent fraud) it may not be

---

3   *Cornwell v Newhaven Port* [2005] EWHC 1469 (Ch); *Gleave v Board of the Pension Protection Fund* [2008] EWHC 1099 (Ch) and *Bestrustees Plc v Kaupthing Singer & Friedlander Ltd* [2013] EWHC 2407 (Ch).

possible for an employer to challenge this figure (but this legal position has been doubted).

After the debt is paid, can the scheme ask the employer for more?

3.1.5   When calculating the *s 75* debt, the scheme's assets are valued at a specific point. This can be before the trustees secure the benefits of the scheme in full. So, for example, if the *s 75* debt is triggered because of the employer's insolvency, the assets are valued at a point immediately before the insolvency event occurred rather than when the benefits are secured (eg on the scheme winding-up).

This leaves the pension scheme vulnerable to the employer paying the *s 75* debt in full, but the trustees later discovering that this is insufficient to buy out all the scheme benefits in full. For example, there may be a decline in the value of the scheme's assets or increase in the cost of buying annuities.

However, *s 75(7)* makes clear that if the trustees have any other right or remedy in respect of a deficiency in the scheme's assets, this is not prejudiced. Whether the trustees will be able to ask the employer to contribute further towards a buy-out deficit will depend on the rules of the scheme.

The statutory funding obligation under the scheme-specific funding obligations in *Part 3* of the *Pensions Act 2004* will generally not apply after a scheme starts to wind up (*reg 17(1)(l), Scheme Funding Regulations*). Nor will any funding obligation (outside *s 75*) apply if the scheme is in an assessment period under the PPF legislation (*PA 2004, s 133*).

Offsetting s 75 payments against the schedule of contributions

3.1.6   In October 2013, the Pensions Regulator issued a statement about 'Double Counting'. In this statement TPR expressed concerns about what it considers to be attempts by some trustees and employers to 'double count' payments made under the schedule of contributions (see **2.1** above) as also satisfying *section 75* debt obligations. TPR stated that it considered that in some circumstances such arrangements could unduly fetter the discretion of trustees on funding and risk causing the scheme to be ineligible to enter the Pension Protection Fund (as being an agreement to reduce the *s 75* debt and so triggering *reg 2(2)* of the *PPF Entry Rules Regulations* - see **5.1.2** below).

The TPR statement expressly states that it does not provide a definitive interpretation of the law and that trustees should seek their own legal advice.

The TPR statement does not deal with a situation where (say) the schedule of contributions expressly provides that future contributions by the remaining employers are to be reduced to reflect a *s 75* payment that has been made by a departing employer.

Such an arrangement seems clearly not to fall foul of the concerns expressed by TPR in its statement (it does not restrict the ability of the trustees to review the schedule of contributions in the light of the exit, nor does it cancel or waive the *s 75* debt). In practice trustees and employers may still consider it appropriate to include such a provision in the schedule of contributions and recovery plan in suitable cases eg where it deals with the potential exit of a small employer in circumstances where a large employer (which is the primary support for the scheme) would remain (indeed the covenant supporting the scheme may improve). TPR may well make comments about such a provision when it reviews the funding arrangements (see **2.2** above), but it seems clear that in suitable cases such a provision can be supported.

3.2   Multi-employer pension schemes and *s 75* debts – the elephant trap

Summary

A *s 75* debt is a debt due from an employer (or former employer) to the trustees of an occupational pension scheme. One trigger in a multi-employer defined benefit pension scheme is if an employment-cessation event (ECE) occurs; this occurs when an employer stops employing one or more active members in the scheme and at least one other employer – in the same scheme – continues to employ at least one other active member.

This section examines possible employment-cessation events and explains some of the pitfalls.

3.2.1   Before insolvency, it is likely that an ongoing employer that participates in a multi-employer defined benefit (DB) pension scheme (eg a corporate group's scheme) will be most concerned about a *s 75* debt being triggered on an employment-cessation event (ECE).

TPR issued guidance on '*Multi-employer schemes and employer departures*' in July 2012.

When do ECEs occur?

3.2.2   ECEs can occur in various circumstances, such as the situations shown in the case studies below.

The case studies show how a *s 75* debt can be triggered in different scenarios involving Company A, Company B and Company C.

Company A owns the shares in Company B and employs active DB members in the ABC pension scheme (a DB scheme). Company C is not in the same group as Company A or B.

Case study 1 – business sale of whole business

If Company B sells (for example) the whole of its business to Company C, this may lead to all Company B's employees transferring to Company

C because of the *Transfer of Undertakings* (*Protection of Employment*) *Regulations 2006* (*Tupe*).

Company B will therefore no longer employ any active members in ABC pension scheme at a time when Company A (ie another participating employer) continues to do so.

There is an ECE and so (depending on the funding level of the scheme at that point) a *s 75* debt is triggered and is the responsibility of Company B.

Company C (the buyer) would not be liable for any *s 75* debt (absent a contractual agreement) because the debt does not, under *Tupe*, transfer with the business.

Case study 2 – part-sale of business

If Company B sells (for example) part of its business to Company C, this may lead to some (but not all) of Company B's employees transferring to Company C as a result of the *Transfer of Undertakings* (*Protection of Employment*) *Regulations 2006*.

If after the transfer Company B still employs active members in ABC pension scheme, there is no ECE and so no *s 75* debt is triggered at this point.

Case study 3 – share sale

Company A sells all its shares in Company B to Company C (ie outside the corporate group) and, as a result, Company B ceases to participate in ABC pension scheme.

Company B will therefore no longer employ any active members in ABC pension scheme at a time when Company A (ie another participating employer) continues to do so.

A *s 75* debt is triggered and is the responsibility of Company B – so Company C (the buyer) will be concerned about having bought a company with a *s 75* liability.

Company C may ask for a lower price for Company B. Alternatively, Company A may agree (see below for discussion on how to implement such an agreement) to retain responsibility for paying the *s 75* debt, particularly where it has agreed to retain responsibility for the transferring employees' past service liabilities (ie there is a 'clean break').

Case study 4 – an internal group reorganisation

If all Company B's employees are moved to Company A, Company B will no longer employ any active DB members in ABC pension scheme at a time when Company A will continue to employ active DB members.

So, there is an ECE and Company B's *s 75* debt is triggered.

Case study 5 – passage of time

Company B's *s 75* debt is triggered if its last active member in the scheme retires or dies at a time when Company A continues to employ active DB members.

This may occur as a result of a passage of time, especially if ABC pension scheme is closed to new DB entrants so younger employees are no longer joining the scheme.

Case study 6 – when reducing pension costs or de-risking

Company B may trigger a *s 75* debt if it transfers all its employees out of ABC pension scheme – so that it no longer employs any active DB members – at a time when Company A continues to employ active DB members in the scheme.

Company B may do such a transfer to try to manage its ongoing liability to ABC pension scheme.

Former employers and frozen schemes

3.2.3   Importantly, an ECE is not triggered if all the employers cease to participate in a multi-employer scheme at the same time (ie the scheme is frozen).

However, all the employers at the time of freezing (ie that previously 'employed persons in the description of employment to which the scheme relates') remain liable (unless they are specifically excluded) for paying the *s 75* debt when it is triggered at a later stage – that is, on the scheme beginning to wind up or a scheme failure notice. Former employers that are excluded from having any further liabilities include those that ceased to participate in an ongoing scheme before it was frozen and later paid their share of the *s 75* debt (or entered into an arrangement under the *Employer Debt Regulations* – see *Dealing with a section 75 debt,* **3.3** below).

Due diligence therefore becomes important when buying a company that used to participate in a pension scheme and could still be 'on the hook' as a former employer for a future *s 75* debt. A buyer may seek protection against such exposure either by way of an indemnity (depending on the strength of the seller's group) or some other form of collateral.

The *Employer Debt Regulations* (after their amendment in April 2008) now look for the ECE trigger to occur when an employer ceases to be the employer of active members in a scheme. Before April 2008, the relevant definition referred to being an employer of 'persons in the description or category to which the scheme relates'. It looks from the cases that this is a wider expression, so that a company can remain an 'employer' for statutory purposes if it has employees (who could join the scheme), even if none of them is an active member – see Peter Smith J in the *Cemex* case[4] and later Warren J in the *Pilots* case.[5] See **2.4** above.

Who is the employer?

3.2.4   All this means that it is important to work out exactly who is an 'employer' for statutory purposes. In some corporate groups this may not be easy (as a factual issue) – employees may have moved from company to company and the records may not be complete. In most issues (at least before insolvency) this has not mattered – but it can now for *s 75* purposes. See **2.4** above.

---

4   *Cemex UK Marine Ltd v MNOPF Trustees Ltd* [2009] EWHC 3258 (Ch), [2010] ICR 732.
5   *PNPF Trust Co Ltd v Taylor* [2010] EWHC 1573 (Ch).

Twelve-month grace period (*extendable to three years*)

3.2.5   Under *reg 6A* of the *Employer Debt Regulations* (as amended in 2008 and in 2012), an employer can serve a notice to be given a 12-month 'period of grace' to re-employ an active member before a *s 75* debt is triggered. The notice must be served before the date that is two months (extended from one month from 2012) after the cessation. From 27 January 2012, the trustees are able to agree to extend the period of grace above 12 months to a later date (but not more than three years). Any extension must be made by the trustees before the period of grace would otherwise expire.

If the employer does not employ an active member within the period of grace and it notifies the trustees of the scheme that it has no intention to employ such persons or becomes insolvent, the period of grace is treated as never having occurred and the *s 75* debt is triggered from the usual time.

Note that this period of grace only applies for *s 75*; it does not affect a former employer's liability (if any) to continue making ongoing payments into the scheme in accordance with the scheme-specific funding regime and/or the scheme's rules.

How is a s 75 debt calculated on an ECE?

3.2.6   Broadly, an employer that ceases to participate in the scheme will be liable for a share of the total buy-out deficit for the whole scheme. The individual employer's share is calculated as a percentage based on:

- the scheme benefit liabilities 'attributable to employment' with the employer, divided by;
- the scheme benefit liabilities 'attributable to employment' with all the current employers,

unless an alternative is agreed, for example, through a scheme apportionment arrangement (see *Dealing with a section 75 debt – apportionment and withdrawal arrangements*, **3.3**).

Section 75 debt for employer X is the Total Debt × A ÷ B

where   ***Total Debt*** = the total *s 75* debt for the whole scheme;

A = benefit liabilities attributable to employment with employer X

B = benefit liabilities attributable to employment with all current employers (including X).

There may be some benefit liabilities that are not attributable to a current employer (eg they may be attributable to a former employer who has now left the scheme). These are commonly called 'orphan liabilities'. The effect of the sharing formula above is that the leaving employer's *s 75* debt includes a share of the deficit for the orphan liabilities.

What does attributable to employment mean?

3.2.7   Clearly benefit liabilities relating to employment with a particular employer are treated for this purpose as 'attributable' to that employer. This includes liabilities arising under the pension scheme as a result of a transfer-in in relation to a member if he or she was employed by that employer at the date of the transfer-in (ie even if the transfer-in related to benefits in another scheme and were not all attributable to the same employer in that other scheme) – *reg 6(4)(b)*.

The *Employer Debt Regulations* give guidance on how scheme benefit liabilities should be allocated if trustees are:

- unable to determine exact benefit liabilities attributable to the exiting employer; or

- able to do so only at disproportionate cost.

This is useful if, for example, the employer has not kept detailed records of intra-group transfers.

Under the *Employer Debt Regulations*, *reg 6(4)(c)* if all allocation is not otherwise possible, then:

- if the exiting employer was a person's last employer, all benefit liabilities of that person are attributed to that employer;

- benefit liabilities in respect of any member that cannot be attributed to any employer are attributed in a 'reasonable manner' to one or more employer (which may or may not include the exiting employer); and

- if the trustees are unable to determine whether the exiting employer was the last employer and benefit liabilities cannot be attributed to any employer, those benefit liabilities are not attributed to any employer (ie they become 'orphan' liabilities).

Orphan liabilities: example of how an exiting employer's debt is calculated

3.2.8   Assume:

Three current employers A, B and C;

3.2.8 *Debt on the employer – section 75 issues*

Total buy-out liability – £100 million;

Total scheme assets – £70 million;

Section 75 deficit (for the whole scheme) – £30 million.

	Benefit liability attributable to employer(say):	*Deficit on share of asset basis*	*Share of s 75 debt*
Employer A's benefit liability in scheme attributable to employment with A	£10m	£3m	£6m
Employer B's benefit liability in scheme	£20m	£6m	£12m
Employer C's benefit liability in scheme	£20m	£6m	£12m
Orphan benefit liabilities in scheme (ienot attributable to employment with A, B or C)	£50m	£15m	
Employer A's (*exiting employer*) *s 75 debt*	1/5× £30m [total scheme deficit] = £6m [NB1/5th of total deficit, even though only 1/10th of members' benefit liabilities attributable to Employer A]		

144

3.3   Dealing with a *s 75* debt – apportionment and withdrawal arrangements

Summary

When an employer leaves a multi-employer defined benefit pension scheme, an employer debt – a *s 75* debt – may arise if the scheme was underfunded.

There are five main arrangements for managing a *s 75* debt. This section explains what they are and the conditions under which they can apply.

Other strategies for dealing with a *s 75* debt are also touched on (eg schemes of arrangement and company voluntary arrangements).

3.3.1   The employment-cessation event trigger (see **3.2** above) aims to reduce the likelihood of employers exiting a scheme in advance (eg of the scheme winding-up) to escape a potential *s 75* liability, leaving the last employer with the whole liability. But *s 75* is a very specific debt provision. It can unnecessarily hinder a restructuring and transaction because it makes limited allowance for the possibility that the scheme will be ongoing, backed by a financially strong employer and funded on an agreed scheme-specific basis (or a recovery plan).

Requiring a lump sum funding payment under *s 75* on the buy-out basis can also be inconsistent with the balance of powers between the trustees and employer that is envisaged by the scheme-specific funding requirements.

One obvious way to deal with a *s 75* debt is to pay it, but this may be an undesirable use of resources within the group, especially if the debt is significant.

There are, however, several mechanisms and easements under the *Employer Debt Regulations 2005* that can mitigate the effects of a *s 75* debt being triggered.

Different arrangements

3.3.2   Under the *Employer Debt Regulations* as amended in 2008 (and again in 2010 and from 2012), there are seven main options for dealing with a *s 75* debt. These are summarised below:

3.3.2 *Debt on the employer – section 75 issues*

1.   Scheme apportionment arrangement (SAA)

This allows trustees to consent to the exiting employer paying the 'scheme apportionment arrangement share', which can be less than the default liability share. The arrangement also needs to be reflected on the face of the rules. One of the remaining employers will usually take over (as a contingent obligation) the exiting employer's unpaid *s 75* debt liability or the exiting employer's benefit obligations. The remaining employers must meet the 'funding test' (see below).

2.   Flexible apportionment arrangement (FAA) (added from 27 January 2012)

The wording of the relevant regulations is very confusing but the aim seems to be very similar to an SAA. An FAA allows trustees to agree with the exiting employer and a receiving employer for the exiting employer to pay a nil or reduced *s 75* debt and the receiving employer agreeing to an increased (contingent) *s 75* debt liability, in that all the exiting employer's scheme liabilities (including benefit liabilities of members with the exiting employer) need to be transferred to the receiving employer. The remaining employers must meet the 'funding test' (see below) and the trustee must be satisfied that an assessment period with the PPF is unlikely to begin within one year.

3.   Regulated apportionment arrangement (RAA)

This is similar to an SAA but is relevant only if the trustees believe there is a reasonable likelihood of the scheme entering an assessment period for the Pension Protection Fund (PPF) in the next 12 months or if an assessment period has already started. The Pensions Regulator (TPR) must issue a notice of approval and the PPF must not object to the proposal.

Unlike under the other four arrangements (SAA, FAA WA and AWA) there is no requirement under an RAA for the remaining employers to meet the statutory funding test.

4.   Withdrawal arrangement (WA)

This does not require TPR's approval. Trustees can agree with an employer that a lower debt (based on the scheme funding deficit rather than the buy-out deficit) is payable, with the difference guaranteed by another employer(s) in the scheme or a third party. The 'funding test' must be met (see below) and the trustees must be satisfied that the guarantors have sufficient financial resources to be able to pay the guaranteed amount when required.

5.   Approved withdrawal arrangement (AWA)

This option is the same as a WA but requires TPR's agreement and can be used if the exiting employer proposes to pay less than the scheme-funding amount share of the debt. TPR must be satisfied that it is reasonable to approve the arrangement, taking into account such matters as it considers relevant, including:

- the potential effects of the employment-cessation event on the method or assumptions for calculating the scheme's technical provisions;

- the financial circumstances of the proposed guarantor;

- the amount of the liability share (if it had applied);

- the amount of the AWA share; and

- the effect of the proposed AWA on the security of members' benefits.

6 and 7   Intra-group easements

Two new easements (for intra-group transactions) were added in 2010. These are the group and *de minimis* easements – see **3.4** below.

What is the funding test?

3.3.3   The statutory funding test is set out in the *Employer Debt Regulations, regs 2(4A)* to (*4D*). To meet the funding test (which needs to be satisfied for four of the five types of the arrangements above, ie excluding an RAA), the trustees must be 'reasonably satisfied' that, when the arrangement takes effect:

- the remaining employers (or employer if only a single employer remains) will be reasonably likely to be able to fund the scheme; and

- that it will have sufficient and appropriate assets to cover its technical provisions (ie any deficit on the scheme specific funding basis under *Part 3* of the *Pensions Act 2004*), taking account of any change in the technical provisions necessary as a result of the arrangement.

Trustees may consider the test met if, in their opinion, the remaining employers are able to meet the relevant payments as they fall due under the schedule of contributions, taking account of any revision necessary.

For an SAA or FAA, trustees must also be reasonably satisfied that there is no adverse effect on the security of members' benefits as a result of:

- a material change in legal, demographic or economic circumstances that would justify a change to method and assumptions; or

3.3.3 *Debt on the employer – section 75 issues*

•   a material revision to an existing recovery plan.

The expression 'reasonably satisfied' is not defined further in the *Employer Debt Regulations*. It seems to envisage a factual test being satisfied. One problem is that third parties (eg a purchaser of an exiting or leaving employer) will not be able to know definitively if the trustees have actually so satisfied themselves (even if they say so in the arrangements, this is presumably not definitive).

To be reasonably satisfied about the funding test, it seems likely that a court would hold[6] that the trustees must:

•   actually hold that view; and

•   be satisfied they have evidence that the facts are sufficient to induce that belief or opinion in a reasonable person.

Should the trustees agree to any apportionments?

3.3.4 Trustees' normal fiduciary duties will apply. The trustees will need to exercise their powers for a proper purpose – often this is in what they consider to be the best interests of the scheme, having regard to the interests of all the beneficiaries (including, in most schemes, the employer).

To comply with their fiduciary duties under trust law, the trustees would need to have good grounds for agreeing to any such apportionment. This can lead to prolonged negotiations.

If the parties applied for clearance from TPR (see *Section 75 debt arrangements and the Pensions Regulator,* **3.5**) the trustees may be able to get significant comfort from this.

Amendment to reflect an apportionment arrangement

3.3.5 Trustees have a statutory power (under *s 68(2)(e)* of the *Pensions Act 1995*) to amend scheme rules 'after consulting such employers in relation to the scheme as they think appropriate' to provide for an employer's share of the difference under one of the options (SAA, WA etc) to be attributed in a different

---

6   There are, as yet, no reported court decisions on the funding test under the *Employer Debt Regulations*. But this analysis fits with the legislation and two Australian decisions (on similar wording) in different legislation say this: *ING Funds v ANZ Nominees* [2009] NSWSC 243, (2009) 228 FLR 444 and *Gypsy Jokers Motorcycle Club v Commissioner of Police* [2008] HCA 4, (2008) 234 CLR 532.

proportion from that which would otherwise apply by virtue of the liability share that would apply under the *Employer Debt Regulations*.

Extra easements from 2010

3.3.6   Since 6 April 2010, the *Employer Debt Regulations 2005* have contained two new limited easements that prevent an employment-cessation event from occurring and therefore no *s 75* debt being triggered.

Broadly, the general easement is meant to allow restructurings that do not entail a weakening in the employer covenant; and the *de minimis* easement applies for small-scale restructurings.

A key feature of both easements is that they can only be used in 'one-to-one' transactions, where one employer (the 'receiving employer') agrees to take over all the other employer's (the 'exiting employer') employees, assets, scheme members and scheme liabilities. The easements are complex to apply and limited in scope – they are not available, for example, in a multiple restructuring across an employer group. See further, *The general and de minimis easements from 2010,* **3.4** below.

Other ways of dealing with a s 75 debt

3.3.7   There are other strategies for dealing with a *s 75* debt outside the *Employer Debt Regulations* that may be helpful in certain circumstances. For example, the trustees of the scheme may agree to compromise the debt as part of:

- schemes of arrangement under *s 895* of the *Companies Act 2006* (formerly *Companies Act 1985, s 425*); or
- company voluntary arrangements (CVAs) under *Part 1* of the *Insolvency Act 1986*.

Generally, trustees will be cautious about agreeing to compromise a *s 75* debt (outside an arrangement under the *Employer Debt Regulations*) because this may make the scheme ineligible for PPF entry.

For more information, see *UK defined benefit pension schemes and corporate restructurings,* **9.1** below.

3.3.8 *Debt on the employer – section 75 issues*

The five main different arrangements for managing a s 75 debt

3.3.8

	Withdrawal arrangement (WA)	Approved withdrawal arrangement (AWA)	Scheme apportionment arrangement (SAA)	Regulated apportionment arrangement (RAA)	Flexible Apportion- ment Arrangement (FAA)
How much must exiting employer pay?	Employer must pay an amount equal to or greater (not less) than Amount A	Yes– Employer must be paying *less* than Amount A	Can be £1	Can be £1	Nil
Who can take a liability?	Anyone	Anyone	Must be an employer	Must be an employer	Must be an employer
Funding test must be satisfied?	Yes	Yes	Yes, unless: 1. SAA share higher than liability share and employer can afford to pay SAA share; or 2. scheme in wind-up and SAA share is lower than liability share and employer could not pay liability share and can pay SAA share	Not applicable	Yes
Trustee consent?	Trustees must be satisfied guarantors can pay amount B	Trustees must notify TPR that funding test is met	Yes	Yes (unless PPF assessment period has commenced)	Yes

	Withdrawal arrangement (*WA*)	*Approved withdrawal arrangement* (*AWA*)	*Scheme apportionment arrangement* (*SAA*)	*Regulated apportionment arrangement* (*RAA*)	*Flexible Apportionment Arrangement* (FAA)
Regulator approval required?	No	Yes. Regulator must consider arrangement reasonable	No	Yes. Regulator must consider arrangement reasonable	No
PPF approval required?	No	No	No	Must not object	No
Timing	Any	Any	Any	Any – however, this option is only appropriate where PPF assessment period has commenced or is likely to.	Any– however, this option is only appropriate where PPF assessment period is not likely to commence within one year.
Notes			Arrangement must be under scheme rules	Arrangement must be under scheme rules	

Amount A is the amount the employer agrees to pay, which is its share of the scheme's deficit on an SSF basis. Amount B is the balance between amount A and the share of the buy-out debt (ie the balance of the *s 75* debt)

Funding test – when arrangement takes effect, remaining employers will be reasonably likely to be able to fund the scheme/will have sufficient and appropriate assets to cover technical provisions

For an SAA or FAA, trustees must also (in practice) be satisfied that there is no adverse effect on the security of members' benefits

3.3.8 *Debt on the employer – section 75 issues*

3.4 *Section 75* – intra-group transfers – the general and *de minimis* easements from 2010

Summary

Since 6 April 2010, employers have been able to use two new easements during corporate restructurings to manage pension scheme debts that can arise under *s 75* of the *Pensions Act 1995*.

This section:

- analyses the changes,

- discusses whether they will be helpful to employers,

- considers how they compare to tried and tested strategies for managing *s 75* debts, and

- considers the role of trustees if employers choose to use these new tools.

The easements are complex to apply and limited in scope. In practice this has meant that they have not much been used.

3.4.1 The *Employer Debt Regulations 2005* were amended from April 2010 to make it easier to carry out some corporate restructurings without triggering a debt under *s 75* of the *Pensions Act 1995*.

The relaxed rules can be used only in one-to-one restructurings between two current employers – and one of the employers must agree to take over all the other's employees, assets, scheme members and scheme liabilities. Other conditions must also be satisfied.

Background

3.4.2 If an 'employment-cessation event' (ECE) occurs, an employer that participates in an underfunded defined-benefit (DB) scheme will be required by statute to pay the trustees their share of the pension scheme's liabilities – these can be substantial when measured on the required buy-out basis. An ECE occurs if an employer stops employing its last active member in a multi-employer pension scheme and another employer continues to employ an active member in the scheme (see **3.2** above).

ECEs can, for example, commonly occur if a company sells its subsidiary so that the subsidiary leaves the corporate group (assuming it ceases to participate in the scheme), or if a company's employees transfer to a new employer on a business sale. This can therefore hinder a restructuring.

The easements added in 2010

3.4.3   On 6 April 2010, the former Labour government amended the employer debt regulations so that it could introduce 'greater flexibility for employers, whilst at the same time maintaining member protection' (September 2009 consultation paper).

The amended employer debt regulations now contain a 'general' and '*de minimis*' easement that can be used in, for example, an intra-group reorganisation. These easements mean that, in some limited circumstances, an ECE that would otherwise occur will not be treated as occurring – therefore, no *s 75* debt is triggered.

Broadly, the general easement is meant to allow restructurings that do not entail a weakening in the employer covenant and the *de minimis* easement applies to small-scale restructurings.

A key feature of both easements is that they can only be used in 'one-to-one' transactions, where one employer (the 'receiving employer') agrees to take over all the other employer's (the 'exiting employer') employees, assets, scheme members and scheme liabilities. The easements are not available, for example, in multiple restructurings across an employer group.

Both employers must already participate in the multi-employer scheme and employ at least one active DB member. The receiving employer must also either be 'associated' (within the meaning of the *Insolvency Act 1986*) with the exiting employer or itself is the 'new legal status' of the exiting employer (see below).

Unlike the apportionment arrangements in the *Employer Debt Regulations* (see **3.3** above), the new easements do not require express trustee consent, nor does the statutory funding test need to be met. They do however set out various prescriptive steps that must be followed.

Who do the easements help?

Only companies that are employers

3.4.4   The easements are only available for restructurings between two parties that employ at least one person who is an active DB scheme member.

3.4.4 *Debt on the employer – section 75 issues*

Companies that do not employ an active DB member in the pension scheme would need to do so before using either easement. If the receiving company is not yet a scheme employer, it would need to become one.

According to the former government, if the receiving employer is newly created it may not be possible for that employer already to be participating in the scheme before completing the restructuring: the policy is, therefore, that the receiving employer only has to employ at least one active member in respect of whom defined benefits are accruing once the transaction is completed.

For restructurings involving newly created employers (and companies that are not yet employers) the trustees may, in practice, be able to veto the transaction. In many schemes, the trustees must consent before a new company becomes a participating employer.

When will the two employers be associated?

3.4.5 The concept of 'associated' will normally catch companies in the same group but can also catch a much broader ranger of entities. For more information see *Who is 'connected' or 'associated'?*, **4.2**.

The employers can cease to be associated after the easements have been used in the restructuring – but this may trigger a *s 75* debt for different reasons.

What is the 'new legal status' of an employer?

3.4.6 The employer debt regulations do not explain what is meant by 'new legal status'. But the former government's September 2009 consultation stated that the effect of this provision is that if a change is made to the legal status of an employer (eg a general partnership becomes a limited liability partnership, which is a body corporate) the parties can use the general easement to ensure no debt is triggered on that change in status. This may perhaps also cover the conversion of a company into a European company (Societas Europaea – SE) under the relevant European legislation.

Under the employer debt regulations, a *s 75* debt may otherwise be triggered where there is a change of legal status. So this provision may be some help.

No record of insolvencies

3.4.7   There is an additional requirement that neither the exiting nor receiving employer must have previously suffered an insolvency event, been voluntarily wound up or had a *s 129* notice made.[7]

This appears overly restrictive. If an insolvency occurred in the past but has since been discharged, there is no obvious reason why the easements should not apply.

A closer look at the changes

Taking over the exiting employer's assets, employees, scheme members and scheme liabilities

3.4.8   To use either the general or *de minimis* easement, the receiving employer is required (on or after 6 April 2010) to use a legally enforceable agreement to take over all the exiting employer's:

- assets ('without exception', even if greater than the exiting employer's liabilities to the scheme);

- employees, regardless of whether they transfer under the *Transfer of Undertakings* (*Protection of Employment*) *Regulations 2006* (*Tupe*);

- pension scheme members; and

- DB liabilities to the scheme (including any liabilities that are not attributable to any employer – ie orphan liabilities – or any scheme funding liabilities under a schedule of contributions or recovery plan).

Presumably, the requirement to transfer all the exiting employer's assets means that the benefit of being able to enforce the legally enforceable agreement against the receiving employer would also have to be transferred to that receiving employer (ie this will give the receiving employer the ability to enforce the transaction against itself). It is not clear if this was the former government's intention.

All the employees need to transfer or cease to be employed. Not one employee can remain with the exiting employer.

---

7   *Section 129* of the *Pensions Act 2004* applies to some employers who cannot enter an insolvency process (eg charities or trade unions). It allows the trustees and pensions regulator to trigger the Pension Protection Fund (PPF) process by a notice to the PPF, if the scheme's employer is unlikely to continue as a going concern.

3.4.8   *Debt on the employer – section 75 issues*

If *Tupe* applies (eg because it is a transfer of the whole of the business of the exiting company), the employees will transfer automatically. *Tupe* allows for employees to refuse to transfer, but the exiting employer will need to treat them as having resigned or as dismissed. In either event, they will cease to be employees of the exiting company so the obligation that the receiving employer takes over all employees will have been met.

If *Tupe* does not apply (which is probably unlikely), the employees will almost certainly need to consent if they are being transferred to the receiving employer. Consent may be relatively easy to obtain, since the exiting employer will presumably cease to trade once the transfer takes place. However, if any employees do refuse to transfer then the exiting employer will either have to persuade them or dismiss them.

The transfers must take place within 18 weeks of the trustees notifying the receiving and exiting employers they are satisfied that either the restructuring test is met (in the case of the general easement) or the relevant thresholds are not exceeded (for the *de minimis* easement). This period can be extended by up to 18 additional weeks if the trustees agree.

Unfortunately, the legislation does not explain how this legally enforceable agreement is meant to operate when taking over the pension scheme members and liabilities.

If it is 'impossible' for the receiving employer to use a legally enforceable agreement to take over 'all' its scheme liabilities, the exiting employer's liabilities have to be 'treated for all purposes as being the responsibility of the receiving employer' instead. Again, the legislation does not explain how this is to be achieved.

General easement

3.4.9   To satisfy the general easement, the trustees and employers are required to carry out seven steps (see table below).

The main financial test is for the trustees to be 'satisfied' that the receiving employer will be 'at least as likely' to meet the exiting employer's scheme liabilities and their own pre-existing liabilities after replacing the exiting employer – the 'restructuring test'.

The former government, in its consultation response, stated that its policy intention is for the trustees to be 'broadly satisfied' (ie 'all things considered and taking one thing with another') that the restructuring test is met and not necessarily 'certain'.

When applying this restructuring test, the employer debt regulations state that trustees must take into account the change in employer covenant – that is,

156

'factors including any material change in legal, demographic or economic circumstances … that would justify a change to the method or assumptions used on the last occasion on which the scheme's technical provisions were calculated [under the scheme-specific funding requirements]'.

Although this easement is only meant to apply to 'one-to-one' restructurings, the former government commented that 'there is no limit on the number of such transactions that can be undertaken by employers for the general easement'. But, in practice it is not clear how attractive it is to repeat the procedure a number of times, given the prescriptive nature of the seven-stage test and the cost of a covenant review to help satisfy the 'restructuring test'.

De minimis easement

3.4.10   The *de minimis* easement is intended to apply only in cases of small-scale corporate restructuring.

To use this easement, the trustees and employers need to take five steps. However, there is no need to satisfy a restructuring test or funding test (as there is for scheme apportionment arrangements – see below).

The former government suggested that this easement may be helpful where, for example, it is inappropriate to use the general easement because of 'potential extra cost that covenant assessments could entail (which could well outweigh the actual level of employer debt)' due to the restructuring test.

The *de minimis* easement states that a *s 75* debt will not be triggered if, among other things, the trustees are satisfied that:

- the scheme is funded up to Pension Protection Fund (PPF) protected levels (see **5.2** below);

- the number of DB scheme members who are attributable to the exiting employer is either no more than 2%, or less than 3% of all the DB scheme members, whichever is greater;

- the total annual amount of accrued pensions of the members that are transferring does not exceed £20,000 in the 2010/11 tax year (this figure increases by £500 in subsequent tax years); and

- in a rolling three-year period the *de minimis* easement is not used to transfer more than five members, or 7.5%, of all the DB scheme members – whichever is larger. The total annual amount of accrued pensions of members who are transferring must also not exceed £50,000 in this three-year period. The former government commented that these restrictions are intended to 'limit the number of times the *de minimis* easement can be used in a multi-employer scheme'.

3.4.11   *Debt on the employer – section 75 issues*

Cut-off date and moral hazard

3.4.11   An ECE will be treated as having occurred as normal (and therefore a *s 75* debt will be triggered) if some of the steps necessary for the general and *de minimis* easement were not carried out properly before a six-year 'cut-off date'.

An ECE will be treated as having occurred if the employers provided incorrect or incomplete information and the trustees are satisfied that they would 'have made a different decision' when deciding if the restructuring test was satisfied for the general easement. This makes accurate and full information fundamentally important. Employers will also not be sure about how much information they must give the trustees, so it would be unreasonable for the trustees to claim that any gaps in the information (that are subsequently discovered) would have been fundamental to their decision.

An ECE will also be treated as having occurred where either easement was used and there has been an incomplete transfer of assets, employees, scheme members or scheme liabilities; or the employers failed to notify the trustees of the transfer. Again this creates some uncertainty because it is not clear how parties are expected to use a 'legally enforceable agreement' to transfer scheme members and scheme liabilities, as discussed above. Also, it is not clear who should be a party to, or be able to enforce, such an agreement as discussed below.

The former government introduced this six-year cut-off date to 'address situations where the general easement could otherwise hamper future corporate mergers and acquisitions if a potential debt continues to hang (for an indefinite period) over a company or companies eg where the group later wishes to dispose of that company or those companies'. However, the many uncertainties discussed in this section will make it difficult for employers that use the easements to be confident that a *s 75* debt will not still be triggered within the six years.

Cost of the restructuring

3.4.12   The trustees or managers may allocate 'any costs' incurred by them because of a restructuring under easement to the exiting, receiving or both employers.

The amended employer debt regulations do not contain any provisions for the employers to dispute these costs.

Are the easements more useful than scheme apportionment arrangements?

3.4.13 The easements do not replace scheme apportionment arrangements (SAAs) under the employer debt regulations. SAAs (and now FAAs) allow trustees to agree to the exiting employer paying an agreed share of the scheme's total *s 75* debt liability, which can be less than their default share. The remaining employers must, however, be able to meet the 'funding test' (see below).

In practice, only the general easement will be relevant to most transactions, given the low thresholds for the *de minimis* easement.

It appears easier for employers to satisfy the restructuring test for the general easement than the funding test for SAAs and FAAs – giving them an important advantage in the limited circumstances under which the easement can be used.

For SAAs and FAAs, the trustees have to be reasonably satisfied that 'the remaining employers will be reasonably likely to be able to fund the scheme' in accordance with the scheme-specific funding requirements. Depending on the scheme liabilities, the employers may have a task on their hands persuading the trustees that they can meet this standard – giving the trustees greater bargaining power in a transaction.

In addition, the trustees' consent is needed for an SAA or FAA.

Conversely, for the general easement the trustees only need to be satisfied that the receiving employer's ability to fund the scheme is no worse than the exiting employer's (even if the outlook is poor for both companies).

However, uncertainties and practical difficulties may undermine the advantage of using the general easement instead of an SAA or FAA.

For the general easement (and the *de minimis* easement), it is unclear who must be a party to and be able to enforce the 'legally enforceable agreement' to take over the receiving employer's assets, employees and pension scheme members. It could be argued that the trustees or pension scheme members should be able to enforce the legally enforceable agreement and/or be a party to it (not just both employers). If this is correct, the trustees and members may have a greater role to play in restructurings. For example, they would have significant discretion when deciding whether to agree to the legally enforceable agreement. This would undermine the supposed benefit of using the general easement instead of an SAA.

However, the drafting of the employer debt regulations suggests that the former government probably did not intend anybody other than the exiting and receiving employer to be a party to the agreement or be able to enforce it.

3.4.13 *Debt on the employer – section 75 issues*

Nevertheless, it would be helpful if it had addressed this point (especially given that we made the former government aware of this uncertainty when it consulted on the changes).

A practical difficulty with the general easement is that the trustees must be convinced that the restructuring test is satisfied right up to the point of transfer to the receiving employer. The employers will therefore need to co-ordinate their signing of the agreement with the trustees' confirmation of their continued satisfaction, To overcome this, the trustees will probably either need to meet (at the point of transfer) to confirm this decision or delegate it to someone who will be present at the time of transfer.

These uncertainties and practical difficulties do not necessarily mean that the general easement is less useful than the SAA, just that it is less tested.

Clearance?

3.4.14   The former government also commented that 'there is nothing in these regulations that would prevent the Pensions Regulator from using its anti-avoidance powers [to issue a contribution notice or financial support direction] where it considers it reasonable to do so, and the legal tests for using those powers have been met'. So clearance from the Pensions Regulator may still be necessary, or at least desirable (see *Section 75 debts and the Pensions Regulator,* **3.5** below).

Should the parties notify the Regulator?

3.4.15   There is probably an obligation to notify the Pensions Regulator when using either of the easements. The requirement for the exiting employer to transfer all its assets and employees will probably mean that it will 'cease to carry on business in the United Kingdom', which must be notified to the Regulator under the *Pensions Regulator (Notifiable Events) Regulations 2005 –* see *Notifiable events*, **13.1**. This notifiable event is not one that benefits from the exemption that applies to some notifiable events if the relevant scheme is funded over the PPF level.

The employer will probably have to notify the Regulator as soon as reasonably practicable after it decides to enter such a transaction, which will be before the transaction is finalised, The Regulator's guidance indicates that this obligation implies urgency: for example, where a trustee is made aware of a notifiable event on a Sunday, the Regulator should be notified on Monday.'

Failure to notify, without reasonable excuse, can lead to a civil fine on the employer (and the directors and officers who cause a company to fail to comply with its obligations). The maximum civil fine is £5,000 for individuals and £50,000 for a company.

The *Pensions Act 2004* also stipulates that failure to report a notifiable event may, in some circumstances, make it 'reasonable' for the Regulator to issue a contribution notice under its moral hazard powers.

For more information see *Notifiable events: Obligations to report certain events to the Pensions Regulator*, **13.1**.

Steps needed for general and de minimis easements

3.4.16

General easement	De minimis easement
Employers should also consider whether it is necessary to notify the Pensions Regulator and/or desirable to ask it for clearance. This may affect the timetable below.	
Step 1 – must take place before step 2 *(exiting employer to decide when)* Exiting employer to write to trustees asking them to make their decision on restructuring test in step 4.	*Step 1 – must take place before step 2* *(exiting employer to decide when)* Exiting employer to write to trustees asking for them to make decision.
Step 2 – must take place 'without undue delay' Both exiting and receiving employer (unless receiving employer not yet created) provide information to trustees. Trustees may request information (which employers must provide).	*Step 2 – must take place 'without undue delay'* Trustees to decide if they are satisfied that restructuring is below the *de minimis* threshold tests.
Step 3 – must take place 'without undue delay' Trustees consult both exiting and receiving employer (unless receiving employer not yet created) about restructuring test in step 4.	*Step 3 – must take place 'without undue delay'* Trustees to notify both exiting and receiving employer (unless receiving employer not yet created) in writing of their decision and reason for decision in step 2.

3.4.16 *Debt on the employer – section 75 issues*

General easement	De minimis easement
Step 4 – must take place 'without undue delay' Trustees to decide if they are satisfied that restructuring test is met.	*Step 4 – must take place within 18 weeks (or up to 36 weeks if trustees agree) of step 3* Receiving employer to take over exiting employer's assets, employees, scheme members and liabilities under a legally enforceable agreement.
Step 5 – must take place 'without undue delay' Trustees to notify both exiting and receiving employer (unless receiving employer not yet created) in writing of their decision and reasons for decision.	*Step 5 – must take place 'without undue delay'* Both employers notify trustees that step 4 is completed and date of completion.
Step 6 – must take place within 18 weeks (or up to 36 weeks if trustees agree) of step 5 Receiving employer to take over exiting employer's assets, employees, scheme members and scheme liabilities under a legally enforceable agreement. Receiving employer decides whether to take step 6, but can only do so if: • trustees decided they were satisfied in step 4; • trustees are satisfied there has been no change that would alter their decision in step 4; and • within 18 weeks (or up to 36 weeks if trustees choose).	
Step 7 – must take place 'without undue delay' Both employers notify trustees that step 6 is completed and date of completion.	

Other legal issues

3.4.17   The other legal implications of a relevant transfer will also need to be considered, including those listed below.

Employee notification and consultation: the transfer is likely to be a transfer within *Tupe*, so appropriate notification and consultation will be needed. In practice, these may be minimal if no changes in employment terms or working conditions are envisaged.

Onward position of exiting employer: the exiting employer will cease to have any assets or employees (it may perhaps retain non-scheme-related liabilities). In practice, this is likely to mean that the exiting employer is technically insolvent, so its directors will aim to transfer all liabilities as well (or perhaps look for some legal support for them from the receiving company).

Implications for benefits under the scheme: in practice, it is likely that benefits will continue as before for the relevant employees (ie their service will be treated as continuous). The terms of the scheme need to be checked to confirm this. Schemes that have closed to new entrants and are relying on the exemption from indirect age discrimination under the relevant regulations will need to check that this exemption continues to be available.

Providing information: the fact that the exiting employer will cease to be an employer probably needs to be notified to the trustees within one month, under the Scheme Administration Regulations 1996 – for background information on these regulations see *When should employers disclose a proposed transaction to trustees or the Pensions Regulator?*, **13.4**. The trustees will want to inform their advisers (eg the actuary and auditor) and consider if any change to, for example, the schedule of contributions is desirable as a result.

3.5   *Section 75* debt arrangements and the Pensions Regulator

3.5.1

Summary

Certain events – such as a reorganisation – can trigger an obligation for an employer to contribute to its defined-benefit pension scheme (a '*s 75* debt').

There are many pitfalls in handling this situation, including some complicated decisions over whether it needs to be declared to or approved by the Pensions Regulator.

This section outlines the issues and how to handle them.

Events such as company reorganisations can trigger an obligation for an employer to contribute to its defined-benefit (DB) pension scheme. This is known as a *s 75* debt, because it arises under *s 75* of the *Pensions Act 1995*. *Section 75: Debt on the employer – overview,* **3.1** above explains more fully. This section deals specifically with the obligation to report arrangements connected with certain *s 75* debts to the Pensions Regulator (TPR) and whether clearance from TPR is necessary or desirable.

The Pensions Regulator's 'moral hazard' powers

3.5.2   TPR is given powers under the *Pensions Act 2004* that aim to discourage employers from abusing corporate structures to avoid their liabilities (including liability under *s 75*) to a DB scheme. These powers are broad and allow TPR to make employers and third parties that are 'connected' or 'associated' with the employer liable for the deficit in an employer's pension scheme (see generally Chapter **4** below).

The definitions of 'connected' and 'associated' are broad and can include other companies in the group, an employer's director or a shareholder with one-third or more of the company's shares.

TPR can issue a contribution notice (CN) requiring a person to make a contribution into the scheme if they were party to an act (or failure to act):

●   that has had a materially detrimental effect on the likelihood of scheme members receiving their accrued benefits; or

- the 'main purpose' of which was to:

    – prevent the recovery of the whole or part of a *s 75* debt; or

    – prevent the *s 75* debt from becoming due or to compromise, settle or reduce the *s 75* debt.

TPR can also require an employer or connected or associated third party to put financial support in place for the scheme.

On the face of it, most attempts to manage or reduce an employer's *s 75* debt may be at risk of a CN either because they may be considered materially detrimental to members' benefits or because their main purpose may be to prevent recovery of the debt or prevent the debt becoming due.

However, the *Pensions Act 2004* contains a formal clearance procedure whereby an employer (or persons connected or associated with the employer) can seek confirmation from TPR that a proposed transaction will not fall foul of the moral hazard provisions.

For more information, see Chapter **4** below, in particular: *Extracting pension scheme funding from third parties: overview*, **4.1** and *Who is 'connected' or 'associated'?*, **4.2.**

Is clearance needed when dealing with a s 75 debt?

3.5.3   TPR's guidance indicates that clearance should be considered for 'type A events'. Broadly, a type A event occurs in circumstances that would be 'materially detrimental to the ability of the scheme to meet its pension liabilities'. This may be because of an employer's legal obligations (eg an obligation to pay a *s 75* debt) to a scheme and/or because its financial strength is so badly weakened – see *Pensions and transactions – applying to TPR for clearance*, **4.13**.

Examples of a type A event listed in TPR's clearance guidance include: 'an agreement entered into by the trustees to compromise the employer's *s 75* debt and reduce the amount that will be paid to the scheme'. The guidance goes on to state that 'any such attempt to compromise will always be a type A event, irrespective of the level of the scheme's deficit before or after the compromise ...'

Scheme apportionment arrangements

3.5.4   However, TPR states in its clearance guidance that the use of a scheme apportionment arrangement (SAA – see *Dealing with a section 75 debt – apportionment and withdrawal arrangements*, **3.3**) will be a type A event, unless:

3.5.4 *Debt on the employer – section 75 issues*

• it increases the *s 75* debt that is immediately payable by an employer, which can afford the increased *s 75* debt;

• the cost and complexity of other alternatives (including calculating the unmodified *s 75* debt or an approved withdrawal arrangement (AWA)) are far greater or disproportionate and the apportionment results in a *s 75* debt that is the scheme actuary's best estimate of the unmodified *s 75* debt and is immediately payable by the departing employer; or

• the *s 75* debt arises in circumstances in which there is no net reduction of employer covenant – for example, on the consolidation of several employers within the employer group in certain circumstances, provided that all employer assets and their pension liabilities transfer.

If the SAA does not have any of the above features it will, in TPR's opinion, be a type A event irrespective of the level of the scheme's deficit.

Withdrawal arrangements

3.5.5 TPR states in its clearance guidance that a regulated apportionment arrangement (RAA) may be a type A event (so clearance may be appropriate as well as approval of the RAA).

It also says that an AWA may be a type A event, particularly if the guarantee does not sufficiently mitigate the effect of a financially strong employer leaving the scheme (apparently, even if the guarantee is sufficient to meet the exiting employer's liabilities to the scheme). Similarly, other forms of withdrawal arrangement (WA) can be type A events, especially if the guarantee does not sufficiently mitigate the fact that a *s 75* debt is not being paid in full.

General and de minimis easements

3.5.6 Employers that use the general or *de minimis* easement to manage the *s 75* debt (see *Section 75:–The general and de minimis easements*, **3.4**) will also need to consider whether to apply for clearance.

Notifiable events

3.5.7 Some events trigger an obligation to notify TPR. The *Employer Debt Regulations* expressly state that if an SAA is entered into *after* an employment cessation event, or if an FAA is entered into (at any time) it will be a scheme-related notifiable event (see *Notifiable events*, **13.1** below). This triggers an obligation on the trustees to notify TPR of the event. Failure to notify can lead to a maximum civil penalty of £50,000 and can influence TPR's decisions on whether to use its moral hazard powers.

Regulation 2(2) of the *Notifiable Events Regulations 2005* also requires the employer or trustees (depending on who makes the decision) to notify TPR of any decision 'which will, or is intended to, result in any debt which is or may become due to the scheme not being paid in full. For this purpose 'debt' can include a contingent debt so is likely to apply to a *s 75* one that is triggered on an employment-cessation event.

The breadth of these provisions suggests that most attempts to compromise a *s 75* debt will be notifiable.

However, an SAA or FAA entered into before the employment-cessation event does not appear to be a notifiable event because, if the necessary circumstances are satisfied, the debt will be the amount payable under an SAA or FAA. If the intention is that the SAA or FAA amount (which is the *s 75* debt) will be paid in full, this means that the decision to enter into the SAA or FAA will not result in any 'debt' that is 'not being paid in full' and therefore neither the trustee nor the employer should be required to notify TPR.

This view is consistent with and supported by the fact that an SAA entered into *after* an employment-cessation event is expressly stated to be a notifiable event.

Similarly, a WA will also not be a notifiable event because the debt becomes the amount that is payable under the WA.

Notification is less of an issue for RAAs and AWAs because TPR will need to approve these arrangements in any case.

There is probably an obligation to notify TPR when using either the general or *de minimis* easements under the *Employer Debt Regulations* – see **3.4**). The requirement that the exiting employer transfer all its assets and employees will probably mean that it will 'cease to carry on business in the United Kingdom', which must be notified to TPR under the *Notifiable Events Regulations*.

For more information on the notifiable events regime see *Notifiable events: obligation to report certain events to the Pensions Regulator*, **13.1**.

3.6   Tax position on payment of a *s 75* debt into a pension scheme following subsidiary sale

3.6.1

Summary

This section considers the tax position where a *s 75* debt is paid on a sale of a company and looks at the implications of guidance from HM Revenue & Customs (HMRC) on this issue.

Overview

3.6.2   The sale of a subsidiary (Target) will, in practice, mean that it ceases to participate in the pension scheme operated by the Seller. Where the scheme is a UK tax registered group defined benefit scheme, this cessation will often trigger a statutory debt obligation on Target (under *s 75* of the *Pensions Act 1995*).

The amount of the *s 75* debt can be substantial (the figure is based on the amount needed to secure liabilities in the scheme on a 'buy-out' basis and is dependent on market conditions etc and so is variable).

Any potential purchaser of Target will look to reduce any purchase price payable to reflect this debt. Given the uncertainties over its amount, there is a risk that any reduction is likely to be an overestimate.

For this reason it is common for a seller to agree to protect the purchaser against any such liability. The payment will go into the Seller-retained pension scheme and will benefit Seller going forward (and not Target).

Generally payments by employers into registered pension schemes give rise to a tax deduction, even if they are of a capital nature, for the employer. But this only applies if the payment is 'wholly and exclusively' for the purposes of the trade of the employer.[8]

Tax authority (HMRC) guidance on this indicates that:

- a tax deduction should be available for Target if it makes the *s 75* payment (although this would probably be spread over up to four years);

---

8   The rules for employers that carry on investment businesses are slightly different, with separate guidance – see **3.6.8** below.

- it is much less likely that Seller would get a deduction for any amount that it pays; and

- there may be some circumstances when Seller could get a deduction particularly if Target could not pay the *s 75* debt and Seller considers that it needs to in order to preserve its business reputation and the morale of its own employees). Even here the deduction may be limited to any liabilities attributable to 'orphan' members of the Seller pension scheme (ie those not attributable to Target).

If correct, this leaves three options.

Target pays

3.6.3   Target makes the *s 75* payment and claims the tax relief. Seller reimburses the Purchaser (or the price is reduced up front) and adjustments are made for the tax relief, usually by way of payments back to Seller, as and when tax relief is saved.

- This is quite complex to document and the tax relief element can be hard to police.

- Payments by the Seller to the Purchaser and adjustment payments the other way risk being taxable on the recipient. To reduce the risk any payments are usually structured as adjustments to the purchase price.

- Target/Purchaser may not have sufficient taxable profits to be able to utilise the tax relief (eg if the purchaser is debt funded and would otherwise have offset taxable profits with interest costs on acquisition debt). It can be hard to determine exactly when the Target/Purchaser makes a real tax saving, and how much that is.

- The Seller scheme ends up with extra funding. This may lead the trustees to revisit the investment strategy in a way that Seller does not want. Otherwise the extra funding should result in a surplus or lower funding obligations on Seller in the future.

Seller pays

3.6.4   Seller arranges for it (or another employer) to make the payment instead of Target (this requires an agreement with the Seller scheme trustees and the Pensions Regulator, but this is unlikely to be a concern if Seller is paying in full on the sale).

3.6.4 *Debt on the employer – section 75 issues*

- HMRC guidance indicates Seller may not get tax relief, unless it can show that Target could not pay and the payment is attributable to orphans. The issue can be tested by seeking formal guidance from HMRC.

- The Seller scheme ends up with extra funding, which may lead the trustees to revisit the investment strategy in a way that Seller does not want. Otherwise, the extra funding should result in lower funding obligations on Seller in the future.

No-one pays, but security offered

3.6.5   If the *s 75* debt were paid, it would just amount to extra security for the benefits under the Seller scheme. Seller could offer security to the trustees instead of all or part of the full immediate payment (eg a parent guarantee/bank letter of credit/charge over cash or assets). Seller group's ongoing contributions to the Seller scheme would not be affected (ie not reduced because there is no *s 75* payment). Security is gradually released over time as general Seller group contributions are made to the Seller scheme.

- This approach requires agreement with the trustees (and probably the Pensions Regulator). They may be concerned at the loss of security (compared to a full payment now), so ask to be offered security with a value of more than the *s 75* debt. The TPR statement from October 2013 on 'Double Counting' may also be relevant (see **3.1.6** above).

- There is an improved prospect of tax relief for Seller for its normal funding payments, but this is a new area and is not guaranteed. HMRC may perhaps take a view that the Seller contributions are delayed payment of the *s 75* debt (and so potentially not deductible for tax purposes). It may well be arguable, however, that contributions would have been payable anyway (separately from the sale of Target) so are not being paid to enhance the sale price (but instead are wholly and exclusively for the purposes of Seller's trade). It will obviously be helpful if the contributions are similar in amount and timing as would have been made absent a sale of Target, with the only change being the provision of security.

- This issue could be tested by seeking formal guidance from HMRC.

Tax deductions for pension contributions on the sale of a company

3.6.6 HMRC guidance was issued in 2007 as new pages in the Business Income Manual (BIM) and has subsequently been updated, most recently in December 2013 – see BIM46000 onwards.[9]

The guidance is not legally binding, but it gives a good guide to the likely stance that HMRC will take. A more definitive view, based on the specific current circumstances, can be sought by writing for specific guidance.

The tax issue is what tax deduction, if any, is available in relation to the payment of a *s 75* debt on a sale by a seller (such as Seller) of the shares in a target company (such as Target) to a third party, where the target participates in a multi-employer defined benefit pension scheme being retained by the Seller Group (such as the Seller pension scheme).

The guidance notes set out HMRC's view of the position. Some key aspects of the guidance are summarised below.

General

3.6.7 In deciding whether a contribution to a registered pension scheme is allowable, the same rules apply as for any other expense (with the exceptions of whether a payment is capital and the timing of the deduction – see BIM46005–10).

In particular, any contribution must be paid wholly and exclusively for the purposes of the trade for it to be deductible (*CTA 2009, s 54(1)(a)*).

It is likely that Target will get a deduction (albeit potentially spread over up to four years) for the *s 75* debt it may pay (see BIM46045).

This allows the potential for Seller to be able to take the benefit of the tax by only agreeing to reimburse the Purchaser for the net of tax cost, although the Purchaser will often only be prepared to pass back tax savings when they are actually made, rather than upfront.

If the *s 75* debt is reallocated (by agreement with the trustees using an SAA or FAA (see **3.3** above) to a retained company (say Seller instead of Target), a deduction for the payment by the Seller-retained company is more difficult.

---

9 See www.hmrc.gov.uk/manuals/bimmanual/BIM46000.htm

3.6.7 Debt on the employer – section 75 issues

HMRC is more likely to say that the payment is not for the purposes of Seller's business, but instead to facilitate the sale – see example 2 in BIM46060.

Example 2 from BIM 46060

Company A decided to sell one of its trading subsidiaries to an unconnected party. The subsidiary operated a registered pension scheme for its employees, which was underfunded at the time of sale. Although the subsidiary was in a position to meet its £25 million liability under, *s 75* in relation to its pension scheme deficit, the former parent believed it could secure an increased sale price for its shares in company B and entered into an approved withdrawal arrangement to meet the £25 million from the proceeds of the sale.

At the time the agreement was entered into Company A did not do so wholly and exclusively for the purposes of its trade, but rather with a non-trade purpose of securing sale of its shares in the subsidiary at an enhanced value.

This example is in contrast to BIM46045 example 3. In that example the only purpose in a parent company meeting the liability of a subsidiary being sold was to underpin the morale of its remaining scheme members. In that case the subsidiary itself was not in a financial position to meet its *Pensions Act 1995, s 75* liability. In that case the parent was able to make a deduction as the contribution was wholly and exclusively for the purposes of its trade.

Example 3 from BIM46045: approved withdrawal arrangement

The entire share capital in Company A was being sold to a previously unconnected company. The financial liquidity of Company A was such that it was unable to meet the *s 75* debt in relation to its pension scheme deficit. The former parent Company B entered into an approved withdrawal arrangement to guarantee £2 million of the pension deficit relating to the liability of Company A, as it wanted to secure the morale of the remaining members of its pension scheme.

At the time the agreement was entered into Company B did so wholly and exclusively for the purposes of its trade. If and when Company B is required to make payment in respect of the guarantee, it will make a deduction for the £2 milion during the period in which the contribution was paid (BIM46065).

A deduction may therefore still be available if the payment can be shown to be for the benefit of the Seller business because Target could not pay the *s 75* debt and Seller wanted to preserve its business reputation and the morale of its own employees.

However, guidance also indicates that a deduction is more likely to be available for contributions that reflect orphan liabilities – see BIM46055 to 46065, including example 4 in BIM46065.

Example 4 from BIM46065: orphan liabilities

Company D decides to sell one of its trading subsidiaries. At the time this decision was taken it was also agreed with the pension trustees that the potential liabilities under *s 75* of the *Pensions Act 1995* (see BIM46045), attaching to the subsidiary in respect of orphan employees, would be reallocated to Company D, who then made a payment of £2 million into the pension scheme prior to the sale of the subsidiary.

Whether Company D decided to meet the pension liability of its subsidiary for the purposes of its own trade is a question of fact. If Company D decided to meet the orphan liability of the subsidiary solely to protect its reputation as an employer, when the subsidiary was not in a position to fund the deficit itself, then relief will be due. The fact that the liability relates to orphan liabilities rather than the pension liabilities relating to current employees of the subsidiary would normally support the reputation purpose.

However if the subsidiary was in a position to fund its own pension deficit and instead Company D took on this liability to increase consideration for the sale of shares in the subsidiary then no deduction will be due as the £2 million was not paid wholly and exclusively for the purposes of the trade of Company D.

Alternatively, if the subsidiary had itself made the £2 million payment, it would have done so wholly and exclusively for the purposes of its own trade and been due a deduction of £2 million.

3.6.8 *Debt on the employer – section 75 issues*

Holding companies

3.6.8 One point that is often worth considering further is that non trading holding companies within a group are subject to a slightly different set of rules, and there is separate guidance for them in the Company Taxation Manual at CTM08340 onwards. This may well be relevant for any contributions made by the Seller or (if different) the group parent. In particular, the 'wholly and exclusively' rule does not apply, but the expenditure must be in respect of the company's investment business. Although the guidance is broadly similar to that for trading companies, and in particular also indicates that the chances of a deduction for Seller would be highest where Target could not meet the *s 75* liability and that liability relates to 'orphans', there are some hints of a more generous approach. This should be considered further on a case by case basis, but could well affect the analysis of which entity or entities should make the contribution, and also what (if any) recharge arrangements should be put in place between Seller group members.

Better route?

3.6.9 The above still seems to allow the remaining employers to obtain a deduction for later payments after the sale if these are part of normal funding. So if, say, it was possible to agree a scheme specific apportionment (SAA) or flexible apportionment arrangement (FAA) with the trustees (see *Dealing with a s 75 debt: Apportionment and withdrawal arrangements*, **3.3**) so that:

- no (or a nominal) debt would be payable by Target; and

- no amount is payable into the scheme now by Seller; but

- instead, say, the *s 75* amount was put in a blocked account (or some other security given – eg a parent guarantee or a letter of credit), then later funding payments by Seller (and its group) would be normal ongoing funding and so look more likely to get a tax deduction. One variant would be for the security to reduce as these later funding payments are made.

This is not dealt with in the HMRC guidance, but seems to give a better prospect of a deduction for the retained company (compared to a straight contribution to the scheme). Obviously a major issue may be getting the trustees to agree to this (but if full security was offered, would they be more likely to agree?).

3.7 *Section 75*: grace periods

Summary

This section looks at the 'period of grace' provisions that can apply in some cases to the debts that arise on employers under *section 75* of the *Pensions Act 1995*.

In a multi-employer scheme, if one employer ceases to employ any active members, a *s 75* debt can arise on that employer. The period of grace provisions allow the employer to serve a notice so that the debt is suspended, giving the employer a period (at least a year, but potentially up to three years if the trustees agree) in which to employ an active member.

If the employer does employ an active member within the grace period, the potential *s 75* debt trigger is cancelled. There are various conditions for this, including service of a notice on the trustees within two months of the cessation date and there being no intention for the scheme to become a frozen scheme.

If the employer fails to employ an active member within the grace period (or enters an insolvency process), the grace period is cancelled and the original *s 75* debt revived.

This section sets out when a period of grace notice can be used, the necessary requirements for an effective period of grace notice and the effect of a grace period.

Section 75 and ECEs

3.7.1   When an employer in a multi-employer defined benefit occupational pension scheme ceases to employ active members of the scheme (eg the last active member employed by that employer leaves employment or retires or dies), an *'employment-cessation event'* (ECE) will usually occur – *2005 Employer Debt Regulations*.[10]

The effect of this is usually to trigger a debt (a *'section 75* debt') under *section 75* of the *Pensions Act 1995*. This is a debt obligation on the leaving

---

10 *Occupational Pension Schemes (Employer Debt) Regulations 2005 (SI 2005/678)*, as amended.

3.7.1 *Debt on the employer – section 75 issues*

employer to pay to the scheme a share of the total funding shortfall (calculated on a buy-out basis) in the scheme. This can result in significant payments becoming due – see *Multi-employer pension schemes and s 75 debts – the elephant trap*, **3.2** above.

An employment-cessation event only occurs at this stage if there is at least one other employer who continues to employ active members in the scheme. So if the scheme freezes (ie all active members cease to be active members at the same time) no employment-cessation event occurs at that time. But the last employers remain deemed to be employers for relevant statutory purposes (eg statutory funding obligations under *Part 3* of the *Pensions Act 2004*) and remain potentially liable for a *s 75* debt if another trigger later occurs (eg the scheme starts to wind-up).

Period of Grace – overview

3.7.2   In order to offer some flexibility to employers when an ECE occurs, regulations introduced from 6 April 2008 (into the *2005 Employer Debt Regulations*) a 'period of grace' for:

- an employer who ceases to employ active members[11] in a scheme, but

- who intends to employ at least one person as an active member within a limited period (originally 12 months, but now extended to up to three years following the amendments to the regulations taking effect in 2012).

The period of grace is designed to protect employers from unintentionally triggering a *section 75* debt when ceasing to employ active members. It may also be useful in respect of employers/workers in seasonal industries.

Under the period of grace provisions, the employer is able to:

- suspend the *section 75* debt by serving a notice (a *period of grace notice*) on the trustee(s) of the scheme; and

- cancel the ECE (and *s 75* debt) if the employer employs an active member during the period.

When such a notice is served, the regulations provide that the employer will be 'treated for a period of grace as if he employed a person who is an active member of the scheme,' subject to certain conditions.

---

11 An active member is a member in pensionable service under the scheme – *s 124* of the *Pensions Act 1995*. It can in some cases be difficult to decide whether or not a person is an active member – eg we consider that a life member (who only qualifies for death benefits) is not an active member, but this is untested.

If the employer fails to employ an active member within the grace period (or enters an insolvency process or changes its intention to employ an active member), the grace period is cancelled and the original *s 75* debt revived (based on the original ECE and cessation date).

Circumstances where a period of grace will be available

3.7.3   A period of grace can be available if a situation arises where:

- an employment-cessation event occurs. This occurs where there is a multi employer scheme and 'the employer has ceased to employ at least one person who is an active member of the scheme and at least one other employer who is not a defined contribution employer continues to employ at least one active member of the scheme'. The date of the ECE is the **cessation date**; and

- the employer gives the trustees a period of grace notice within the relevant time.

  - The notice must be given to the trustees before or on the cessation date or before the date which is two months after the cessation date.

  - A period of grace notice is a written notice that the 'employer intends during the grace period to employ at least one member who will be an active member of the scheme'; and

- the employer intends to employ at least one person who will be an active member; and

- the scheme is not a frozen scheme and there is no intention for it to become one during the grace period – see **3.7.7** below.

Requirements for serving a valid period of grace notice

3.7.4   The employer must notify the trustee(s) or manager(s) of the scheme of its intention to 'employ at least one person who will be an active member of the scheme.'

This notice must be in writing and given by the employer to the trustee(s) or manager(s) either before, on or within two months after the cessation date.

3.7.5   If an employment-cessation event has occurred (and so a *s 75* debt has been triggered) but this is not discovered until more than two months has elapsed, the grace period provision will not be available. The trustee has no power to agree an extension of this initial two month time limit.

If the two month time limit was missed, the employer would need to pay the *s 75* debt or seek to agree an apportionment arrangement with the trustee (if possible). See *Dealing with a s 75 debt – apportionment and withdrawal arrangements,* **3.3** above.

For this reason, where it is contemplated that a grace period may be needed, without the date of triggering the *s* 75 debt being known, a form of grace notice may be provided to the trustees in advance to preserve the position.

3.7.6 There is no requirement for the trustees to consent to the period of grace. The trustees merely have to be given the notice. But trustee consent is needed:

- if the grace period is to last for longer than one year; or

- if trustee agreement is needed because the scheme needs to be amended to allow a new entrant.

There is no requirement to notify the Pensions Regulator.

Frozen and closed schemes

3.7.7 If all the employers have already ceased to have active members in the scheme, this will mean that the scheme will be a 'frozen scheme' and the period of grace will not be available. In practice if a scheme freezes there is usually no need for a grace period as an employment-cessation event (the relevant *s* 75 trigger) cannot occur.

In addition, a period of grace notice can only relate to a scheme where the employer 'is not aware of any intention for [the scheme] to become a frozen scheme during the period of grace'.

It is not clear from the drafting of the Regulations who needs to have such an intention (eg does it refer only to the intention of the employer itself, or is it all of the employers in the scheme? Or the principal employer only?).

The grace period provisions will be more difficult where a multi-employer scheme is closed to new entrants (but still has active members – so is a closed scheme rather than a frozen scheme).

- One solution would be if the employer can arrange to employ someone who is already an active member of the scheme, such as an employee of another group company.

- The alternative may be to arrange for the scheme to re-open to a new entrant, but care needs to be taken in such a case:
  - an amendment to the scheme may be needed if the scheme has been formally closed. Often such an amendment will need the agreement of the trustee;

– the exemption from the prohibitions on age discrimination for a scheme or section closed to new joiners (see **16.1.10** below) may cease to apply. The impact of this would need to be considered.

3.7.8

Chart on availability of grace periods

Establishing if Grace Period is available:

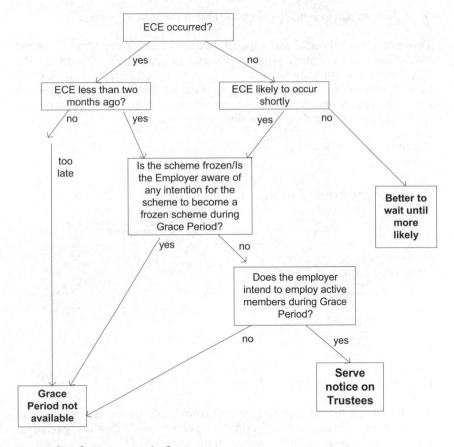

Length of grace period

3.7.9   The grace period runs for the longer of:

- up to 12 months starting from the employment-cessation event; and

- a longer period (up to 36 months) if the trustees agree – this was a change introduced in 2012.

The grace period ends if the employer starts to employ an active member of the scheme. This means that a new grace period must be started if that member ceases to be an active member even before the end date for what would have been the old grace period.

The grace period can only last for longer than one year, if:

- the trustees nominate a longer period in writing; and

- the nomination is made before the end of the current grace period.

This means that any initial extension beyond the 12 month default grace period would need to be agreed prior to the end of the 12 month period. The Regulations also allow further extensions to be agreed (subject to the overall limit of 36 months post the employment-cessation event), provided again that the extension is nominated in writing before the end of the previously applicable end date for the grace period.

3.7.10

Timeline for grace periods:

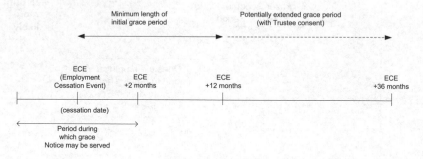

Effect of grace period

3.7.11   During the grace period the (ex) employer is treated as remaining an employer for *s 75* purposes and during that period no *s 75* debt is triggered on the employer ceasing to employ active members.

However, the grace period will be ineffective (and a *s 75* debt will arise as at the original cessation date) if the employer:

- does not employ an active member in the scheme before the end of the grace period; or

- enters an insolvency process in the UK (eg liquidation, administration); or

- changes its intention during the grace period to employ an active member. In this instance, the employer must notify the trustee(s) that it no longer intends to employ any active members.

In these three scenarios, the grace period will end. The *s* 75 debt will be calculated as if the grace period had never applied and will arise as at the date of the original employment-cessation event.

Therefore, it is not possible for employers to use a grace period to alter the time at which the *s* 75 debt is calculated if no active member is ultimately employed during the grace period.

There is no provision for interest to be paid on *s* 75 debts, so the effect of the grace period ending (with the *s* 75 debt reviving) is not to increase the amount payable. The leaving employer will usually be deemed to remain an employer for statutory purposes (eg moral hazard powers, employer-related investment) until the *s* 75 debt is actually paid.

Once the employer employs an active member of the scheme, either before or after notice is given, the period of grace comes to an end and the employer is treated as though the original employment-cessation event had not occurred. As the employer remains an employer in the scheme, it has a contingent *s* 75 debt in the future if a later trigger occurs (eg a further employment-cessation event or an insolvency event of the employer).

3.7.12 *Debt on the employer – section 75 issues*

3.7.12

Outcomes of grace periods

During Grace Period:

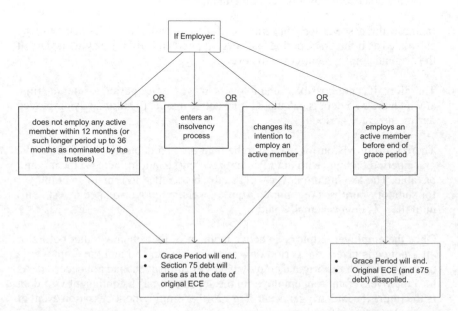

Moral hazard powers

3.7.13 *Section 38* of the *Pensions Act 2004* provides that the Pensions Regulator (**TPR**) may issue a contribution notice on an employer of a defined benefit pension scheme if TPR is of the opinion that the employer was a party to act in relation to which one of the main purposes is to prevent the recovery of the whole or part of the *s 75* debt due from the employer, or the act has the effect of preventing such a debt becoming due or otherwise settling or reducing the amount of such debt.

Where the grace period provisions are used but do not, in the end, apply to defer the *s 75* debt (because the employer is unable to employ at least one active member within the grace period), the original *s 75* debt will be calculated as at the employment cessation event date. It seems, therefore, that in this scenario and in relation to the use of the grace period alone, there would be little scope for TPR to argue to that it is able to exercise its moral hazard powers. This is because the use of the grace period does not ultimately reduce or prevent the *s 75* debt from arising.

Similarly, where the grace period provisions are successfully used to defer a *s 75* debt, the regulations provide that no *s 75* debt is deemed to have arisen. There therefore seems to be little scope for TPR's moral hazard provisions to apply simply because a grace period notice is given.

Summary of factors to be taken into account when considering whether to issue a period of grace notice

3.7.14   As explained above, the grace period is intended to alleviate the accidental triggering of an employer's *s 75* debt. This helps reduce the risk for employers with only few active members if they were all to leave and the employer then having to pay the debt when new employees are still expected to join in the near future.

Therefore, if an employer's intention is to defer triggering the *s 75* debt, the period of grace acts as a useful mechanism to do so. It is not however, a mechanism by which an employer can circumvent or eradicate the *s 75* debt. Employers will therefore need to be careful to use the period of grace provisions in the appropriate manner.

Timing is also a very important issue for employers when considering when to issue a period of grace notice. There are no restrictions on when an employer can issue the notice before an employment-cessation event occurs. But when an employment cessation event does occur, the employer will only have two months from the date of the employment-cessation event to issue the notice.

The grace period provisions will be more difficult where a multi-employer scheme is closed to new entrants. They could still apply if (say) the employer can employ someone who is already an active member, such as an employee of another group company.

If the employer expects to become insolvent, or is likely to have difficulty in employing an active member within the grace period, the grace period will potentially only be useful in delaying the debt, given that the debt will be treated as having arisen as at the date of the original cessation event if an insolvency event occurs in relation to the employer or if no active member is ultimately employed during the grace period.

183

3.8 *Section 75* **and relevant transfer deductions**

Summary

This section looks at the legal provisions dealing with the potential for a leaving employer from an occupational pension scheme to reduce its *section 75* debt by using the 'relevant transfer deduction' under the *2005 Employer Debt Regulations*.

In a multi-employer scheme, if one employer ceases to employ any active members, a *s 75* debt to the scheme can arise on that employer. The relevant transfer deduction provisions allow the employer to serve a notice on the trustees that it envisages transfers out to another scheme within a year. This notice means that:

- the *section 75* debt process is suspended pending the relevant transfers; and

- if within the next year members with benefits 'attributable to the employer' transfer-out, all or part of the employer's *s 75* debt is reduced by the amount by which the transfer value is less than the full *s 75* liability amount for the transferring members.

In practice the relevant transfer deduction provisions are quite complex and have a number of uncertainties. So they are not much used. But the deduction does not depend on the consent of the trustees (although usually trustee consent to the transfer being made and the transfer amount will be needed).

This section looks at the requirements for the deduction to be available and explains how the deduction is calculated.

Background

3.8.1   When an employer in a multi-employer defined benefit scheme (the scheme) ceases to employ active members of the scheme (eg the last active member employed by that employer leaves employment or retires or dies), an 'employment-cessation event' (ECE) can occur. The date of the ECE is called the *cessation date*.

The effect of this is to trigger a *section 75* debt which puts an obligation on the leaving employer to pay a share of the funding shortfall (calculated on a buy-out basis) in the scheme. This can result in significant payments becoming due – see *Multi-employer pension schemes and s 75 debts – the elephant trap*, **3.2** above.

In some cases, the leaving employer from the scheme may intend to seek to arrange a transfer of some or all of its members in the scheme to a new pension scheme (the Receiving Scheme).[12] Where such a transfer occurs within one year of the cessation date, it is possible to reduce the amount of the *section 75* debt by the Relevant Transfer Deduction.

Employer liability share

3.8.2 Broadly, the *s 75* debt for an employer that ceases to participate in a scheme is its share of the total buy-out deficit for the scheme. The individual employer's share of the total scheme deficit is calculated as a percentage based on:

1. the scheme benefit liabilities 'attributable to employment' with the employer, divided by;

2. the scheme benefit liabilities attributable to employment with all the current employers,

unless an alternative is agreed, for example, through a scheme apportionment arrangement – see *Dealing with a s 75 debt – apportionment and withdrawal arrangements*, **3.3** above.

The total *section 75* debt for the departing employer is:

Total Debt × (A/B), where

- **Total Debt** means the total *s 75* debt for the scheme as a whole;

- *A* means the scheme benefit liabilities attributable to employment with the departing employer; and

- *B* means the scheme benefit liabilities attributable to employment with all current employers (including the departing employer).

---

12 Often (eg on a de-merger) this will be to a new 'mirror' DB scheme established by the employer where those members would be credited with their full current benefits in the form of transfer credits.

3.8.2 *Debt on the employer – section 75 issues*

There may be some scheme liabilities that are not attributable to employment with a current employer (eg they may be attributable to a former employer who has now left the scheme). These are commonly called 'orphan liabilities'. The effect of the sharing formula above is that the leaving employer's *s 75* debt includes a share of the deficit for the orphan liabilities. For more detailed commentary on the attribution of orphan liabilities, see *Multi-employer pension schemes and s 75 debts – the elephant trap*, **3.2** above.

Relevant transfer deduction

3.8.3   *Regulation 6(6)* of the *Occupational Pension Schemes (Employer Debt) Regulations 2005* (the *Employer Debt Regulations*) provides that a leaving employer can notify the trustees of the scheme that a Relevant Transfer Deduction will apply to its liability share.

The Relevant Transfer Deduction effectively gives credit for a transfer out of liabilities from the scheme and reduces the *section 75* debt due by the amount by which the assets transferred are less than the corresponding buyout liabilities.

The Relevant Transfer Deduction will apply on the departing employer's exit to reduce its *section 75* debt to the scheme provided the transfer of assets and liabilities is completed within 12 months of the cessation date. The Relevant Transfer Deduction will be referred to on the actuary's certificate where it is applicable.

The formula for calculating a departing employer's *s 75* debt to the scheme assuming that a transfer out of some or all of its members is made within one year of its cessation of participation in the scheme is therefore as follows (definitions as above):

[Total Debt x (A/B)] – Relevant Transfer Deduction

3.8.4

Worked example

Transferring members' benefit liabilities in the scheme:

Cash equivalent transfer value[13]	Technical provisions basis	Buy-out basis
30	50	90
Transfer assets (say):	30	RTD = 90–30 = 60
	40	RTD = 90–40 = 50

1   Assume the scheme has two employers (Y and Z) and Y triggers an employment cessation event. Y will agree to the transfer of its members (or potentially some of its members – see 4 below) into the Receiving Scheme, where those members will receive transfer credits to reflect their benefits in the scheme. The table above sets out the different measures of the transferring members' benefit liabilities in the scheme.

3.   The amount of the Relevant Transfer Deduction under the *Employer Debt Regulations* is calculated by:

   • subtracting the value of the assets transferred out to the Receiving Scheme;

   • from the buy-out value of the benefit liabilities transferred and attributable to Y (ie here attributable to the transferring employees).

   The Relevant Transfer Deduction is then subtracted from Y's *section 75* debt (so that Y owes a smaller *section 75* debt to the scheme).

4.   On the basis of the simplified figures in the table, if assets valued at 30 (ie equal to the cash equivalent transfer value) were transferred, the value of the Relevant Transfer Deduction would be 60 (ie the buy-out value of the transferred liabilities, being 90, minus the transfer value of 30). 60 can therefore then be subtracted from Y's section 75 debt.

---

13   The cash equivalent transfer value (CETV) is the amount that the trustees would agree to transfer if the member exercised his statutory transfer right under the *Pension Schemes Act 1993*.

> 5. Depending on the class of members who transfer-out, Y may still have a *section 75* debt to the scheme. If, for example, Y does not intend to transfer to the Receiving Scheme any inactive members whose employment is attributable to it, no Relevant Transfer Deduction will be available in respect of those inactive member liabilities.

3.8.5 Note that if the Receiving Scheme is to grant mirror benefits by way of a transfer credit, a deficit on the technical provisions basis in respect of the transferred members will arise in the Receiving Scheme (in the example above it is only receiving assets worth 30, but the technical provisions liabilities are 50). This will need to be addressed by the employer in the Receiving Scheme at some stage.

The timing in respect of making up this shortfall will depend to some extent on negotiations with the Receiving Scheme trustees, ie they may require that the benefits are topped up to be fully funded on the technical provisions basis as a requirement of accepting the transfer, or the deficit may fall to be paid over time in line with the Receiving Scheme's recovery plan.

3.8.6 In some respects for the employer, it may not make much arithmetic difference whether or not a higher transfer value is negotiated with the trustees of the scheme – while this would mean that less of a top-up is required to reach the statutory funding objective in respect of these liabilities in the Receiving Scheme, the corresponding Relevant Transfer Deduction as regards the *section 75* debt would then be reduced. The negotiation of the transfer value may therefore depend on the position of the Receiving Scheme trustees and also any cash flow concerns.

In the example, if the Trustees of the scheme agreed an enhanced transfer value (say a share of fund) of eg 45, then:

6. the top-up required by the Receiving Scheme may be less (say $50 - 45 = 5$); but

7. the Relevant Transfer Deduction would be reduced to 45 (ie 90 – 45) instead of 60, so Y's *s75* debt would increase by that amount,

so that Y pays: (i) 15 less to the Receiving Scheme (perhaps over time), but (ii) 15 more as a *section 75* debt to the scheme.

Orphan liabilities

3.8.7   The position in relation to orphan liabilities in the scheme is more complicated. The Relevant Transfer Deduction arguably does not take any account of the orphan liabilities, even if these are also transferred.

Regulation 2 of the *Employer Debt Regulations* defines the Relevant Transfer Deduction by referring to 'liabilities attributable to a departing employer that are transferred'. Arguably orphan liabilities are not 'attributable' to the departing employer. The wording differs from that used in calculating the employer's liability share, where the reference is to 'liabilities attributable to employment with the employer'. So the argument arises that some liabilities for orphan benefits are attributable to the departing employer in that its *s 75* debt is calculated including a share of such liabilities.

3.8.8   Taking a further worked example to demonstrate the issue:

	Benefit liabilities (on buy-out cost)	Proportional share of assets	Section 75 debt
Y	100	40	75
Z	100	40	75
Orphans	50	20	N/A
Total	250	100	150

Y transfers all liabilities associated with its employees and former employees (but not its share of the orphan liabilities) into the Receiving Scheme on the basis of a transfer value of 40. Y would then remain liable to pay a *s 75* debt of 15 to the Scheme.

- This is calculated as Y's *section 75* debt of 75 minus a Relevant Transfer Deduction of 60 (the buy-out liabilities of 100 minus the transfer value of 40).

However, in the circumstance where Y takes a transfer of all liabilities associated with its employees and former employees *and* its share of the orphan liabilities, it is not clear that the Employer Debt Regulations gives credit to Y for taking a transfer of the orphan liabilities.

While one would expect that it should be possible to reduce Y's *s 75* debt to the Scheme to zero (subject to the value of the assets transferred to the Receiving Scheme) if it transfers all of its member liabilities and its share of the orphan liabilities, it is unclear whether or not the orphan liabilities are 'liabilities attributable to' Y, and therefore whether or not the transfer of these liabilities can be accounted for in the Relevant Transfer Deduction.

Practical points in relation to Relevant Transfer Deductions

3.8.9   **Notice:** The departing employer must serve a notice to the Trustees of the scheme that the Relevant Transfer Deduction provisions apply. The Employer Debt Regulations do not require this to be in writing, but it is obviously prudent to serve a written notice. There is no express time limit for this notice, but in practice the leaving employer should be reasonably prompt after the ECE has occurred.

3.8.10   **Calculation date:** The Trusees of the scheme are unable to issue the *section 75* certificate in respect of the departing employer while the Relevant Transfer Deduction notice is outstanding. Note, however, that the wording of *reg 6(6)(b)* of the *Employer Debt Regulations 2005* is obscure in terms of the relevant date as at which the liabilities are calculated. The correct reading of this regulation as regards the calculation of the Relevant Transfer Deduction is also confusing.

3.8.11   **Transfer values:** The transfer values will usually need to be negotiated with the Trustees of both the scheme and the Receiving Scheme.

3.8.12   **Timing of transfer:** Transfers must be completed within 12 months of the cessation of participation in the scheme. This 12 month period can also be important where any transferring active members benefit from tax protections.

3.8.13   **Member consent:** There is no requirement that the consent of the members be given to the transfer. Such consent will be needed, unless the transferring trustees agree to a transfer without consent (and the relevant actuarial certificate is obtained). Such a certificate is not usually possible if the benefits credited to the transferring members are to differ substantially from those under the transferring scheme.

3.8.14   **Transfer to DC?:** There is no express requirement that the receiving scheme grant similar benefits to the transferring scheme or even defined benefits (DB). In principle it may be possible for the transfer to be to a DC scheme (indeed the definition of 'relevant transfer liabilities' refers to a transfer to a personal pension scheme). In practice express member consent would be needed for such a transfer. (as compared to DB benefits).

3.8.15   **Transfer of liabilities:** In order for the Relevant Transfer Deduction to be available, the *Regulation 2* of the *Employer Debt Regulations 2005* requires that the liabilities are 'transferred' in the definition of 'relevant transfer liabilities'. This could mean that it is argued that the benefits in the Receiving Scheme need to be the same as those in the scheme in order to make use of the Relevant Transfer Deduction.

Chapter 4

Pensions Regulator – moral hazard powers

4.1 TPR: moral hazard powers: extracting pension scheme funding from third parties: overview

Summary

The *Pensions Act 2004* gave the Pensions Regulator (TPR) far-reaching powers to make third parties connected with an employer liable to contribute to or support an underfunded defined benefit pension scheme.[1] The *2004 Act* gives TPR powers to issue a contribution notice (CN) or financial support direction (FSD) in some circumstances. These powers are often referred to as TPR's 'moral hazard' powers.

These powers are aimed at discouraging the abuse of corporate structures to avoid pension liabilities, or entry into material transactions without taking into account the potential impact on the pension scheme. They are also aimed at reducing the risk of employers shifting their pension liabilities onto the Pension Protection Fund (PPF).[2]

This section gives an overview of the moral hazard powers.

---

1 Consequently any reference to a 'pension scheme' or a 'scheme' in this chapter is a reference to a defined benefit (DB) pension scheme.
2 For a summary of the role of the PPF and the compensation it would provide to scheme members in the event of employer insolvency, see *PPF protected benefits*, **5.2**.

4.1.1   *Pensions Regulator – moral hazard powers*

Which pension schemes can give rise to a claim?

4.1.1   Generally, TPR powers will only apply if the scheme can potentially fall within the PPF, and is one to which the employer debt obligation in *s 75* of the *Pensions Act 1995* (the so-called '*s 75* debt') can apply. The schemes below are excluded.

Excluded schemes

4.1.2   Excluded schemes are as follows:

- money purchase schemes (ie providing only money purchase benefits, ignoring death benefits);

- schemes not registered with HM Revenue & Customs (HMRC) under the *Finance Act 2004*;

- most public sector schemes; and

- schemes just for overseas employees (*s 615* schemes).

Maximum liability

4.1.3   When assessing the maximum potential liability of a person (ie individual or corporation) under a contribution notice (CN) or financial support direction (FSD) to provide funding towards a scheme's deficit, this deficit is measured on a buy-out basis – the basis on which an employer's *s 75* debt liability is calculated. Broadly, this tests whether there would be sufficient assets to secure the benefits with matching insurance policies.

The liability on a buy-out basis is usually significantly greater than the liability assessed on other measures – for example the funding basis used under the scheme-specific funding regime for ongoing schemes, or the accounting basis reflected in company accounts under international accounting standard (IAS) 19 or financial reporting standard (FRS) 17. Schemes are only rarely funded at the buy-out level, so this basis will usually reveal a substantial deficit in the scheme. As a consequence, the potential exposure under a CN or FSD can be large.

Conditions for issuing CNs and FSDs

4.1.4   Liability under a CN or FSD is not automatic. Whether one is issued will depend on an essentially discretionary judgment by TPR. There are three tests that need to be met for a CN or FSD to be issued:

- the target must be connected or associated with an employer (or former employer) in relation to the pension scheme;

- the relevant test for a CN (an act with a main purpose of avoiding a pension liability or act that has detrimentally affected the security of the scheme benefits) or an FSD (the employer is insufficiently resourced or a service company) must be met; and

- TPR must consider that the issue of a CN or FSD is 'reasonable'.

This section looks further at each of these tests below.

'Connected' or 'associated'

4.1.5   FSDs and CNs can be used (in some circumstances) to make the employer or a third party who is 'connected' or 'associated' with the employer (or former employer) liable for all, or some of the deficit in an underfunded pension scheme.

The test for when a company or individual is connected or associated is taken from the *Insolvency Act 1986*. It is widely drawn and will, for example, catch other companies in the same corporate group as the scheme's employer or a one-third shareholder (with voting rights) in the employer's parent company. The target of a CN or FSD does not need to be directly linked to the scheme.

For more information see *Who is 'connected' or 'associated'?*, **4.2** and *TPR: Who is within reach?*, **4.3** below.

What is the test for issuing a CN?

4.1.6   TPR can issue a CN if it believes a connected or associated person has been a party to an act or failure to act as set out in the table below.

Timing	Type of act or omission
Occurred on or after 27 April 2004	The 'main purpose', or one of the main purposes, of the act or omission was to prevent the recovery of any part of an employer's *s 75* debt, to prevent the debt from becoming due or to compromise or otherwise settle or reduce the amount of such a debt that would otherwise become due.

193

4.1.6 *Pensions Regulator – moral hazard powers*

Timing	Type of act or omission
Occurred on or after 14 April 2008[3]	Irrespective of intention, the act or omission has detrimentally affected in a material way the likelihood of accrued scheme benefits being received.

In either case, the recipient can only be issued with a CN in respect of an act or failure to act that occurred in the six years prior to the issue of the CN (the *Pensions Act 2011* has, since 3 January 2012, applied the six-year period so that it ends when a warning notice is issued by TPR – **4.9**).

A person is treated as being party to a relevant act or failure to act if he knowingly assisted in it.

What is the test for issuing an FSD?

4.1.7　In contrast to CNs, FSDs are not event driven. TPR can issue an FSD against a person even if there is no specific act or failure to act to which it would relate. Broadly, FSDs allow TPR to require an associated third party to financially support a scheme if the participating employer does not appear able.

An FSD can be issued against a person if a participating employer in the scheme falls within either of the two categories in the table below, assessed as at a date which is not more than two years prior to the issue of the FSD (the *Pensions Act 2011* has, since 3 January 2012, applied the two year period so that it ends when a warning notice is issued by TPR – see **4.9**).

A service company	The employer's turnover, as shown in its latest accounts, is solely or principally derived from providing services to other companies in its corporate group – probably an indication that the employer will not have sufficient assets
Insufficiently resourced	The net assets of the participating employer are less than 50% of its share of the buy-out deficit in the scheme, in circumstances where one or more other companies that are connected or associated do have sufficient net assets to meet the difference.

3　See *PA 2008, Sch 9, para 15.*

194

Reasonableness

4.1.8   Even if the specific tests for issuing a CN or FSD (discussed above) are satisfied, for example if an act has caused a material detriment to scheme benefits, TPR would still need to decide it 'reasonable' to exercise its powers.

The *Pensions Act 2004* directs TPR to consider a number of factors in deciding whether or not issuing a CN or FSD would be reasonable – see *The reasonableness test – what are the factors that affect liability?*, **4.10**. In brief, these factors include the degree of connection an entity has had with the scheme, any benefits the person has received from an employer or the scheme and (in the case of CNs) the purpose of the particular act or failure to act.

Process

4.1.9   The likelihood of a person becoming the target of a CN or FSD is largely dependent on whether, on the individual facts of the case, the following apply.

- TPR needs to investigate the circumstances of the case. It may be alerted by the pension trustees or investigate following a notification of a notifiable event or breach of law. Alternatively, it may act on its own volition (it is known to monitor developments affecting corporate groups with major pension schemes).

- Having considered the position and gathered information (for this purpose it may use its statutory powers to obtain information from interested parties) TPR then decides whether or not to seek a CN or FSD.

- If TPR wants to go ahead, it must then issue a 'warning notice' of its intention to issue a CN or FSD. This is issued to interested parties (including the trustees). It gives details of TPR's reasons why the CN or FSD should be issued.

- The decision as to whether to issue the CN or FSD must then be made by TPR's determinations panel. This is a statutory body within TPR that operates separately from TPR's investigatory function, and functions much like a tribunal. TPR's investigatory staff must make the case to the panel for the issue of the CN or FSD.

- The parties can make representations to the determinations panel about the contents of the warning notice and TPR's arguments for issuing the CN or FSD. An oral hearing can be requested. The panel will then consider the warning notice and the representations of the parties, and decides whether or not it is reasonable to issue the CN or FSD.

195

- The determinations panel considers the warning notice and the representations of the parties and decides whether or not it is reasonable to issue the FSD or CN.

- An appeal to the Upper Tribunal (Chancery and Tax) can be made. This operates as a new hearing. The arguments for and against can be made again and new evidence produced.

See further *Procedure for issue of a contribution notice or financial support direction*, **4.9**.

Clearance

4.1.10   TPR is able to issue 'clearance' under a statutory process that confirms it will not issue a CN or an FSD on an applicant in relation to a particular action or set of circumstances.

However, TPR will only generally give clearance where it considers there has been what it refers to as a 'type A' event. Broadly, this is an event that has a materially detrimental effect on a pension scheme's ability to meet its liabilities. Type A events can include large returns of capital, inter-company loans or asset transfers that are not on arm's-length terms or a change to the structure of the corporate group that has the effect of reducing the covenant strength of a participating employer.

TPR will usually require the trustees of the scheme to support an application for clearance. For them to do so, they must often have taken independent financial advice. It is also our experience that TPR will usually require some 'mitigation' for the impact of a type A event (eg increased funding or financial support for the scheme), before it will give clearance. In other words, there is usually a 'price' for obtaining clearance.

See *Pensions and transactions: applying to the Pensions Regulator for clearance*, **4.13**.

TPR's guidance on clearance is available on its website at www.thepensions regulator.gov.uk/guidance/guidance-clearance.aspx.

Summary of CNs and FSDs

4.1.11

	Contribution notice	*Financial support direction*
Is fault on the part of the recipient a necessary precondition?	No. The recipient of the CN must have been a party to an act or failure to act. This includes knowingly assisting the act. But since 14 April 2008 the act or failure to act need not have been for the main purpose of avoiding pension liabilities.	No. An FSD is not based on any specific act or omission. It can potentially be issued if the employer is a service company or insufficiently resourced. But under the reasonableness test the actions of the FSD target can have an important bearing on whether the FSD will be issued.
Must the recipient be (or have been) connected or associated with an employer?	Yes	Yes
Can an individual be targeted?	Yes. But an insolvency practitioner is exempt if 'acting in accordance with his functions as an insolvency practitioner'.	No, unless the targeted individual is a participating employer in the scheme (though a non-corporate employer will be rare in large transactions and restructurings).
Does the 'reasonableness' test apply?	Yes. The list of factors that must be considered by TPR under the reasonableness test for CNs is different from those that must be considered under the test for FSDs (though some common factors apply).	Yes. The list of factors that must be considered by TPR under the reasonableness test for FSDs is different from those that must be considered under the test for CNs (though some common factors apply).

4.1.11 *Pensions Regulator – moral hazard powers*

	Contribution notice	*Financial support direction*
Is there a look-back period	Yes. Even if the recipient has now ceased to be connected or associated, TPR can serve a warning notice to issue a CN for acts or failures to act that occurred within the previous six years and either: • on or after 27 April 2004 under the 'main purpose' test; or • on or after 14 April 2008 under the 'material detriment test'	Yes. TPR must select a test date in the last two years before a warning notice is issued and the recipient needs to be connected or associated at that date. TPR may select a date in the look-back period that makes it more likely that it can issue an FSD (egit may choose a reference date at which it knows the relevant employer was insufficiently resourced).

4.2 Who is 'connected' or 'associated'?

4.2.1 Summary

This section explains why the definitions of 'connected' and 'associated', as contained in the *Insolvency Act 1986*, are important in pensions law. It then outlines the statutory provisions and highlights some difficult areas of law.

Pensions and insolvency legislation uses the test in the *Insolvency Act 1986* for assessing whether a person is 'connected' or 'associated' with another.

This test is important because various statutory provisions use it, especially in limiting the persons whom the Pensions Regulator can make responsible for pension scheme deficits under the 'moral hazard' powers in the *Pensions Act 2004*.

This section gives an outline of the statutory provisions and points to some difficult areas.[4]

Why is this relevant?

4.2.2   The *Insolvency Act 1986* includes a definition of someone who is 'connected' with a company (*IA, s 249*) or 'associated' with an individual or company (*IA, s 435*).

The insolvency legislation has special rules dealing with situations involving an insolvent person and someone who is connected or associated with that person. For example, it is easier for an insolvency practitioner to challenge transactions that took place with an associated person before insolvency as transactions at an undervalue or preference etc.

The pensions legislation uses these definitions from the *Insolvency Act 1986* in various areas, including the following:

- The Pensions Regulator (TPR) can make a moral hazard order (contribution notice or financial support direction) only against a person who is associated or connected with an employer (see *Pensions Regulator: moral hazard powers,* **4.1**).

---

4   For a more detailed review see David Pollard's article in (2009) 22 *Insolvency Intelligence* 33 and Chapter 70 in *Corporate Insolvency: Employment and Pension Rights* (5th ed, Bloomsbury Professional, 2013).

- There are restrictions on employer-related investment by pension schemes. This is defined as investment in an employer or in someone associated or connected with an employer.

- The scheme actuary or auditor must generally not be associated or connected with a trustee.

The concept of associated or connected persons is also used in relation to independent trustees on insolvency, Pension Protection Fund guarantees, lien rules, pensions provision on 'Tupe' transfers (ie on a relevant transfer of all or part of a business in the UK), cross-border schemes and notifiable events.

Some general points

4.2.3

- All wholly owned companies in a group are associated.

- Directors are associated with the company on whose board they sit, but not necessarily with its subsidiaries.

- A company is associated with each of its directors, officers and employees.

- Significant shareholders (over one-third) will have 'control' and so are associated with the company and its subsidiaries.

Overview of ss 249 and 435 of the Insolvency Act 1986

Adapted from the TPR's guidance on clearance.

Associated persons

A person is an associate of an individual if that person is, for example:

- the individual's husband, wife or civil partner;

- a relative of the individual;

- a relative of the individual's husband, wife or civil partner;

- the husband, wife or civil partner of a relative of the individual; or

- the husband, wife or civil partner of a relative of the individual's husband, wife or civil partner.

References to a husband, wife or civil partner include a former husband, wife or civil partner and a 'reputed' husband, wife or civil partner.

A person is an associate of any person with whom he is in partnership and of the husband, wife, civil partner or relative of any individual with whom he is in partnership. A Scottish firm is an associate of any person who is a member of the firm.

A trustee is associated with beneficiaries of the trust (but excluding pension schemes and employees' share schemes).

A person is an associate of any person whom he employs or by whom he is employed. Any director or other officer of a company is to be treated as employed by that company.

If a person is associated with another person then they are associates of each other.

A company is an associate of another company if:

- the same person has control of both or a person has control of one and persons who are his associates, or he and persons who are his associates, have control of the other; or

- a group of two or more persons has control of each company and the groups either consist of the same persons or could be regarded as consisting of the same persons by treating (in one or more cases) a member of either group as replaced by a person of whom he is an associate.

A company is an associate of another person if that person has control of it or if that person and persons who are his associates together have control of it.

There are special rules for members of a limited liability partnership.

Control

A person is to be taken as having control of a company if:

- the directors of the company or of another company that has control of it (or any of them) are accustomed to act in accordance with his directions or instructions; or

- he is entitled to exercise, or control the exercise of, one-third or more of the voting power at any general meeting of the company or of another company that has control of it.

If two or more persons together satisfy either of the above conditions, they are to be taken as having control of the company.

> *Connected persons*
>
> A person is connected with a company if that person is:
>
> - a director or shadow director of the company;
> - an associate of such a director or shadow director; or
> - he is an associate of the company.

Is there a chain of links?

4.2.4 The 'associate' test does not generally link – that is, if A is associated with B and B is associated with C, this does not mean that A is associated with C.

But there are two exceptions to this:

- if A controls B and B controls C, this usually means A controls C (and so A is associated with C); and
- if A is associated with B and B is a director (or shadow director) of C, this means A is connected with C.

Control = one-third of the voting power

4.2.5 A person has control of a company if he has one-third or more of the voting power in it at any general meeting. Such control may be possible through a voting agreement. It is also possible that separate holdings of separate shareholders can be added together to give joint control (particularly if the shareholders are associated).

Common directors

4.2.6 The 'connected' test will mean that person A is connected with company B if any of B's directors is associated with A (eg if the director is a director or employee of A).

But this connection will not on its own mean that A is associated or connected with B's subsidiaries (in the absence of some other link). See example below.

Example

A bank or venture capital fund that has nominated one of its employees to be a director of a company (perhaps to protect its interests as minority shareholder) will be connected with that company.

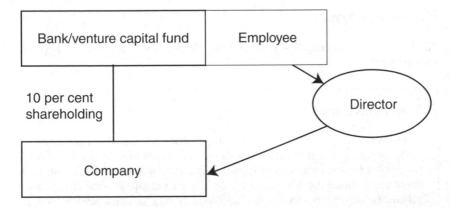

Do nominated directors give control?

4.2.7   If person A appoints a nominee (B) to a company's board of directors, A will be connected with the company if A is an associate of B (eg if A employs B or B is a director of A).

If B is accustomed to act in accordance with A's directions, this may also give A control of the company (it is unclear whether control of the whole or a majority of the board of directors is needed – or if control of just one director is enough). If A has 'control' of the company, it will also be associated with the company's subsidiaries.

See further *Nominating Directors to a board – is there a pensions risk?*, **4.4**.

Share mortgages

4.2.8   A mortgagee over shares in a company may take control of the voting powers under the mortgaged shares. If the mortgaged shares represent more than one-third of the voting shares in the company, it is likely that the mortgagee will 'control' the company if the mortgagee has the voting power.

It is probable (but not certain) that a mortgagee will avoid this (at least up to a declaration of default by the mortgagee) if the mortgage instrument provides that the mortgager retains the voting rights (at least up to that event) – see the reasons (January 2012) of TPR's determinations panel for the FSD determination in the *Box Clever* case (but this may be challenged on appeal) – see **4.16** below.

Overseas companies

4.2.9   The 'associated' test applies to bodies corporate wherever incorporated.

Some terms defined

'Employer' means 'the employer of pensions in the description of employment to which the scheme relates' and is extended by regulations (eg to cover some former employers). This can be a difficult test in some cases (eg if there are life members or if a participating company in a scheme has employees, but none is an active member of the scheme) – see *Who is the employer?*, **2.4** above.

'Shadow director' means 'a person in accordance with whose directions or instructions the directors of the company are accustomed to act' (but not if the person is a professional advisor) – *s 251, Insolvency Act 1986*. It seems that all the board (or a majority) must so act.

'Director' generally includes 'any person occupying the position of director, by whatever name called'. So it covers a *'de facto'* director – *s 251, Insolvency Act 1986*.

'Company' includes a body corporate (whether incorporated in the UK or overseas).

4.3   TPR: who is within reach?

Summary

'TPR's Moral Hazard powers: Extracting pension scheme funding from third parties', **4.1** gives an overview of the 'moral hazard' powers of the Pensions Regulator to make third parties liable to fund occupational pension schemes in some circumstances.

This section looks further at some of the persons and companies who may potentially become liable.

Connected persons and associates

4.3.1   A contribution notice (CN) or a financial support direction (FSD), broadly speaking, may be issued against an employer participating in a pension scheme and/or persons who are (or have been in the relevant period) connected to or associated with a participating employer.

The terms 'connected person' and 'associate' are imported from *ss 249* and *435* of the *Insolvency Act 1986*. The definitions are complex and obscure in places.

The following categories of persons are associated:

- other group companies (eg the parent);

- shareholders who have a large stake in the employer (ie one-third) or more of the 'voting powers' at a general meeting either directly or indirectly); and

- directors (and shadow directors) and employees of the employer.

The term 'connected' person also includes persons who are 'associated' with a director of the employer – who could have a very tenuous connection to the employer, such as:

- a company that also has as one of its directors or employees a person who is a director (or shadow director) of the employer;

- a grandchild of the ex-wife of a director of the employer; and

- a person who is in partnership with a director of the employer.

For more information see *Who is 'connected' or 'associated'?*, **4.2**.

4.3.2 *Pensions Regulator – moral hazard powers*

Individuals (*eg directors*)

4.3.2   The Pensions Regulator (TPR) can issue an FSD against an individual, such as a director, only if that individual is an associate of a non-corporate employer. A non-corporate employer will be rare in large transactions and restructurings.

However, individual directors (and their relatives) are potentially at risk of a CN if TPR considers it reasonable – this will depend on a number of factors, including any benefit derived by the individual from the relevant company.

The Determinations Panel (DP) determined to issue CNs against two shareholder/directors in the *Desmonds* case (being appealed) – see *CNs against directors: Desmond & Sons*, **4.15** below. Otherwise, no CN has to date been reported as issued against an individual (TPR's request for one in the *Bonas* case was refused by the Determinations Panel – see *Bonas: Judicial guidance on CNs*, **4.8**).

Partnerships and limited liability partnerships

4.3.3   *Section 57* of the *Pensions Act 2004* allows regulations to be issued on moral hazard powers in respect of partnerships and limited liability partnerships (LLPs). However, as yet none have been.

Therefore LLPs and partnerships may be at risk of a CN or FSD if connected or associated with the employer in the usual way. For the purposes of pension legislation, an LLP is treated in some respects in the same way as a company, but each member (ie 'partner') of an LLP is treated as associated with every other member.

External investors

4.3.4   TPR is able to issue CNs against persons where it is of the opinion that the person 'was a party to an act or a deliberate failure to act' that satisfies either the 'main purpose' test or 'material detriment' test.

If an investor received a substantial payment (eg dividends) from an employer participating in a pension scheme (or perhaps its parent) that materially weakens the ability of the employer financially to support the pension scheme the investor may potentially be seen as a party to the act and at risk of a CN.

However, a person that is a party to the act or failure to act will be at risk of a CN only if they are connected or associated with the employer (eg due to a large (over one-third) voting shareholding in an employer (or its parent) or being associated with a director of the employer).

There is no requirement for an act or failure to act to have occurred in relation to an FSD. TPR is able to issue an FSD where an employer is insufficiently resourced or a service company. Therefore receipt of a payment from the employer by an investor is not an issue in the same way as for CNs. However, receipt of a dividend or payment from an employer by an investor may still be relevant for an FSD on the question of whether it is reasonable to issue an FSD (assuming the investor is connected or associated with an employer of the pension scheme).

TPR also has a separate power to 'claw back' an asset if given as a gift or if the party received it at a significant under-value – *s 51* of the *Pensions Act 2004*.

Insolvency practitioners

4.3.5   Insolvency practitioners are individuals and so cannot be fixed by an FSD (at least in relation to a corporate employer).

A limited carve-out relating to who can be issued a CN offers some protection to UK insolvency practitioners who may have been party to an act or failure to act with the main purpose of avoiding pension liabilities.

To fall within the carve-out, the insolvency practitioner must have been 'acting in accordance with his functions as an insolvency practitioner' – *s 38(3)(c)* of the *Pensions Act 2004*.

For the purposes of the carve-out, an insolvency practitioner means a liquidator, provisional liquidator, administrator, administrative receiver or nominee or supervisor under a voluntary arrangement. It does not apply to fixed charge receivers or *Law of Property Act 1925* receivers who, depending on the nature of their appointment (eg if the charge is over a controlling interest in the shares of an employer), may be exposed to liability for CNs.

In October 2009, the Department for Work and Pensions wrote to the Financial Markets Law Committee (FMLC) confirming that this protection does not extend to receivers. It however suggests that the terms of the security can be written so that the receiver's liability will be conditional on clearance being obtained from TPR.

Turnaround specialists or 'company doctors'

4.3.6   Company 'doctors' who are brought in to assist a company in financial difficulties may face potential liability under the moral hazard provisions. Their liability is likely to be limited to CNs. FSDs will be a concern only if the employer is an individual, non-corporate entity (which is rare, given the nature of restructurings involving company doctors). The risk arises if a company doctor is appointed to the board of directors (eg as chief restructuring officer), or takes an equity stake.

However, they will have the protection afforded by the requirements of reasonableness – see *The reasonableness test – what are the factors that affect liability?*, **4.10.** In particular TPR is required to consider 'the likelihood of 'relevant creditors' being paid and the extent to which they are likely to be paid' when deciding whether to issue a CN.

The previous government commented in parliament that this provision should provide additional comfort to company doctors who 'cause detriment to a pension scheme, which, in the particular circumstances, was reasonable in the context of the outcome for other creditors' and those who behave reasonably (eg not wilfully ignoring available information or recklessly taking risks that a reasonable company doctor would not have taken).

Despite this additional comfort, company doctors may want to seek directors and officers' liability insurance to protect themselves from any additional risk and carefully review any pre-existing cover.

Companies located outside the UK

4.3.7   The fact that a company is incorporated in a foreign jurisdiction does not, as a matter of English law, prevent TPR from serving an FSD or CN against it.

TPR maintains the public position that it will be able to enforce a CN or FSD outside the UK (particularly within other EU Member States).

However, it is not clear whether TPR would be able to enforce an FSD or CN in a foreign court if a person refused to comply with the FSD or CN.

Only a few FSDs and CNs have been issued to date. One (Sea Containers) was enforced (by agreement) in a US court, but another (Nortel) was rejected by both a Canadian and a US court (mainly because the relevant companies were already in an insolvency process and so subject to a moratorium on legal process, which was held to include proceedings before TPR).

4.4 Nominating directors to a board – is there a pensions risk?

Summary

Investors taking shares in an investee company (the Company) which is part of a group containing a UK defined benefit pension scheme will be aware of the potential liability risk if the Investor becomes 'connected' or associated' with the Company as a result.

This risk arises because the *Pensions Act 2004* gives the UK Pensions Regulator powers, if relevant conditions are met, to make third parties liable to fund or contribute to a pension scheme. These are the 'moral hazard powers' – see **4.1** above.

This section looks at the risk of the Investor becoming connected with the Company if the Investor appoints one or more persons to the board of directors of the Company.

The Investor will become associated if any of the directors of the Company is associated with the Investor (eg is an employee or director of the Investor).

The 'associated' issue

4.4.1   If the Investor is associated with an employer, it will fall within the class of persons against whom the Pensions Regulator may (if other conditions are met) be able to issue a 'moral hazard' order under the *Pensions Act 2004* – a contribution notice (CN) or financial support direction (FSD).

A moral hazard order can oblige the target (here the Investor) to support or contribute to a relevant UK defined benefit pension scheme of the Company (or its group). For further details on CNs and FSDs see the other parts of Chapter **4**.

If the Investor does not become connected to, or associated with, an employer of a pension scheme, then TPR has no power to issue a CN or FSD against the Investor in relation to that scheme.

For a further discussion of the moral hazard powers, see the other parts of this chapter.

What if the Investor appoints a director to the Company board?

4.4.2   Take a typical situation:

- the Investor (and its associates) will after the investment have less than one-third of the voting rights at a general meeting of the Company;

- the Investor wants be able to appoint one or more directors into the Company;

- the nominated person (the Individual) becoming a director may be an employee of the Investor or a director of the Investor;

- the Company (or one of its subsidiaries) is an employer (or former employer) in a UK defined benefit pension scheme.

Could there be a pensions issue for the Investor in these circumstances?

Broadly TPR's moral hazard powers are not automatic just because a third party is associated or connected (contrast the ERISA rules in the US). Additional tests would need to be satisfied – in particular that the Pensions Regulator considers it reasonable to make an order against the third party.

But the clearest 'safe haven' for an Investor is to try to ensure that it does not satisfy the connected or associated test. The issues on this are now discussed in the rest of this section **4.4**.

Associated or connected?

4.4.3   The concern for pension purposes is whether the Investor (or a company in its group) ends up as being 'connected' or 'associated' with a company in the group which is an 'employer' (for statutory purposes) in relation to the Company pension scheme (an employer for this purpose generally means a company which employs active members of the pension scheme, but can also include former employers).

The test for being associated or connected is quite complex – for an overview, see *Who is connected or associated?*, **4.2**.

One-third voting control

4.4.4   The main way in which a third-party Investor would be associated would be if the Investor had a large enough number of voting shares to be deemed to have 'control' of the Company.

The first limb of control is defined[5] in the legislation as being entitled to exercise[6] *one third or more of the voting powers* at a general meeting of the Company. Presumably the Investor can check that this does not apply here. There may be issues if the Investor usually has less than one-third of the votes, but can have more voting rights in some limited circumstances.

Director 'accustomed to act' on directions

4.4.5   The second limb of 'control' is if a director of the Company is *accustomed to act* in accordance with directions or instructions from the Investor.

This is similar to the 'shadow director' test for insolvency and corporate law – but it is unclear if this could apply if just one director so acts, or whether the whole board (or a majority) must so act.

Given that the Individual, as one of the directors of the Company:

- will have been nominated/appointed by the Investor; and

- may have an ongoing information/discussion role with the Investor (and can be seen for some purposes as representing the Investor to the Company),

there may well be more risk of a claim that the Individual falls within this 'accustomed to act' limb of the control test.

The Investor should take care that the Individual acts and is seen to act independently. This will help to reduce any 'shadow director' risk as well.

Director is 'associated' with Investor

4.4.6   The connected/associated test includes a specific provision that a person (here the Investor) is deemed connected with a company (here the Company) if that person is associated with a director (or shadow director) of the Company.

If the Investor is 'associated' with any of the directors of the Company (including the Individual), that will mean that the Investor is connected with the

---

5   *Insolvency Act 1986, s 435(10).*
6   Note that it is likely that the Investor would become entitled to exercise voting power if it controls the voting rights, even if it does not fully own the shares (eg if there is a charge over the shares in favour of the Investor or one of its associated entities) – see the reasons (January 2012) of TPR's determinations panel for the FSD determination in the *Box Clever* case (but may be challenged on appeal).

Company, so the issue may become whether or not the Investor is 'associated' with the Individual?

The main grounds for an Individual being associated with the Investor are if the Individual is:

- a director (includes a *de facto* or shadow director) of the Investor. This will include if the Individual is a non-executive director of the Investor (or the Company); or

- an officer or employee of the Investor; or

- controls the Investor or is in partnership with it (or involved in trusts etc).

If the only connection of the Investor with the Individual is that he or she is a self-employed consultant then this is not enough to make the Investor associated with the Individual.

Company is not a pension scheme employer?

4.4.7 If the Investor is connected with the Company by this 'common director' route, the Investor will be connected with the relevant Company, but not (absent something else (eg deemed control of the Company)) with the subsidiaries of the Company.

So if the actual employers in the group pension scheme are the subsidiaries and not the Company, the connection with the Company will not be a connection with an 'employer' and so will not (on its own) be enough to allow a moral hazard power order against the Investor.

The position will differ if the Company is still deemed to be an employer for statutory purposes – see **2.4** above – (eg in some circumstances if it used to be an employer under the pension scheme in the past).

Other points to note

4.4.8 The Investor needs to consider its group structure. Interests of any associated person (eg other group companies) can also be relevant. Interests of associates (eg other Investor group companies) can be aggregated (eg for the voting control test). This may also apply to other third parties too.

The Individual, as a director of the Company, will be associated with the Company and so in the same way as any director or employee (potentially) may be the subject of a CN (although probably not an FSD). This may be a factor for the Individual in accepting appointment. The Investor should consider carefully the implications and extent of any comfort it may give to the Individual (eg an indemnity).

The connected/associated test applies to companies incorporated outside the UK as well as in the UK.

4.5 Enforcement against foreign targets

Summary

This section considers the legal obstacles that could block the ability of the UK Pensions Regulator to use its moral hazard powers to impose liabilities on companies outside the UK.

Introduction

4.5.1   As a matter of UK law, the Pensions Regulator's moral hazard powers to impose liability to fund defined benefit pension schemes extend to overseas targets. However, it will be a question of local law as to whether it can enforce its powers against these targets. Significant obstacles are likely to arise under private international law.

Even if the UK is party to a treaty for the mutual enforcement of judgments in civil and commercial matters, the Pensions Regulator (TPR) is likely to face considerable difficulty in persuading a foreign court that its orders come within that treaty.

Similar objections are likely to arise under each country's private international law, given the courts' usual tendency to refuse to enforce public law and public powers of other countries.

TPR's powers

4.5.2   The importance of UK pensions as an issue in corporate finance transactions was dramatically increased with the passage of the *Pensions Act 2004*. The *2004 Act* conferred on TPR powers, if certain conditions are met, to make:

- an employer who participates in a defined benefit pension scheme; or

- third parties who are connected or associated with that employer;

liable to contribute to or support the scheme where there is a deficit. These third parties need not have incurred any direct legal obligation to the scheme to be made liable – see **4.1**.

From its inception, one of the key questions raised by this regime has been the extent to which TPR is capable of imposing these liabilities on companies outside the UK. If this power is lacking, there would be a significant gap in TPR's ability to protect pension schemes. For example:

- many major UK businesses with pension schemes have foreign parents;

- before the 2008 financial crisis, there was significant takeover activity among UK public companies by offshore private equity funds; and

- for some UK corporate groups, much of their value resides in their overseas holdings.

Instances of overseas action by TPR

4.5.3   TPR's powers are not limited to companies that are incorporated or have assets in the UK. On paper at least, TPR can serve an FSD or CN against any company in the world, and it has consistently claimed that its powers do extend beyond the UK. Until 2010, this proposition had not been extensively put into practice, as TPR had formally exercised its powers in just one publicly known instance, in 2007. This changed in 2010, when TPR exercised its powers on at least three occasions (see *TPR builds a track record*, **4.11**). It is notable that four of the six publicly known cases of TPR exercising its powers has involved an overseas target:

- *Sea Containers* – in which an FSD was issued to a Bermudan company undergoing a Chapter 11 bankruptcy proceeding in the US;

- *Nortel* – in which FSDs were determined to be issued to companies in Canada, the US, Europe and Africa;

- *Lehman Brothers* – in which FSDs were determined to be issued to companies in the US; and

- *Bonas* – in which a CN was determined to be issued to a company in Belgium.

Although each case has involved (or is expected to involve) significant litigation, as yet the question of whether the TPR order can be enforced under the private international law of the relevant jurisdiction has yet to be tested fully. Given the sudden increase in live cases and the prospect of TPR continuing to adopt a more aggressive and interventionist stance in the future, it is unlikely that this will remain untested for long.

Below we look at some of the legal obstacles that may be thrown in TPR's path. In any event, whether a TPR order can be enforced in a particular jurisdiction will of course be governed by the law of that jurisdiction. Nonetheless, it is possible to look at some general conflict of laws principles that are likely to apply. Initially, we will consider the position under some of the treaties that the

4.5.3 *Pensions Regulator – moral hazard powers*

UK has entered into for mutual enforcement of judgments, concentrating on the arrangements put in place for EU Member States. We will follow this with some observations on general conflict of laws principles that may apply in the absence of such a treaty.

When can TPR impose liability?

TPR may issue:

- a contribution notice (CN) which can be issued to either a company or an individual: It would require the target to pay a sum of money to the pension scheme. TPR will specify that sum and its amount will depend on the individual circumstances of the case, but it may be anything up to the full buy-out deficit in the scheme. A CN maybe issued where the target has been party to an act intended to avoid a pension liability or act that has detrimentally affected the security of the scheme benefits; or

- a financial support direction (FSD), which can usually only be issued to a company. The target would have to give financial support (eg a guarantee) of the employer's statutory liabilities to fund the scheme, in a form approved by TPR. An FSD may be issued if the employer does not have enough assets to fund the scheme from its own resources. If the target fails to comply with the FSD, TPR may then issue a CN.

TPR must also consider it reasonable to issue the CN. In making this decision, it must consider a non-exhaustive list of relevant factual matters, which primarily go to the level of the target's involvement with and responsibility for the pension scheme and its sponsoring employer, and any 'benefits' that it may have received from either.

TPR can only impose liability on a person who is 'connected' or 'associated' with an employer in relation to the pension schemes. But this can include (as a matter of UK law at least) person from outside the UK.

See further *TPR: Moral hazard powers*, **4.1**; and *Who is 'connected' or 'associated?'*, **4.2.**

Treatment of TPR orders under mutual enforcement treaties

4.5.4 For TPR to enforce a CN or FSD issued against a foreign company in its home jurisdiction, or a jurisdiction in which it has substantial assets, it would ultimately need to apply to that jurisdiction's courts. Those courts would determine the matter on the basis of the principles of the private international law of that jurisdiction, but in many instances, the UK will have entered into a reciprocal enforcement of judgments treaty with the country in question. Notable examples include the arrangements for enforcement of judgments:

- within the EU, under *Council Regulation (EC) 44/2001* (the *Brussels Regulation*);

- within the European Free Trade Area, under the *Lugano Convention*; and

- in another Commonwealth country, under the relevant treaty between the UK and the country in question (eg treaties are in place with both Canada and Australia).

The provisions of the relevant treaty (assuming that they have been properly incorporated into domestic law) should be considered first in any given case. Because of the extensive body of European jurisprudence on the subject, it is useful to focus on the provisions and interpretation of the *Brussels Regulation*. However, in certain respects the key principles are very similar across all of the above treaties.

The Brussels Regulation – a 'civil and commercial' claim?

4.5.5   The *Brussels Regulation* has applied in most EU Member States since 1 March 2002, though in many respects it reflects principles that were previously agreed in the *Brussels Convention* of 1968. Its purpose is to provide for the recognition and enforcement of 'judgments' by the courts of Member States in 'civil and commercial matters'. If a judgment is shown to be eligible for recognition under *Chapter III* of the *Brussels Regulation*, its enforcement will be, if not automatic, at least very likely. In this respect, there are three key questions that must be considered.

4.5.6   The first question is whether a TPR order can be treated as a 'judgment'. As *Art 32* of the *Brussels Regulation* defines this as the judgment of a court or tribunal, it may be difficult for TPR to show that a CN or FSD comes within this description. Although the TPR's determinations panel – the body that actually makes the decision to issue the CN or FSD – in some respects resembles and functions like a tribunal, it is clearly not a tribunal. However, TPR may be able to get around this obstacle by seeking to enforce its orders in a UK court and obtaining a judgment debt against the target, and then seeking to enforce that judgment debt in the foreign jurisdiction.

4.5.7   The second question is whether the issue of a CN or FSD by TPR is a civil or commercial matter, rather than a 'revenue, customs or administrative matter', which is expressly excluded by *Art 1(1)*. This condition for

and statute. However, such an argument would seem to have poor prospects of success with a target that is merely connected or associated with an employer. If such a person would only have liability to the pension scheme by reason of the *Pensions Act 2004* and the action taken by TPR under that Act, this would seem to undermine fatally any attempt to treat the issue of a CN or FSD as civil and commercial under the *Brussels Regulation*.

Private international law where no mutual enforcement treaty applies

4.5.11   In the absence of a reciprocal enforcement of judgments treaty between the UK and the country in which TPR is seeking enforcement, or if a treaty does apply but the TPR order is not eligible for recognition and enforcement under it (eg because it fails the civil and commercial test) the courts of that country will determine the matter on the basis of the general principles of private international law that apply in that jurisdiction.

This would be the case if, for example, TPR were to take action against a US company, as there is no relevant treaty between the UK and the US. Indeed, within the US a distinct body of private international law applies in each state.

4.5.12   Local law advice will of course be needed to confirm the position in any given case. However, as a general matter, it is fair to say that in almost every jurisdiction, the courts will not accept jurisdiction to enforce the penal, revenue or (possibly) 'public' or 'administrative' law of another country.

Depending on how these terms are interpreted in local law, a TPR order is unlikely to be viewed as revenue-related, and (though the position is less clear) it should often be possible to put forward reasonable arguments as to why the order is not 'penal'. However, it will be more difficult for TPR if the relevant jurisdiction does not recognise a broader residual category of 'public' or 'administrative' laws. As discussed above on the *Brussels Regulation*, a TPR order may well be viewed as being essentially public in nature.

4.5.13   That said, because TPR's powers straddle public and private interests, there may be scope to rebut such a view. Certainly in some jurisdictions (such as England and Australia) there have been instances of the courts recognising actions by public regulatory bodies, which are exercising public statutory powers, where these have been viewed as not amounting to a 'governmental interest' that cannot be enforced. An interesting example is the Australian case *Robb Evans of Robb Evans & Associates v European Bank* [2004] NSWCA 82, in which the New South Wales courts enforced action by a receiver appointed by the United States Federal Trade Commission to recover the proceeds of a credit card fraud, using powers provided to it under a US statutory consumer protection regime that were intended to enable it to compensate victims of fraud

4.5.13 *Pensions Regulator – moral hazard powers*

(the case is discussed approvingly by the English Court of Appeal in *Government of the Islamic Republic of Iran v Barakat Galleries* [2007] EWCA Civ 1374).

4.5.14 If these arguments have found acceptance in the country in question, TPR's argument may well give emphasis to the role of its powers in ensuring that pension benefits that have been promised are paid in full. If there is flexibility to entertain such arguments, then (perhaps surprisingly) TPR may have more prospect of success when arguing on the basis of such general principles than it would when seeking to have its orders recognised under a mutual enforcement treaty.

Conclusion

4.5.15 It is far from clear whether TPR would be successful if it sought to enforce its orders in a foreign jurisdiction, and this was challenged on private international law grounds.

A large part of the value of TPR's powers in protecting pension schemes and the PPF lies in their deterrent effect, as interested parties (both UK-based and foreign) often structure their affairs and put measures in place for the pension scheme in question at least partly to mitigate the risk of later TPR intervention.

To avoid the risk of undermining this deterrent effect, TPR may well find it prudent to avoid foreign enforcement legal proceedings as much as possible.

4.6 Financial support directions (FSDs)

4.6.1

Summary

The *Pensions Act 2004* gave the UK Pensions Regulator (TPR) 'moral hazard' powers that allow it to bypass corporate structures and fix a liability on third parties that are connected or associated to an employer of an under-funded defined-benefit scheme.

TPR can issue either a contribution notice or a financial support direction (FSD) making the third party pay a specified amount into the scheme or put financial support in place for the scheme. This section looks at FSDs in more detail.

Test for issuing financial support directions

4.6.2   The UK Pensions Regulator (TPR) can issue either a contribution notice (CN) or a financial support direction (FSD) making the third party pay a specified amount into the scheme or put financial support in place for the defined benefit (DB) scheme – for more information on CNs see *Contribution notices (CNs)*, **4.7**.

For an overview of TPR's powers see *TPR Moral hazard powers: Extracting pension scheme funding from third parties*, **4.1**.

FSDs require that the target put reasonable financial support in place.

TPR is able to issue an FSD against another employer or person (other than an individual, in most cases) 'connected' to or 'associated' with the employer in relation to an occupational pension scheme (see *Who is connected or associated*, **4.2**).

The employer must be or have been:

- a service company (ie a company with accounts showing its turnover principally derived from providing services to other group companies); or

- insufficiently resourced – ie it did not have sufficient assets to meet 50% of the employer's debt under *s 75* of the *Pensions Act 1995* (broadly, the deficit found by measuring benefit liabilities on a buy-out basis) in relation to the scheme and at that time there:

- – was a connected or associated person who did have sufficient resources to meet the shortfall to the 50% level; or

- – were two or more persons who were connected with each other and their combined resources were sufficient to meet the shortfall to the 50% level (the 'alternative test' for issuing FSDs).

As with CNs, TPR must consider it 'reasonable' to issue an FSD, having regard to factors such as the degree of connection an entity has had with the DB scheme and any benefits the person has received from a DB employer or scheme. See *The reasonableness test – What are the factors that affect liability?*, **4.10**.

A person who is the subject of an FSD is required to put in place financial support (broadly, funding or guarantees) within a specified period and maintain it throughout the life of the scheme (see further **4.6.5** below).

FSDs can require arrangements to be put in place where all group companies are jointly liable or a suitable holding company is liable.

Time limits

4.6.3   TPR is able to 'look back' in time when deciding whether to issue an FSD. The determinations panel of TPR can decide to issue an FSD if the financial test was satisfied at a date it chooses within the previous two years (the relevant person must have been connected to or associated with an employer at the date chosen).

The *Pensions Act 2011* has from 2 January 2012 extended this time period so that the two-year period (within which the chosen relevant date must lie) runs up to the date of issue of the relevant Warning Notice – instead of the date of the decision by the determinations panel (for the process see *Procedure for issue of a CN or FSD,* **4.9**).

So even if a third party is no longer connected or associated with an employer, they may still be at risk if they were connected or associated within this look-back period with an employer that was a service company or insufficiently resourced. For example, a third party cannot escape an FSD simply because the effect of a recent sale is that it is no longer connected or associated with the scheme's employer.

If a person fails to comply with an FSD, TPR may seek to enforce a monetary obligation by issuing a CN – *s 47*.

Practical effect of the test

4.6.4 TPR may issue an FSD, for example, if a restructuring or sale has resulted in the employer becoming a service company or insufficiently resourced.

But its powers can potentially be used in broader circumstances than a transaction. This is because a person does not need to have committed an act or omission before TPR can issue an FSD against them – contrast this with the position for CNs, which can be issued only against a person that is a party to an act or failure to act. TPR's FSD power can be triggered merely by the fact (regardless of the reason) of an employer becoming a service company or insufficiently resourced.

The then pensions minister, Malcolm Wicks, commented in the standing committee debate on the Pensions Bill 2004 that FSDs could apply 'even where the company structures have been set up for perfectly legitimate reasons'.

What kind of financial support?

4.6.5 An FSD, once issued, requires that the named target puts in place financial support for the scheme within a time specified in the direction and keeps it in place for the remainder of the scheme's existence.

It is for the parties to decide the precise arrangements for this, subject to the need for TPR to approve the arrangements as reasonable. For example, the companies within the group can be jointly and severally liable for the employer's pension liabilities, the group's holding company can be liable or parties can enter into a legally enforceable agreement to support the scheme.

Companies that are served with an FSD will have to consider carefully the most appropriate type of financial support to provide. Agreeing that all group companies will be jointly and severally liable could cause problems with later transactions.

The FSD is only complied with if TPR approves the arrangements. TPR will only do so if it is satisfied that it is reasonable in those circumstances.

A party against whom an FSD is issued must, going forward, notify TPR of certain notifiable employer events (eg breach of banking covenants – see *Notifiable Events: Obligation to report certain events to the Pensions Regulator*, **13.1**), their insolvency or failure to comply with the FSD.

If a target fails to comply with an FSD (eg fails to give financial support), TPR can, through its determinations panel (if it considers it reasonable) issue a CN requiring that the target pays a specified amount to the scheme – *s 47* of the *Pensions Act 2004*. This CN is enforceable as a debt claim.

The determinations panel has decided to issue FSDs in four public cases to date: *Sea Containers, Nortel, Lehman Brothers and Box Clever/ITV*. See *TPR builds a track record*, **4.11**.

Maximum amount

4.6.6 If the Pensions Regulator exercises its 'moral hazard powers' under the *Pensions Act 2004* by issuing a contribution notice (CN) or financial support direction (FSD) against a target, the question can arise as to the maximum liability that can be imposed on a target (or group of targets) as a result.

In the case of an FSD, this does not of itself impose a monetary liability. Instead the target is directed to put in place financial support within a period and to maintain it. If the target fails to do this, ultimately enforcement for failure to comply is by the Regulator issuing a CN, which imposes a debt obligation on the target. The amount of a CN is set as the amount considered by the Regulator to be reasonable.

Individual maximum = *s 75* debt due as at time of non-compliance

The legislation is relatively clear, in a case where the employer has already triggered a debt obligation to the scheme (under *Pensions Act 1995, s 75*), that the maximum amount of an individual CN is the relevant section 75 debt due at the time of non-compliance by the employer to the scheme (called the 'shortfall sum').

Interaction with other liabilities?

The inter-relation of the potential liability with other amounts being claimed or recovered by the scheme (e g from the employer, or from a guarantor or from another FSD target) is complex.

Storm Funding

4.6.7 In December 2013, the High Court ruled in *Re Storm Funding Ltd* [2013] EWHC 4019 (Ch) on maximum liabilities where more than one FSD or CN is issued.

David Richards J concluded that multiple enforcement CNs (each for up to the 'shortfall sum') could be issued in relation to one or more FSDs, permitting a recovery in aggregate (amongst multiple targets) in excess of the shortfall sum – i e the certified but historic *s 75* debt. This would allow the actual scheme deficit (if now greater than the historic *s 75* debt, due to liability drift) to be supported.

This decision relates to an application brought by the relevant UK insolvency practitioners (administrators) of 14 companies in the Lehman Brothers group seeking directions as to their potential scheme liabilities under an FSD (if one is ultimately issued – a reference to the Upper Tribunal from the decision of the Regulator's determinations panel is pending).

David Richards J ruled that:

- the Regulator may issue multiple contribution notices to Lehman Brothers companies that in aggregate exceed the value of the employer's *s 75* debt.

- payment by one target does not reduce the liability of the other (unless the FSD or CN was issued on a joint and several basis, which is a matter for the Regulator to decide when issuing them).

Implications on aggregate liability

4.6.8   If the judgment of David Richards J is upheld (an appeal has been filed), this means that a group where more than one company could have a liability under an FSD:

- could potentially face total aggregate liabilities under all the FSDs greater than the individual cap which applies to each enforcement of an FSD;

- the individual cap on each target is:

   (i)   the employer's historic *s 75* debt amount (scheme deficit) at the relevant insolvency date – *s 48, Pensions Act 2004*; less

   (ii) (seemingly[7]) any amounts already paid towards that debt (by the employer or a third party) before the relevant 'time of non-compliance' with the FSD; and less

   (iii) any reduction agreed by the Regulator following a payment made by a third party after the 'time of non-compliance' (on an application made as soon as reasonably practicable after the payment is made) – *s 50(7), Pensions Act 2004*.

In *Storm Funding*, the Lehman trustees and the Regulator accepted (see para [57]) that the aggregate amount recoverable under the CNs should not

---

7   This point is not discussed in *Storm Funding*.

exceed the amount needed to meet the scheme's pension liabilities – i e presumably the scheme's relevant buy-out deficit at the later date (it is not clear when this would be checked – at the time of issue of the CN or at the time of payment). This was stated to be part of the 'reasonableness' test, but could perhaps also involve the *s 50(7)* discretion.

In *Storm Funding*, an appeal to the Court of Appeal has been lodged. It is clearly possible that the Court of Appeal may take a different view to that of David Richards J on the maximum aggregate liability point.

4.7   Contribution notices (CNs)

Summary

The *Pensions Act 2004* gave the UK Pensions Regulator (TPR) 'moral hazard' powers that allow it to bypass corporate structures and fix a liability on third parties that are connected or associated with an employer of a defined benefit (DB) pension scheme.

TPR can either issue:

- a contribution notice (CN) making the third party pay a specified amount into the scheme; or

- a financial support direction making the third party put financial support in place for the scheme.

This section focuses on the potential exposure of third parties to liability under CNs.

Introduction

4.7.1   The 'moral hazard' powers of the TPR under the *Pensions Act 2004* allow it to bypass corporate structures and fix a liability on third parties that are connected or associated with an employer of a defined benefit pension scheme. For an overview of these powers, see *TPR: Moral hazard powers: Extracting pension scheme funding from third parties*, **4.1**.

TPR can either issue a contribution notice (CN) or a financial support direction (FSD) making the third party pay a specified amount into the scheme or put financial support in place for the scheme. For more information on FSDs, see *Financial support directions (FSDs)*, **4.6**.

Contribution notices

4.7.2   A contribution notice (CN) requires the recipient to pay a specified amount to the pension scheme and – unlike most FSDs – it can be issued against individuals (eg a director of an employer), as well as companies. However, there is an exemption for an insolvency practitioner acting in the course of his or her duties.[8]

TPR can issue a CN under:

- the 'material detriment test', which was introduced with effect on and from 14 April 2008; or

- the 'main purpose' test, which was introduced with effect on and from on 27 April 2004.

We discuss these two tests at (A) and (B) below.

CNs issued under the 'material detriment' test

4.7.3   The *Pensions Act 2008* modified the *Pensions Act 2004* to give TPR the power to issue a CN when an act or failure to act (or series of acts or failure to act) has, in its opinion, detrimentally affected in a material way the likelihood of accrued scheme benefits being received. To date, as far as we are aware, no CN has yet been issued on this basis.

As with CNs issued under the 'main purpose' test (which is discussed at **4.7.8** below), TPR is only able to issue a CN against a person if, in its view (ie the view of the separate determinations panel or DP), it is 'reasonable' to impose a CN. It must have regard to factors such as the degree of connection an entity has had with the scheme, any benefits the person has received from an employer/ scheme and the purpose of the particular act.[9]

The power to issue CNs under the material detriment test can be used in relation to acts or failures to act that occur on or after 14 April 2008 and within six years of the determination by the DP that a CN be issued. The recipient must have been connected to or associated with an employer at any time during that period. The *Pensions Act 2011* has, on and from 3 January 2012, changed the six-year period so that it ends on the date TPR issues its warning notice.

The previous Labour government commented that the material detriment test requires a before and after comparison of the effect of the act (or failure to act) based only on the circumstances prevailing at the time. There is no requirement on TPR to show that the detrimental effect on the security of scheme benefits

---

8   For information on who may be issued with CNs and FSDs, see *Who is connected or associated?*, **4.2** and *TPR: who is within reach?*, **4.3**.

9   For information on the 'reasonableness' test, see *The reasonableness test: what are the factors that affect liability?*, **4.10**.

was a purpose of the act or failure to act (as is required under the original main purpose test).

Clearly, a test based on material detriment could potentially be satisfied in a very wide range of circumstances, putting persons at risk of liability under CNs despite the lack of any intention to avoid liabilities to pension schemes. For example, an employer could invest resources in a flawed business strategy or in a manner that loses money and – simply by weakening the financial position of the employer – this decision could be interpreted as satisfying the material detriment test.

In response to this concern, the previous government and TPR introduced the following safeguards:

- additional 'reasonableness test' factors that TPR must consider before it exercises its power to issue a CN under the material detriment test;
- a statutory defence to a CN issued under the material detriment test;
- a code of practice on when TPR will exercise its power to issue a CN under the material detriment test; and
- illustrative examples from TPR.

The stated aim of these safeguards was to reassure the industry that this new power will not be used in 'normal business transactions' (although this has not been specified as such in the actual legislation).We discuss these safeguards below.

Additional factors that TPR must consider under the 'reasonableness test' before it exercises its power to issue a CN under the material detriment test

4.7.4   For details of these factors, see *The reasonableness test – what are the factors that affect liability?*, **4.10.**

Statutory defence to a CN issued under the material detriment test

4.7.5   The *Pensions Act 2008* introduced a statutory defence to CNs sought on the basis of the material detriment test. The defence is intended to prevent TPR from issuing a CN against any person if TPR is satisfied that the person has shown that:

- before becoming a party to the relevant act or failure to act, the person (following reasonably diligent enquiries and other necessary steps) gave due consideration to the extent to which the act or failure to act might detrimentally affect in a material way the likelihood of accrued scheme benefits being received; and either:

– in any case where, as a result of that consideration, the person considered that the act or failure to act might have such a detrimental effect, the person took all reasonable steps to eliminate or minimise the potentially detrimental effects of the act or failure to act; or

– having regard to all relevant circumstances prevailing at the relevant time, it was reasonable for the person to conclude that the act or failure to act would not detrimentally affect in a material way the likelihood of accrued scheme benefits being received.

TPR's approach to its power to issue a CN under the 'material detriment' test – code of practice

4.7.6   TPR's power to issue a CN under the 'material detriment test' is accompanied by a statutory code of practice, Code of Practice 12, which was issued in June 2009. It outlines the circumstances in which TPR expects to issue CNs on the basis of the material detriment test. In it, TPR has said that it would only issue such a CN if any of the following circumstances are present:

- a transfer of the scheme out of the jurisdiction (ie out of the UK);

- a transfer of the sponsoring employer out of the UK, or the replacement of the sponsoring employer with an entity that does not fall within that jurisdiction;

- sponsor support being removed, substantially reduced or becoming nominal;

- a transfer of liabilities of the scheme to another pension scheme or arrangement which leads to a significant reduction of the:

  – sponsor support in respect of these liabilities; or

  – funding to cover these liabilities; or

- a business model or a manner of operating the scheme, which creates (or which is designed to create) from the scheme a financial benefit for:

  – the employer; or

  – some other person,

where proper account has not been taken of the interests of the members of the scheme, including where risks to members are increased.

TPR's illustrative examples

4.7.7   Although TPR's Code of Practice 12 was intended to reassure the industry that the new power will not be used in response to most normal business transactions, it has been criticised for setting out a list of circumstances that is too broad – especially the reference to sponsor support being 'removed, substantially reduced or [becoming] nominal'.

Circumstances where TPR will not issue a CN under the 'material detriment' test:	*Circumstances where TPR may issue a CN under the 'material detriment' test:*
Payment of dividends to parent company Company A is trading profitably and the associated pension scheme has a deficit which is being addressed by an appropriate recovery plan. As part of the recovery plan directors make a routine annual dividend payment to shareholders in the normal course of business.	*Removal of covenant* Company P is moderately profitable, and is a sponsor of a scheme with a large deficit. The parent company, which has no legal link to the scheme, substitutes it with Company Q, which is a shell company with a materially weaker covenant than Company P, as sponsoring employer. Company P is sold off and the proceeds from the transfer pass directly to the parent company and its shareholders.
Buyouts and annuities The trustees of Scheme B have chosen to buy out pensioner liabilities by annuities. The trustees discharge the scheme liabilities through the purchase of annuities from a regulated insurer, so that the insurer assumes responsibility for making payments of members' benefits. The trustees took proper account of members' interests in deciding to insure the scheme liabilities. They reconciled the respective interests of different classes of member to ensure all are fairly treated, and conducted due diligence when selecting a product and insurer.	*Risking members' benefits* Sponsoring employer R is a company with a very weak covenant and is not able to fund the scheme beyond ongoing expenses. The employer and trustees decide to take an inappropriate investment strategy which will provide profit for the employer and shareholders if a surplus is generated. However, if a deficit is created, any call on the employer for payments will force the company's insolvency. This will in turn cause the scheme and its members to enter the Pension Protection Fund and therefore receive reduced benefits.

4.7.7 *Pensions Regulator – moral hazard powers*

Circumstances where TPR will not issue a CN under the 'material detriment' test:	*Circumstances where TPR may issue a CN under the 'material detriment' test:*
General poor trading Employer C has experienced poor trading as a result of market conditions, and consequently has lost a major customer to its competitors.	*Restructure and transfer — weakened covenant* Company S has transferred its employees and their respective pension liabilities to Company T. Company T is highly leveraged and offers a much weaker supporting covenant to the scheme than Company S. No mitigation has been provided to the scheme or its membership for the weakening position.
Granting of security Employer D grants security in the form of a first charge over some of its assets to renegotiate its borrowings with the bank. In so doing, the employer engages with the scheme trustees and provides appropriate mitigation to the scheme for the reduction in covenant.	
Investment strategy The trustees of Scheme E and representatives of the sponsoring employer agree an investment strategy in light of the employer's ability to cover any shortfall. This ensures a properly chosen, compliant investment strategy with prudent assumptions taking into account the employer's ability to cope with adverse experience.	
TPR cautions that the situations listed above, taken together with other acts or failures to act, might constitute a series of acts which could be considered materially detrimental	
Source: TPR Code related Guidance re material detriment test. See www.thepensionsregulator.gov.uk/codes/code-related-material-detriment-test.aspx	

CNs issued under the 'main purpose' test

4.7.8   CNs can be issued under the 'main purpose test' if:

- the person is an employer or person 'connected with' or 'an associate of' the employer – these are broad terms and can, for example, catch companies within the same group, one-third shareholders and directors;

- there was an act or deliberate omission (or 'series of acts or failure to act' (ie a course of conduct)) that occurred within the last six years. The recipient must have been connected to or associated with an employer in that period (not necessarily at the time of the act or omission);

- that person was a party to (or 'knowingly assisted' in) the act or omission;

- TPR thinks it is reasonable to impose the CN on that person; and

- TPR is of the opinion that the 'main purpose' (or one of the main purposes) of the act or failure to act was to prevent:

    – the recovery of the whole or part of a statutory debt under *s* 75 of the *Pensions Act 1995*; or

    – the *s* 75 debt from becoming due or to compromise, settle or reduce the *s* 75 debt.

Originally, 'good faith' was, in some circumstances, a defence to the issue of a CN on the basis of the main purpose test. Due to changes in legislation introduced by the *Pensions Act 2008*, this is no longer the case.

The first CN to be decided by the determinations panel of TPR issued on this basis was in the *Desmonds* case in April 2011 – see **4.15** but the decision was kept confidential until 2012. The first public case was the *Bonas Group Pension Scheme* case in June 2010 (see **4.8**).

The meaning of 'main purpose'?

4.7.9   For TPR to issue a CN under the 'main purpose' test it has to be of the opinion that a main purpose (but not necessarily the only purpose) of the act or failure to act was to avoid or reduce a *s* 75 debt.

Unfortunately, the concept of 'main purpose' is not defined in the *Pensions Act 2004*. In *Bonas Group Pension Scheme* (2010), the Determinations Panel of TPR held that the 'purpose' of an act should be ascertained objectively but accepted that subjective intention was also relevant if the objective 'purpose' of an act was not 'plain'.

In practice, if the employer is aware of the impact that an act may have on the pension scheme, it may be more difficult to show that this is not one of the main purposes of the act.

To mitigate the risk of a CN being issued under this test, the purpose of undertaking transactions such as internal restructurings, or changing the principal or a participating employer, should be documented, in order to help rebut any later suggestion that the main purpose was to avoid *s 75* liabilities. Parties would need to show an alternative reason for the transaction, which is sufficiently compelling and material, to make the removal of liability to the scheme a peripheral concern.

Preventing the recovery of a *s 75* debt

4.7.10   A key feature of CNs under the main purpose test is that TPR can only issue a CN against a party if they take part in an act the purpose of which is to prevent the recovery of a debt under *s 75* of the *Pensions Act 1995* from an employer or former employer.

In *Bonas Group Pension Scheme*, the determinations panel of TPR interpreted this provision widely. On the basis of that case it would appear that not involving trustees or TPR in negotiations early on in a transaction (thereby denying them the opportunity to negotiate the provision of some funding as a condition of agreeing to the transaction), may be seen as equivalent to preventing the recovery of some or all of a *s 75* debt which might become due. This provided the determinations panel with the basis to issue a CN, although it is a contentious interpretation. Bonas appealed to the Upper Tribunal (Tax and Chancery Chamber), which on a strike-out hearing criticised the test used by the determinations panel (see *The Bonas case*, **4.8**)

Any broadening of the circumstances in which TPR can issue CNs under the main purpose test is perhaps less significant for future actions now that TPR can issue CNs on the seemingly easier basis of 'material detriment'. However, the *Bonas* case is still important because:

- TPR can issue CNs under the main purpose test for acts as far back as 2004, whereas it can only issue CNs under the material detriment test for acts since 2008;

- TPR now has experience issuing a CN under the main purpose test and was (at least initially) successful, which may make it more ready to do so; and

- it is not known how difficult, in practice, TPR will find it to issue a CN under the material detriment test (it may need to rely on detailed financial and actuarial advice to prove material detriment). Conversely, and in contrast to the main purpose test, TPR does not need to show any objective intention in proving the material detriment test.

4.8   The *Bonas* case: judicial guidance on CNs

4.8.1

Summary

In 2010 in the *Bonas* case TPR's determinations panel had issued a CN against the Belgian parent company. The company appealed and applied to the Upper Tribunal to strike out TPR's case.

In 2011, the Upper Tribunal's tax and chancery chamber ruled that a contribution notice should compensate the pension scheme for detriment suffered. It should not actively penalise the target.

The case was due to have gone on to a full hearing before the Upper Tribunal but was subsequently settled in May 2011. The Upper Tribunal's holdings in the strike-out hearing are likely to carry much weight in future cases.

This section outlines:

- the background and summarises the main points that may affect future cases involving contribution notices; and

- the terms of the settlement and TPR's comments.

4.8.2   The first public issue of a CN by TPR was in the Bonas case.

The facts at a glance

- VDW was the ultimate parent of Bonas (a UK company). Bonas was the employer and sponsor of the Bonas Group pension scheme.

- VDW financially supported Bonas, but ultimately decided this could not continue and Bonas went into administration (with a pre-pack sale of its business and assets for £40,000 to another subsidiary of VDW).

- The Bonas Group pension scheme was left behind as the major (unsecured) creditor of Bonas.

- The PPF shortfall was about £5 million. The *s 75* buy-out shortfall was about £20 million. The scheme was taken over by the PPF.[10]

- TPR sought a CN against both VDW and Mr Beauduin, a director (of Bonas and VDW). The determinations panel decided (in May 2010):

  – to issue a CN against VDW for about £5 million; and

  – not to issue a CN against Mr Beauduin.

- VDW appealed the determinations panel decision to the Upper Tribunal. TPR's statement of case sought to follow the determinations panel decision but increase the amount of the CN against VDW and make a CN against Mr Beauduin. VDW applied (in effect) to strike out part of the TPR case

Strike-out application rejected

4.8.3 In January 2011, the Upper Tribunal (tax and chancery chamber) rejected a strike-out application by the target of the first public contribution notice (CN) issued by the Pensions Regulator (TPR).[11]

In June 2010, TPR confirmed that the DP had determined to issue a CN against a Belgian company, Michel Van De Wiele (VDW), the parent company of Bonas UK (*Bonas*), the sponsoring employer of the Bonas Group Pension Scheme. Bonas had entered administration in 2006 and then had its business sold to another subsidiary of VDW under a pre-pack insolvency process, leaving the scheme to be taken over by the Pension Protection Fund (PPF). The CN would, if issued, order VDW to pay just over £5 million to the PPF.

VDW appealed to the Upper Tribunal and made an interlocutory application to strike out TPR's case. Although the application was refused, Mr Justice Warren, the president of the tax and chancery chamber, criticised the amount specified in the CN, stating that some of the determinations panel's reasoning as to the relevant amount was 'unsustainable'.

Warren J reasoned that the purpose of a CN should be to compensate the scheme for the detriment suffered rather than actively penalise the target. Any

---

10 This means that even if an FSD were to be issued, it could not be enforced by a CN under *s 47* of the *Pensions Act 2004* – see *s 47(5)* and Briggs J in *Re Nortel GmbH* [2010] EWHC (Ch) 3010 at para [36].

11 *In the matter of the Bonas Group Pension Scheme; Michel Van de Wiele NV v the Pensions Regulator*, 17 January 2011, Warren J, Upper Tribunal (Tax and Chancery chamber), FS/2010/0007. The judgment (52 pages) is available at http://www.bailii.org/uk/cases/UKUT/TCC/2011/B3.html

recovery of additional amounts should be obtained through the financial support direction (FSD) regime. On the facts presented, Warren J felt that if TPR could show that (for example) the assets of Bonas had been sold at an under-value (as part of the pre-pack administration) the appropriate amount for a CN would be no more than the difference between the market value of the business and the price obtained.

The case was then due to proceed to a full hearing before the Upper Tribunal, but the issue was settled in May 2011.

Implications of the decision

4.8.4   This decision is definitely a shot across TPR's bows by Mr Justice Warren – it is not strictly binding on a future tribunal but is likely to be given lots of weight. The main points include the following.

- The statute says that any CN award must be reasonable. Mr Justice Warren considered that this means the amount must not be penal and so it is 'not easy to see' how it should exceed the amount of the *s 75* debt avoided by the relevant act (ie the obligation to contribute to the scheme under *s 75* of the *Pensions Act 1995*, triggered by an event such as a company reorganisation). This means it is very difficult to justify the £5 million CN based on just (say):

  - VDW failing to inform the trustees or TPR of its proposals; or

  - (even if shown) the sale of Bonas's assets at an under-value (given that the asset value was probably no more than £100,000).

- These limits on a CN probably do not apply to an FSD. This is likely to mean that in future TPR is even more likely to look for an FSD ahead of a CN (but note the more restrictive time limits).

- TPR cannot itself appeal against the determinations panel's decision (eg here the panel decided not to grant a CN personally against one of the directors):

  - but if there is an appeal (eg by the company or trustees as a directly affected party), TPR could argue for an increased CN (ie as here against the parent company); and

  - this is a point that targets will need to bear in mind if they are thinking of appeal – it could result in a larger award.

There was no strike-out here on most of the points because they will depend on the factual evidence (still to be finalised and heard). But the judgment contains pretty strong hints by Mr Justice Warren that the evidence is not enough to justify the £5 million CN previously determined.

4.8.5   *Pensions Regulator – moral hazard powers*

Background – the appeal to the Upper Tribunal

4.8.5   TPR's determinations panel decided in May 2010 that a CN for about £5 million should be issued against VDW. It also decided not to issue a CN against one of the directors of Bonas, Mr Beauduin.

VDW appealed to the Upper Tribunal against the decision against it and applied to strike out part of TPR's claim.

Mr Justice Warren, the president of the Upper Tribunal (tax and chancery chamber) gave judgment in January 2011. This was a preliminary strike-out application (and not a full hearing of the appeal).

Points to consider for future CNs

4.8.6   Warren J's decision is the first real appeal hearing from a determinations panel decision in a moral hazard case. It includes several important points, as discussed below.

The appeal is a new decision

4.8.7   An appeal to the Upper Tribunal operates as a new decision. It is not necessary to show that the determinations panel was in error (para 38).

New facts can be introduced

4.8.8   New facts can be introduced by all the parties, including the target of the CN and TPR (para 39). The Upper Tribunal may be reluctant to hear all the evidence that has already been given (but could decide to) (para 40).

TPR cannot appeal alone

4.8.9   TPR cannot itself appeal a decision of the determinations panel, but the target or another 'directly affected' person (eg the pension trustees) can (para 66).

enforcement may well prove to be a significantly more challenging obstacle to TPR, as the broad principle that emerges from the case law is that if the claim made is one by a public body, which only a public law body could make, it will not fall within the *Brussels Regulation*.

This principle was stated in *LTU v Eurocontrol* (Case 29/76) [1976] ECR 1541, in which the body responsible for regulating European civil aviation brought an action in Belgium to recover unpaid invoices rendered by it to Lufthansa. The ECJ ruled that this action was not a civil or commercial matter and so fell outside the then-applicable *Brussels Convention*. Similarly, in *Netherlands v Ruffer* (Case 814/79) [1980] ECJ 3807, a sunken barge was removed by a Dutch government body, using its specific powers under Dutch law. That body then brought a claim against a German defendant in the Dutch courts under the Dutch private law of tort to recover the cost of the operation. As the government body was making the claim in the course of carrying out its public functions, the ECJ held that this was not a civil and commercial matter.

4.5.8 How likely is a court to take a similar view of TPR exercising its powers? It could be argued by TPR that it is merely acting on behalf of the trustee of the pension scheme in question and, in essence, ensuring that the employer's obligations to fund the scheme are met in full and that benefits are paid as promised. Under such an argument, TPR's role is to ensure financial recovery by and on behalf of private interests, the trustee and the scheme members. However, an obvious weakness in this argument is that the protection of those private interests would be sought by TPR under a public policy, using unique powers that are granted to it for this purpose.

4.5.9 This point leads neatly into a crucial aspect of the ECJ's interpretation of 'civil and commercial'; it is essentially the flipside of the 'public body/public powers' issue discussed above. It is the requirement that TPR (or any governmental body seeking to enforce its orders) must not be making any claim, or imposing any liability, that would not arise or be available to individuals making a claim under private law. This issue was considered by the ECJ in *Preservatrice fonciere TIARD (PFA) v Netherlands* (Case C-266/01) [2003] ECR I-4867, in which the Netherlands government was seeking to enforce a guarantee provided by an insurer (PFA) on behalf of a Dutch association of carriers. The provision of the guarantee was a condition imposed by the Netherlands government for granting authorisation to the carriers to carry out certain functions. However, although the guarantee was given in a public and regulatory context, it nonetheless arose under and was governed by private law, and was therefore enforceable under the *Brussels Convention*.

4.5.10 TPR may have some scope to argue that its powers do no more than reflect and allow for the enforcement of existing private law obligations – but, it seems, only if the recipient of the CN or FSD is a participating employer in the scheme, which has incurred liability to the pension scheme under private law

Entirely new claims cannot be brought

4.8.10   A new claim probably cannot be introduced. TPR probably cannot claim a new measure not in the original warning notice (para 70).[12]

TPR can argue for a higher amount

4.8.11   If there is an appeal, TPR can seek a CN for a higher amount than was decided by the determinations panel (para 70).

Each determination is separate

4.8.12   Each target is the subject of a separate decision by the determinations panel, so the appeal by VDW is not an appeal in the case involving the director, Mr Beauduin. No appeal had been made in Mr Beauduin's case, so it was not possible for the Upper Tribunal to issue a CN against Mr Beauduin (para 199).

The requirements for a 'main purpose CN' were analysed

4.8.13   There is some analysis of the meaning of the CN legislation (*s 38* of the *Pensions Act 2004*), but note this was dealing with the *2004 Act* before the amendments made in 2008 (by the *Pensions Act 2008*).

In particular Warren J reviewed:

- when there would be a 'failure to act'. Warren J thought this did not require a failure to do something under a positive duty (para 88);

- how the 'main purpose' would be identified. Warren J thought this would probably have a subjective element (what the person intends) as well as an objective element (the act must be able to prevent recovery of a *s 75* debt) (paras 90 and 91); and

- recovery of all or part of a *s 75* debt can be prevented only if the person is liable to pay an amount (eg the employer or a guarantor). It is not enough to prevent a voluntary payment (paras 93 and 94).

---

12   This is now of even more importance now that the changes to the time limits for CNs and FSDs have been brought into effect from January 2012 under the *Pensions Act 2011*. The two-year (FSD) and six-year (CN) time limits have changed so that they now run up to the date of issue of a warning notice by TPR – a change from the previous time period, which ended at the date of the determination by the determinations panel.

4.8.14   *Pensions Regulator – moral hazard powers*

'Walking away' does not justify a CN

4.8.14   Warren J considered that a failure to negotiate with TPR about clearance cannot itself be an act or failure justifying a CN (paras 159 to 161). Failure by VDW to engage with the trustees or TPR was 'not of great significance' because it did not prejudice TPR from issuing a CN later (para 163).

But non-engagement could be relevant to establish subjective intention. So TPR can still in this case seek to rely on the 'walking away' evidence (para 164).

Sale at under-value can be discussed

4.8.15   TPR is allowed to produce evidence that the sale by the administrator of Bonas of its business to another VDW group company was at an under-value (ie the company was worth more than the £40,000 paid).

- But it is now quite late for such evidence to be introduced (it was produced too late to be discussed before the determinations panel and still had not been produced in the proceedings before the Upper Tribunal). Leave would be needed from the Upper Tribunal.

- Warren J thought it likely to be 'hard to contend' that the market value should have been more than £100,000 (para 178). So any CN based on such a sale at an under-value would probably be limited to £60,000. He commented:

  '178. It is a different matter, however, whether it would be reasonable to issue a contribution notice on that basis for a sum of £5.089 million let alone any higher figure. If no further evidence is adduced, the most that the Regulator could say is that the sale price was at the bottom end of the range. Even if one takes a very generous view in favour of the Regulator, it appears to me to be hard to contend on the evidence so far that the market value was more than £100,000. In that case, it is difficult to see how the Regulator could properly form the view, by reference to the sale at undervalue point, that it would be reasonable for the contribution notice to specify an amount more than the difference between that sum and the price actually paid.'

Whether the sale prevented recovery of the s 75 debt is a matter for factual investigation

4.8.16   TPR argued that putting Bonas into a pre-pack administration prevented the payment of future contributions by Bonas.

Warren J rejected TPR's argument that VDW's failure to continue funding Bonas meant that it avoided the payment of the ongoing contribution payments and so prevented payment of a *s 75* debt (paras 162 and 180).

Warren J discussed an alternative argument that this also meant that VDW had prevented the recovery of contributions that would have reduced the *s 75* debt. He considered that this raised a difficult factual case for TPR – it would have to show that Bonas would have paid the ongoing contributions, but he suspected that instead Bonas would have gone into liquidation (para 186). But this was a matter for factual investigation, so Warren J decided that no bar should apply at this stage. He did comment that:

> '187. Whether it is possible to issue a contribution notice to VDW on the basis that it could have chosen voluntarily to support Bonas and thereby the Scheme but chose not to do must be highly questionable. It is the territory of the FSD regime to impose liabilities on associated companies in such circumstances. To say that VDW has prevented payment by Bonas of part of the *s 75* debt by declining to support Bonas when it was not obliged to do so would represent an extreme interpretation of section 38. As with the first difficulty, I do not consider that I can properly resolve this issue on this application. I consider that it should be resolved only after a full investigation of the facts. The facts may reveal that it would not be reasonable to issue a contribution notice at all based on the failure by VDW voluntarily to support Bonas in which case it may be unnecessary to rule one way or the other on this second difficulty. Reasonableness, however, is a matter which can only be dealt with at a full hearing.'

Amount of a CN – it should reflect loss, not be a penalty

4.8.17   There should be no penalty element to a CN. Recovery of any amount more than the loss caused by the act or omission is more a matter for the FSD regime[13] (paras 100, 121 and 187).

In this case the evidence was that the legal advice to VDW was that if it had sought clearance from TPR, this would probably have involved a contribution to fund the scheme to the PPF level – about £8 million. Warren J considered it 'frankly inconceivable' that VDW would have agreed to this (paras 123 and 144).

The legislation specifies that a CN must be reasonable (see *The reasonableness test: what are the factors that affect liability*, **4.10**). Warren J considered that

---

13   An FSD was not being claimed in this case.

this means that there must be no penalty element (para 100) and that it is 'not easy to see' how TPR could impose liability for a whole debt if only part has been prevented from being paid (paras 96 to 98):

> '96 ... Section 38(5) refers to the recovery of the whole or any part of the debt. If an act or failure to act prevents payment of only part of the debt, then the case falls within the subsection. The person preventing that payment is then exposed to the risk of a contribution notice being issued against him. But the liability which can be imposed is restricted, under section 38(3)(d) to the sum which the Regulator considers that it is reasonable to impose. Since payment of part only of the debt has been prevented by the act or failure to act under consideration, it is not easy to see how the Regulator could properly be of the opinion that it is reasonable to impose a liability for the whole debt. To take an extreme case, the act or failure to act might have prevented recovery of only £1,000. It would be very surprising if the Regulator was able to impose a liability under section 38 for £1,000,000 being the total section 75 debt.'

The amount of any CN must reflect the amount that the act or failure has made irrecoverable, except in the 'most exceptional circumstances' (para 193). The determinations panel's reasoning in imposing a CN for £5 million based on the PPF funding level was 'unsustainable':

> '192. My analysis of section 38 shows that this reasoning on the part of the Panel is unsustainable. VDW has not, by failing to negotiate openly, prevented payment of any part of the section 75 debt any more than if it had negotiated but failed to reach a negotiated settlement. If it had negotiated but failed to arrive at an agreed figure, it cannot be suggested that some sum, which the Regulator or the Panel or the Tribunal thinks would have been a reasonable negotiated figure, represents part of the section 75 of which VDW has prevented payment. Instead, the focus must be on what Bonas has been prevented from paying.

> '193. More generally, section 38(5)(a)(i) applies where the relevant act or failure to act has as one of its main purposes to prevent recovery of the whole or part of the section 75 debt. The purpose of this provision (in contrast with the different regime of FSDs) must, I suggest, be to enable the Trustees to recover from the persons concerned the amount which the act or failure to act has resulted in becoming, or possibly becoming, irrecoverable. It is no part of section 38 to make him liable for a large sum (£20 million in the present case, according to the Regulator) when, but for his acts, the section 75 debt would not have been recoverable, in whole or in part, quite apart from those acts. The section is concerned with

recoverability and the extent to which the relevant act or failure to act prejudices that recoverability.'

2011: Bonas settlement

4.8.18   The case was due to proceed to a full hearing before the Upper Tribunal, where it was hoped that Warren J's comments would be considered in further detail and clarification over the scope of the CN regime provided.

However, on 9 June 2011 TPR published a report confirming that it had reached a settlement in the *Bonas* case by agreeing to issue a CN for a significantly reduced figure of £60,000.[14]

The settlement: a big climb down?

4.8.19   At first it would appear that TPR may have taken Warren J's comments on board in deciding to settle; however, the contents of its report suggest otherwise.

In particular, the TPR has indicated that:

- It did *not* consider that the comments of Warren J limited TPR's power to issue a CN to the amount of detriment caused (as those comments related to the particular facts and should not be relied on in other cases); and

- The *Bonas* case will *not* cause the TPR to change its approach to taking appropriate and proper regulatory action in other cases.

In effect, the TPR said it will be operating 'business as usual' in its approach to investigating and enforcing avoidance activity.

The *Bonas* settlement looks to be a big climb-down by TPR. It was originally seeking a CN for the full *s* 75 deficit of £20m. The determinations panel of TPR then decided only to issue one for the PPF deficit of about £5m. This figure in itself seemed large, given the stated facts of the case (with the parent apparently having purchased a subsidiary in distress and then supported that subsidiary and hence the scheme in its, ultimately unsuccessful, attempts to turn it around).

It was clear on the strike-out application that Warren J felt much the same, although reserving the final decision to a full hearing (given that the precise facts are relevant).

---

14   The Determinations Panel had issued the CN for £60,000 on 8 June 2011, following an order from the Upper Tribunal on 16 May 2011. See www.thepensionsregulator.gov.uk/docs/ DN1932061.pdf

4.8.19   *Pensions Regulator – moral hazard powers*

The suspicion is that TPR thought it would lose on the appeal and did not want to run that risk. From VDW's perspective, it may be that it thought that £60,000 was worth paying to avoid the costs (and risks) of an Upper Tribunal hearing. The Upper Tribunal rules[15] do allow for costs to be awarded against TPR, but only if the tribunal considers that a party has acted unreasonably or that the determination panel's decision was unreasonable.

It is possible that TPR is seeking, in its statement, to throw doubts on the comments made by Warren J in the earlier proceedings. As noted above, it comments that 'they should not be relied on in other cases' (and notes that the relevant comments from Warren J are not technically binding on future cases).

However, it remains to be seen how the determinations panel will apply the decisions and comments of Warren J in future cases. Warren J is a respected pensions judge, this is a reasoned judgment and is so far the only judicial comment available as guidance on the issue of how the amount that TPR may obtain when seeking a CN can be constrained to the detriment/loss caused by the target company to the relevant pension scheme.

TPR's report indicates that it will continue to push to test the limits of its powers. The clear warning is that TPR will try again.

4.8.20

Extracts from Report under s 89 of the Pensions Act 2004 – issued by the Pensions Regulator in relation to the Bonas Group Pension Scheme (June 2011)

The sum of a CN

In the regulator's opinion, there is the potential for some of Mr Justice Warren's comments about the appropriate sum of a CN to be misunderstood. First, it should be remembered that the comments are *obiter dicta*. Second, Warren J's comments should not be taken out of context; they relate to the particular facts of the *Bonas* case and should not be relied on in other cases.

It is plain that the jurisdiction of the regulator's power to issue a CN in a particular sum is not limited to compensation for the detriment caused (although this will often be one of the factors that the regulator will taken into account when assessing reasonableness). Warren J's *obiter* comments concern the question of a reasonable amount that might be specified in the CN in this particular case. The regulator does not consider that Warren J meant to restrict,

---

15 *Upper Tribunal Rules, reg 10(3).*

in all cases, the amount of a CN to the detriment suffered by a pension scheme which could be demonstrated to be caused by the specified act or failure to act. Certainly, that is not how the regulator will approach the sum of a CN in existing and future cases, including cases involving pre-pack administration.

The *Bonas* case will not cause the regulator to change its approach to taking appropriate and proper regulator action in other cases. In effect, the regulator will be operating 'business as usual' in its approach to investigating and enforcing avoidance activity.

The regulator's powers were strengthened by the introduction of a material detriment test as a group for issuing a CN. This particular ground may be available for acts on or after 14 April 2008 (after the acts specified in the *Bonas* case).

The Regulator will seek to use its so-called 'moral hazard' powers in a reasonable manner whenever appropriate.

4.9 Procedure for issue of a CN or FSD

Summary

This section looks at the procedure followed by the Pensions Regulator (TPR) when seeking the issue of a contribution notice (CN) or financial support direction (FSD) under its 'moral hazard' powers under the *Pensions Act 2004*.

It looks at the standard process, including determination by TPR's Determinations Panel (DP) and the potential for appeals to the Upper Tribunal (Tax and Chancery) Chamber.

4.9.1

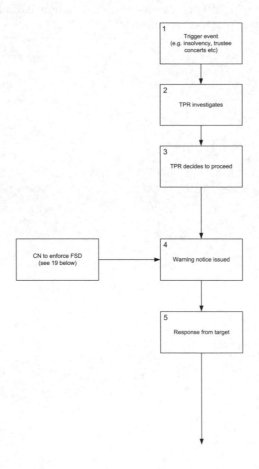

1. TPR will investigate the issue, having been made aware of it (eg by the pension scheme trustees or through notification of a notifiable event – see **13.1**).

2. TPR may (but does not have to) seek to liaise directly with the potential target during the investigation to see whether a solution can be agreed. TPR also has powers to require production of information (subject to an exclusion where legal privilege applies).

3. TPR will consider the evidence and decide whether to proceed.[16]

    FSD: TPR needs to fix a relevant date to test for the employer being 'insufficiently resourced' or a service company. In an 'insufficiently resourced' case, TPR may write seeking to fix the financial test.[17] CN: TPR needs to identify the relevant act or omission triggering a CN.

4. TPR issues a 'warning notice' to the potential target (and other interested parties (eg the trustees)) indicating that it is asking the DP to issue a CN or FSD. The warning notice explains why TPR thinks the CN or FSD should be issued; it is accompanied by documentation/witness statements etc. These documents can be lengthy.

    The warning notice must be issued within the relevant period under the statute (two years for an FSD, six years for a CN).[18]

5. The potential target (and other interested parties) will have the opportunity to make representations to the DP about why the CN or FSD should or should not be issued. Representations are copied to other parties. The DP does not have power to compel parties to disclose documentation or give evidence. Confidentiality will not automatically be protected under the determinations process (the DP publishes its findings and may hold a public hearing).

TPR guidance is that parties should usually have at least 14 days to respond to a warning notice, although time extensions can be requested.[19]

6. The DP may decide to hold an oral hearing. Parties may request an oral hearing, too, which should be done before the deadline for responding to

---

16 There is no formal appeal from a decision of the TPR not to proceed.

17 *2005 FSD Regulations (SI 2005/2188), reg 12.*

18 The *Pensions Act 2011* has, on and from 3 January 2012, altered this six year and two year requirement so that the period ends on the date of issue of the warning notice. This was a change from the previous provision where the period ended on the date of the determination of the DP.

19 According to press reports, in 2010 Lehman Brothers sought judicial review of attempts by TPR to set harsh time limits within which the targets had to respond to extremely complex warning notices. Before the judicial review hearing, TPR abandoned the deadline it had imposed and the DP set a new deadline that provided the targets with more time available to respond to the warning notice.

4.9.1 *Pensions Regulator – moral hazard powers*

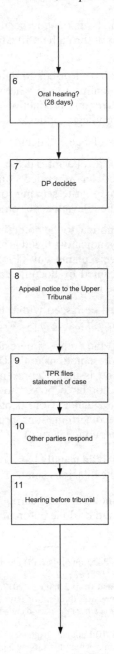

the warning notice. The DP decides whether one will be held. The parties can be represented, for example, by lawyers, and witnesses can give evidence and be cross-examined. All public DP determinations on CNs and FSDs to date have been made after an oral hearing.

7. The DP will consider all the representations (oral and written) of all concerned parties. The DP decides and notifies the parties in writing. The notice explains what powers are being exercised, what facts were used to reach the decision and the reason for the decision. (The reasons may follow the formal notice.)

FSD or CN is not finally issued until the appeal period expires (see below).

8. If the DP determines that a CN should be issued to the potential target, the potential target may object by appealing to the Upper Tribunal. Reference notice for an appeal must be filed with the Upper Tribunal within 28 days[20] of the determination.[21] If an appeal is made, the CN or FSD cannot be issued until the appeal is complete.

9. TPR issues a statement of case to the Upper Tribunal and the other interested parties. The time limit is within 28 days[22] of the reference (8 above) being made and notified to TPR by the Upper Tribunal.

10. The potential target (and other interested parties) has 28 days (from receipt of TPR's statement of case) to respond. The Upper Tribunal has the power to order disclosure by the parties etc.

11. There is usually an oral hearing. The Upper Tribunal may consider all matters of law and fact, including evidence relating to the determination notice, and whether or not the evidence was available to TPR at the time – *Pensions Act 2004, s 103(3)*.

12. The Upper Tribunal must determine what, if any, appropriate action TPR should take.

The Upper Tribunal must pass the matter to TPR with such directions to TPR as it considers appropriate for giving effect to the determination, including:

- confirming, varying or revoking TPR's determination and any order, notice, direction made, issued or given as a result;

---

20 The Upper Tribunal can waive this requirement and grant time extensions etc – *Upper Tribunal Rules 2008 (SI 2008/2698, as amended), r 7*.
21 *Upper Tribunal Rules 2008 (SI 2008/2698, as amended), Sch 3, para 2(2)*.
22 The Upper Tribunal can waive this requirement and grant time extensions etc – *Upper Tribunal Rules 2008 (SI 2008/2698, as amended), r 7*.

4.9.1 *Pensions Regulator – moral hazard powers*

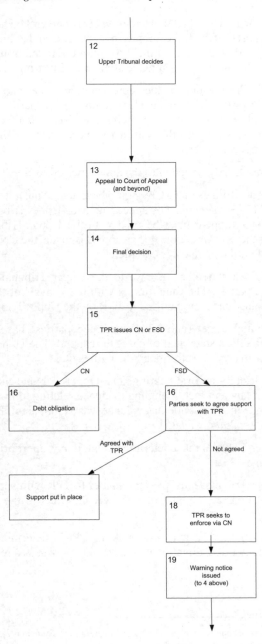

- substituting a different determination, order, notice or direction; or

- making such savings and transitional provisions as the tribunal considers appropriate.

TPR must obey the directions of the Upper Tribunal. The Upper Tribunal's order may be enforced as if it were an order of a county court.

13. A party to a reference to the Upper Tribunal may, with permission, appeal to the Court of Appeal on a point of law (not fact) arising from the Upper Tribunal's decision.

   Permission is needed from the Tribunal or, if refused by the Tribunal, from the Court of Appeal.

14. On appeal, the Court of Appeal may pass the matter to the Upper Tribunal for a rehearing and determination or may make its own determination.

   Leave to appeal to the Supreme Court is needed to appeal the decision of the Court of Appeal.

15. If the potential target has exhausted all rights of appeal, TPR may issue the CN or FSD.

16. CN: a CN specifies an amount payable and is enforceable as a debt obligation.

17. FSD: an FSD specifies that the target must put in place financial support within a specified period.

18. If financial support is not put in place, TPR can seek a CN.[23]

Details of TPR's procedure are on its website:
http://www.thepensionsregulator.gov.uk/regulate-and-enforce/determinations.aspx

Publication of DP determinations

4.9.2   Determinations (and the reasons) are usually published by TPR as soon as practicable following the determination by the DP. TPR's published procedure states that exceptions to publishing a determination, or publishing it in full, will be considered where publication would give rise to one or more of the following:

- an adverse effect on market behaviours – which can include commercial and/or price sensitivity;

- issues that prejudice investigations by other bodies;

---

23 *Pensions Act 2004, s 47.*

- disclosure of information protected under the *Official Secrets Act* or unrelated restricted information;

- risk to individual safety or mental health (in relation to reputational and civil liability); or

- disclosure of sensitive personal data.

Costs

4.9.3   There is no provision for costs to be awarded in relation to proceedings before the DP.

If there is an appeal to the Upper Tribunal, costs can be awarded if the tribunal considers that:

- a party has acted unreasonably; or

- the decision of the DP was unreasonable.[24]

---

24   *Upper Tribunal Rules 2008* (SI 2008/2698, as amended), *reg 10(3)*.

4.10   The reasonableness test – what are the factors that affect liability?

Summary

In this section we outline the factors that are relevant when looking at whether or not it is 'reasonable' for the UK Pensions Regulator (TPR) to issue a financial support direction (FSD) or contribution notice (CN) against a person (Potential Target).

These powers are often referred to as TPR's moral hazard powers.

We also touch on factors that might influence TPR's decision to reduce or increase the Potential Target's liability under a CN.

Introduction

4.10.1   This section outlines the issues for a person (the Potential Target) and the factors that are relevant when deciding whether or not it would be 'reasonable' for the UK Pensions Regulator (TPR) to issue a financial support direction (FSD) or contribution notice (CN) against the Potential Target. The powers to issue FSDs and CNs are often referred to as TPR's 'moral hazard' powers. It also briefly discusses factors that might influence TPR's decision to reduce or increase the Potential Target's liability under a CN.

For further detail on TPR's moral hazard powers, see the other sections of this chapter.

This section assumes that the other two tests for the issue of a CN or FSD have been met (ie that the Potential Target is connected or associated with an employer and that the financial test (FSDs) or event test (CNs) has been satisfied). The issue that is discussed here is the circumstances in which the issue of a CN or FSD against the Potential Target may be reasonable in the opinion of TPR.

This section does not focus on any of the issues that arise because the relevant company may be incorporated or carry on business outside the UK. Nor does it look in depth at the interaction with the insolvency laws.

Outline of CNs and FSDs

4.10.2   A CN or FSD can only be issued against a person who is connected or associated with an employer in relation to a particular occupational pension scheme. See *Who is 'connected' or 'associated'?*, **4.2**.

FSDs

4.10.3   TPR can issue an FSD where another participating employer is or was a 'service company' (ie a company with accounts showing its turnover principally derived from providing services to other group companies) or is 'insufficiently resourced'. An FSD requires a person to put in place financial support for the scheme.

CNs

4.10.4   TPR can issue a CN where a person acts or fails to act:

- on or after 27 April 2004 with a main purpose of preventing the recovery of the whole or any part of an actual or contingent *s 75* debt payable by a participating employer to a scheme – the 'main purpose' test for issuing CNs; or

- on or after 14 April 2008 and the act or failure to act has 'detrimentally affected in a material way the likelihood of accrued benefits being received' – the 'material detriment' test for issuing CNs.

Reasonableness

4.10.5   If one of the three tests above has been satisfied, the likelihood of an exercise of a moral hazard power will depend on whether TPR considers it 'reasonable' to do so, which is largely a factual question.

The likelihood of an exercise of a moral hazard power will depend on whether:

- TPR's investigatory staff consider it reasonable to seek a determination, by issuing a 'warning notice'; and

- the determinations panel at TPR, which is a separate body from the investigatory function at TPR and which functions in a manner similar to a tribunal, considers it reasonable to issue the determination exercising the power. The target is usually given the opportunity to make representations to the panel before a decision is made.

Both are largely factual questions and, as the circumstances of each case will vary, they essentially involve the exercise of a discretion by TPR.

Relevant factors for assessing reasonableness

4.10.6 'Reasonableness' will have its ordinary meaning in this context. But the *Pensions Act 2004* also requires TPR to consider a non-exhaustive list of factual matters when deciding whether it would be reasonable to issue an FSD or a CN.[25] The factors that must be considered differ for FSDs and CNs, though a number of them are the same for each power. TPR is also required to consider an additional list of factors when deciding whether to issue a CN under the new 'material detriment' test.

The factors that must be considered in relation to each power are set out below:

Factor (with comments in italics)	FSDs	CNs (main purpose test)	CNs (material detriment test)
The degree of involvement of that person in the act or failure to act; (*eg did the person sanction the business deal?*)		✓	✓
The relationship the person has or had with the employer; *for example, is the person a director or a senior executive of the employer? Is the person a company that is the parent company of the employer?*	✓	✓	✓
Any connection or involvement the person has or had with the scheme; *for example, is the person a trustee of the scheme or an employer in relation to it?*	✓	✓	✓
Whether the act or failure to act was a notifiable event that the person had a duty to notify to TPR but failed to do so (CN).		✓	✓
All the purposes of the act or failure to act, including whether a purpose was to prevent or limit loss of employment (CN).		✓	✓

---

25 *Pensions Act 2004: s 43(7)* in respect of an FSD, *s 38(7)* in respect of a CN.

Factor (with comments in italics)	FSDs	CNs (main purpose test)	CNs (material detriment test)
The financial circumstances of the person; *for example, TPR may consider that it is appropriate for less than the full s 75 debt to be required if contributions to another scheme would otherwise be materially affected.*	✓	✓	✓
The value of any 'benefits' that, directly or indirectly, the person receives or is entitled to receive from the employer or under the scheme.	✓	✓	✓
The likelihood of 'relevant creditors' being paid and the extent to which they are likely to be paid.		✓	✓
Further factors (see below).		✓	✓

The concepts of 'benefit' and 'relevant creditors' (see **4.10.17** below) are discussed further below.

These factors are not an exhaustive list. TPR may consider other factors as well. In practice, the determinations panel will look at each factor when giving its reasons.

Circumstances where TPR may issue a CN under the alternative 'material detriment test'

4.10.7   TPR is required to consider the additional list of factors below when deciding whether to issue a CN under the post 2008 'material detriment' test:[26]

- the value of the assets or liabilities of the pension scheme;

- the effect of a person's act, or failure to act, on the value of those assets and liabilities;

- the obligations of any person to the pension scheme;

---

26   *Pensions Act 2004, s 38A* (inserted by the *Pensions Act 2008*).

- the effect of an act, or failure to act, on any person's obligation to provide funding to the scheme (including whether the act or failure causes the country or territory in which any of those obligations would fall to be enforced to be different); and

- the effect of an act, or failure to act, on any person's ability to discharge those obligations.

The statutory factors above are defined very broadly and it is important to note that the test of 'reasonableness' is not a solely objective test. Rather, it is 'in the opinion of the Pensions Regulator'[27] – effectively the view of the determinations panel. If the panel's decision is appealed, the Upper Tribunal (Tax and Chancery Chamber) will decide (see *Procedure for issue of a CN or FSD*, **4.9**).

Objectives of TPR

4.10.8 The relevant objectives of TPR in exercising its functions (eg determining to exercise its moral hazard powers) are stated in *s 5(1)* of the *Pensions Act 2004*:

- to protect the benefits under occupational pension schemes of, or in respect of, members of such schemes;

- to reduce the risk of situations arising which may lead to compensation being payable from the PPF; and

- to promote, and to improve understanding of the good administration of work-based pension schemes.

Pre-2004 events

4.10.9   The relevant circumstances are not expressly limited to events or actions after 27 April 2004, when the moral hazard powers came into force. There is no express time limit on the factors that may be relevant for the reasonableness test.

In practice, TPR has referred to facts and circumstances prior to 2004 and it may look back on actions, or a course of conduct, that occurred many years in the past. This contrasts with primary tests for issuing FSDs or CNs – which are based on the financial position of the employer (in the case of FSDs) or any specific act or failure to act by the target (in the case of CNs) – and which are subject to express time limits.

---

27   *Pensions Act 2004, ss 38(3)* and *42(5)*.

This retrospective approach (considering events before 2004) was challenged in submissions before the determinations panel in the *Box Clever* case – see **4.16**. But the DP rejected this challenge[28] and allowed pre 2004 events to be a factor in assessing reasonableness (this could be challenged on appeal).

'Benefits' received from the employer?

4.10.10 One major factor will be the level of benefits that the Potential Target may have received from the employer, either directly or indirectly. This is not the only relevant factor – influence or control over the actions of the employer may also be very material – but it is often likely to be a crucial factor.

TPR's clearance guidance says that the following is an example of 'benefits' that a person may have received directly or indirectly from an employer:

'... assets or dividends from the employer, or shared common security or cash flow arrangements or gained tax advantages ...'

In March 2006, TPR published an article entitled 'Anti-avoidance and clearance: the bigger picture'. In this article, TPR specified that by 'benefits' it means:

'... not only cash, assets and loans, but also associations, names, knowledge, tax advantages, rent and common ownership benefits such as a division into an operating and a property company to make assets safe'.

It goes on to say that:

'The funding of the scheme, the schedule of contributions, the length of the person's connection with the scheme and the terms of the scheme membership will also be considered.'

The Sea Containers case

4.10.11 In June 2007, TPR's determination panel issued FSDs against Sea Containers (a Bermudan company) in relation to UK pension schemes that were sponsored by its wholly owned UK subsidiary. This was the first public instance

---

28 See the DP reasons issued in January 2012 at para [130]. On TPR's website at http://www.thepensionsregulator.gov.uk/docs/DN2084757.pdf

of the moral hazard powers being exercised. The panel's reasons[29] provide some guidance on when TPR may consider it 'reasonable' to issue FSDs in the future.

The panel held that it was reasonable in the circumstances to issue FSDs against Sea Containers because:

- the principal employer of the schemes (the UK subsidiary of Sea Containers) was wholly owned and controlled by Sea Containers;

- Sea Containers received 'benefits' from the principal employer;

- Sea Containers was closely connected to the scheme and many of its officers acted as trustees; and

- the principal employer was insufficiently resourced, whereas Sea Containers had substantial assets.

In deciding that Sea Containers had received 'benefits' from the principal employer of the pension schemes, TPR interpreted the definition of 'benefits' very widely to include:

- services it received from the principal employer that it was not required to repay within any prescribed time; and

- the overall benefit it received from the corporate group structure. Specifically, Sea Containers was held to have benefited because it was able to trade from Europe through its UK subsidiary but retain tax advantages from the Bermudan tax regime.

The Bonas case

4.10.12 In June 2010, the determinations panel issued a CN against the parent of Bonas, a UK company that sponsored a pension scheme. Bonas had been put into a 'pre-pack' administration and its business was then sold to another subsidiary of the parent. The CN was issued despite the fact that the parent appeared to have supported the subsidiary financially over the years and had not derived income or a profit from the company. The parent did have the benefit of having the subsidiary within its group (it ended up as a group marketing company).

As the facts pre-date the introduction of the 'material detriment' test for CNs in 2008, the reasons given by the panel focus on the 'main purpose' test for issuing

---

29 See *The Sea Containers 1983 and 1990 Pension Schemes: Reasons of the Determinations Panel of the Pensions Regulator in Relation to the Determination Notices Issued on 15 June 2007* (TM222/TM1495).

the CN. The determination was remarkably brief on the 'reasonableness' issue, dealing with it in just three paragraphs. Interestingly, the panel refused the application by TPR to issue a CN against an individual who was a director of both the subsidiary and the parent. It noted that he had acted as a director for and on behalf of the parent, rather than in a personal capacity, and had been concerned with ensuring continuation of employment of the subsidiary's staff.

On appeal, Mr Justice Warren in the Upper Tribunal was critical of the determinations panel's reasoning and the case ultimately settled (at a relatively small amount) – see *The Bonas case*, **4.8**

The Caparo Automotive case

4.10.13 The approach of the determinations panel in the *Bonas* case contrasts with TPR's decision not to seek the issue of a CN or FSD in the case of *Caparo Automotive*. Details of this case were published in a report of the Parliamentary Ombudsman in June 2010 (there has been no report by TPR).[30]

In the *Caparo* case, a pension scheme member made a complaint to the Parliamentary Ombudsman that TPR had failed to exercise its discretion reasonably in declining to issue a CN or FSD against Caparo Group Limited, the parent company of Caparo Automotive, a company that sponsored a pension scheme. The member's complaint was that this amounted to maladministration by TPR. It was argued that TPR should have issued a CN or FSD against the parent company on the basis that it:

- had received a benefit from the pension scheme because the employer company had taken a contribution holiday;

- had deliberately sought to avoid the debt by placing the employer into a pre-pack insolvency process, to enable it to buy back the employer's assets free of the pension liability;

- had impliedly accepted responsibility for the employer's liability by making a compromise offer to pay a sum of money to the scheme, which had been refused; and

- had substantial assets.

However, the Parliamentary Ombudsman found that there was no evidence that TPR had failed to exercise its powers properly. Although it was not possible for the ombudsman to set out any detailed reasoning for this (as the evidence that had been considered was still subject to the confidentiality restrictions

---

30 See the Parliamentary Ombudsman's report (HC 169) at: www.ombudsman.org.uk/__data/assets/pdf_file/0004/4198/PHSO-0097_to_web.pdf

applicable to information provided to TPR), she noted that the reason TPR had given to the trustees for its decision was that:

'... the overwhelming flow of benefit had been from Caparo Group Limited to the participating employer rather than vice versa'.

This contrasts with the approach of TPR in the *Bonas* case, where the history of financial support given to the employer by the parent was not apparently given very much weight.

The Nortel case

4.10.14 In June 2010, the determinations panel decided to issue FSDs against 25 companies in the Nortel Networks group in Canada, the US, Africa, the Middle East and Europe. All of the entities were in insolvency proceedings at the time.

The reasoning of the panel in this case is less convincing than in the Sea Containers case, in particular because the target entities did not appear before, or make submissions to, the panel, so the factual claims made by TPR to the panel were not contested (or indeed proved).

The panel accepted TPR's submissions and, in relation to the reasonableness test, it referred to:

- the integrated nature of the Nortel group and its businesses;

- the sharing of technical standards within the group (which was significant as the companies operated in the telecommunications sector);

- the control exercised by the Canadian parents over the UK employer;

- the intra-group loans made within the group;

- the economic benefit derived from the contributions holiday taken by the employer before 2002;

- the provision of management services by the employer to other group companies; and

- the existence of transfer pricing agreements between the various group companies.

The panel's reasons show the potential breadth of the reasonableness test and the concept of 'benefits': what are, essentially, normal practices within an integrated corporate group with a global business can easily be viewed as benefits derived from the scheme employer for these purposes.

The Lehman Brothers case

4.10.15   In September 2010, the determinations panel decided to issue FSDs against various companies in the Lehman Brothers group.

Following an oral hearing, the panel determined on 13 September 2010 to issue an FSD against six companies in the Lehman Brothers group following the entry of most of the group into insolvency on 15 September 2008. The six companies were the three main UK operating companies and three of the holding companies of the main employer, Lehman Brothers Ltd (LBL). TPR dropped claims against 29 other group companies before the hearing and the panel refused to issue an FSD against a further 38 group companies based on the lack of specific evidence involving those companies.

Unlike in the *Nortel* case, four of the target companies appeared at the oral hearing and representatives of most of the others submitted at least some representations.

The panel determined to issue the FSDs based on the relationship of the six companies with LBL. The group operated on an integrated global basis.

LBL was a service company and employed the majority of the UK employees and they were seconded to three operating companies (who tended not to have any direct employees). The panel considered that the three operating companies had benefited from the services of the employees (there were cost-sharing arrangements but no uplift for LBL in some cases and payments due under the arrangements were left outstanding) and that in reality the operating companies were the employers 'for all practical purposes'.

The group had operated a general cash sweep-out of all group accounts into the holding company's account. There had also been some benefit to the operating companies through provision by LBL of directors, use of LBL as a property and asset holding company, it taking the lead for tax purposes.

In relation to the holding companies, although the ultimate holding company had given a (limited) guarantee to the pension scheme, the panel considered that it had benefited (perhaps indirectly) from the arrangements between LBL and the operating companies and had been the ultimate source of funding for the contributions to the scheme.

The two intermediate holding companies were considered to be 'passive holding companies operated as conduits for money and control', but took benefits by virtue of their ownership of the operating companies. The panel considered that this was enough to determine that an FSD be issued.

The panel decided to issue the FSDs even though it expressly noted that there was 'no allegation that the Lehman group acted in any way improperly or even poorly towards' the LBL pension scheme.

The point was raised that the relevant companies are generally in insolvency processes. The panel considered that this made it even more reasonable, in the context of a complex multi-jurisdictional group to impose FSDs.

For further details see http://www.thepensionsregulator.gov.uk/docs/DN 1784039.pdf

Great Lakes

4.10.16 The Pensions Regulator announced in July 2011 that it has withdrawn moral hazard proceedings against Chemtura Manufacturing UK Limited (CMUK) and its US parent, Chemtura Corporation. This follows an agreement being reached by Chemtura with the trustees of the Great Lakes UK Limited Pension Plan (the Plan) over its funding package.

In June 2009, the trustees of the Plan – sponsored by the solvent CMUK – approached TPR over concerns relating to the financial position of the Plan. Chemtura Corporation and a number of other entities within the group had recently filed for *Chapter 11* bankruptcy protection in the US. The Plan's deficit, calculated on a buy-out basis, was an estimated £95 million. TPR began investigating whether or not it was appropriate to issue an FSD under *s 43* of the *Pensions Act 2004*.

In November 2010, the parties agreed, as part of the *Chapter 11* proceedings,[31] to a 'stipulation' allowing contribution and financial support claims to be 'passed through' the *Chapter 11* bankruptcy. Subsequently, in December 2010, TPR issued CMUK and various Chemtura companies with a warning notice setting out its intention to seek an FSD from the determinations panel (DP).

Relevant parties, including the target companies and the trustees were invited to make representations in relation to the facts set out in the warning notice. The matter was due to be heard by the determinations panel in June 2011.

However, in the course of ongoing negotiations between the target companies and the trustees of the Plan, a funding package was agreed, to the satisfaction of TPR, in May 2011. Under the agreement:

- CMUK will make cash contributions of £60 million over three years, starting with an initial contribution of £30 million;

- CMUK will also provide contributions for any possible additional liabilities connected with equalisation; and

---

31   See http://www.kccllc.net/documents/0911233/0911233101130000000000004.pdf

- entities in the Chemtura Group (including Chemtura Corporation) have entered into guarantee and security agreements to protect the Plan against any further liabilities it may incur.

In its report, TPR stated that it will no longer pursue the matter as it is satisfied that the funding package 'was broadly equivalent to what might have been achieved if an FSD had been issued'.

TPR's two page report is online at:www.thepensionsregulator.gov.uk/docs/section-89-great-lakes.pdf

Box Clever

4.10.17 The determinations panel made a determination in December 2011 to issue an FSD against ITV (and some of its subsidiaries) in relation its 50% stake in the Box Clever group of companies (that went into insolvency in 2003). TPR commented that:

> 'The regulator's Determinations Panel ("the Panel") found that it was reasonable for Granada UK Rental & Retail Limited, Granada Media Limited, Granada Group Limited, Granada Limited and ITV plc to provide financial support for the Box Clever Group Pension Scheme. The Box Clever group become insolvent in 2003 leaving the pension scheme with a deficit of approximately £62m at the end of 2009, on the section 75 "buy-out" basis.'

Under UK pensions law, an FSD requires the recipient to secure that reasonable financial support is put in place for a particular pension scheme. The precise form of that support is not prescribed and in practice there is significant flexibility for FSD recipients.

The 'target' companies in this case have referred the decision to the Upper Tribunal. The regulator cannot issue FSDs whilst appeal proceedings are pending.

The regulator's executive director for defined benefit regulation, Stephen Soper, said:

> 'The Panel found that the target companies received valuable financial benefits from the creation and structure of the Box Clever joint venture. A highly leveraged structure was used, leaving the sponsoring employers in a weak position.'

Relevant creditors

4.10.18 'Relevant creditors' means creditors of the employer and of any other person who has a liability or other obligation (including a contingent debt or one that otherwise might fall due) to make a payment or a transfer of assets to the scheme.

In October 2008, the government commented that this factor would be particularly relevant for companies in distress and is intended to allay concerns of pension schemes becoming 'super-creditors' (with priority over other unsecured creditors of the employer).[32] Presumably this means that TPR should arguably be less willing to issue a CN where this would affect other unsecured creditors of an employer in financial difficulties.

In parliamentary debates on the *Pensions Bill 2008*, the then government minister commented that this factor would reduce the risk of 'company doctors' (who are brought in to assist a company in financial difficulties) becoming the subject of a CN. The minister stated that:

> 'First where a company doctor has to make hard decisions in an attempt to save a company, these factors would protect the position of a company doctor who had to cause detriment to a pension scheme, which, in the particular circumstances, was reasonable in the context of the outcome for other creditors. Secondly, TPR would need to take into account that, in some circumstances, decisions must necessarily be rapid, as the noble Lord has indicated, and perfect data to inform the decision may not be available. Provided that the company doctor has behaved reasonably and has not, for example, wilfully ignored available information or recklessly taken risks that a reasonable company doctor would not have taken, I believe that members of organisations such as R3 and the Institute for Turnaround should take significant comfort from these provisions.'[33]

Amount of liability under a CN or FSD

4.10.19 If TPR decides to issue a CN or FSD, it has a discretion to specify a sum that is either a whole or part of the employer's *s 75* debt (or expected debt if it is not yet due).

---

32 Amendments to the anti-avoidance measures in the *Pensions Act 2004*: government response to the consultation – October 2008. On the DWP website.
33 See statement by Lord McKenzie, *Hansard*, House of Lords, third committee sitting, report stage, col 1584, 29 October 2008.

4.10.19   *Pensions Regulator – moral hazard powers*

The *Pensions Act 2004* does not list the factors that TPR would have to consider when exercising its discretion. However, the government emphasised that under public law there is an overriding obligation for TPR to 'act proportionately and only where reasonable'.[34]

Presumably alluding to this public law obligation, the then government minister commented in 2008 that if TPR issued a CN under the material detriment test:

> 'TPR would then be bound to act reasonably in its assessment of how much of this sum should be payable by the party to the transaction.
>
> The transaction itself and any benefit from it may not be the only factor here, and may not be the most important factor. Some factors may increase the amount that should be payable towards the upper limit; for example, the history of that person's involvement with the scheme or the employer. However, other factors might decrease the amount. For example, that person's degree of involvement in the transaction may have been limited, and there may have been other parties to the act. That person may be an individual who acted merely as an agent for a corporate entity that was party to the act, or other purposes of the act may have meant that the person's actions were reasonable in the circumstances.
>
> Another factor that is likely to be relevant is the position of the scheme following the transaction. Of course, considering what amount would be reasonable is entirely a matter for TPR, who must examine each case on its own merits and is required to consider anything that is relevant, disregarding anything irrelevant. I hope that it is a comfort to know that simply having deep pockets should not make a person the target of a contribution notice. It is more constrained than that.'[35]

Clearly TPR is not bound to act in accordance with the above ministerial statement. Nevertheless, it provides some helpful guidance.

In the *Bonas* case (see **4.8** and **4.10.12** above), the amount of the CN that the Determinations Panel determined to issue was limited to the amount needed to enable the scheme to fully secure the Pension Protection Fund (PPF) protected level of benefits (see **5.2**), rather than the greater amount that would have been needed to fully fund the scheme on an insurance buy-out basis. This was based on the panel's view that – had the parent company entered into prior negotiations with the pension scheme trustees (with a view to implementing the pre-pack administration of *Bonas* with the trustees' consent and potentially

---

34   Ibid, seventh committee stage, col 1275, 16 July 2008.
35   Ibid, third committee sitting, report stage, col 1585, 29 October 2008.

seeking TPR clearance), the payment of the deficit on the PPF basis would, most likely, have been sufficient to obtain that consent.

On the strike-out appeal, Mr Justice Warren later held that any CN should 'normally' be limited to the amount of the loss derived from the relevant act or omission – see *The Bonas case judicial guidance on CNs*, **4.8**.

In June 2012, TPR subsequently issued a statement about its intentions in an insolvency situation – see **4.12** below.

4.11   TPR builds a track record

Summary

This section summarises the Pensions Regulator's public exercises of moral hazard powers to date.

It also looks at threatened exercises (based on the limited publicly available information).

Cases so far

4.11.1   Proceedings of the Pensions Regulator (TPR) are not usually made public unless and until published by TPR, generally in the form of determinations by its determinations panel. The following determinations have been published of exercises of moral hazard powers to issue a contribution notice (CN) or financial support direction (FSD).

Case	TPR Power exercised or sought to be exercised	Date
Sea Containers	FSD issued (service company)	June 2007
Bonas Group pension scheme	CN decided	May 2010
	Appeal settled	May 2011
Nortel	FSD decided (insufficiently resourced)	June 2010
Lehman Brothers	FSD decided (service company)	September 2010
Box Clever	FSD decided (insufficiently resourced)	January 2012
Desmonds	CN decided	April 2010

There are also the following reported threatened exercises of the moral hazard powers.

Case	TPR power exercised or sought to be exercised	Date
Duke Street Capital	Threatened use	September 2008
Reader's Digest	CN considered	February 2010
Visteon	Threatened use	May 2010
Caparo Automotive	Requested use	June 2010
Great Lakes	Threatened use	Settled – June 2011
Carlyle Group	Potential use	September 2011
MF Global UK Ltd	Threatened use	October 2013

For further detail on the moral hazard powers, see:

- *TPR: Moral hazard powers: Extracting pension scheme funding from third parties*, **4.1**;

- *Financial support directions (FSDs)*, **4.6**; and

- *Contribution notices (CNs)*, **4.7**.

Reasonableness

4.11.2   Once one of the threshold tests for a CN or FSD has been satisfied, the likelihood of an exercise of a moral hazard power will depend on whether TPR considers it 'reasonable' to do so, which is largely a factual question.

This section analyses previous exercises (and threatened exercises) of moral hazard powers, specifically the rationale for 'reasonableness', and derives a list of factors that TPR has considered when deciding whether to use these powers and determining the quantum of liability.

The likelihood of exercise of a moral hazard power will depend on:

- whether TPR considers it reasonable to seek a determination (by issuing a 'warning notice'); and

- whether the determinations panel at TPR (a separate body from the investigatory function at TPR) considers it reasonable to issue an order (the target usually having been given the opportunity to make representations).

Both of these are largely factual questions. (See generally *The reasonableness test – what are the factors that affect liability?*, **4.10**.

269

4.11.3 *Pensions Regulator – moral hazard powers*

Sea Containers (FSD issued) – June 2007

4.11.3   In February 2008 (following an initial determination process in June 2007) TPR confirmed that it would issue two FSDs on Sea Containers Ltd (Sea Containers), a Bermudan company in US bankruptcy proceedings. TPR had initially sought to issue the FSDs in June 2007, but Sea Containers had appealed, causing a delay.

The FSDs required Sea Containers to provide financial support for two pension schemes sponsored by its London-based UK subsidiary Sea Containers Services Ltd (SCS).

Sea Containers was clearly associated with SCS. The financial test for an FSD was met (this does not seem to have been contested).

The determinations panel of TPR held that it was reasonable to issue FSDs against Sea Containers because:

- SCS (the principal employer of the schemes) was wholly owned and controlled by Sea Containers;

- SCS is a service company employing much of the group's management;

- Sea Containers received 'benefits' from SCS;

- Sea Containers was closely connected to the pension schemes and many of its officers acted as trustees; and

- SCS was insufficiently resourced whereas Sea Containers had substantial assets.

In deciding that Sea Containers had received benefits from SCS, the determinations panel interpreted the definition of 'benefits' widely to include:

- services it received from SCS that it was not required to repay within any prescribed time; and

- the benefit it received from the group structure (in this case Sea Containers was held to have benefited because it was able to trade from Europe through SCS but retained tax advantages from the Bermudan tax regime).

The panel also stated that it did not consider the fact that Sea Containers had entered insolvency proceedings (Chapter 11 proceedings in the US) as a reason not to issue the FSDs. (For further information, see www.thepensionsregulator. gov.uk/press/PN08–02.aspx)

Bonas Group Pension Scheme (CN determination) – May 2010

4.11.4 On 29 June 2010 (following an initial determination process in May 2010) TPR confirmed that it had issued its first CN. The CN was issued against a Belgian company, Michel Van De Wiele NV (VDW), the parent company of Bonas UK Ltd (Bonas), the sponsoring employer of the Bonas Group pension scheme.

The CN was issued under the 'main purpose' provision of the *Pensions Act 2004* (it related to actions before changes to CNs were made in 2008) – and the panel took the view that a main purpose of the act was to avoid or reduce a pension liability.

VDW had arranged for Bonas to go into administration and then for the administrators to sell its business to another subsidiary of VDW. In TPR's view, VDW had used the pre-pack sale to retain Bonas's business 'while avoiding the pensions liability … and had not engaged openly with pension trustees or the Regulator'.

However, the panel refused to issue a CN against an individual who was a director of both Bonas and VDW.

Refusal to issue a CN against an individual

4.11.5 The panel decided not to issue a CN against an individual (Mr Beauduin) who was a managing director of Bonas and chairman of VDW. It felt that it would not be reasonable to issue a CN because:

- he had acted as a director for VDW rather than in a 'personal capacity'; and

- he was personally concerned with ensuring the 'continuation of employment of Bonas' staff.

It is not clear what is meant by the first point because the panel did not further explain its reasoning. However, the panel may have been suggesting that it was not reasonable to target Mr Beauduin because he did not personally receive a benefit from VDW's decisions (as opposed to receiving a benefit through VDW).

Nor did the panel expand further on the second point. However, this reason may be a reference to the *Pensions Act 2004* requirement that TPR must consider whether the 'purpose of the act or failure was to prevent or limit loss of employment' when deciding whether to issue a CN under the main purpose test.

271

Decision to issue a CN against VDW

4.11.6   The panel accepted that VDW had performed 'acts', within the meaning of the CN provisions in the *Pensions Act 2004*, by:

- 'walking away without engaging openly with the Trustees or Regulator'; and

- 'retaining the business while avoiding the pension liability'.

It came to the conclusion that there had been such acts by VDW because:

- the evidence, in the panel's view, proved VDW had implemented the pre-pack sale of Bonas with the aim of retaining Bonas's business but in a new company that had no liability towards the scheme; and

- VDW had caused knowledge of the pre-pack sale to be withheld from the trustees and had itself avoided informing the trustees or TPR of the sale 'so that it could walk away from the scheme, taking the risk of a CN being sought by TPR rather than face an FSD or a CN being swiftly imposed'.

It is worth noting that it was Bonas, rather than VDW, that had carried out some of the actions that led to the CN. However, the panel was satisfied that 'VDW was controlling the decision-making process relating to the future of both Bonas and the Scheme'. For this reason, the panel appeared not to draw a distinction between acts carried out by VDW and those carried out by its subsidiary.

The panel was further satisfied that a CN could be issued because it came to the view that a main purpose of the act of walking away described above was 'to prevent the recovery of the whole or any part of a debt which was, or might become, due from the employer in relation to the scheme under *section 75* of the *Pensions Act 1995*' – see *s 38(5)* of the *Pensions Act 2004*. The panel was satisfied that this was the case because 'VDW's purpose was to minimise the amount it would have to pay into the Scheme, either quickly or at some undefined, later, stage'.

The panel's view was that by not engaging with the trustees or TPR, VDW had denied the trustees the opportunity to seek some form of mitigation as part of any clearance application and denied them the ability to ask TPR to issue an FSD or CN at that point. It was held that this was equivalent to preventing the recovery of some or all of a *s 75* debt that might become due.

Finally, the panel, as required by statute, was satisfied that it was reasonable to issue a CN against the parent company, VDW, for £5.089 million because this was the amount needed to take the scheme up to a position of solvency on the PPF basis. It appeared to be satisfied that this was the appropriate sum because, in its view (based on documents disclosed during the proceedings), VDW had believed that it had taken action that would avoid it funding the scheme up to the PPF funding level.

The panel also took account of VDW's financial position, its close degree of involvement with the relevant act, its close association (through its funding of Bonas) with the scheme and its control of Bonas (in particular over all aspects of its administration, the pre-pack sale and the abandonment of the scheme).

We understand that TPR had actually asked the panel to impose a CN in the amount of the buy-out deficit of the scheme, rather than the deficit calculated on the PPF basis. The buy-out measurement would most likely have shown a larger deficit in the scheme. However, the panel refused to use the buy-out measurement.

For further information, see www.thepensionsregulator.gov.uk/press/pn10–11.aspx. An appeal was due to be heard in 2011. A preliminary hearing was held earlier in 2011 and the Regulator then settled its claim by agreement – for details see *The Bonas case: judicial guidance on CNs*, **4.8**.

Nortel (FSD Determination) – June 2010

4.11.7   On 8 July 2010, the panel published a determination to issue an FSD against 25 companies in the Nortel group in Canada, the US, Europe and Africa.

In practice, the decision here is less strong than in other cases. The Nortel companies refused to appear at the oral hearing held by the panel. In the case of the Canadian and US companies, this was on the basis that the insolvency courts in those countries had made orders confirming that the TPR proceedings were invalidated by the stay (under Canadian or US law) on legal proceedings.

The panel concluded that it would be reasonable (based solely on the evidence submitted by the trustees and TPR) to impose the FSD. The employer of the Nortel Networks UK pension plan. Nortel Networks UK Ltd (NNUK), had entered administration in January 2009, with several, other entities worldwide. NNUK was found to be insufficiently resourced. This is the required test for an FSD. The panel agreed to base this test on the financial information available on 30 June 2008 (ie before the Nortel group entered insolvency proceedings in January 2009).

An important aspect of the determination was evidence (uncontested before the panel because the Nortel companies did not appear) that from the early 1990s the Nortel group was run as a single integrated global entity, with the Canadian parent companies – Nortel Networks Corporation and Nortel Networks Ltd – having effective control of NNUK.

4.11.7   *Pensions Regulator – moral hazard powers*

This (it was found) included control of the amounts contributed to the pension plan, which had been 'woefully inadequate' to repair its deficit – this was estimated to stand at £2.1 billion on a buy-out basis at the time NNUK entered administration.

The panel accepted, in the absence of any contesting submissions or evidence, that the Nortel group:

- derived significant benefit from NNUK's research and development, management, sales and marketing activities, for which NNUK was not adequately compensated; and

- further benefited from a growing interest-free loan (reaching a peak of £467 million by late 2007), which NNUK was obliged to enter into by its immediate Canadian parent company as a means of dealing with unpaid transfer pricing adjustments.

For further information, see www.thepensionsregulator.gov.uk/press/pn10–13.aspx.

Lehman Brothers (FSD determination) – September 2010

4.11.8   Following an oral hearing, the determinations panel decided on 13 September 2010 to issue an FSD against six companies in the Lehman Brothers group following the entry of most of the group into insolvency on 15 September 2008. The six companies were the three main UK operating companies and three of the holding companies of the main employer, Lehman Brothers Ltd (LBL). TPR dropped claims against 29 other group companies before the hearing and the panel refused to issue an FSD against a further 38 group companies based on the lack of specific evidence involving those companies.

Unlike in the *Nortel* case, four of the target companies appeared at the oral hearing and representatives of most of the others submitted at least some representations.

The panel determined to issue the FSDs based on the relationship of the six companies with LBL. The group operated on an integrated global basis.

LBL was a service company and employed the majority of the UK employees and they were seconded to three operating companies (who tended not to have any direct employees). The panel considered that the three operating companies had benefited from the services of the employees (there were cost-sharing arrangements but no uplift for LBL in some cases and payments due under the arrangements were left outstanding) and that in reality the operating companies were the employers 'for all practical purposes'.

The group had operated a general cash sweep-out of all group accounts into the holding company's account. There had also been some benefit to the operating companies through provision by LBL of directors, use of LBL as property and an asset holding company, it taking the lead for tax purposes.

In relation to the holding companies, although the ultimate holding company had given a (limited) guarantee to the pension scheme, the panel considered that it had benefited (perhaps indirectly) from the arrangements between LBL and the operating companies and had been the ultimate source of funding for the contributions to the scheme.

The two intermediate holding companies were considered to be 'passive holding companies operated as conduits for money and control', but took benefits by virtue of their ownership of the operating companies. The panel considered that this was enough to determine that an FSD be issued.

The panel decided to issue the FSDs even though it expressly noted that there was 'no allegation that the Lehman group acted in any way improperly or even poorly towards' the LBL pension scheme.

The point was raised that the relevant companies are generally in insolvency processes. The panel considered that this made it even more reasonable, in the context of a complex multi-jurisdictional group to impose FSDs.

For further details see www.thepensionsregulator.gov.uk/docs/DN1784039.pdf

Box Clever (FSD Determination) – December 2011

The Determinations Panel issued its reasons in the Box Clever case in late January 2012.[36]

The determinations panel made a determination in December 2011 to issue FSDs against ITV (and some of its subsidiaries) in relation its 50% stake in the Box Clever group of companies (that went into insolvency in 2003). TPR commented that:

> 'The regulator's Determinations Panel ("the Panel") found that it was reasonable for Granada UK Rental & Retail Limited, Granada Media Limited, Granada Group Limited, Granada Limited and ITV plc to provide financial support for the Box Clever Group Pension Scheme. The Box Clever group become insolvent in 2003 leaving the pension

---

36   See http://www.thepensionsregulator.gov.uk/docs/DN2084757.pdf

scheme with a deficit of approximately £62m at the end of 2009, on the section 75 "buy-out" basis.'

Under UK pensions law, an FSD requires the recipient to secure that reasonable financial support is put in place for a particular pension scheme. The precise form of that support is not prescribed and in practice there is significant flexibility for FSD recipients.

The 'target' companies in this case have referred the decision to the Upper Tribunal. The regulator cannot issue FSDs whilst appeal proceedings are pending.

The regulator's executive director for defined benefit regulation, Stephen Soper, said:

'The Panel found that the target companies received valuable financial benefits from the creation and structure of the Box Clever joint venture. A highly leveraged structure was used, leaving the sponsoring employers in a weak position.'

For further discussion – see **4.16.**

Commentary on the cases so far

4.11.9   As noted above, the justification for the reasonableness of issuing an FSD in the Sea Containers determination turned significantly on the level of corporate benefit obtained by the parent company from the employers to the scheme, without sufficient support given to the pension scheme.

The reasoning was similar in the subsequent Nortel determinations, although as noted this is the weaker of the precedents in that no contesting evidence or views were produced. The Nortel companies were seen to draw a net benefit from the UK employer and there were accusations that Nortel used its position as ultimate owner to divert cash away from the UK employer, and accordingly away from the pension scheme.

Conversely, the determination in relation to the Bonas Group UK pension plan is more extreme. There, the rationale supporting the reasonableness of issuing a CN appears to be premised on the history of support by the parent company for the subsidiary (and indirectly the pension scheme) and the subsequent removal of that support. Further, the panel clearly considered the fact that the transaction had been concluded without consultation with the trustees or TPR as supporting the decision to issue the CN.

The result of the *Bonas* determination was that it seemed much easier than previously thought for TPR to be able to convince the panel that a CN or FSD should be issued. This may mean that in any case it is more likely than previously thought that TPR may try to get a CN or FSD. However, as discussed in **4.8**, it remains to be seen how the determinations panel will act in future given the decision and comments of Mr Justice Warren on the later appeal.

However, the report of the parliamentary ombudsman in the *Caparo* case does give some indication that (unlike the apparent approach in Bonas), a potential target may have some prospect of convincing TPR that it would be unreasonable to impose a CN or FSD if it can show that the benefit flow has overwhelmingly been from the target to the employer or the scheme rather than vice versa.

The *Lehmans* determinations show clearly that an integrated group is at risk of an FSD where (as will often be the case) benefits flow round the group. Even if there are agreements in place between the various companies, it may not be possible to demonstrate that they are on third-party terms (and so no benefit has flowed, particularly without a suitable uplift over 'cost' (or if the cost is paid and not left outstanding).

It will be a struggle to be able to displace the presumption of the determinations panel that an FSD is appropriate 'to protect the interests of members' (para 122). *Lehmans* also indicates that holding companies can be seen to benefit just by owning their subsidiaries (also a theme in the *Bonas* case). This seems to be going too far.

The *Desmonds* determinations shows the DP willing to act even where the actions taken did not trigger a *s 75* debt at the time. Similarly in *Box Clever/ITV*, the DP relied on actions of ITV and its predecessors before the moral hazard regime was on the statute books.

CNs as a priority claim in insolvency

4.11.10 In both the *Nortel* and *Lehman's* cases, the decision of the Determinations Panel to issue FSDs against group companies in administration proceedings in the UK was appealed. This appeal has not yet been heard, but in the meantime the administrators were concerned about how any liability on the company should be treated if an FSD (and a later enforcement CN) was later issued.

The Court of Appeal held in 2011 that any such liability should rank as an expense of the insolvency proceedings – ie ahead of the general creditors and any floating charge – but this was reversed by the Supreme Court in 2013[37] – see *Moral hazard powers of TPR – how do they rank against a company in*

---

37 *Re Nortel GMBH (in administration)* [2013] UKSC 52, reversing [2011] EWCA Civ 1124.

insolvency? **4.12**. If the Court of Appeal decision had been upheld it may have encouraged the Regulator to seek an FSD or CN in insolvency cases on the basis that a priority claim may result (see *Pension debts – priority of claims*, **9.3**)

Threatened use of CNs or FSDs

4.11.11 In addition to the cases outlined above, there are various examples of TPR threatening the use of its moral hazard powers and where the parties have reached an agreement (usually in the form of an additional contribution or guarantee to the pension scheme) on the basis that TPR stops pursuing the matter. Threatened uses of power are not generally made public, so it is difficult to obtain the full set of facts and circumstances (the analysis below is based on media reports and press releases). It is also likely that there are other relevant examples of which we are unaware.

Duke Street Capital – September 2008

4.11.12 In September 2008, media reports suggested that TPR sought to use its powers to recover a pension fund deficit from a private equity owner (Duke Street Capital) after it had sold the Focus DIY business to Cerberus Capital Management in June 2007.

TPR did not formally issue a CN or FSD against Duke Street Capital. It is believed that it threatened to use its powers but withdrew action because Duke Street Capital agreed to pay a sum (£8 million) into the Focus DIY pension fund.

Duke Street was targeted, it is thought, rather than the then owner because of the way in which it refinanced the Focus DIY business – paying itself a dividend on a leveraged recapitalisation some time before the sale. It is not clear whether a view was taken in the circumstances that it was best to complete the sale of Focus DIY and address TPR's issues subsequently.

Reader's Digest – February 2010

4.11.13 It was reported in February 2010 that TPR had rejected a compromise proposed by the Reader's Digest Association in respect of liabilities owed to the under-funded defined-benefit pension scheme of its subsidiary and that the subsidiary later entered administration.

TPR said that it was 'now considering its next steps, including use of its powers'. It is presumed that TPR's rejection of the compromise is based on an expectation that either the trustees will be able to get better recovery proving for the *s* 75 debt in the administration or that TPR will be able to exercise its moral hazard powers to recover funds in excess of what was offered as part of the compromise from other group companies.

Previously TPR has indicated its preference for parties reaching agreement among themselves, rather than exercising its powers. However, this case represented a direct rejection of an agreement that had been reached between the other parties (presumably on the basis that an exercise of moral hazards powers may prove more fruitful).

Visteon – June 2010

4.11.14 Following the insolvency of Visteon UK, which was the sponsoring employer of the Visteon UK pension plan, the trustees of that pension scheme are reported to have lodged a contingent claim against the us parent entities in Chapter 11 proceedings, on the basis that an exercise of TPR's moral hazard powers would result in a provable debt for the trustees in the Chapter 11 proceedings.

However, this contingent claim was withdrawn by the trustees after reports that the parent company had provided net financial benefits to Visteon UK. It is not possible to determine whether this purported net flow of benefits towards the sponsoring employer was the reason for the withdrawal of the contingent claim or whether in fact there were difficulties with other elements of the purported claim, such as an inability to satisfy the insufficiently resourced test.

Caparo Automotive/Armstrong Group – June 2010

4.11.15 The panel's approach in the *Bonas* case contrasts with its decision not to seek the issue of a CN or FSD in another case – *Caparo Automotive*. Details of this case were published as a report of the parliamentary ombudsman in June 2010 (there has been no report by TPR).

In the *Caparo Automotive* case, a pension scheme member made a complaint to the parliamentary ombudsman that TPR had failed to exercise its discretion reasonably in declining to issue a CN or FSD against Caparo Group Ltd, the relevant parent company. The member's complaint was that this was maladministration by TPR. It was argued that TPR should have made a CN or FSD on the basis that:

- the parent company had received benefit from the pension scheme because the employer company had taken a contribution holiday (and had impliedly accepted responsibility for the debt by making a compromise offer, which had been refused);

4.11.15 *Pensions Regulator – moral hazard powers*

- the parent company had deliberately sought to avoid the debt by placing the employer into an insolvency process in order to buy back the employer's assets (free of the pension deficit); and

- the parent company had substantial assets.

However, the Parliamentary Ombudsman found that there was no evidence that TPR had failed to exercise its powers properly.

Although it was not possible for the Parliamentary Ombudsman to set out any detailed reasoning for this (because the evidence that had been considered was still subject to the confidentiality restrictions applicable to information provided to TPR), she noted that the reason TPR had given to the trustees for its decision was that 'the overwhelming flow of benefit had been from Caparo Group Limited to the participating employer rather than vice versa'.

The trustees had considered bringing judicial review proceedings against TPR, but had decided not to proceed with this after TPR gave the trustees a summary of its analysis that underpinned the reasons it had not taken regulatory action.

For further details see the parliamentary ombudsman's report issued in June 2010 (HC 169).[38]

Great Lakes – June 2011

4.11.16 Information on the Great Lakes case was made publicly available by TPR through a report under *section 89* of the *Pensions Act 2004*. This allows TPR to publish an explanation of how it has exercised its powers in a specific case.

TPR first began to investigate whether or not it was appropriate to issue an FSD against Chemtura Corporation (the US parent of Chemtura Manufacturing UK (CMUK), which was the sponsoring employer of the Great Lakes UK Limited Pension Plan) and potentially other entities within the Chemtura group following an approach in June 2009 by the trustees who were concerned about the financial position of the Plan. The Plan had approximately 1,270 members and the Plan's deficit, calculated on a buy-out basis, was an estimated £95m.

In November 2010, the relevant Chemtura entities emerged from Chapter 11 bankruptcy protection in the US following a financial restructuring. The parties agreed to a 'stipulation' allowing contribution and financial support claims to be 'passed through' the Chapter 11 bankruptcy. In December 2010, TPR issued

---

38   http://www.ombudsman.org.uk/__data/assets/pdf_file/0004/4198/PHSO-0097_to_web.pdf

CMUK and various Chemtura companies with a warning notice setting out its intention to seek an FSD from TPR's Determinations Panel.

During ongoing funding negotiations between CMUK, Chemtura Corporation and the trustees of the Plan, a funding package was agreed to the satisfaction of TPR, in May 2011. Under the agreement:

- CMUK will make cash contributions of £60m over three years, starting with an initial £30m (which was paid before TPR's press release);

- CMUK will also provide contributions for any possible additional liabilities connected with equalisation (if necessary); and

- entities in the Chemtura Group (including Chemtura Corporation) have entered into guarantee and security agreements to protect the Plan against any further liabilities.

In its Report, TPR has stated that it will no longer pursue the matter because it is satisfied that the funding package 'was broadly equivalent to what might have been achieved if an FSD had been issued'.

What lessons can be learned?

4.11.17 Although any settlement approved by TPR will depend on its particular facts, useful points can be drawn from TPR's announcement:

- first, the press release clearly states that TPR would prefer to see negotiated settlements reached rather than have to take enforcement action; and

- second, although some details of the settlement are given, the Report is not clear on what level of support the US parent was required to provide by way of guarantee/security. (For example, there is no indication of the value of the security package or whether the guarantees were capped or otherwise limited.) The statement does, however, suggest that protection was given to all liabilities of the pension plan.

The key point is that the *Great Lakes* case (like the 2007 *Sea Containers* case) shows how the use or, indeed, threat of TPR's moral hazard powers can be enough to secure additional financial support for a UK scheme from an overseas parent company.

4.11.18 *Pensions Regulator – moral hazard powers*

Carlyle Group – September 2011

4.11.18 The *Financial Times*[39] reported on 22 September 2011, that TPR was looking at making use of its 'moral hazard' powers to force a division of the Carlyle Group, a private equity firm, to make good on a pension shortfall at Brintons [Ltd], a Worcestershire carpet manufacturer whose scheme it is trying to pass to the Pension Protection Fund.

In early September 2011, Carlyle Strategic Partners, a global fund, acquired the roughly £18m of senior debt of struggling Brintons and launched a pre-pack administration. Under a pre-pack a company is put into, and brought out of, administration quickly, reaching terms with all creditors. In this case, however, Carlyle held discussions with the trustees of the Brintons pension scheme but never reached agreement.

In commenting on the case TPR was reported as noting 'In this case, discussions involving the regulator and PPF never resulted in a realistic offer which treated the pension scheme fairly with regards to the position of other creditors.'

The case highlights concerns that TPR has about the potential for pre-pack insolvencies to be used to offload pension liabilities cheaply. Bill Galvin, chief executive of TPR, said that TPR was already investigating some earlier cases of pre-pack administration arrangements and was considering enforcement actions in those cases as well.

In light of TPR's statutory duty to limit claims on the PPF, it may be that the case will result in greater scrutiny by TPR of pre-pack administrations if they have the effect of offloading the pension scheme onto the PPF.

Anti-avoidance and clearance: the bigger picture

4.11.19 In March 2006 TPR wrote an article ('Anti-avoidance and clearance: the bigger picture') in which it gave examples of situations where it had refused clearance (ie confirmation that it would not issue a CN or FSD (see extract below)). These two examples give an indication of the circumstances in which TPR has, in practice, considered that it may be reasonable to issue a CN or FSD (but presumably did not).

> 'In one of these cases, an arm's-length management buy-in, the relatively robust position of the pension creditor (which had

---

39 Report by Norma Cohen, Economics Correspondent, *Financial Times* dated 22 September 2011.

282

previously ranked *pari passu* with all other creditors) was considerably diluted by a "money out" deal financed by a bank debt secured by fixed and floating charges. The regulator took into account a report from the trustees' financial advisers who were unable to recommend acceptance of the proposed transaction, and noted that the trustees were affected by a conflict of interest which had not been resolved. Ultimately, the lack of mitigation (eg through a reduced period for eliminating the deficit, or the provision of good security) meant that the regulator was not totally satisfied that it would be unreasonable to issue a contribution notice or financial support direction.

The second case was a complex restructuring and sale transaction in which a number of employers and schemes were involved. In summary, the affected schemes were not offered immediate cash payments toward the reduction of deficits; the only security offered to trustees was dependent on the future success of the restructured group. At the same time, an exceptional dividend was to be paid to some shareholders, and a certain amount of secured debt was to be paid down.'

It seems that since the economic downturn TPR has been taking increasingly tough positions about the extent of its moral hazard powers and when to invoke those powers.

MF Global UK Limited – October 2013

4.11.20 In October 2013, TPR issued a *section 89* report detailing its investigation and threatened use of an FSD against MF Global UK Limited (MFGUK).

MFGUK was a UK based broker-dealer business, MF Global UK Services Limited (MFG Services) provided employee and pension services for the UK operations of the MF Global Group. MFGUK and MFG Services went into administration on 31 October 2011, and MF Global Holdings Limited (MFGUK's parent) filed for Chapter 11 bankruptcy protection in the US on the same day.

MFG Services was the principal (and only) employer of the MF Global UK Pension Fund (the MFG Scheme) which had a deficit of £35 million on a buy-out basis at the time of the group's insolvency. The MFG Scheme entered the PPF assessment period following MFG Services insolvency.

TPR in the report noted that following an investigation to determine whether it would be appropriate to issue an FSD to MFGUK and other entities within the

MF Global Group, a warning notice was drafted, alerting directly affected parties that the DP may be asked (on or before 30 October 2013)[40] to consider whether to issue an FSD.

Running parallel to TPR's investigation, the trustees of the MFG Scheme were in discussion with KPMG (as the special administrator) in an attempt to reach an early settlement of their claim against MFGUK. All parties were aware of TPR's investigation and the intention to issue a warning notice.

On 16 October 2013, it was announced that a settlement had been reached with a significant payment being made into the MFG Scheme. This allowed the trustees to secure a buy-out with an insurer (Pension Insurance Corporation) and the MFG Scheme will wind up outside the PPF, with members receiving benefits broadly equivalent in value to those that they had been promised prior to the insolvency. It has been reported in the media that the buyout transaction was completed on 15 October 2013 and the MFG Scheme will now fully exit its PPF assessment period having received full co-operation from the PPF.

In light of the settlement TPR considered that it would not be appropriate to issue its warning notice. As TPR sets out in the *section 89* report, this case shows that TPR's moral hazard powers can prove influential in affected parties reaching a settlement without the need for formal regulatory action.

---

40 This date would be two years from the date of the insolvency of MFG Services and therefore (in practice) the last date available for TPR to issue a warning notice for an FSD.

4.12   Moral hazard powers are a provable debt: *Nortel/Lehman*

Summary

Third parties associated with an employer may find themselves liable to contribute to the employer's occupational pension scheme. Where a pension scheme is in deficit, the Pensions Regulator has powers – so-called 'moral hazard' powers – that can require a third party to give financial support or a specific payment to the pension scheme.

If the third party target company is already in insolvency proceedings (eg administration) when TPR starts to act, how does any resulting CN or FSD rank as against the insolvent target? The Supreme Court has held, reversing the Court of Appeal, in the *Nortel* case (July 2013), that such a debt is a provable debt (ranking alongside other unsecured claims) and does not constitute as an expense of the insolvency (and so ahead of ordinary unsecured creditors and creditors with floating charges).

This section looks at the Supreme Court decision and its implications.

4.12.1   On 24 July 2013, the Supreme Court handed down its long-awaited judgment in the Nortel/Lehman case: *Re Nortel Companies* [2013] UKSC 52. The court looked at the position where a contribution notice (CN) or financial support direction (FSD) was issued by the Pensions Regulator (TPR) on a company that is already in insolvency proceedings in England (eg administration). How does the relevant obligation rank in the order of priority of payment?

The Supreme Court held that liabilities arising under the 'FSD regime' usually rank as a provable debt (at least where the relevant situation relied on by the Regulator pre-dates the start of the insolvency process).

The judgment overturns the decisions reached by both the Court of Appeal (CA) and Briggs J in the High Court[41] that such a debt ranks as an expense of the insolvency and so ahead of unsecured creditors, creditors with floating charges and various other expenses including, importantly, the insolvency officeholder's own remuneration.

---

41   *Re Nortel GMBH (in administration)* [2011] EWCA Civ 1124, upholding Briggs J [2010] EWHC 3010 (Ch).

4.12.1 *Pensions Regulator – moral hazard powers*

The Supreme Court ruling will be welcomed by creditors and insolvency practitioners alike, for whom the implications of the lower courts' arguably surprising decisions were serious and wide-ranging.

Background

4.12.2 TPR has, under the *Pensions Act 2004*, so-called 'moral hazard' powers to make third parties liable to provide support or funding to a defined benefit occupational pension scheme in certain circumstances.

Various companies in the Lehman Brothers and Nortel groups entered into administration in England in September 2008 and January 2009 respectively.

In June and September 2010 TPR's Determination Panel determined that it would be reasonable to issue an FSD against companies in the Nortel and Lehman groups.

The administrators of the relevant Nortel and Lehman companies applied to court for directions as to where, in the statutory order of priority of payment, liabilities arising in respect of compliance with an FSD/CN should rank in circumstances where the FSD/CN was issued when the target company was already in insolvency proceedings.

4.12.3 The High Court and CA held that:

- based on previous cases on provable debts, an FSD issued after insolvency proceedings start is not a provable debt in a company's insolvency (even where the facts giving rise to the FSD occurred before the insolvency commenced);

- the liability arising in respect of compliance with an FSD made on a company in administration ranks as an administration expense. So it would have 'super priority' over all other unsecured claims of creditors (and those secured by a floating charge) and also (subject to the potential for the court to rank them ahead) the administrators' remuneration;

- for administrations commenced prior to 5 April 2010 only (such as those in Nortel/Lehman themselves), a CN issued on a company to enforce the obligations of an FSD issued while the company was in administration, will, on the company entering liquidation, not be an expense but instead rank as a provable debt in the company's liquidation; and

- for administrations commenced after 5 April 2010 (and due to a change in the relevant legislation which took effect then), an FSD/CN issued on a company in an administration will rank as an expense of the administration or subsequent liquidation.

Provable debt, expense or 'black hole': the arguments before the Supreme Court

4.12.4   Pensions legislation is silent as to how FSDs and CNs should be treated if they are issued in an insolvency (although it does specifically state that the underlying *s 75* debt on the employer which crystallises the pension deficit is not a preferential debt and, as it is taken to have arisen just before the employer's insolvency, ranks as a provable debt, not an expense). Accordingly, it is necessary to look to the insolvency legislation to find the answer.

Four possibilities on how liabilities in relation to the 'FSD regime' could rank in a company's insolvency were argued before the Supreme Court:

- option 1: that the lower courts were right and that an FSD/CN is an expense of the administration or liquidation (that is given 'super priority' over all other creditors and the insolvency officeholder's own remuneration);

- option 2: as a provable debt (that would rank alongside other unsecured, non-preferential creditors);

- option 3: as a non-provable claim payable (if at all) only out of any surplus available after all other creditors have been paid in full (the so called 'black hole' as it is assumed that payment in these circumstances is highly unlikely);[42] or

- option 4: as a non-provable claim (ie 'black hole') but with the court under its residual discretion directing the administrators to treat the FSD claim more favourably. This was a new option advanced in the Supreme Court. The argument advanced in the lower courts that the court should direct an officeholder to comply with an FSD/CN under the principle of ex parte James was no longer put forward.

Option 1: provable debt

4.12.5   *Rule 13.12* of the *Insolvency Rules 1986* defines what constitutes a 'debt' for the purpose of proving in an insolvency. The Supreme Court held that there were in summary two types of debt set out in this rule: liabilities to which the company is already subject at the start of the insolvency (set out in

---

42 In fact, since the litigation started in 2010, both the Lehman and Nortel administrations have progressed considerably and in the latest Lehman progress report (12 April 2013) the administrators have suggested that there may be sufficient funds to settle in full all provable claims, excluding claims by shareholders and claims for interest. This is, however, a highly unusual situation.

4.12.5 *Pensions Regulator – moral hazard powers*

rule 13.12(1)(a)) and those to which it may become subject after the insolvency by reason of any obligation incurred before (*rule 13.12(1)(b)*).

The court found that an FSD/CN claim issued after the insolvency is not capable of falling within *rule 13.12(1)(a)* and the issue was whether it falls within rule *13.12(1)(b)*. While the court stated that it would be dangerous to try and suggest a universally applicable formula for a company to have incurred an obligation under *rule 13.12(1)(b)*, three conditions must normally be met [paragraph 77]:

- it must have taken, or been subjected to, some step or combination of steps which have a legal effect. Here, this was met because on the administration date the companies had been a member of the respective Lehman/Nortel group for the relevant look-back period under the *Pensions Act 2004* (two years). Membership of a group of companies was 'undoubtedly' a significant relationship in terms of law and therefore fulfilled the first condition;

- the steps must have resulted in the company being vulnerable to the liability in question, such that there is a real prospect of that liability being incurred. The court held that if, on the administration date, the groups included either a service company (Lehman) or an insufficiently resourced employer company (Nortel) then the target companies were precisely the type of entities that were intended to be rendered liable under the FSD regime. The target companies 'were not in the sunlight, free of the FSD regime, but were well inside the penumbra of the regime, even though they were not in the full shadow of the receipt of an FSD, let alone in the darkness of the receipt of a CN';

- it must be consistent with the regime under which the liability is imposed to conclude that the step or combination of steps gives rise to a liability under the rule. Here the court considered that the FSD/CN regime should give rise to a liability but that this should be similar to a (provable) *s 75* debt.

In reaching its decision, the Supreme Court overruled the earlier decisions (made mostly in the context of personal bankruptcy) which had constrained the lower courts. These earlier decisions held that where an order for costs was made (in litigation) against a bankrupt person after the insolvency process began, this did not arise from an obligation which had arisen before the bankruptcy, even where the litigation had been started before the insolvency. The lower courts considered the same reasoning to apply to the FSD regime. The Supreme Court was clear that (in line with its ruling on the FSD regime) an order for costs made against a company in insolvency will be a provable debt where proceedings were begun before the insolvency.

Option 2: insolvency expense

4.12.6 If the FSD/CN liabilities rank as a provable debt, all sides accepted that the liabilities would not be expenses. In light of this, the court did not strictly have to analyse whether they would have been an insolvency expense. However, Lord Neuberger held that even if the FSD/CN was not considered to be a provable debt, it would not fall within the scope of a 'necessary disbursement' under the expenses regime as set out in *rule 2.67(1)(f)* (administration) or *rule 4.218(3)(m)* (liquidation) for these reasons:

- the liability did not result from any act or decision taken by the insolvency officeholder (unlike, for example, the decision to remain in premises which are subject to commercial rates); and

- the mere fact that an event occurs during the administration which under statute gives rise to a debt is not, of itself, sufficient to render payment of the debt an insolvency expense.

The Supreme Court held that the lower courts had misinterpreted the 2002 House of Lords decision in *Re Toshoku*.[43] Lord Neuberger held that *Toshoku* did not hold that where a statutory claim is not a provable debt it must be an expense under the 'necessary disbursement' heading (if it does not fit neatly within any other head of expenses). The Supreme Court held that where a statutory liability is one that can be imposed both before and after insolvency and where the statute is silent on ranking, the liability can only be an expense (assuming that it is not a provable debt) if the nature of the liability is such that it must reasonably have been intended by parliament that it should rank ahead of provable debts.

The Supreme Court distinguished *Toshoku* as relating to a tax liability that was specifically imposed on a liquidator (not the company) and as it specifically applied to a company which had gone into liquidation. However, the Supreme Court held that even in such a case it would be appropriate for a court to consider whether parliament intended the liabilities to rank as an expense.

Option 3: non-provable claim (and not an expense) – 'black hole'

4.12.7 The Supreme Court was clear that if it had decided that the FSD/CN liability was not a provable debt, it would not have held that the FSD/CN liability was, by default, an administration expense. In this case it would have simply fallen down the black hole.

---

43   *Re Toshoku Finance UK plc* [2002] UKHL 6, [2002] 3 All ER 961.

Option 4: court's residual discretion

4.12.8 Again, in light of the provable debt decision, this point was technically moot. However, the court held that a court does not have the power to order an administrator to treat an FSD liability as a provable debt – even where it would otherwise fall down the black hole.

Commercial implications of the CA decision – avoided

4.12.9 In reaching its decision the Supreme Court was clearly guided by what it considered the 'sensible and fair answer' that liabilities under an FSD/CN should be treated as a provable debt. By ruling in favour of the provable debt option, the Supreme Court avoided the 'oddities, anomalies and inconveniences' of the CA decision, for example:

- an FSD/CN issued just before a company enters administration or liquidation would be a provable debt, and so rank alongside all other non-preferential unsecured creditors. But an FSD or CN issued just after a company enters an insolvency process would count as an expense and be given 'super priority'. The Supreme Court acknowledged that 'It appears somewhat arbitrary that the characterisation and treatment of the liability under the FSD regime should turn on when the FSD or CN happens to have been issued …';

- if a CN were issued to enforce an earlier FSD that was issued before the company entered administration or liquidation, the CN would be a provable debt and not an expense; and

- while a *s 75* debt is a provable debt in the insolvency of an employer, an FSD/CN liability aimed at reducing the *s 75* debt would be payable with much higher priority, namely as an expense. Again, the Supreme Court grasps this anomaly by the head and acknowledges that:

  > 'It would be strange if the employer company's statutory obligation to make good a shortfall in its employees' pension scheme ranked lower in its insolvency than the more indirect statutory obligation of a target to make that deficiency good ranked in the target's insolvency.'

Comment

4.12.10 In adopting a 'compromise' outcome that falls between the two extremes of insolvency expense and black hole, the Supreme Court has reached a pragmatic and commercial solution. The court was clearly driven by the policy rationale that all possible liabilities, within reason, ought to rank as a provable debt to achieve equal justice to all creditors.

The consequences of the Supreme Court decision for each stakeholder:

Insolvency practitioners: should take care when complying with or settling an FSD liability to ensure that the parties agree that such settlement/compliance does not give rise to an administration expense but remains a provable debt;

Banks: may breathe a sigh of relief – to the extent that the fixed charge security does not cover the amounts owed, the floating charge realisations are now no longer diluted – or indeed entirely wiped out – by a large FSD/CN claim; and

TPR: issued a press release shortly after the Supreme Court decision was released stating that it welcomed the decision and was 'pleased that the Supreme Court has decided that an FSD issued against an insolvent target is effective'. Although it sought (in a press release issued shortly after the CA judgment and a subsequent formal statement in July 2012 on FSDs and insolvency) to provide reassurance that it was not TPR's intention to hamper the legitimate work of the administration and restructuring process, it was inevitable that concern and uncertainty had remained. Now TPR no longer has to face the conflict between maximising recovery for pension scheme members (and schemes) and seeking to be 'reasonable' and not interfere with commercial restructurings.

4.12.11   The judgment also fixes the anomaly that a *s 75* debt ranks as a provable debt, whilst an FSD/CN liability aimed at reducing the *s 75* debt would be payable with much higher priority, namely as an expense. Employment specialists will also take note of the Supreme Court's endorsement of the decision in *Day v Haine*[44] holding that a protective award issued by an employment tribunal following the start of an administration is a provable debt.

---

44   [2008] EWCA Civ 626.

4.13 Pensions and transactions – applying to TPR for clearance

Summary

The Pensions Regulator has wide-ranging 'moral hazard' powers under the *Pensions Act 2004* to make third parties liable to fund pension schemes.

The risk of these powers being used can make it safer to apply for statutory clearance during a transaction, particularly if the transaction has a materially detrimental effect on the likelihood of a defined benefit pension scheme's ability to meet its liabilities.

This section explains the Pensions Regulator's clearance procedure and when it should be sought.

Introduction

4.13.1 The *Pensions Act 2004* provides a formal, voluntary clearance procedure that allows parties to seek confirmation from the Pensions Regulator (TPR) that a proposed act, or failure to act, will not lead to it using its 'moral hazard' powers.

Under its moral hazard powers, TPR can issue a contribution notice (CN) or a financial support direction (FSD) against a participating employer (or third party), making that party contribute or provide financial support for its defined benefit (DB) pension scheme. See *TPR Moral hazard powers: Extracting pension scheme funding from third parties*, **4.1**.

These powers are extensive and can catch third parties connected or associated with an employer; for example, other companies in the same group, persons that own over a third of the voting rights in the employer or a director (including shadow director). For more information, see *Who is 'connected' or 'associated'?*, **4.2**. Therefore, the availability of this clearance procedure can be a significant comfort to an array of parties during a transaction.

Clearance is also an attractive option because of the uncertainty caused by changes in 2008 to TPR's clearance guidance and the *Pensions Act 2004*. In April 2008, TPR updated its clearance guidance by moving away from applying prescriptive tests and adopting a more principle-based approach. In its March 2008 consultation report, TPR recognised the 'concerns around the lack of certainty' with this new approach.

Furthermore, the *Pensions Act 2008* significantly expanded TPR's moral hazard powers under the *Pensions Act 2004* and added more uncertainty. In particular, it removed a defence of 'good faith' against CNs and created an alternative objective test based on 'material detriment' for issuing CNs. Further minor revisions were made to TPR's clearance guidance in December 2008, June 2009 and March 2010, respectively to reflect the enactment of the *Pensions Act 2008* and to take account of the introduction of the material detriment test. For more information on this test, see *Contribution notices*, **4.7**.

Voluntary process

4.13.2   The Regulator's guidance on clearance is on its website at www.thepensionsregulator.gov.uk/guidance/guidance-clearance.aspx.

However, clearance is a voluntary process and need not always be sought, even though it can be the safest option. Some features in the clearance procedure may deter parties from applying (eg employers are required to share information at an early stage with trustees, the application can take several weeks and parties will almost always have to offer the scheme some form of mitigation for any perceived detrimental effect). Furthermore, there may be instances where clearance is not appropriate or would be of little value. Parties will need to balance all these issues when deciding whether to apply for clearance.

When is clearance appropriate? – Type A events

4.13.3   In its 2010 guidance on clearance, TPR states that clearance is appropriate only for a 'Type A' event. Type A events are described as 'all events that are materially detrimental to the ability of the scheme to meet its pension liabilities'. These can either be related to the actions of the employer (employer-related events) or to the scheme (scheme-related events).

Employer-related events

4.13.4   The TPR clearance guidance contains a non-exhaustive list of employer-related type A events. Examples given include a change in priority, return of capital and change of group structure (including change of control), granting and repaying of inter-company loans and business and assets sales from the employer.

In its November 2009 scheme funding analysis, TPR said that the most employer-related clearance activity it had witnessed in financial year 2008 to 2009 had been:

4.13.4   *Pensions Regulator – moral hazard powers*

- company restructurings (12% of cases);

- employment-cessation events (12% of cases)

- loss of priority to new money (9% of cases);

- sales of the employer (8% of cases);

- loss of priority – old money (6% of cases);

- return of capital (5% of cases);

- employer insolvencies (5% of cases);

- asset sales (5% of cases).

Transaction types that each accounted for less than 5% of activity were business acquisitions, sales of parent companies, conversions/IPOs, and sales and leasebacks.

In a similar analysis (*Recovery plans: Assumptions and triggers*) for the financial year 2009/10, TPR said that there had been a year-on-year reduction in the number of clearance and withdrawal applications since its inception. In its Annual Report and accounts for 2010/11 the Regulator confirmed that the number of clearance statements issued in relation to CNs dropped from 55 in 2009/10 to 40 in 2010/11 while the number of clearance statements issued in relation to FSDs increased slightly from 37 in 2009/10 to 38 in 2010/11. The Regulator attributes this reduction to two factors: first, that activities that would previously have been addressed through clearances are now being dealt with within recovery plans, and second, that there has been a decrease in business activity (mergers and acquisitions in particular) over the period. TPR's corporate plan for 2011/14 confirms that 44 clearance applications were received in the financial year April 2010 to March 2011 and predicts that 70 applications will be received in the financial year April 2011 to March 2012.

An employer-related event is broadly only considered to be a Type A event if:

- it results in a weakening of the employer's covenant to such a degree that it could be considered materially detrimental to the ability of the scheme to meet its liabilities; and

- the scheme has a 'relevant deficit', which is measured on the highest of the:

  – employer's accounting basis under Financial Reporting Standard 17/International Accounting Standard 19;

  – PPF valuation basis;

  – scheme-funding basis; or

  – ongoing basis.

A higher basis may be used to measure the 'relevant deficit' where:

- the event is significantly materially detrimental to the scheme's ability to meet its liabilities (including a significant weakening in employer covenant); or

- there are going concern issues, the scheme is in wind-up or there is scheme abandonment (when *s 75*/buy-out is the appropriate basis).

The TPR clearance guidance expressly envisages that there may be events that weaken the employer covenant but that result from 'normal commercial activity' and may not be within the employer's control, such as losing a key supplier or customer contract. By themselves these are not generally Type A events but trustees and employers are still advised to consider their impact on the scheme.

Scheme-related events

4.13.5   The clearance guidance also states that clearance will be appropriate for scheme-related Type A events. Examples given include compromise agreements, certain apportionments of scheme deficits, and arrangements that have the result of preventing a *s 75* debt from triggering.

TPR notes that it would not expect all 'withdrawal arrangements' under the employer debt regime to come to it for clearance. However, there may be appropriate cases, namely where a withdrawal arrangement could itself be detrimental to the ability of a scheme to meet its pension liabilities, for example, if the guarantee does not sufficiently mitigate the fact that a *s 75* debt is not being paid in full.

In its November 2009 scheme-funding analysis, TPR said that the most scheme-related clearance activity in financial year 2008/09 was as follows:

- cessation events (over 12% of cases);

- scheme apportionments (over 8% of cases);

- cases where the Pension Protection Fund was involved (over 5% of cases); and

- compromises (over 2% of cases).

Agreeing a price for clearance

4.13.6   In its November 2009 scheme-funding analysis, TPR stated that in the financial years 2006/07, 2007/08 and 2008/09 it granted in excess of 400 clearance applications and rejected only three. This striking ratio is partly indicative of the number of applications that are withdrawn once made. But it can also be explained by TPR's general willingness to grant clearance where parties provide adequate support to the pension scheme to mitigate the detrimental effect of the Type A event on the scheme (ie TPR will give clearance but only at the right 'price').

TPR states in its clearance guidance that its 'preference is to be a referee in most transactions, rather than a player'. It indicates that it will generally grant clearance, with minimum interference, if:

- the trustees are involved in discussions about the Type A event (eg during a proposed transaction) as soon as reasonably practicable;

- any issues with conflict of interests are dealt with;

- the trustees support the transaction;

- the trustees obtain independent professional advice (in some circumstances, even to help with negotiations); and

- the most appropriate form of mitigation is agreed.

However, the case studies published by TPR and our experience show that TPR will not simply 'rubber stamp' agreement reached between the trustees and employers – see *Case studies on clearance from the Pensions Regulator*, **4.14**. Instead it will examine the proposal (and mitigation), relying to a large extent on advice given to the trustees. TPR may contact the relevant parties for further information. The case studies show that TPR can sometimes be a player in a transaction. If TPR deems mitigation to be unacceptable, it will hold meetings with the trustees and participating employers and seek to extract additional mitigation before granting clearance.

Similarly, TPR may facilitate negotiations between trustees and employers if discussions have broken down. In its case studies on clearance, it has even suggested that it may grant clearance where mitigation is adequate but the trustees have refused to support the application.

The level and type of mitigation that TPR will deem appropriate will depend on the nature, circumstances and impact of the Type A event on the funding of the scheme, taking into account the 'relevant deficit' – see above. TPR's expectation is that a mitigation package will include a cash payment to address the detrimental effect of the Type A event, but parent company guarantees and other forms of security often form part of the agreed mitigation.

If a transaction results in a highly leveraged employer, TPR is likely to require stronger mitigation perhaps even on a self-sufficiency basis (ie 'a cash payment to the scheme that would allow benefits to be met by existing assets and investment returns with minimal amounts of investment risk').[45] The Regulator has also said that 'the presence of private equity in a transaction is not a consideration for TPR. However, the degree of leverage and the timing of potential further ownership change will be key factors that are taken into account.[46]

Similarly, TPR will expect stronger mitigation if the sponsoring employer is severing links with the scheme without providing the scheme with adequate funds or assets to compensate for loss of the employer's ongoing support. TPR refers to this as 'abandonment' and states that in such cases 'As a starting point trustees should always consider whether it is appropriate for the employer to pay its full liability share.'[47]

See *Case studies on clearance from the Pensions Regulator*, **4.14** for case studies provided by TPR on how it operates its clearance procedure.

Making an application and timescales

4.13.7   Before making a formal application, a likely applicant (or the trustees) can contact TPR's corporate risk management team for preliminary enquiries. These can be made on a unnamed basis if necessary, although the level of guidance will be limited accordingly.

But enquiries are not a substitute for clearance, and TPR cautions that if an enquiry develops into an application, its view may change as new information is provided.

Formal applications can be made by parties at risk of a CN or FSD (ie an employer of the scheme or persons connected or associated with the employer (see above)). If there is more than one applicant in respect of the Type A event, TPR prefers for all applicants to be included on one application form.

The clearance guidance suggests that, in TPR's view, it is not usually appropriate for trustees to apply for a clearance statement. However, trustees should continue to consider the need for clearance when they are dealing with Type A events.

Clearance applications usually take at least three to four weeks from TPR being supplied with a full application (ie including financial reports etc). This time frame can be reduced by taking a number of actions:

---

45 *Scheme-funding: an analysis of recovery plans and clearance applications* – December 2008.
46 Ibid.
47 *Multi-employer schemes and employer departures guidance*, para 67 – July 2010.

- making a preliminary enquiry (see above);

- informing TPR of any timescales;

- sharing information with trustees early on;

- dealing with potential trustee conflict of interests; and

- discussing and agreeing proposals to mitigate a type A event.

TPR can also be willing to reduce its time frame for granting clearance in urgent circumstances.

Comfort letters

4.13.8   If the parties to a transaction do not believe that there is a Type A event (or do not want to formally confirm that they believe there may be a Type A event), they may be able to persuade TPR to provide a comfort letter, instead of clearance, confirming that TPR does not believe there to be a Type A event. We are aware of previous circumstances where TPR has issued a comfort letter.

It is not legally binding on TPR but it would, in our view, often be difficult for it subsequently to use its moral hazard powers for the relevant transaction. A comfort letter (given to another party) is mentioned in the DP's reasons for deciding on an FSD in the *Box Clever* case.[48]

Does clearance have value?

Full, accurate and up-to-date disclosure

4.13.9   Applications for clearance should include a full and accurate disclosure if clearance is to have any value. Failure to provide full and accurate information may render clearance worthless because it can be set aside if the circumstances described in the application are not the same as those arising and this is material – see *ss 42(5)* and *46(5)*, *Pensions Act 2004*.

A difficulty can arise because TPR often requests information regarding the specific Type A event. This makes it difficult to obtain clearance if a deal is continuously changing.

If clearance is granted but the facts change, confirmation can be sought from TPR on whether a change is material. If it is material, a new clearance application may be needed.

---

48   See para [164] at http://www.thepensionsregulator.gov.uk/docs/DN2084757.pdf

FSDs

4.13.10 Clearance provides comfort that neither a CN nor an FSD will be issued. However, in practice it is difficult to obtain clearance as protection from a future FSD because, unlike CNs, these can be issued even if a party has not taken part in an act that detrimentally affected the pension scheme. TPR may attempt to issue an FSD on the basis of how the corporate group is structured and operates day to day. TPR may, for example, seek an FSD because the pension scheme employer is insufficiently resourced or a service company at a time when other companies in the group are financially strong.

So it can be difficult exhaustively to describe (or even identify) the facts within a clearance application that would provide sufficient cover against an FSD (eg should the parent company ask TPR to sanction its entire corporate structure and all intra-group dealings?) Clearly, this would be impractical. For more information on FSDs, see *Financial support directions*, **4.6**.

In an article published in 2005, TPR suggested that it would be willing to give ongoing clearance (sometimes called 'squash court rules') to parties at risk of FSDs. Broadly, such clearance would be given in advance for a series of future dealings by, for example, a new owner with the employer, provided various conditions are met (eg on funding level of the scheme and net worth of the group). However, it is not clear how many such clearances have actually been granted (we are only aware of one) and such a procedure was not mentioned in TPR's updated clearance guidance or in the 2010 analysis of recovery plans and clearance applications.

If clearance only protects a party against a CN, and not an FSD, then clearance will be less valuable.

Are there any other options?

4.13.11 Applying for clearance will be the safer option in most cases, especially since the *Pensions Act 2008* extended TPR's powers (see above) and TPR has begun to focus more on conflicts – see *Conflicts of interest: the Pensions Regulator's guidance*, **12.1**. However, it is not the only option.

If clearance is not a realistic option, parties should consider seeking to minimise the risk of it being reasonable for TPR to later issue a CN or an FSD. For example, the parties can ensure that sufficient mitigation is offered or document decisions that they make so that they can later rely on the defence to CNs issued under the material detriment or main purpose test.

If applying for clearance is impractical (eg due to a short time frame), the parties can still apply for clearance retrospectively after the Type A event has occurred, although, in these circumstances, there is a risk that the price of clearance (ie mitigation required) may be disproportionately high.

The employer and other interested parties may simply make the decision that clearance is not necessary. If the trustees are happy with the proposal and they believe that adequate mitigation is offered, then all parties may decide that the transaction is not materially detrimental to scheme benefits, so reducing the risk of a CN or an FSD. The benefit of acting without TPR's endorsement is that the parties will be able to make their own commercial decisions without TPR shaping the transaction.

Getting agreement with the trustees and deciding that there is no material detriment is not, of course, a statutory defence to a CN or an FSD, but may be indicators helping defend any subsequent claim that could arise.

Will the trustees demand clearance?

4.13.12 Trustees may insist that the company obtains clearance, particularly if they have an actual or perceived conflict of interest (eg trustees who are also company employees). Trustees may believe that clearance will provide objective justification that the decisions taken by them were reasonable, reducing the risk of them being held to be in breach of their own duties in court. This also avoids the risk of TPR sanctioning the trustees, for example, by replacing them with independent trustees.

However, there are alternative strategies to clearance that trustees can use to become comfortable with agreeing to a transaction.

There are also a number of ways to manage conflicts (eg withdrawing from the decision-making process) – see *Should the Finance Director be a pension trustee?*, **12.2**.

4.13.13 The Regulator's guidance on corporate transactions (see www.thepensionsregulator.gov.uk/guidance/guidance-corporate-transactions. aspx) contains the following flowchart on employer decision-making when contemplating a transaction:

Flowchart: employer considerations in respect of the material detriment test

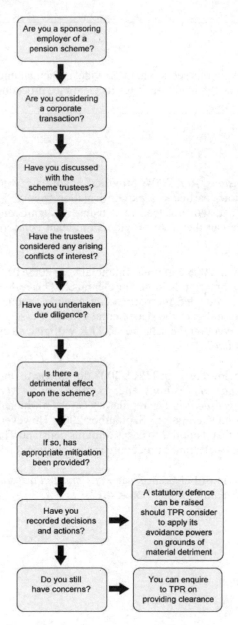

4.14   Case studies on clearance from the Pensions Regulator

Summary

The case studies in this section help provide a practical understanding of how the Pensions Regulator operates its clearance procedure.

Case studies

4.14.1   The *Pensions Act 2004* provides a formal, voluntary clearance procedure that allows parties to seek confirmation from TPR that a proposed act, or failure to act, will not lead to it using its significant 'moral hazard' powers. Clearance can therefore provide significant comfort, especially in a transaction.

Since its inception in 2005 and up to financial year 2009/10, TPR is known to have rejected only three applications for clearance. This reflects its willingness to grant clearance, provided the parties can provide adequate support to the pension scheme to mitigate the detrimental effect of a scheme-related or an employer-related event on the scheme (ie TPR will give clearance but usually only at the right 'price').

The case studies below are from TPR's 2008 document *An analysis of recovery plans and clearance applications* and its 2005 article *Anti-avoidance and clearance: the bigger picture*. The regulatory cases on which these case studies are based were completed before September 2008. However, TPR has stated that the principles that it applies to cases remains constant. The examples show how TPR operates its clearance procedure and the mitigation it expects.

For a general overview of clearance, see *Pensions and transactions – applying to the Pensions Regulator for clearance*, **4.13**.

Case study A: return of capital	*Case study B: change in priority – new money*
The employer was sponsor to a number of separate defined benefit pension (DB) schemes of which one was open to future accrual. The employer had a strong financial covenant and was a subsidiary of an overseas parent. As part of the global group restructuring plan, a number of businesses, in both the UK and elsewhere, had closed and the assets were sold. As a result, the schemes (other than the one that remained open) became frozen with no active members.	Clearance was requested for the refinancing of a largeplc group, which would result in the new lenders acquiring significant security where previously there had been none. The group was the sole sponsoring employer of the DB scheme that was open to future accrual.
Assets were gradually sold with the intention of passing the proceeds back to the parent company by way of dividends. The employer obtained legal advice and applied for clearance as the dividends were seen to represent a Type A event. The original plan was to inject funds only into the scheme with active members.	The group's proposed mitigation, which the trustees supported, was for a cash payment to be made into an escrow account when the group sold its entire shares in another company. As the mitigation on offer was future and contingent, TPR's team felt it was not acceptable in view of the risk to the scheme going forward should the refinancing proceed.
TPR considered that all of the pension schemes should be treated equally. As a result, mitigation to offset the reduction of the employer's balance sheet strength was paid to each of the schemes. The trustees of all the schemes were able to support the clearance application.	TPR met the group and the trustees, and the mitigation finally offered was for a third charge to be given to the scheme (thereby improving its outcome in the event of employer insolvency), to be reduced when the sale of its ownership in the other company materialised, and for the cash payment previously discussed to go straight into the scheme. In addition, a negative pledge was given to the trustees that no further extension to the group's borrowings would be made without their agreement and that cash payments over a fixed period would be made into the scheme to reduce the deficit.

Case study C: highly leveraged merger	*Case study D: special dividend payment*
Clearance was sought for the merger of two private equity-owned groups. Funding for the transaction was being provided by way of borrowing secured on the assets of the companies in both groups.	Clearance was sought by a listed company to make an extraordinary dividend to its shareholders. To combat rising production costs, the company had outsourced manufacturing to the Far East and had become a design and distribution company. As a result, the company had sold off surplus property and manufacturing equipment and was consequently cash rich. Shareholders bought into the company in anticipation of a special dividend expected to be greater than the cost of the shares.
Two multi-employer pension schemes were affected by the transaction. Both schemes were open to future accrual and both were in surplus on the financial reporting standard 17 (FRS17) and technical provisions bases but in deficit on the buy-out basis.	

In accordance with TPR's reminder and guidance of March 2007 on highly leveraged transactions, the trustees negotiated appropriate mitigation for the detriment to each scheme. This took the form of security for the schemes ahead of the bank debt at an appropriate level for each scheme, which was above technical provisions but below buyout. The schemes' security was equal, the schemes ranking with each other. The scheme trustees also obtained a guarantee from the ultimate parent of the merged group for the full buy-out (*s 75*) debt. Parallel negotiations took place with the two sets of trustees that resulted in two successful clearance applications being submitted to TPR.	The company was the principal employer of a DB pension scheme, which was open to future accrual. The scheme had a deficit of over £15 million on a *s 75* full insurance buyout basis, an FRS17 valuation of around £7 million and a *s 179* valuation of just under £10 million. The trustees were all ex-senior management of the employer from its time as a manufacturer and believed that it could not survive in its new guise. Consequently, the trustees took the view that they would not agree to the clearance application unless there was mitigation to the *s 75* level. The trustees had obtained an independent review of the employer covenant by a leading accounting firm, which did not identify material risks to the viability of the employer. TPR reviewed the covenant report and the latest unqualified audited accounts. There was no evidence to indicate that the employer would not continue trading as normal. The clearance guidance indicated *s 75* was only the appropriate level of mitigation where there was doubt as to whether the employer would continue as a going concern.
	Negotiations between the parties, facilitated by TPR, led to an impasse. The employer, recognising its responsibilities to the scheme, offered a package of cash and security to the trustees up to the *s 179* level. The trustees did not support this level; however, TPR felt it to be a reasonable and appropriate level, and provided clearance.

Case study E: highly leveraged transaction (private equity)

Clearance was sought for a private equity investor to acquire a large UK company. Under current ownership, the majority of debt was unsecured.

The company was the parent of a group of companies operating a DB scheme that was open to future accrual but closed to new members. As at March 2007, the scheme had a surplus on an FRS17 basis but an estimated deficit of around its total net assets on a full insurance buyout measure.

As a result of the proposed acquisition, new borrowing would be secured on the assets of the company, and it was accepted by all parties that this would have a significantly detrimental effect to the position of the scheme, both in terms of the ongoing ability to meet contributions and in an insolvency situation.

In line with TPR's guidance and reminder of March 2007 on highly leveraged transactions, the vendors, purchasers and trustees based initial discussions on the mitigation to the scheme on the basis of 'self-sufficiency' (ie a cash payment to the scheme that would allow benefits to be met by existing assets and investment returns with minimal amounts of investment risk).

The mitigation package finally offered by the vendor to the trustees was on a self-sufficiency basis and was structured as such, incorporating a recovery plan:

- an immediate payment of cash on completion of the transaction;

- annual contributions over ten years, supported by a bank standby letter of credit;

- a final payment payable after ten years and secured over valuable receivables; and

- the benefit of a package of prior ranking and *pari passu* security.

TPR's team concluded that this package represented sufficient mitigation for the detrimental effect of the transaction, and clearance was granted.

Case study F: multi-national group companies

This case centres on a multi-national group of companies, of which two UK employers sponsored DB pension schemes. The employers had common ownership but no trading relationships.

The schemes had significant key differences. The first was far larger in respect of scheme size and number of members. Furthermore, that scheme was still open with many active members, many of whom were some way from retirement age. The trustees were anxious to work with the directors regarding the scheme as future and continuing employment was a key issue for those members.

The employer for the second scheme had effectively ceased to trade and the scheme was closed with no active members. The scheme rules allowed the trustees to set the level of contributions. In the absence of a solvent trading employer, the trustees of this scheme felt the most appropriate measure of the pension scheme deficit was at the buy-out level. Despite lengthy discussions with the employer group, this could not be agreed and the trustees effectively served demand for settlement of the entire deficit.

Enforcement of this debt would be sufficient to bring about the insolvency not only of the employer of the second scheme but potentially of other UK-based companies (given the inter-company positions), including the sponsor of the first scheme.

It was at this point that TPR became involved in the discussions. It was not in the interests of either trustee board to see a situation where either or both schemes entered the PPF.

It was agreed after detailed independent legal and actuarial advice that the schemes should merge. This represented a very pragmatic solution for the trustees of the second scheme.

4.14.1   *Pensions Regulator – moral hazard powers*

Case study G: two examples of refusal to grant clearance

In one of these cases, an arm's-length management buy-in, the relatively robust position of the pension creditor (which had previously ranked *pari passu* with all other creditors) was considerably diluted by a 'money out' deal financed by a bank debt secured by fixed and floating charges. TPR took into account a report from the trustees' financial advisers, who were unable to recommend acceptance of the proposed transaction, and noted that the trustees were affected by a conflict of interest that had not been resolved. Ultimately, the lack of mitigation (egthrough a reduced period for eliminating the deficit, or the provision of good security) meant that TPR was not totally satisfied that it would be unreasonable to issue a contribution notice or financial support direction.

The second case was a complex restructuring and sale transaction involving a number of employers and schemes. In summary, the affected schemes were not offered immediate cash payments towards the reduction of deficits; the only security offered to trustees was dependent on the future success of the restructured group. At the same time, an exceptional dividend was to be paid to some shareholders, and a certain amount of secured debt was to be paid down.

Source: TPR website

An analysis of recovery plans and clearance applications (December 2008):
www.thepensionsregulator.gov.uk/docs/scheme-funding-analysis-2008.pdf

Anti-avoidance and clearance: the bigger picture (2006)

Further reading on the TPR website

4.14.2   www.thepensionregulator.gov.uk

Clearance guidance – March 2010.

Scheme funding: an analysis of recovery plans – November 2010.

Multi-employer schemes and employer departures – November 2010.

Code of Practice No 12: Circumstances in relation to the material detriment test – May 2009.

Regulatory Guidance – Corporate transactions – June 2009.

Anti-avoidance and clearance: the bigger picture – May 2005.

4.15 Desmond & Sons: contribution notice against two directors and appeal by the Pensions Regulator to the Upper Tribunal

Summary

The Upper Tribunal has ruled that it can increase sums already decided under a determination of the Pension Regulator's determinations panel to issue a contribution notice.

In its interim decision in Desmond & Sons, the tribunal also rejected an attempt to bring in another party who had not been made a target under the decision of TPR's determinations panel.

In this section we outline the background of the Desmond & Sons case and how this latest decision shows the Upper Tribunal's jurisdiction to reconsider the Pensions Regulator's decisions.

Contribution notices

4.15.1   Under the *Pensions Act 2004* the Pensions Regulator has the power to issue a contribution notice to a company or individual for certain acts or deliberate failures to act. The notice can demand that the target pays a sum to the trustees of the pension scheme.

The Pensions Regulator's Determinations Panel exercises these 'moral-hazard powers', and an appeal to the Upper Tribunal can challenge its decision. The Determinations Panel has only issued a contribution notice once before – in the Bonas Group Pension Scheme [2011].

Desmond and others v The Pensions Regulator and Garvin Trustees Ltd [2010]

4.15.2   After an oral hearing in April 2010, the Determinations Panel decided to issue a contribution notice against two director/shareholders, Mr Desmond and Mr Gordon (almost six years after the events). If issued, the contribution notice would order Mr Desmond to pay £900,000 and Mr Gordon to pay £100,000 into Desmond & Sons Ltd Pensions & Life Assurance Scheme.

The Pensions Regulator delayed publishing the panel's decision until an embargo on the tribunal decision was lifted. It made the determination notice and the Determination Panel's reasons to issue contribution notices public on 13 March 2012.

Background – Desmond & Sons' pensions scheme

4.15.3   Desmond & Sons set up its occupational pension scheme in 1969. The scheme provided final salary benefits, with Desmond & Sons as its only employer.

Desmonds, a clothing manufacturer in Northern Ireland, relied on Marks & Spencer as its only customer. The relationship was based on 60 years' loyalty and trust, rather than a formal contract. In February 2004, Marks & Spencer gave Desmonds 24 months' notice that it intended to deal directly with the factories that supplied Desmonds, cutting the company out of the picture.

In June 2004 Desmonds' shareholders placed the company into members voluntary liquidation (MVL). The pensions scheme had a funding shortfall on a buyout basis estimated at £10.9m. But Northern Ireland legislation at the time provided for the statutory *s 75* debt payable when a company enters liquidation to be calculated on an MFR basis. So the scheme's liabilities were calculated on a minimum funding requirement basis, rather than the more expensive buyout valuation basis.

The Determination Panel's findings

4.15.4   The targets argued that the MVL was an inevitable result of Marks & Spencer's decision to end business with Desmonds. But the Determinations Panel decided that the MVL exploited existing legislation, by ensuring that the debt due to the scheme was calculated on an minimum funding requirement basis rather than a buyout basis. This enhanced shareholder value to the detriment of the pension scheme.

The Determinations Panel accepted evidence that the director shareholders were aware that new legislation was planned and that the calculation basis would change. The Panel also found that the director shareholders had misled the trustees by suggesting that the scheme would continue. In doing so, they had prevented the trustees from negotiating other funding for the scheme.

The Panel also ruled that it was not reasonable to impose liability on two other shareholders. Although as shareholders they were parties to the MVL, they were not involved with the decision-making process that led Desmonds into the MVL in any meaningful way.

Appeal to the Upper Tribunal

4.15.5   Mr Desmond and Mr Gordon appealed against the use of the contribution notices to the Upper Tribunal. They argued that the Panel should not have issued a notice against either of them or that the amounts should have been zero.

4.15.6   The scheme trustees also referred the matter to the Upper Tribunal. They challenged that the amount of the notice imposed should have been the full buyout shortfall and that Mrs Desmond should also be a liable target under a contribution notice. The Pensions Regulator filed a statement of case to support the trustees' position.

4.15.7   Both the targets and Mrs Desmond submitted interim applications to the tribunal. They asked:

- for Mrs Desmond not to be added to the contribution notice. They argued that not only was the Pensions Regulator outside the time limit to issue a contribution notice against her, but that the Upper Tribunal had no power to decide the referral for her; and

- for some issues to be struck out. They argued that;

  - the tribunal could not increase the sum issued under the contribution notice;

  - the allegations were not in the Determinations Panel's original decision; and

  - they referred to a series of acts rather than a single act prescribed by the legislation.

The Upper Tribunal's decision

4.15.8   The Upper Tribunal upheld Mrs Desmond's application, but dismissed the other strike-out applications.

It ruled that:

- the Upper Tribunal can increase the contribution notice amount as part of its statutory role;

- the statutory function of the Tribunal is to reach its own decision and it can depart from the Panel's findings – as recognised in *Bonas*. The parties can raise fresh arguments or reintroduce points from the original decision, if new factual matters relate to the act;

4.15.8 *Pensions Regulator – moral hazard powers*

- a contribution notice can relate to a series of events as an 'act'. The tribunal could conclude whether the targets' actions relied on by the trustees and regulator were collectively an act ending with the MVL; and

- there was no prospect of the trustees' case succeeding against Mrs Desmond. The regulator was out of time to issue a contribution notice against her and the Upper Tribunal could not now order the Determinations Panel to issue a contribution notice.

What this means

4.15.9 The Upper Tribunal's decision is notable. Until now, the contribution notice imposed in *Bonas* was believed to be the first since the regulator got its anti-avoidance powers. With the original hearing in February 2011, this decision predates the Bonas notice.

The decision highlights the Upper Tribunal's extensive jurisdiction to reconsider the Pension Regulator's decision. It also illustrates the stringent limit periods that applied to contribution notices.

The Tribunal has not said that the amount of the contribution notice is unreasonable and has clarified that it can increase the sum. So it seems likely that any settlement would represent the buyout deficit in the scheme.

The Pensions Regulator's press release on 13 March 2012 suggests a full hearing of the main issues before the Upper Tribunal will follow.

The Regulator took an appeal against the Tribunal's refusal to add another target to the contribution notice on limitation grounds to the Court of Appeal in Northern Ireland.

4.15.10 In November 2013, the Court of Appeal of Northern Ireland handed down its decision in *The Pensions Regulator v Desmond*.[49]

The Court of Appeal of Northern Ireland allowed TPR's and the trustee's appeal. It held that it is for the Upper Tribunal to determine whether it should substitute a decision to exercise the power to issue a CN. In determining the appropriate action for TPR to take, the Upper Tribunal will consider whether the statutory conditions for issuing a CN are satisfied taking into account the new material before it and 'basing its conclusions on time by reference to the date on which the Panel made its decision'.

---

49 [2013] NICA 62.

310

Therefore, the Upper Tribunal was not constrained by the six year look-back period in which the Determinations Panel of TPR can exercise its power to issue a CN. The matter will now be heard by the Upper Tribunal in due course.

This decision is consistent with the outcome in the *Lehman Brothers*[50] FSD case handed down in June 2013, which considered similar issues as they applied to FSDs. The Northern Ireland Court of Appeal recognised in its reasoning that the statutory provisions in that case is somewhat different but that the court considered that 'the outcomes are broadly consistent'.

In any event the outcome is not of much wider assistance. For cases since 3 January 2012, the *Pensions Act 2011* applies the relevant the six-year period for CNs so that it ends when a warning notice is issued by TPR (rather than as previously on the DP's determination) – see **4.9** above.

---

50 *LB Re Financing No 1 Ltd and 36 others v Lehman Brothers Pension Scheme Trustees and another* [2013] EWCA Civ 751 (21 June 2013).

4.16   Box Clever: FSD proceeding against ITV

Summary

On 21 December 2011 the Pensions Regulator's Determinations Panel determined to issue financial support directions (FSDs) to five companies in the ITV group, based on their ownership of a 50% stake in the Box Clever joint venture. ITV has appealed, but if ultimately issued, the FSDs would require them to put in place financial support for the Box Clever pension scheme, which has an estimated *s 75* deficit of £62m.

ITV has since lodged an appeal to the Upper Tribunal, claiming the FSD was 'wholly unreasonable' as it never participated in the scheme and had no control over the growth of its deficit.

The move by the Regulator to seek an FSD basing 'reasonableness' on business transactions before 2004 sets a number of precedents that could have wide implications. Those implications are looked at in this section.

Box Clever time line

4.16.1

2000

Box Clever established as joint venture (50/50 owned by Granada and Thorn)

Granada and Thorn sell businesses to Box Clever

Box Clever borrows from banks to fund acquisition

Box Clever sets up a new pension scheme for future service

2003

Box Clever companies owe £860m to banks

Box Clever placed in administrative receivership (default declared under security document)

2004

ITV established as the new holding company for Granada

312

2005

Box Clever business sold to private equity buyer

Legal ownership of shares in 3 (of 5) employers transferred to bank nominee

2009

ITV applies for clearance; TPR refuses and says it's investigating

31 December: relevant date for FSD test as chosen by TPR

2011

TPR issues warning notice on ITV companies (September)

Oral hearing before the determinations panel (December)

Determinations panel determines to issue FSDs (December)

ITV companies appeal to the Upper Tribunal (FSD is not issued, pending the outcome of appeal)

2012

Upper Tribunal allows pension trustees to be party to the appeal

The Box Clever pension scheme

4.16.2   The scheme was established following the setting up in 2000 of Box Clever as a joint venture group that acquired and then merged Granada's and Thorn's television rentals businesses. Box Clever paid cash for the businesses and borrowed from banks to fund this. The new Box Clever scheme provided future service defined benefits for former active members of the Granada and Thorn pension funds now employed under the joint venture, reflecting the benefits under those schemes.

In 2003, it became clear that Box Clever was unable to service its £860m debt owed to WestDeutsche Landesbank (WestLB). In September 2003, partners at PricewaterhouseCoopers were appointed administrative receivers over the business.

4.16.3   In 2005, Box Clever's business was sold to a private equity buyer. This new owner was not involved with the receivers, the pension scheme or the deficit. The administrative receivers subsequently reorganised the joint venture and at the end of 2009 the scheme's assets were £14.4m. With buyout liabilities of £76.5m (needed to provide pensions for its 3,000 members), the scheme was left with an estimated deficit of more than £62m.

Steps leading to the FSD determination

4.16.4 On 18 November 2009, ITV applied for clearance from the regulator to clarify that it would not engage its powers to issue a financial support direction (FSD) or contributions notice in relation to the scheme. However, the Pensions Regulator told ITV it could not provide a clearance statement and was instead investigating the matter.

4.16.5 In September 2011, the regulator issued a warning notice to five companies in the ITV group (Targets) indicating that it considered it appropriate to issue FSDs against them in relation to the scheme. The Targets were Granada UK Rental & Retail, Granada Media, Granada Group, Granada and ITV. Following an oral hearing on 21 December 2011, the Determinations Panel decided it was reasonable to impose FSDs. The Determinations Panel said: 'Overall it seems to us that this is a case where the Scheme's principal employer, BCT, was set up by the Granada and Thorn groups as part of a transaction that aimed to extract value from the consumer rentals businesses of those groups, but leave them able to share in any future profit.'

4.16.6 ITV has lodged an appeal to the Upper Tribunal, claiming the FSD was 'wholly unreasonable' as it never participated in the scheme and has no control over the growth of its deficit.

A preliminary issue (whether the trustee should be involved in the proceedings) was heard by the Upper Tribunal in April 2012 (FS/2012/0001–5).

Financial support directions

4.16.7 The Pensions Regulator may issue an FSD against an employer under, or persons connected or associated with an employer under, a funded tax-approved defined benefit scheme where it considers that the employer in relation to the defined benefit scheme is either a service company or 'insufficiently resourced', as defined in *s 44* of the *PA 2004*. If used, an FSD requires the target to put in place financial support for the scheme.

4.16.8 The Regulator can only issue an FSD if it is satisfied that the employer was either a service company or insufficiently resourced at the 'relevant time'. Until statutory changes on 3 January 2012, this was the period of two years before the determinations panel reached its decision to impose an FSD. Changes made by the *Pensions Act 2011* now mean that in future the two-year look-back period runs back from the date the Regulator issues its warning notice. This means the Regulator has longer to prepare its case.

4.16.9 Under the *Pensions Regulator (Financial Support Directions, etc) Regulations 2005*, 'insufficiently resourced' applies where:

- the value of 'resources of an employer' is less than 50% of its estimated *section 75* debt to the scheme; and

- another associated or connected person has sufficient resources that, when added to those of the employer, result in aggregate resources of at least 50% of the estimated *section 75* debt.

4.16.10 For an FSD to be issued, the Pensions Regulator (and its DP) must consider that it is reasonable to impose an FSD. The Pensions Regulator will have regard to the following factors:

- the financial circumstances of the person;

- the value of any benefits received directly or indirectly by that person from the employer;

- the relationship that the person has or has had with the employer (eg a parent company); and

- any connection or involvement that the person has or has had with the scheme (eg a trustee).

For further details, see *Financial Support Directions, 4.6*.

Procedural issues

4.16.11 Two main procedural issues were raised by the Targets at the hearing.

Shortage of time

4.16.12 Whether the shortage of time available for them to prepare for the hearing was unfair. The Targets had two months and two weeks to prepare from the service of the warning notice to the hearing itself. They argued that they were put at a serious disadvantage in comparison to the Regulator, which had substantial time to prepare its case over the preceding years, and the case should therefore be thrown out.

The panel ruled that the Targets had, by a narrow margin, been given reasonable time and opportunity to respond to the case being brought against them. The panel accepted the submissions of the Regulator that the Targets had known of the possibility of an FSD being issued since at least November 2007.

Changes in the case

4.16.13 Whether changes in the Regulator's case between service of the warning notice and the hearing was unfair. In particular, the Regulator amended its arguments relating to the ownership of the Targets after receiving further information from the administrative receivers in early December 2011.

As for the changes to the Regulator's case, the Determinations Panel ruled against the Targets again. As a matter of principle, the Regulator could in presenting its case to the Panel depart from the arguments and evidence contained in the warning notice. Whether this principle applied in a particular case would depend on the specific facts. The Panel wished to avoid a case being 'ossified' in the warning notice and perhaps being deprived of up-to-date evidence. The Regulator could rely on new evidence so long as it met certain tests:

- evidence adduced after service of a warning notice must be adduced in circumstances where all parties could fairly take account of it;

- the parties were given a fair opportunity to respond meaningfully to any new arguments raised on the basis of that evidence; and

- those new arguments remained within the scope of the warning notice.

Note that the Determinations Panel did not deal with changes where it had become too late to issue a warning notice – this may become more important following the time limit statutory changes in January 2012.

Effect of bank security

4.16.14 The security granted by the Box Clever companies to the banks included provision for the shares in the five employer companies (all subsidiaries of Box Clever Technology Limited, the holding company) to be mortgaged to the security agent (JP Morgan). In 2005, the shares in three of the employers were transferred to JP Morgan so that it became the registered holder of the shares.

The DP noted that the evidence about ownership and voting powers was not full but held that the security agent held the shares as mortgagee. so that the beneficial ownership remained with the relevant Box Clever companies.

4.16.15 The DP also interpreted the voting provisions in the bank security document as meaning that the Box Clever companies retained a right to vote the shares (or direct the security agent how to vote the shares) even though a 'Declared Default' had occurred in September 2003 (when the administrative receivers were appointed). This meant that the Box Clever holding companies retained 'control' of the employers and so the ITV companies (as 50% shareholders in Box Clever Technology Limited) remained associated with the employers.

The DP held that the ability of the security agent to serve notice removing the Box Clever companies power to exercise votes did not mean that control had passed to the security agent (at least before such a notice was given).

Reasonableness

4.16.16 In relation to whether it was reasonable to issue the FSDs, the Targets argued that relying on events between eight and ten years ago amounted to retrospective application of the legislation. The panel did not accept the Targets' reliance on a presumption against retrospection. Noting there was no temporal limitation on the factors that had to be considered in *section 43(7)* of the *Pensions Act 2004*, the panel said 'we consider it clear that Parliament intended the Regulator to have regard to all relevant matters when deciding upon reasonableness under *section 43*, no matter when they occurred'. Moreover, noting that negotiations over the key issues had been ongoing since 2009, the panel said the length of the negotiations should not affect the regulatory position.

4.16.17 The Regulator listed the factors it considered when assessing 'reasonableness'. In terms of the individual factors, the panel concluded that the factors that 'weighed most heavily' were the value of benefits received by the Targets from the employers and the Targets' relationship with those employers.

In this case, the value of benefits received by the Targets from the employers was considered to be 'crucial' as the joint venture had resulted in substantial financial returns for both Thorn and Granada. Furthermore, when BCT offered a defined benefit scheme instead of a defined contribution scheme to transferring employees, this showed that Granada Group had a relatively close connection and involvement with the creation and development of the scheme.

Comment

4.16.18 The Pensions Regulator is still feeling its way with FSDs, so this decision is likely to be a significant one. We have already seen the Regulator use its moral hazard powers against large insolvent companies such as *Nortel* and *Lehman*; however, this will be the first time it has decided on a joint venture (particularly a JV that was established long before the FSD legislation came into force).

317

4.16.18   *Pensions Regulator – moral hazard powers*

So far, the panel has provided some useful guidance regarding procedural issues, focusing principally on any retrospective application of the FSD regime and the ability of the Regulator to alter its case before the panel.

4.17 Kodak: Pensions Trustees' 'Loan to Own' strategy: a trend to come?

Summary

Eastman Kodak Corporation (Kodak US), the US parent of the Kodak group, filed for chapter 11 protection in the United States in January 2012. It successfully emerged from bankruptcy in September 2013 as a new restructured technology company focused on imaging for businesses. Many other Kodak companies throughout the world were able to avoid following in their parents' footsteps and were maintained as going concern businesses whilst the US bankruptcy process was ongoing.

As a result of a restructuring deal agreed between the English Kodak entity, Kodak Limited (Kodak UK), Kodak US and the UK Kodak Pension Plan (KPP) (and approved by the US bankruptcy court), the KPP acquired the global Kodak Personalised Imaging and Document Imaging businesses. The consideration for the purchase consisted of both cash and a settlement of KPP's claims against Kodak US and Kodak UK. As part of the deal, Kodak UK is now free of all liabilities to the KPP.

Impact of the parent guarantee and interplay with the Chapter 11 process

4.17.1 Kodak UK maintained a final salary pension plan for its employees, the KPP, which had developed a significant funding deficit. As is increasingly common in pension structures, Kodak UK's parent, Kodak US, had agreed to provide certain funding support regarding Kodak UK's liabilities to the KPP. When Kodak US entered into bankruptcy proceedings, the KPP filed a claim in the US process and was the largest unsecured creditor in those proceedings with potential claims against Kodak US and Kodak UK in excess of US$2.8bn.

Agreeing the KPP restructuring deal was therefore a key component to Kodak US successfully emerging from bankruptcy and the deal required the approval of the US bankruptcy court. The UK Pensions Regulator was involved in negotiations between the trustees of the KPP and Kodak US from an early stage. Clearance from the Pensions Regulator of the deal (ie confirmation that it would not use its 'moral hazard' powers against the Kodak group) and confirmation from the Pension Protection Fund (PPF) that it would not object to the Pensions Regulator's clearance were conditions precedent to completion of the transaction. Unusually, the Pensions Regulator effectively gave advance clearance at the signing stage of the acquisition of the Kodak businesses on

26 April 2013 when details of the business acquisitions (and the underlying transaction documents) were not yet fully settled.

The advance clearance was important for the Chapter 11 process and meant that at the time the Chapter 11 disclosure statement in respect of the US emergence plan was filed in court by Kodak US (June 2013), the KPP deal had already been approved and signed on a conditional basis.

The Pensions Regulator reserved the right to object if the transaction changed materially between signing in April and completion in early September. Ultimately, the Pensions Regulator did not object to any changes and the transaction successfully closed on 3 September, as planned.

Settlement of Kodak's pension liabilities in exchange for two businesses

4.17.2 The KPP was able to purchase two large Kodak businesses with reduced cash paydown by using debts owed by the Kodak group as consideration, thus mirroring 'loan to own' strategies and rationale from the private equity world.

It is unusual for pension trustees to give up all claims against the employer group and settle its pension claims by way of consideration for a business. In this case, the KPP bought the businesses to hold them under a separate vehicle. The KPP created a new company, Kodak Alaris, in which to hold the business under a licence.

In the past, it has been more usual for trustees to accept cash and shares in the restructured employer group. It is however not unprecedented for pension trustees to invest in assets in which the wider group has a stake – in 2012, the UK Coal Pension Scheme invested its own funds to acquire a majority interest in the property division of the UK Coal group.

Restructured KPP – reduced benefits but higher than PPF

4.17.3 As a result of the restructuring, members of the KPP will be given the chance to transfer to a new pension scheme, which is not expected to enter the PPF (at least in the short term). Under the new scheme, scheme benefits for members will be lower than the unsustainable levels under the old KPP, however such benefits would still exceed the benefits members could expect if the KPP were to enter the PPF. The new scheme will be entitled to receive dividends from the two businesses acquired from Kodak and a share of the KPP's existing assets.

Any members who do not wish to transfer to the new scheme will remain in the KPP, which, it is anticipated, will enter the PPF in due course. It has now been confirmed that more than three quarters of members of the KPP have agreed to transfer to the new pension scheme.

Does the Kodak settlement herald a new trend of pension plan trustees acquiring business assets from the plan's sponsor to settle large pension debts?

4.17.4 It remains to be seen whether other pension funds see sufficient value/income generation potential in the businesses related to their employer groups to seek to acquire them at a heavily discounted price by using the debts owed by the employer group to them as part consideration.

For smaller schemes with little investment potential, this is unlikely. It is possible that the Pensions Regulator was willing to agree to an innovative, unusual solution for Kodak at least in part due to the sheer size of the deficit and the strain this would have placed on the PPF had the KPP failed. It may well be that – perhaps counter-intuitively – the Pensions Regulator will continue to take a more conservative approach with smaller schemes in financial difficulty.

However, recently larger pension scheme trustees do seem to have been acting as one would expect any interested commercial players to act and to be willing to take a more active role in restructuring the employer group.

Chapter 5

Pension Protection Fund (PPF)

5.1 The Pension Protection Fund

Summary

The *Pensions Act 2004* provided for the establishment of the Pension Protection Fund (PPF). This aims to provide members with a certain level of protection in the event of scheme insolvencies.

This section considers two areas:

- the establishment of the Board of the PPF and its functions;
- how the PPF operates – what schemes it covers, how it will assume responsibility for a scheme.

Establishment and operation of the PPF

5.1.1   The *Pensions Act 2004* established the Pension Protection Fund (PPF) with effect on and from 6 April 2005.

The Board of the PPF is established as a body corporate under the *Pensions Act 2004*. The *Pensions Act* provides that the Board is not to be regarded as a servant or agent of the Crown, or as enjoying any status, privilege or immunity of the Crown.

The Board's primary function is to 'hold, manage and apply' the PPF and the Fraud Compensation Fund.

The Board may delegate any of its functions to any executive members of the Board, any staff member of the Board or any of the Board's committees or sub-committees.

5.1.1 *Pension Protection Fund (PPF)*

Broadly, the PPF is designed to provide a safety net for eligible occupational pension schemes. If a scheme is eligible and a qualifying insolvency event occurs (ie the employer enters formal insolvency in Great Britain after 5 April 2005), an 'assessment period' will start.

Eligible schemes

5.1.2   The *Pensions Act 2004* envisages that the PPF will cover all 'eligible schemes'.

An eligible scheme is defined as an occupational pension scheme which:

- is not a money purchase scheme;
- is not a prescribed scheme or a scheme of a prescribed description; and
- is not being wound up immediately before a prescribed date (fixed as 6 April 2005).

The PPF does not, therefore, apply retrospectively to schemes already being wound up or whose winding up has been completed before April 2005.

Schemes which are not eligible schemes include unfunded public service pension schemes, schemes which have a ministerial guarantee, schemes which are not tax registered and schemes with fewer than two members.

A scheme may also cease to be eligible if its trustees enter into a binding agreement with an employer to reduce the amount of a *s 75* debt that is recoverable.

Assessment period

5.1.3   During the assessment period the PPF will look at the scheme to see if it has sufficient funds to meet the protected level of benefits provided by the PPF.

If the scheme does not, and the insolvency practitioner states that a scheme rescue is not possible, the scheme will enter the PPF (the first schemes entered in December 2006).

On entering the PPF, all the assets and liabilities (other than defined benefit liabilities to and in respect of members) of the scheme are transferred (under the *Pensions Act 2004*) to the PPF, which will:

- take over responsibility for the transferred external liabilities; and

- (in theory) take over responsibility for any money purchase benefits; and

- provide compensation at a protected level of benefits to the members who were entitled to defined benefits.

Insolvency event

5.1.4   An insolvency event is defined in *s 121* of *PA 2004* and *reg 5* of the PPF Entry Rules Regulations.[1] The definition is important as it is used for much of *PA 2004* and for the amended employer debt provisions in *s 75* of the *PA 1995* – see *s 75(6C)(a)*.

An insolvency event (in relation to a company) is:

- a nominee submitting a report for a voluntary arrangement under *Pt 1* of the *Insolvency Act 1986 (IA 1986)*;

- the directors of a company filing or lodging with the court documents and statements under *para 7(1)* of *Sch A1* to *IA 1986* dealing with the moratorium on directors proposing a voluntary arrangement;

- an administrative receiver within *IA 1986, s 251* being appointed;

- the company entering administration within the meaning of *para 1(2)(b)* of *Sch B1, IA 1986*;

- a resolution being passed for the voluntary winding-up of the company without a declaration of solvency under *IA 1986, s 89*;

- a creditors' meeting being held under *IA 1986, s 95* to convert an MVL (members' voluntary liquidation) into a CVL (creditors' voluntary liquidation);

- an order for the winding-up of the company being made by the court under *Pt 4* or *5* of IA *1986*;

- an administration order being made by the court in respect of the company by virtue of any enactment which applies *Part 2* of *IA 1986* (administration orders) (with or without modification);

- a notice from an administrator under *para 83(3)* of *Sch B1* to *IA 1986* (moving from administration to creditors' voluntary liquidation) in relation to the company being registered by the registrar of companies;

---

1   *The Pension Protection Fund (Entry Rules) Regulations 2005, SI 2005/590* (the *PPF Entry Rules Regulations*).

5.1.4 *Pension Protection Fund (PPF)*

- the company moving from administration to winding-up pursuant to an order of the court under *r 2.132* of the *Insolvency Rules 1986* (conversion of administration to winding up – power of court); or

- an administrator or liquidator of the company, being the nominee in relation to a proposal for a voluntary arrangement under *Pt 1* of *IA 1986* (company voluntary arrangements), summoning meetings of the company and of its creditors to consider the proposal, in accordance with *IA 1986, s 3(2)* of (summoning of meetings).

The definition of 'insolvency event' includes any winding-up by the court. Such a winding-up could occur in relation to a solvent employer.

The statutory list in *PA 2004, ss 121(2) to (4) and in any regulations under s 121(5) is definitive.*

Although not listed in *PA 2004* or the PPF Entry Rules Regulations, the various insolvency regimes under the *Banking Act 2009* will also count as an insolvency event for these purposes. The same applies to building societies – see the *Building Societies (Insolvency and Special Administration) Order 2009 (SI 2009/805).*

Note that the following are *not* an insolvency event under *s 121*:

- a resolution being passed for a voluntary winding-up with a declaration of solvency (ie a members' voluntary liquidation);

- appointment of a provisional liquidator;

- appointment of a receiver who is not an administrative receiver (eg an LPA receiver);

- entry of the company into a non-UK insolvency proceeding.

Note that a members' voluntary liquidation (MVL) involves a declaration of solvency being given by the directors and so (in principle) the company is not insolvent. MVLs are generally outside the new definition of an 'insolvency event' in the *Pensions Act 2004*, but an MVL triggers a *s 75* debt (see *Debt on the employer*, **3.1** above).

The definition of an 'insolvency event' relates only to insolvency proceedings under the *Insolvency Act 1986* and so will not apply to an insolvency proceeding outside the UK even if applying to a UK company (eg under the *Cross-Border Insolvency Regulations 2006 (SI 2006/1030)*). See *Olympic Airlines*, **9.5** below.

Generally a scheme can only enter an assessment period (or ultimately the PPF) if the employer (or for a multi-employer scheme all the employers) have a qualifying insolvency event occur in relation to them.

Qualifying insolvency event

5.1.5   A qualifying insolvency event in relation to an employer of an eligible scheme is an insolvency event that occurs on or after 6 April 2005. This is irrespective of any previous insolvency event prior to this date.

In addition, in order to be an eligible scheme for entry into the PPF, the scheme must not have commenced wind-up before 6 April 2005.

The guidance on the PPF website summarises the position.

Where there is a multi-employer scheme, the definition of 'qualifying insolvency event' can be modified).

Entering the PPF outside insolvency – s 129

5.1.6   But there is an alternative route available in some (limited) cases. *Sections 128* and *129* of *PA 2004* allow the trustees of a scheme to apply to the PPF if they become aware that the employer in relation to the scheme is unlikely to continue as a going concern. This does not require a formal insolvency of the employer in the UK, but is only available where the prescribed circumstances in *reg 7* of the PPF Entry Rules apply. These are limited to public bodies, charities and trade unions in relation to which it is not possible for an insolvency event (as defined in *PA 2004, s 121*) to occur.

PPF protected benefits

5.1.7   The PPF protected benefits are summarised as set out in the table below (based on a summary on the PPF website):

Compensation

If you are already receiving compensation from the Pension Protection Fund and want information on your personal entitlements, please click here to go to our members' site, where you will find this information and frequently asked questions (FAQs).

The PPF pays different levels of compensation, depending on your circumstances:

If You Have Retired

You will have been receiving a pension from your scheme before your former employer went bust.

5.1.7 *Pension Protection Fund (PPF)*

If you were beyond the scheme's normal retirement age when your employer went bust, the Pension Protection Fund will generally pay 100 per cent level of compensation, which means we will generally pay you the same amount in compensation when your scheme enters the PPF.

Your payments relating to pensionable service from 5 April 1997 will then rise in line with inflation each year, subject to a maximum of 2.5 per cent a year. Payments relating to service before that date will not increase.

This information may also apply if you retired through ill-health or if you are receiving a pension in relation to someone who has died.

If You Retired Early

If you retired early and had not reached your scheme's normal pension age when your employer went bust, then you will generally receive 90 per cent level of compensation based on what your pension was worth at the time. The annual compensation you will receive is capped at a certain level.

The cap at age 65 is, from 1 April 2013, £34,867.04 (this equates to £31,380.34 when the 90 per cent level is applied) per year. The earlier you retired, the lower the annual cap is set, to compensate for the longer time you will be receiving payments.

You can view a full list of the compensation caps for each age here.

Once compensation is being paid, then payments relating to pensionable service from 5 April 1997 will rise in line with inflation each year, subject to a maximum of 2.5 per cent. Payments relating to service before that date will not increase.

If You Have Yet to Retire

When you reach your scheme's normal retirement age, we will pay you compensation based on the 90 per cent level subject to a cap, as described above.

Until you reach retirement age and your compensation is put in payment, your compensation entitlement will rise in line with inflation each year, subject to a cap. See our FAQ about revaluation of compensation while you are a deferred member.

Once compensation is being paid, then payments relating to pensionable service from 5 April 1997 will rise in line with inflation each year, subject to a maximum of 2.5 per cent. Payments relating to service before that date will not increase.

If You Die

After your death, we will pay compensation to any children you may have who are under 18 years old, or under 23 if they are in full-time education or have a disability.

We will also generally pay compensation to any legal spouse, civil partner or other relevant partner. However, individual circumstances may differ depending on the rules of the former pension scheme.

Please read our leaflet on Compensation for Survivors & Children (this link will take you to our member site).

If You Are Divorced

A member's compensation can be shared with their ex-spouse or former civil partner if the court makes a pension compensation sharing order. Please read our leaflet on Compensation and Divorce and information on the associated PPF Divorce Charges for more information. The charges for dealing with a Pension Sharing Order may be different, so you should contact the PPF for more details on these.

Please note, levels of compensation can be altered by the Secretary of State on the advice of the PPF.

Source: PPF website: http://www.pensionprotectionfund.org.uk/Pages/ Compensation.aspx

The Pension Protection Fund has the ability to alter the levy to meet its liabilities. However, in extreme circumstances compensation could be reduced:

● Revaluation and indexation could be reduced by the Pension Protection Fund if circumstances required it.

● Levels of compensation could be reduced by the Secretary of State on the recommendation of the Pension Protection Fund.

Summary of PPF role

5.1.8   The PPF Board summarises its role in its guidance to scheme trustees as follows:

The assessment period

If a qualifying insolvency event occurs in relation to an employer of an eligible scheme, this will trigger the beginning of an assessment period. During this period the Pension Protection Fund will assess whether or not it must assume responsibility for the scheme.

What happens during an assessment period?

During the assessment period the Pension Protection Fund looks to determine whether a scheme is eligible for entry. During this period the scheme continues to be administered by its trustees, subject to various restrictions and controls.

During the assessment period the Pension Protection Fund will look to establish the answer to two main questions:

1   Can the scheme be rescued? (For example, can the original employer continue as a going concern, or is another employer going to take the original employer over and assume responsibility for the scheme?); and

2   Can the scheme afford to secure benefits which are at least equal to the compensation that the Pension Protection Fund would pay if it assumed responsibility for the scheme?

If the answer to either of these questions is 'yes' then the Pension Protection Fund will cease to be involved with the scheme once the relevant processes and procedures have been completed.

However, if the answer to both the questions is 'no', and the relevant process and procedures have been completed, then the Pension Protection Fund will assume responsibility for the scheme and compensation will then become payable.

A Pension Protection Fund assessment period is likely to last a minimum of one year and could be longer, depending on the complexity of the financial situation of both the employer and the scheme, and the possibility of a scheme rescue.

The role of trustees

During an assessment period, the trustees of the scheme retain responsibility for the administration of the scheme and for communicating with and making pension payments to scheme members. The trustees must continue to act in the interests of all the scheme members.

However, during an assessment period, various restrictions and controls will apply in relation to the scheme. In particular, pensions will be restricted to Pension Protection Fund compensation levels [see 'compensation' for more details].

The role of the Pensions Regulator

Once a scheme enters an assessment period, the Pension Protection Fund will work closely with the Regulator, keeping it informed of any relevant developments relating to the scheme. The Regulator may use its powers when problems arise on individual schemes.

For further information on the Pensions Regulator, visit its website at www.thepensionsregulator.gov.uk.

The role of the Pension Protection Fund

During an assessment period, the Pension Protection Fund will undertake a monitoring role in relation to the trustees of the scheme. This is to ensure that the trustees maintain the scheme in an appropriate manner for potential entry to the Pension Protection Fund. In certain circumstances, the Pension Protection Fund can issue directions to trustees in relation to areas such as the investment of the scheme's assets, the incurring of expenditure and the bringing or conduct of legal proceedings.

The Pension Protection Fund will also monitor the progress of the insolvency proceedings, liaising closely with the insolvency practitioner.

Where the Pension Protection Fund ultimately assumes responsibility for a scheme, arrangements will then be made to pay compensation to the scheme members.

Source: PPF website.

Assessment period

5.1.9   An assessment period starts when a qualifying insolvency event occurs. This may well be before the trustees receive the notice from the insolvency practitioner.

The PPF will only confirm that it considers the scheme to be eligible after it receives the notice from the insolvency practitioner (its guidance indicates that it will try to do this within 28 days of receipt of the notice and relevant information, but this validation period is not a fixed period in the legislation).

5.1.9 *Pension Protection Fund (PPF)*

The effect will be to confirm that the assessment period started when the relevant insolvency started.

During the assessment period:

- the PPF Board considers whether or not it needs to take over the pension scheme;

- accrual of benefits and the powers of the trustees are limited during this period:

  - No new members can be admitted.

  - No further contributions can be paid to the scheme – save as prescribed in regulations (or which fell due and payable before the assessment period). Regulations allow an employer to pay further contributions where those contributions relate to:

    (a) all or any part of that employer's liability for any debt due from him to the scheme under *s 75* of *PA 1995* which has not yet been discharged; and

    (b) the value of an asset of the scheme arising from a debt or obligation referred to in *PA 2004*, *s 143(5)(a)* to (*d*) (Board's obligation to obtain valuation of assets and protected liabilities). *Section 143(5)* relates to statutory obligations on an employer under various provisions, including *s 75* of the *PA 1995* and under contribution notices, financial support directions or restoration orders issued by the Pensions Regulator under *PA 2004*.

  - No benefits can accrue, save for an increase which would otherwise accrue in accordance with the scheme or an enactment. This seems to envisage that there will be no additional pensionable service. Money purchase benefits can also accrue.

  - The board of the PPF can give directions to the trustees (or employer or scheme administrator) regarding exercise of his powers in relation to investment of scheme assets, expenditure, conduct of legal proceedings and amendments to the scheme.

  - Schemes cannot start to wind up unless this is ordered by the Pensions Regulator.

  - Transfers out of the scheme can only be made in prescribed circumstances.

  - Contribution refunds (for members whose pensionable service terminates with less than two years qualifying service).

  - Payment of scheme benefits are limited to the amounts that would be protected by the PPF.

- The Board of the PPF is able to validate actions that would otherwise be prohibited (and so void).

- The PPF Board takes control of all rights of the pension scheme trustees as creditors. All relevant documents about creditor status (eg notices of creditor meetings and proof of debt forms) should be sent to the PPF (and not the trustees).

- All payments from the employer should go to the PPF.

The trustees remain responsible for the administration of the scheme.

End of assessment period

5.1.10 The PPF Board ceases to be involved with the scheme (and the assessment period ends) if a withdrawal event occurs. A withdrawal event includes the issuing by an IP of a withdrawal notice confirming that a scheme rescue has occurred.

A withdrawal notice requires the IP to confirm that a scheme rescue has occurred.

An assessment period ends when:

- the PPF Board assumes responsibility for the scheme; or

- a withdrawal notice becomes effective (eg that a scheme rescue has occurred).

According to the PPF guidance for trustees:

The assessment period will conclude with the Board of the Pension Protection Fund assuming responsibility for a scheme when the following conditions have been met:

- A pension scheme rescue is not possible and a scheme failure notice is binding;

- A *section 143* valuation shows that the pension scheme's assets are not sufficient to secure the Pension Protection Fund protected liabilities; and

- The Board of the Pension Protection Fund's approval of the *section 143* valuation is binding.

Within two months of the *section 143* valuation becoming binding the Pension Protection Fund is required to issue a transfer notice.

5.1.10   *Pension Protection Fund (PPF)*

> On receipt of the notice the trustees are discharged of their
> responsibilities for administering the scheme and the assets and
> prescribed liabilities are transferred to the Board of the Pension
> Protection Fund.
>
> The pension scheme is then treated as having wound up.
>
> *Source:* PPF Guidance for Trustees.
> www.pensionprotectionfund.org.uk/TrusteeGuidance/DetailedTrustee
> Guidance/Pages/ResponsibilityforSchemeAssumed.aspx

End of assessment period

5.1.11   At the end of the assessment period:

- If the valuation shows that the scheme assets are sufficient to pay at least
  protected liabilities, the PPF has no further involvement with the scheme
  and the scheme is required to wind-up outside of the PPF.

- If the valuation shows that the scheme assets are insufficient to pay
  protected liabilities, the scheme enters the PPF. The property, rights and
  liabilities transfer to the Board of the PPF and the trustees or managers
  are discharged of their responsibilities towards the scheme and the
  scheme is treated as if it were wound-up.

Source: PPF guidance for trustees: www.pensionprotectionfund.org.uk/index/
TrusteeGuidance/DetailedTrusteeGuidance/Pages/OverviewoftheAssessment
Period.aspx

Pensions and a company entering administration – an overview

5.1.12   The position can get quite complex depending on how many
participating employers are in the scheme and what the scheme rules say.

Assuming that a company is the only employer and it enters administration, the
following happens in relation to the pension scheme:

1   The scheme enters an 'assessment period'. The scheme is frozen during
this period meaning that there is no further accrual of benefits, no
contributions that were not already due are payable (save for any *s 75* debt
– see 5 below) and benefits are only payable out of the scheme at the PPF
protected level. In practice this means that the administrator will stop
deducting contributions from pay. The PPF protected level of benefits is

334

Overview of the assessment period

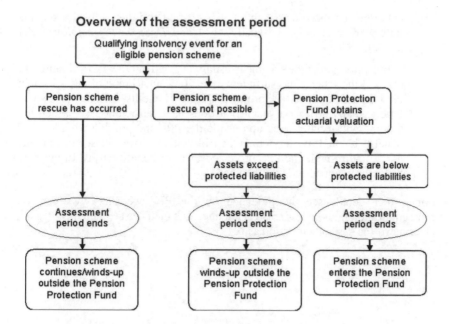

(broadly) 100% of pension (for those aged over the NPA) and 90% of benefits, subject to a cap (of £31,380.34 from 1 April 2013) for those aged under NPA (even those who have retired early). There are special rules on ill-health pensions and on pension increases.

2   The administrator has to notify the trustees, the Pension Protection Fund (PPF) and the Pensions Regulator of his appointment and which schemes are in place. The Regulator may (but does not have to) appoint an independent trustee under *section 23* of the *Pensions Act 1995*. Where they do so, any power vested in the trustees of the scheme and exercisable at their discretion may be exercised only by the independent trustee. See **9.4** below.

3   The trustees stay in place but are subject to direction by the PPF. Any payments due have to be to the PPF.

4   The administrator needs to decide in due course whether or not a scheme rescue will be possible. If it is he serves a 'scheme rescue notice'. A scheme rescue would be if the company exited administration in a solvent form or if someone came in and took over the scheme. If a scheme rescue is not possible, the administrator serves a 'scheme failure notice'.

5   Entry into administration triggers a debt payable by the company under *s 75* of the *Pensions Act 1995* (this is unsecured and non-preferential). The debt is fixed by regulations (and quantified by the scheme actuary) as being the amount needed to fund the scheme up to full buy-out level. This

debt does not become payable until certified and then only if a scheme failure notice has been issued (see 4 and *Debt on the employer*, **3.1** above).

6   A full valuation of the scheme is usually carried out (a *s 143* valuation) to check if the scheme has sufficient assets (taking account of any *s 75* debt recovery) to fund the PPF protected level of benefits. This can take some time (usually at least a year). If it does have sufficient assets, then the scheme will usually wind up outside the PPF and provide what level of benefits it can. If it cannot then the PPF will take over the scheme and its assets and provide the PPF protected level of benefits itself. Either way the assessment period will then end.

For further details see the guidance on the PPF website: www.pension protectionfund.org.uk/index/TrusteeGuidance/DetailedTrusteeGuidance/Pages/OverviewoftheAssessmentPeriod.aspx

5.2 PPF protected benefits

5.2.1

Summary

This section looks at the level of protected benefits currently provided under the Pension Protection Fund when it takes over a scheme (usually following an employer insolvency).

The level of protection can also be relevant before an insolvency – the level of PPF benefit cover is relevant for the levy payable to the PPF and for the priority of benefits on a winding-up.

Schemes which are over 100% funded on the PPF benefit basis may also be exempted from some notifiable events (see *Notifiable events*, **13.1**).

Issues for employers and trustees

5.2.2   The *Pensions Act 2004* established the Pension Protection Fund (PPF) from 6 April 2005. This provides compensation for members of defined benefit (DB) pension schemes which begin winding up after April 2005 where the sponsoring employer is insolvent and leaves unfunded liabilities in the scheme. Employers and trustees need to understand what benefits are protected by the PPF, both where a pension scheme is ongoing and where a pension scheme starts to wind up.

Ongoing scheme

5.2.3   There are two key issues where a scheme is ongoing.

- The PPF imposes a risk-based levy on pension schemes. The calculation of this includes an assessment of the difference between a scheme's assets and its protected liabilities. Trustees have to obtain actuarial valuations addressing this.

- Disclosure requirements require information to be given to members about PPF protection.

5.2.4   *Pension Protection Fund (PPF)*

Scheme in wind-up

5.2.4   Where a scheme winds up with insufficient assets to meet the protected level of liabilities (eg because the employer is insolvent) the assets of the scheme will transfer to the PPF, which will assume responsibility for providing the PPF protected level of benefit to members.

If, however, the scheme has sufficient assets to meet the PPF protected level of liabilities the scheme will not be taken on by the PPF. The trustees will then need to wind up the scheme in accordance with the statutory order of priority. This was amended by the *Pensions Act 2004* so that (generally) priority is given to the protected PPF benefits before other DB benefits.

Benefits payable by the PPF

Basic principles

5.2.5   The protected benefit provisions are set out in *Sch 7* to the *Pensions Act 2004*. The table below summarises the compensation payable to different categories of member.

The broad approach is that the PPF protected benefits will replicate some scheme-specific characteristics for a member's basic benefit (ie based on pension accrued to the start of the assessment period based on accrual rates, pensionable salary and pensionable service as defined in the scheme).

However, the PPF is not intended to replicate all a member's rights and benefits under the scheme. On issues such as dependants' pensions, pension increases and revaluation, the *2004 Act* has taken a 'broad brush' approach (so the same PPF benefit applies to all, regardless of specific scheme rules). This was considered in 2004 by the then government to be 'equitable and ... simpler to administer' (see Malcolm Wicks, Standing Committee B, Hansard, 30 March 2004, column 475).

The PPF protected benefits are summarised as set out in the table below:

Compensation

If you are already receiving compensation from the Pension Protection Fund and want information on your personal entitlements, please click here to go to our members' site, where you will find this information and frequently asked questions (FAQs).

The PPF pays different levels of compensation, depending on your circumstances:

If You Have Retired

You will have been receiving a pension from your scheme before your former employer went bust.

If you were beyond the scheme's normal retirement age when your employer went bust, the Pension Protection Fund will generally pay 100 per cent level of compensation, which means we will generally pay you the same amount in compensation when your scheme enters the PPF.

Your payments relating to pensionable service from 5 April 1997 will then rise in line with inflation each year, subject to a maximum of 2.5 per cent a year. Payments relating to service before that date will not increase.

This information may also apply if you retired through ill-health or if you are receiving a pension in relation to someone who has died.

If You Retired Early

If you retired early and had not reached your scheme's normal pension age when your employer went bust, then you will generally receive 90 per cent level of compensation based on what your pension was worth at the time. The annual compensation you will receive is capped at a certain level.

The cap at age 65 is, from 1 April 2013, £34,867.04 (this equates to £31,380.34 when the 90 per cent level is applied) per year. The earlier you retired, the lower the annual cap is set, to compensate for the longer time you will be receiving payments.

You can view a full list of the compensation caps for each age here.

Once compensation is being paid, then payments relating to pensionable service from 5 April 1997 will rise in line with inflation each year, subject to a maximum of 2.5 per cent. Payments relating to service before that date will not increase.

If You Have Yet to Retire

When you reach your scheme's normal retirement age, we will pay you compensation based on the 90 per cent level subject to a cap, as described above.

5.2.5 *Pension Protection Fund (PPF)*

Until you reach retirement age and your compensation is put in payment, your compensation entitlement will rise in line with inflation each year, subject to a cap. See our FAQ about revaluation of compensation while you are a deferred member.

Once compensation is being paid, then payments relating to pensionable service from 5 April 1997 will rise in line with inflation each year, subject to a maximum of 2.5 per cent. Payments relating to service before that date will not increase.

If You Die

After your death, we will pay compensation to any children you may have who are under 18 years old, or under 23 if they are in full-time education or have a disability.

We will also generally pay compensation to any legal spouse, civil partner or other relevant partner. However, individual circumstances may differ depending on the rules of the former pension scheme.

Please read our leaflet on Compensation for Survivors & Children (this link will take you to our member site).

If You Are Divorced

A member's compensation can be shared with their ex-spouse or former civil partner if the court makes a pension compensation sharing order. Please read our leaflet on Compensation and Divorce and information on the associated PPF Divorce Charges for more information. The charges for dealing with a Pension Sharing Order may be different, so you should contact the PPF for more details on these.

Please note, levels of compensation can be altered by the Secretary of State on the advice of the PPF.

Source: PPF website www.pensionprotectionfund.org.uk/Pages/ Compensation.aspx

Schedule 7, Pensions Act 2004: compensation payable by PPF

5.2.6

	Pensioners over NPA (or ill-health) on assessment date	*Pensioners under NPA on assessment date (not ill-health)*	*Pension benefits postponed after NPA on assessment date*	*Active[2] and deferred members over NPA on assessment date*	*Active members under NPA on assessment date*
Position for member[3]	Entitled to periodic compensation from assessment date for life at 100% (of the annual rate of pension entitlement under the scheme's admissible rules).	Entitled to periodic compensation from assessment date for life at 90% of annual protected pension rate under the scheme's admissible rules.	Entitled to periodic compensation from assessment date for life at 100 % (of the annual rate of pension entitlement under the scheme's admissible rules).	Entitled to periodic compensation from assessment date of 100% (of the annual rate of pension entitlement under the scheme's admissible rules).	Where member survives to NPA, entitled to periodic compensation at 90% of protected notional pension rate (plus revaluation) from NPA for life. The entitlement is revalued between the assessment date and NPA by LPI (capped at 5% for pensionable service to April 2009, and 2.5% for pensionable service after that date).

---

2   Scheme freezes as at the start of the assessment period.
3   The 90% and 100% levels can be changed by regulations enacted by the Secretary of State.

5.2.6   Pension Protection Fund (PPF)

	Pensioners over NPA (or ill-health) on assessment date	Pensioners under NPA on assessment date (not ill-health)	Pension benefits postponed after NPA on assessment date	Active[2]and deferred members over NPA on assessment date	Active members under NPA on assessment date
Compensation cap?[4]	No	Yes	No	No	Yes
Widow/ widower	Entitled upon death of member (on or after assessment date) to half the annual rate/accrued amount that the member was entitled to, save in prescribed circumstances.				
Lump sums on retirement	Not applicable.		Where entitlement to a scheme lump sum is postponed, member entitled to 100% of accrued amount under scheme rules, as long as NPA reached.		Member entitled to 90% of accrued amount (plus revaluation).
Commutation	Not applicable.		Can opt to commute for a lump sum up to 25% of periodic compensation.		
Early payment	Not applicable.			Regulations to prescribe circumstances when can have payment prior to NPA. The cap is reduced to reflect early payment. Board to determine actuarial reduction applicable.	
Dependants[5]	Regulations may provide for compensation for partners and dependants of prescribed descriptions.				
Increases to benefits in payment[6]	Annual increases of lesser of RPI (CPI from 1 January 2012) and 2.5% on post-1997 service only.				

Limitations on compensation payable

5.2.7   There are four important limitations on the compensation payable under the PPF:

---

4   Initially £25,000 pa. Usually increased each year. £31,380.34 (from 1 April 2013) after the 90% has been applied.
5   *The Pension Protection Fund (Compensation) Regulations 2005.*
6   The rates of revaluation or indexation can be changed by the PPF Board.

- Generally, members who have not reached normal pension age (NPA) at the date the scheme enters the PPF process will receive compensation at a rate of 90 per cent of their benefit (as opposed to 100% for members who have already reached normal pension age or ill-health pensioners at that date).

  Normal pension age is defined as the age specified in the scheme as the earliest age at which the pension or lump sum becomes payable without actuarial adjustment (disregarding ill-health rules).

- Members who have not reached normal pension age (and who are not ill-health pensioners), as at the date assessment begins (unless they are in receipt of a pension on the grounds of ill-health) are also subject to a compensation cap.

  At age 65, the cap is, from 1 April 2013, £34,867.04 (this equates to £31,380.34 when the 90% level is applied). The cap is adjusted according to the age at which compensation comes into payment.

- The basic benefit provisions of the scheme rules will apply only to the extent that they are 'admissible'. This excludes recent rule changes, if those rule changes and recent discretionary increases have the combined effect of increasing the protected liabilities of the scheme.

  - 'Recent rule changes' means changes which were made or took effect in the three years before the assessment date and any scheme rules which are triggered by the winding-up of the scheme or insolvency of the employer.

  - 'Recent discretionary increases' are increases which came into effect in the three years before the assessment date.

- Increases to pensions in payment are limited to 2.5% Limited Price Indexation on post-1997 service. This is a lower rate of increase than the scheme was previously required to provide for post 5 April 1997 service under the *Pensions Act 1995*, see *Indexation*, **14.8** below. It may also not reflect rights that the members had under the rules of the old scheme.

The Secretary of State and PPF Board have wide powers to change the compensation payable under the PPF by:

- changing the percentages specified to calculate benefits (ie the 100% and 90% mentioned above); and

- changing the revaluation rate for deferred benefits and/or the level of pension increases.

5.2.8 The *Pensions Bill 2014* envisages changes being made to the PPF compensation limits so that those with longer service (over 20 years) will have an increased limit. Clause 47 and Schedule 19 provide for a revised

5.2.8   *Pension Protection Fund (PPF)*

compensation cap dependent on a person's age and length of pensionable service when the person first becomes entitled to compensation.

If enacted, *Schedule 19* will amend the *Pensions Act 2004* to insert a new paragraph setting out how the compensation cap will be calculated for future compensation calculations. There will be a standard amount (which is expected to be calculated in the same way as the current compensation cap amount) for anyone with pensionable service of 20 years or less. For anyone with 21 years or more pensionable service, the cap will be increased by 3% for each full year, to a maximum of double the standard amount.

5.3   *ITS v Hope*: **High Court rejects a cunning plan to protect pension scheme members**

5.3.1

Summary

In *Independent Trustee Services v Hope,* the High Court held that trustees may not arrange to seek to make a transfer out of a scheme before it entered the PPF with a view to getting better benefits for the transferring members than they would get under the PPF. Such a transfer would not reduce benefits for the remaining members (as the level of their PPF benefits would not be affected), but the court ruled that such a transfer would not be for a proper purpose.

This judgment is likely to cause difficulties with many future actions of trustees and employers. They may need to be judged against a vague and uncertain 'proper purpose' test.

In *Independent Trustee Services v Hope,*[7] Henderson J, in the High Court, held that the trustees of the Ilford pension scheme, a defined-benefit (DB) scheme, could not seek to improve the position of some of the members by buying out part of their benefits with an insurer. The trustees were not allowed to take into account the potential protection of the Pension Protection Fund (PPF) when seeking to partially buy out benefits.

Broadly, the PPF can take over underfunded eligible DB pension schemes if the sponsoring employer has suffered a qualifying insolvency event. The PPF will then use the scheme's assets and its own assets (as a 'top-up') to compensate scheme members by providing benefits, but only up to a protected level. Generally, only members who have reached normal pension age (or retired early due to ill-health) will receive 100% compensation – for further information see *PPF protected benefits,* **5.2**)

Facts of the case

5.3.2   In this case, the scheme was significantly underfunded, the employer was insolvent and the trustees intended to take steps later to cause the scheme to enter the PPF.

---

7   *Independent Trustee Services v Hope* [2009] EWHC 2810 (Ch).

5.3.2 *Pension Protection Fund (PPF)*

The trustees asked the court to rule on whether they could (in an extreme version of the proposal) use all the scheme's assets to buy out benefits for members who would have had a reduced and capped compensation if the scheme entered the PPF.

This would have secured higher benefits for these members than they would have received under PPF compensation. But the buyout would leave no (or disproportionately reduced) assets in the scheme with which to secure benefits for members who had not had their benefits bought out.

In effect, the trustees were proposing this buy-out in the knowledge that once they had taken steps to transfer the scheme to the PPF, the PPF would need to use more of its own assets to protect members who had not been bought out. The buyout would cause a net higher cost for the PPF.

Decision

5.3.3 Henderson J held that the buyout was unlawful for the following main reasons.

- The buyout would use a share of the assets that did not 'fairly represent' the benefits of the members bought out. It would consume a disproportionate amount of the scheme's assets, which (if the PPF did not exist) would prejudice members who had not been bought out. For this to be allowed under the scheme rules it would 'need the clearest possible justification, and equally clear language'.

- The proposed buyout was a 'blatant attempt to undermine or circumvent the policy of the PPF legislation' and was 'inimical to public interest'. This was because the proposal sought to 'minimise, if not eliminate, the Scheme assets which will vest in the PPF, at a time when the Scheme is seriously underfunded'. Furthermore, the proposal treated 'the availability of PPF compensation as though it were an advantage to be exploited for the Scheme's benefit, whereas Parliament clearly intended the PPF to be a funder of last resort which will step in if, and to the extent that, the Scheme is unable to fund PPF level benefits with its own assets'.

- The trustees did not have to consider the PPF's interest because it was not a contingent beneficiary of the scheme. But, in light of the public interest argument, it was a matter of law, in the context of the present case, that 'the prospective availability of compensation under the PPF, if and when the Scheme enters the PPF, is not a relevant factor for the Trustee to take into account' in the exercise of their discretionary powers, and would not be relevant in 'any instance where trustees seek to take advantage of the existence of the PPF as a justification for acting in a way which would otherwise be improper'.

Comment

5.3.4   The facts of this case are unusual because the employer had become insolvent without triggering a qualifying insolvency event for the purpose of PPF protection, and the trustees were the only creditors who had an interest in forcing a further insolvency event. This gave the trustees an unusual ability to control when the employer would suffer a 'qualifying insolvency event', without which the scheme could not enter the PPF. Therefore they had sufficient time to formulate a buy-out proposal before the qualifying insolvency event. Usually the employer itself or another contingent creditor would trigger the insolvency event, which would leave the trustees with insufficient time to formulate a buyout. The judge acknowledged that 'typically, a period of between 15 and 24 months is needed' for a buyout.

Standing back, it seems reasonable (as the judge decided) to protect the PPF in the specific circumstances of this case. Having said that, Henderson J was obviously struggling to find a legal way of reaching his decision. The members pointed out that parliament has enacted a range of protections for the PPF but did not think it necessary to block this route.

The problem with the judgment is that it raises many uncertainties. Henderson J wanted to deter any future attempt to 'take advantage of the existence of the PPF' and held that there was a 'principled basis upon which the court can intervene to nip behaviour of this kind in the bud'. So this decision could have wider relevance. For example, this case may prevent the trustees of a scheme that is funded below the PPF protected level from taking a 'Las Vegas gamble' by making high-risk investments knowing that even if the investments fail, the scheme members will still be protected up to the PPF level.

If this case has wider application, Henderson J's reliance on the 'public interest' arguments creates some uncertainty. It is not clear when this principle can be invoked in the future. For example, it may not always be clear when trustees are allowed to take the PPF into account when buying out benefits, allocating assets during a partial wind-up (eg if only some sections of the scheme are eligible for PPF entry), during a merger (trustees compare the PPF level before and after the merger), commuting pensions for cash or investing the scheme's assets. But this decision will probably not affect buy-ins, because a buy-in policy will still be an asset of the scheme that is available to the PPF.

An odd aspect of this case is that the judge did not explain why a different approach was adopted by the Court of Appeal in the earlier case of *Eastearly v Headway*[8] [2009] (Henderson J did not even refer to this case). In *Eastearly*, the Court of Appeal allowed a different cunning plan – that is, for the trustees to

---

8   *Easterly Ltd v Headway plc* [2009] EWCA Civ 793, [2010] ICR 153. Followed in *Sarjeant v Rigid Group Ltd* [2013] EWCA Civ 1714.

5.3.4 *Pension Protection Fund (PPF)*

carry out a partial buy-out that increased the employer's liability to the scheme. Perhaps there may be less public interest in protecting an employer than in protecting the PPF? But it would have been better if the judgment in *ITS v Hope* had at least dealt with this.

The safest course of action for trustees will be to ask themselves whether it would be reasonable for them to make a particular decision even if the PPF did not exist. Trustees should carefully minute these decisions so that they can later prove that the PPF's existence was not a factor in their decision. If trustees cannot ignore the PPF's existence, they will need advice based on the specific facts of their situation.

In a more recent case, *Dalriada Trustees Ltd v Faulds*[9] Bean J followed a similar proper purpose approach to an investment power (this time to invalidate actions by trustees designed to get round tax rules).

---

9   *Dalriada Trustees Ltd v Faulds* [2011] EWHC 3391 (Ch).

Chapter 6

Corporate transactions (sales, purchases and corporate activity)

6.1 Intra-group transfers – moving employees within a group – pensions implications

Summary

Transfers of employees between companies within a corporate group are common.

This section looks at the implications of a corporate reorganisation should the employees include members of a UK occupational pension scheme maintained by the group.

Reorganisations

6.1.1   It is common for employees to move employment from one company to another within a group. This could be part of:

- a transfer of a business from one group company to another – in this case the relevant employees 'assigned' to that business would usually move under the *Transfer of Undertakings (Protection of Employment) Regulations 2006 (Tupe)*; or

- a transfer of employees from one company to another (without there being a business transfer) – for example as part of a promotion or new group structure.

If there is a UK occupational pension scheme within the group, then the implications of the reorganisation on the group (and the employees) need to be considered. There can be implications even where (say) the benefits and rights

349

of employees are not intended to be changed as a result of the transfer or where the transfer of assets is intended to be broadly neutral from a group perspective.

This section looks at the pensions issues should there be a transfer of employees which is intended to be on a broadly neutral basis with no change to pension benefits. In practice the intention may be to be able to say to the employees that the transfer will not change their pension benefits (and that they will remain active members of the group pension scheme).

Transfer of a business from one group company to another, including employees

6.1.2   *Tupe* will apply if there is a business transfer from one company to another. It is clear that *Tupe* applies in relation to employees where there is a transfer of a UK-based business, even if the transfer is within a wholly owned group of companies.

The general principle of *Tupe* is that rights under or relating to an occupational pension scheme do not transfer (*reg 10*). Benefits which are not for old age, invalidity or survivors (eg redundancy pensions) may transfer under the *Beckmann* principle[1] (see *Tupe and pensions: transfer of early retirement benefits*, **6.6**)

This does not prevent the employers agreeing that pension continuity should be provided. See for example *Whitney v Monster Worldwide Ltd*.[2]

The following pension issues should be considered:

---

1   *Beckmann v Dynamco Whicheloe Macfarlane Ltd* (C-164/00) [2002] ECR I-4893.
2   [2010] EWCA Civ 1312.

	Issue	Legal analysis	Action
1.	Participation in group pension scheme	The new employer will need to be (or become) a participating employer in the group pension scheme.	Check if new employer participates. If not, deed of participation will be needed (trustee consent is commonly required) – see the further practical issues outlined below and *Participation in pension schemes: new group company participation legal issues,* **10.2.**
2.	Continuity of benefits	Does move from one participating employer to another maintain continuity of benefits?	Common rule – but need to check scheme rules.
3.	Enhanced benefit trigger?	Some schemes give enhanced benefits to members in certain circumstances, including perhaps redundancy or cessation of employment at the request of the employer. Such provisions should be considered as to whether they could be triggered by an intra-group transfer, potentially (although this is less common) even if the employees transfer under *Tupe* (and so are not dismissed) and/or retain their membership of the existing pension scheme.	Consider scheme rules.

6.1.2 *Corporate transactions (sales, purchases and corporate activity)*

	Issue	Legal analysis	Action
4.	*Pensions Act* obligations re benefits	The *Pensions Act 2004* imposes obligations on transferee employers where there is a transfer under *Tupe* of members who were active in an occupational pension scheme before the transfer.	Check if benefit level satisfies *Pensions Act* requirements.
		The obligation is to offer a minimum level of pension benefits for future service.	
		If the group scheme is contracted out on a salary-related basis, then the continuing membership of the scheme with the new employer should satisfy these requirements.	
		But if the scheme is not contracted out, then an obligation may arise under the *PA 2004* provisions.	
		Similarly, if the scheme is money purchase, the obligation under the *2004 Act* is for matching benefits up to 6percent of pay. This would apply even if it is greater than the previous level of money purchase obligations – but the position will change if/when the *Transfer of Employment (Pension Protection) (Amendment) Regulations 2013* (which have currently only been published in draft) come into force. These will amend the requirements under the *PA 2004* provisions so as to give the transferor a choice between matching the contributions made by (a) the transferor immediately before the transfer or (b) the transferring employee (still subject to the 6% cap).	
		For further details see *Tupe and Pensions: Pensions Act 2004 obligations*, **6.4**.	

	Issue	Legal analysis	Action
5.	Consultation with employees	*Pensions Act*: if the relevant employees remain members of the same pension scheme as before, there will be no obligation to consult under the *Pensions Act 2004* consultation requirements. However, if benefits are to change (or the scheme is to change) a consultation obligation may arise– see *Pensions Act 2004: employers' consultation obligations*, **15.1**. *Tupe*: if any 'measures' are proposed in relation to pensions, a consultation obligation may arise under *Tupe* (the consultation obligations apply to pension benefits even though the transfer provisions generally do not).	Consider if any pension benefit changes envisaged. Consider employee communications carefully (can have contractual implications).
6.	Wages deductions	If the pension scheme is contributory, continuing authority is needed to make deductions from employees' wages for the purposes of *Part 2* of the *Employment Rights Act 1996*. Any existing authorisation may well not transfer under *Tupe*.	Check authority terms.
7.	Notice to Trustees	The transfer of employees may be a material event (egif no active members remain with the old employer or if material change in employer covenant). Employers are obliged to inform trustees of material events within one month (*Scheme Administration Regulations 1996, reg 6*). May need trustee consent (egif new employer needs to become a participating employer – see 1 above – or need to deal with *s 75* debt – see 9 below).	Consider informing trustees before transfer. Consider any express employer/trustee information agreements.
8.	Notice to Pensions Regulator	If the current employer is to cease carrying on business in the UK (egbecause all its current business is to transfer) then this is a notifiable event requiring notification (when the decision is made) to TPR (see *Pensions Act 2004, s 69* and *Notifiable Events: Obligation to report certain events to the Pensions Regulator*), **13.1**.	Give notice to the Regulator. Consider likely *s75* issue – see 9 below.

6.1.2 *Corporate transactions (sales, purchases and corporate activity)*

	Issue	*Legal analysis*	*Action*
9.	*Section 75 debts?*	Is the effect of the transfer that the current employer ceases to have any employees who are active members of the relevant occupational scheme (whether or not other employees may remain with the existing employer)? If so, and the scheme is multi-employer, this will be an employment-cessation event (ECE) under *s 75* of *the Pensions Act 1995* (as amended) and a debt is likely to arise on the current employer. The *s 75* debt will need to be paid, apportioned or modified – see *Multi-Employer Pension Schemes and Section 75 Debts,* **3.2.** If the current employer is the only employer, the scheme will not be a multi-employer scheme and so there will be no ECE. Similarly, if all members in the pension scheme are currently deferred or pensioner members and there are no active members, then the cessation of employment and move to the new employer will not be an ECE.	Check if *s 75* debt is triggered. If it is, consider how to deal with it (eg utilise grace period).
10.	Impact on employer covenant	The trustees may be concerned about the impact of the transfer on the strength of the sponsoring companies supporting the scheme. This will depend on the financial circumstances of the current employer compared with the new employer.	Consider impact. Inform or consult with trustees as appropriate.
11.	Impact on security/ funding agreements etc	Does the transfer impact on any existing security or the funding arrangements? Any existing contingent asset security for the trustees (eg a guarantee from another group company) will need to be considered – if the new employer was not previously a participating employer, does it need to be included within the ambit of any existing security? If the security is Pension Protection Fund (PPF) qualifying, the PPF may need to be told of the change	Consider impact. Inform or consult with trustees or PPF as appropriate.

	Issue	Legal analysis	Action
12.	PPF levy	The change of employer may result in a change to the relevant rating score of the employers for PPF levy purposes. This needs to be considered. The change in employer may be an event requiring notification to the PPF?	Consider impact on PPF scores/levy.

6.2   Corporate sales and purchases – overview

Summary

This section gives a broad overview of the implications for the parties to a sale or purchase of a company or business where there is an existing occupational pension scheme.

Further details are in the other sections in this chapter.

Company and business sales

6.2.1   In the UK, pension schemes can be a key focus of negotiations on mergers and acquisitions. The comments below relate only to tax-registered occupational pension schemes but issues also arise with unapproved schemes and group personal pensions (GPPs).

The effect of a disposal on the employees' contracts of employment and their pension entitlements will depend on whether it is a company sale (where the issued share capital (stock) of a company or group of companies is sold) or an asset sale. Where a sale of assets amounts to the sale of a business or 'undertaking', the *Transfer of Undertakings (Protection of Employment) Regulations 2006 (Tupe)*, the UK regulations which implement the *EU Acquired Rights Directive*, may apply to transfer employees (and their contracts of employment) to the purchaser and protect their employment rights, see *Tupe: the general rules*, **6.3**. The general principle of *Tupe* is that rights under or relating to an occupational pension scheme do not transfer (*reg 10*). However, following the judgments of the European Court of Justice in *Beckmann* and *Martin* it is now clear that some pension rights also transfer automatically on a business sale (see *Tupe and Pensions: Transfer of early retirement benefits*, **6.6**). Employers cannot opt out of the application of *Tupe*.

The treatment of the pension scheme on a sale depends on whether the scheme has one or more participating employers and, if more than one (a multi-employer scheme), whether or not the employer being sold is the principal employer for the scheme. The pension scheme attaches to the principal employer.

Where the pension scheme goes across with the principal employer

6.2.2   Where the principal employer itself is sold (a share sale), the pension scheme stays with the principal employer and so automatically goes across with that company to the purchaser's group. If more than one employer participates in the scheme, any participating employers retained by the seller will in practice cease participating, and must make alternative arrangements. On a business sale, if all or most of the employees participating in the plan transfer to the purchaser, it may make sense for the purchaser to adopt the plan as well, by a substitution of principal employer.

The seller and purchaser should account for the funding position of the scheme (ie whether it is in surplus or deficit) as part of the valuation of the company or business and setting the purchase price. Alternatively, funding indemnities may be agreed and the scheme valued after the sale has completed.

Where the pension scheme does not transfer with the employer

6.2.3   If the company being sold is part of a group pension scheme and is not the principal employer, or there is a business sale where employees transfer to the purchaser, the general principle is that the transferring employees will cease to participate in the seller's scheme for future service. There are a number of options for dealing with future pension arrangements and, separately, with the benefits employees have already accrued prior to the sale.

Do nothing

6.2.4   The sale agreement could be silent on pension matters. Transferring employees with vested rights would automatically have their benefits preserved in the seller's pension scheme until they reach retirement age. In a final salary scheme, their pension benefits would be based on their service and salaries at the time of sale, revalued broadly in line with inflation until actual retirement. In a defined contribution (DC) scheme, the member's account remains invested until retirement age.

Members may be able to elect for a transfer value (based on their past service benefits) to their new employer's arrangement in the future, or to a personal pension plan.

The purchaser would still need to consider what to do for the future, taking into account any contractual rights of the employees, *Tupe* requirements and general human resources issues (including any issues relating to obligations under the automatic enrolment legislation – see *Auto-enrolment: issues for employers,* **19.1**). If the purchaser already has pension arrangements in place, they may be offered to the transferred employees. If there is no existing scheme, it is becoming common for employers to favour group personal pension arrangements for the future.

The seller will also need to consider the effect on its retained workforce of appearing not to protect transferring employees' interests.

Arrangements for the past: transfer payments

6.2.5 The parties can agree in the sale agreement that a bulk transfer payment will be made from the seller's pension scheme to transfer past service liabilities of the transferring employees to a purchaser's replacement scheme. Member consent to the transfer is normally sought and it is usually only active employees who are involved.

From the employees' perspective, this allows their past service benefits to be joined up with future service benefits and, in a defined benefit (DB) scheme, to apply future salary increases to the whole of their accrued service entitlement. This used to be a popular method of dealing with pension scheme liabilities but is now less common.

The terms for the transfer are usually set out in a schedule to the sale agreement, which will also specify how the payment should be calculated (usually in an annexed actuary's letter). There is a wide range of practice in the UK on how the transfer payment could be calculated. The actuarial assumptions and methodology to be used are negotiated between the seller's and the purchaser's actuaries.

Assumptions which are appropriate to the asset and liability profile of the transferring fund may produce a deficit or surplus in a receiving fund with a different profile.

As noted above, the pension fund is a separate entity from the seller and usually the trustees who administer the pension fund will not be party to the sale agreement. However, they often have control over the ultimate transfer payment to the purchaser's scheme (eg because the making of transfer payments is subject to trustee consent under the rules of the pension scheme). This can lead to a potential problem if the trustees refuse to make the payment on the terms agreed in the sale agreement (eg if the funding level of the scheme has dropped by the time the transfer is finally due, which can be some time after the original sale occurred). A common solution to this risk is for the sale agreement to include a shortfall clause – the seller underwrites any shortfall in the actual amount transferred by the trustees compared with the negotiated transfer amount. Historically seen simply as part of delivering value for the purchase price, these guarantees are now beginning to bite as fund values drop.

The parties will also negotiate the level of benefits which must be provided in the receiving fund in return for the transfer. These could be benefits which mirror those transferred, benefits of equivalent value to the benefits transferred, or benefits equivalent in value to the transfer payment. However, if the agreed valuation basis does not match the basis on which the receiving scheme actually funds benefits, there may be a funding shortfall in the receiving scheme.

Special arrangements may be needed for individual benefit promises given to highly paid individuals.

Arrangements for the future: future service benefits

6.2.6   The seller may, for human resources reasons, wish to require the purchaser to provide a particular type of pension arrangement for future service by the purchaser. It is usual to limit the period for which future benefits will be as specified.

If the transfer is a *Tupe* transfer, the purchaser may also be required to provide a certain level of future service benefits under the *Pensions Act 2004* requirements (see **6.2.7** below).

Pensions Act 2004 requirements if there is a Tupe transfer

6.2.7   Where the transferred employee was accruing benefits in a DB scheme before the transfer, or was accruing benefits in a defined contribution (DC) scheme to which the employer made contributions (or, in either case, if they were eligible to be a member or in a waiting period), the purchaser is obliged to offer either a DB or DC scheme for the accrual of future service benefits after the transfer.

Where the employee qualifies for protection, it is up to the transferee employer to choose what type of pension provision to make: *either* a DB scheme of a specified standard or a DC scheme to which the employer contributes at a specified rate.

If a DC scheme is offered, the purchaser must match employee contributions up to 6% of the employee's basic pay.

But the position will change if/when the *Transfer of Employment* (*Pension Protection*) (*Amendment*) *Regulations 2013* (which have currently only been published in draft) come into force. These will amend the requirements under the *Pensions Act 2004* provisions so as to give the transferor a choice between matching the contributions made by: (a) the transferor immediately before the transfer or (b) the transferring employee (still subject to the 6% cap).

If a DB scheme is offered, the purchaser must provide a scheme giving a certain level of benefit accrual. Broadly this is satisfied if either:

6.2.7 *Corporate transactions (sales, purchases and corporate activity)*

- the value of the benefits is at least 6% of pensionable pay per year of service in addition to the member's contribution (and the employees are not required to contribute (if at all) more than 6% of pensionable pay); or

- the purchaser makes matching contributions of up to 6% of the employee's basic pay.

The employee and the transferee employer (purchaser) may agree to contract out of these obligations and agree alternative arrangements. They can do this at any time *after* the employee becomes employed by the transferee.

See further *Tupe and pensions: Pensions Act 2004 Obligations*, **6.4**.

Temporary participation

6.2.8 It is possible for a company or business being sold to continue to participate in the seller's scheme for a temporary period following the completion of the sale, even though it is no longer related to the principal employer. This is commonly known as an interim period or a transitional participation period. This allows the buyer time to set up replacement pension arrangements and minimise disruption to employees' benefit arrangements. The terms of any such extended participation will need to be negotiated between the parties to the sale, and each will need certain assurances and protections against actions of the other during that period which might have cost implications for them.

Funding issues

6.2.9 Where an employer leaves a multi-employer scheme or otherwise ceases to have active members in the scheme and that scheme is in deficit on the buy-out basis (ie the level required to purchase annuities with an insurance company for all scheme members), an immediate statutory withdrawal debt is triggered on the departing employer (known as a *s 75* debt or employer debt, from *s 75* of the *Pensions Act 1995*). The debt is owed by the departing employer to the trustees of the scheme, and is a proportion of the total deficit in the scheme – see *Multi-employer pension schemes and section 75 debts*, **3.2** above. The parties to the sale may negotiate for the liability to be reallocated as between the parties. If there is a transitional participation period, the debt, if any, will be triggered at the end of this period, rather than on completion of the deal, as this is when the employer actually leaves the scheme.

This is a key issue on sales as potentially very large debts can be triggered. There are ways of mitigating the debt which may be relevant in particular circumstances. They would usually involve the consent of TPR and are likely to be negotiated with the trustees, which may have timing implications.

Whether or not there is a *s 75* debt and whether the whole scheme transfers or a transfer payment is made to a replacement scheme, the true underlying value of the company or business being acquired will be affected by any surplus or deficit in the seller's scheme. Future pension costs (ie the employer contributions which may be needed in the future) may differ significantly from historical experience. Pension costs should be carefully considered when fixing the purchase price for a business. In addition, warranties may be appropriate in order to flush out any unknown liabilities not already taken into account in the valuation of the pension fund.

6.3 *Tupe* – the general rules

Summary

The *Transfer of Undertakings (Protection of Employment) Regulations 2006 (Tupe)* protects employees' rights on business transfers (and service provision changes) in the UK. *Tupe* itself is based on the *Acquired Rights Directive*. As a result, its application is influenced not only by UK case law but also by decisions of the ECJ.

This section summarises when *Tupe* applies and its consequences for both employer and employee.

Glossary	
Tupe	*Transfer of Undertakings (Protection of Employment) Regulations 2006*
Acquired Rights Directive (ARD)	Directive No 2001/23 on the approximation of the laws of the Member States relating to the safeguarding of employees' rights in the event of transfers of undertakings, businesses or parts of businesses (as amended)
ECJ	European Court of Justice
EAT	Employment Appeal Tribunal

When does Tupe apply?

6.3.1 *Tupe* applies automatically to any transfer of all or part of a trade or business situated in the UK, as long as the business constitutes an economic entity that retains its identity after the transfer. An economic entity is defined as 'an organised grouping of resources which has the objective of pursuing an economic activity'. Courts and tribunals take a wide view on what constitutes such a transfer. It is not possible to contract out of the application of *Tupe*.

Tupe can apply to business transfers in any form, including:

- transfers of commercial and non-commercial ventures;

- contracting out (where an owner of a business entrusts another to take over the provision of services or switches between contractors) or subsequently takes a service back in-house;

- intra-group reorganisations;

- transfers of part of an undertaking – even though the part may be ancillary to the transferor's overall business (eg transfer of the operation of a canteen by a manufacturing business); and

- a transfer involving a change in the person responsible for carrying on the business (who also assumes the role of employer of the employees concerned) irrespective of whether or not ownership in the business is transferred and whether or not any property is transferred. This could include the termination and re-grant of a franchise or concession.

Tupe will *not* apply:

- to a transfer of shares in a company (see Appendix at **6.3.29** for a comparison of the principal employment law issues on share sales and business transfers); or

- to a transfer of assets alone (without a business that could constitute an 'economic activity') – sometimes it can be difficult to distinguish between a sale of mere assets and the transfer of a business.

Contracting out of services

6.3.2   *Tupe* can also apply to the contracting out of services (where the owner of a business appoints another to take over the provision of services), second-generation or subsequent outsourcing (where there is a change of contractor) and contracting in (where the owner takes the service back in-house). These are each called a 'service provision change'.

Any 'service provision change' will amount to a transfer if:

- there is an 'organised grouping' of employees;

- the 'principal purpose' of which is to carry out activities on behalf of the client; and

- the activities continue after the transfer and are not in connection with a single specific event, or task, of short-term duration.

These conditions should ensure that *Tupe* operates wherever an organised grouping of employees provides a service to a particular client (eg provision of a staff canteen for a particular organisation). Situations where a customer is serviced by a variety of employees on an ad hoc basis, or where a dedicated team provides services to a number of different clients, are not caught.

6.3.3   *Corporate transactions (sales, purchases and corporate activity)*

The principal effects of Tupe

6.3.3   If *Tupe* applies to a business transfer (or service provision change):

- the contracts of employment of employees of the transferor engaged in the business (or providing the service) automatically transfer to the transferee;

- all the employer's rights, powers, duties and liabilities (subject to certain narrow exclusions) under or in connection with such contracts pass to the transferee;

- employees' continuity of employment is preserved;

- employees have a right to object to transferring to the transferee;

- any dismissals made where the reason (or principal reason) is the business transfer will be automatically unfair;

- both the transferor and transferee have obligations to inform and, in some cases, consult representatives of their respective employees; and

- collective agreements and recognition arrangements entered into by the transferor with trade unions will normally transfer to the transferee.

Who transfers?

6.3.4   *Regulation 4* operates to transfer to the transferee the contracts of employment of all employees employed by the transferor in the business immediately before the transfer 'whose employment would otherwise have been terminated by the transfer'.

Employees the transferor wishes to retain

6.3.5   There is an argument that a transferor is not required to part with employees whom he wishes to continue to employ after the business transfer because their employment with the transferor continues notwithstanding the business transfer. Provided that the ongoing duties of these employees fall within the duties agreed to under their existing contract of employment, it may be that such employees cannot insist on transferring with the business.

In the *Sunley Turiff case*,[3] however, the EAT held that a transferor intending to retain an employee employed in the business to be transferred should obtain his express consent. Certainly, where the retained employee will be required to

---

3   *Sunley Turriff Holdings Ltd v Thomson* [1995] IRLR 184.

364

perform different duties following the transfer, the employer should gain his express consent to prevent *Tupe* from transferring him (and his employment) to the transferee.

Mismatched employees

6.3.6 *Regulation 4* applies to employees 'employed by the transferor'. Accordingly, it could be argued that mismatched employees – those who technically have no contract of employment with the transferor but who nevertheless work in the transferring business – will not be transferred by *Tupe*. This issue often arises in corporate structures where all the group's employees are employed by a service company. Unless resolved, the transferor risks being overmanned after the transfer and possibly facing a redundancy programme. In contrast, the transferee may be left without key members of the workforce.

Alternatively, even if mismatched employees agree to accept employment with the transferee, they may not be transferred by the operation of *Tupe*. In that case they might become entitled to statutory (or contractual) redundancy payments from the transferor following the termination of their employment. Intra-group employee transfers can usually be structured so that they do not trigger statutory redundancy entitlements.

In practice, the courts are likely to adopt a flexible approach to the issue of mismatched employees. In several cases, tribunals and courts have ignored the formal legal position and looked at whether the employee was actually working for the part of the business transferred.[4] However, tribunals will not necessarily be consistent in their approach especially if it is to employees' advantage to argue that they have not transferred (eg to benefit from severance payments).

Until this issue is resolved, the safest action is to 'match up' the mismatched employees with the business in which they work. This is achieved by obtaining the employees' agreement to an intra-group transfer before the business transfer. It is important to address the issue before the transfer to preserve employees' continuity of employment.

Employees with split duties

6.3.7 As *reg 4* applies to employees 'assigned' to the economic entity being transferred, difficulties can arise in determining the application of *Tupe* to employees with split duties and responsibilities. Such employees perform some

---

4 See the decision of the ECJ in *Albron Catering BV v FNV Bondgenoten* (C-242/09) [2011] 1 CMLR 1267.

duties in the business being transferred and other duties in the business retained by the transferor.

Although it will be necessary to consider each situation on its own facts, the ECJ in *Botzen*[5] confirmed that the *Acquired Rights Directive* does not apply to employees of the transferor who are assigned to other departments or divisions that are not themselves included in the business to be transferred (such as general administration or personnel). Accordingly, such employees will not automatically transfer with the business even where they had previously performed some duties for the transferred departments or divisions. This still leaves open the question of how to determine to which part of the undertaking a person is assigned.

In *Duncan Web Offset (Maidstone) Limited v Cooper*[6] the EAT indicated that there were no hard and fast rules, but that the following factors would be relevant:

- the amount of time spent in differing parts of the business;

- the amount of value given to the part;

- the terms of the contract; and

- how the cost of the employee's service had been allocated in the company accounts.

In *Northern General Hospital NHS Trust v Gale*[7] the Court of Appeal held that an employee who simply happened, at a particular time, to be temporarily employed at a hospital could not be said to be assigned there at the time of transfer.

Employees dismissed immediately before the transfer

6.3.8   *Tupe* applies to employees 'employed … immediately before the transfer or who would have been so employed' if they had not been dismissed:

- because of the transfer; or

- for a reason related to the transfer that was not an economic, technical or organisational reason entailing changes in the workforce.

The transferee will usually become liable for claims arising out of such dismissals.

---

5   *Botzen v Rotterdamsche Droogdok Maatschappij BV* (C-186/83) [1985] ECR 519.
6   *Duncan Web Offset (Maidstone) Ltd v Cooper* [1995] IRLR 633.
7   [1994] ICR 426.

Employee's right to object

6.3.9   Employees have the right to object to the transfer under two separate provisions.

- *Regulation 4(9)* expressly allows an employee to resign from his employment and treat himself as dismissed if the transfer 'involves or would involve a substantial change in working conditions to his material detriment'.[8] This right is more extensive than has previously been available (eg extending to changes in opportunities to earn non-contractual commission) and allows an employee to treat himself as dismissed even though there has been no breach of his contract of employment. Therefore an employer must be careful if it changes working conditions (eg altering employees' duties or the basis of exercising any discretion, such as discretionary bonuses) in connection with a *Tupe* transfer. If changes are to the employees' material detriment, the employer risks facing unfair dismissal claims.

- *Regulation 4(7)* confers a right on an employee employed in the business to be transferred to object to becoming an employee of the transferee even where there are no changes to working conditions.

Regulation 4(8) provides that the employment of an employee who exercises the right to object under *reg 4(7)* will be terminated but the employee 'shall not be treated, for any purpose, as having been dismissed by the transferor'. In other words, they are effectively treated as having resigned and no claims can arise for statutory redundancy pay or unfair dismissal. For this reason, employees are likely to find this option unattractive. However, the Court of Appeal ruled in *University of Oxford v Humphries*[9] that an objecting employee could succeed with an unfair dismissal claim against a transferor if the transfer would result in a breach of the employee's terms and conditions (and their right to resign and claim constructive dismissal is now covered in *reg 4(11)*). This may surprise an unwary transferor, as employees can bring actions against it on the basis of anticipated actions by the transferee, even if the transferor made no changes to terms and conditions itself. Obtaining indemnity protection will be important for transferors in this situation.

If employees exercise their right to object, the transferee could be deprived of key personnel whose experience may be crucial to the future success of the undertaking.

Depending on the circumstances, a transferee may consider seeking binding commitments from key employees before the transfer confirming their

---

8   But not extending to changes in occupational pension schemes – see *reg 10(3)*.
9   [2000] 1 All ER 996, [2000] IRLR 183.

intention to transfer. From a practical point of view, the transferee may want to consider offering incentives to ensure that key employees remain with the business post-transfer.

However, employers should be wary of using the right of objection in *reg 4(7)* to circumvent *Tupe*. In *Senior Heat Treatment v Bell*,[10] employees of the transferor of a business were given three options: they could be re-employed by the transferor, transfer to the purchaser on existing terms, or exercise their right to object to the transfer and accept a severance package. Employees who chose the last option signed a form stating that they objected to the transfer. Many of them also accepted jobs with the purchaser and, when they were subsequently made redundant by the purchaser, they claimed redundancy payments based on their service with both the transferor and transferee. The EAT decided that because the employees had accepted jobs with the purchaser before the business transfer took place, they could not be said to have objected to their employment transferring under *Tupe* and their transfer to the purchaser did not therefore break the continuity of their employment. Redundancy payments therefore had to be calculated by reference to the original start date. In practice, the safest course is often to dismiss the employee and enter into a settlement agreement for his unfair dismissal claim.

Employees not told about the transfer

6.3.10 In *Secretary of State for Trade and Industry v Cook*[11] the EAT confirmed that *Tupe* will operate to transfer an employee's contract to the transferee even where the employee is not given notice of the transfer or the identity of the transferee. It refused to follow a previous case that *Tupe* did not apply in these circumstances because an employee could not exercise his right to object to the transfer unless he had been told about it.

What rights and liabilities transfer?

6.3.11 All rights, powers, duties and liabilities under the employee's contract transfer, subject to certain exclusions. This includes liabilities arising before the transfer (eg unpaid wages). For this reason the transferee will normally require the transferor to warrant that there are no outstanding liabilities and/or undertake to indemnify the transferee against any such liabilities.

---

10 *Senior Heat Treatment Ltd v Bell* [1997] IRLR 614.
11 [1997] ICR 288, [1997] IRLR 150.

Due diligence

6.3.12 *Tupe* contains a legal obligation on the transferor to provide certain information about transferring employees to the transferee. The information that has to be provided is set out in *reg 11* and covers:

- the identity and age of the employees concerned;

- their particulars of employment;

- details of any disciplinary procedure taken by an employer or any grievance procedure initiated by an employee in the last two years;

- details of any court or tribunal proceedings brought by an employee against the employer in the past two years;

- information of any reasonable grounds the employer has to believe an employee may bring court or tribunal proceedings arising out of his employment; and

- information relating to any collective agreements that apply to those employees and that will have effect after the transfer.

Information has to be provided at least 14 days (to be extended to 28 days from 31 January 2014)[12] before completion of the transfer, unless it is not reasonably practicable to do so. Any changes to the information, once notified, must be given in writing.

If a transferee successfully complains about a failure to provide information, the employment tribunal will award it 'just and equitable' compensation having regard to any loss attributable to the matters complained of (*reg 12*). Minimum compensation of £500 per employee in respect of whom information has not been provided will be awarded, unless it is just and equitable to award a lesser sum. There is no upper limit on compensation.

It is not uncommon in transactions for the parties to agree that the indemnities and warranties in the sale agreement will be relied on for the purposes of any action about failure to provide the information envisaged by *reg 11* (to the exclusion of the right under *reg 12*).

Liabilities that will not transfer

6.3.13 These include:

- criminal liabilities of the transferor in relation to the employees; and

---

12 *The Collective Redundancies and Transfer of Undertakings (Protection of Employment) (Amendment) Regulations 2014 (SI 2014/16).*

- occupational pension scheme rights (see below).

Originally it was thought that a transferor's liability for a failure to comply with his statutory obligations to inform and consult employees would not pass to the transferee under *Tupe*. However, more recent cases make it clear that such liability transfers. Purchasers are likely to require indemnity protection.

Dismissal rights

6.3.14 Statutory rights (eg to unfair dismissal or redundancy) will not normally be triggered by a *Tupe* transfer. This is because there is no dismissal. However, *Tupe* may not be effective to exclude rights of transferring employees to contractual redundancy schemes or severance pay. In any particular case, the wording of the relevant scheme should be considered carefully: if, for example, severance rights are payable on the 'cessation of employment' with a particular company or corporate group, the 'cessation test' may be satisfied even if an employee's employment is transferred by *reg 4* to the new owners. As he will 'cease to be employed' by his previous employer, his entitlement to contractual redundancy or severance pay may be triggered.

Pensions

6.3.15 An employee's right to participate in an occupational pension scheme does not transfer under *Tupe* with the rest of his employment rights. However, since April 2005, transferees have been obliged under the *Pensions Act 2004* and underlying regulations to provide pension benefits for transferring employees if there was an occupational pension scheme in place before the transfer. The transferee can choose to put either a defined benefit or a defined contribution scheme in place as long as certain minimum standards are met. For more information, see *Tupe and pensions: Pensions Act 2004 obligations,* **6.4**.

However, there may still be some situations in which an employee can claim pre-transfer pension benefits. The exclusion in *reg 10* relates only to occupational pension schemes and not to personal pension schemes. Therefore, if the transferor has contracted to contribute to an employee's personal pension scheme, the exclusion in *reg 10* will not apply and the transferor's obligation to contribute to such an arrangement will be transferred to the transferee.

Moreover, the exclusion in *reg 10* is limited to ensure that *reg 4* will still apply to any provisions of an occupational pension scheme 'which do not relate to benefits for old age, invalidity or survivors'.

For example, in the public sector (but not generally in the private sector), it is common for pension schemes to include additional rights on redundancy of employees. *Regulation 10* aims to put beyond doubt the fact that employee rights to redundancy compensation automatically transfer by virtue of *reg 4* even if contained in a pension scheme. Various decisions of the ECJ have also indicated that non 'old age' benefits will transfer because these do not fall within the excluded categories. It had been suggested, although the point has never been considered by the courts, that where a transferee makes no, or reduced, future pension provision, employees could bring claims (under *reg 4(9)* – see above) for constructive dismissal on the basis that there has been a substantial change in their working conditions to their detriment. *Regulation 10(3)* now makes it clear that such claims will not be successful against a transferor. See further *Tupe – transfer of non 'old age' benefits: Beckmann, Martin and Procter & Gamble*, **6.6**.

Collective agreements

6.3.16   Collective agreements entered into by the transferor with recognised trade unions are transferred and have effect as if originally made between the transferee and the trade unions concerned (*reg 5*). Trade union recognition arrangements are also transferred, provided that the undertaking transferred maintains a distinct identity in the future (*reg 6*). In any case, under *reg 4*, the transferee may still be bound by any terms of collective bargaining agreements that have been incorporated into employees' contracts.

In *Whent v Cartledge*[13] employees' pay was determined by an industry-wide collective agreement. The transferee de-recognised the union after buying the business and told employees that pay would in future be determined on an individual basis. However, the EAT decided that because of the wording of the contractual entitlement the transferee was obliged to pay the rates determined by the collective bargaining agreement until such time as it negotiated variations to the employees' contracts. In practice the decision of the House of Lords in *Wilson v St Helen's Borough Council*[14] may make such negotiations very difficult (and see **6.6.10** below).

In 2013, the ECJ ruled in *Alemo-Herron v Parkwood Leisure Ltd*[15] that employees who have *Tupe* transferred are not entitled to benefit from collectively agreed terms where such terms are agreed after the date of transfer and where the transferee is not a party to the collective negotiations. This decision, which endorsed the 'static' interpretation of collective agreements on a *Tupe* transfer, was welcomed by employers. With effect from 2014, the

---

13   *Whent v T Cartledge Ltd* [1997] IRLR 153.
14   *Wilson v St Helens Borough Council* [1999] 2 AC 52.
15   C-426/11, [2013] IRLR 744, [2013] ICR 1116.

government has amended[16] *Tupe* to provide expressly for a static approach to the transfer of terms derived from collective agreements.

Recognising the burden imposed on businesses that inherit onerous terms and conditions derived from collective bargaining agreements, the government has also decided from 2014 to limit the period during which terms derived from collective agreements must be observed to one year after the transfer.[17] After that period, variations may be made to those terms, even where the reason for seeking to change them is the transfer, provided that overall the changes are no less favourable to employees. However, where terms and conditions derived from collective agreements are incorporated into employment contracts (as is commonly the case in the UK), the usual restrictions on post-transfer changes to terms and conditions will continue to apply.

Bonus scheme, profit-related pay and share schemes

6.3.17   Particular consideration may need to be given to the provisions of any bonus schemes (including relevant targets) and profit-related pay arrangements. Although the employees may have a contractual right to these forms of remuneration, the actual scheme may not operate easily after the transfer (eg because the previous profit targets related to a group of businesses of which the business is no longer part or because HMRC approval cannot be obtained). However, failure to maintain the terms of the schemes will technically be a breach of contract. Employers may seek to reduce such risks by putting in place equivalent schemes.

It may be easier for transferees to manage discretionary schemes. Here it can be argued that the discretion transfers and therefore the transferee inherits the previous flexibility that the transferor previously had. Any discretion will, however need to the exercised by the transferee having regard to the usual relevant factors, including the obligation not to exercise the discretion unfairly or capriciously.[18]

Restrictive covenants

6.3.18   The transferee may need to consider redrafting any restrictive covenants in the employees' employment contracts to reflect the transferee's

---

16   *The Collective Redundancies and Transfer of Undertakings (Protection of Employment) (Amendment) Regulations 2014 (SI 2014/16)*.

17   *The Collective Redundancies and Transfer of Undertakings (Protection of Employment) (Amendment) Regulations 2014 (SI 2014/16)*.

18   See eg *Commerzbank AG v Keen* [2006] EWCA Civ 1536, [2007] ICR 623.

business activities (including the location of the operation) and the employees' new responsibilities within it. In practice, amendments may be difficult to introduce for the reasons set out in the section on harmonising terms and conditions.

Non-contractual claims

6.3.19 The Court of Appeal has ruled[19] that the transferor's liability to its employees for personal injury or negligence transfers to the transferee under *Tupe*. As the transferor's right to claim under its liability insurance policy in respect of the transferred employees also transfers this is unlikely to be a significant problem in most transactions. However, an indemnity may be needed in public sector transfers, where transferors are not obliged to maintain employers' liability insurance. Transferors and transferees are jointly and severally liable in such a situation (*reg 17*), so transferees should be able to obtain a contribution reflecting the transferor's fault.

Dismissing employees on a business transfer and harmonising terms and conditions

Dismissal

6.3.20 The dismissal of any employees (of either the transferor or the transferee and either before or after the transfer) is automatically unfair under *reg 7(1)* if the transfer or a reason connected with it (which is not an economic, technical or organisational reason entailing changes in the workforce) is the reason or principal reason for the dismissal.

Regulation 7(2) provides that where the reason for the dismissal is connected to the transfer but constitutes 'an economic, technical or organisational reason entailing changes in the workforce of either the transferor or the transferee before or after a relevant transfer' (an ETO reason), the dismissal will not automatically be unfair.

The government intends[20] to amend *Tupe* from 2014 so that protections will only apply where the reason for the dismissal is the transfer itself and not a reason connected with the transfer.

The exception should, for example, cover dismissals resulting from genuine redundancy programmes.

---

19 *Bernadone v Pall Mall Services Group* [2000] 3 All ER 544, [2000] IRLR 487.
20 *The Collective Redundancies and Transfer of Undertakings (Protection of Employment) (Amendment) Regulations 2014 (SI 2014/16).*

6.3.20 *Corporate transactions (sales, purchases and corporate activity)*

However, the following should be noted:

- the exception normally only applies if there are reductions in the numbers of employees (as opposed merely to changes in the individuals making up the workforce) or a change in job functions;

- dismissals effected by the transferor at the transferee's request (which may be included as a term of the business transfer agreement) will not automatically fall within the exception;

- the exception means only that the dismissal will not be automatically unfair. The employer will still be liable for an unfair dismissal claim if he is unable to satisfy an employment tribunal that the dismissal was for a potentially fair reason (eg redundancy) and that he acted reasonably in all the circumstances. In this regard, particular consideration may need to be given to the 'pool' from which any genuine redundancies are to be selected.

Although the courts have yet to consider the point it is likely that, following the transfer, the transferee will be required to consider including its existing workforce in the pool, as opposed to confining it to the transferring employees. A failure to select from the proper pool may give rise to claims for unfair dismissal from redundant employees on the grounds that the selection criteria were unfair.

The House of Lords decision in *Wilson v St Helen's Borough Council*[21] established that dismissals that are connected with a transfer are effective to terminate the employment relationship. Consequently, liability for dismissals occurring before a transfer will become the responsibility of the transferee if there is no ETO reason. If a dismissal is connected with the transfer and so is unfair, employees will be entitled to an unfair dismissal award (provided they have sufficient continuous service to be eligible to bring a claim – currently two years' continuous service).

It may well not be possible for the transferor to dismiss ahead of any transfer, seeking to rely on the transferee's potential ETO reason following the Scottish case of *Hynd v Armstrong*.[22]

Harmonising terms and conditions

6.3.21 Many transferees will wish to harmonise the terms and conditions of employment of incoming employees with those of their existing workforce. This can be difficult and employers should bear in mind the following points:

---

21   *Wilson v St Helens Borough Council* [1999] 2 AC 52.
22   [2007] CSIH 16, [2007] IRLR 338.

- Since employers may not unilaterally vary a contract of employment (in the absence of an express power to vary in the employment contract), any variation will need to be with the employee's consent. Any dismissal of an employee for failure to agree to a change will almost inevitably be automatically unfair if it is connected with a transfer.

- *Regulation 4(4)* makes it clear that changes where the sole or principal reason is the transfer or a reason connected with the transfer that is not an ETO reason will be void. Transfer connected changes will only be valid if they are for an ETO reason. Where the aim of a change is to harmonise terms and conditions, it is often difficult for an employer to point to changes in employee numbers or functions, so while there may be an ETO reason for the change, this will often not involve changes in the workforce.

- This means that even where the employee has apparently agreed to a contractual package that is more favourable overall than that in place before the variation, an employer will not be able to enforce an individual term that is detrimental (eg a new restrictive covenant) if the reason for the variation was connected with the transfer and is not an ETO reason.

- A transfer-connected dismissal will be effective to terminate employment, whether or not there is an ETO reason. In such circumstances, the employee's remedy is an unfair dismissal claim. Employers could dismiss employees on notice and offer new terms and conditions of employment post-transfer to be sure that the changes are effective. However, the dismissals will be automatically unfair if they are connected with the transfer and such an approach is clearly unattractive from an employee relations perspective.

As with dismissals (**6.3.20** above), the government has amended[23] *Tupe* from 2014 so that protections will only apply where the reason for the change is the transfer itself and not a reason connected with the transfer.

A mere wish to introduce changes does not constitute an ETO reason. Where the transferee cannot point to an ETO reason, the following may help to reduce the risk of any changes being held to be connected with the transfer:

- establishing a reason for the changes that is independent of the transfer (this may be easier if the transferee can show that non-transferring employees were also affected);

- applying changes to the contracts of all employees, not just to those of the transferring employees;

---

23 *The Collective Redundancies and Transfer of Undertakings (Protection of Employment) (Amendment) Regulations 2014 (SI 2014/16).*

- leaving as much time as possible between the transfer and the changes to avoid the suggestion that they are connected (although the mere passage of time itself will not prevent the change from being connected with the transfer). Because the reason for the change is the key factor, there is no particular amount of time after a transfer that will enable an employer to safely introduce changes. Even a two-year delay between transfer and the change was found to be insufficient to break the link between the transfer and the variation in one case.

Information and consultation obligations

6.3.22   *Regulation 13* imposes a duty on the transferor and transferee to inform and, depending on the precise circumstances, to consult appropriate representatives of their affected employees. There may be separate, additional, information and consultation obligations if either the transferor or transferee has a works council or other employee representative body.

The obligations under *reg 13* are as follows:

- The transferor must inform appropriate representatives 'long enough before a relevant transfer to enable consultations to take place'. In summary, the appropriate representatives must be supplied with written information as to:
    - the timing and reasons for the transfer;
    - the 'legal, economic and social implications' of the transfer; and
    - the measures envisaged by either the transferor or the transferee in connection with the transfer.
- Each party must consult the appropriate representatives where measures are envisaged by that employer. *Regulation 13(6)* requires that consultations must be conducted 'with a view to seeking agreement to measures to be taken'.
- The transferee is required to provide the transferor with details of any measures it envisages taking following the transfer (*reg 13(4)*).

These duties relate to 'affected employees', which includes any employee of the transferor or the transferee who may be affected by the transfer. In other words, information and consultation may be required with employees who work outside the business being transferred.

Whose obligation?

6.3.23   The transferor must inform and consult regarding:

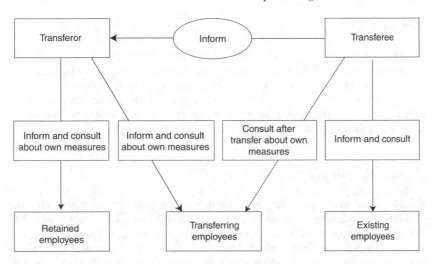

- its retained employees (who will not be transferring) if they are affected by the transfer; and

- its employees who will transfer.

Consultation is only about measures that the transferor envisages taking; the transferor is under no duty to consult about measures that the transferee may take. It does, however, have a duty to inform representatives about such measures.

Similarly the transferee must inform and consult regarding its existing workforce if they will be affected by the transfer. The transferee has no obligation to inform or consult directly regarding the transferring employees before the transfer.

What are 'measures'?

6.3.24   The term 'measures' is not defined in *Tupe*. However, it will generally include proposed dismissals or any significant alteration in existing terms and conditions of employment or working practices. If something is to be a 'measure', the employer must have formulated some definite plan or proposal that it has in mind to implement. It is not enough that a possibility be contemplated.

Measures will include changes to occupational pension arrangements, even if these are excluded from transferring under *Tupe* – see **6.6.1**.

6.3.25   *Corporate transactions (sales, purchases and corporate activity)*

Timing

6.3.25   *Tupe* does not specify time limits or provide any practical guidance on when consultation should start or how long it should last. The obligation is to inform 'long enough before the transfer to enable consultation to take place'. The precise length of time will therefore depend on the circumstances and in particular on the impact of the transfer on employees. Where the impact is minimal, a shorter period of consultation is likely to be sufficient.

Failure to comply

6.3.26   The maximum sanction for failing properly to comply with the obligations under *reg 13* is an award to each employee of 13 weeks' pay. The statutory cap on a week's pay for other employee claims (eg unfair dismissal and redundancy) does not apply. *Sweetin v Coral Racing*[24] confirms that, where there has been a complete failure to consult, the proper approach is to award the maximum penalty unless there are mitigating circumstances that make it just and equitable to decrease the award.

As indicated earlier, liability for a transferor's failure to inform and consult will pass to the transferee under *Tupe* and the transferee will generally require indemnity protection against this. Liability for this to the employee is now joint and several under *Tupe* but an indemnity will provide better protection than subsequently applying to the court for a contribution from the transferor.

Appropriate representatives

6.3.27   The employer should consult with 'appropriate representatives' of the affected employees, namely:

- where an independent trade union is recognised, representatives of the trade union; and
- where no union is recognised, either:
    - persons elected by employees for the purposes of the employer's information and consultation obligations; or
    - persons appointed or elected by employees for another purpose but whom the employer can appropriately consult.

It is for the employer to choose with which of the latter categories to consult.

---

24   *Sweetin v Coral Racing* [2006] IRLR 252.

Rules on the election of employee representatives

6.3.28 *Tupe* sets out various conditions that elections of representatives for information and consultation purposes must meet. The requirements are as follows:

- The employer must make such arrangements as are reasonably practical to ensure the election is fair.

- The employer must decide the number of representatives to be elected and ensure that there are sufficient representatives to represent the interests of all affected employees.

- The employer must decide whether the affected employees should be represented by representatives of all affected employees or by representatives of particular classes of those employees.

- The employer must decide the term of office of employee representatives, which must be sufficient to enable information and consultation obligations to be completed.

- All candidates for election as representatives must be affected employees on the date of the election.

- No affected employee can be unreasonably excluded from standing as candidate.

- All affected employees at the date of the election are entitled to vote and may vote for as many candidates as there are posts to be filled.

- The election must be conducted so that votes are accurately counted and so that as far as reasonably practicable those voting do so in secret.

Employee representatives have rights and protections, including rights of access to employees, a right to use appropriate facilities and accommodation, a right not to be dismissed or suffer detriment because of their position and a right to paid time off to carry out their duties.

If employees fail to elect representatives within a reasonable time of being asked to do so, the employer must give the information directly to the affected employees themselves.

6.3.29 *Corporate transactions (sales, purchases and corporate activity)*

Appendix: summary of principal employment law issues

6.3.29

Issue	Share sale	Business sale
Consultation obligations	No legal obligations[25]	Yes[26]
Secretary of state notification	No legal obligations	No legal obligations
Effect on employment contracts	No dismissal: continuity preserved. No change of employer.	No dismissal: continuity preserved. New owner takes over as new employer.
Consultation on making employees redundant on completion of sale	Yes[27]	Yes[28]
Changes to terms and conditions of employment following completion of sale	With employee consent[29]	Not unless there is a dismissal or the changes are unconnected with the transfer or connected but there is an ETO reason.[30]

25 The terms of relevant trade union, information and consultation or European works council agreements should be checked to ensure that they do not contain any obligations to inform and/or consult employees (or their representatives) on a share sale.

26 Obligations begin with a duty to inform appropriate representatives of the business sale 'long enough before' the sale to enable consultation to take place. Consultation must then take place where any measures are envisaged in relation to the employees. There is no specific timetable (see **6.3.25**).

27 Obligations under the *Trade Union and Labour Relations (Consolidation) Act 1992* are to begin consultation 'in good time' with appropriate representatives. Legislation sets out minimum periods of consultation in connection with redundancies of 30 or 45 days (depending on the number of proposed redundancies). Consultation could be challenged in its entirety as a 'sham' if decisions on redundancies are finalised before consultation commences (in particular, consultation should begin well in advance of the issue of notices of termination to redundant employees).

28 See footnote above.

29 An employer may not unilaterally change his employees' terms and conditions of employment. If employees' consent to the changes cannot be obtained, the employees may be given notice of termination in accordance with their contracts and offered new contracts on the amended terms. However, termination for this reason constitutes a redundancy for some purposes and the employer would have to consult appropriate representatives of the employees about the changes. Dismissals may also be unfair.

6.4 *Tupe* and pensions: *Pensions Act 2004* obligations

Summary

The *Pensions Act 2004* requires a minimum level of future pension provision to be provided following a *Tupe* transfer where the transfer includes employees who were previously members of an occupational pension scheme (or eligible to join).

This section summarises the obligations under *PA 2004* on providing pension benefits following a business transfer.

Introduction

6.4.1   This section summarises the requirements under the *Pensions Act 2004* for pension provision following a *Tupe* transfer taking place on or after 6 April 2005.

The position before 6 April 2005

6.4.2   Before 6 April 2005 rights and obligations relating to 'old age, invalidity or survivors' benefits' under an occupational pension scheme did not transfer on a transfer of an undertaking (or part of an undertaking) to which the *Transfer of Undertakings (Protection of Employment) Regulations 1981 (Tupe)* applied.

However, following the European Court of Justice (ECJ) cases of *Beckmann* (2002) and *Martin* (2003), this general rule has been interpreted in a narrow way so that benefits that are payable before normal retirement age which are triggered by, for example, redundancy, may transfer. For more information, see *Tupe and pensions: transfer of early retirement benefits,* **6.6.**

---

30   Following the decision of the House of Lords in *Wilson v St Helen's Borough Council* a variation in terms and conditions of employment that is by reason of a business transfer covered by *Tupe* may be held to be invalid so that employees are entitled to be employed on their original terms.

6.4.3   *Corporate transactions (sales, purchases and corporate activity)*

The position from 6 April 2005

6.4.3   Under the *Pensions Act 2004*[31] (and the regulations[32] made under it), from April 2005, transferee employers are obliged to provide pension benefits for transferring employees where the following conditions are satisfied:

- there is a *Tupe* transfer resulting in the transfer of employment of the employee from the transferor employer to the transferee employer; and

- immediately before the employee becomes employed by the transferee there is an occupational pension scheme in relation to which the transferor is the employer and the employee is:

  - an active member of the scheme; or

  - eligible to be such a member; or

  - in a waiting period to become eligible to be a member.

What is the protection under the Pensions Act 2004?

6.4.4   Where the employee qualifies for protection, it is up to the transferee employer to choose what type of pension provision to make, either:

- a DB scheme of a specified standard; or

- a money purchase (DC) occupational scheme (including stakeholder) to which the employer contributes at a specified rate.

Future money purchase benefits

6.4.5   The transferee company must secure that the employee is (or is eligible to be) an active member of an occupational money purchase pension scheme or a stakeholder scheme into which the transferee employer makes (or, in the case of a stakeholder scheme, offers to make) 'relevant contributions'.

The regulations provide that these must be matching contributions of up to 6% of the employee's basic pay.

---

31   *Sections 257* and *258* of the *Pensions Act 2004*.
32   *The Transfer of Employment (Pension Protection) Regulations 2005 (SI 2005/649)*.

Future DB scheme

6.4.6 The transferee employer must secure that the employee is or is eligible to be an active member of an occupational DB pension scheme which satisfies one of the following:

- the statutory reference scheme test (for contracting-out purposes). In practice this will be clear if the scheme holds a contracting-out certificate (on a salary-related basis); or

- the value of the benefits provided under the transferee's scheme is at least 6% of pensionable pay (as defined by the scheme rules) for each year of employment together with the total amount of the employee's contributions and employees are not required to contribute (if at all) at a rate exceeding 6% of pensionable pay; or

- the transferee employer must make 'relevant contributions' (ie matching contributions of up to 6% of the employee's basic (not pensionable) pay).

Timing

6.4.7 The transferee employer must provide the employee with the applicable pension provision with effect from either: (a) the date of the *Tupe* transfer; or (b) the end of the applicable waiting period, as appropriate.

Opting out

6.4.8 The *Pensions Act 2004* does allow the employee and the transferee employer to agree to contract out of these obligations and agree alternative arrangements. They can do this at any time *after* the employee becomes employed by the transferee – an agreement before the transfer would seem to be ineffective.

Anti-avoidance provisions

6.4.9 The 2004 Act contains anti-avoidance protection. The condition that immediately before the *Tupe* transfer there is a scheme in respect of which the employee is an active member/eligible to be one/in a waiting period will be regarded as being satisfied in any case where it would have been satisfied but for any action taken by the transferor by reason of the transfer.

6.4.10 *Corporate transactions (sales, purchases and corporate activity)*

Transfer of early retirement benefits

6.4.10   The changes made by the 2004 Act and the regulations do not affect the potential for the transfer of some early retirement rights under *Tupe* following the ECJ's decisions in the cases of *Beckmann* and *Martin* – see **6.6.**

6.5   *Tupe* – telling employees about benefits: the dangers inherent in communication: *Hagen v ICI Chemicals*

Summary

In a business transfer the transferring employer must take care to ensure that employees are given accurate information about their pensions benefits under the new employer.

In *Hagen v ICI Chemicals*, ICI were found liable for damages to employees who claimed that they would have opposed their transfer to a purchaser had they been given the correct information about changes to their pension benefits.

Hagen v ICI Chemicals and Polymers Ltd

6.5.1   The decision in 2001 of Mr Justice Elias (as he then was) in *Hagen v ICI Chemicals and Polymers Ltd*[33] highlighted the need for employers to ensure accuracy in all communications to employees about their employment and pension benefits.

Hagen was a dispute on the question of transfer of employment under *Tupe* from one company, ICI, to another, RES. The employees claimed that ICI had misrepresented the employment conditions, job security and pension rights they would have with RES. They claimed that they would have opposed the transfer had they been given correct information. Elias J held that an individual employee acting alone could not have resisted the transfer and remained with ICI. But he also found that the employees had collectively relied upon the representations made by ICI and that collective opposition to the transfer could have derailed the whole transaction.

Elias J found that the employees had not made out their claims relating to statements about job security and general terms and conditions. However, he held that ICI had honestly but negligently misstated the pension benefits that RES would provide.

He held that employers had a duty to take reasonable care in making statements, at least where:

● the employer was proposing that the employees transfer their employment;

---

33   [2002] IRLR 31.

6.5.1 *Corporate transactions (sales, purchases and corporate activity)*

- the transfer would impact upon the future economic interests of employees (as it almost always would);

- the transfer would be unlikely to take place if a significant body of the employees objected;

- the employer had access to certain information unavailable to the employees; and

- the employer knew that its information or advice would carry significant weight with the employees.

Elias J found that ICI had told employees their pension benefits in the new RES scheme would be broadly similar to the ICI scheme benefits. It was alleged that ICI had said that the benefits provided in the RES scheme would be within 0.5% of those provided under the ICI scheme. In fact, on an individual basis, the pension benefits provided by the RES scheme were up to 5% less generous than those provided by ICI.

Further pension information was later given to the employees and ICI argued that they had had the opportunity to take advice from either RES or independent pensions experts on the differences between the benefits. Elias J held that this did not negate the misleading impression given by the 0.5% statement. Once a false impression had been created it was up to the maker of the statement unambiguously to correct it.

Elias J held that each employee affected should receive damages from ICI so that they were not more than 2% worse off in the RES scheme than they would have been had they remained members of the ICI scheme. In doing so he appears to have accepted evidence from actuarial experts that this was the test they would apply in assessing whether benefits were 'broadly comparable'.

Broadly comparable pension benefits

6.5.2   A key point is the examination of the meaning of 'broadly comparable' in the representations made by ICI about the pension benefits that the employees would be entitled to accrue after the transfer of their employment under *Tupe*.

A purchaser will sometimes contract to provide future service pension benefits for employees transferring to them which are 'broadly comparable' to those under the employees' former pension arrangements.[34] Actuaries acting on either side will usually be required to agree whether the proposed benefits meet this test. This case may inform those discussions but will not determine them.

Hagen turned, not on the terms of a formal agreement, but on the interpretation of written and oral announcements made to members. One interpretation of this case might be that an employer which tells a transferring workforce that their pension benefits will be 'broadly comparable' to the benefits they had before ought to ensure that those benefits are no more than 2% worse to avoid claims being brought. This is probably too simplistic. Elias J followed expert actuarial advice in reaching the conclusion that 2% reduction in actuarial value was the appropriate test in this case. Other judges and actuaries may reach different conclusions even when considering similar language.

Transfer of liability under Tupe

6.5.3   Elias J confirmed that *Tupe* would not transfer to a purchaser liability in relation to statements made by a vendor about pension benefits. The transfer provisions in *Tupe* (now *reg 10*) exclude liabilities for occupational pension schemes. However, purchasers of businesses should consider asking for indemnification from vendors about any statements they may make (for pension arrangements or otherwise).

No positive duty to inform on benefits

6.5.4   Elias J rejected a claim that there was an implied duty on ICI to take reasonable steps to keep employees informed of their benefits and pension rights. Counsel for the employees had argued that this was a positive duty (outside the statutory duty under *Tupe*) on the employer to inform employees, rather than simply to take care over information actually given. Elias J considered that no such duty arose under previous case law[35] or the general obligation of trust and confidence owed by an employer but, that, if employers chose to give information, they should ensure it was correct to avoid the risk of a claim.

Under *Tupe* a vendor of a business must inform trade unions or employee representatives of any measures (broadly, changes to terms and conditions or working practices) which either it or the purchaser of the business envisages taking in relation to the transfer. This covers changes to pensions.

---

34 Some purchasers may give a contractual commitment to employees about levels of future pension benefits – eg in *Whitney v Monster Worldwide Ltd* [2010] EWCA Civ 1312 a transferee was held liable under a 'no detriment' guarantee.
35 Eg *Scally v Southern Health and Social Services Board* [1992] 1 AC 294.

6.5.5   *Corporate transactions (sales, purchases and corporate activity)*

Getting it right

6.5.5   Employers should take care with pension communications. This case highlights how employees and their representations can easily misunderstand oral communications. Employers should therefore provide clear, written materials and keep records of what is said at presentations (written Q&As are helpful).

Vendors should ask purchasers to give details of pensions proposals to pass on to employees (perhaps with indemnities in the agreement if any liability flows as a result of these being incorrect). Similarly, purchasers will look for confirmation from vendors that information given out was accurate.

Is this a special case?

6.5.6   Clearly, the best way for employers to avoid claims is to get communications right. But if they go wrong, will liability flow? The finding that ICI and RES would not have gone ahead with the transaction had a large number of employees objected was crucial to the liability of ICI.

How often will this occur in the future? There may be an evidential issue for employees in showing that pensions were so important that they would have objected strongly to adverse changes. If they can show this, it may be difficult for an employer to defend a claim on the basis that the deal would have happened anyway. The courts may find that employers are really not that bad – for instance, would they really want to buy a business if the workforce was very agitated about pensions?

6.6   *Tupe* – transfer of non 'old age' benefits: *Beckmann, Martin and P&G*

Summary

This section discusses what pension benefits may transfer as part of a *Tupe* transfer – in particular benefits which are not 'old age, invalidity or survivors'. The decisions of the ECJ in *Beckmann* (2002) and *Martin* (2003) are discussed, together with the more recent High Court decision in *Procter & Gamble* (2012).

Generally, rights and liabilities under or in connection with an occupational pension do not transfer under *Tupe* with the transfer of a business.

The ECJ held, in both *Beckmann* and *Martin*, that some benefits payable by a pension scheme before normal retirement age (eg benefits after age 50 on the redundancy of an employee) potentially do transfer under *Tupe* as, not being 'old age benefits', they fall outside of the *Tupe* exclusion. More recently, the High Court has also provided some much needed guidance in *Procter & Gamble*.

These three decisions have wide-ranging implications for employers, sellers and purchasers to consider when transferring a business. The issues remaining after these three cases are discussed at **6.7** below.

The Tupe pension exception

6.6.1   *The Transfer of Undertakings (Protection of Employment) Regulations 2006 (Tupe)* govern the position of employees if a business is transferred. They replaced the previous 1981 regulations (but these were similar to the 2006 regulations in this area).

Tupe, and the underlying European directive, the *Acquired Rights Directive* (ARD) generally transfers all employment-related rights and liabilities to the new employer but the Directive (and *reg 10* of *Tupe*) exclude from transfer liabilities relating to occupational pension scheme 'benefits for old age, invalidity or survivors'.

Tupe raises various complex issues, but before *Beckmann*, buyers and sellers of businesses may have been comforted by one area of relative certainty: pension rights do not transfer.

This general statement is a little too wide:

389

6.6.1 *Corporate transactions (sales, purchases and corporate activity)*

- Rights relating to personal pensions do transfer – only occupational pensions are excluded.

- The obligation to inform and consult employee representatives (*regs 10 and 11* of *Tupe 2006*) applies to pensions as well as other employee benefits.

- It was also possible that if a purchaser changes pension benefits, this could be an adverse change to terms and conditions which might give transferring employees the right to object to the transfer and claim constructive dismissal (*reg 4(9)* of *Tupe 2006*), but there is now a clear exclusion for such claims in *reg 10(3)* of *Tupe 2006*.

Old age, invalidity and survivors exclusion

6.6.2 The exclusion in *reg 7* of *Tupe 1981* (now reg 10 of *Tupe*) was narrowed in 1993 to bring *Tupe* into line with the ARD. The pension exclusion was limited so that, from 1 August 1993, it only applies to benefits under an occupational pension scheme which relate to: 'benefits for old age, invalidity or survivors'.

These words are taken from the *ARD*.[36] As ever with European drafting, they are not particularly clear. There were concerns that benefits triggered by, say, redundancy would not fall within the exclusion. This is often an issue for *Tupe* transfers from the public sector, as many public sector schemes include redundancy rights (some payable from as early as age 40).

But even in relation to such redundancy benefits it was arguable that what was being paid was still a pension, payable for life (usually) and so was still an 'old age' benefit even if it was triggered by an event (eg redundancy) and payable for a comparatively early age. So it was not a surprise that in 1999 the Employment Appeal Tribunal held that the *Tupe* exclusion wording applied to benefits in a pension scheme triggered by redundancy – *Frankling v BPS Public Sector*.[37]

This certainty was swept away by the European Court of Justice. On 4 June 2002, in *Beckmann v Dynamco Whicheloe Macfarlane*,[38] the ECJ found that benefits payable by a pension scheme after age 50 on the redundancy of an employee are not 'old age benefits'. So the rights to those benefits did transfer and the new employer was liable to pay them.

---

36 *Article 3(3)* of the *Acquired Rights Directive (77/187)*.
37 [1999] ICR 347, [1999] IRLR 212.
38 *Beckmann v Dynamco Whicheloe Macfarlane* (C-164/00), [2002] ECR I-4893.

Beckmann: the background

6.6.3   Mrs Beckmann had been employed by the NHS and was a member of the NHS superannuation scheme. She transferred from the NHS to Dynamco Whicheloe Macfarlane (DWM) as part of a transfer of an undertaking that was governed by *Tupe*. DWM did not become a party to the NHS superannuation scheme and the rights under that scheme were not mirrored.

Mrs Beckmann was later made redundant by DWM and she claimed to be entitled to be paid the same benefits by DWM as would have been paid by the NHS superannuation scheme.

The NHS scheme provided for a special early retirement pension to be payable in cases of redundancy (and similar) on after age 50. This special benefit was payable up to normal retirement age.

Martin v South Bank University

6.6.4   In 2003, the European Court of Justice (ECJ) gave judgment in *Martin v South Bank University*.[39] The effect of the decision was to widen the extent to which pension obligations may transfer under *Tupe*. However, as is the case with many ECJ judgments, in answering some questions, it leaves others unanswered and raises yet further questions.

As with *Beckmann*, the case concerned the scope of the exclusion in *Article 3(3)* of the ARD (and hence *reg 10* of *Tupe*). The case also considers whether transferring employees can waive the rights that transfer and whether the new employer can offer less favourable benefits to transferring employees.

Martin: the background

6.6.5   Ms Martin, Mr Daby and Mr Willis were employed as nursing lecturers under conditions of employment of the General Whitley Council (GWC), which adopted the terms of a collective bargaining agreement. They were members of the NHS Pension Scheme. In 1994 the college became part of South Bank University (SBU), which then became their employer under *Tupe*.

Unable to remain members of the NHS Pension Scheme, they joined the Teachers' Superannuation Scheme (TSS). Instead of accepting the terms and conditions of employment of SBU, they took up the option of remaining on the terms and conditions of their existing employment contracts at the time of the

---

39   *Martin v South Bank University* (C-4/01) [2003] ECR I-12859.

6.6.5 *Corporate transactions (sales, purchases and corporate activity)*

transfer. In particular, it was claimed that their rights under section 46 of the GWC's conditions of service still applied.

Section 46 provided for an immediate payment of enhanced retirement pension and compensation in specified circumstances, including early retirement 'in the interests of the efficiency of the service'. The Employment Tribunal found that Ms Martin and Mr Daby had taken early retirement in these circumstances.

Although early retirement had been offered by SBU on specific terms, Ms Martin and Mr Daby claimed entitlement to enhanced benefits in accordance with the terms of *section 46*, which were more favourable than those offered by SBU. (Certain elements of compensation were mandatory under the GWC terms but discretionary under the SBU terms.) The Employment Tribunal referred to the ECJ a number of questions aimed at clarifying whether the obligation to pay early retirement benefits passes to the transferor on a business sale.

Beckmann and *Martin*: The decisions of the ECJ

Scope of the exclusion for 'old age' benefits: *Beckmann*

6.6.6   The ECJ held that a right to benefits under a pension scheme, payable on redundancy, transfers under the *ARD* (and hence *Tupe*) to the purchaser of a business. This was because the exclusion in the *ARD* (and hence *Tupe*) for pension benefits relating to old age does not apply to benefits paid early.

The ECJ held that:

* the pension exclusion must be interpreted narrowly (see para 30 of the ECJ judgment); and

* 'only benefits paid from the time that an employee reaches the end of his normal working life as laid down by the general structure of the pension scheme in question … can be classified as old age benefits, even if they are calculated by reference to the rules for calculating normal pension benefits' (see para 31).

In *Beckmann* it found that benefits payable by a pension scheme after age 50 on the redundancy of an employee were not old age benefits.

Scope of the exclusion for 'old age' benefits: *Beckmann*

6.6.7   The ECJ subsequently decided in *Martin* that rights contingent upon either dismissal or early retirement by agreement with the employer should be treated no differently from benefits payable on redundancy: neither falls within

392

the scope of the old-age benefits exception and therefore both transfer to the transferee on a business sale. The ECJ stated that this is the case even though the obligations which are transferred derive from statutory instruments, as in the case of the TSS.

This is in line with the ECJ's reasoning in *Beckmann* on the meaning of 'old age' benefits.

In *Martin* the ECJ held that the rights under section 46 were early retirement rights contingent on dismissal rather than on reaching a certain age.

Waiver of rights

6.6.8   The ECJ was asked in *Martin* whether, if these rights did transfer, the transferred employees, by joining their new employer's pension scheme (regardless of whether or not they transferred their accrued rights under the old scheme), had waived their rights to the better benefits under the NHS scheme which were not available from SBU.

The ECJ found that, in accordance with previous case law (*Tellerup v Daddy's Dance Hall*).[40] an employee cannot waive rights which arise under the *ARD*. The purpose of the *ARD* is to safeguard the rights resulting from a contract of employment, an employment relationship or a collective agreement with transferred employees. This protection is a matter of public policy and cannot therefore be varied by the parties to a contract of employment in a manner unfavourable to employees.

However, in accordance with national law, an employee can agree to his employment benefits being altered, provided that the transfer of the undertaking is not the reason for the change.

Benefits offered by the transferee

6.6.9   The ECJ was asked in *Martin*, if the effect of *Article 3* of the *ARD* is to preclude the transferee from offering transferred employees early retirement benefits on a less favourable basis than existed prior to the transfer, what the consequences were for employees who nevertheless accepted an offer from their employer on the less favourable basis.

The ECJ found that such an offer would be in breach of the public policy obligations imposed by *Article 3* and that it would be for the transferee to ensure

---

40   *Tellerup v Daddy's Dance Hall* (C-324/86) [1988] ECR 739, [1988] IRLR 315.

6.6.9 *Corporate transactions (sales, purchases and corporate activity)*

that those employees were accorded early retirement on the terms to which they were entitled under their employment relationship with the transferor.

However, an employer can, if permitted under national law, vary terms and conditions of employment if such changes are unconnected with the transfer and are made for an economic, technical or organisational reason.

6.6.10 A grey area had been created by the fact that *section 46* of the GWC conditions of service is the product of a collective agreement.

Article 3(2) of the *ARD* requires the transferee to continue to observe the terms and conditions of any collective agreement on the same terms applicable to the transferor under that agreement, until the date of termination or expiry of the collective agreement or the entry into force or application of another collective agreement.

The ECJ held that therefore, if the collective agreement giving rise to the provision had, as a matter of national law, ceased to apply to Ms Martin and colleagues when they accepted early retirement on terms other than those laid down by *section 46* of the GWC conditions of service, they would have lost the right laid down by that section.

6.6.11 The ECJ in *Beckmann* held that the *ARD* pensions exclusion meant (for example) that rights in a public sector pension scheme to early retirement pensions payable on redundancy were capable of transferring under *Tupe*. However, prior to the *Procter & Gamble* decision in 2012 there has been considerable uncertainty about the extent to which it is possible to confine *Beckmann* to its facts. This has had significant implications for commercial transactions, with indemnities often being negotiated by purchasers to cover these potential liabilities.

Procter & Gamble (2012)

6.6.12 The High Court's decision in May 2012 in the *Procter & Gamble* case has shed some much-needed light on the question of what early retirement or redundancy benefits (so-called 'Beckmann benefits') transfer with employees under *Tupe*.

In *Procter & Gamble Co v Svenska Cellulosa Aktiebolaget*,[41] Hildyard J considered both *Beckmann* and *Martin* and held that:

- *Tupe* applies to transfer some pension rights under a private sector, trust style scheme, but

---

41   [2012] EWHC 2839 (Ch) (Hildyard J).

394

● the rights that transfer are limited to any enhanced pension actually payable over the period from drawing to the normal retirement date (and not any pension payable after NRD).

Leave to appeal to the Court of Appeal was given to SCA in October 2012, however the parties have since settled the case.

6.6.13   Hildyard J decided in *Procter & Gamble* that:

● an early retirement or redundancy right under a private sector pension scheme could transfer under *Tupe*;

● if such a benefit was discretionary or required employer consent, a right to be considered in good faith for the early retirement benefit could transfer;

● the purchaser would only assume liability in relation to any enhanced element (i.e. the amount over and above any deferred pension that remains payable from the seller's scheme);

● only benefits payable over the period from retirement to the normal retirement date (NRD) can transfer, not any benefits payable from or after the NRD. A limited interpretation must be given to the ECJ decision in *Beckmann*, so that even if a pension initially comes into payment earlier than the scheme's NRD, when the employee reaches NRD under the scheme the instalments of pension payable after the NRD are 'old age' benefit and so fall outside the scope of *Tupe*.

Procter & Gamble – **background**

Procter & Gamble **concerned the interpretation of Beckmann in a private sector context**

6.6.14   As part of a sale of assets by P&G, a number of UK employees transferred under *Tupe* to an SCA group company. The employees had, before transfer, participated in the P&G final salary pension scheme, under which certain enhanced early retirement benefits were available.

It appears that the parties were aware of the possibility that these early retirement rights might transfer under *Tupe* to SCA (following *Beckmann*). A price adjustment mechanism was therefore negotiated, under which SCA would benefit from a reduction to the purchase price to reflect any liabilities and benefits accrued under the P&G fund before the *Tupe* transfer (to the extent that those liabilities transferred under *Tupe* to SCA).

The dispute arose from the failure by the parties to agree the appropriate price adjustment amount. SCA's actuaries calculated that SCA's exposure to

6.6.14   *Corporate transactions (sales, purchases and corporate activity)*

Beckmann risk was significant in financial terms. P&G's actuaries disagreed and calculated the risk to be nil, leaving a £19 million gap.

6.6.15   Hildyard J considered and decided on the following issues:

Should a price adjustment be made on the basis that Tupe operates to transfer some pension 'liabilities' even if employer consent is needed?

6.6.16   P&G pointed out that, under the P&G scheme rules, it had the power to amend the scheme and so could remove the right to take early retirement. In addition, employees required P&G's consent to take early retirement, so they did not have an unqualified right to retire early. P&G argued that this meant that there was therefore no liability under the employment contract which could transfer to SCA under *Tupe*.

SCA argued that the employees were pension scheme members as a result of their employment and any rights were therefore rights under, or in connection with, their employment contracts. The need for employer consent, and the ability of P&G to remove the early retirement rights under the rules, did not prevent there being 'rights or obligations' within *Tupe* and so therefore transferring under *Tupe*.

Hildyard J held that, in principle, a right to request early retirement on enhanced terms could transfer under *Tupe*. Where early retirement is subject to employer consent, what transfers is simply an expectation by the relevant employees of being fairly treated in exercising their entitlement to be considered for early retirement benefits.

Hildyard J held that the employees did not get any greater rights as a result of the *Tupe* transfer. So any requirement for consent remains, although subject to being exercised in good faith – ie in accordance with the contractual or implied limits on the employer (eg the '*Imperial*' duty of trust and confidence).

In *Procter & Gamble*, because the parties had agreed to fix a value to any transferring liabilities, Hildyard J concluded that it was possible (within that framework) to value the expectation of employees in this context, even though employer consent may well still be needed. Not discussed in this case, but other agreements could have a different effect. In other cases, an employee right, which is subject to employer consent, could be seen as being outside any agreement between the seller and the purchaser as being under the control of the purchaser/transferee and so not triggering a liability (eg if an indemnity given by a seller to a purchaser provides that nothing is payable if the liability results from an act of the purchaser after the transfer – in this case the giving of consent).

Where early retirement under the seller scheme is not subject to employer consent, it seems easier to see that an employee right could transfer under *Tupe*.

In both cases (whether employer or trustee consent is needed for early benefits or not) a right or liability will only transfer under *Tupe* if the benefit is not an 'old age' benefit. Hildyard J indicated that his view was that 'normal' early retirement benefits (ie ones triggered by the employee, rather than the employer) may still be old age benefits and so not transfer under *Tupe*. – see further **6.7.5** below.

If early retirement rights do transfer, what account is taken of the deferred rights in the seller's scheme?

6.6.17   Hildyard J accepted that any deferred pension payable to an employee under the P&G Scheme would go towards satisfying his entitlement or right to a benefit from SCA as purchaser. Only the enhanced element (over and above the usual deferred pension payable by the P&G scheme) would become an obligation of SCA (as the transferee) under *Tupe*.

If early retirement rights do transfer, what happens when an employee reaches normal retirement age (NRA) under the scheme?

6.6.18   One of the reasons for the ECJ's decision in *Beckmann* that redundancy pension rights could transfer under *Tupe* was that these rights did not relate to 'old age'.

In *Beckmann*, this distinction was easy to draw: the redundancy pension in question was a 'bridging pension' payable from the date of redundancy until NRA. At NRA, the bridging pension would stop, and the normal retirement pension would start. In a private sector context, however, this distinction is less easily made out. Under most private sector schemes, early retirement pensions come into payment and carry on until death: they are a substitute for normal retirement pensions, rather than an addition to them.

P&G argued that if early retirement rights transferred to SCA, only rights in respect of the period between the date of early retirement and the NRA under the P&G scheme would transfer (that is, once the employees reached NRA, SCA's liabilities would cease). SCA argued there was no basis on which to argue that only a partial liability would transfer under *Tupe*.

Hildyard J decided that, even if a pension comes into payment earlier than the scheme's NRA, when the employee reaches NRA under the scheme, that pension then becomes an 'old age pension' and the post NRA payments therefore fall outside the scope of *Tupe* (and so do not transfer).

6.7 *Tupe* and pensions: issues remaining after *Beckmann*, *Martin* and *Procter & Gamble*

Summary

This section follows from the previous section and discusses some of the issues remaining as regards the pension liabilities that may transfer as part of a *Tupe* transfer.

It is clear that occupational pension benefits which are not 'old age, invalidity or survivors' can transfer . This section discusses some of the various potential issues in the light of the decisions of the ECJ in *Beckmann* (2002) and *Martin* (2003) and the more recent High Court decision in *Procter & Gamble* (2012).

The position is still uncertain in a number of areas.

The Tupe pension exception

6.7.1 *Discussion of cases:*

Following *Beckmann*[42] and *Martin*,[43] in transactions where *Tupe* applies, it seems that:

- redundancy benefits under occupational pension schemes can transfer under *Tupe*;

- voluntary redundancy benefits payable before normal retirement may also transfer (eg if a scheme gives a right to retire early, that right may also transfer).

6.7.2 Hildyard J decided in *Procter & Gamble*[44] that:

- an early retirement or redundancy right under a private sector pension scheme could transfer under *Tupe*;

- if such a benefit was discretionary or required employer consent, a right to be considered in good faith for the early retirement benefit could transfer;

---

42 *Beckmann v Dynamco Whicheloe Macfarlane* (C-164/00), [2002] ECR I-4893.
43 *Martin v South Bank University* (C-4/01) [2003] ECR I-12859.
44 *Procter & Gamble Co v Svenska Cellulosa Aktiebolaget* [2012] EWHC 2839 (Ch) (Hildyard J).

- the purchaser would only assume liability in relation to any enhanced element (ie the amount over and above any deferred pension that remains payable from the seller's scheme);

- only benefits payable over the period from retirement to the normal retirement date (NRD) can transfer, not any benefits payable from or after the NRD. A limited interpretation must be given to the ECJ decision in *Beckmann*, so that even if a pension initially comes into payment earlier than the scheme's NRD, when the employee reaches NRD under the scheme the instalments of pension payable after the NRD are 'old age' benefit and so fall outside the scope of *Tupe*.

Hildyard J's decision in *Procter & Gamble* is a first instance decision only. It is not strictly binding on later judges even at first instance (although they will normally follow a previous decision unless convinced that it is clearly wrong). Leave to appeal to the Court of Appeal was given, but the case settled by agreement before any appeal was heard.

6.7.3   A number of legal issues remain outstanding following these three decisions. These are discussed in this section.

6.7.4   Public sector only? Benefits which are not contractual?

Both *Beckmann* and *Martin* were concerned with public sector schemes under which not only is a pension payable from normal retirement age (NRA) but also, in certain circumstances of early retirement, a separate 'compensation' pension is payable until NRA. There may still be arguments that pension rights do not transfer in the private sector because:

- it is not clear from the ECJ judgments whether their scope is limited to the 'compensation' pension payable until NRA under a public service scheme or whether it extends to all types of retirement pension;

- in the case of many private sector schemes there is a separate trust and less of a contractual promise; and

- private sector early retirement benefits are usually payable for life (not as a separate supplement or compensation payment only up to normal retirement date).

The employer, DWM, argued in *Beckmann* that pension benefits did not transfer because they were payable by the NHS scheme under the relevant regulations governing that scheme, not by the employer. However Mrs Beckmann pointed out that she was entitled to these benefits under her contract of employment with the NHS. The ECJ referred back to the English Court to decide whether the benefits 'arose from her contract of employment', but held that it was not material that the benefits were payable under separate regulations.

399

6.7.4   *Corporate transactions (sales, purchases and corporate activity)*

It is arguable that this should not apply to a private sector pension scheme where the employer's contractual obligation may be much more limited. However, it must be doubtful that the ECJ would appreciate the distinction.

In *Procter & Gamble*, Hildyard J held that rights under a private sector pension scheme (ie under a trust and not just in a contract or regulations) would transfer under *Tupe*.

6.7.5   Scope of old age exclusion? Are early retirement rights outside?

Where an employee takes early retirement under scheme rules which do not require employer consent, this is not redundancy (*Beckmann*) nor 'in the interests of the efficiency of the service' (*Martin*); does such a right therefore not transfer under *Tupe*?

The ECJ's judgment in *Beckmann* is notable in not expressly limiting its effect to pension benefits triggered by redundancy. This left it arguable in future cases that the ECJ's decision in *Beckmann* should be limited to its particular facts (eg to cases of redundancy benefits where there is an obligation in the employment contract and where the relevant pension is stated to be separate and only payable to normal retirement date). But the ECJ's judgment did not state that these are the grounds on which it decided the case.

In *Martin* the ECJ held that the benefit transferred where it was triggered on early retirement 'in the interests of the efficiency of the service'. However in practice this looks to be a broadly similar trigger to redundancy.

In *Procter & Gamble*, Hildyard J held that a benefit right could transfer even where this was just retirement with the consent of the employer.

It now seems to be arguable that *Tupe* transfers the right to receive all pension scheme benefits payable before normal retirement age. It may (for example) also apply to some early retirement benefits payable with employer or trustee consent. Incapacity pensions are probably still excluded (see below), but it seems arguable that any other early retirement right may transfer.

The EU Commission seems to have argued in *Beckmann* that 'normal' retirement rights did not transfer (see paras 25 and 26 of the ECJ judgment). The advocate general had based part of his reasoning in his advisory opinion to the ECJ on the fact that the NHS benefits were payable only up until normal retirement date – see para 79 of the Opinion of Advocate General Alber given on 13 December 2001. However the ECJ did not make the same distinction.

In *Procter & Gamble*, P&G conceded that benefits payable before NRD were not old age benefits. Having referred to this, Hildyard J referred to the Advocate General's opinion in *Martin* and considered that this supported a view that a benefit payable before NRD may still be an old age benefit. This was on the basis that a benefit that is:

(i) payable through life;

(ii) only after the attainment of a given minimum age in line with the accepted norms for early retirement (for example, 55 being the minimum acceptable to HMRC);

(iii) without any other qualifying or triggering event except the agreement of the employer,

would be an 'old age benefit'.[45]

But Hildyard J did not have formally to decide this given the concession by P&G.

Time limits? Consent by employee?

6.7.6   There is no specific time limit for employees to bring claims relating to rights that have transferred under *Tupe*. Under *Tupe*, the rights transfer automatically and continue to exist between the employees and their new employer until their employment terminates.

Purchasers may, at the time of the transfer, have made clear to employees what redundancy benefits (and possibly other benefits) would be given in the future. However in many circumstances this will not exclude any existing rights that have transferred. This is for several reasons.

• British courts are reluctant to construe merely continuing to work as being acceptance by an employee of changed terms if the changes do not affect day-to-day working – see, for example, the EAT in *Jones v Associated Tunnelling Co*[46] (1981) and Lightman J in *Re Leyland DAF*[47] (1994).

• British courts also consider that employees cannot waive their rights under *Tupe*. So even express consent to new terms is legally void if the change is by reason of a *Tupe* transfer – see *Martin*, the Court of Appeal in

---

45 See para [150], citing the A-G's opinions in *Martin* paras AG62 and 63 and in *Beckmann* para 73.
46 *Jones v Associated Tunnelling Co* [1981] IRLR 477.
47 *Re Leyland DAF* [1994] 4 All ER 300.

6.7.6   *Corporate transactions (sales, purchases and corporate activity)*

Credit Suisse First Boston (Europe) v Robert Lister[48] (1998) and the decision of the EFTA court in *Viggosddottir v Iceland Post*[49] (2002).

- Even if a voluntary redundancy package is agreed at the time of a particular redundancy, the court may hold that the employee's agreement to a smaller package is invalidated by a mistake (eg see Jonathan Parker J in *Spooner v British Telecommunications*.[50]

So current employees may be able to look back to their old terms even if the *Tupe* transfer was many years ago. Employees who have left employment may also still be able to claim. Since these are likely to be contractual claims, the usual six year limitation period will generally apply. But if the relevant policy (eg redundancy) is expressly linked to statutory redundancy, the normal statutory periods for bringing claims before the employment tribunal may apply (three to six months, depending on the claim).

Pre-1993 transfers?

6.7.7   A further issue raised is whether, initially, the *Acquired Rights Directive* was correctly implemented in 1981. Before 1993, *Tupe* did not qualify the exclusion of occupational pension rights from transferring under *Tupe*. It is therefore arguable that before 1993 all benefits from occupational pension schemes were excluded from transferring. It is untested whether *Tupe* transfers that took place before 1 August 1993 could now be revisited on the grounds that certain rights (eg redundancy and early retirement benefits) should have transferred to the new employer.

What about future service benefits?

6.7.8   If the employee had been an active member of the seller's plan up to the transfer date, he or she would have continued (had they not transferred to the buy) to accrue further benefits for their future service after the transfer date (future service benefits). In a DB scheme these are commonly extra benefits by reason of the extra periods of pensionable service and also a linkage to the employee's ultimate final salary.

Such extra benefits were not considered by Hildyard J in *Procter & Gamble* as they were not relevant to the contract in that case, neither in relation to future accrual of service nor salary linkage.

---

48   *Credit Suisse First Boston (Europe) v Robert Lister* [1998] IRLR 700.
49   *Viggosddottir v Iceland Post* Case E-3/01 (2002). http://www.eftacourt.int/images/uploads/E-3–01_Judgment_EN.pdf
50   *Spooner v British Telecommunications* [2000] OPLR 189.

So there must be a risk that a purchaser takes on an obligation to provide such an early retirement benefit in relation to future service/salary linkage.

But Hildyard J did comment to the effect that there may well be arguments that a normal early retirement benefit payable before NRA at the member's option (or with employer consent) before NRA may still be an 'old age benefit' (and so not transfer) – see **6.7.5** above. If Hildyard J's comments are right, then only an employer triggered benefit (eg on redundancy) would potentially transfer.

Ill-health benefits

6.7.9 In *Procter & Gamble*, Hildyard J did not deal with these, save to mention (at para [21]) that early retirement benefits through disability under the P&G scheme (these are not specified) count as 'invalidity' benefits and so are expressly excluded from transfer. See also the ECJ in 2000 in *Buchner v Sozialversicherungsanstalt der Bauern*[51] that an invalidity benefit is not an old age benefit if granted:

'only to persons who are incapable, following an illness or other infirmity or weakness of their physical or mental powers, of continuing to work' – para [20]

Death benefits

6.7.10 Death benefits are commonly provided by occupational schemes. They envisage a lump sum and pension being payable to the member's spouse, civil partner, or dependants following the member's death (lump sum benefits can also be paid to a wider class than this). Such benefits are not mentioned in any of the three judgments. So there is no comment on whether liability for benefits payable on death (eg a spouse pension) would transfer.

For example, in *Procter & Gamble* it is not clear whether the actuarial valuation of the benefits for the purposes of the deduction under the sale agreement would only relate to benefits payable to member or perhaps also include benefits payable to their spouses etc?

Such benefits look clearly to fall within the 'survivors' exclusion in *Tupe* and the *ARD*. this means that only the benefit payable to the employee transfers, leaving the survivor's benefits (applicable to a deferred member) behind. This seems odd, but looks clear on the wording of *Tupe* and the *ARD*.

---

51   (C-104/98) [2000] ECR I-3625, [2002] 1 CMLR 1126, ECJ.

6.7.10   *Corporate transactions (sales, purchases and corporate activity)*

How is account taken of the employee's retained rights in the seller scheme?

6.7.11   How are retained benefits in any pension scheme of the seller/ transferor taken into account? Does the purchaser/transferee have to pay the full transferred benefit ignoring the retained rights, or does the employee retain their rights against the old pension scheme (which must be deducted form any claim against the purchaser)?

In *Procter & Gamble* Hildyard J accepted that any deferred pension payable to an employee under the P&G Scheme would go towards satisfying the employee's entitlement, so that only the enhanced element (over and above the usual deferred pension) would become an obligation of the purchaser/ transferee under *Tupe*.

This was in the context of a seller scheme (the P&G Scheme) which was presumably on-going and so that solvency was not mentioned as an issue. In an insolvency situation, other issues may come into play – see further **6.7.13** below.

If early retirement rights do transfer, what happens when an employee reaches normal retirement age (NRA) under the scheme?

6.7.12   One of the reasons for the ECJ's decision in *Beckmann* that redundancy pension rights could transfer under *Tupe* was that these rights did not relate to 'old age'.

In both *Beckmann* and *Martin*, this distinction was easy to draw: the redundancy pension in question was a 'bridging pension' payable from the date of redundancy until NRA. At NRA, the bridging pension would stop, and the normal retirement pension would start. In a private sector context, however, this distinction is less easily made out.

Under most private sector schemes, early retirement pensions come into payment and carry on until death: they are a substitute for normal retirement pensions, rather than an addition to them.

In *Procter & Gamble*, P&G argued that if early retirement rights transferred to SCA, only rights in respect of the period between the date of early retirement and the NRA under the P&G scheme would transfer (that is, once the employees reached NRA, SCA's liabilities would cease). SCA argued there was no basis on which to argue that only a partial liability would transfer under *Tupe*.

Hildyard J decided that, even if a pension comes into payment earlier than the scheme's NRA, when the employee reaches NRA under the scheme, that pension then becomes an 'old age pension' and therefore at that falls outside the scope of *Tupe*. This means that the liability to make payments on and from NRA does not transfer under *Tupe*.

In practice this does make it difficult for the purchaser/transferee to provide the transferred benefits through a tax registered scheme (as the tax rules generally require a pension to be paid for life and so should continue after NRA. There are some limited exceptions for bridging pensions).

What happens if the seller plan winds up or becomes insolvent?

6.7.13   This was presumably not an issue on the facts in *Procter & Gamble*, so Hildyard J did not discuss this. He held that the obligations of P&G (and indeed SCA) to provide the deferred vested benefits accrued before the transfer was satisfied by the obligations under the P&G Fund.

It seems to be implicit in this that P&G (and hence SCA) had met their obligation by providing the benefits under the P&G Fund – this does not seem to depend on whether or not the benefits were actually provided under the P&G Fund.

Change to seller scheme post-transfer

6.7.14   Logically, it seems unlikely that there should be an obligation on the purchaser if the seller later changes its scheme in relation to pension benefits, but this could be tied in with the debate currently taking place in relation to the impact of *Tupe* on collective terms – see **6.3.16** above and *Parkwood Leisure Ltd v Alemo-Herron*[52] in the ECJ.

On pensions, the EAT, in *Worrall v Wilmott Dixon Partnerships Ltd*,[53] had earlier (2010) held that changes made to the old scheme of the seller after the transfer should be ignored.

Purchaser/transferee power to amend scheme

6.7.15   There seems to be no good reason why the purchaser (transferee) cannot exercise the relevant powers under the seller's scheme in the same way as the seller could before the transfer. This would be consistent with the principle that *Tupe* is not intended to improve the position of employees.

There is perhaps a tension here with the rule that changes cannot be made to contract terms with the agreement of the employee, if the reason for the change is the transfer itself (see *Martin*). But it seems right to say that powers already in the contract/employment relationship can continue to be exercised after the transfer.

---

52   C-426/11.
53   (2010) UKEAT/0521/09/DM; [2010] All ER (D) 107 Jul), EAT.

6.8   Joint ventures

Summary

This section looks at the provision of pension benefits for employees of a joint venture company (JVC).

In particular it looks at pension benefits for any who are transferred to (or join) a JVC and discusses the implications should a JVC set up its own scheme or participate in a scheme of a joint venture party.

Overview

6.8.1   Where a joint venture is to be established, terms relating to onward pension provision for employees of the joint venture company (JVC) need to be considered:

- What pension provision will apply for new hires?

- If there is to be a transfer of employees from one or more of the joint venture parties to the JVC, will *Tupe* apply and what pension arrangements will apply (both for the future and the past)?

Practical questions arise where the parties to a joint venture wish to provide for the JVC to put in place pension arrangements for its employees which are similar (or, if feasible, identical) to those they enjoyed when employed by the joint venture party:

- Should the joint venture employees remain in the existing pension scheme of the joint venture party, if possible? or

- Should a new scheme be set up by the JVC perhaps with a transfer payment (based on the value of the accrued rights of the employees in that scheme up to the transfer) made into it from the schemes of the joint venture parties?

Tupe

6.8.2   There is an exclusion from the *Tupe* provisions in the UK in relation to occupational pension rights and obligations. However, the *Pensions Act 2004* introduced a minimum standard of future service pension to be given to all transferred employees who were members of an occupational pension prior to a *Tupe* transfer.

Sections 257 and *258* of the *Pensions Act 2004* provide that the minimum level will be either:

(i) a final salary scheme which satisfies the reference scheme test for contracting-out purposes; or

(ii) a money purchase scheme under which the employer matches employees' contributions up to 6% of basic pay.

See generally *Tupe and pensions: the Pensions Act 2004 obligations,* **6.4.**

Using existing scheme of a joint venture party

6.8.3   One option that may be available is for the JVC to participate in the existing group pension arrangements of one (or more) of the joint venture parties. This may be attractive in relation to the employees supplied by that joint venture party.

In the UK there has not, since April 2006, been a tax requirement that companies participating in the same pension scheme must be in the same corporate group or have a sufficient 'business association'. There may, indeed, be a number of advantages of continued participation in existing pension arrangements of a UK joint venture party. There is less need to set up new arrangements. It is easier to explain to transferring employees (in particular, the consultation on any *Tupe* transfer should be more straightforward). Possible economies of scale can be achieved. It is possible for the JVC to share in any current contribution reduction (compared to normal costings) in the joint venture party's scheme.

It is possible to arrange for the JVC to participate in the joint venture party's pension scheme either on a permanent or temporary basis. This can be structured as an interim solution to enable time for the JVC to set up its own scheme and seek consents to transfer. Where the JVC participates in the joint venture party's scheme, care needs to be taken to deal with any residual liabilities which arise (by statute or under the terms of the scheme) in relation to funding of the old scheme. Indemnities and/or confirmations may be desirable.

However, there are a number of potential disadvantages to such a route which need to be considered:

●   The JVC is likely to have a potential funding liability in respect of the joint venture party's scheme – see *Scheme-specific funding requirements,* **2.1** above.

●   There will be a need to document the terms of the participation by the JVC. What level of contributions will it pay? Will it be able to take advantage of any contribution reduction or holiday? Will it have to pay additional contributions if liabilities increase (eg larger pay rises than anticipated, or discretionary benefits such as early retirement/ redundancies granted)? See further *Moving employees within a group,* **10.1** below.

Special terms can be agreed in the relevant deed of participation that JVC will, in practice, need to execute with the scheme's trustees and the principal employer or company. Special terms in such a deed on funding obligations are more difficult, as JVC will in any event become subject to the statutory funding provisions (ie scheme specific funding under *Part 3* of the *Pensions Act 2004* and the debt on employer provisions under *s 75* of the *Pensions Act 1995*), which will in practice apply despite any agreement with the Trustee to the contrary (the JVC could agree special terms outside the scheme with the principal employer, but these would not bind the trustees). The JVC may be able to agree special terms with the trustees and the principal employer in other areas (eg amendments, partial winding-up provisions).

- The parties will need to consider the implications if the JVC should ultimately cease to be associated with the sponsoring employer for the pension scheme.

- At that stage, the JVC would usually want to cease to participate in the pension scheme, and the exit terms may need to be negotiated from the outset (eg if the exit occurs involuntarily as a result, say, of option rights applying under the joint venture agreement, or if sale or subsequent flotation is a realistic possibility).

- Should a termination trigger partial winding-up provisions in the pension scheme?

- What special provisions should apply for the transfer of pension liabilities?

- How should any existing funding deficit in the scheme be covered? The JVC may fall under a statutory obligation to fund, if necessary, part of the deficit in the scheme, being a share of the total deficit for the scheme.

When the JVC ceases to participate in the pension scheme, a statutory debt obligation will often be triggered on the JVC under s 75 of the *Pensions Act 1995*, this debt obligation is calculated on a share of the scheme's buy-out deficit (ie the deficit based on the cost of securing benefits based on purchasing annuity policies from an insurer). It is possible, in some circumstances, to modify this *s 75* debt (eg by a scheme apportionment arrangement under the *Employer Debt Regulations 2005*). See further *Multi-employer pension schemes and section 75 debts,* **3.2** above.

JVC's own scheme

6.8.4   If it is decided that employees of the JVC should not remain in a scheme of one of the joint venture parties, the alternative route is to review the possibility of the JVC establishing its own pension arrangements. Much will depend on the laws and practice of the relevant jurisdiction of the JVC. Actuarial advice on the costs involved in this should also be obtained.

In the UK, it was common to negotiate for an enhanced transfer payment from the pension scheme of the joint venture party in relation to those employees who transfer to the JVC and who consent to a transfer of their pension benefits being made. This was designed to enable the JVC to offer broadly equivalent benefits to such employees, notwithstanding that they cease to remain in pensionable service in the joint venture party's scheme.

If such special transfer terms are not negotiated, there is a risk that if the previous scheme of the joint venture party is a final salary (DB) scheme that the employees will be left in their existing scheme with statutory minimum preserved benefits and statutory cash-equivalent transfer rights. These are calculated on the basis of salary at the date of leaving the existing scheme and may well result in a reduction of anticipated benefits for the employees concerned (given that their benefits previously were tied to their ultimate final salary).

If a bulk transfer is agreed, it is usual for the terms of the transfer to be set out in a pension schedule in an agreement between the JVC and the relevant joint venture party. This schedule will include a set of actuarial assumptions detailing how the transfer payment ought to be calculated. Actuarial advice should be taken on this by both parties.

Joint venture party liability for JVC pensions

6.8.5   The Pensions Regulator has powers under the 'moral hazard' provisions of the *Pensions Act 2004* to ignore the corporate veil and impose funding obligations on third parties in relation to occupational pension schemes of an employer. These provisions are designed to protect pension benefits. See *TPR Moral hazard powers*, **4.1** above.

Joint venture parties may potentially be at risk of such funding orders in relation to the pension benefits of the JVC's employees.

- Broadly, TPR is able to issue contribution notices and financial support directions imposing liability on a person 'connected with or an associate of' the employer. Such connected and associated persons are widely defined (see *Who is 'connected' or 'associated'?* **4.2** above). and include

409

6.8.5 *Corporate transactions (sales, purchases and corporate activity)*

members of the same group of companies, a shareholder holding at least one-third of the company's voting capital and companies who are connected to a director of the JVC (eg because the JVC director is also an employee or director of the joint venture party). In relation to a corporate JVC employer, associated parties will therefore often include the joint venture parties themselves.

● Liability is not automatic just because a party is connected or associated with the employer. The relevant notices and directions can only be issued if the Pensions Regulator (TPR) considers it to be reasonable. In determining reasonableness, the Pensions Regulator will consider, amongst other factors, the degree of involvement of that party, the relationship that party has with the employer and the party's financial circumstances. The reasonableness requirement means that, in practice, liability is only likely to be imposed if the connected person has been actively involved with the employer or has benefited from the activities of the employer.

The determinations panel of TPR decided to issue an FSD against various ITV companies in relation to a pension scheme of a joint venture, Box Clever, in which ITV held a 50% stake. see *Box Clever – FSD proceeding against ITV*, **4.16** above.

The potential for liability under the 'moral hazard' provisions should be considered in the context of the arrangements for establishing the JVC. It may be that the financial consequences of any risk can, and should, be reduced by indemnities from the relevant joint venture party. In addition, it is possible to seek (on a voluntary basis) clearance from TPR that it would not be reasonable for it to exercise its power to issue contribution notices or financial support directions in the particular circumstances described in the application (such a clearance will tend only to apply to existing circumstances – a clearance covering future actions/dealings is likely to be very difficult to obtain).

The parties may want to consider the implications of the moral hazard powers. In practice they may be primarily concerned as to whether any party becomes associated with another party's pension scheme, such that the moral hazard powers could apply.

Examples of moral hazard analysis

6.8.6 Assume there are no special voting rights attaching to the shares and that A and B are not otherwise connected or associated.

6.8.7   1.   A and B have DB schemes. JVC sets up its own scheme but does not become an employer in relation to the A or B schemes.

Company A will be associated with JVC. Its 80% shareholding will give it 'control' of JVC.

- A will not be connected or associated with B (in the absence of some other connection) and so no moral hazard orders are possible on A in relation to the B group pension schemes.

Company B will not be associated with JVC by reason only of its 20% shareholding in JVC.

- But B could be connected with JVC if it is associated with a director of JVC. So if Company B has power to appoint one or more directors of JVC and one director is an associate of B (eg a director, officer or employee of B), then B will be connected with JVC (see *s 249* of the *Insolvency Act 1986*).

- Similarly if B becomes a shadow director of JVC (or perhaps its director is or becomes accustomed to act in accordance with B's directions) – see *s 435(10)* of the *Insolvency Act 1986*.

- B could also be associated with JVC if its link with A is sufficient to mean that the aggregation wording at the end of the definition of control in *s 435(10)* applies.

- B will not be connected or associated with A (in the absence of some other connection) and so no moral hazard orders on B are possible in relation to the A group pension schemes.

JVC will be associated with Company A (by reason of the 80% shareholding). So JVC could be made liable for a moral hazard notice in relation to relevant pension schemes of the Company A group.

- If JVC becomes connected or associated with B, then moral hazard orders on JVC are possible in relation to the B group pension schemes.

- If JVC does not become connected or associated with B then no moral hazard orders on JVC are possible in relation to the B group pension schemes.

6.8.8   2.   A and B have DB schemes. JVC becomes an employer in relation to the A and B schemes.

Company A will be associated with JVC. Its 80% shareholding will give it 'control' of JVC.

- This means that A will be connected or associated with an employer in the B scheme and a moral hazard order is possible on A in relation to the B group pension schemes.

Company B will not be associated with JVC by reason only of its 20% shareholding in JVC.

- But B could be connected with JVC if it is associated with a director of JVC. So if Company B has power to appoint one or more directors of JVC and one director is an associate of B (eg a director, officer or employee of B), then B will be connected with JVC (see *s 249* of the *Insolvency Act 1986*).

- Similarly if B becomes a shadow director of JVC (or perhaps has its director accustomed to act in accordance with B's directions) – see *s 435(10)* of the *Insolvency Act 1986*.

- B could also be associated with JVC if its link with A is sufficient to mean that the aggregation wording at the end of the definition of control in *s 435(10)* applies.

- If B does become connected or associated with JVC, this means that B will be connected or associated with an employer in the A scheme and a moral hazard order is possible on B in relation to the A group pension schemes.

- If B is not connected or associated with JVC, B will not be connected or associated with A (in the absence of some other connection) and so no moral hazard orders on B are possible in relation to the A group pension schemes.

JVC will be an employer in both the A and B schemes. So JVC could be made liable for a moral hazard order in relation to relevant pension scheme in which it participates (either of the Company A group or Company B group).

6.8.9   3.   If the JVC pension scheme is a subsidiary of JVC (and JVC is not an employer), how does the position change?

The main change is that B may not be connected or associated with the JVC subsidiary (and hence not with an employer in the JVC scheme) if the only link is the director connection.

6.9   Pensions issues on paying dividends

Summary

This section outlines the UK pension implications for an employer (Employer) and its parent company (Parent) of:

- a dividend to shareholders by the Parent; and

- an intra-group dividend by the Employer to its Parent (eg to fund the Parent to pay its own dividend).

Both the companies and the trustees may need to consider the implications of the payment of such dividends on the security for the pension scheme, in particular whether dividends would mean:

- the existing funding arrangements need revision; or

- the Pensions Regulator's moral hazard powers could apply.

Dividends can affect the strength of the support (covenant) available to a pension scheme. As a result, the Employer may need to agree new ongoing funding arrangements with the trustee of the Scheme. If there is a material adverse change, the trustee may look at its options to agree new on-going funding arrangements. Dividends will also be relevant when trustees look at the affordability of deficit contributions.

A dividend could also trigger the Pensions Regulator looking to see if it should use its 'moral hazard' powers to issue a contribution notice or a financial support direction in connection with (or as a result of) the proposed dividend.

There are various actions that the Parent and the Employer could undertake to limit any Trustee concerns regarding the impact of the proposed dividend on the Scheme.

The potential disclosures obligations in relation to a proposed dividend also need to be considered.

Overview

Pensions issues on proposed dividends

6.9.1   Companies will often want to pay dividends to shareholders – whether:

6.9.1 *Corporate transactions (sales, purchases and corporate activity)*

- by a parent company out of the group (to ultimate shareholders); or

- within a group, from (say) the employer to the (non-employer) parent company.

A (simple) example is:

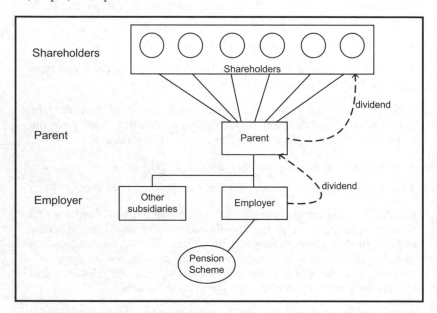

6.9.2   Pension schemes are direct creditors of the relevant Employer (by reason of the statutory funding obligations under the *Pensions Act 2004* and the debt on employer provisions in *section 75* of the *Pensions Act 1995*). Schemes are not automatically direct creditors of other companies in the group (absent a direct guarantee or the Pensions Regulator exercising its moral hazard powers) – see *Pension debts – priority of claims,* **9.3** below.

6.9.3   Dividends can affect the strength of the support (covenant) available to a pension scheme. Proposed dividends raise three main pensions issues:

- does any change in the strength of the covenant impact on ongoing funding arrangements?

- does any dividend raise potential risks of the Pensions Regulator exercising its moral hazard powers?

- what are the disclosure and notification obligations? How is any conflict of interest dealt with?

414

Trustee and funding

6.9.4   The Employer may need to agree new ongoing funding arrangements with the trustee of the Scheme (the Trustee). The Trustee is likely to take a dividend into account when assessing the strength of the Employer as the principal employer of the Scheme, and any additional support that could be expected from the Parent. The effect of:

- a dividend from the Employer to the Parent, is to weaken the strength of the Employer, but this may be counterbalanced (to a degree) by the extra strength given to the Parent (depending on what the Parent plans to do with the proceeds of the dividend and the degree of support that the Trustee sees from the Parent as part of the Employer's 'wider group').

- A dividend from the Parent to its shareholders, is to weaken the strength of the Parent. The materiality of that to the Scheme will depend on the size of the dividend and the degree of support that the Trustee sees from the Parent as part of the Employer's 'wider group' (as opposed to the shareholders who may not be).

Depending on size and materiality, the dividend can affect the level of contributions which the Trustee seeks from the Employer.

Potential moral hazard risk

6.9.5   The Pensions Regulator (TPR) could use its moral hazard powers[54] to issue a contribution notice (CN) or a financial support direction (FSD) in connection with (or as a result of) the proposed dividend.

In order to issue a CN or an FSD against someone that is not a participating employer of the Scheme:

- that third party must be connected or associated with a participating employer;

- the relevant conditions for issuing a CN or an FSD must be met; and

- TPR must consider it reasonable to issue such a notice.

The following entities/persons, in particular, would be potential targets for TPR's moral hazard powers:

- Parent and other entities in the Parent group; and

- the directors of the Employer.

---

54   See *TPR: Moral Hazard Powers*, **4.1** above.

6.9.6   *Corporate transactions (sales, purchases and corporate activity)*

Disclosure/Conflicts of Interest

6.9.6   The Employer and the individual directors of the Trustee board have certain duties to disclose information to the Trustee board.

Limiting any Trustee concerns

6.9.7   The Parent and the Employer could undertake the following actions to limit any Trustee concerns regarding the impact of the proposed dividend on the Scheme:

Explain the group's dividend policy to the Trustee

This action does not seek Trustee consent, but merely clarification that the Trustee board is aware of the position. This may also allow the company to claim that dividends are not material (either for moral hazard purposes or scheme funding). It also reduces the potential for the Trustee seeking changes to the current ongoing funding arrangements.

However, it must be remembered that this offers no express clearance or exemption from moral hazard powers.

Agree the dividend with the Trustee

The dividend policy of the Employer/Parent could be agreed with the Trustee, at the time or in advance (eg as part of the scheme funding negotiations). This should allow the company to claim that dividends within that policy are not material (either for moral hazard purposes or scheme funding).

Mitigate any reduction in the Employer covenant

In relation to a material dividend from the employer to the parent, mitigation could be offered – eg a parent company guarantee may result in no overall covenant reduction (and could improve the scheme's PPF levy situation), but would also formally tie the Parent to the Employer and Scheme. Furthermore, a parent company guarantee would not then be available for future negotiations if needed.

Seek clearance from TPR

Formal clearance from TPR will provide comfort to the parties on TPR's moral hazard powers (but only to the extent of the facts as disclosed). TPR or the

Trustee may also want extra funding in return and the clearance may not cover all future events.

Funding implications

6.9.8   As part of the scheme specific funding arrangements (under the *Pensions Act 2004*), the Trustee will need to consider the strength of the employer covenant supporting the plans when assessing scheme specific funding. Trustees increasingly look for a formal covenant review and the proposed dividend will be relevant to this assessment.

Dividend from the Employer

6.9.9   An intra-group dividend from the Employer to the Parent would have the effect of reducing the net assets of the Employer. The Scheme would be (if an insolvency occurred) an unsecured creditor of the Employer. Depending on the financial impact, the Trustee may consider a dividend to be a material change when looking at covenant issues. This will have an effect on the negotiation of future funding.

The impact of this may in some cases be reduced, given that the Parent is part of the Employer's 'wider group' and so may (depending on the circumstances) be an entity that the Trustee may look to for support in any event.

Dividend from the Parent

6.9.10   As noted above, schemes are not automatically direct creditors of other companies in the group (absent a direct guarantee or the Pensions Regulator exercising its moral hazard powers).[55] But schemes may have an interest in the strength of the Parent for various reasons:

- the Employer may be creditor of the Parent (eg if it has lent funds to the Parent). So the strength of the Employer depends (in part) on the ability of the Parent to repay that debt;

- the Parent may have given security or support direct to the Scheme;

- the Scheme may consider that TPR could exercise its moral hazard powers (see below) and force the parent to contribute or give security to the Scheme;

---

55 See *Pension debts – priority of claims*, **9.3** below.

6.9.10 *Corporate transactions (sales, purchases and corporate activity)*

- the Parent will form part of the 'wider group'[56] on which the Employer or the Scheme may be able to rely (to a degree) in practice even absent a formal legal obligation.

What can the Trustee do?

6.9.11 The Trustee's powers, when faced with a dividend (or notice of a potential dividend), to raise employer contributions, depend on the terms of the scheme and the funding arrangements already agreed:

- Some schemes give the Trustee a unilateral power to fix contributions – in such cases, where the dividend has a potentially material impact, the Trustee may consider exercising that power and raising contributions.

- In other schemes, the rules provide for contributions to be fixed by the employer or by agreement – here the Trustee does not have a unilateral power to increase contributions, but it may be able to seek agreement with the Employer on a revision to the funding arrangements in light of the dividend. The scheme specific funding provisions under the *Pensions Act 2004* include provision for a scheme's recovery plan to be reviewed 'and if necessary revised' where the trustees 'consider that there are reasons that may justify a variation to it'.[57] If the Trustee and the Employer do not agree, then the Pensions Regulator may have power to impose a new schedule of contributions (*s 231* of the *Pensions Act 2004*).

TPR's views on dividends

6.9.12 TPR's guidance on 'Monitoring employer support' suggests that trustees and employers should consider increasing scheme security by using contingent assets, including:

> 'negative pledges, whereby an employer makes a commitment not to do something such as grant new security without the agreement of trustees or not to increase dividends'.

TPR's statements on funding indicate that it expects the funding of the pension scheme to be taken into account by companies, when looking at dividend policy. It discourages increases in dividend payments at a time when recovery

---

56 See TPR's 'Clearance guidance' (2009) at para 172 and 176. Also TPR's guidance (Nov 2010) on 'Monitoring employer support' at para 32.
57 *Reg 8(5)* of the *Occupational Pension Schemes (Scheme Funding) Regulations 2005*. TPR's Code of Practice 03 on *'Funding Defined Benefits'* suggests it will usually be appropriate to commission an early actuarial valuation and review in the light of that (para 137).

plan periods may be looking to be extended. Its general guidance is for trustees to look for contributions based on the amount that companies can reasonably afford.

TPR Statement (April 2012) Pension scheme funding in the current environment

24. Where deficits have increased, some employers will be in a position to accommodate deficit repair contribution increases in their business plans. Others will have significant competing demands making cash contribution increases difficult. Servicing of other debts and facilitation of appropriate capital expenditure are necessary features of successful businesses as part of ensuring ongoing employer support.

25. The pension scheme should, however, be equitably treated among the competing demands on an employer (eg to balance the business dynamics for capital investment and dividends payments with obligations to service debt). Where cash is being used within the business at the expense of what otherwise would have been affordable pension contributions, it is important that it is being used to improve the employer's covenant – rather than benefits accruing disproportionately to other stakeholders.

26. Most employers can afford appropriate dividend payments without prejudice to the funding of the pension scheme. However, if there is substantial risk to the likelihood of the pension scheme delivering the benefit entitlements promised within it, then dividend payments need to be re-assessed in light of the obligations to the pension scheme, and other creditors.

27. Where the employer's covenant has weakened and it cannot afford to continue contributions at previously agreed levels, or is unable to pay more in respect of a larger deficit, trustees may need to agree to a longer recovery plan. A material extension to the recovery plan end date will require sound justification.

Moral hazard powers

6.9.13 The moral hazard powers of TPR include powers to make third parties liable for pension deficits/funding etc in certain circumstances. Such third parties must be connected or associated with an employer, the relevant conditions for issues or issue of an FSD or CN must be met and TPR must consider issue of such a notice to be reasonable.

A dividend has two potential impacts on the risk of a CN or FSD:

6.9.13 *Corporate transactions (sales, purchases and corporate activity)*

- the dividend could itself be a trigger for a CN as being an act that supports a CN; or

- in the case of a dividend payable to the Parent, the fact of the dividend having been paid, reinforces the connection of the Parent with the Employer. It is an example of the Parent having drawn a benefit from the Employer and so could make it more reasonable to make a CN or FSD against the Parent. See for example the reasons given by the determinations panel of TPR in the *Box Clever* determination in 2011.[58]

CNs

6.9.14　TPR has the power to issue a CN where either:

- a person has been a party to an act/omission since April 2004, the main purpose of which or one of the main purposes of which was to avoid or reduce the *s 75* pension liability;[59] or

- an act/failure to act since April 2008 has detrimentally affected in a material way the likelihood of accrued scheme benefits being received.

6.9.15　In both FSD and CN cases TPR must consider it reasonable to issue a CN having regard to factors set out in the legislation.

A CN can be issued on a person who is (or has been) connected or associated with the employer[60] – eg an individual (eg a director of the Employer) or a company (eg Parent) – who was a 'party to' (or 'knowingly assisted') in the relevant act or omission. The warning notice needs to be issued within six years of the relevant act or omission.

FSDs

6.9.16　The primary test for an FSD is financial – is the employer a service company or 'insufficiently resourced'? An FSD cannot be made against an individual (where the employer is a company).

58　Determination against ITV and others on 21 December 2011 at para 41. See *Box Clever – FSD proceeding against ITV*, **4.16** above.

59　This test may mean that an event affecting the Parent is not an event potentially triggering a CN under this limb – as the Parent does not directly owe a *s 75* debt to the Scheme. This is untested. It may be arguable that the existing obligations of the Parent to the Employer (eg an intercompany loan owed to the Employer) could be enough to trigger this limb (because it can impact on the assets of the Employer and so indirectly on the recoverability of the *s 75* debt from the Employer). In any event the newer (2008) 'material detriment' limb of the CN test looks wider in referring to the 'likelihood of accrued scheme benefits being received' (and not to a *s 75* debt being recovered).

60　See *Who is 'connected' or 'associated'?*, **4.2** above.

Who is potentially liable?

6.9.17   An FSD in a group situation can only be issued against other group companies. It cannot be issued against individuals. CNs can be issued against connected companies (eg Parent) but also against individuals who are associated or connected with an Employer (eg directors or employees of the Employer).[61] They need to be 'party to' (including those who 'knowingly assist') the relevant act or omission that triggers the CN.

There is a statutory defence (*s 38B* of the *Pensions Act 2004*) available to the 'materially detrimental' CN test – where a target (eg a director):

- gave due consideration to how the scheme might detrimentally be affected; and

- took all reasonable steps to minimise any detriment; and

- reasonably concluded that the act or failure 'would not detrimentally affect in a material way the likelihood of accrued scheme benefits being received'.

Disclosure/conflicts of interest

6.9.18   There may be two potential disclosures which arise in relation to a proposed dividend:

- disclosure by the Employer (or Parent) to the Trustee; and

- disclosure by individual members of the Trustee board (who may hold senior positions in the Parent) to the Trustee board.

Employer disclosure/discussion

6.9.20   One issue for the Employer is when to discuss the proposed dividend with the Trustee.

Partly this depends on whether there is any formal disclosure protocol that has already been agreed. There is a statutory obligation on an employer to disclose material events to trustees within one month of them happening. In addition, the Employer is required to disclose material information if requested by the Trustee (*Reg 6* of the *Scheme Administration Regulations 1996*).

---

61   But not directors of the Parent, if that is their only connection with the Employer.

6.9.20   *Corporate transactions (sales, purchases and corporate activity)*

There is no obligation to inform the Pensions Regulator about a dividend – dividends are not within the notifiable event obligations.[62]

Trustee disclosure

6.9.21   The position where a member of the Trustee board is aware of a proposed dividend (eg by virtue of his position within the Employer or Parent) depends on the materiality of the proposal and on the disclosure/conflicts provisions of the Scheme (or the articles of association of the trustee company).

The conflicts policy that has been adopted by the Trustee (following the *Companies Act 2006* and TPR guidance on conflicts at about the same time) needs to be considered.

---

62   See Notifiable events – *Obligation to report certain events to the Pensions Regulator*, **13.1** below. The notifiable event relating to a change in employer credit rating was abolished from April 2009.

Chapter 7

Scheme mergers

7.1 Merging pension schemes – introduction

Summary

This section summarises the major issues arising in relation to a merger of two occupational pension schemes. It gives an outline of the major issues from the perspective of the company and of the two (or more) sets of trustees. It concludes with a view of the legal and administrative issues involved.

These sections are necessarily only an overview of the legal principles. Each merger requires individual examination.

Overview

7.1.1   It may be desirable from an employer's perspective to merge pension schemes in order to save costs or rationalise.

When two or more occupational pension schemes are merged there is a transfer of assets from one scheme (the transferring scheme) to the other (the receiving scheme) and the transferring scheme is then wound up. It is not usually necessary to seek members' consent for the transfer although this may be sought from active members. Consent must be sought from the trustees of the scheme. Employers, although under a duty to consider the effects on staff, will generally act in their own interests, while trustees are under an obligation to act for a proper purpose, usually the purposes of the pension scheme.

Trustees from both pension schemes will have a number of issues that they must consider before giving consent to a merger and employers should bear these in mind during the process of merging. Trustees will generally find it easier to approve a merger if a benefit improvement is included as part of the package.

7.1.1   *Scheme mergers*

In any merger it is almost inevitable that one scheme will be better funded than the other and that (absent extra funding from the employer) the merged scheme will be funded somewhere in the middle of the two schemes. Both sets of trustees will look at the benefits in the receiving scheme. Trustees from the transferring scheme will also look at how the balance of powers and solvency levels compare, and what the motive for the merger is. Receiving scheme trustees will want to know about hidden liabilities and, again, motive.

Both sets of trustees need to check they have the required powers to consent to the merger – the transferring trustees will need a bulk transfer or winding-up rule and receiving trustees must confirm they are able to admit transferring members and grant them the transfer credits for the power service envisaged.

The merger document itself should set out the conditions to be met before the merger takes place, what will happen when the merger takes place, the nature of benefits to be granted to transferring members, any indemnities given by the employers or trustees and any amendments to the schemes.

Once the asset transfer has taken place, all holders of the assets must be notified and the trustees of the receiving scheme will need to decide how the assets are to be managed in the future. Members must be told of the transfer (and divorced ex-spouses of members) and various regulatory bodies must also be notified.

What is a merger of pension schemes?

7.1.2   A merger of pension schemes occurs when two (or more) pension schemes of an employer are merged together.

Legally this process occurs by the transfer of the assets of one scheme (the 'transferring scheme') to the other (the 'receiving scheme'). The receiving scheme agrees to grant benefits (under and on the terms of the receiving scheme) to the members of the transferring scheme in exchange for the assets transferred. Active members (ie those still in pensionable service) under the transferring scheme will usually continue to accrue further benefits under the receiving scheme. The transferring scheme will then usually be wound up.

Member consents?

7.1.3   Usually such mergers take place without seeking the consent of the members of the transferring scheme. This is allowed in many cases by the

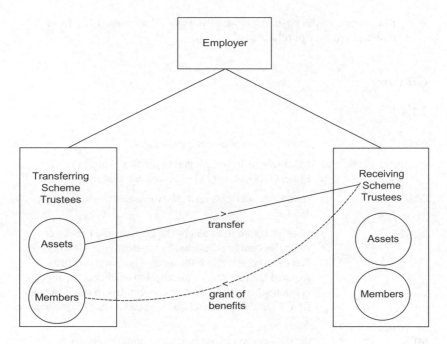

relevant legislation,[1] subject to the actuary of the transferring scheme giving a certificate – formerly called a GN16 certificate (see **7.3.19**).

It is usually considered to be impractical to seek consent from all the pensioners and deferred members.

Consent from all affected active members may be sought. In practice, the consent of active members will be needed for continued deduction of contributions (now payable to the receiving scheme instead of to the transferring scheme). However if an active member does not consent, in practice he or she will then be treated as though they have opted out of pensionable service. This means that he or she will be treated as a deferred pensioner and so transferred in any event.

Consent may be necessary in some cases if a merger is to take place. For example:

● if changes to the benefits are envisaged which fall outside the 'broadly no less favourable' wording in the actuarial certificate; or

---

1   *Occupational Pension Schemes (Preservation of Benefit) Regulations 1991, reg 12.*

7.1.3 *Scheme mergers*

- if a change in the basis for contracting out is envisaged (eg from salary related to money purchase).

Glossary

7.1.4

AVC	additional voluntary contributions
contracted-out rights	rights in substitution for part of the state pension scheme. Either GMPs, or *s 9(2B)* rights or protected rights
GMPs	contracted-out rights on a salary related basis before 6 April 1997
GN16	Guidance Note 16 issued by the Institute and Faculty of Actuaries (and later adopted by the Board for Actuarial Standards) dealing with the form of actuarial certificate required for a transfer of members to another occupational pension scheme without their consent. GN16 ceased to apply from 1 October 2011 and was replaced by the Transformations TAS
MFR	the statutory minimum funding requirement under the *Pensions Act 1995*
PPF basis	the statutory funding basis used by the Pension Protection Fund (PPF). Also called the *s 179* basis
Section 9(2B) rights	contracted-out rights on a salary related basis after 5 April 1997
TAS	Technical Actuarial Standard, as adopted by the Board for Actuarial Standards

7.2   Mergers: the employer's perspective

Summary

This section looks at the issues for mergers of pensions schemes from the perspective of the employer. It looks in particular at:

- the rationale for a merger
- the benefits to be offered in the receiving scheme
- consultation obligations
- Pensions Regulator impact
- costs
- contacting-out; and
- trustee issues

Why merge pension schemes?

7.2.1   The main reasons for merging pension schemes from an employer's perspective tend to be:

- a desire to rationalise pension schemes so as to reduce the number of schemes being operated;
- a desire to save costs;
- a desire to increase uniformity of benefit provision.

Rationalisation

7.2.2   Employers can find themselves with a number of separate occupational pension schemes for various reasons:

- if the employer has acquired companies with their own pension arrangements, these often will have continued (perhaps closed to new entrants);
- it was quite common in the past for a separate executive scheme to be set up for senior employees;
- works and staff schemes (with separate benefit structures) were also a feature in the past.

427

7.2.2   *Scheme mergers*

Rationalising all these schemes by merging them into one may have the following benefits:

- easier administration (a need to keep track of only one scheme for legal and statutory compliance);

- a saving of costs (lower administration, less need for separate meetings and compliance etc);

- savings through having a common pool of assets (perhaps a lower investment management fee);

- more stability and a larger fund (less likely to have variations in regular costs).

Employers' aims

7.2.3   Employers commonly look to mergers of pension schemes to achieve:

- a common pool of assets supporting all benefits (not separate pools of assets);

- an agreed benefits structure;

- uniform administration arrangements going forward.

The process of merger

7.2.4   Careful planning is necessary to ensure that the process to complete a merger runs smoothly. In practice the employer will usually be the one who instigates the merger process. However, the need to obtain consent of the trustees of each of the relevant pension schemes means that their position needs to be considered from the outset.

Employers generally consider pension benefits to be part of a remuneration package. Accordingly, they generally look at mergers in the context of the employer – employee relationship. Although the courts imply a mutual duty of trust and confidence in relation to the employees (and ex-employees) generally, this still allows employers to consider their own position.

Conversely, trustees will have a fiduciary duty to exercise their powers for a proper purpose – usually for the purposes of the pension scheme. Commonly this will mean that they have a fiduciary duty to act in what they consider to be the best interests of the beneficiaries of the scheme. Although the employer's interests may be included within the range of matters to which the trustees should have regard, in practice the employer will be part of the process and will be able to look after its own interest. In practice this means the trustees tend to look to act in what they consider to be the best interests of the members (and other beneficiaries) of their particular scheme.

Both sets of trustees will need to consider a number of issues. Employers should recognise this from the outset and seek to manage the process so that control of the merger process is retained. This is particularly important if the employer is agreeing to pay the costs of the merger. In practice this management process involves:

- identifying what is on offer;
- identifying the issues the transferring and receiving trustees may raise;
- identifying possible solutions to those issues;
- the employer submitting a written proposal to the trustees;
- setting timescales;
- the employer being aware of trustees' requirements;
- the employer trying to keep control of the process (and its costs).

Benefits to be offered

Improvements?

7.2.5 Generally it will usually make a merger proposal easier for trustees to agree if a benefit improvement is included as part of the package. Historically many employers agreed to do this. This could, depending on the circumstances, include an agreement to convert a current discretionary benefit (eg pension increases) into one, which is guaranteed in the future. Such a benefit improvement would make it easier for trustees to agree to a merger.

Obviously the employer will need to take actuarial advice on the likely costs of any benefit improvement. Even if the improvement is already costed for in the normal ongoing funding assumptions and statutory transfer (cash equivalent) calculations (eg a particular level of discretionary pension increases), converting the benefit to one which is an entitlement, will increase liability in some measures – eg winding-up or PPF liability (which does not include discretionary benefits).

However, it is now less common for employers to propose, or agree to, benefit improvements as part of a merger. If no benefit improvements are on offer (and trustees may ask for them to show that they have sought to argue for the best deal available), this does not necessarily mean that a merger cannot take place. In practice the employer would need to put forward good reasons for why the trustees should agree to a merger.

7.2.6 *Scheme mergers*

Benefits to be offered: past service

7.2.6 In practice it is common for the existing past service benefits in the transferring scheme to be mirrored in the receiving scheme. This makes it easier for the trustees to agree to the merger. If the benefit structures between the two schemes differ (which is fairly common), this will mean that the receiving scheme will need to establish a separate benefit structure for the transferring members (to mirror the benefit structure in the transferring scheme). The administrative implications of this will need to be considered.

Such a separate benefit section could be backed by its own separate ring-fenced assets. In this case cross subsidy is avoided (but the scheme will be treated as if it were two separate schemes for many purposes). More common is for there to be separate benefit sections, but only one, merged, pool of assets for all benefits sections.

Care needs to be taken to identify which benefits are to be continued. In practice it should be clarified:

- that only pension and lump sum benefits are included. This is to avoid later claims that other issues (eg choice of AVCs, how trustees are elected etc) are also benefits that have been continued;

- whether any benefits that have been given in the transferring scheme as a matter of practice are also being given (as of right?) in the receiving scheme;

- whether discretionary benefit practices will also continue.

Employers need to consider the implications of giving any benefit improvements or agreeing that past practices are to now become rights.

In practice it is helpful for any formal merger agreement to identify the specific benefit provisions of the transferring scheme that are being continued in the receiving scheme. This should avoid any later doubts as to which existing provisions of the receiving scheme (eg amendment provisions, transfer-out powers, winding-up provisions, general administrative provisions etc) will apply to the benefits granted to the transferring members as part of the merger.

It may be possible to make (limited) changes even to the benefits for past service as part of the merger. Generally this will be easiest with active members where their express consent is given (the trustees will still be concerned that these members have been given proper information).

430

Limited changes may also be possible for non-consenting members. The preservation legislation and the actuarial certificate[2] (see *Appendix A* at **7.3.30**) requires the actuary to certify that the benefits in the receiving scheme are 'broadly no less favourable' than those in the transferring scheme.[3] This gives some flexibility to change benefits (assuming that the trustees agree). An example would be a change to the date on which pension increases are given.

Discretionary benefits and practices

7.2.7   Some indication of the employer's intention in relation to discretionary benefits may need to be given to the transferring trustees as part of the merger process. This may be required in order for the actuarial certificate to be given. The transferring trustees may also look for it in any event.

These discretionary issues can include:

● the employer's practice in relation to agreeing to discretionary pension increases;

● what actuarial factors are used (eg on transfers or commutation);

● how cash equivalent transfer values are calculated;

● what AVC choices are made available for members;

● how trustees are appointed and elected.

Employers should consider carefully the legal implications of any statements they make at the time. Generally all that may be required are statements of current intention. It will be important to clarify that these are not intended to be legally binding and that practices may change in the future.

Future service benefits

7.2.8   It may be possible to change the future benefits of the transferring active members so that they move to the receiving scheme's benefit structure for future service benefits.

The trustees of the transferring scheme may have some concerns about this if benefits are reduced.

In addition if a change in benefits is envisaged the employer will need to consider if the active members have any contractual rights to a particular level

---

2   Commonly called a GN16 certificate after the (now revoked) actuarial guidance note GN16.
3   Note that this is more flexible than the no 'detrimental modification' wording required in the actuarial certificate for scheme amendments under *s 67* of the *Pensions Act 1995* (as amended by the *Pensions Act 2004*).

7.2.8 *Scheme mergers*

of benefits. A change is also more likely to trigger an obligation on the employer to consult with active members (under the *Pensions Act 2004*).

Consultation with members

7.2.9 The *1991 Preservation Regulations* require written notice of at least one month to be given to the relevant members before there is a transfer without their consent. This should be factored into the timetable.

The *Pensions Act 2004* also imposes consultation obligations on employers if there is a 'listed change' to the benefits envisaged under pension schemes. Closure and winding up of the transferring scheme technically may arguably amount to a listed change, even if benefits are continued unchanged in the receiving scheme.

While there does not seem to be any public example of any case where TPR or the members have taken this point, generally, if the timetable allows, it will be safer to inform and consult with the active members.

Consultation under the *Pensions Act 2004* involves providing relevant information to the affected members at least 60 days before any decision is made and then consulting with relevant representatives (or the members themselves) – see *Pensions Act 2004: Employers' consultation obligations*, **15.1**.

Notifying the Pensions Regulator

Clearance

7.2.10 A full scheme merger is unlikely to be an event with a potential material adverse effect on the support for the pension schemes so that clearance is required from the Pensions Regulator in relation to its 'moral hazard' powers under the *Pensions Act 2004*. There may be circumstances in which clearance may be more desirable (eg if one or more employers who support the transferring scheme are not becoming employers in the receiving scheme).

The issue on clearance needs to be considered in the light of the individual facts.

Notifiable events

7.2.11 A scheme merger is not a notifiable event requiring the employer to notify the Pensions Regulator, but it may well be an event requiring the trustees to notify the Regulator – see *Notifiable events*, **13.1**.

In any event, informing the Pensions Regulator of a proposed merger is often helpful to keep the Regulator informed of events affecting the scheme.

Costs

7.2.12   The costs of the merger process need to be considered.

In many respects it is easier for the employer to agree to pay the transferring and receiving trustees' legal and other costs:

- this may give the employer more control over the level of those costs;

- the receiving trustees have a better idea of the level of assets they are going to receive;

- finally, given that some of the costs will only be incurred after the merger date, it avoids the need for an estimate of costs to form a retention by the transferring trustees.

In practice even if the trustees' costs (including merger costs) generally come out of the fund, ultimately these will reduce the fund and may well increase the contribution rate for the employers. Generally, this reinforces the need, from the employer's perspective, for it to control the process and the costs being incurred.

Hidden liabilities

7.2.13   It is important to anticipate, as part of the merger process, what (if any) unrecorded liabilities there may be in the transferring scheme.

In practice are there any liabilities not shown in the actuarial valuations that may be of concern to the receiving scheme trustees? Examples could be:

- practices which are considered to be discretionary (but in fact have become a legal right over time);[4] or

- where mistakes have been made in documenting benefits etc; or

- potential extra equalisation liabilities following changes made after the *Barber* case in 1990; or

- the cost of equalising GMPs or allowing access to part-timers etc; or

---

4   It may well be difficult for a member to succeed with a claim that a discretionary practice has become a right over time – see eg *Prudential Staff Pensions Ltd v The Prudential Assurance Co Ltd* [2011] EWHC 960 (Ch).

- the cost of equalising to reflect age discrimination requirements.

From the employer's prospective it may be important to check for these in advance to avoid them coming out a long way down the merger process. At that stage there may be pressure to agree to the practices becoming rights etc in order to avoid the merger failing.

Advisers

7.2.14 Each set of trustees will need their own legal and actuarial advice. Commonly they will look to use their existing advisers. Often these advisers are the same as those advising the employer. In practice it may well be possible for the advisers to continue to advise both parties (possibly with different individuals at the adviser providing the advice). However, each party (the various sets of trustees and the employer) will need to be aware of (and agree to) the different roles being played by the advisers.

There may be costs savings in having the same advisers involved acting for more than one party, but it is useful also to consider the perception that is raised. If the merger is ever the subject of a challenge, it is helpful for the trustees to be able to point to the fact that they have had independent legal and actuarial advice.

There is no one answer to this issue. It is for the parties to consider the advantages and disadvantages.

Contracting out

7.2.15 The technical requirements of contracting out will need to be considered and complied with. If both schemes are COSR schemes, that is, contracted out on a final salary basis (either through GMPs or *s 9(2B)* rights), it is possible to make transfers between the schemes without member consent.

The situation becomes more difficult where other sorts of contracting-out rights are involved. These can stop a merger in its tracks, so it is important they are considered in advance. A brief summary is given below:

- A scheme which is not contracted-out cannot receive contracted-out rights. Thus if the receiving scheme is a contracted-in scheme, it cannot receive contracted-out rights from the transferring scheme. Either the receiving scheme must become contracted out (which involves having active members who are contracted out – this could be a small group) or the contracting-out liabilities must be left behind in the transferring scheme (perhaps being bought out with insurance policies etc).

- If the transferring scheme includes benefits contracted out on a protected rights (money purchase) basis (COMP), a transfer of these rights can be made without the consent of the member concerned to another occupational pension scheme (but it must be a COMP or a COMB).

- If the transferring scheme is contracted out on a salary-related basis, but the receiving scheme is or was contracted out on a money purchase basis, a transfer of GMPs and *s 9(2B)* rights cannot be made without the consent of the members concerned. This either means those rights must be left behind (and bought out) or the receiving scheme will need to also become contracted out on a salary-related basis (a contracted-out mixed benefit scheme or COMB). Such contracting out will require a number of active members who are contracted out on that basis into the future (this could be only temporary and they could later cease to be contracted out on that basis).

- Contracting-out on a money purchase basis (either through a COMP or a COMB) ceased to be possible from 6 April 2012.

Transfers: contracting-out issues

Can contracted-out rights be transferred?

7.2.16

Transferring Scheme	Receiving Scheme (for transfer before 6 April 2012)			
	Not C-O	COSR	COMP	COMB
COSR (GMPs, *s 9(2B)* rights)	Not possible	Member consent or actuarial certificate	Member consent	Member consent or actuarial certificate
COMP (protected rights)	Not possible	Member consent	Member consent or actuarial certificate	Member consent or actuarial certificate

7.2.16 *Scheme mergers*

Transferring Scheme	*Receiving Scheme* *(for transfer before 6 April 2012)*			
	Not C-O	*COSR*	*COMP*	*COMB*
COMB:	Not possible			
(a) GMPs, *s 9(2B)* rights	Not possible	(a) member consent or actuarial certificate	(a) member consent	(a) member consent or actuarial certificate
(b) protected rights	Not possible	(b) member consent	(b) member consent or actuarial certificate	(b) member consent or actuarial certificate

Statutory deficits

7.2.17 *Section 75* of the *Pensions Act 1995* triggers a potential debt on an employer in certain circumstances. These include when a scheme winds up or the employer ceases to have any active members in the scheme. This will of course happen in relation to the transferring scheme following the transfer of the members out of the scheme. Broadly, under *s 75* as currently enacted, no debt is triggered if all the active members in the transferring scheme stop accruing benefits and the transfer is made out of the transferring scheme before it starts to wind up.

It may happen that a winding up of the transferring scheme is needed to be triggered before the merger date. (This may be necessary to give power to make transfers without consent.)

Accordingly it is important at an early stage to check on the funding position of the transferring scheme. If it is less than 100% funded on the statutory buy-out basis, then a debt will be triggered on the employer. In effect this may be a cash-flow issue. It means that the employer will have to fund the deficit at the time of the merger (instead of having a period of years in which to fund).

There may be ways of structuring the merger so as to avoid such a funding requirement. However they suffer from looking slightly artificial and would need careful consideration.

One method would be to do the merger in two stages:

- transfer all but a handful of active employees (who remain in the transferring scheme). Assets are left behind in the transferring scheme sufficient to cover the liabilities for those remaining employees on a 100% buy-out basis; and

- once the first transfer has been made, the remaining active employees can transfer to the receiving scheme (perhaps with their consent). No debt is triggered on the basis that the transferring scheme is then 100% funded on the buy-out basis.

In practice the trustees of the transferring scheme may be reluctant to proceed if this looks like a way of avoiding the *s 75* deficit. In addition the receiving scheme may have issues about receiving under-funded transfers in.

Obtaining clearance from the Pensions Regulator may need to be considered – see *Pensions and transactions – applying to TPR for clearance*, **4.13**.

Indemnities for the trustees

7.2.18   The trustees of the transferring scheme may well look for protection in relation to their personal position. Prior to the merger taking effect they will usually have an indemnity for liabilities they properly incur out of the assets of the transferring scheme. Once those assets are transferred to the receiving scheme they will lose that indemnity. They may well look for indemnities from the receiving scheme, but it is generally easier if the employer gives any indemnities. This may be no more than a repetition (inserted into the face of the merger agreement) of the existing indemnities from the employer in the transferring scheme documents (perhaps extended to make it clear that the merger itself is being covered). Conversely, the trustees of the receiving scheme may be reluctant to give indemnities.

This is one area mainly where there may well be more difficult negotiations between the parties. Accordingly it is important for the employer to consider the implications in advance. Such indemnities may well avoid the need for payment of insurance premiums by the transferring trustees (which will mean a saving of those premiums and hence a benefit in terms of funding for the employer).

It is possible that the receiving scheme trustees may well also look for indemnities from the employer in relation to the merger transaction (and/or confirmation of onward funding particularly in relation to hidden liabilities and/or under-funded transfers).

Generally any indemnities given by the employer should be limited to cover liabilities incurred by the trustees in good faith. Employers should also consider if they should also be expressed not to apply to the extent that the trustees can

7.2.18 *Scheme mergers*

recover from any third party (eg under an insurance policy) – see *Trustee directors: exonerations, indemnities and insurance*, **11.7** below.

Transferring trustees may also look for insurance cover to be continued.

Trusteeship

Conflict issues

7.2.19   Generally the employer must recognise that any trustees who are appointed by the employer must not be treated as though they are representatives of the employer. They must perform their trustee role properly, making any decision ignoring any other interests they may have.

Onward selection

7.2.20   The employer will also want to consider how the merger may affect the composition of the trustee body in the merged (receiving) scheme. Will this need to be changed to reflect the new membership? Will the members of the transferring scheme (and its trustees) look for some form of representation in the merged scheme?

Summary of issues for the employers

7.2.21   Generally when considering a pension scheme merger, employers should seek to:

● establish clear objectives;

● address any potential problem areas at the outset;

● be realistic about the needs of the trustees;

● seek to control and manage the merger process (eg by agreeing an action plan and a timetable of regular meetings).

7.3 Mergers: the trustees' perspective

Summary

This section looks at the issues for mergers of pensions schemes from the perspective of the receiving and transferring trustees. It looks in particular at:

- the impact on the funding position of the schemes

- trustee powers

- trustees fiduciary duties

- actuarial certificates; and

- indemnities

7.3.1   Even in a simple merger (one scheme into the other), the perspective of the two sets of trustees will usually differ.

In practice it is almost inevitable that one scheme will be better funded than the other. This means that the ongoing merged scheme will be funded somewhere in the middle (ie better funded than one of the original schemes, less well funded than the other).

Example

7.3.2   It is helpful to look at a simple example of a merger.

Let us assume an employer has two separate schemes. One is an executive scheme, the other is a main scheme. Both are final salary (defined benefit) occupational pension schemes. Let us assume that the latest estimate of the funding position is:

Scheme	*IAS 19 funding*	*Ongoing funding (technical provisions)*	*PPF funding*
Executive	105%	98%	84%
Main	130%	125%	112%
Merged	125%	120%	105%

439

7.3.2 *Scheme mergers*

Because the executive scheme is much smaller than the main scheme, the scheme that would result from a merger is only slightly worse funded than the existing main scheme.

Issues for the trustees

7.3.3　There are a number of issues that both sets of trustees need to consider before going ahead and agreeing to a merger. The questions are the same both for the transferring scheme and the receiving scheme.

The main issues are:

- Should the trustees agree to the merger?
- Do the trustees have power to agree to the merger?
- What can be done to protect the scheme members?
- What can be done to protect the trustees?

Should the trustees agree to the merger?

7.3.4　Broadly the trustees of both schemes need to satisfy themselves that the merger is in the best interests of the beneficiaries of the scheme.

In practice, in a merger this usually means the members (and their spouses and dependants etc); the position of the employers is protected by the need for their express consent to the merger (acting through the principal company).

This may actually be taking too cautious a view. It may well be the case that legally trustees are entitled to consider the interests of the employers (as quasi beneficiaries of the scheme). However it is safest, given the need for the consent of the principal company, for the trustees to look at the position of the members.

The trustees need to consider the implications of the merger (having taken proper advice and considered appropriate information). Having done that do they consider that the merger is in the best interests of the members?

The issues to be addressed will depend on the precise terms of the merger.

In our example, from the perspective of the executive scheme (being wound up and transferring its liabilities to the main scheme), the main issues are:

- benefit issues;
- balance of power comparisons;

440

- funding issues;

- motive for the merger.

Transferring scheme

What benefits are to be granted in the receiving scheme?

7.3.5 In practice it is common for existing benefits to be mirrored precisely in the receiving scheme. If any changes are in fact proposed, they will still have to be made either with the express consent of the members or within the limits allowed by the actuarial certificate. Obviously the trustees need carefully to consider the implications of any proposed adverse changes (or indeed changes which may or may not be adverse – eg a change to the guaranteed level of pension increases or to the date on which increases are made).

If benefit improvements are proposed as part of the merger, this can be a factor weighing quite heavily in the mind of the trustees in favour of agreeing to a merger. In practice even if the transferring scheme is well funded (and in surplus), it is common to find that there is no unilateral right for the trustees to be able to improve benefits as a result (at least prior to a winding up). Accordingly there may be no expectation of the employer agreeing to benefit improvements if the merger did not take place.

Although a benefit improvement helps the trustees to agree to the merger, it is not necessarily a conclusive factor. Conversely, the absence of a benefit improvement is also not a conclusive factor against a merger. Other factors also need to be considered and weighed in the balance.

How does the balance of powers compare?

7.3.6 What level of employer control is there in the main scheme when compared to the executive scheme? When can the trustees act without any need for employer consent and when is employer consent needed (or can the employer direct the trustees)?

This is relevant because, even if the benefits are the same, it may be that the trustees in the executive scheme had greater control over its assets and benefits etc than is possessed by the trustees in the main scheme. For example, one set of trustees may have the ability to use surplus on a winding-up to increase benefits without any need for employer consent.

In practice the legal advisers should draw up a table of the main control points and discretions in relation to the schemes and make a comparison.

441

How do the solvency levels compare?

7.3.7   In practice one scheme is going to be better funded than the other. In our example, the main scheme is better funded than the executive scheme. This means that, from the perspective of the executive scheme trustees, the merged scheme will be better funded on the three measures available.

This means that the ultimate provision of benefits to the members of the executive scheme should be more secure in the merged scheme than it would have been in the executive scheme (in marginal cases it may be appropriate to ask the actuary to consider the security position for each class of beneficiary, given that the winding-up rule in the merged main scheme may prefer one class over another).

Conversely, the receiving scheme trustees will be concerned to consider the impact of the potential reduction in the solvency level. Is this material? Will the employers make it up by providing extra funding? Is security available?

This may not be an issue if the assets are held in the merged scheme in separate segregated pools after the merger. The merged scheme would then be treated in effect as two separate schemes for many purposes (but this may mean that some of the advantages of a merger fall away).

What is the motive for the merger?

7.3.8   The executive scheme trustees need to consider the motive of the employer in requesting the merger. If this were (say) to gain access to surplus that it could not otherwise gain access to, this may mean that the merger is for an improper purpose and hence not a correct use of the merger power in either scheme.

This is a difficult area in which, frankly, it is difficult to discover any consistent underlying principle from the decisions of the courts. The particular circumstances of each merger will need to be considered carefully.

Notifying the Pensions Regulator

7.3.9   A scheme merger is not a notifiable event requiring the employer to notify the Pensions Regulator, but a decision to transfer out as part of a merger may well be an event requiring the transferring trustees to notify the Regulator. It is a notifiable event if:

- a decision is made for more than 5% of the scheme's assets to be transferred (or assets of more than £1.5 million); and

- the scheme is not fully funded on the PPF basis or a report has been made the Regulator in last 12 months about a failure of the employer to pay contributions.

See generally *Notifiable events*, **13.1**.

In any event, informing the Pensions Regulator of a proposed merger is often helpful to keep the Regulator informed of events affecting the scheme.

Receiving scheme trustees

7.3.10   From the perspective of the trustees of the receiving scheme, the same issues also arise.

What benefits are granted in the main scheme?

7.3.11   In relation to *benefits* it will obviously be easier for the trustees of the main scheme to agree to the merger if a benefit improvement is proposed for the members of the main scheme (and this would not otherwise be available as a unilateral act by the trustees).

In our example, the effect of the merger will be to reduce the solvency in the main scheme. However it would seem to remain adequately funded. Actuarial advice on this should be sought.

The reduction in solvency may well only be a reduction in the security for benefits (rather than necessarily reducing the benefits themselves). If, as in our example, the transferring scheme is quite small, the trustees of the receiving scheme may be able to decide that the reduction in solvency is relatively small and hence it is appropriate to agree to the merger.

Conversely, if the trustees are not satisfied about the potential adverse impact on solvency, they could consider a formal undertaking from the principal company in relation to funding to cover the reduction. This could reinforce any existing funding obligation on the employers.

Hidden liabilities: benefits

7.3.12   The main scheme trustees also have to consider whether there are any 'hidden liabilities' being transferred to them. In practice the executive scheme trustees will look for all liabilities to provide benefits to members to be transferred to the main scheme. This is so that they can wind up the executive scheme (and it will also assist the actuary in giving the actuarial certificate).

7.3.12   *Scheme mergers*

The trustees of the main (receiving) scheme should consider whether there are any 'hidden liabilities' not reflected in the actuarial valuation. Examples include:

- any potential liability to equalise benefits are triggered as a result of unequalised benefits – eg *Barber*, guaranteed minimum pensions (GMPs) or age discrimination claims;

- any liability towards part-time members;

- any liability as a result of mis-statements or mis-recordings of data etc;

- potential liability under the age discrimination regulations.

Hidden liabilities: others

7.3.13   It is possible that the executive scheme trustees also have other liabilities (eg if they have failed to exercise their investment powers properly and this has resulted in a diminution of assets in the scheme).

These liabilities will not transfer as a result of an acceptance by the main scheme of the benefit liabilities of the executive scheme. However the executive scheme trustees may seek an indemnity for the main scheme trustees covering such liabilities. This is discussed further below. The main scheme trustees when deciding whether or not to agree to the merger should consider the implications of such an indemnity.

Motive

7.3.14   Lastly, the motive of the employers in seeking the merger is also relevant as regards the proper exercise of the power of the main scheme trustees to agree to the merger.

Actuarial advice

7.3.15   It is important for both sets of trustees to have relatively up-to-date figures on the solvency of the two schemes.

It will also be important that both sets of solvency figures are assessed by reference to the same actuarial assumptions (or any differences made clear and the effect of them advised on by the actuaries).

Do the transferring trustees have power to merge?

7.3.16 In relation to the executive scheme trustees (the transferring trustees in our example), the main issue is whether there is a bulk transfer rule allowing transfer of members without any requirement for their consent.

If there is not a suitable rule, is there a transfer rule on a winding up of the scheme or could a bulk transfer rule be introduced now?

Powers on winding-up

7.3.17 In relation to bulk transfers on a winding-up, there is a statutory implied transfer power now under *s 74* of the *Pensions Act 1995*. However this route will require a winding-up of the transferring scheme and it may be that this gives more control to the trustees (eg a discretion as to what happens on surplus). The implications of this would need to be considered.

In addition, winding-up a scheme will usually trigger an immediate requirement on the employers to make up any deficit on the buy-out basis.[5]

Amendment before winding-up

7.3.18 If the transferring scheme needs to be amended to introduce a power to make transfers without consent, the regulations under *s 67* of the *Pensions Act 1995* make it clear that the inclusion of such a power is not prohibited by that section (it still leaves open the question about whether or not the exercise of a power to transfer is still a potential amendment within that section).

Actuarial Certificate

7.3.19 In order to make transfers without consent, the preservation requirements under the *Pension Schemes Act 1993* need to be complied with. *Reg 12* of the *1991 Preservation Regulations* allows a bulk transfer without consent of the members concerned, but only where there is part of a reorganisation of (broadly) pension schemes relating to the same group of employers and where the actuary to the transferring scheme gives a certificate.[6]

The Board of Actuarial Standards (BAS) has replaced the Faculty and Institute of Actuaries as the relevant regulator. BAS took over the guidance note to

---

5   See *s 75* of the *Pensions Act 1995*.
6   *Regulation 12* of the *Occupational Pension Schemes (Preservation of Benefit) Regulations 1991 (SI 1991/167*, as amended). See Appendix B at **7.3.31**.

actuaries on when they should issue the certificate. This was Guidance Note 16 (hence the common name GN16 certificate). GN16 ceased to apply from 1 October 2011 and was replaced by the Transformations TAS. The form of the certificate is now set out in *Schedule 3* to the *1991 Preservation Regulations* (see Appendix A below).

Broadly, the actuary to the transferring scheme (in our example the executive scheme) has to be able to confirm that:

- the transfer credits in the receiving scheme will be broadly no less favourable than the rights to be transferred – note they do not have to be identical, just broadly no less favourable (eg not materially inferior);

- discretionary benefits or increases in benefits of the receiving scheme can be taken into account for this purpose and need to be compared with discretionary benefits or increases under the transferring scheme.

A copy of an actuarial certificate, derived from that which used to be in GN16, is set out in Appendix A at **7.3.30**.

Discretionary practices

7.3.20 The actuarial certificate requires the actuary to look at the discretionary practices of the transferring scheme and compare them to the benefits being granted as an entitlement or discretionary practice in the receiving scheme.

If the receiving scheme has no relevant historical practice for the actuary to consider, GN16 used to indicate that the actuary could take into account announcements by the employer (or trustees) to the members or the actuary about their intended future practice in this area. This practice is likely to continue.

Winding-up position

7.3.21 In addition, GN16 itself (but not the preservation regulations) used to require the actuary also to consider the position of the benefits of the transferring members in the main scheme. If the main scheme were wound up shortly after the transfer, would those benefits be materially less than those payable from the transferring scheme?

This will involve the actuary considering the relative funding levels of both schemes and also looking at who has any discretion (on winding-up) over any surplus in the transferring scheme and the receiving scheme.

Ring fencing

7.3.22   If there is an issue here (eg if the receiving scheme were better funded than the transferring scheme or the transferring scheme gave a discretion to the trustees on winding-up whereas the receiving scheme does not), it may be possible to meet the concerns of the actuary in relation to the GN16 certificate (and indeed the fiduciary concerns of the sets of trustees) by providing for a degree of 'ring fencing' in the receiving scheme.

Ring-fencing is often designed particularly to deal with a concern that should the receiving scheme wind up shortly after the merger, then one set of beneficiaries is materially worse off than they would have been had the merger not taken place. Such winding up may not be anticipated, but the ring fencing at least can go towards alleviating its impact.

In practice it is often sought to make ring fencing only apply if a winding-up actually occurs (ie it is not intended to keep the funds segregated in the receiving scheme – at least prior to a winding-up).

Ring fencing is often limited in time. The actuary to the transferring scheme (in our case the executive scheme) may consider that ring fencing is only needed for the period over which any surplus could be used up by an employer contribution holiday in any event. Actuarial advice on this is needed. In practice it may impossible notionally to recreate ring fencing if it is intended to apply after too long a period.

Ring fencing also needs to be considered in the light of the statutory overriding priority on winding-up under *s 73* of the *Pensions Act 1995*. In practice this may mean that only any surplus over the PPF or winding-up solvency level is available for allocation as part of ring fencing.

Contracting-out issues

7.3.23   Finally, if the transferring (executive) scheme is contracted out, the statutory requirements in relation to contracting out will need to be complied with (see above in relation to employer's issues).

In practice, the trustees of the executive scheme will be looking to ensure that the transfer discharges their liabilities to provide contracted-out benefits. Some of the problems of this are discussed earlier.

Further regulatory issues are discussed below.

Powers of the receiving scheme trustees

7.3.24   The receiving scheme trustees need to check that they have power to:

447

- admit the transferring members; and

- grant them the transfer credits for power service that is envisaged.

Some amendments may be needed to the deeds of the receiving scheme to achieve this.

The transferring scheme trustees may be looking for entrenchment of some discretionary practices or powers that are in the transferring scheme. These will need to be documented in the receiving scheme.

Conversely, the receiving scheme trustees may want to ring-fence some of their surplus (or to think about requesting benefit improvements) before agreeing to the transfer.

The receiving scheme trustees may also look for a funding guarantee from the employer (in relation to any reduction of solvency that occurs as a result of the merger) or for any hidden liabilities. This could run for a limited period.

Notifying the Pensions Regulator

7.3.25 A scheme merger is not a notifiable event requiring the employer to notify the Pensions Regulator, but a decision to transfer-out as part of a merger may well be an event requiring the transferring trustees and the receiving trustees to notify the Regulator. It is a notifiable event if:

- a decision is made for a transfer-in of more than 5% of the scheme's assets (or assets of more than £1.5 million); and

- the scheme is not fully funded on the PPF basis or a report has been made the Regulator in last 12 months about a failure of the employer to pay contributions.

In addition it is a notifiable event for receiving trustees to make a decision to grant additional benefits under the scheme without either:

- seeking advice from the scheme actuary; or

- securing additional funding if such funding was advised by the scheme actuary.

There is no exemption from this notifiable event if the scheme is well funded etc.

See generally *Notifiable Events*, **13.1**.

In any event, informing the Pensions Regulator of a proposed merger is often helpful to keep the Regulator informed of events affecting the scheme.

Trustee protections and indemnities

Transferring trustees

7.3.26   The transferring (executive) scheme trustees may well have existing exoneration clauses and/or indemnities either out of the fund or from the employers. By transferring the assets of the executive scheme to the main scheme they will be losing the protection of the indemnity out of the assets of the fund.

This should lead them to consider what protections should be given in relation to the merger. A restatement of any indemnity from the employer would be helpful. If there is not an existing indemnity from the employer, then the executive scheme trustees may well look for an indemnity from the employer.

Depending on the financial status of the employer, the executive scheme trustees may also look for indemnities from the receiving scheme trustees.

Insurance?

7.3.27   One protection would be for the transferring (executive) trustees to seek insurance cover for any claims that may arise. However there will be a cost involved in this (this is one factor leading the employer to be more likely to agree to give an indemnity).

It may be appropriate to advertise for missing beneficiaries in the executive scheme. Some limited protection against unknown claims is given to the trustees if this is done under *s 27* of the *Trustee Act 1925*.

Receiving trustees

7.3.28   From the perspective of the receiving scheme trustees, they may also look for indemnity and/or funding covenants from the employer.

It is more difficult for receiving scheme trustees to grant an indemnity to the transferring trustees. They could perhaps feel that there is sufficient surplus being transferred as part of the merger process and that this justifies them granting such an indemnity.

Obviously if the two schemes have been run side by side for some period as part of the employers pension arrangements, the trustees may be feel it easier in giving indemnities.

7.3.29   *Scheme mergers*

Merger costs

7.3.29   The expenses of the merger need to be considered. In practice it may be easier for the employer to agree to meet these direct on the basis that this means the actuarial figures available to the two sets of trustees are less likely to be reduced.

Appendix A – Actuarial Certificate from Schedule 3, Preservation Regulations (formerly called a GN16 Certificate)

7.3.30

Inserted from 6 April 2011 by *SI 2011/672, reg 3(1), (3), Sch 1.*

Actuarial Certificate for the purposes of Regulation 12 of the Occupational Pension Schemes (Preservation of Benefit) Regulations 1991

Actuary's Certificate

Given for the purposes of regulation 12(3) of
the Occupational Pension Schemes (Preservation of Benefit) Regulations 1991.

THIS CERTIFICATE IS SUBJECT TO THE NOTES BELOW

The name of the transferring scheme is:

The reference number of Her Majesty's Revenue and Customs for that scheme is:

The name of the receiving scheme is:

The reference number of Her Majesty's Revenue and Customs for that scheme is:

1   I certify that in my opinion, the transfer credits to be acquired for each member under the receiving scheme in the categories of member covered by this certificate are, broadly, no less favourable than the rights to be transferred.

2   Where it is the established custom for discretionary benefits or increases in benefits to be awarded under the transferring scheme, I certify that in my opinion, there is good cause to believe that the award of discretionary benefits or increases in benefits under the receiving scheme will (making allowance for any amount by which transfer credits under the receiving scheme are more favourable than the rights to be transferred) be, broadly, no less favourable.

In making this certification:

— I used these benefits:

— I used this data:

— I used these key actuarial assumptions to value the rights, transfer credits, any discretionary benefits and any discretionary increases in benefits:

— I used these documents:

The categories of member covered by this certificate are:

Signature:

Date of signature:

Name:

Qualification:

Address:

Name of employer (if applicable):

Notes:

Phrases used in this certificate have the same meaning as in the Occupational Pension Schemes (Preservation of Benefit) Regulations 1991 ('the 1991 Regulations').

The certification in paragraph 1 was made in accordance with regulation 12(4) of the 1991 Regulations. The certification in paragraph 2 was made in accordance with regulation 12(4A) of the 1991 Regulations.

This certificate is valid only for the purposes of the 1991 Regulations.

This certificate must not be taken by the trustees or managers of the scheme as authority to make a transfer without members' consents. It must also not be taken as a recommendation to make a transfer without members' consents. The trustees or managers of the scheme need to satisfy themselves that making the transfer is consistent with their duties to the transferring members and the remaining members. The trustees of the scheme need to satisfy themselves that making the transfer is consistent with their responsibilities and powers under trust law.

7.3.30 *Scheme mergers*

The actuary is not expressing in this certificate an opinion on whether or not the amount of the transfer value is reasonable.

The actuary has taken account of the benefits accrued by the date of this certificate. The actuary has not taken account of any differences between the terms and conditions of any benefits that may accrue in the future under the transferring scheme and the receiving scheme.]

Inserted by SI 2011/672, reg 3(1), (3), Sch 1.

Appendix B – Regulation 12 of the Occupational Pension Schemes (Preservation of Benefit) Regulations 1991 (SI 1991/167, as amended to 6 April 2013)

7.3.31

12   Transfer of member's accrued rights without consent

(1)   For the purposes of section 73(4) of the Act, a scheme may provide for the member's accrued rights to be transferred to another occupational pension scheme (as described in section 73(2)(a)(i) of the Act) without the member's consent where the conditions set out in paragraphs (2) and (3) of this regulation are satisfied.

(1A)   For the purposes of section 73(4) of the Act, a scheme may provide for a transfer payment to be made to another occupational or personal pension scheme (as described in section 73(2)(a)(i) of the Act) without the member's consent where the conditions set out in paragraph (6) of this regulation are satisfied.

(2)   The condition set out in this paragraph is that the rights of a member are being transferred from the transferring scheme to the receiving scheme and either:

(a)   the transferring scheme and the receiving scheme relate to persons who are or have been in employment with the same employer; or

(b)   the transferring scheme and the receiving scheme relate to persons who are or have been in employment with different employers, the member concerned is one of a group in respect of whom transfers are being made from the transferring scheme to the receiving scheme, and either:

    (i)   the transfer is a consequence of a financial transaction between the employers; or

452

(ii) the employers are companies or partnerships bearing a relationship to each other such as is described in regulation 64(2) of the Occupational Pension Schemes (Contracting-out) Regulations 1996 (meaning of expression 'connected employer').

(3) The condition set out in this paragraph is that—

(a) the relevant actuary gives a certification, by completing the certificate in Schedule 3, in relation to the members' rights in the receiving scheme;

(b) the relevant actuary sends that certificate to the trustees or managers of the transferring scheme;

(c) the transfer takes place within 3 months of the date of the relevant actuary's signature in the certificate; and

(d) there are no significant changes to the benefits, data and documents used in making the certificate (see the benefits, data and documents specified in the certificate) by the date on which the transfer takes place.

(4) For the purposes of making the certification in paragraph 1 of the certificate in Schedule 3, where long service benefit in the transferring scheme is related to a member's earnings at, or in a specified period before, the time when he attains normal pension age then, in the case of a member in pensionable service at the date of transfer, the value of the rights to be transferred shall be based on pensionable service (including any transfer credits) in the transferring scheme up to that date and projected final pensionable earnings.

(4A) For the purposes of making the certification in paragraph 2 of the certificate in Schedule 3, the relevant actuary shall, in considering whether there is good cause, have regard to all the circumstances of the case and in particular—

(a) to any established custom of the receiving scheme with regard to the provision of discretionary benefits or increases in benefits; and

(b) to any announcements made with regard to the provision of such benefits under the receiving scheme.

(4B) Where it is proposed that a member's accrued rights are to be transferred in accordance with this regulation, information about the proposed transfer and details of the value of the rights to be transferred (including rights in respect of death in service benefits and survivors' benefits) shall be furnished to the member not less than one month before the proposed transfer is due to take place.

(5) In this regulation 'the relevant actuary' means—

7.3.31 *Scheme mergers*

(a)   where the transferring scheme is a scheme for which an actuary is required under *section 47* of the *Pensions Act 1995* to be appointed, the individual for the time being appointed in accordance with subsection (1) of that section as actuary for that scheme;

(b)   in any other case, a Fellow of the Institute and Faculty of Actuaries or a person with other actuarial qualifications who is approved by the Secretary of State, at the request of the trustees or managers of the scheme, as being a proper person to act for the purposes of this regulation in connection with the scheme.

(6)   The conditions set out in this paragraph are that—

(a)   the transferring scheme is or has been a stakeholder pension scheme, within the meaning of section 1 of the Welfare Reform and Pensions Act 1999 or Article 3 of the Welfare Reform and Pensions (Northern Ireland) Order 1999, and the receiving scheme is such a scheme;

(b)   the transferring scheme has commenced winding-up; and

(c)   the transfer payment is of an amount at least equal to the cash equivalent of the member's rights under the scheme, as calculated and verified in a manner consistent with regulations made under section 97 of the 1993 Act (calculation of cash equivalents).

7.4 Mergers: carrying out the merger

Summary

This section looks at the mechanics of carrying out a merger of pension schemes. It involves looking at various stages including:

- deciding on the merger and on advisers
- drafting agreements
- obtaining relevant consents
- finalising advice
- holding meetings of the trustees
- giving information to members
- finalising the asset transfers

Advisers

7.4.1   Both sets of trustees (and the employer) are going to need advice on the actuarial issues on funding in relation to a merger. In the vast majority of cases an actuarial certificate is also going to be needed.

Legal advice is also going to be needed for both sets of trustees – do they have power to carry out the merger? What are the legal implications?

In practice it is common for the trustees to look for the existing advisers to be used. It is common for the advisers to advise both the employer and the trustees in relation to ongoing trustee matters. Can this continue in relation to a merger?

7.4.2   There is no single answer to this. If the parties have separate independent advisers, this may help from a perception issue. If the merger is ever the subject of a challenge, it is helpful for the trustees to be able to point to the fact that they have had independent legal and actuarial advice. This may be particularly important if some or all of the trustees have conflicting roles (eg as trustees of the other scheme or as senior management of the employer). Conversely, the use of independent advisers is likely to increase costs.

In relation to legal advisers, professional obligations may restrict the ability of one set of solicitors to act, even with express consent. The code policed by the Solicitors' Regulation Authority needs to be considered.

7.4.3   *Scheme mergers*

Documentation

7.4.3   Once the broad outlines of the merger have been discussed, there is a need for a merger agreement to document the actual merger process. It is not a particularly long document. It will deal with:

- conditions before the merger takes place;
- what will happen on the merger (transfer of assets and grant of benefits);
- the nature of the benefits to be granted to the transferring members;
- any indemnities given by the employers or by the trustees;
- any amendments to the schemes.

Documenting the benefits

7.4.4   In relation to benefits, it is helpful to set out in the merger agreement the individual rules from the transferring scheme that will apply to define the benefits in the receiving scheme. This clarifies which rules from the transferring scheme will apply and which rules from the receiving scheme will apply. For example, it is common for the winding-up provision in the receiving scheme to apply (and not the winding-up provision in the transferring scheme).

This avoids any later arguments about this issue. In practice such an exercise will have to be carried out at some stage in order to document the benefits in the receiving scheme. It will be helpful to carry it out sooner to avoid dispute later.

Amending the rules in the receiving scheme

7.4.5   Some particular rules that may need amending in the receiving scheme are:

- the employer lien rule;
- the death nomination rule;
- the winding-up rule in relation to any ring-fencing.

Lien rule

7.4.6   Occupational schemes often have a lien rule entitling the employer to claim a charge over benefits of a member in limited circumstances (this was allowed by the preservation laws and now by the *Pensions Act 1995*). This lien generally cannot apply to transfer credits, but this prohibition on the lien applying to transfer credits does not apply in (generally) circumstances of a merger. There may need to be an amendment of the lien rule in the receiving scheme to clarify that the existing lien in the transferring scheme can continue. See further *Lien and forfeiture rules*, **14.1**.

Death benefit nominations

7.4.7 Schemes often provide for members to be able to give (non-binding) nominations in relation to the destination of lump sum benefits following death. These often envisage that the trustees of the scheme must have received any nomination before the member's death. If the rule in the receiving scheme is written in this way, it will obviously mean that the trustees of the receiving scheme cannot consider nominations received (before the merger date) by the trustees of the transferring scheme. It is a helpful to include a provision in the merger agreement to amend the receiving scheme so that the trustees can consider and rely on nominations given to the transferring trustees before the merger date. This avoids the risk of a transferring member dying shortly after the merger without having updated his or her nomination form.

Ring fencing

7.4.8 If ring-fencing is envisaged (see above) the amendments to the receiving scheme should also be documented in the merger deed.

Pensions Regulator

7.4.9 It is often prudent to let the Pensions Regulator know about the proposed merger (to keep it informed).

Notifiable event

7.4.10 A decision by either set of trustees to transfer/receive assets representing more than 5% of the assets of a scheme or of more than £1.5 million will be a notifiable event unless the scheme is funded to the PPF level so that the funding exemption applies (and there has been no default in the payment of contributions).

The receiving trustees will have a notification obligation if they grant benefits without both taking advice from the scheme actuary or do not secure any additional funding advice.

See generally *Notifiable events*, **13.1**.

7.4.11 *Scheme mergers*

Clearance

7.4.11 A full scheme merger is unlikely to be an event with a potential material adverse effect on the support for the pension schemes so that clearance is required from the Pensions Regulator in relation to its 'moral hazard' powers under the *Pensions Act 2004*. There may be circumstances in which clearance may be more desirable (eg if one or more employers who support the transferring scheme are not becoming employers in the receiving scheme).

The issue on clearance needs to be considered in the light of the individual facts. See generally *Pensions and transactions – applying to TPR for clearance*, **4.13**.

Consents

7.4.12 Various consents to a merger are going to be needed:

- the transferring scheme actuary;
- possibly the receiving scheme actuary;
- both sets of trustees;
- possibly the transferring members; and
- the principal employers.

Tax: HM Revenue & Customs

7.4.13 The consent of the Pension Scheme Office (PSO) of the Inland Revenue used to be needed (before 6 April 2006) where the schemes were revenue approved. Consent from HMRC is no longer required, but the trustees and the employer will be concerned:

- to ensure that the transfer is an authorised payment out of the transferring schemes (ie that both the transferring and receiving schemes are tax registered);
- that the transfer-in does not count towards the annual allowance for the transferring members; and
- that any existing transitional tax protections (eg primary protection, lump sums, ability to retire at 50) are preserved and not lost by the merger.

One way for comfort to be given in this area is for the employer to agree to pay any increased tax costs etc incurred by members that would not have been paid but for the merger.

Tax: anti-forestalling

7.4.14   The anti-forestalling tax regime introduced by the *Finance Act 2009* applied for tax years 2009/10 and 2010/11 to impose an additional tax charge in some circumstances on accrual of benefits for persons with income of over £130,000pa. There were some exemptions if (broadly) the pattern of benefit contributions/benefit accrual has not changed from previous years. The impact of the merger on the transferring employees (who will now be accruing in a new scheme) needed to be considered.

Actuarial certificate

7.4.15   An actuarial certificate will be required to make a transfer of members without their consent. This was before 2011 called the GN16 certificate. This certificate is envisaged by the preservation legislation.[7] GN16 ceased to apply from 1 October 2011 and was replaced by the Transformations TAS and the certificate at *Schedule 3* to the *1991 Preservation Regulations*.

A copy of the form of certificate is included at **7.3.30**.

In addition, the actuary will need to give any certificate relating to changes in either of the two schemes. If the receiving scheme is contracted-out on a salary related basis, then a certificate has to be given by the actuary (under *s 37* of the *Pension Schemes Act 1993*) if any rule change is made that changes any *s 9(2B)* rights.

If there are other changes to benefits etc then a certificate under *s 67* of the *Pensions Act 1995* may also be needed.

Trustee consent

7.4.16   The trustees will also need to consent to the merger in practically all cases. It is perhaps conceivable there could be circumstances where the scheme does not require the consent of the trustees to bulk transfers, but this is very unusual. In any event employers will probably seek trustee consent.

Consent of the principal company (or employer) will almost certainly be needed under the rules of each scheme either relating to bulk transfers or in relation to amendments. The scheme deeds will need to be considered as to

---

7   See *reg 12* of the *Occupational Pension Schemes (Preservation of Benefit) Regulations 1991* (*SI 1991/167*, as amended).

whether or not consent or the individual employers (rather than the principal company) will also be needed.

Member consent

7.4.17   In practice it is common to circulate the active members to seek their consent to the transfer. This is on the basis that often their consent to joining the receiving scheme as active members will be sought in any event (particularly if the receiving scheme envisages member contributions – an authority for deduction from wages will be needed under *Part 2* of the *Employment Rights Act 1996*).[8]

Such a request for consent of the active members can make the point that if they do not consent then they will be treated as a deferred member. This will mean that their benefits will be transferred in any event (under the actuarial certificate) and they will not accrue any further pensionable service in the new receiving scheme after the merger date.

This approach can also be helpful if there are any amendments to benefits envisaged as part of the merger process that could be considered to be adverse to the transferring active members. Their consent to such changes can be sought.

This may make it easier for the actuary to give the actuarial certificate on the basis that it would only relate to pensioners and deferred members and not to the active members who have consented. If this approach is followed care needs to be taken to deal with the situation should an active member die or become a deferred member after having given consent (but before the merger date).

Contracting-out

7.4.18   The merger will need to comply with the various requirements of the contracting-out legislation in relation to discharge of existing contracted-out liabilities in the transferring scheme.

In practice this will often require the receiving scheme to be contracted-out itself. If the receiving scheme is a new scheme or is not already contracted-out, the trustees of the transferring scheme may only look to make a new transfer once a contracting-out certificate has actually been received by the receiving scheme (the alternative would be for the trustees of the transferring scheme to rely on indemnities from the employer/receiving scheme trustees).

---

8   Formerly the *Wages Act 1986*.

In practice this means that notices of contracting-out will need to be given to the members well in advance of the merger date (three months if there is a trade union unless it agrees to a shorter one-month period, otherwise one month) and time allowed for the relevant returns to be made to the contracting-out authorities. If requested, they can act quickly to grant a contracting-out certificate once they have received the forms.

Divorce orders

7.4.19　From 1 December 2000, schemes have found themselves having to act on pension-sharing orders made by the divorce courts. These have the effect of reducing the benefits payable to members and to give a pension credit in favour of the ex-spouse. This will need to be dealt with in the merger agreement to cover two situations:

- a merger during the implementation period for a pension credit;
- a merger where the transferring scheme has granted internal pension credit benefits to an ex-spouse.

Implementation period

7.4.20　The legislation allows an implementation period (usually four months) between receipt of the sharing order from the court and its final implementation by the scheme. There will need to be consideration as to what happens should the merger occur during that period.

Pension credit members

7.4.21　If the sharing order is implemented by a transfer out, then the ex-spouse will not be a member of the scheme so need not be considered further.

If, however, the pension credit is secured by the grant of a credit of benefits within the transferring scheme, the ex-spouse will count as a 'pension credit member' for the purposes of the scheme. Accordingly those benefits will also need to be transferred as part of the merger process. The relevant divorce regulations dealing with such pension credit benefits allow transfers without consent to another occupational pension scheme in a similar way to those under the preservation regulations.

7.4.21 *Scheme mergers*

However (for no obvious reason) there are some differences in approach. Additional requirements[9] in relation to pension credits include that:

- the trustees consider the transfer to be reasonable to be made without the pension credit members' consent;

- 30 days' written notice has been given to the pension credit members; and

- there is no outstanding transfer notice by the pension credit member seeking a transfer out of the scheme at the date the merger is agreed.

Earmarking orders

7.4.22 If there are any existing divorce earmarking orders then notifications of the merger need to be given by the trustees of the transferring scheme to:

- the ex-spouse; and

- the trustees of the receiving scheme.[10]

Trustees' meetings

7.4.23 Both sets of the trustees will need to approve the merger.

Meetings

7.4.24 Meetings of both sets of trustees will need to be convened to approve the merger and merger agreement. The usual requirements for trustees' meetings will need to be complied with. (The *Pensions Act 1995* usually requires at least ten days notice for a meeting of individual trustees.)

Conflicts

7.4.25 It will be prudent to check the terms of the scheme trust deed (and any articles of association of a corporate trustee) to see how conflicts of interests are dealt with. It is commonly the case that some trustees have a conflict as being also a trustee of the other scheme and/or interested in the employer.

---

9 See generally *reg 10* of the *Pension Sharing (Pension Credit Benefit) Regulations 2000* (*SI 2000/1054*).
10 In relation to earmarking orders see *reg 4* of the *Divorce Etc (Pensions) Regulations 2000* (*SI 2000/1123*).

In any event it is prudent to declare interests or conflicts like this at the relevant meetings so that everybody is aware of them.

It is prudent to check that the meetings comply with the requirements of the member-nominated trustee legislation. For example are the right number of member-nominated trustees present as envisaged by the legislation (or any opt-out)? If an individual were seeking to challenge the merger at a later date, they may seek to do so on the basis that the scheme has failed to comply with this legislation.

Decision

7.4.26   The meeting should then consider the merger proposal and the advice from both the actuaries and the lawyers.

Having done this, the trustees should make a decision about whether or not to agree to the merger and to execute the merger agreement. It may be appropriate to delegate power actually to carry out the merger to a committee of trustees at this stage (a delegation provision could be useful and be included in the merger agreement as well).

Actuarial advice

7.4.27   The advice to be considered from the actuaries will include:

- advice on the funding of the schemes. It is prudent to have it on an ongoing, PPF and buy-out basis;

- whether the relevant actuarial certificate will be granted;

- that any relevant certificates for amendments of the scheme (*PSA 1993, s 37* or *PA 1995, s 67*) are available;

- whether any potential liability arises on winding-up of the transferring scheme under *s 75* of the *Pensions Act 1995* (based on the buy-out basis);

- whether any changes are needed to the schedule of contributions etc as a result of the merger;

Any advice needed in relation to any change in the statement of investment principles (SIP) may usefully come from the actuary as well (see below).

Legal advice

7.4.28   The legal advice needs to confirm that:

- the trustees have power to agree to the merger;

- the merger complies with the relevant legislation and that the required consents are being obtained;

- the merger will comply with the provisions of the trust deeds governing the schemes;

- the factors mentioned are those that the trustees should be considering in relation to the merger;

- the trustees will, in the lawyers' view, be acting properly if they agree to the merger having considered the factors mentioned in the advice letter.

Ultimately whether or not to proceed with the merger is a decision for the trustees, but they should take it based on proper advice.

Information to members

Consultation

7.4.29   The *Pensions Act 2004* introduced a new obligation on employers to inform and consult employees about 'listed changes'. It is arguable that this includes a scheme merger (because there is a reduction in the accrual rate in the existing scheme). The converse argument is that if there is no change in the benefits for the members involved, the consultation requirements are pretty meaningless. This may perhaps need to be considered with the Pensions Regulator.

Under the *2004 Act*, consultation must be for at least 60 days before a relevant decision is made.

See generally *Pensions Act 2004: Employer's consultation obligations*, **15.1**.

Preservation regulations

7.4.30   The preservation regulations require notice of at least one month to be given to all members where there is a transfer without their consent. The sanction for failure to comply with this without reasonable excuse is potentially a fine on the transferring trustees from the Pensions Regulator.

Somewhat strangely there is no provision expressly exempting the trustees from the obligation to notify a member merely because they do not have his or her address (this will usually only apply to a deferred member). However failing to inform such person because of a lack of address may well be a reasonable excuse. Failure to comply with this notification obligation is not expressly stated to invalidate the transfer as part of the merger.

Ex-spouses of divorced members will also need to be informed of the merger. If they are benefiting from an earmarking order this obligation applies under *reg 4* of the *Divorce Etc* (*Pensions*) *Regulations 2000* (*SI 2000/1123*).

If the ex-spouse is a pension credit member then the requirement to give notice arises under the *Pension Sharing* (*Pension Credit Benefit*) *Regulations 2000*. The notice to be given must give notice of intention to transfer the rights to another scheme unless the pension credit member exercises a right to give a transfer notice out of the scheme (under *s 101F* of *PSA 1993*). Slightly oddly, under these regulations[11] giving this notice is a precondition to allow a transfer without consent.

In addition, the transferring members must, as new members, be given the usual information about the receiving scheme within two months of their becoming members of the scheme. This arises under the 2013 *Disclosure of Information Regulations* (before April 2014, the *1996 Regulations*). It will not apply if the transferring members are already members of the receiving scheme before the merger (if the transferring scheme is a top-up scheme).

The employer will also need to consider amending any references to the transferring scheme in the contract of employment.

Transfer of assets

7.4.31 Broadly a complete merger of one scheme into another will involve the transfer of all the relevant funds of the transferring scheme to the receiving scheme. The simplest way of achieving this is a global transfer of all assets of the transferring scheme into the receiving scheme.

The only exception to this should be that the transferring trustees should retain the benefit of any indemnities etc given to the transferring trustees. If the transferring trustees are retaining any funds to meet expenses etc this should also be carved out of the asset transfer.

Stamp duty/SDRT

7.4.32 Generally it is important to ensure that the asset transfer is stamped with a fixed £5 stamp duty. This will then avoid any potential charge to stamp duty reserve tax (SDRT) in relation to marketable securities etc. SDRT is normally charged as a percentage (0.5%) of the value of the assets being transferred. This can be significant, so it is important that this charge does not apply.

---

11 See *Reg 10* of the *Pension Sharing* (*Pension Credit Benefit*) *Regulations 2000* (*SI 2000/1054*).

7.4.32 *Scheme mergers*

A problem had arisen in relation to unit trust and open ended investment companies (OEICs). A change in stamp duty legislation has meant that stamp duty is no longer payable on the transfers of units in unit trusts or shares in OEICs. Instead stamp duty reserve tax (SDRT) is chargeable. In 2005, the Inland Revenue confirmed, in relation to pension fund mergers, that SDRT should not be payable where the assets transferring from the transferring scheme include unit trusts or OEICs.

Similarly stamp duty land tax should not be payable if land is transferred between the two schemes (see the HMRC SDLT manual at SDLTM31800).

Notification to asset holders

7.4.33 Having executed an asset transfer, notification must be given to the holders of the assets (eg fund managers, custodians, banks etc). This notification should confirm that the relevant assets have now been assigned to the new trustees and that instructions should be taken from the new trustees in the future.

Ongoing fund management

7.4.34 The trustees of the receiving scheme will need to decide how they want to manage the assets in the future. In practice it is relatively common for the existing fund managers to be retained for a period after the merger until any required review or rationalisation can be carried out.

If this course is to be followed then it will be important to novate the existing fund management agreements to ensure that the fund managers have been appointed properly (in particular in compliance with the requirements in relation to professional advisers under *s 47* of the *Pensions Act 1995*).

Statement of investment principles (SIP)

7.4.35 In addition, the fund managers will be required under the *Pensions Act 1995*, to seek to comply with the statement of investment principles of the receiving scheme.

This may mean a change to the receiving scheme's SIP is needed. Previously the transferring scheme's fund managers would have been following the SIP of the transferring scheme. One way of dealing with this point (on an interim basis) is to amend the SIP for the receiving scheme to deem it to include the SIP for the transferring scheme in relation to the transferring assets. Suitable advice will be needed in relation to the SIP and this change.

Relevant bank signatories and management mandates will need to be changed as well.

Post-merger notifications

7.4.36   Following the merger and completion of the transfer of assets, grant of new benefits etc various notifications remain to be completed. These include:

- telling the members about the transfer (and that they are now members of the receiving scheme);
- telling divorced ex-spouses of members;
- telling HMRC about the transfer and that the transferring scheme will now be wound up;
- telling the contracting-out authority about the transfer of contracting-out liabilities;
- telling the Pensions Registry about the winding-up of the transferring scheme;
- dealing with any re-elections for contracting out and any deeds of adherence etc;
- asking members to update death nominations and to consider reconfirming any choices they have made in relation to money purchase benefits such as AVCs.

Winding up of the old scheme

7.4.37   This will involve:

- obtaining final scheme accounts;
- notifying HMRC;
- closing the relevant files of the contracting-out authority (ie satisfying them that the contracting-out liabilities have been appropriately secured by the transfer to the receiving scheme);
- notifying the Pensions Registry of the winding-up;
- considering whether to advertise in newspapers for missing beneficiaries or claims (*s 27* of the *Trustee Act 1925*);
- considering taking out any insurance.

The ongoing issues in the receiving scheme include:

7.4.37 *Scheme mergers*

- consents from active members to deductions from pay;
- review of death nominations;
- amending the receiving scheme trust deed to document any new benefits;
- updating the booklets etc;
- updating data protection consents etc.

Chapter 8

Cross-border schemes

8.1 Cross-border pension schemes in the EU

Summary

Special rules came into force on 30 December 2005 for UK occupational pension schemes operating cross-border in another EU Member State.

This chapter looks at the main impact of these provisions and at the Pensions Regulator's approach to implementing them.

The requirements include that a cross-border scheme:

- is fully funded;

- has obtained authorisation and approval from the Pensions Regulator;

- obtains full actuarial valuations annually; and

- complies with the 'social and labour laws' of the other relevant Member State.

Introduction

8.1.1   *Sections 287* to *295* of the *Pensions Act 2004* contain provisions intended to comply with the cross-border requirements of the *Directive on the Activities and Supervision of Institutions for Occupational Retirement Provision*[1] (the *Iorp Directive*).

---

1   *Directive 2003/41/EC.*

8.1.1 *Cross-border schemes*

The relevant regulations are the *Occupational Pension Schemes* (*Cross-border Activities*) *Regulations 2005*[2] (the *Cross-border Regulations 2005*). These came into force on 30 December 2005 for occupational pension schemes operating cross-border in another EU Member State.

These were amended in November 2007 to include the three non-EU EEA states (Iceland, Liechtenstein and Norway).[3]

They set out the conditions that an occupational pension scheme located in the UK must meet before it can begin to operate as a cross-border scheme. Serious concerns were expressed during the government consultation on the draft regulations, published in August 2005.

The deadline for EU Member States to comply with the *Iorp Directive* was 22 September 2005. Only nine out of the (then) 25 Member States met this deadline (the UK was not one of them). However, the provisions of the *Cross-border Regulations 2005* have, broadly, an effective date of 22 September 2005 – there are numerous references to time periods beginning on that date, as noted below.

What can a cross-border scheme do?

8.1.2 Under the *Iorp Directive*, occupational pension schemes established in one EEA state can engage in 'cross-border activity' (ie accept contributions from a European Employer (an employer under a cross-border scheme) and scheme members in other EEA states).

This is subject to certain conditions, including prior authorisation and approval by the relevant competent authority (the Pensions Regulator (TPR) in the case of the UK). For example, a multinational operating in a number of EEA states through subsidiary companies might wish to consolidate its pension arrangements in one EEA state or an employer in one EEA state might have commercial reasons for locating its pension scheme in another EEA state.

Guidance is available on the TPR website on TPR's approach to implementing the cross-border requirements.[4]

Trustees are liable to a civil penalty if they receive contributions from a European Employer:

---

2   *SI 2005/3381.*
3   *Occupational Pension Schemes* (*EEA States*) *Regulations 2007* (*SI 2007/3014*).
4   *www.thepensionsregulator.gov.uk/guidance/guidance-cross-border-schemes.aspx*

- in the absence of approval and authorisation as a cross-border scheme; and

- without relevant notifications from TPR.[5]

What is a cross-border scheme?

8.1.3   A cross-border scheme is one which has 'European members' or 'European survivors' (the latter meaning the survivors of European members who are entitled to benefits or have a right to future benefits under the scheme).

European members are (broadly) employees (or self-employed persons):

- who are 'qualifying persons' (ie those whose place of work under his contract is (or was) sufficiently located in another EEA state (other than the UK)) 'so that his relationship with his employer is subject to the social and labour law relevant to the field of occupational pensions';

- who are not 'seconded workers' – see box below; and

- in respect of whom contributions were made to the scheme by a 'European Employer' (ie the entity which employs the 'qualifying persons').

The definition is quite complex and there are some areas of doubt yet to be resolved. It is clear that:

- a scheme with active members outside the UK and only in other countries outside the EEA (eg the US, Singapore, Japan or Australia) does not qualify as a cross-border scheme; and

- active members in the UK (eg Scotland or Northern Ireland) or in parts of the British Isles not within the EEA (eg the Channel Islands or the Isle of Man) do not count – this is confirmed by the TPR guidance – whereas employees in the Republic of Ireland do.

Schemes which used to have active members outside the UK but which ceased to do so before 30 December 2005 seem likely to fall outside the cross-border regime. There is no express exemption in the legislation, but in practice it seems unlikely that the former employer will make contributions to the scheme in respect of them (and the specific provision in *reg 3(3)* dealing with former employers applies only to European Employers which have been approved by TPR).

---

5   *Pensions Act 2004, s 287.*

8.1.3 *Cross-border schemes*

EU countries (all also part of the EEA)		*Non-EU EEA countries*	*Examples of non-EU countries*
Austria	Italy	Iceland	Jersey
Belgium	Latvia	Liechtenstein	Guernsey
Bulgaria	Lithuania	Norway	Isle of Man
Croatia*	Luxembourg		Canada
Cyprus	Malta		Australia
Czech Republic	Netherlands		Singapore
Denmark	Poland		Switzerland
Estonia	Portugal		USA
Finland	Romania		Japan
France	Slovakia		Hong Kong
Germany	Slovenia		
Greece	Spain		
Hungary	Sweden		
Ireland	UK (and Gibraltar)		

* As at the date of writing, Croatia's accession to the EEA continues, pursuant to its EU accession, to be negotiated. For the purposes of UK legislation, however, it is deemed to be an EEA state by virtue of its EU membership.[6]

Deferred members and pensioners?

8.1.4 Having deferred members or pensioners who, having been employed in the UK, are now outside the UK and in another EEA state should not of itself make the scheme a cross-border scheme if they are no longer employed by a scheme employer (even if they are employed by an associated employer).

The position is less clear if a deferred member or pensioner was in fact working in the other EEA state for a scheme employer. It is possible that they could

---

6   *Interpretation Act 1989, Schedule 1* (definition of 'EEA state'); *European Communities Act 1972, Schedule 1, Part II* (definition of 'Member State').

(even though no longer active members) fall within the definition of a 'qualifying person'. There is nothing in the legislation that expressly requires a link between the employment and qualifying for benefits under the scheme. Instead the link is whether contributions are paid to the scheme by the employer 'in respect of' that member.

In practice it seems odd to categorise the employment of a deferred member as potentially qualifying a scheme as cross border. It will often be unlikely that a European Employer is making contributions to the scheme 'in respect of' a deferred member or pensioner (even general deficit contributions should be difficult to categorise in this way).

The TPR guidance only says that:

> 'Trustees and employers should be mindful of the position of all members, including deferred members and pensioners, when considering whether their scheme should be seeking authorisation and approval.'

Life members?

8.1.5   It is not clear whether offering life cover to members outside the UK could mean that the scheme qualifies as cross-border.

One area of concern with the draft regulations was that they envisaged that if an employer were a UK company with branches (and employees) elsewhere in the EU, the scheme would be treated as a cross-border scheme even if all the scheme members employed outside the UK were not members of the scheme.

The final regulations dealt with this by clarifying that to be a cross-border scheme (and have a European Employer), the employer must be making contributions to the scheme in respect of the non-UK employees. (In practice this is unlikely unless the non-UK employees are active members of the scheme.)

The final regulations also made it clear that seconded workers (see box below) are to be disregarded in determining whether an employer is a 'European Employer'. A scheme will not be carrying on cross-border activity if its only active members employed in another EEA state are seconded workers. This means that fewer schemes fall within the cross-border definition.

Auto-eject rule – stopping overseas workers being members

8.1.6   Given the potentially onerous requirements should a scheme become cross-border (see below), some schemes have included an 'auto-eject' rule

8.1.6   *Cross-border schemes*

(ie an express rule that a member will automatically cease to be an active member if he or she starts to work in an EEA state (unless the secondment provisions apply)).

This helps reduce the risk of an inadvertent contravention if there is a change in employment location of a member. As noted above, it relies (to a degree) on such a member becoming a deferred pensioner on his or her relocation and so not becoming a 'European member' (because the employer ceases to contribute in respect of him or her).

It has not yet been tested whether such an auto-eject rule is compatible with the prohibition, in *s 66A* of the *Pensions Act 1995*, on scheme provisions that treat a member differently, as regards contributions, benefits or eligibility, depending on whether or not the member works in the UK or outside.

All occupational schemes

8.1.7   There is no restriction of the cross-border requirements to defined benefit (DB) tax-registered schemes. A cross-border scheme can be:

- defined contribution (DC);

- a scheme without tax registration; or

- a *s 615* scheme (established only for employees outside the UK).

Seconded workers

8.1.8   The *Cross-border Regulations 2005* expressly exempt seconded workers from counting as a European member. TPR's guidance is in the box below. See further *Cross border schemes – seconded employees*, **8.2**.

Who are 'seconded employees'?

If employees are sent by a UK employer to work overseas for a period in another [EEA state],[7] and at the end of that period intend to return to resume work for that employer in the UK or intend to retire, then:

---

7   The guidance is not completely up-to-date at the time of writing, but does make clear that 'references to EU states in this guidance include EEA states …'.

- if they were sent to the other [EEA state] for a limited period; and

- they were sent for the purpose of providing services on behalf of the UK employer; and

- they intend at the end of that period either to return to the UK to work for the same employer, or to retire,

they are counted as seconded employees.

The characteristics of a secondment are:

- the employee being sent to work overseas from the UK;

- the employee providing services on behalf of the UK employer;

- the limited period; and

- the expectation either to return to the UK or to retire (in the UK or otherwise) at the end of that period.

Source: TPR guidance

http://www.thepensionsregulator.gov.uk/guidance/guidance-cross-border-schemes.aspx

TPR has published a decision tree to help decide whether or not a scheme falls within the cross-border provisions.[8]

---

8   Note that this flowchart predates the accession of the non-EU EEA states to the cross-border regime, and so references to 'EU member states' should be read accordingly.

8.1.8 *Cross-border schemes*

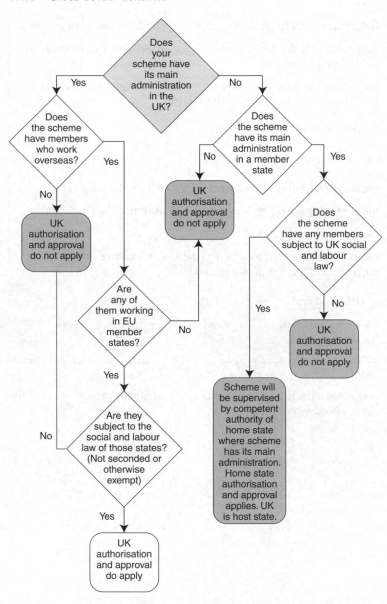

Source: TPR website *http://www.thepensionsregulator.gov.uk/guidance/guidance-cross-border-schemes.aspx*

Cross-border requirements ceasing

8.1.9 TPR's guidance points out that the cross-border requirements will cease to apply if all the liabilities for any European members (or survivors) are bought out in full or transferred to another arrangement.

Fully funded requirement

8.1.10 In the event of cross-border activity with another Member State, the *Iorp Directive* requires that an occupational pension scheme 'shall at all times be fully funded'.

Unlike a domestic scheme, a cross-border scheme is not permitted to rectify its underfunding through the use of a recovery plan, although the *Cross-border Regulations 2005* envisage a very limited recovery period in certain circumstances: schemes entering into cross-border activity will have to obtain annual valuations and to make up within 24 months of the effective date of a deficit valuation any shortfall identified in it on the statutory funding objective basis (under *s 222* of the *Pensions Act 2004*).

TPR's Code of Practice 03 points out that where a cross-border scheme's actuarial valuation reveals that the technical provisions are not covered, the trustees must send a valuation summary to the Pensions Regulator within a reasonable period.[9] The Code goes on to state that 'the reasonable period for sending the valuation summary to the Pensions Regulator is within ten working days of the date the related schedule of contributions is certified by the actuary. The schedule should be sent at the same time'.[10]

As a transitional provision, the final cross-border regulations gave existing cross-border schemes (those already engaging in cross-border activity on 22 September 2005) until 22 September 2008 to show that they are fully funded; this is an extra year from that envisaged in the draft regulations.

TPR has power to revoke the cross-border approval of schemes that fail to meet this funding requirement. To demonstrate compliance with the fully funded

---

9   See *paragraph 6(2)(b)(i)* of *Schedule 2* to the *2005 Scheme Funding Regulations*.
10   *Code of Practice 03*, paras 170 and 171.

8.1.10 *Cross-border schemes*

requirement, cross-border DB schemes will have to carry out annual (rather than triennial) valuations.

The regulations did not change to address one major area of concern. The government considered that the *Iorp Directive* requires an entire cross-border scheme (including the UK element) to be fully funded, whereas many respondents to the consultation interpreted the *Iorp Directive* as allowing this requirement to apply only to the cross-border element of a scheme. The final regulations, like the draft regulations, apply the fully funded requirement to the entire scheme (although TPR does have power to order the ring-fencing of assets if it has concerns (eg of misappropriation)).

This means that a scheme with just one (non-UK) scheme member employed at a branch in another EEA state would be brought within the cross-border provisions and have to be fully funded at all times. This is likely to deter many schemes from taking advantage of the cross-border provisions.

Furthermore, as noted above, the basis to be used for ascertaining whether a cross-border scheme is fully funded is the statutory funding objective, which may be more onerous than in many other EEA states.

EU/EEA social and labour laws

8.1.11 A cross-border scheme must comply with the 'social and labour laws' of the other relevant EEA state (*Pensions Act 2004, s 291*).

TPR is required to notify the relevant applicant at the scheme of details of the applicable social and labour laws that it has received from its corresponding regulator in the other EEA state (*Pensions Act 2004, s 290*).

At present, TPR has no definite intention to provide guidance on what 'compliance with the social and labour laws' means in each EEA state, as this information will become available gradually as applications are received from schemes to act cross border in each EEA state; in the meantime, schemes considering cross-border operation would be advised to take legal advice on the issue.

UK provisions 'not to apply'

8.1.12 Various provisions of the UK pension legislation are stated not to apply to European members (or survivors) in relation to their 'accrued European rights' – generally the rights that result from service as a European Member.

These excluded provisions include (for European Members who first become European Members of the scheme after 30 December 2005):

- preservation;
- revaluation;
- transfer values;
- indexation of pensions; and
- assignment, forfeiture etc.

Formalities: a brief outline

8.1.13   Broadly, before a scheme can operate cross-border in the EEA, TPR must have:

- authorised it to engage in cross-border activity generally; and
- approved it to receive contributions in respect of a specific employer from a specified different Member State.

Each time a scheme takes on its first member in a Member State for which it has no approval, or for a new employer in a Member State for which it already holds approval but in respect of a different employer, a further application for approval must be made. In addition, certain time limits apply in relation to information required to be exchanged between TPR and its counterpart in the other Member State(s).

Transitional arrangements applied to schemes already operating cross border in 2005 (TPR thought these were mainly Anglo-Irish). The table below shows when schemes must apply for authorisation and approval (an online application form is available on TPR's website) and when they must satisfy TPR that they are fully funded.

The application for authorisation (to have cross-border members) must include confirmations by the trustees on compliance with UK legal requirements on:

- registrable information;
- disclosure;
- investment; and
- trustee knowledge and understanding.

The trustees must also certify that the scheme is established under trust and supply the funding valuation and a copy of the most recent statement of funding principles (or, for DC schemes, an up-to-date payment schedule).

8.1.13 *Cross-border schemes*

The application for approval (to receive contributions) can be made simultaneously, including information on the employer in the host state whose employees will be contributing to the scheme based in the home state.

The *Iorp Directive* requires TPR to be satisfied about the 'good repute and professional qualifications or experience of the persons running the institution'. This is neither expressly reflected in the regulations nor in TPR's guidance, but TPR's consultation document stated: 'Our focus will be on the trustees of the scheme, although we may also seek information about the scheme advisers.'

TPR says in its guidance that:[11]

> 'We will base our decision on the information contained in the application form and any other data about the scheme which is available to the regulator.'

	Existing cross-border schemes in 2005	*Existing 2005 schemes wishing to operate cross-border in future*	*New schemes (no members yet)*
Apply when?	By 29 March 2006	Before start to operate cross-border	Before start to operate cross-border
Show fully funded (provided valuation) when?	By 22 September 2008	At time of application	Within two years of date of application

Sanctions

8.1.14 If a scheme operates as a cross-border scheme without the required approval and authorisation, TPR can impose a civil penalty on each trustee who has failed to take reasonable steps to secure compliance (*Pensions Act 2004, s 287*). This penalty is up to £5,000 for an individual and £50,000 for a company. Trustee directors may also be subject to a civil penalty if the relevant breach was with their consent or connivance or neglect (*Pensions Act 1995, s 10(5)*).

---

11 *http://www.thepensionsregulator.gov.uk/guidance/guidance-cross-border-schemes.aspx*

8.2 Cross-border schemes – seconded employees

Summary

The first section of this chapter outlined the position for occupational pension schemes that are within the cross-border provisions. The legislation imposes more onerous obligations on such schemes, in particular on funding.

The legislation provides that an employee who is seconded to work outside the UK, but within the EEA, does not count as a 'European member' and so will not, on their own require a scheme to become authorised and approved.

This section looks at the 'secondee' exemption in more detail and discusses the TPR guidance.

Seconded employees

8.2.1 The *Occupational Pension Schemes (Cross-border Activities) Regulations 2005*[12] (the *Cross-border Regulations 2005*) expressly exempt a 'seconded' worker from counting as a European member. This means that the employer is not treated as a 'European employer' and so the scheme should not be treated as being cross border (and needing to comply with the cross-border legislation).

The *Cross-border Regulations 2005* define a 'seconded worker' for a secondment starting after 2005 as follows:

'Seconded worker' means a person:

(a) who –

    (i) is employed under a contract of service by an employer established in the United Kingdom and whose habitual place of work under that contract is located in the United Kingdom, or

---

12 *SI 2005/3381.*

481

> (ii) immediately before the commencement of the period of secondment was employed under a contract of service by an employer established in the United Kingdom and whose habitual place of work under that contract was located in the United Kingdom,
>
> (b) who ... is posted ... for a limited period to an EEA state other than the United Kingdom for the purpose of providing services on behalf of his employer, and
>
> (c) who –
>
> (i) at the time when that posting began expected to return to the United Kingdom to work for the employer described in (a)(i) or (ii) after the expiry of that period, or
>
> (ii) expects to retire from employment immediately after the expiry of that period.
>
> *Regulation 2(1)* of the *Occupational Pension Schemes (Cross-border Activities) Regulations 2005 (SI 2005/3381)*

TPR has published guidance on the position of seconded employees. This is available on its website and is in the box below.

Who are 'seconded employees'?

If employees are sent by a UK employer to work overseas for a period in another EU Member State, and at the end of that period intend to return to resume work for that employer in the UK or intend to retire, then if :

(i) they were sent to the other EU Member State for a limited period; and

(ii) they were sent for the purpose of providing services on behalf of the UK employer; and

(iii) they intend at the end of that period either to return to the UK to work for the same employer, or to retire,

they are counted as seconded employees.

The characteristics of a secondment are:

(i) the employee being sent to work overseas from the UK;

(ii) the employee providing services on behalf of the UK employer;

(iii)   the limited period; and

(iv)   the expectation either to return to the UK or to retire (in the UK or otherwise) at the end of that period.

If an overseas posting has these characteristics, it may be regarded as a secondment. Cases which do not have these characteristics (if, for example, no limited period was expressed, or there was no expectation of return to the UK or retirement at the end of the limited period) should not be regarded as secondments.

If employees are working in another EU Member State but are not seconded, perhaps because they work in more than one state, it does not automatically follow that they are subject to the other state's social and labour law. It depends on whether their place of work is sufficiently located in the other member state.

The main characteristic of a limited period is that it will end on a specified date although it is also possible for a period to be 'limited' if it ends when a specific event, such as the completion of a project, takes place.

If employees work abroad for an indefinite period, or for their entire career, that should not be regarded as a secondment.

If a member of a scheme is seconded overseas and, at the end of that secondment is seconded again, either to the same or to another EU Member State, this should be regarded as a 'fresh start' rather than a single secondment. Each secondment must maintain the characteristics of a secondment.

If the question of extending an existing secondment arises, the trustees should be sure that the secondment is really for a limited period, and that the total period of secondment is not in fact a permanent posting.

It is up to the trustees to determine whether any members of the scheme who work in EU Member States other than the UK are seconded employees.

The fact that an employer has seconded employees in its pension scheme does not mean that the scheme is accepting contributions in respect of European members. If the only employees working overseas are seconded employees then this guidance does not apply. UK employers should make sure that they are aware of all employees who are posted to other EU Member States, and should be clear whether they are 'seconded employees' so that the trustees of the relevant schemes can have this information to hand.

Source: TPR guidance *http://www.thepensionsregulator.gov.uk/ guidance/guidance-cross-border- schemes.aspx*

8.2.2 *Cross-border schemes*

Background: Overseas members

8.2.2   Many schemes do not generally allow non-UK employees into active membership, but may allow employees who are seconded to work outside the UK to remain as active members of the scheme.

Pre-2006 tax rules

8.2.3   Under the tax laws before April 2006, this was allowed by the Inland Revenue in the UK:

● for an unlimited period, if the member remained employed by the UK employer; or

● for a limited period (of up to ten years) if the employee became employed by a non-UK employer.

Post-2006 tax rules

8.2.4   These limits ceased under the new tax rules in force from 6 April 2006, so that the tax laws now do not prohibit or limit overseas employees or employers in a tax-registered occupational pension scheme.

Iorp

8.2.5   The *Iorp Directive* makes no express reference to seconded workers.

Limited period

8.2.6   The original draft cross-border regulations envisaged that an employee's secondment to another EU Member State for more than 12 months brought the scheme within the cross-border regime and would therefore be subject to the fully funded requirement (see **8.1.10**). Many respondents to the consultation commented that, far from encouraging the free movement of workers, this provision would potentially inhibit even short-term secondments.

It appeared at one stage that the government intended to extend the 12-month period to five years; however, the final regulations contain no express time limit, merely stipulating that the secondment must be for a limited period.

The Pensions Regulator issued guidance on who could be a secondee. The first set of guidance expressly stated that secondments for a period of five years or less would have the characteristics of a secondment, if the other characteristics were present, and that secondments for longer periods could also retain these characteristics, but it would become increasingly hard not to consider such secondments to be permanent postings the more the limited periods become extended.

The most recent version of the TPR guidance (from June 2007) no longer refers to the five-year period.

The latest set of guidance is set out in the box above. The relevant extract provides:

'The main characteristic of a limited period is that it will end on a specified date although it is also possible for a period to be "limited" if it ends when a specific event, such as the completion of a project, takes place.

If employees work abroad for an indefinite period, or for their entire career, that should not be regarded as a secondment.

If a member of a scheme is seconded overseas and, at the end of that secondment is seconded again, either to the same or to another [EEA state],[13] this should be regarded as a "fresh start" rather than a single secondment. Each secondment must maintain the characteristics of a secondment.

If the question of extending an existing secondment arises, the trustees should be sure that the secondment is really for a limited period, and that the total period of secondment is not in fact a permanent posting.

It is up to the trustees to determine whether any members of the scheme who work in [EEA states] other than the UK are seconded employees.'

Timing of expectation

8.2.7   The 'expectation of return or retirement' test, to be applied at commencement of the secondment, is intended to cater for the fact that individuals do not always return to the UK upon completion of a secondment but may move to another EEA state.

---

13   The guidance is not completely up-to-date at the time of writing, but does make clear that 'references to EU states in this guidance include EEA states ...'.

8.2.7 *Cross-border schemes*

The definition also recognises that employees are sometimes on secondment as their last posting before retirement (retirement is, intriguingly, not defined for this purpose – a cautious approach would be to envisage retirement from work generally, not just leaving the current employer/group).

Onward transfer to another Member State?

8.2.8   In 2006, TPR confirmed that, provided a secondment was for a limited period and satisfied the 'expectation of return or retirement' test, the fact that a worker was seconded to first one and then another EEA state outside the UK without returning to the UK between postings would not cause TPR to regard this as a permanent posting overseas rather than a secondment – as long as the total secondment period was not excessive. TPR further confirmed that the five years mentioned in its guidance is only an indicative period; 'however if a number of postings each of five years had been in question the Regulator may have come to a different view'.

It is not clear what happens if the original posting is extended or if the expectation to return to the UK changes. It may be arguable that, as the test is expressly stated to apply at commencement of the secondment, a last-minute change of plan should not bring the scheme within the cross-border provisions. The safer course would perhaps be for the employee to return to the UK to work for the same employer for a period before commencing a further period of secondment.

Continue to work for the UK employer?

8.2.9   The definition in the *Cross-border Regulations 2005* looks to be wide enough to cover an employee who, while on the secondment ceases to be employed by the UK employer and becomes employed by another company (eg another group company in the Member State). The definition in the Regulations requires the employee to be posted 'for the purpose of providing services on behalf of his employer'.

It seems to us to be arguable that the 'employer' mentioned here could be the new employer (and not the original UK employer). But TPR takes a different view in its guidance (see above) instead envisaging that the employee must provide services on behalf of the UK employer.

TPR's views are not legally determinative on this – ultimately it is a question of the legal interpretation of the regulation. However, TPR is the relevant enforcement body, so its views are highly relevant as to whether it would bring proceedings for what it saw as a breach. The safest course may be to leave the employee as being employed by the UK company during his secondment.

Return to the UK

8.2.10   The expectation must be that the employee would return to the UK to work for his seconding UK employer. An expectation of a return to the UK, but for another UK company (even within the same group) seems not to be enough.

A change in expectation during the secondment seems not to matter. So, this may still qualify if there was a new agreement near the end of the secondment that the employee actually returned to the UK to work for another employer.

Overview

8.2.11   The definition of seconded worker is complex and needs to be carefully checked in individual cases. For example, it would seem not to cover:

- an employee who is hired from outside the group and who does not work for the UK employer immediately before the posting; or

- an employee who is posted for non-work reasons (eg study leave) and so is not posted 'for the purpose of providing services on behalf of his employer'.

Evidence

8.2.12   It would be prudent for employers and schemes with secondees to obtain suitable evidence of compliance with the seconded workers definition (eg written statements from the employee about his or her expectations of return to the UK or to retire).

Extensions to a secondment

8.2.13   It will be a fact-specific question as to whether an extension to a secondment stops qualifying as a seconded worker. It does not turn on a particular length of time (although clearly the longer the period of time, the less likely it is to be a secondment rather than a permanent posting).

In a case where it is an extension to the original secondment, the employer and trustees will need to consider the following:

1   Does it look like a genuine extension to a secondment or rather is it becoming a permanent posting?

2   Is the extension for a limited period (this will be helpful – in fact necessary for the purposes of the legislation)?

8.2.13 *Cross-border schemes*

3   What is the combined length of the secondment plus extension (similar to point 1 – ie this will help determine whether it still looks like a secondment)?

4   All the other aspects of a secondment must be met (ie the employee must be providing services on behalf of the UK employer, for a limited period, and there is the expectation that the individual will either return to work for the UK employer in the UK or retire at the end of the period).

Sources

8.2.14

- *The Iorp Directive* – the *Directive on the Activities and Supervision of Institutions for Occupational Retirement Provision (Directive 2003/41/EC).*

- *Sections 287* to *295* of the *Pensions Act 2004.*

- *The Occupational Pension Schemes (Cross-border Activities) Regulations 2005 (SI 2005/3381).*

- *The Occupational Pension Schemes (EEA States) Regulations 2007 (SI 2007/3014).*

- TPR guidance (see *http://www.thepensionsregulator.gov.uk/guidance/ guidance-cross-border-schemes.aspx*).

Chapter 9

Restructuring, insolvency and pension schemes

9.1 UK defined benefit pension schemes and corporate restructurings

Summary

This section explains why pension deficits can be a critical issue in a corporate restructuring and how pension scheme trustees, the Pensions Regulator and the Pension Protection Fund can be key players in the process and outcomes.

Introduction

9.1.1   A prominent aspect of the most recent wave of restructuring is the significant role often played by defined benefit (DB) pension liabilities. This can partly be explained by the following:

●   Poor investment returns, the loss of significant tax relief to pension funds in 1997, low bond yields and increased longevity have all contributed to larger funding deficits in DB pension schemes. For some companies their pension scheme will be one of their largest creditors or at least comparable with obligations owed to banks and other holders of corporate debt. Furthermore, pension liabilities can be highly volatile.

●   Pension liabilities are reflected on the corporate balance sheet, but the accounting treatment of those liabilities is increasingly viewed as unreliable. The basis on which the liabilities are valued will often be the focus of negotiations in restructurings.

489

- The risk of triggering *s 75* of the *Pensions Act 1995* heightens the importance of pensions in restructurings. *Section 75* imposes a debt obligation on employers if (broadly) the pension scheme starts to wind up or the employer enters liquidation or ceases to participate in the scheme. The debt is the shortfall in the scheme funding measured on a buy-out basis, which tests whether there would be sufficient assets to secure liabilities with insurance policies – this will usually show a larger deficit than scheme specific funding under *PA 2004* or when measured on an FRS17 or IAS19 accounting basis. Many DB schemes will have substantial buy-out deficits (sometimes, even if there is an FRS 17/IAS19 surplus). Furthermore, the last underlying full scheme valuation can be up to three years out of date (depending on when the last triennial valuation took place), so may not reveal the true deficit. See further *Debt on the employer – an overview of s 75*, **3.1**.

- Pension scheme trustees are subject to special rules and not necessarily able to negotiate and settle liabilities on a commercial basis.

- If a restructuring leaves the pension scheme worse off, this may trigger the Pensions Regulator's (TPR) 'moral hazard' powers under the *Pensions Act 2004*. These powers allow TPR, in certain circumstances, to make third parties that are 'connected' or 'associated' with the employer liable for a pension scheme deficit (eg other group companies, directors and investors with a one-third or greater shareholding). TPR exercised these powers at least three times during 2010. Given the size of pension scheme deficits and TPR's activist approach, the risk of being made liable will be a serious concern to a number of parties in a restructuring. See further *TPR: Moral hazard powers*, **4.1**.

- If the employer suffers a 'qualifying insolvency event' the Pension Protection Fund (PPF) may assume the rights of the pension scheme as a creditor. The PPF's powers and policies can exercise a major influence in the restructuring or rescue of an insolvent company.

The pension scheme trustees

Why is it important to include trustees in negotiations?

9.1.2   The practical effect of the *Pensions Act 2004* and TPR's moral hazard powers is that the trustees are often given significant leverage in negotiations. For example, because trustees need to agree to a proposal if the parties are seeking clearance from TPR (ie confirmation that TPR will not later use its powers (see *Pensions and transactions – applying to TPR for clearance*, **4.13**).

Trustees may also have significant power under the scheme's governing documents (but this will turn on the terms of the deed). For example, the trustees may have the power to wind up the scheme (triggering a *s 75* debt). Inviting trustees into negotiations at an early stage may reduce the likelihood of trustees later taking actions that delay or frustrate a restructuring.

How will trustees act in negotiations?

9.1.3   TPR expects that when negotiating with an employer, trustees should generally adopt the approach of a bank that has advanced a large unsecured debt.

TPR comments[1]:

> 'If it is in deficit on any basis, the scheme is a creditor of the employer. Usually, because of the size of the deficit, it is a material creditor. Although a scheme is not identical to a large unsecured bank loan, it does (particularly because of the long-term nature of the pensions obligation) have many similarities in the form of:
>
> • its size relative to other unsecured creditors; and
>
> • its importance to the company.'

Trustees are expected to assess how the transaction would affect the pension scheme as an unsecured creditor and negotiate with the employer or, if they lack the necessary negotiating skills, instruct independent professional advisers to assist them in negotiations.

What result do trustees want from a negotiation?

9.1.4   A key objective for trustees will be to protect the pension scheme members. If a restructuring weakens an employer's financial ability or legal obligation to fund the scheme, then trustees will often seek some mitigation. TPR in its clearance guidance gives a non-exhaustive list of the types of mitigation that trustees can consider. These include: additional employer contributions of cash or assets; fixed or floating charges; escrow accounts; letters of credit, guarantees or insurance; and parental and intra-group guarantees.

There may be circumstances in which the trustees may agree to compromise a *s 75* debt or perhaps give up a cash guarantee from an external institution (or perhaps replace it with alternative securities). The trustees may be willing to

---

1   Para 98 of TPR's guidance on clearance. See www.thepensionsregulator.gov.uk/guidance/guidance-clearance.aspx

agree to this if they consider that it is likely to achieve a larger amount for the scheme than the trustees would obtain on the employer becoming insolvent and the scheme entering the PPF. The trustees may also be more amenable to such a proposal if it would prevent the employer from entering insolvency altogether – this is especially so given TPR's February 2009 statement on repairing pension scheme deficits.[2] TPR stated that 'the best outcome for scheme and employer is a viable sponsor that will continue to support the scheme'. Also the Court of Appeal in *Foster Wheeler v Hanley*[3] (2009) stated that trustees should act fairly towards the employer.

How can an employer implement an agreement with the trustees?

9.1.5   Schemes of arrangement under the *Companies Act 2006* and company voluntary arrangements (CVAs) under the *Insolvency Act 1986* can bind trustees to a compromise of the pension scheme debt if they are parties to it. However, a decision to compromise a pension scheme debt gives rise to a duty on the employer and the trustee to notify TPR (*s 69* of the *Pensions Act 2004*). See *Notifiable Events*, **13.1**.

This may lead to a review of the proposed transaction by TPR. Unless clearance is obtained in respect of the compromise, it is possible that TPR may use its moral hazard powers (see below).

In addition, trustees will be unwilling to enter any agreements if doing so leads to the pension scheme becoming ineligible for entry into the PPF. If there is a legally enforceable agreement that has the effect of reducing a *s 75* debt (eg a compromise of a scheme debt) the scheme may be excluded from the scope of the PPF. This does not apply to an agreement under a Companies Act scheme of arrangement.

There are also a number of statutory mechanisms under the *Employer Debt Regulations 2005* (*SI 2005/678*) that allow an employer, which is exiting a group scheme, to agree with the trustees for it to pay a lower share of a *s 75* debt.

For example, a regulated apportionment arrangement (RAA) can be used if the trustees are of the opinion that there is a reasonable likelihood of the scheme entering the PPF assessment period in the next 12 months (ie the trustees believe that there is a reasonable likelihood of the employer becoming insolvent) or an assessment period has already started.[4] Such RAAs may help

---

2   www.thepensionsregulator.gov.uk/docs/statement-to-employers-feb-2009.pdf
3   *Foster Wheeler Ltd v Hanley* [2009] EWCA Civ 651, [2010] ICR 374 at para [36].
4   The other forms of apportionment arrangement or withdrawal arrangement may not be suitable as the statutory 'funding test' is required to be satisfied and this may not be possible.

stave off a full *s 75* debt (and so insolvency) for one employer but will need to pass the *s 75* liability to another employer and:

- will need approval from TPR (in practice a clearance application is needed); and

- the PPF must also not object (in practice this means that the PPF must approve the transaction – see **9.1.8**).

See *Dealing with a s 75 debt*, **3.3**.

TPR and its 'moral hazard' powers

9.1.6   TPR has significant statutory powers to make third parties that are 'connected' or 'associated' with the employer liable to an employer's pension scheme. 'Connected' or 'associated' persons can include a range of parties including companies in the employer's corporate group, the directors of controlling entities and investors with a one-third or greater shareholding in the employer (in a restructuring, this may concern a bank that is considering a debt-for-equity swap).

Financial support directions (FSDs) require a person to put in place, and maintain, financial support (broadly, funding or guarantees) for an employer's scheme if the employer is 'insufficiently resourced' or 'a service company'.

Alternatively, TPR may try to issue a contribution notice (CN) requesting that a person make a contribution to the scheme. TPR can issue a CN in the following circumstances:

- *main purpose test*: if TPR is of the opinion that the person was a party to an act or failure to act that occurred within six years, a 'main purpose' of which was to prevent or reduce the recovery of, or the amount of, any debt payable by the employer to the scheme under *s 75* of the *Pensions Act 1995*; or

- *material detriment test*: if an act or failure to act has occurred on or after 14 April 2008 and, in TPR's opinion, it has detrimentally affected in a material way the likelihood of accrued scheme benefits being received.

The effect of the material detriment test, which was introduced in 2008, is that CNs can now potentially be issued in a wider range of circumstances. Simply weakening the financial position of the employer, even if unintended, could be interpreted as satisfying the material detriment test.

During 2010, TPR used its power on at least four occasions, all in a distress or insolvency context (Nortel, Bonas Group, Desmonds and Lehman Brothers) –

9.1.6 *Restructuring, insolvency and pension schemes*

see *TPR builds a track record,* **4.11** and *TPR: moral hazard powers,* **4.1**. This activist approach has significantly increased parties' appreciation of the risk of TPR interaction in a corporate restructuring.

However, there are a number of safeguards in the legislation and steps that can be taken to minimise this moral hazard risk. For example:

- FSDs cannot be issued against individuals (which will be of comfort to 'company doctors' and insolvency practitioners (IPs)).

- A CN cannot be issued against an IP who is 'acting in accordance with his function as an insolvency practitioner'.

- The parties can apply to TPR for statutory clearance – ie confirmation that it will not use its moral hazard powers– see *Pensions and transactions – applying to TPR for clearance,* **4.13**).

- TPR must consider a number of 'reasonableness' factors before issuing a CN or FSD – in particular, if relevant, the position of the employer's other creditors before issuing a CN. See *The reasonableness test,* **4.10**. The previous government said that this was intended to allay concerns of pension schemes becoming a 'super-creditor' in an insolvency situation. The pensions minister in 2008 also said that this factor would protect 'company doctors' who cause detriment that was reasonable in the context of the outcome for other creditors and have behaved reasonably (eg not wilfully ignoring information or taking reckless risks).

- Directors can carefully minute the purpose of decisions that might weaken the strength of the participating employer's ability (or obligation) to fund the pension scheme. This is so that they can later prove that a main purpose of an act was not to prevent or reduce a *s 75* debt.

- Parties may be able to rely on a defence to a CN under the material detriment test. Broadly, the defence will be available to a person who considers the effect of an act on scheme benefits, takes all reasonable steps to eliminate or minimise the risk and it is reasonable for that person to conclude that an act is not materially detrimental to scheme benefits. Again, directors should take care when minuting decisions; this will make it easier later to rely on this statutory defence. See *Contribution Notices,* **4.7**.

Nortel – Moral hazard orders treated as provable debt in an insolvency

9.1.7   Where a CN or FSD is issued against a target after a liquidation or administration in the UK has started over that target, the relevant debt claim will be treated as a provable debt in the insolvency proceedings. This is a difficult area and has been considered by the courts in the *Nortel/Lehmans* litigation – see: *Moral hazard powers are a proveable debt: Nortel/Lehman*, **4.12**

The PPF and distressed restructurings

9.1.8   If an employer with an eligible DB scheme enters into a formal insolvency then the PPF will assess whether it should take over responsibility for the pension scheme. During this assessment period the rights and powers of the scheme trustees are exercisable by the PPF and it has the power to participate, on behalf of the pension fund, in the restructuring or rescue of an insolvent company.

The PPF can agree to compromise the employer's *s* 75 debt (and all other liabilities to the scheme). To enable this, it is necessary for the employer to have a qualifying insolvency event (eg administration or a CVA).

The PPF may in some circumstances be in a better position than trustees to engage in a restructuring. Trustees cannot invest more than 5% of the scheme's assets by value in their employer[5] (or an associated or connected person), whereas the PPF can accept a sizeable equity stake in the employer – allowing it to agree a debt-for-equity swap and avoid a prolonged and value-destructive insolvency process.

In its guidance for insolvency practitioners[6] (updated May 2010), the PPF board states that it will only participate in a restructuring or rescue if:

- insolvency is inevitable; and

- the scheme receives consideration that is significantly better than the dividend that would be received if the company went into an ordinary insolvency;

- what is offered is fair given what the other creditors and shareholders are to gain as a consequence of the rescue. The example given in the PPF guidance is

    'ie the insolvency return might be £0 and we are offered £500,000 in respect of a £100 million pension debt. However, the expectation is that after the restructuring, the irrecoverable bank debt of £100 million would become fully recoverable over time because the pension debt is no longer in the company. In such a case, we would seek to extract a suitable "price"

---

5   See *Employer-related investment limits*, **17.5**.
6   See Part 5. On the PPF website at: www.pensionprotectionfund.org.uk/DocumentLibrary/ Documents/insolvency_guidance.pdf

from the bank for allowing it the opportunity of getting its money back over time';

- the scheme is given 10% of the equity where the future shareholders are not currently involved with the company and 33% if the parties are currently involved:

  - (The PPF says that this is a form of anti embarrassment protection to ensure that the PPF does not find itself with a large pension liability and not much to go with it and whilst the purchaser goes off with a very valuable business because there was some golden nugget in it which no one on the PPF's side of the deal spotted or was told about at the time);

  - The PPF has a standard form of shareholder agreement and articles of association to protect the pension scheme's interests (as the PPF takes non voting equity);

- TPR would not be able to use its moral hazard powers to generate more money for the scheme than the deal the PPF has negotiated;

- TPR is prepared to clear the deal;

- the banks' fees are reasonable, if the deal involves a refinancing;

- the other party pays the PPF's and the trustees' legal fees for documenting and executing the deal; and

The PPF says that a draft clearance application must have been submitted to and considered by, TPR before the PPF will engage in discussions (the PPF will work with TPR to consider the proposition).

In the past, the PPF has been reluctant to move from its rule (see above) of asking for more equity if there is 'old money' involved in the restructuring (note that if there is a mixture of 'new' and 'old' money, the PPF may ask for between 10% and 33% equity). Knowing that the PPF will insist on an 'equity price', calculated according to its rigid rules, can actually speed up a restructuring because it avoids protracted negotiations and parties can plan ahead before approaching the PPF.

Conversely in the BMI restructuring in 2012, there was a restructuring with the pension scheme entering the PPF. It seems from TPR's report that no equity stake was given to the PPF (see the TPR report in May 2012).[7]

---

7   On TPR's website at: http://www.thepensionsregulator.gov.uk/docs/section-89-bma.pdf.

9.1.9   In January 2014, the PPF issued a fact sheet titled 'Restructuring and Insolvency – the PPF Approach', setting out its policy on restructuring and insolvency.[8]

This is stated in rigid terms. It says:

'So, we will only take part in restructures or rescues if certain principles are met. These are designed to make sure that we are in a much better position than we would have been if we had done nothing.

Most negotiations will take place alongside the Pensions Regulator which usually needs to "clear" the deal before any agreement can be made.'

The seven principles listed are the same as those set out in Part 5 of the PPF guidance for insolvency practitioners.

As such the PPF fact sheet is not saying anything new. In particular this means that it seems to only envisage a PPF restructure if there is an equity stake for the PPF (principle 4). Some recent restructures have not in fact involved an equity stake (e g Cattles, BMI and, arguably, Kodak). These are not mentioned. It does mean that it is difficult to see when the PPF will agree to a deal with an equity stake and when not.

9.1.10   Other issues include:

- The principle that there must be a 'fair' dividend for the scheme (compared to other creditors) is re-stated. So an offer (say) that results in an increased payment to the scheme (compared with the insolvency dividend) may still be refused. Indeed the example in the PPF case study and in principle 3 still envisages an 'appropriate price' being necessary. Just more for the scheme than would be achieved in insolvency seems not necessarily to be enough.

- The PPF principles may only come into play if PPF approval for a deal is needed. Under the legislation this looks only to be required where either:

    (a)   the PPF has taken over the pension trustee's rights (because the pension scheme has entered a PPF assessment period) and trustee approval is needed – eg as part of a creditors' voluntary arrangement (CVA); or

    (b)   if a Regulated Apportionment Agreement (RAA) is needed (in practice if it is desired to apportion any potential debt owed to the

---

8   http://www.pensionprotectionfund.org.uk/DocumentLibrary/Documents/Restructuring_and_
     Insolvency.pdf

trustee under *s 75* of the *Pensions Act 1995* away from an employer or former employer – in practice because the restructure will not involve that employer entering a formal UK insolvency process). If the restructure does not need an RAA – e g because it involves the employerentering insolvency (e g a pre pack), then PPF approval is not needed under the pensions legislation.

- But the PPF position may still be relevant if clearance is wanted from the Pensions Regulator (TPR) in relation to its 'moral hazard' powers to issue contribution notices (CNs) or financial support directions (FSDs) against associated third parties (under the *Pensions Act 2004*). It is likely that, before agreeing to clearance, TPR will take into account the impact of a restructure on the PPF. Para 149 of the TPR clearance guidance states: 'Where the insolvency of the employer is likely and the scheme may be assessed by the PPF, then the PPF may be included in any discussions with the applicants and trustees. The PPF is a separate body from the regulator.' So It is possible that TPR may look to apply the same principles as set out by the PPF, but this is not stated in the TPR guidance on clearance.

The Reader's Digest case

9.1.11   In February 2010, Reader's Digest Association stated that TPR 'would not support an agreement already reached between [its UK subsidiary], the trustees of its pension plan and the UK Pension Protection Fund (PPF) to settle a longstanding pension plan liability'. The UK subsidiary subsequently went into administration.

TPR may have rejected this compromise because it expected that more could be recovered either by the trustees pursuing a *s 75* debt in the administration or by TPR exercising its moral hazard powers to recover funds from other connected or associated companies.

The *Reader's Digest* case shows that the PPF's requirement that TPR 'clear the deal' is more than a formality, even if all other parties are in agreement. Previously TPR has indicated that it preferred being 'a referee not a player'; it would allow parties to reach agreement among themselves, rather than exercise its powers. However, this case represented a direct rejection of an agreement reached between the other parties (including the PPF).

Kodak

9.1.12   In 2013 the trustees in the Kodak case successfully negotiated a settlement of their claims against Kodak, including purchasing a business from Kodak. See *Kodak restructuring*, **4.17** above.

Concluding thoughts

9.1.13   This area of law will be daunting for many. It is complex and there have been frequent changes.

But the main thing to remember is that DB pension schemes can be large creditors. This can make pension scheme trustees, TPR and the PPF key players in restructurings and they may need to be invited to the negotiating table early on.

9.2 Employer insolvency and pension schemes – overview

Summary

This section examines how pension schemes are affected when companies become insolvent and what outstanding employer contributions can be claimed. It does not review the PPF implications – these are outlined in Chapter 5.1

Summary of key points:

- Under insolvency law, the employment of employees and their active membership of a company pension scheme is only automatically terminated if a liquidator or receiver is appointed by the court.

- Often the insolvency of the company will trigger the entry of the pension scheme into a PPF assessment period and the winding-up of the pension scheme.

- There is a statutory obligation (*s 75*) for employers to make up part of any deficit in a pension scheme if a liquidator or administrator is appointed or the scheme is wound up, but this only ranks as an unsecured claim and such creditors frequently receive little or nothing.

- Members' pension contributions deducted from their pay and employer contributions for contracting-out in respect of the last year rank as preferential debts on insolvency. Broadly the same amounts of members' contributions are also guaranteed by the state out of the national insurance fund, but the guarantee in relation to employer contributions is wider.

- If receivers or administrators arrange for a company to continue to employ company employees beyond 14 days after their appointment, salaries and pension contributions for this additional service are given top priority. However, the extent of the 'super-priority' given to pension funding is unclear in relation to final salary pension schemes.

UK insolvency regime

9.2.1   The UK's statutory insolvency scheme was introduced in order to make possible various different (and sometimes conflicting) objectives. These include allowing:

- the winding-up of a corporate body (whether solvent or insolvent);

- a creditor to call in security it holds (usually under a receivership arrangement);

- breathing space to attempt a company rescue (administrations);

- arrangements to be reached between creditors to keep a company going (voluntary arrangements); and

- the termination of an insolvent undertaking (corporate or individual) and an equitable division of the assets among creditors (insolvent liquidation or bankruptcy).

These objectives must always be kept in mind when considering the different effects of the various insolvency regimes on employees, occupational pension schemes and, indeed, on other parties. The following pages briefly describe the various types of liquidations and receiverships and the role of an insolvency practitioner (IP).

What types of liquidation are there?

9.2.2   A liquidation involves the termination of the existence of a company (or other corporation).

Such a termination may be desired where the company is solvent. In this case the position of creditors is of less concern (because, by definition, if the company is solvent, all creditors will ultimately be paid their debts). Conversely, termination of the company may be required because the company is insolvent. In this case the position of creditors will be of more concern, given that they will not be wholly repaid. This distinction is reflected in the greater degree of control and influence given to creditors in an insolvent liquidation.

Liquidations are also divided between court winding-up (CWU) and voluntary winding-up (VWU) under the *Insolvency Act 1986*.

Court liquidations

9.2.3   Court liquidations involve an order being made by the court to wind up the company.

A petition may be presented by various parties – usually the company or a member (effectively a shareholder) or by a creditor. In practice, a creditor cannot force a VWU and the only remedy is to proceed by way of a CWU. Actions against the company are automatically stayed under the *Insolvency Act 1986* if a winding-up order is made by the court.

9.2.3 *Restructuring, insolvency and pension schemes*

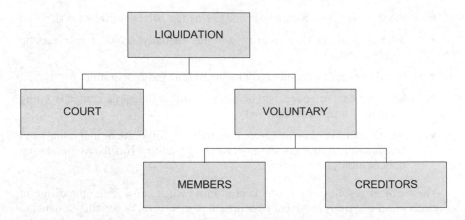

The court may also, after the presentation of a winding-up petition, appoint a provisional liquidator. The person appointed will usually (depending on the terms of the order of appointment) take over the management of the company as an interim measure pending an ultimate winding-up order (eg where it is desired to displace the existing management or in order for the company to continue to trade).

Voluntary liquidations

9.2.4   A shareholder resolution is needed for this. A VWU may be either a:

- members' (shareholders) voluntary winding up – MVL; or
- creditors' voluntary winding-up – CVL.

A VWU will be a creditors' voluntary liquidation (CVL) unless a declaration of solvency has been sworn by the directors and filed with the Companies Registry. A members' voluntary liquidation (MVL) may be converted to a creditors' voluntary liquidation if it later becomes apparent that the company is in fact insolvent. A VWU can also be converted to a CWU.

In an MVL, control of the winding-up generally remains with the shareholders (eg the appointment of a liquidator and the approval of actions). In a CVL control passes to the creditors (the right to override appointment of a liquidator by the members, for example, and the appointment of a liquidation committee to oversee the liquidator).

All liquidations

9.2.5   The effect of appointing a liquidator is that the powers of the directors cease (unless empowered to continue in an MVL).

The company must cease to carry on business from the date of winding-up order or resolution, unless continuing with the business will aid the winding-up process and help maximise return to creditors. The sanction of the court is needed for the liquidator to continue carrying on business in a CWU.

The liquidator must gather in the assets of the company (assets subject to a fixed or floating charge are not included as these will have been used to guarantee liabilities, such as loans or the provision of goods or services). Creditors then have to demonstrate what they were owed at the date the company went into liquidation.

The liquidator realises the assets and distributes them in accordance with the prescribed order:

- liquidation expenses;
- preferential debts;
- debts secured by a floating charge;
- ordinary, unsecured debts;
- post-liquidation interest; and
- any deferred claims.

Special rules apply to secured creditors, foreign currency claims and contingent or future claims. There are also special rules for the liquidation of partnerships.

What types of receiverships are there?

9.2.6   The term 'receiver' will mean different things in different circumstances and it is important to be aware of the precise meaning in any given situation.

Court receivers

9.2.7   These are relatively rare. The appointment of a receiver by the court is an interim measure devised by the courts. In the same way an interim injunction may be granted, a receiver is appointed by the court to take charge of property or a company in order to preserve the position pending resolution of some dispute.

Contractual receivers

9.2.8   These are a contractual device included within security documents (usually fixed and floating charges used to guarantee liabilities) as a means of

9.2.8   *Restructuring, insolvency and pension schemes*

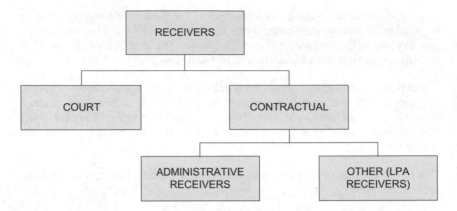

realisation and enforcement of the security. Contractual receivers take charge of the company in a similar manner to court receivers but without the need for a court order.

Essentially, the security will provide that, in certain circumstances, the security holder is able to appoint a receiver and manager to receive income and manage the property of the company which gave the security. Obviously the primary purpose of the appointment of such a receiver and manager is to recover the relevant secured amount. However, the security document will generally provide that receivers are the agent of a company so that they are able to manage its assets and continue its business.

Generally, where a receiver has been appointed under a floating charge (where all the company's assets are used to guarantee a loan) the receiver will take control of the business and assets of the company and the directors will retain some residual authority.

Unsecured creditors (such as employees) rank behind the security and will not usually seek to enforce their claims unless they wish to place the company in liquidation (eg in order to contest the validity of the security under which the receiver is appointed). The receiver's agency to carry on the business of the company will terminate if the company enters liquidation.

Administrative receivers

9.2.9   This is a categorisation, first introduced in 1986, of certain types of contractual receivers appointed in relation to a company under a floating charge covering all, or substantially all, of the company's assets. Administrative receivers should not be confused with administrators (see below).

Administrative receivers must be IPs and are given certain enhanced duties and powers under the *Insolvency Act 1986*.

Since 2003, the capacity of a floating charge holder to appoint an administrative receiver has been drastically reduced. It only survives for charges created before 15 September 2003 (and some finance structures). Instead floating charge holders have a power to appoint an administrator.

What is an administration?

9.2.10   Administration was first introduced as an insolvency process in 1986. It is designated to help the rescue of companies and to avoid liquidation if possible. The administrator is given power to seek remedies previously only available to a liquidator. The reason for introducing the new procedure was that a liquidation can force the cessation of a continuing business, in view of the fact that liquidators have only limited powers to keep the business running.

Administration is designed as a mechanism to freeze enforcement of security or the presentation of winding-up petitions. It is intended to give a breathing space for negotiations to take place to see if the company or its business can be saved (or its assets more beneficially realised) without the irrevocable step of a winding-up.

Before 2003 an administration was only an interim measure. It was followed by liquidation or, if it succeeded, the return of the company as a going concern or an arrangement with creditors. Since 2003, administrators have power, in some circumstances, to pay dividends to creditors. They look more like liquidations.

An administrator is appointed:

- out of court: or
- by order of the court following a petition presented by a creditor or, more usually (given the requirement to provide various types of information to support the petition), by the directors of the company.

Common features of insolvency procedures

9.2.11   Insolvency proceedings contain various common features (despite their differing aims):

- management of the company is in general taken away from the directors and given to an IP (whether a liquidator, administrator or administrative receiver); and
- the relevant office holder (liquidator, administrator or administrative receiver) must be a qualified IP. An IP will be an accountant (or perhaps a solicitor) who has been specially licensed by the relevant professional body.

9.2.12 *Restructuring, insolvency and pension schemes*

Position of the insolvency practitioner

9.2.12 In all these insolvency proceedings, the relevant officer appointed to take over management of the affairs of the company or individual will be responsible for carrying out the purposes of the insolvency proceeding. In a liquidation, this will be realising assets and distributing the proceeds to creditors and shareholders. In an administration, it will be to preserve the position of the company for an interim period. In the case of receivership, it will be to realise assets to repay the secured debt.

The IP, in carrying out these duties, commonly acts as agent of the company concerned. As far as the position of an employee (as a creditor and contracting party) is concerned, if the company is insolvent the employee's claims against the company may have little value (unless they are preferential). The pension scheme will be in a similar position.

However, if the employee (or other creditor) can establish a liability or responsibility to them on the part of the IP, then the chances of recovery are much enhanced. Either the IP will be personally liable to the employee, or a claim can be established as an expense of the insolvency proceedings. Such expenses usually rank ahead of all other claims on the assets of the insolvent company. The effect of this will be to prefer the claim of the employee or pension scheme ahead of even some secured creditors.

In practice, IPs will be more willing to accept that a claim will rank as an insolvency expense than to accept that the IP has personal liability. Although an IP will usually have the right to be indemnified out of the assets of the insolvent company, he will be reluctant to incur possibly unlimited liability to a creditor (such as an employee) when this might not be covered by the relevant assets.

Effect on employees and pension schemes

9.2.13 The effect of the appointment of an IP over a company can be summarised as follows:

- *Court liquidator*: All employees are automatically dismissed. The liquidator may offer new employment but in practice has only limited powers to continue the business.

- *Voluntary liquidator*: Employment is not terminated automatically but the liquidator has only a limited power to continue the business, so dismissal is likely to follow shortly thereafter.

- *Court receiver* (rare): All employees are automatically dismissed.

506

- *Out-of-court receivers*: No automatic termination of employment. Receivers will usually try to continue to trade if they consider this the most likely way to raise most money from the assets of the company.

- *Administrations*: Again, no automatic termination of employment – depending on the reason for the appointment, the administrator may arrange for the company to continue to trade.

The effect of the insolvency of an employer company on its pension scheme can depend on which type of insolvency proceedings have been taken. Naturally if employees are dismissed, their active membership of any occupational pension scheme ceases. However, if they remain in employment, even if only temporarily, their membership of the pension scheme will normally continue unchanged (subject, since 2005, to the freezing of pension accrual when a scheme enters a PPF assessment period – see *Pension Protection Fund*, **5.1**).

9.3 Pension debts – priority of claims

Summary

Employers (and others) will owe various liabilities to fund defined benefit pension schemes. It can be important to know how that liability ranks as a matter of priority compared to other claims on the employer.

This can be important in insolvency but also when trustees look at the 'strength of employer covenant'.

This section looks at the general position of priority of pension claims.

Pension liabilities

9.3.1 The general rule is that employers have liability (under statute or the terms of the pension scheme itself) to fund defined benefit occupational pension schemes. This obligation can either be on an ongoing basis or as a termination debt on a relevant trigger (scheme winding-up or employer entering insolvency etc).

The funding obligations under the trust deed and rules of the scheme are underpinned by the statutory obligations:

- For an ongoing scheme this is the scheme-specific funding provisions in *Part 3* of the *Pensions Act 2004*. See *Scheme specific funding requirements,* **2.1**.

- On a termination, this is the debt on the employer provisions under *s 75* of the *Pensions Act 1995*. See *Debt on the employer – an overview of s 75 of the Pensions Act 1995,* **3.1**.

Priority of claims

9.3.2 It is clear that in general, the obligations on employers to fund pension schemes are unsecured and non-preferential. This means that they rank alongside other unsecured creditors of the employer. For example on a liquidation of the employer, the order in which available assets are used to meet outstanding claims generally envisages that secured claims (fixed or floating charge) and preferential claims are met ahead of unsecured non-preferential claims.

The general rule is that pension claims are unsecured and non-preferential. However there are exceptions to this:

- Some outstanding pension obligations are preferential debts under the *Insolvency Act 1986*. The amount of these is however relatively small – see further discussion below.

- Pension debts will have an increased priority if express security is given by the employer. For example a fixed or floating charge over assets. These have become more common in recent years – there can be a saving from the levy charged by the Pension Protection Fund (PPF).

- Some priority may apply to pension obligations that arise after a formal insolvency process (eg a liquidation or administration) starts. Some obligations can get an increased priority as being 'adopted' employee claims or as being expenses of the insolvency. This is a complex area. It is discussed further below.

The scheme is usually an unsecured creditor of the employer. The insolvency priority of an unsecured creditor, with regard to the realisation of the assets of a company in the event of insolvency and when compared to other creditors, is broadly summarised below:

- creditors with fixed charges;

- insolvency expenses (within the *Insolvency Rules 1986*);

- preferential creditors;

- creditors with floating charges;

- unsecured creditors (usually including the pension creditor);

- subordinated creditors;

- equity/share capital.

Source: Adapted from TPR guidance on 'Monitoring employer support'. See www.thepensionsregulator.gov.uk

---

Claims against third parties

9.3.3   Third parties (ie entities which are not the employer) can also have liabilities to fund pension schemes. In practice this is most likely to arise:

- If the third party has given a direct guarantee or security to the pension scheme – this can be used to reinforce the employer 'covenant' and can help with funding discussions with trustees and with the PPF levy.

- If liabilities are imposed on the third party by TPR using its 'moral hazard' powers under the *Pensions Act 2004*. See generally *TPR: Moral hazard powers: Extracting Pension Scheme Funding from Third Parties: Overview*, **4.1**.

- If the third party has given a funding commitment to the employer (eg as part of service arrangements for the use of employees). This would tend to be an obligation on the third party to pay an amount to the employer (and not to the trustees etc).

Broadly the level of commitment on the third party, as a question of priority for its debts will depend on the nature of the claim. A simple guarantee or moral hazard order from TPR will rank as an unsecured claim. However priority for what would otherwise be an unsecured debt may arise if:

- the third party itself grants security (eg a mortgage or charge over assets); or

- the claim arises as after the start of insolvency and becomes an expense of the insolvency – see further below.

Structural subordination

9.3.4 When dealing with groups of companies, the general rule is that each member of the group is liable for its own debts. If the companies are (as is common) limited liability entities, there is no general liability of (say) a holding company for the debts or obligations of its subsidiary. A liability can arise in extreme circumstances, but this is difficult and unusual, absent an express guarantee from the parent.

This means that it can be important to know which entity has relevant assets and which entity has the relevant claims against it. A claim (say) against a parent company may be of lower value than the same claim against a subsidiary (with assets) if the parent company's only assets are shares in subsidiaries and all the real assets are in the subsidiaries. This would mean that:

- a claim against a subsidiary would rank for a dividend against the assets in that subsidiary;

- but a claim against a parent would only rank against the assets of the parent. In practice if the parent's only assets are shares in the subsidiary, then a dividend will only be payable to the parent's creditors if there is a flow of assets from the subsidiary to the parent (eg the subsidiary is solvent and pays a dividend up to the parent).

This means that a comparison between a claim against the parent and a claim against the subsidiary is that the parent claim will only be payable out of the subsidiary's assets behind any direct claim against the subsidiary (ie it is less likely to be paid than the subsidiary claim). This is sometimes called 'structural subordination' and needs to be kept in mind when looking at claims in a group of companies.

Preferential debts

9.3.5   The *Insolvency Act 1986* provides for some classes of claims against an insolvent company to be preferential debts. These are payable ahead of unsecured claims and claims which are secured by a floating charge (they rank behind a fixed charge). They can also have a special status in other proceedings (eg voluntary arrangements).

Various claims by the Crown for tax used to be preferential debts, but this preference was abolished in 2003. The main remaining category of preferential debt are some employee claims (but generally these are limited to £800) and some pension claims.

The pension claims that are given preferential status are (broadly):

- *Employee contributions*: Contributions deducted by the employer from the employee's pay but not yet paid to an occupational pension scheme. This is limited to the four months before the insolvency date.

- *Employer contributions*: Contributions due from the employer to an occupational pension scheme in the 12 months preceding the insolvency date. But this is limited so that it only applies to amounts due to a contracted-out scheme and then to a specific percentage of earnings within a band. This means in practice the obligation is limited.

Claims on an employer arising under the statutory schedule of contributions are classified as a debt – *s 228(3)* of the *Pensions Act 2004*. Claims arising under the employer debt provisions in *s 75* of the *Pensions Act 1995* are also a debt, but are clearly stated *not* to be preferential debts for *Insolvency Act* purposes – *s 75(8)* of the *Pensions Act 1995*.

The preferential debts are therefore limited to unpaid contributions broadly during the period before the insolvency.

- *Employee contributions*: In relation to unpaid employee contributions, there is no limit on the amount that can be preferential. But in practice amounts may be fairly limited. For relevant tax-registered schemes there are relatively tight rules under pension legislation giving time limits for the employer to pay employee contributions to the pension scheme. Contributions deducted during a particular month from a member's pay must be paid before the 19th of the following month to the scheme – see generally *Employer failure to pay pension contributions*, **2.3**.

511

- *Employer contributions*: Unpaid employer contributions are only a preferential debt if they were due to a contracted-out occupational pension scheme. The amount of the preference is limited to a percentage of the band earnings applicable for national insurance purposes – see box below.

Employer contributions – preferential amount

For a contracted-out salary related scheme, the amount of the preference is limited to a percentage of the band earnings applicable for national insurance purposes The percentage is 3% or 4.8% (depending on whether or not the members pay contributions).

This means that for tax year 2013/14 the maximum amount of preferential debt is about £1,650 (approx) per member. This maximum only applies for a scheme that is:

- contracted out;

- does not require employee contributions; and

- where the member earns over the 'upper accrual point' (UAP) for national insurance purposes of £40,040.

The maximum amount per contracted-out member is 4.8% of the annual UAP of £40,040 less the lower earnings limit (LEL) of £5,668 (ie 4.8 per cent of £34,3724).

In relation to a contracted-out money purchase scheme (COMP) the preferential debt is equal to the minimum payments payable by the employer as part of the contracting-out rebate in the 12 months before the relevant insolvency date.

Insolvency expenses

9.3.6   When a company enters insolvency proceedings (eg liquidation or administration), the *Insolvency Rules 1986* provide for the expenses of the insolvency to be payable out of the assets of the company ahead of unsecured creditors (and ahead of claims secured by a floating charge).

In addition, the *Insolvency Act 1986* gives a super priority to some employment claims where the contracts of employment of the relevant employees are 'adopted' by an administrator.

The adoption priority only applies to claims arising under a contract of employment (not statutory claims) and which relate to liabilities arsing after the date of the insolvency (*para 99, Sch B1* to the *Insolvency Act 1986*). In practice these limits, combined with the freezing of benefits and contributions under the *Pensions Act 2004* where a scheme enters a PPF assessment period following insolvency of an employer, mean that pension liabilities are unlikely to fall within the adoption super priority.

Given the specific provisions for preferential debts and adoption expenses, it is unlikely that pension contributions (particularly deficit contributions for periods before an insolvency) will be eligible to be insolvency expenses, even if the debt only arises after the insolvency starts.

The position of moral hazard orders made by TPR against a company in administration (or liquidation) has been clarified by the Supreme Court. In *Re Nortel GmbH*,[9] the Supreme Court held in July 2013 that such orders rank as a provable debt (at least where the relevant situation relied on by the Regulator pre-dates the start of the insolvency process). The judgment overturned the decision reached by both the Court of Appeal and Briggs J in the High Court that such a debt ranks as an expense of the insolvency and so ahead of unsecured creditors, creditors with floating charges and various other expenses including the insolvency officeholder's own remuneration. See *Moral hazard powers are proveable debts: Nortel/Lehman*, **4.12**.

---

9   [2013] UKSC 52.

9.4 The independent trustee regime on employer insolvency

Summary

A new independent trustee (IT) regime on employer insolvency for all occupational pension schemes came into force on 6 April 2005 under the *Pensions Act 2004*.

The 2005 regime:

- obliges insolvency practitioners (IPs) to inform certain parties in writing of the appointment of an IP;

- repealed the duty on IPs to ensure there is an IT in place; and

- allows TPR to decide whether to appoint an IT and to order that the fees and expenses of an IT appointed on or after 6 April 2005 are borne by the employer.

The post-2005 regime

9.4.1   Insolvency practitioners (liquidators, administrators, administrative receivers etc) (*IPs*) had become familiar with the requirement under the *Pensions Act 1995* to ensure that there is an independent person to act as an independent trustee (*IT*) in relation to an occupational pension scheme (subject to exceptions) following an insolvency appointment over an employer.

Under the *Pensions Act 2004*, a new regime came into force on 6 April 2005.

The main changes were as follows:

- The 2005 regime applies to all occupational pension schemes (defined benefit and defined contribution, death benefit only, unapproved, overseas schemes etc). The exemptions for various schemes that applied previously have been repealed.

- The IP is obliged, under the new version of *s 22* of the *Pensions Act 1995* (as substituted by the *2004 Act*), to give written notice to TPR, the PPF and the trustees of each pension scheme of the company informing them of the IP's appointment (there is a similar, but separate, notification obligation on IPs under *s 120* of the *Pensions Act 2004* – both notifications need to be given).

- The duty on the IP to ensure that there is an IT in place has been repealed.

- TPR now has discretion over whether or not to appoint an IT.

- TPR can decide to order that the fees and expenses of an IT appointed on or after 6 April 2005 are borne by the employer. It is unclear if this obligation counts as an insolvency expense or just an unsecured potentially provable claim.

Implications

9.4.2   The process of TPR deciding whether or not to appoint an IT may be slow. It is unclear how the Regulator will operate in practice. A delay could affect the willingness of pension trustees to make decisions in the interim.

There is now no point in employers appointing their own IT before the insolvency starts. The power given to TPR to appoint an IT will remain (although the fact that there is an existing independent person in place may perhaps influence TPR in deciding whether or not to appoint).

The obligation on an IP to provide information to pension trustees on request remains (*s 26* of the *Pensions Act 1995*). This obligation applies whether or not an IT has been appointed. From 6 April 2005 it applies to all occupational pension schemes. The exemptions in the *1997 Regulations* (for money purchase schemes, unapproved schemes etc) no longer apply.

Sources

9.4.3

- *Pensions Act 1995, ss 22 to 26*, as amended by *s 36* of the *Pensions Act 2004*.

- *The Occupational Pension Schemes (Independent Trustee) Regulations 2005 (SI 2005/703)*.

- David Pollard *Corporate Insolvency: Employment and Pension Rights* (5th ed, Bloomsbury Professional, 2013).

- 'Dear IP' letter issued by the Insolvency Service of the then Department of Trade and Industry with guidance on the *Pensions Act 2004* – see www.insolvency.gov.uk/whatsnew/whatsnew.htm .

- PPF website: Guidance for Insolvency Practitioners – see www.pensionprotectionfund.org.uk/DocumentLibrary/Documents/ insolvency_guidance.pdf

9.5 *Olympic Airlines*: Problems with PPF entry for companies in insolvency outside the UK

Summary

The Court of Appeal's judgment in *The Trustees of the Olympic Airlines SA Pension & Life Insurance Scheme v Olympic Airlines SA*[10] has clarified what is required to fall within the definition of an 'establishment' for the purposes of the EC Insolvency Regulation[11] (the *Insolvency Regulation*).

The *Insolvency Regulation* provides that once insolvency proceedings have been opened in a member state where the company has its centre of main interests (COMI), secondary insolvency proceedings can only be opened in another member state if the company has an establishment in that member state.

The Court of Appeal held that it is not sufficient for a company to have a branch or office that fulfils no function, other than to assist in the winding up of a company. Instead, there must be a business operation with economic activity that is external and market facing. On the facts, the Court of Appeal (overturning the High Court) held that Olympic Airlines did not have an establishment in England and so no secondary proceedings could be opened.

Various UK protection statutes (eg employee claims on the National Insurance Fund and pension scheme entry into the Pension Protection Fund) depend on there being a UK insolvency started over the relevant employers. This decision exposes a big hole in this protection – oddly only applying to companies with a COMI in an EU member state. For companies outside the EU, the problem does not arise. A bizarre effect of the *Insolvency Regulation* is that the Olympic Airlines pension fund is unable currently to be transferred to the Pension Protection Fund.

While not directly the ratio decidendi of the case, *Olympic* confirms the decision in *Office Metro*[12] that the relevant time for deciding whether a company has an establishment is the date of the application to court to open secondary proceedings. The decision in *Olympic* also confirms

---

10 [2013] EWCA Civ 643.
11 Council Regulation (EC) 1346/2000 on insolvency proceedings.
12 *Trillium (Nelson) Properties Ltd v Office Metro Ltd* [2012] EWHC 1191 (Ch).

> that the existence of an establishment can disappear rapidly. By analogy it should be possible to set up an establishment (as long as it is non transitory and external, market facing) rapidly as well.

Background

9.5.1   Olympic Airlines was a Greek state-owned airline that commenced operations in December 2003. On 17 September 2008, the European Commission held that it had received illegal state aid from the Greek state. As a consequence, Olympic Airlines ceased all commercial operations on 28 September 2009 and entered 'special' liquidation in Greece on 2 October 2009. Olympic Airlines carried on business in England. It had a head office in London and premises at both Heathrow and Manchester. Olympic Airlines employed 27 employees in England, all of whom were members of its pension and life assurance scheme, which had a deficit in excess of £15m.

The pension scheme trustees wished to ensure that the Pension Protection Fund (PPF) assumed responsibility for the scheme so that its members would receive a protected level of pension benefits despite the scheme's underfunding. Under the *Pensions Act 2004* only certain events are classified as 'qualifying events' which allow a scheme to enter the PPF. An order for the winding up of a company made by the court under the *Insolvency Act 1986* is a qualifying event, but the Greek liquidation does not constitute a qualifying event. As such, the trustees of the pension scheme presented a petition to the High Court in England for a winding up order in respect of Olympic Airlines, based on the debt due by Olympic Airlines to it and its inability to pay.

As Olympic Airlines had its COMI in Greece, the Greek special liquidation proceeding is the main proceeding for the purposes of the *Insolvency Regulation*. Once main proceedings have been opened, a court in a different member state (such as the UK in this instance) can only open so called 'secondary' proceedings. A prerequisite to the opening of secondary proceedings is that the company has an 'establishment' in the territory of the member state. *Article 2(h)* of the *Insolvency Regulation* defines an establishment as 'any place of operations where the debtor carries out a non-transitory economic activity with human means and goods'.

At first instance the judge (the Chancellor, Morritt C) concluded that at the time of the pension trustees' application to court (following *Re Office Metro*) this is regarded as the relevant date), Olympic Airlines had an establishment. He therefore made the winding up order.

The Appeal

9.5.2   Olympic Airlines appealed the finding that an establishment was present at the relevant time. It argued that the mere winding down of a business could not amount to an establishment for the purposes of the *Insolvency Regulation*, but that there had to be more than transitory economic activity which was external and market facing.

Prior to Olympic Airlines entering into special liquidation, it had an establishment in the UK. Between the date of the Greek liquidation (October 2009) and the date of the trustees' petition (July 2010) the operations were wound down:

- the ticket office at Heathrow was closed;

- the premises in Manchester were vacated;

- the company's bank in England was instructed to cancel all direct debits and standing orders with immediate effect; and

- the employment contract of all 27 employees in England were terminated.

Only the English branch's financial manager and an assistant were re-employed on a short term contract to assist with the liquidation. However, the office still had telephone and internet services until the end of 2010, the branch's bank accounts were only frozen in August 2010 and the final closure was not until December 2011.

9.5.3   On 6 June, the Court of Appeal overturned the High Court's decision and found that the London premises were not an establishment for the purposes of the *Insolvency Regulation*. In doing so, they relied heavily on *Virgós-Schmit* report on the *Insolvency Regulation* and its reference in paragraph 71 to 'economic activity' being activity 'exercised on the market (ie externally).'

In giving his judgment, Sir Bernard Rix (with whom the other judges agreed) emphasised that:

> 'what is being looked for is a location where there is still, at the critical date, a business operation ("a place of operations" performing "economic activity") such as will justify secondary proceedings in a state outside the state of the centre of main interests.'

Therefore, when considering the definition of 'establishment', it is necessary to identify more economic activity than the mere process of winding up.

Moreover, he held that economic activity has to be 'exercised on the market (ie externally)'. A dormant branch, one which has not yet started economic activities or one which has fallen into economic inactivity (such as here) will not suffice. At the time of the presentation of the petition, only a skeleton operation remained for the purposes of winding up. Most importantly, nothing which was happening at the relevant date seemed to have any external economic function other than as part of a desultory liquidation.

For that reason, the Court of Appeal found that Olympic Airlines did not have an establishment in England, and there was therefore, under the *Insolvency Regulation* no jurisdiction to order a winding up.

Implications

Meaning of establishment

9.5.4   The judgment has expanded on the definition of 'establishment' set out in the *Insolvency Regulation* and as interpreted by the courts.

In *Interedil*[13] [2011], the European Court of Justice (ECJ) held that for there to be an establishment there must be 'a minimum level of organisation and a degree of stability necessary for the purpose of pursuing an economic activity'. In that case, the presence of goods alone did not meet the definition. In *Interedil* the ECJ also held that an establishment must be determined on the basis of objective factors which are ascertainable by third parties (as is the case in the determination of COMI).

The Court of Appeal has now taken this further and has introduced the requirement that the economic activity must also be exercised on the market, ie externally. In doing so, the Court of Appeal relied on the *Virgós-Schmit* report which the Court accepted as authoritative commentary on the *Insolvency Regulation*. It is interesting that the English courts have adopted this slightly higher test and it will be interesting to see if other member states will adopt the same approach.

Relevant date

9.5.5   There are multiple points in time when the court could decide whether an establishment is made out. These are the date of:

1.   a particular transaction (this was argued but expressly rejected by Mann J in *Re Office Metro*[14]);

2.   the opening of the main proceedings;

---

13   *Interedil SRL (in liq) v Palimento Interedil SRL* (C-396/09); [2011] ECR I-9915.
14   *Re Office Metro Ltd* [2012] EWHC 1191 (CR).

3.   the application to court for secondary proceedings; or

4.   the court hearing to determine whether to open secondary proceedings.

It is clear that the outcome of the determination can be very different at each of those dates. In the *Olympic* case, had (2) been the relevant date, Olympic Airlines' London office would have been likely still to satisfy the establishment test. However, following the case of *Re Office Metro* (and *Interedil* in relation to the date for the determination of a company's COMI) both the Chancellor and the Court of Appeal found it to be common ground that the relevant date is the date when the request for the opening of proceedings is lodged.

9.5.6   However, the *Insolvency Regulation* is in the process of being revised and the draft text (that is currently with the European institutions for discussion) will change this position. The draft text states that:

> 'where insolvency proceedings have been opened in accordance with paragraph 1, any proceedings opened subsequently in accordance with paragraph 2 shall be secondary proceedings. In such a case, the relevant time for assessing whether the debtor possesses an establishment within the territory of another member state shall be the date of the opening of the main proceedings'.

Had the draft text been in force now, the outcome for the Olympic Airlines pension fund would probably have been different. It is likely that a winding up order could have been made and so that the fund would have been transferred into the PPF.

Taking the time of the opening of the main proceedings as the relevant date also avoids a race to the court – with a pension fund often needing to file quickly on becoming aware of main proceedings being opened, so as not to risk the loss of economic activity.

Given that the relevant date is one particular date and not a period of time, it is clear that the existence of an establishment can change from one day to another. One day an establishment could be in the process of being set up (but not yet classified as such because not yet engaged in market facing activities), while the next day it could be fully operative and classified as an establishment (as long as its operations are non transitory). A sudden wind down of operations could however make the establishment disappear within days. This analysis must also hold true for the determination of a company's COMI.

Unnecessary secondary proceedings

9.5.7   The simplest answer to this problem would be if the *Pensions Act 2004* included as qualifying events (for PPF entry) main proceedings that have been opened in other EC member states and which are afforded automatic recognition under *Articles 3 and 17* of the *Insolvency Regulation*. In this case, the Greek special liquidation would then have been sufficient for the PPF to assume responsibility for the pension scheme.

A similar change would also resolve the issue in relation to claims by employees on the UK National Insurance Fund (where generally, under the *Employment Rights Act 1996*, a UK insolvency is also needed).

This approach would have been not only in line with the aim of the *Insolvency Regulation* (and, indeed, the proposed draft new *Insolvency Regulation*) to avoid multiple insolvency proceedings which are disruptive and value destructive but also would have given *Article 17* of the *Insolvency Regulation* its proper meaning. *Article 17* states that a judgment opening main insolvency proceedings:

> 'shall, with no further formalities, produce the same effects in any other Member State as under this law of the State of the opening of proceedings …'.

9.5.8   Given the fact that the coming into force of the reformed text of the *Insolvency Regulation* (if the final version of the draft includes the new reference to the relevant date) is some way off yet, an amendment to the pensions (and employment) legislation would be the quickest (and indeed, most appropriate) fix for the current situation to avoid a race to the court to open (potentially entirely unnecessary secondary proceedings).

Chapter 10

Multi-employer schemes

10.1   Moving employees within a group: pensions implications

Summary

Transfers of employees between companies within a corporate group are common.

This section looks at the implications of a corporate reorganisation when the employees include members of a UK occupational pension scheme maintained by the group and where membership of that scheme is to be continued. This section broadly repeats **6.1**, but includes further practical issues.

Reorganisations

10.1.1   It is common for employees to move employment from one company to another within a group. This could be part of:

- a transfer of a business from one group company to another – in this case the relevant employees 'assigned' to that business would usually move under *Tupe*; or

- a transfer of employees from one company to another (without there being a business transfer) – for example as part of a promotion or new group structure.

If there is a UK occupational pension scheme within the group, then the implications of the reorganisation on the group (and the employees) need to be considered. There can be implications even where (say) the benefits and rights of employees are not intended to be changed as a result of the transfer or where the transfer of assets is intended to be broadly neutral from a group perspective.

This section looks at the pensions issues should there be a transfer of employees which is intended to be on a broadly neutral basis with no change to pension benefits. In practice the intention may be to be able to say to the employees that the transfer will not change their pension benefits (and that they will remain active members of the group pension scheme).

Transfer of a business from one group company to another, including employees

10.1.2 *Tupe* will apply if there is a business transfer from one company to another. It is clear that *Tupe 2006* applies in relation to employees where there is a transfer of a UK-based business, even if the transfer is within a wholly owned group of companies.

The general principle of *Tupe* is that rights under or relating to an occupational pension scheme do not transfer (*reg 10*). Benefits which are not for 'old age, invalidity or survivors' (eg redundancy pensions) may transfer under the *Beckmann* principle[1] (see *Tupe and pensions: transfer of early retirement benefits: Beckmann, Martin and P&G*, **6.6** and *Tupe and pensions: Iissues following Beckmann, Martin and Procter & Gamble*, **6.7**).

This does not prevent the employers agreeing that pension continuity should be provided. See for example *Whitney v Monster Worldwide* (2010).

The following pension issues should be considered:

	Issue	Legal analysis	Action
1	Participation in group pension scheme	The new employer will need to be (or become) a participating employer in the group pension scheme.	Check if new employer participates. If not, deed of participation will be needed (trustee consent is commonly required) – see the further practical issues outlined below and see *New group company participation legal issues*, **10.2.**

---

1   *Beckmann v Dynamco Whicheloe MacFarlane Ltd* (C-164/00) [2002] ECR I-4893.

10.1.2 *Multi-employer schemes*

	Issue	*Legal analysis*	*Action*
2	*Continuity of benefits*	Does move from one participating employer to another maintain continuity of benefits?	Common rule – but need to check trust deed.
3	*Enhanced benefit trigger?*	Some schemes give enhanced benefits to members in certain circumstances, including perhaps redundancy or cessation of employment at the request of the employer.	Consider scheme rules.
		Such provisions should be considered as to whether they could be triggered by an intra-group transfer, potentially (although this is less common) even if the employees transfer under *Tupe* (and so are not dismissed) and/or retain their membership of the existing pension scheme.	
4	*Pensions Act obligations re benefits*	The *Pensions Act 2004* imposes obligations on transferee employers where there is a transfer under *Tupe* of members who were active in an occupational pension scheme before the transfer.	Check if benefit level satisfies *Pensions Act 2004* requirements
		The obligation is to offer a minimum level of pension benefits for future service.	
		If the group scheme is contracted out on a salary-related basis, then the continuing membership of the scheme with the new employer should satisfy these requirements.	
		But if the scheme is not contracted out, then the test may be more difficult to meet.	
		If the scheme is money purchase, the obligation under the *2004 Act* is for matching benefits up to 6percent of pay. This would apply even if it is greater than the previous level of money purchase obligations.	
		For further details see *Tupe and Pensions: Pensions Act 2004 obligations*, **6.4**.	

	Issue	Legal analysis	Action
5	Consultation with employees	*Pensions Act 2004:* if the relevant employees remain members of the same pension scheme as before, there will be no obligation to consult under the *Pensions Act 2004* consultation requirements. However, if benefits are to change (or the scheme is to change) a consultation obligation may arise – see *Pensions Act 2004: employers' consultation obligations,* **15.1**. *Tupe:* if any 'measures' are proposed in relation to pensions, a consultation obligation may arise under *Tupe 2006* (the consultation obligations apply to pension benefits even though the transfer provisions generally do not).	Consider if any pension benefit changes envisaged. Consider employee communications carefully (can have contractual implications).
6	Wages deductions	If the pension scheme is contributory, continuing authority is needed to make deductions from employees' wages for the purposes of *Part II* of the *Employment Rights Act 1996* (formerly the *Wages Act*). Any existing authorisation may well not transfer under *Tupe 2006*.	Check authority terms.
7	Notice to Trustees	The transfer of employees may be a 'material event' (eg if no active members remain with the old employer or if the reorganisation gives rise to a material change in employer covenant (see also 10 below)). Employers are obliged to inform trustees of material events within one month (*Scheme Administration Regulations 1996*). May need trustee consent (egif new employer needs to become a participating employer – see 1 above – or need to deal with *s 75* debt – see 9 below).	Consider informing trustees before transfer. Consider any express employer/trustee information agreements
8	Notice to Pensions Regulator	If the current employer is to cease carrying on business in the UK (eg because all its current business is to transfer) then this is a notifiable event requiring notification (when the decision is made) to the Pensions Regulator (see *Pensions Act 2004, s 69* and *Notifiable events: Obligation to report certain events to the Pensions Regulator,* **13.1**).	Give notice to the Regulator. Consider likely *s 75* issue – see 9 below

10.1.2 *Multi-employer schemes*

	Issue	*Legal analysis*	*Action*
9	*Section 75 debts?*	Is the effect of the transfer that the current employer ceases to have any employees who are active members of the relevant occupational scheme (whether or not other employees may remain with the existing employer)?	Check if *s* 75 debt is triggered If it is, consider how to deal with it.
		If so and the scheme is multi-employer, this will be an employment-cessation event (ECE) under *s* 75 of the *Pensions Act 1995* (as amended) and a debt is likely to arise on the current employer.	
		The *s* 75 debt will need to be paid or modified – see *Multi-employer pension schemes and section 75 debts,* **3.6.**	
		If the current employer is the only employer, the scheme will not be a multi-employer scheme and so there will be no ECE. Similarly, if all members in the pension scheme are currently deferred or pensioner members and there are no active members, then the cessation of employment and move to the new employer will not be an ECE.	
10	*Impact on employer covenant*	The trustees may be concerned about the impact of the transfer on the strength of the sponsoring companies supporting the scheme.	Consider impact Inform or consult with trustees as appropriate.
		This will depend on the financial circumstances of the current employer compared to the new employer.	
11	*Impact on security/funding agreements etc*	Does the transfer impact on any existing security or the funding arrangements?	Consider impact Inform or consult with trustees as appropriate.
		Any existing contingent asset security for the trustees (eg a guarantee from another group company) will need to be considered – if the new employer was not previously a participating employer does it need to be included within the ambit of any existing security?	
		If the security is PPF qualifying, the PPF may need to be told of the change.	

	Issue	Legal analysis	Action
12	*PPF levy*	The change of employer may result in a change to the relevant rating score of the employers for Pension Protection Fund levy purposes. This needs to be considered. The change in employer may be an event requiring notification to the PPF.	Consider impact on PPF scores/levy.
13	*Auto enrolment duties*	The move of employees from their current employer to Newco may also trigger a renewed obligation on Newco to arrange for auto-enrolment to apply (depending on Newco's staging date), even where the employees have previously opted out.	Consider auto-enrolment notifications (as if employees were new hires).

Practical issues if the new employer needs to become a participating employer

10.1.3   If the new employer is not already a participating employer in the group scheme then some further issues may flow from it starting to participate:

- A deed of participation/adherence will usually be needed (see **10.2.1**). Commonly this needs to be executed by the new employer, the principal employer and the trustees.

- The contracting-out certificate may need to be amended to reflect the change (a further election made and notice given to employees and any recognised trade unions). There are exemptions available where employees remain in the same scheme and there is no change in their contracted-out status – *Contracting-Out Regulations 1996, reg 10*;

- Any deed of adherence involving the new employer may need to involve an update to any existing authorisation for the principal employer to act on behalf of all employers – see *Multi-employer pension schemes: giving authority to the principal company,* **10.3**.

- Any existing contingent asset security for the trustees (eg a guarantee from another group company) will need to be considered – if there is a new participating employer it is more likely that an amendment will be needed so that it is covered by the existing security. If the security is PPF qualifying, the PPF may need to be told of the change (see **10.1.2** above, point 11).

10.1.3 *Multi-employer schemes*

- Inserting a new employer will require (ultimately) notification to HMRC and the Pensions Regulator (as the body running the register of occupational pension schemes).

See also *New group company participation in pension schemes: legal issues,* **10.2**.

Non-Tupe transfers

10.1.4   The same issues will generally arise even if the employment transfer is not part of a *Tupe* transfer. Such a transfer is more likely to involve agreement with the employees. Note that some of the issues noted above will only apply if there is a *Tupe* transfer (eg consultation under *Tupe* and the *Pensions Act 2004* obligations following *Tupe*).

Age discrimination exemption for closed schemes

10.1.5   One final technical point – if the scheme is closed to new members, it may be relying on the relevant exemption from the age discrimination obligations under the *Equality Act 2010*. See *Age discrimination and pensions,* **16.1**. This exemption could be lost if new members are allowed to join the scheme (unless they join a separate section as a result of a *Tupe* transfer).

In practice we take the view that, if the transferring employees are already members of the group scheme, their remaining within the scheme will not count as their being new 'joiners' (which otherwise could potentially mean the exemption is lost).

10.2 New group company participation in pension schemes: legal issues

Summary

Occupational pension schemes often operate on a group-wide level. This section looks at the legal issues to be considered if a company in the same group as the scheme sponsor (principal company or principal employer) is to start participating in the pension scheme (eg as part of an internal reorganisation or following a purchase).

Participation in pension schemes

10.2.1   If a group company (Newco) is to start to participate in the pension scheme (eg as part of an internal reorganisation or following a purchase), it will need to execute a deed of participation (sometimes called a deed of adherence).

The scheme rules will set out what needs to be in this deed. Usually it will require Newco to agree to be bound by the terms of the scheme. Often a deed of participation (or side letter) will include an authority from Newco, usually in favour of the principal company or employer, nominating one company as its agent to act on its behalf for specified purposes – see *Multi-employer pension schemes: Giving authority to the principal employer*, **10.3**.

Special terms

10.2.2   The deed of participation may set out any special terms on which the Newco is to participate. Typically this can include separate or modified benefits or no admission to Newco employees who only join the company (or apply) after a particular date.

Special terms on funding obligations are more difficult, as Newco will in any event become subject to the statutory funding provisions (ie scheme-specific funding under *Part 3* of the *Pensions Act 2004* and the debt on employer provisions under *Pensions Act 1995, s 75*),[2] which will in practice apply despite any agreement with the trustees to the contrary (Newco could agree special terms outside the scheme with the principal employer, but these would not bind the trustees). Newco may be able to agree special terms with the trustees and the

---

2   See *Scheme specific funding requirements*, **2.1** and *Debt on the employer*, **3.1**.

principal employer in other areas (eg amendments, partial winding-up provisions).

Special terms are more common if the Newco is not a wholly-owned member of the same group of companies as the principal employer.

Newco bound by future changes

10.2.3 By entering into a deed of participation, Newco is very likely (absent any specific agreed special terms) committing to be bound by future changes to the relevant trust deed and rules of the scheme, even if they impose further liabilities on Newco (at least while it is an employer) – see the *Pilots*[3] (2010) and the *Stena*[4] (2011) cases.

Effective date of participation

10.2.4 Strictly, any deed of participation should be put in place before Newco starts to participate. In practice, however, if all concerned have treated Newco as participating from an earlier date (eg Newco and its employed members have paid contributions), this can be included in the deed as the effective date of participation. Note that the deed itself will not be backdated, but instead it will be stated to take effect from the earlier date.

The consent of the trustees will probably be needed for backdated participation even if ordinarily trustee consent is not required for participation. Conceivably, HMRC could object to backdating participation (arguing that filling in the gap between the stated effective date and the actual date of the deed of participation just takes effect as an augmentation). This could have adverse tax effects. In practice, however, this is unlikely to be raised.

Trustee and principal employer consent

10.2.5 The scheme will usually require that the participation of a new company needs the approval of the trustees and the principal employer. (Some schemes require only the consent of the principal employer). In practice, this consent is usually evidenced by having the relevant deed of participation executed by the trustees and the principal employer.

---

3   *PNPF Trust Co Ltd v Taylor* [2010] EWHC 1573 (Ch).
4   *Stena Line Ltd v Merchant Navy Ratings Pension Fund Trustees Ltd* [2011] EWCA Civ 543.

Issues for the trustees in giving consent

10.2.6   In practice, the only significant issue for the trustees is whether the participation of Newco will affect the ability of each individual employer to fund the scheme. For example, could the trustees be concerned that the participation of Newco will result in a reduced 'covenant' compared to that of the previous employers? This may usually be regarded as unlikely. However, in some cases the trustees may look for some comfort on this (eg a guarantee from the principal company of the obligations of the individual subsidiaries).

Tax implications

10.2.7   Before April 2006, the Inland Revenue (now HMRC) needed to approve participation of every company in a group scheme. In practice, the Revenue always agreed to the participation of a company in a group scheme where it is a subsidiary of the principal company. This requirement for Revenue approval ceased when the new tax laws under the *Finance Act 2004* started to apply in April 2006.

HMRC should be notified of the new participating employer within 180 days of the end of the relevant scheme year in which participation commences. It is not necessary to file a copy of the deed of participation.

If Newco is not resident in the UK

10.2.8   If Newco is not resident in the UK for tax purposes, the Inland Revenue used (before April 2006) to require membership of the scheme to be limited to those employees who are subject to tax in the UK on their employment income (old 'Schedule E'). This may have been made a term of the scheme.

This limitation is no longer required by the post-2006 tax laws. But care is needed to consider the implications of an overseas company participating in the scheme – in particular the tax implications for the members and the potential for the scheme to be become a 'cross-border' scheme if any of the members end up working in another EU member state (see *Cross-border pension schemes in the EU*, **8.1**).

Continuity of benefits for existing scheme members transferring to Newco

10.2.9   Unless the scheme rules provide otherwise or unless specific provision is made, the aim will usually be that any individual employees who are already members of the scheme and who transfer to a new participating employer as a result of an internal reorganisation (here, Newco) will maintain continuity of service for benefits etc. In a defined benefit scheme, any subsequent pay rise given by Newco will therefore apply for all benefits (ie it will not be limited to benefits after the transfer date).

See *Moving employees within a group: pensions implications*, **10.1**.

Admission of Newco employees as new members?

10.2.10   Care should be taken to check the admission rule of the scheme. It may be that any existing (non-member) employees of Newco or any (non-member) employees joining Newco as a result of the reorganisation or purchase could be given a right to join the scheme under the general admission rule.

If this is not intended (eg if it is not intended to give any current employees who have not previously joined the scheme a (new) right to join when they move to become employed by Newco), provision about this needs to be included in the deed of participation.

Another point to consider is whether future employees of Newco will be able to join the scheme on the usual basis.

Care needs to be taken if the scheme is closed to new entrants (eg so that the express exemption under the age discrimination laws applies)

Tax limits on members

10.2.11   Under pre-2006 tax rules, the tax status of any existing scheme members who transferred to Newco and remained in the scheme should not have been affected (unless there is a break in pensionable service). For example, any members who were pre-1989 joiners and so not subject before the transfer to the Revenue's 'earnings cap' on benefits would have remained exempt (because they were not changing pension scheme).

The tax simplification from April 2006 has broadly the same effect. Under the *Finance Act 2004*, existing members who join Newco and stay in the scheme should have the same tax treatment as if they had not moved (eg they will retain any transitional exemptions, such as primary protection and the right to retire at age 50). This applies to moves both before and after April 2006.

Contracting out

10.2.12   If the scheme is contracted out of the state second pension, contracting-out notices may need to be issued to relevant employees who are moving to become employees of Newco. These notices can be sent individually or put on notice boards etc. If there is a recognised trade union, it will also need to be informed and consulted to comply with *regs 3* and *4* of the *Occupational Pension Schemes (Contracting-out) Regulations 1996 (SI 1996/1172)*.

If the only employees affected are those existing members of the scheme who are moving to Newco, there is no need to notify or consult with the employees (or any unions) and the relevant election can follow a relatively short form (see *reg 10* of the *1996 Contracting-out Regulations*). The contracted-out status of the individual employees is not changing; only the identity of their employer is changing.

Newco will need to be added to the contracting-out certificate for the scheme. The relevant forms will need to be completed and submitted to the Elections Section of HMRC.

If an existing employer ceases to participate

10.2.13 If the participation of Newco is part of an internal group reorganisation, care needs to be taken if any of the existing employers ceases to be an employer for statutory purposes (ie cease to be 'the employer of persons in the description or category of employment to which the scheme relates').

Such a cessation of participation in a multi-employer scheme (or ceasing to have any employees who are active members of the scheme) will usually trigger a debt due to the scheme by that employer under *s 75* of the *Pensions Act 1995* – see below and *Moving employees within a group: pension implications* **10.1**.

Impact on schedule of contributions

10.2.14 Newco will become bound to contribute to the scheme as envisaged in the scheme's funding rule and by the existing schedule of contributions.

Thought should be given as to whether this needs to be modified to reflect the new group structure. For example, would it be more appropriate for an individual contribution rate to be assessed for each employer instead of (say) a common percentage rate for all employers? Such a sharing of liability can be required in corporate accounts under accounting standard IAS19 (which can have a different effect to the UK standard, FRS17 on this point).

Specific s 75 funding on cessation?

10.2.15 If a participating employer ceases to participate, a funding check under *s 75* of the *Pensions Act 1995* will usually be triggered. If the funding check reveals a deficit, a proportion of the debt will be payable by the employer which ceases to participate (or which is not sold but ceases to have any active employees employed by it).

This cessation debt has, for cessations on or after 2 September 2005, been calculated looking at the scheme deficit based on the cost of insurance company buy-outs. For further details, see *Multi-employer pension schemes and section 75 debts,* **3.6.**

Mechanics of execution of deeds of participation

10.2.16 As noted above, the requirements for adding the new participating employer to the group's contracting-out certificate must be complied with.

In addition, the following matters in **10.2.17** to **10.2.25** (inclusive) below must be dealt with:

Execution and dating

10.2.17 If more than one new employer is to start participating, it may be easier to have separate deeds of participation for each new employer, rather than one deed to be executed by all the new employers, depending on the location of the employers and any timing issues.

The deed of participation will usually need to be executed by the trustees, the principal company and Newco. It should be dated on the cover page and the first page only when the last person has executed it.

Authorisation

10.2.18 Execution by the companies should comply with their respective constitutional documents (usually their memoranda and articles of association). The relevant articles of association should be checked, but commonly they require a board resolution to authorise the use of the common seal of the relevant company. Statutory alternatives are for signature (without a seal being used) on behalf of the company by:

- two directors or a director and the secretary; or

- by one director (but attested by a witness).

Any unusual execution mechanics should be accurately provided for in the execution pages.

Where any of the directors of the relevant company are also interested in the scheme (eg as members of the scheme or as directors of the trustee company), care should be taken to comply with the relevant statutory requirements and provisions in the articles relating to transactions in which directors have an interest. In particular:

- all directors with an interest should declare the nature of their interest at the board meeting in order to comply with *ss 177* and *182* of the *Companies Act 2006* (formerly *s 317* of the *Companies Act 1985*);

- as a transaction in which directors are interested, it must fall within the relevant authorising provision in the articles, and any conditions in that article (eg disclosure to the board) must be complied with; and

- the provisions in the articles dealing with the quorum for the board meetings and whether directors can vote on transactions in which they are interested must be complied with.

Individual trustees

10.2.19 Where there are individual trustees rather than a sole corporate trustee, it is usual for all trustees to be party to, and execute, a deed of participation. (It can be easier to get deeds executed by a corporate trustee instead of individuals.)

Where some (or all) of the trustees are individuals, they need to sign the deed in the presence of a witness (who should not be another party to the deed (eg not another trustee) and should preferably not be the spouse of a trustee). The witness must also sign the deed as a witness.

Stamp duty

10.2.20 No stamp duty is payable on a deed of participation (fixed duties were abolished, except on land and securities, from 1 December 2003).

It was previously not clear whether or not stamp duty of £5 was payable on a deed of a participation (or deed of amendment) as being a form of declaration of trust. We tended to avoid any doubt by usually arranging for the £5 fixed duty to be paid (it added much-needed colour to the document).

Pensions registry

10.2.21 The Pensions Regulator (as operator of the register of occupational pension schemes) must also be informed of the change in participating employers.

This may usually be done on the next annual return form that the Regulator sends out (but that return must be filed on time). Alternatively, a simple letter to the Regulator is sufficient. No fee is payable.

Other advisers

10.2.22 It is desirable to inform the scheme's actuary and auditor as well as any other relevant adviser of the new employer's participation. It would be helpful to send them a copy of the deed of participation when executed for their records. Often this is something required in their appointment letters.

Notice to members

10.2.23 There is no requirement under the *Occupational Pension Schemes (Disclosure of Information) Regulations 2013* (before April 2014, the *1996 Regulations*) to notify the members generally of the participation of a new employer. Obviously, the members transferring to Newco will need to be told of the change in employer and if there is any change in their benefits.

If they have not already received this, Newco needs to ensure that the relevant employees of Newco are notified of their membership of the scheme (*Employment Rights Act 1996, s 1*) and the trustees need to arrange for them to be given basic information about the scheme (*2013 Disclosure Regulations, Sch 1*).

The trustees will be required to provide a copy of the deed of participation if a member requests a copy of the scheme documents under the *2013 Disclosure Regulations* (before April 2014, the *1996 Regulations*).

Auto-enrolment

10.2.24 The move of employees from their current employer to Newco may also trigger a renewed obligation on Newco to arrange for auto-enrolment to apply (depending on Newco's staging date), even where the employees have previously opted out.

Original deeds

10.2.25 Original deeds are usually retained by the trustees. Sometimes the principal company also keeps an original of all schemes documents, in which case the deed is executed in duplicate.

10.3   Multi-employer pension schemes: Giving authority to the principal company

Summary

Trustees of occupational pension schemes are required by legislation to obtain the consent of, or to consult with, the employer in various circumstances. This section looks at how the required consultations and consents of participating employers in a multi-employer scheme can be channelled through the principal company.

The *Pensions Act 2004* brought in a number of new consultation and consent requirements. Principal companies should review the position to ensure that authorities are in place and consider whether new authorities are needed to replace any existing authorities.

Introduction

10.3.1   There are various statutory requirements in the pension legislation which require trustees of occupational pension schemes to obtain the consent of, or to consult with, 'the employer'. Examples are:

- the member-nominated trustee (MNT) provisions;

- the statement of investment principles (SIP); and

- the schedule of contributions.

A fuller list appears at the end of this section, see **10.3.10**.

The legislation tends to be written on the basis that there is only one employer. The position is then modified for multi-employer schemes by regulations. Commonly, these regulations envisage that, if there is more than one employer, the relevant consent or consultation must be from or with all of the employers.

Getting this wrong (eg leaving out an employer) can have serious repercussions. For example, failure to consult with all employers may well invalidate a SIP, as in *Pitmans Trustees Ltd v The Telecommunications Group Plc*[5] (2004), where the High Court held that a failure by a trustee properly to consult with a sole employer about a SIP invalidated it, even though there was no evidence that the consultation would have made any difference to the end result.

---

5   *Pitmans Trustees Limited v The Telecommunications Group* [2004] EWHC 181 (Ch).

10.3.1 *Multi-employer schemes*

However, the legislation often envisages that one employer can be nominated to act on behalf of the other employers for this purpose. There also seems to be no reason why an individual employer should not be able to authorise another person to act on its behalf.

Since 1997, when the *Pensions Act 1995* introduced the first of these requirements, it has been common to provide for a form of 'Pensions Act Authority' to be given by participating employers to the principal company. This authorises the principal company to act on the other participating employers' behalf in respect of the consultation and consent requirements of the *1995 Act* (this is often included as part of the deed of participation). Such an authority enables the matters it covers to be agreed by the principal company, so avoiding the need for each individual employer also to be involved (indeed it can go on to say that the participating employers must not get involved or exercise any discretion).

The *Pensions Act 2004* extended the range of statutory areas where employer involvement is needed. Any pre-2004 authorities still in place should therefore be revised to cover the additional requirements. Where no authority is in place, the opportunity should be taken to put one in place.

Ambit of authority

10.3.2 Such an authority should usefully be expressed to give a general authority to the principal company to agree matters and exercise discretions under the pension legislation.

However, it may be convenient to give a wider authority, for example to provide for the principal company to give consent or agree on behalf of the participating employers for:

- matters under the trust deed and rules, eg the powers of the employer to agree to late joining or to early retirement; or

- all matters connected with the scheme (but this may be thought to be too wide).

A power of attorney can be included to allow the principal company to execute documents on behalf of the participating employer.

Who should give an authority?

10.3.3 Given that the scope of the statutory provisions requiring employer consultation or agreement has been widened by the *Pensions Act 2004*, all participating employers who will not be involved in the processes should sign an authority. In some circumstances, a more limited authority might be appropriate (eg an employer might want to be involved only in the schedule of contributions).

In practice, it is probably easier for an authority to be given by wholly-owned subsidiaries in favour of their parent. If any of the participating employers is not wholly owned (eg there is a minority shareholding or it is a joint venture), then an authority may be less appropriate (the employer may look to be more involved in the pension scheme etc).

Do all the employers have to give an authority?

10.3.4 There is no requirement for all employers to give an authority. Commonly, an authority will work just for those employers which have given the authority. The others which have not will need to consent or be consulted as appropriate.

Some of the relevant pieces of legislation envisage that all employers need to authorise one of their number but other legislation does not (or refers to a majority). In any event, the power of attorney in the authority form should enable the principal company to act on behalf of the employer concerned.

How is such an authority given?

10.3.5 For new employers, the authority is most easily documented in the relevant deed of participation (eg as a separate schedule).

However, it can just as easily be in a separate authorisation document. This would need to be done for those employers already participating.

Who should be given the authority?

10.3.6 The principal company or employer under the scheme will usually be the right company to have the authority. Depending on the scheme, that company may well have various discretions already (eg power to agree to amendments, transfer payments, participation etc).

It helps if the principal company is also a participating employer. But this does not seem to be crucial if a power of attorney is also included.

The authority should be expressed to remain in place until changed by the principal company and the individual participating employer. It can be expressed to be irrevocable, though it is unclear if this will be effective (eg even on the insolvency of the participating employer). A power of attorney can be made irrevocable if it secures a proprietary interest of the donee (here the principal company) or an obligation owed to the donee (see *Powers of Attorney Act 1971, s 4*), but this may not apply here.

If there were subsequently to be a disposal of the participating employer, a relevant purchaser may well look for this authority to be terminated or modified.

Who should be a party to the authority?

10.3.7   The trustees do not have to be a party to the authority. The authority can be a simple document (two or three pages) executed by the participating employer (as a deed to give a power of attorney to the principal company).

The trustees should be given a copy of the authority. This allows them to check that consultation/consent by the principal company is all that is needed.

Does the principal company owe any duties to the participating employers as a result?

10.3.8   The nature of any duties that could be owed generally by a principal company to the participating employers is not one that has yet been examined by the courts. For example, a power of amendment is commonly left with the principal company, but the participating employers are bound by changes made.

In practice, it is helpful if this issue can be dealt with in the authority (eg expressly provide that the principal company owes no duty to the participating employer).

Implications of an authority

10.3.9   Delegating powers and responsibilities to a principal company is fairly common in group multi-employer schemes. However, there are possible implications:

- potentially an increased exposure to the Pensions Regulator (TPR) using its moral hazard powers against the principal company (see Chapter **4**);

- potentially an increased chance of the principal company being considered a shadow director of the participating companies; and

- potentially issues about whether the principal company should be considered the actual employer instead of the nominal participating employer.

In practice, depending on the facts and circumstances, these issues may well be unlikely to be material (but companies should be aware of them).

Particular cases of principal company authority to act

10.3.10

Matter	Statute
Methods and assumptions to be used in calculating the scheme's technical provisions	*Sections 222(4) and 229 of the Pensions Act 2004* *Para 2, Sch 2 of the Occupational Pension Schemes (Scheme Funding) Regulations 2005*
Statement of funding principles	*Sections 223 and 229 of the Pensions Act 2004* *Para 2, Sch 2 of the Occupational Pension Schemes (Scheme Funding) Regulations 2005*
Schedule of contributions	*Sections 227 and 229 of the Pensions Act 2004* *Para 2, Sch 2 of the Occupational Pension Schemes (Scheme Funding) Regulations 2005*
Recovery plan	*Sections 226 and 229 of the Pensions Act 2004* *Para 2, Sch 2, Occupational Pension Schemes (Scheme Funding) Regulations 2005*
Modification of the scheme for future accrual of benefits	*Section 229(2) of the Pensions Act 2004* *Para 2, Sch 2, Occupational Pension Schemes (Scheme Funding) Regulations 2005*
Consultation about 'listed changes' to future benefits etc	*Section 259, Pensions Act 2004* *Occupational and Personal Pension Schemes (Consultation by Employers and Miscellaneous Amendment) Regulations 2006* *Occupational Pension Schemes (Consultation by Employers) (Modification for Multi-employer Schemes) Regulations 2006*
Power to amend the scheme, including to extend the class of person who may receive benefits in respect of the death of a member	*Section 68(2)(a), Pensions Act 1995*

10.3.10 *Multi-employer schemes*

Matter	Statute
Age discrimination – benefits based on length of service	*Reg 32*, and *para 3A* of *Sch 2* of the *Employment Equality (Age) Regulations 2006* *Para10, Sch 9* of the *Equality Act 2010*: *Article 6* of the *Equality Act (Age Exceptions for Pension Schemes) Order 2010*
Consultation about scheme amendments to accrued rights	*Sections 67* to *67I* of the *Pensions Act 1995* *Occupational Pension Schemes (Modification of Schemes) Regulations 2006*
Statement of investment principles and investment matters	*Section 35(3), Pensions Act 1995* *Occupational Pension Schemes (Investment) Regulations 2005*
Payments to employers	*Section 37, Pensions Act 1995* *Section 251, Pensions Act 2004* (as amended by the *Pensions Act 2011*)
Member-nominated Trustees and Directors	*Sections 241* to *243* of the *Pensions Act 2004* *Occupational Pension Schemes (Member-nominated Trustees and Directors) Regulations 2006*

Chapter 11

Trustees

11.1 Member-nominated trustees (MNTs)

Summary

A new regime for member-nominated trustees (MNTs) and member-nominated directors (MNDs) came into force in 2006. Previous opt-outs remained valid until their expiry, or 31 October 2007, if earlier.

Broadly relevant schemes are required to make arrangements for at least one-third of the trustee board to be member-nominated, by a process settled by the trustees. The new law is more flexible than the old process under the *Pensions Act 1995*, but allows for fewer exceptions from the basic rule.

This section looks at the requirements under the *Pensions Act 2004*.

Introduction

11.1.1   The current regime for member-nominated trustees/directors (MNTs/MNDs), introduced by *ss 241 to 243* of the *Pensions Act 2004* and the *Occupational Pension Schemes (Member-nominated Trustees and Directors) Regulations 2006* (*SI 2006/714*) came into force on 6 April 2006. This replaced (after a transitional period) the previous MNT/MND rules under the *Pensions Act 1995*.

In addition to the legislation, the Pensions Regulator (TPR) issued in November 2006 a Code of Practice 08: *MNT/MND – putting arrangements in place*. In

11.1.1 *Trustees*

August 2006 TPR also issued guidance for trustees, covering timings and transitional issues. Both are available in the Codes of Practice section of TPR's website.[1]

The requirements are broadly the same for MNTs and MNDs (differing only where a company is trustee of more than one scheme). This section will use the expression MNTs to encompass both unless specified otherwise.

The requirements apply to all occupational schemes unless they are exempted. The list of exempted schemes has changed slightly from that of the *Pensions Act 1995* (see box on next page). Trustees of schemes previously exempt should therefore have checked whether their scheme remained exempt, and keep exemptions under review (eg a scheme with one member is exempt but an increase to two would end the exemption).

TPR has powers to investigate any alleged breaches of the MNT requirements and take corrective or punitive action.

Key changes from the Pensions Act 1995 regime

11.1.2   The basic requirement is still that at least one-third of the total number of the trustees of an occupational pension scheme be MNTs. (The Secretary of State has power to prescribe that this will in future increase to one half.) However, the current regime has significant differences from the *Pensions Act 1995* regime:

- the 'MNT opt-out' (facility for employers to make alternative arrangements) has been abolished; but

- subject to the one-third requirement, the legislation is less prescriptive and intended to be more flexible (eg there is no specified term of office) – TPR's code of practice explains that trustees are now expected to decide on their arrangements on the basis of three principles:

    - proportionality – the costs and nature of the approach chosen should be appropriate to the scheme's circumstances (eg method of communication with members);

    - fairness (but this does not mean that all classes of member have to be treated the same); and

    - transparency (eg the outcomes of the nomination and selection processes and the method of selection should be communicated to all members involved) – see **11.1.7** below.

---

1   See www.thepensionsregulator.gov.uk/codes/code-mnt-mnd-arrangements.aspx

The legislation requires the trustees of an occupational scheme to ensure that:

- arrangements are put in place which provide for at least one-third MNTs – this involves nomination and selection processes;

- those arrangements are implemented; and

- each step takes place within a 'reasonable period', set out in the code of practice (see below).

Exemptions from requirement for MNTs

- Schemes with fewer than two members.

- Schemes within *s 22* of the *Pensions Act 1995* (ie employer is insolvent or within an assessment period – whether or not a statutory independent trustee has been appointed).

- Schemes not registered for tax purposes.

- Stakeholder schemes.

- Small insured schemes (fewer than 12 members with fully insured benefits).

- Relevant centralised schemes.

- Where the scheme is a direct payment, paid-up insurance scheme.

- Former 'old code' schemes.

- *Section 615(6)* schemes (ie schemes established only for employees outside the UK).

- Relevant small occupational pension schemes (fewer than 12 members, all members are trustees/directors of trustee company and there is an independent trustee).

- Schemes where all trustees are independent of both the employer and employees.

- Schemes independent of the employer because employer was dissolved/liquidated pre-6 April 2005.

- Parliamentary schemes, some coal industry schemes and schemes where the trustee is governed by church legislation.

- Relevant executive pension scheme (company is sole employer and sole trustee; members are current or former directors of company and include at least one-third of the current directors) (MNDs only).

11.1.2 *Trustees*

- Relevant wholly insured scheme (scheme has a sole trustee; all benefits are insured, some or all with an insurer who is, or is connected with, the sole trustee but is not, and is not connected with, the employer) (MNDs only).

- NEST (as a scheme established under *s 67* of the *Pensions Act 2008*.

Timing: from when do the MNT requirements apply?

11.1.3 Trustees were required to put arrangements in place within a reasonable period of the commencement date for their scheme. Transitional arrangements were in place when the *2004 Act* came into force, but the new arrangements should have come into force by 31 October 2007.

Putting in place arrangements providing for at least one-third MNTs

11.1.4 Trustees should review the arrangements every three to five years. They should ask themselves at least the following questions:

- Which requirements apply to the scheme – MNT or MND (see table on next page)?

- How many MNTs are required?

  – Check legal requirement (eg total of ten trustees, at least four must be MNTs).

  – Do the scheme rules require more? Where the rules provide for more than the –minimum one-third MNTs, the legislation does not override this.

- Is it proposed to have more than one-third MNTs but the scheme rules do not provide for it? If so, employer consent will be required.

- How many MNT vacancies are there, taking into account the number of MNTs already in post (including those appointed under the *Pensions Act 1995*)?

- Are any current arrangements still appropriate or are new ones needed? (Remember to comply with the principle of proportionality as regards the cost for the scheme of running the selection process as well as the principles of fairness and transparency.)

- Is it proposed that non-members should be eligible for nomination and selection? The employer has the right to require its consent to the nomination and selection of non members. Trustees should therefore discuss in advance with the employer whether it will require this; if it will, this should be reflected in the arrangements.

- What if there are fewer nominations than vacancies: will the nominees be deemed to be selected or will a selection process still be run?

- If there are unfilled vacancies because of insufficient nominations, how soon should the nomination and selection processes normally be re-run (see **11.1.13** below)?

- How should responsibilities under the arrangements be allocated?

- What systems should be put in place to implement the arrangements?

MNT or MND?	
Which requirements apply depends on the composition of the trustee board:	
MNT	*MND*
Individual trustees	Sole corporate trustee
Individuals and corporate trustees	More than one corporate trustee (unless an independent trustee and no individual trustees)
Each corporate trustee counts as one trustee for purpose of calculating total number of trustees.	MND requirements apply separately to each company.

Implementing arrangements: the nomination and selection processes

Nomination

11.1.5 The nomination process must involve all active and pensioner members or organisations adequately representing them. The code gives guidance on how to assess this and points out that if representative organisations only are involved (ie no individuals) it is likely that actives and pensioners will need separate representative organisations.

If there are no active or pensioner members, at least some of the deferred members must be eligible to participate: 'at least such deferred members as the trustees determine are eligible to participate' – *reg 5(6)*.

Members or representative organisations should be given sufficient time to consider who they want to nominate.

11.1.5 *Trustees*

Trustees may decide to use constituencies in the nomination process (eg by site, category of member or section of the scheme) but they should have regard to the principles of proportionality, fairness and transparency. For example, it would not, in general, be fair for a constituency of 100 members to nominate two MNTs, and a constituency of 10,000 members to nominate only one.

Selection

11.1.6   The arrangements must provide for a selection process if:

- there are more nominations than vacancies; or

- the trustees decide to have one, even if in the event there are fewer nominations than vacancies.

The arrangements should also provide for the appointment of the MNTs selected (or deemed to be selected).

The selection process must involve at least some of the members or their representative organisations. If selection is by a panel or group, trustees must ensure that these include some scheme members.

The methods of selection may vary according to the circumstances of the scheme. They are likely to be affected by the number of scheme members trustees choose to involve in selection. It may be appropriate to adopt a combination of methods (eg in the case of constituencies it may be appropriate to have a member committee per site for active members and a ballot for pensioner members).

TPR gives examples of selection methods:

- ballot;

- selection panels;

- selection by member representative committees;

- selection by pension management committees;

- selection by trade unions; and

- selection by existing trustees.

Communication with members/representatives

Content of communication

11.1.7 See box below for the minimum information which the code recommends communicating to all members involved in the nomination and selection processes.

Communication with members/representatives about nomination and selection – code of practice recommended minimum

Nomination

- Number of MNTs scheme should have.

- Number of MNTs in place.

- Number of MNT vacancies.

- Short explanation of role of a trustee and any available training (could include reference to first module of TPR's trustee toolkit).

- Any eligibility criteria.

- What will happen if number of nominations is less than or equal to number of vacancies.

- Details of selection process to be used if more nominations than vacancies, or if trustees have decided to hold one anyway.

- How to nominate someone for selection as an MNT.

- Any applicable time limits.

- Contact for queries.

Selection

11.1.8

- What those involved in the selection process need to do.

- Outcome of nomination process.

- Method of selection.

Method of communication

11.1.9 The Code says trustees should consider using their established means of communicating with members, as these will often be effective and less expensive. However, the method may vary according to the circumstances of the scheme, eg:

- a scheme of a large company on multiple sites might place a prominent announcement in its regular pensions bulletin or in a staff magazine;

- a small scheme with active members only, all employed on one site, may be able to use a staff notice board; or

- for a mature scheme with a large number of deferred and pensioner members the postal system may be more appropriate.

'Reasonable periods'

11.1.10 All the steps involved in the new MNT arrangements must be carried out within a 'reasonable time'. The reasonable periods stated in the code of practice are set out below.

Putting arrangements in place – six months

11.1.11 The period may vary according to the size, structure and circumstances of the scheme. TPR expects most schemes to take less than six months but is aware that large schemes with members employed at many locations could need longer.

Nomination and selection of MNTs – six months

11.1.12 This should take place, but need not necessarily be completed, within six months.

Re-running the nomination process due to an unfilled vacancy because of insufficient nominations – maximum three years

11.1.13 But if a significant change occurs to the scheme membership (eg a bulk transfer-in of new members), trustees should consider an earlier re-running of the nomination and selection processes.

Reviewing arrangements (to establish whether they remain appropriate for the scheme) – every three to five years

11.1.14 TPR makes it clear that it is not suggesting this will automatically result in changes to the arrangements: if the outcome is that they remain appropriate there is no need for any changes.

Trustees should consider an earlier review if there is a material change to the scheme's circumstances and/or membership (eg a bulk transfer-in or a large number of redundancies).

Trustees may consider including deferred members when re-running the processes if they were not included when they were first run.

Action

11.1.15 Trustees should consider what new arrangements are needed well before expiry of current arrangements. It is worth making checklists of what needs to be in the arrangements and of what is in the current arrangements. Can any of the current arrangements for MNTs and MNDs be retained, in whole or in part?

Trustees should keep a record of the steps taken to comply with new MNT requirements. The code of practice notes that trustees may wish to keep records of the material matters they took into account during their deliberations.

11.2 Advantages and disadvantages of a separate trustee company

Summary

Using a trustee company rather than individual trustees for an occupational pension scheme can involve less bureaucracy because it is generally easier to get deeds executed and the transfer of trust assets is simpler. The directors can also shelter behind the trustee company's corporate personality.

However, returns must be made to the Companies Registry and there may be slightly less transparency. It is also more difficult to entrench a particular trustee structure with a corporate trustee.

This section outlines the main advantages and disadvantages of having a separate trustee company.

11.2.1   UK private sector occupational pension schemes need a trustee, either a group of individual trustees or a trustee company. A trustee company board can be formed by the individuals who would have been trustees, but they would instead now be directors rather than trustees. The advantages and disadvantages of having a corporate trustee are set out below.

A trustee company is generally easier to operate and can give some additional protection to individuals on the trustee board.

Advantages

11.2.2

- The transfer of trust assets is simpler. The legal title to assets and contracts remains with the trustee company if there is a change of director and there is no need to seek to renew contracts or transfer assets.

- There is less formality involved in a change of a trustee director than in a change of a personal trustee. There is also less need for deeds of appointment or removal so fewer deeds are involved. Fewer notifications are needed – the only requirement is a notification to the Companies Registry within 14 days.

- The duties and responsibilities of the party appointing and removing trustee company directors (usually the employing company) are clearer than those of individual trustees.

- Using a trustee company avoids the problem of being unable to have more than four trustees as legal owners of land under *s 34* of the *Trustee Act 1925*.

- Companies usually provide full majority voting by directors. However, the articles can provide for something else (eg weighted voting for directors in some circumstances). The general rule for individual pension trustees now is that decisions can be made by a majority of the trustees unless the trust deed allows otherwise.

- It is generally easier to get deeds executed. Once a matter has been approved by the board it usually needs only the signatures of: one director provided a witness attests the signature; two directors; or a director and a secretary. There is no need to involve all the directors.

- The trustee company's directors can shelter behind the separate corporate personality of the trustee company, at least in relation to ordinary creditors (eg fund managers, third party contractors, creditors etc) – see further below.

- There are advantages in terms of more flexibility in the investment provisions in the *Pensions Act 1995*.

- Certain transactions between directors and the company are prohibited by the Companies Acts. If directors of the employer company were also individual trustees, these sections could cause difficulty with some types of transaction between the employer company and the individual trustee, even though in most cases there would be exceptions for trustees of the company pension scheme.

- Delegation by individual trustees is not generally permitted unless expressly authorised by the trust instrument. However, delegation by companies' boards of directors (including corporate trustees) is generally permitted and will usually be expressly dealt with under the articles of association, if not elsewhere. Directors' and officers' insurance cover may be easier to extend to directors of a subsidiary trustee company.

Disadvantages

11.2.3

- A separate trustee is needed to give receipts for the proceeds of sale or other capital moneys arising under a trust for sale of land (under *Trustee Act 1925 s 14* and *Law of Property Act 1925 s 27*).

11.2.3 *Trustees*

- Additional paperwork is involved and it is necessary to submit returns to the Companies Registry. These are not onerous.

- A trustee company will probably count as a dormant company under the Companies Acts. A dormant company is exempt from the requirement to have audited accounts but shareholders can give a notice requiring the company to obtain an audit of its accounts for a financial year. A dormant company will also not need to appoint auditors. It will, however, still be required to deliver (unaudited) accounts of the company (as opposed to the scheme) to the Registrar of Companies and circulate copies of annual accounts to every member of the company, every holder of the company's debentures and every person who is entitled to receive notice of general meetings. If the dormant company also qualifies for the small companies regime it will only need to prepare 'abbreviated accounts'.

- Under the *Companies Acts* and the disclosure rules for listed companies, a body corporate controlling the trustee company is deemed to be interested in shares held by the trustee company (even if they are held on trust for the pension scheme). If the trustee company is a subsidiary of one of the employers, this means that the employer (and any other companies having control of the employer) will be treated as being interested in shares held by the trustee company.

- It may be necessary to check that any exclusion or limitation clauses affecting the trustees' general liability are expressly applicable to directors of a trustee company.

- There is perhaps less transparency – individual trustees may be more visible to employees.

- The 'usual residential address' of each director of the trustee company must be included in the details filed at Companies House (provisions in the *Companies Act 2006*, which came into force in October 2009, allow directors to use a service address instead of their usual residential address on the company's register of directors. The director's residential address will still need to be provided to Companies House but this will be kept on a separate secure register). For individual trustees, the only registration requirement is with the Pensions Registry and there is no obligation to give residential addresses.

- The maximum civil penalties that TPR can levy are generally greater for trustee companies than for individual trustees.

- It is harder to entrench a particular trustee structure with a corporate trustee.

- If one director becomes disqualified from acting as a trustee, the whole trustee company is disqualified until that director leaves the board – so the articles of association should state that a director automatically ceases to hold office if he becomes disqualified.

554

• If the trustee company is a subsidiary of an employer, this may mean that potential liability to the carbon reduction commitment (CRC) needs to be considered – see *Trustees and Carbon Reduction Commitment*, **11.5** below. Registration on a 'disaggregated' basis may deal with any potential CRC liability.

Director liability

11.2.4   In practice the individuals acting as directors of a trustee company will often consider themselves to be the trustees and may even call themselves this. But, legally, the company is the trustee, not the individuals.

This means that the directors owe the usual fiduciary and statutory duties to the trustee company. But they will not automatically owe any duties to third parties such as creditors or members of the pension scheme. This has been confirmed by case law in *Gregson v HAE Trustees*[2] (2008) and *HR v JAPT*[3] *(1999)*. Liabilities to third parties (eg members) can arise in some circumstances (eg knowing assistance in a breach of trust), but generally trustee directors are better protected than individual trustees. This is particularly against contractual claims, which can be significant if (say) investments contracts are involved.

Indemnities and exonerations in trust documents in favour of trustees need to be checked to see that they extend to directors of a trustee company. The *Companies Acts* also include some limitations on indemnities (see **11.3**).

---

2   *Gregson v HAE Trustees Ltd* [2008] EWHC 1006 (Ch); [2008] 2 BCLC 542.
3   *HR v JAPT* [1997] OPLR 123.

11.3 *Companies Act 2006*: **Duties and indemnities: What do directors of pension corporate trustees need to know?**

Summary

This section outlines the implications of the *Companies Act 2006* for directors of corporate trustees of occupational pension schemes.

Introduction

11.3.1   The *Companies Act 2006* (the *2006 Act*) was passed on 8 November 2006. Its provisions have come into force at different times since then.

Previously the rules governing directors came from several sources, including the common law (developed by case law) and the *Companies Act 1985*.

The *2006 Act* sets out, in *sections 170* to *181*, a new statement of directors' duties – described as their general duties – in place of the common law and replaced (and to some extent re-wrote) the relevant provisions of the *Companies Act 1985*.

General duties

11.3.2   There are seven general duties in the *2006 Act*. The most relevant for a director of a pension scheme trust company are:

- a duty to promote the success of the company for the benefit of its members, including factors to be taken into account when making board decisions – this requirement came into force on 1 October 2007;

    - a duty to avoid conflicts of interest – this came into force on 1 October 2008.[4]

- a duty to declare to the company's other directors any interest he has in a proposed transaction or arrangement with the company – this came into force on 1 October 2008; and

---

4   Previously, if a director allowed his personal interests or his duties to another person to conflict with his duty to the company, unless the articles allowed, or the shareholders consented to, the conflict: (i) the company could avoid any relevant contract; and (ii) he had to account to the company for any profit he made.

• a duty to exercise 'independent judgement' – this came into force on 1 October 2007.

These duties are considered in more detail below.

Factors to take into account when making board decisions

11.3.3 The 2006 regime obliges a director to 'act in the way he considers, in good faith, would be most likely to promote the success of the company for the benefit of its members as a whole'.

In deciding how to promote the success of the company, the directors are required to have regard 'amongst other matters' to:

• the likely long-term consequences of their decisions;

• the interests of the company's employees;

• the need to foster the company's business relationships with suppliers, customers and others;

• the effect of the company's operations on the community and the environment;

• the desirability of maintaining a reputation for a high standard of business conduct; and

• the need to act fairly as between members of the company.

These matters should be considered when making decisions (and those involved in preparing board papers should also bear them in mind).

In June 2007, the then Department of Trade and Industry (DTI) issued a collection of ministerial statements on director's duties in the new legislation. The examples include a comment from Lord Goldsmith in the Lords' Grand Committee on 6 February 2006, when he discussed the duty to promote the success of the company in the context of a non-commercial company. He said:

> 'What is success? The starting point is that it is essentially for the members of the company to define the objective they wish to achieve. Success means what the members collectively want the company to achieve. For a commercial company, success will usually mean long-term increase in value. For certain companies, such as charities and community-interest companies, it will mean the attainment of the objectives for which the company has been established.'

Directors of a trustee company may also in certain circumstances have fiduciary duties such as taking account of all relevant factors and excluding irrelevant factors.

11.3.4 *Trustees*

Conflicts of interest

11.3.4   There are four provisions in the *2006 Act* dealing with conflicts of interest and their disclosure. They distinguish between:

- interests in transactions and arrangements with the company (which must be disclosed but not approved by the board); and

- all other conflicts (which normally require approval by the board).

In relation to the conflicts requiring approval – which are likely to be the most relevant for directors of corporate trustees – the *2006 Act* contains a broad general duty to avoid situations in which a director has an interest that conflicts or may conflict with the company's interests. This applies to the exploitation of any property, information or opportunity, whether or not the company could have taken advantage of it.

Board approval is not required if:

- the conflict arises in a situation that cannot reasonably be regarded as likely to give rise to a conflict; or

- the conflict is authorised by the articles of association of the company; or

- the matter has been authorised by the directors.

Board authorisation can be given only if:

- it is not invalidated by the company's articles;

- any quorum is met without counting the interested director(s); and

- the matter is agreed without counting any vote cast by the interested director(s).

Changes to the articles of association

11.3.5   Corporate trustee companies should consider taking advantage of the provision in the *2006 Act* that allows them to deal with conflicts of interest in their articles of association. Any action taken in accordance with such a provision will not be a breach of the conflict.

It will therefore be possible to make provision for particular areas in which conflicts are likely to arise (eg by providing that a director who is also a director or employee of the sponsoring employer (or associate) will not be regarded as being in breach of the no-conflict rule and need not disclose confidential information received by virtue of that directorship).

It would also be prudent to have a similar provision in the articles of the employer.

Duty to exercise independent judgement

11.3.6 There is no exactly equivalent duty in common law. However, directors are generally under an obligation not to fetter their discretion to act or take decisions and this aspect of the general duty replaces this obligation.

There have been concerns that this requirement may prevent individual directors from relying on the judgement of others in areas in which they are not expert. The government has confirmed in debate that directors will continue to be able to do this – and to delegate matters to committees – provided they exercise their own judgement in deciding whether to follow advice or accept someone else's judgement on a matter.

Directors of a trustee company have separate duties under *s 248* of the *Pensions Act 2004* and trust law to have sufficient knowledge and understanding of relevant law and the governing documentation of their scheme.

Indemnities to pension scheme trustee directors

11.3.7 The previous statutory prohibition on exoneration clauses covering negligence, default, breach of duty or breach of trust by a director in relation to the company of which he is director (or an associated company) has been re-enacted in the 2006 Act (*s 232*) with effect from 1 October 2007.

However, indemnities for directors are permitted in certain circumstances, including if they are:

- a permitted type of insurance; or
- a 'qualifying pension scheme indemnity provision' (QPSIP) – *s 235*. This is a provision indemnifying a director of a company that is a trustee of an occupational pension scheme against liability incurred in connection with the company's activities as trustee of the scheme.

This addresses a concern that an indemnity provided by an employer for a director of a pension scheme trustee company would be void if that person were also a director of the employer. Any indemnity in favour of the trustee directors by the trust company itself may also need to be a QPSIP (although it is arguable that this is not an indemnity from the trustee company itself but a right to claim on the fund directly).

A sponsoring company of a pension scheme can therefore use a QPSIP to indemnify a trustee director of a corporate trustee against liability incurred in connection with the company's activities as trustee of the scheme.

Requirements of a QPSIP

11.3.8   The QPSIP is similar to the qualifying third-party indemnity provision exemption previously available. For example, the indemnity must not cover:

- liability to pay a fine imposed in criminal proceedings;

- any sum payable to a regulatory authority as a penalty for non-compliance with a regulatory requirement; or

- any liability of a director in defending criminal proceedings in which he is convicted.

In contrast with a qualifying third-party indemnity provision, QPSIPs may cover costs in defending civil proceedings brought against the director by the company or an associated company in which judgment is given against him.

Disclosure

11.3.9   QPSIPs must be disclosed in the directors' reports of the trustee company and the company providing the indemnity. A copy of the QPSIP must be kept at the registered office and available for a year after it has expired or terminated. This may involve companies' keeping copies of extracts from scheme trust deeds if the QPSIP is in the trust document.

In addition, shareholders have a right to request a copy of the QPSIP.

Pensions Act position

11.3.10   The *Pensions Act 2004* (*s 256*) prohibits indemnities out of the assets of a pension trust to the extent that they cover criminal fines or civil penalties under pension legislation.

Requirement to retire at age 70

11.3.11   There was a maximum age threshold of 70 years (at the time of appointment) for directors of public companies and their subsidiaries (which could include the pension scheme trustee), unless the articles provided otherwise. This requirement has been repealed from 6 April 2007 and the upper age limit of 70 years abolished.

Company websites and e-mails

11.3.12 Regulations[5] that came into force on 1 January 2007 require companies to ensure that:

- the company's name is 'mentioned,' in legible characters, on its websites and in electronic documents, including letters, order forms, receipts and invoices; and

- certain additional details are included on its websites and in electronic business letters and order forms, including the company's place of registration, registered number and registered office.

These regulations will apply to pension scheme websites if the trustee is a corporate trustee.

---

5   *The Companies (Registrar, Languages and Trading Disclosures) Regulations 2006.*

11.4   Pension schemes: paying trustees

Summary

This section considers whether pension scheme trustees can be paid and, if so, whether they should be paid.

Issues include whether:

- paid trustees have a higher duty of care (and consequent increase in personal liability); and

- it is in the interests of the members that trustees be paid.

Introduction

11.4.1   'In general, paying trustees for the performance of their duties is good practice.' This was one of the conclusions reached by Paul Myners in his March 2001 report, 'Institutional Investment in the United Kingdom: a Review'. In his view, this would help to:

- foster a culture in which pension fund management is carried out in a businesslike manner; and

- address the problem of lack of investment expertise among trustees of occupational pension schemes.

The government's response to this review indicated that, to the extent that trustees are retaining responsibility for investment matters, they are fulfilling a complex and important role and that, at the very least, serious consideration should be given to paying trustees for fulfilling the role.

However, a 2003 poll indicated that at that point out of the FTSE 50 companies, only one paid its employee trustees.[6] Some companies pay external trustees and fewer still pay an independent trustee chairman.

Legal considerations

11.4.2   The two main legal considerations that arise in relation to paying trustees (or directors of a trustee company) are:

---

6   FTfm survey, *Financial Times*, 6 January *2003*.

- *can* the trustees be paid? and, if so

- *should* the trustees be paid?

Can the trustees be paid?

The employer can, of course, pay the trustees out of its own resources (subject to some of the practical considerations).

If however their fees are to be paid out of the assets of the pension scheme, the position is more complex.

The general law position is that a trustee has no right to be paid for his time and efforts. The reason given in the case law for this is that if a trustee were paid, his interest in doing as much paid work as possible could prevail over his fiduciary duty of undivided loyalty to the beneficiaries.

The general rule is modified, however, if the trust deed contains an express power to remunerate the trustees.

There is now an implied power under the *Trustee Act 2000* for trustees to be paid for services (but generally only if acting in a professional capacity).

Does the trust deed contain the power to pay trustees?

11.4.3 If the trust deed does not contain an express power to pay trustees for their services (as distinct from reimbursing their expenses), the scheme rules will need to be amended to insert such a power.[7] If the change requires trustee consent, the trustees will need to consider very carefully why such a change would be for a proper purpose.

This is a similar issue to payment of insurance premiums for trustees. It may be possible to justify payment of trustees on the basis of encouraging people to act as trustees – but some evidence may be needed that otherwise appropriate people are not willing to serve. See, for example, the Scottish case of *Dollar Academy v Lord Advocate*[8] (1995).

Should the trustees be paid?

11.4.4 Even where there is an express power to pay trustees, the question remains as to whether it should be used.

---

7   The limited implied power to pay professional (but not lay) *trustees* under s 28, *Trustee Act 2000* can apply in some cases.

8   1995 SLT 596 (Lord Hope).

11.4.5 *Trustees*

Benefit to scheme

11.4.5 The trustees would need to be able to show some benefit to the scheme as a result of the payment (particularly in a money purchase scheme, where the payment will reduce not only members' security but also their benefits). This might be hard to do, particularly if there is a willing and able supply of volunteers in the workforce. One possible *quid pro quo* is incentivising trustees to obtain better qualifications and paying them only when they do so.

Higher duty of care

11.4.6 However, paid trustees may well have a higher duty of care in exercising their powers and discretions and indemnity/exoneration clauses would need to be checked to see whether they are sufficient for the increase in liability (see for instance the 1980 decision of Brightman J in *Bartlett v Barclays Bank Trust Co*).[9]

Disclosure

11.4.7 It would be prudent for trustees to disclose the payment to members as soon as possible. Payments would need to be shown in pension scheme accounts and possibly also in company accounts (if the trustees are also directors).

Structure of payment

11.4.8 Care should be taken to ensure that the payment is structured only as compensation for the role of trustee. If it is too closely connected with investment services provided, there is a danger that there may be a breach of the authorisation requirements of the *Financial Services and Markets Act 2000*.

Practical issues

11.4.9 A number of practical questions arise:

● Employee trustees already have a right in law (under the *Employment Rights Act 1996*) to paid time off to carry out their duties in relation to their employer's scheme. Employers may be unwilling to pay more.

---

9   *Bartlett v Barclays Bank Trust Co Ltd (No 2)* [1980] 2 All *ER* 92.

- There is no useful guidance on what an appropriate level of payment would be. How then should any payment be structured? Should non-management trustees be paid more to compensate for the higher pay for the same time given to management trustees? How should pensioner trustees be compensated? Would it be on an annual basis (similar to non-executive directors) or, for example, on an hourly basis?

- Should there be a two-tier trustee board (ie some trustees with requisite qualifications being paid and some not)?

- Would a higher duty of care and consequently an increased personal liability for paid trustees be likely to deter potential member-nominated trustees from volunteering to act as trustees?

- There may be some impact on the cost of trustee liability insurance because of the potentially higher duty of care of paid trustees. Would the trustees be expected to pay for their insurance out of their fees?

- Tax implications should be considered. Payments will generally be chargeable to tax (under what was Schedule E) and the PAYE deduction system will need to operate.

Conclusion

11.4.10   As with many pension issues, the question of paying trustees is not as straightforward as it may at first appear. Any decision to pay trustees should be considered in the context of a proper purpose – what is in the best interests of the scheme? In other words, payment should result in a benefit to the scheme.

11.5   Trustee companies and Carbon Reduction Commitment (CRC)

Summary

This section looks at the position of a pension scheme trustee company that is a subsidiary of the employer.

It considers the implications for such a trustee company of the obligations under the UK CRC Energy Efficiency Scheme (the CRC Scheme).

Carbon reduction commitment – impact on pension trustee companies

CRC Scheme

11.5.1   Broadly, groups of companies are given obligations under the CRC Scheme, including registering and purchasing allowances sufficient to meet the companies' annual carbon emissions from energy consumption. The CRC Scheme came into operation on 1 April 2010, though was substantively amended in 2013 with the intention of simplification. The First Phase (previously known as Phase One) is currently operating and runs until 31 March 2014. The Initial Phase (previously known as Phase Two) will run from 1 April 2014 to 31 March 2019.

In November 2013, the Department of Energy and Climate Change (DECC) published a consultation on proposals for the CRC Scheme to incentivise the uptake of on-site renewable energy, exclude metallurgical and mineralogical processes, clarify the way in which the CRC Scheme applies to landlords and tenants, and allow more flexibility for a subsidiary company to participate in the CRC Scheme independently from its parent organisation (termed 'disaggregation'). These further changes are expected to come into force by 1 April 2014, in time for the commencement of the Initial Phase.

Liability on a trustee company

11.5.2   The obligations under the CRC Scheme are applied to groups of companies. Rather unusually, the legislation makes each company in a group jointly and severally liable for the obligations of the group. In addition, directors of a company in a group can be liable in some circumstances.

Indemnities?

11.5.3 It will often not be absolutely clear if any such liability on the trustee company (or its directors) is covered by any indemnity out of the pension plan's assets under the rules of the pension plan or by any indemnity from the employers. If the indemnity applies, this may encourage the relevant authority to look to the trustee (or its directors) if a liability arises. Alternatively, if the indemnity does not apply, the trustee and its directors may be concerned that they have a liability but no matching assets.

Steps to take?

11.5.4 There are various steps that the trustee can consider to deal with this:

- seek an indemnity from the employer to cover any liability – this provides protection while the employer is solvent (the employer can be asked to estimate what amounts the group is paying under the CRC Scheme);

- 'disaggregate' the trustee company's CRC Scheme group registration, so that it participates in the CRC Scheme in its own right and is no longer jointly liable for the obligations of the employer's CRC Scheme group;

- de-group the trustee company so that it is no longer a group company. The implications of such de-grouping would need to be considered. It could have a knock-on effect on other areas (e g investment, insurance, etc). This is unlikely to be necessary given recent amendments to the CRC Scheme which allows 'disaggregation' as noted above; and/or

- amend the plan indemnity to clarify that the trustee shall have no claim on the pension scheme's assets regarding CRC Scheme liabilities.

We suggest that the trustee's steps are:

- to check on the size of the potential liability;

- if this is significant, ask the employer for an indemnity;

- consider whether to 'disaggregate' the trustee from the group before the commencement of the Initial Phase before 31 January 2014 (or if this deadline is missed, keep under review DECC's proposal to allow disaggregation during a phase); and

- keep the matter under review.

If the plan holds any direct investment in land, the implications of this on the group's CRC Scheme position should also be considered.

CRC Scheme: nature of liability

11.5.5 The relevant legislation is the *CRC Energy Efficiency Scheme Order 2011* (SI 2010/768) as amended by the *CRC Energy Efficiency Scheme (Amendment) Order 2011* (SI 2011/234), which came into force on 1 April 2011. The 2010 Order was further amended by the *CRC Energy Efficiency Scheme Order 2013* (SI 2013/1119) which came into force on 20 May 2013. The 2013 Order replaces the 2010 Order, except in respect of certain provisions which are necessary for completion of the First Phase of the Scheme. References below are to articles in the 2013 Order.

The CRC Scheme is a mandatory climate change and energy saving scheme that first came into force in the UK on 1 April 2010. The Qualification Year for the Initial Phase is 1 April 2012 to 31 March 2013 and the deadline for registration for the Initial Phase is 31 January 2014. The entire registration process, which can take a number of weeks, must have been completed by the registration deadline.

11.5.6 The CRC Scheme currently applies to an 'undertaking' or a 'group of undertakings' (each as defined) that, in the relevant qualification year (which is 1 April 2012 to 31 March 2013 for the Initial Phase), was supplied with electricity measured by a Settled Half-Hourly Meter (SHHM) and had a total annual electricity consumption of over 6,000 megawatt-hours, excluding certain types of electricity use (eg for domestic accommodation) – see *arts 3* and *24* and *para 1* of *Sch 3*. (At 2012/13 market rates, depending on electricity pricing arrangements between customers and utilities, this is equivalent to an annual electricity bill of between about £500,000 and £700,000.)

As a result of the simplification of the CRC Scheme by the 2013 Order, the rules regarding an organisation that qualifies for the Initial and subsequent Phases are as follows:

(a)   Qualification is assessed only on electricity supplies through SHHMs. Organisations do not have to consider supplies through other types of Half Hourly Meter when deciding if they qualify. This is unlike the First Phase, where organisations had to take account of supplies through SHHMs, Non-settled Half Hourly Meters and 'Dynamic Supply'.

(b)   Unconsumed supplies can only be deducted from supplies when assessing qualification for the Initial Phase provided that the unconsumed supply is metered.

(c)   Unlike in the First Phase, supplies to Climate Change Agreement facilities and EU ETS installations are excluded when assessing qualification.

(d)   Supplies that an organisation requests to be delivered to another organisation will be the responsibility of the requesting organisation. In the First Phase this point was unclear.

Where an entity such as the trustee company is part of a 'group of undertakings' for the purposes of the consumption requirements referred to above, all members in that group are subject to the relevant CRC Scheme requirements – see *art 24*. The group test is based on the test for parent and subsidiary undertakings contained in the *Companies Act 2006* (see *para 1* of *Sch 4*). All entities meeting the group test will be grouped together regardless of whether or not their parent undertaking has any presence in the UK. However, companies are entitled to 'disaggregate' for their group, and participate independently. Importantly, the 2013 Order has made the rules on organisational structures more flexible: there is now no minimum threshold for disaggregation, so any group may disaggregate subsidiary undertakings or groups of subsidiary undertakings of any size. The remainder of the group will still have to participate in the CRC Scheme even if it no longer meets the qualification amount of 6,000 annual megawatt-hours.

Disaggregation is currently only available at the time of registration, however following the November 2013 Consultation, it is expected that by the start of the Initial Phase in April 2014, participants will be permitted to disaggregate subsidiary undertakings at any stage during a Phase.

11.5.7   The CRC Scheme imposes a range of obligations on undertakings (including groups of undertakings). The key aspects of the regime are set out below.

Undertakings that qualify for the CRC Scheme ('participants') must register for the Initial Phase by 31 January 2014 using the CRC Registry. Undertakings which participated in the First Phase of the CRC Scheme will have some details auto-populated in the Registry, however will need to re-enter their organisational structure. This is because in the First Phase, undertakings were required to identify 'significant group undertakings' in their structures. For the Initial Phase onwards, these are replaced by 'participant equivalents'. A significant group undertaking or participant equivalent is a single undertaking that, were it not part of a group, would have qualified for the CRC Scheme in its own right.

The First Phase of the CRC Scheme started on 1 April 2011. The 2010 Order required participants to purchase sufficient 'allowances' from the government in July 2012 (which were unlimited and available for £12 each during The First Phase) to cover the amount of CO_2 they emitted in the UK in the preceding Scheme year. There was a further retrospective sale of allowances for 2012/2013 emissions in July 2013. In the Initial Phase, there will be two sales per scheme year: one cheaper prospective or 'forecast' sale and one more expensive retrospective or 'buy to comply' sale. Applications for the prospective sale will take place in April of the relevant year (e g in April 2014 for the 1 April 2014 to 31 March 2015 year) and applications for the retrospective sale will take place in June of the following year (e g June 2015 for the 1 April 2014 to 31 March 2015 year). The price applicable to the retrospective sale will be higher in order that there can be a trading of allowances on a secondary market.

11.5.8 The Environment Agency previously published annual league tables ranking the CO_2 efficiency performance of all participants. The 2013 Order abolished the league tables, and instead provides for the publication by the Environment Agency of annual reports regarding the operation of the CRC scheme. The first annual report was published in November 2013 and contained unranked information about participants obtained from information submitted annually by participants in compliance with the CRC Order.

11.5.9 The key point at which a participant faces liability is at the end of each year, when participants have to surrender sufficient allowances to cover the carbon emissions of the year to the relevant administrator (the Environment Agency in England). Civil penalties apply if insufficient allowances are surrendered, which may consist of having the failure publicised by the relevant administrator, blocking a participant from trading allowances, and fines at a rate significantly higher than the price per allowance.

During the Initial Phase, the requirement for predicting likely emissions in order to buy sufficient allowances in the prospective sale may result in participants overestimating the allowances required in order to avoid having to 'top up' in the more expensive retrospective sale. These allowances can be sold to other participants on a secondary market.

11.5.10 Civil penalties may also be imposed on a participant for a range of offences, such as failing to register, failing to comply with annual reporting requirements, providing inaccurate information and failing to maintain records.

The trustee's potential scope for liability

11.5.11 If the employer or parent has been CRC Scheme registered it is likely that the trustee (as a subsidiary) forms part of the employer's CRC Scheme group. Unless the trustee is disaggregated, this exposes it to joint and several liability in respect of the liabilities of other members of the CRC Scheme group – see *Art 8*.

It should be noted that this only applies to civil penalty-related liabilities – the CRC Scheme creates a number of criminal offences (e g knowingly filing misleading information), but the joint and several liability provisions do not apply to criminal offences.

In line with the analysis above, the key types of liability that the trustee could therefore assume under the CRC Scheme include:

- liability for the cost of allowances for carbon emissions for which the plan (and, potentially, all members of the employer's group) are responsible, which are payable on an annual basis in arrears; and

- the cost of meeting any civil penalties imposed on any members of the employer's CRC Scheme group regarding any non-compliance with the CRC Scheme (e g failure to provide annual reports).

Indemnification – pension scheme liability out of the fund?

11.5.12 In this section, we look at whether the pension scheme could end up with a payment obligation that relates to the employer's CRC Scheme liabilities, given that the trustee is a subsidiary of the employer (and provided that the trustee is not disaggregated).

As discussed above, under the CRC Scheme Order the group members are jointly and severally liable.

Indemnities in trust deeds often permit the trustee (and its directors) to have an indemnity:

- out of the assets of the plan for liabilities incurred in good faith, etc; and/or

- from the employers, again for liabilities incurred in good faith to the extent that such liabilities cannot be recovered from the fund or from a third party.

Depending on the wording of the indemnities, it may well be that the trustee has no direct right to recoup any liabilities from either the plan or the employers resulting from the employer group's CRC Scheme obligations (e g if the indemnities only allow it to reimburse itself out of trust assets for liabilities 'arising out of or in connection withthe Plan …').

However, if the trustee (acting in its capacity as trustee of the plan) has electricity consumption for CRC Scheme purposes (e g if it has entered into electricity contracts for direct investment property held in its own name), it may be more difficult to argue that there is no right of indemnity out of trust assets for that CRC Scheme liability. The Environment Agency has published guidance on the application of the CRC Scheme to trust structures generally and the only assets believed to be relevant are real property and shareholdings in companies that own real property.

11.5.13   *Trustees*

Position of the trustee directors

11.5.13   If there is no indemnity out of the assets of the pension plan, this could leave the trustee directors in a difficult position. The trustee could have a liability, but no matching asset in the form of the indemnity from the assets of the pension plan.

This could potentially cause issues for the trustee directors – if a liability ever arose on the employer group, this could leave the trustee company technically insolvent (as it could not pay). The directors may become concerned that they are directors of an insolvent company.

Way ahead?

11.5.14   To provide more protection for the pension plan and the trustee (and for the directors of the trustee, who could, in certain circumstances, have personal liability for CRC Scheme obligations), while seeking to reduce any risk that liabilities resulting from other members of the employer's CRC Scheme group could be met from the pension plan's assets, the trustee could agree with the employer (for example):

- to be given an indemnity from the employer essentially so that, in practice, while the employer remains solvent, the trustee (and its directors) will have no liability for the CRC Scheme obligations (or no liability beyond that relating to the plan's own electricity consumption);

- to disaggregate the trustee from the employer so that it is no longer jointly liable with the remaining members of the employer's CRC Scheme group for any obligations or liabilities of the group. If the trustee is disaggregated, it is possible for any subsidiaries of the trustee to remain with the employer's CRC Scheme group in order that the trust becomes liable exclusively for its own obligations;

- to de-group – for example, enough of the shares in the trustee could be transferred to (say) the trustee's directors (and other amendments could be made to the trustee's structure) so that the trustee no longer constitutes part of the employer's CRC Scheme group.

However, the implications of such de-grouping would need to be considered. It could have a knock-on effect on other areas (e g investment, insurance, etc);

- to amend the indemnity provisions in the plan's trust deed (set out above) to clarify that the trustee shall have no claim on the pension scheme's assets for CRC Scheme liabilities. However, the trustee may then have a CRC Scheme liability for which it has no assets (and the trustee's directors could still, in theory, be personally liable if certain requirements under the CRC Scheme legislation are met). As a result, the trustee's directors may prefer the option in the first bulleted point above to be used in conjunction with this point, if this is to be used.

11.6 Things you may not know about Trustee Liability

Summary

Trustee liability: good news and bad news

Potential liability is an extremely important issue for the trustees of occupational pension schemes and, unfortunately, is also an especially complicated area of law. The aim of this section is to highlight some important things that you may not know about trustee liability – both good and bad.

To make sense of some of the twists and turns in the law on trustee liability, it is necessary to understand the underlying legal framework. This section begins with a brief overview of the duties and obligations of pension scheme trustees and the protections from liability generally afforded to them.

It then moves on to cover some important things that trustees may not be aware of, starting with what could be called 'bad news' items:

- six more unusual potential liabilities; and

- six limitations on indemnity / exoneration protection.

The aim however is to redress the balance by highlighting eight 'good news' items that trustees may not know of, in particular areas where:

- trustees have more protection than you might expect; or

- trustee protection can be improved.

Further details on protections is given in *Trustee directors: exonerations, indemnities and insurance,* **11.7** below.

Reminder: the duties and obligations of pension trustees

11.6.1   It is fair to say that being a pension scheme trustee is a tricky job, and is a role that is becoming increasingly onerous.

There is no general codification of the law relating to pension scheme trustees; no single rule book that a trustee can turn to in order to learn about his or her obligations. Instead, the rights and obligations of pension trustees are derived from a whole range of sources:

- the trust deed and rules of the pension scheme and other scheme documents;

- the general law relating to trusts, both legislation and case-law;

- the rafts of specific pensions legislation, both in statute and regulations; and

- other general law (eg contract law, data protection law, derivatives law).

Just taking one source of pension trustee obligations illustrates how onerous the obligations are. At the heart of the general law of trusts are the core duties of skill and care, including:

- the duty to act with prudence in investment matters, taking such care as an ordinary businessman would take in managing his own affairs if he were under a moral obligation to provide for others;

- the duty to act in accordance with scheme documentation, no matter how complex or obscure; and

- the duty to act for a proper purpose, often in the best interests of the scheme beneficiaries.

But the key cause for concern for trustees is not the (potentially overwhelming) extent of these duties, but the consequences of breaching them. This is because the general principle is that a trustee will have personal liability for loss caused by breach of duties.

Reminder: protection available for pension trustees

11.6.2   Of course, if pension scheme trustees were required to risk personal liability without any form of protection, you would never get anyone to be a pension scheme trustee. Fortunately, trustees can and do benefit from considerable protection that enables them to avoid personal liability when things go wrong.

There is a wide range of protection commonly available, including:

- exoneration clauses in scheme rules, which provide that trustees are exempted from personal liability for breach of duty;

- indemnities in the scheme rules which allow the trustees to be reimbursed from scheme assets for any liability;

- indemnities from scheme employers, under which the trustees are reimbursed by the employers for liability for breach of duty (for example, if scheme assets are insufficient); and

- trustee insurance, which provides protection that is not dependent on the sufficiency of scheme assets or on the employer's ability to pay. This may be obtained both to provide an additional layer of protection in an on-going scheme or to provide run-off protection following the winding-up of a pension scheme.

If all those avenues fail, there is also a court discretion to excuse trustees from personal liability in *section 61* of the *Trustee Act 1925*. This allows the court to excuse a trustee where he or she has acted honestly and reasonably and ought fairly to be excused. This is a fairly high threshold and relief may not be available in many cases.

'Bad news' items: more unusual potential liabilities

11.6.3 The summary above might lead a trustee to feel quite comfortable with their position. However, numerous twists and turns in the law relating to trustee liability may make a trustee feel rather uneasy again.

The perils of joint and several liability

11.6.4 It is often forgotten that when trustees breach their duties of care and skill, they will be 'jointly and severally' liable for the loss caused to the pension scheme. Joint and several liability means that all trustees will be potentially liable for the whole of the loss suffered, regardless of whether the trustee participated in, or even knew about, the breach.

Joint and several liability continues to apply to former trustees, who remain liable for breaches during their time as trustee and can extend to new trustees who fail to remedy a breach. It also applies to all trustees regardless of their particular status (eg whether they are member-nominated trustees or professional trust corporations).

Because each trustee could be liable for the whole of the loss suffered, the share of the liability ultimately met by a particular trustee will depend on a number of factors, such as:

- whether the other trustees have the benefit of exoneration clauses (eg if an exoneration clause distinguishes between protection given to lay/professional trustees); and

- the financial resources of other trustees (with 'rich' trustees inevitably risking taking a greater share).

Note that the share of the liability may bear no resemblance whatsoever to the degree of culpability of the particular trustee for the wrongdoing in question.

This is illustrated rather dramatically by a recent Australian case: *Shail Superannuation Fund*[10] (2011).

In *Shail*, a husband and wife were both the trustees and the only two members of their joint pension scheme. The husband then absconded with most of the pension scheme assets (essentially stealing his wife's pension fund) and the removal of the assets from the scheme also resulted in a significant tax charge being levied (in excess of AUS$2m).

Despite being entirely innocent of wrongdoing, the wife (as pension scheme trustee) was also liable for the tax due to the tax authorities under the principle of joint and several liability – and, of course, was left to foot the whole of the bill because her husband (the trustee at fault) had vanished without trace.

Liability for civil penalties

11.6.5 Whilst it might, perhaps, seem unfair and onerous, the principle of joint and several liability is at least aimed at addressing losses to scheme beneficiaries or liabilities of the scheme to third parties. There are, however, a wide range of statutory obligations in pensions legislation where the Pensions Regulator can issue a civil penalty (essentially akin to a fine) against trustees for a breach of that obligation, even though no loss has been caused.

A small sample of the statutory obligations in pensions legislation where the Pensions Regulator can issue a civil penalty for breach indicates the breadth of this power and the range of sometimes major but also sometimes seemingly quite trivial areas covered:

- failure to report notifiable events and breaches of the law;
- failure to provide required information to the Pensions Regulator (eg scheme returns);
- breach of investment and funding legislation (eg failure to obtain advice); and
- relying on improperly appointed advisers (eg where *section 47* of the *Pensions Act 1995* has not been complied with).

There are more than 70 different statutory provisions (covering all areas, many of which are quite technical) where breach can result in a civil penalty.

Civil penalties can be awarded against individual trustees, trustee companies and against trustee directors (who will then be personally liable). The

---

10 *Re Shail Superannuation Fund and Commissioner of Taxation* [2011] *AATA* 940.

maximum liability (for each civil penalty) is £5,000 for an individual and £50,000 for a company.

Trustees in the 'net' for the Pensions Regulator's moral hazard powers

11.6.6 Not only does the Pensions Regulator have the power to issue civil penalties, it can also make certain third parties liable for the deficits in defined benefit pension schemes using 'contribution notices' (which require payment of a particular sum to the pension scheme) and 'financial support directions' (which require financial support, such as payments or guarantees, to be put into place). These powers are commonly known as the Pensions Regulator's 'moral hazard' powers – see Chapter **4**, *Moral Hazard powers* above.

The Pensions Regulator can use its moral hazard powers against any company (and, in the case of contribution notices, any individual) that is 'connected or associated' with the employer of the pension scheme. It is important to remember that this will include many trustees (both individual trustees and trustee directors) – for example if they are directors or employees of the employer company.

Unhelpfully, although clearance is available to provide protection to third parties, the Pensions Regulator has also said that it will not give clearance to trustees who are concerned that their actions might expose them to this risk.

This is rather odd, particularly as there is nothing in the legislation that precludes trustees from seeking clearance. Generally speaking, while trustees are unlikely to be directly involved in action that might lead to a contribution notice being issued, this will not always be the case – particularly in circumstances where there is a restructuring of pension liabilities – and it seems rather unfair that all the other parties are able to seek the formal certainty of clearance.

Crime and punishment

11.6.7 There is, however, an even worse possibility than any form of civil liability or financial penalty – that of criminal liability for trustees.

It is likely that all trustees would accept that they would be exposed to criminal liability if they were to act fraudulently (just like they would in any aspect of their lives). However, there are also some breaches of technical statutory obligations that are a criminal offence and do not require fraudulent action by the trustees.

Examples include:

- breach of the restrictions on making employer-related investments;

- failure to provide information to the Regulator or Pension Protection Fund, or providing them with misleading information;

- using pension fund assets to meet civil penalties; and

- carrying on regulated activity while unauthorised/not exempt (under the *Financial Services and Markets Act 2000*).

The penalties attached to these breaches are potentially extremely severe as these are indictable offences that carry up to two years in prison, or a fine, or both.

Trustee company liabilities

11.6.8   It is clear that being a trustee director can provide additional protection over and above the protection available for individual trustees (see below). However, being a trustee director also brings with it a whole raft of corporate responsibilities.

This is because trustee directors owe duties to the trustee company, for example general duties such as skill and care (under the *Companies Act 2006*) plus more specific potential exposure to liability, such as liability for wrongful trading (under the *Insolvency Act 1986*).

Employer liabilities

11.6.9   Finally, on unusual liabilities, it is worth noting that if the trustee is an employer (eg of in-house administrators) there will be the usual statutory employment liabilities. Further, some of these (eg unlawful discrimination) can result in personal liability not just for individual trustees but for trustee directors as well.

Trustees likely also owe duties of care to pension scheme employers, as well as members. For example, with investment decisions it will be the employer (who has to fund the scheme) rather than the scheme members who will generally lose out when poor investments have been made in breach of the investment requirements.

More 'bad news': when trustee protection simply doesn't work

11.6.10 Six more unusual areas of trustee liability have now been covered. The second area of bad news is that the wide trustee protection we described earlier often simply doesn't work because there are significant legal restrictions on the scope of the protection. Here are six key examples.

Third party liabilities

It is often overlooked that exoneration clauses in pension scheme documentation can only limit a trustee's liability to beneficiaries of the trust (ie the employers and members). Such exoneration clauses will have no effect on a trustee's liability to third parties, such as advisers, investment managers and derivatives counter-parties. Unless the relevant third party contract is expressly limited, individual trustees will have personal liability.

Statutory duties

Statutory duties under the pensions legislation are probably not limited by an exoneration clause in the trust deed.

Investment functions

Under *section 33* of the *Pensions Act 1995*, exoneration provisions and indemnities out of the fund do not work in relation to a trustee's duties to take care or exercise skill in the performance of investment functions. *Section 33* also means that indemnities from the employer may not work for investment matters either – leaving a significant gap in trustee protection.

Fines and penalties

Indemnities out of the fund (and insurance paid for out of the fund) cannot cover criminal fines and civil penalties because this is prohibited by *section 256* of the *Pensions Act 2004*. As noted above, breach of *section 256* is a criminal offence, although rather bizarrely *section 256* only applies to reimbursement of a trustee (and not expressly to reimbursement of a trustee director).

Breaching other duties

Trustee indemnities out of the fund may also not work if the trustee has broken another duty and owes money to the fund. This can be a concern for third parties, such as derivatives counterparties (particularly if there is a sole corporate trustee), as they have to rely on the indemnity from the fund to ensure that the trustee can meet its obligations under the derivative instrument but they could find that the indemnity is not available to the trustee (and hence not available to them) because of a completely unrelated breach of trust by the trustee.

Companies Act 2006

An indemnity from an employer to a trustee (or director of a trustee company) who is also a director of the indemnifying employer needs to comply with the *Companies Act 2006* limitations. This means that it cannot cover fines/civil penalties or the cost of defending criminal proceedings when the director is convicted. If the indemnity attempts to cover such liabilities, the whole indemnity may be void.

Some 'good news': lesser known helpful facts

11.6.11 This section has so far focused on bad news trustee liability issues. However, there are some less well-known points on trustee liability that are helpful in providing protection to trustees or in making it possible to obtain better protection for trustees.

Exonerations generally do work

This section has focused on some key limitations on trustee exonerations above, but it is important to remember that (aside from those limitations), exonerations will generally apply in accordance with their terms.

Those terms can be extremely broad, although it will depend on the exact wording in the particular trust deed. While exoneration clauses cannot apply in cases of actual fraud, they can be drafted to effectively excuse a trustee of anything less culpable including, for example, gross negligence: see *Spread Trustee v Hutcheson*[11] (2011).

Former trustees are protected

Former trustees will usually remain covered by indemnity and exoneration clauses although, again, the extent of the protection will depend on the particular wording used.

Helpfully, former trustees will be protected by an exoneration clause regardless of whether former trustees are expressly covered by the terms of the clause: see *Seifert v Pensions Ombudsman*[12] (1996).

---

11   *Spread Trustee Co Ltd v Hutcheson* [2011] UKPC 13, [2012] 2 AC 194.
12   *Seifert v Pensions Ombudsman* [1997] 1 All ER 214.

11.6.11   *Trustees*

No liability for actions of fund manager

Although the ability of exoneration and indemnity clauses to protect trustees from liability for investment matters is severely restricted (see above), *section 34(4)* of the *Pensions Act 1995* provides valuable protection for trustees for actions that have been delegated to the fund manager.

Section 34(4) provides that there will be no personal liability for the actions of the fund manager, provided the trustees take all reasonable steps to:

- ensure that the fund manager has appropriate knowledge and experience; and

- appropriately monitor the fund manager's performance.

Indemnities and exonerations can be broadened

11.6.12 If the protection provided to the trustees in the trust deed appears to be inadequate, it may well be possible to amend the provisions to provide better or more comprehensive protection. Generally speaking, indemnities and exonerations may be widened if this is for a proper purpose (for example if it is necessary in order to attract new trustees), provided there is no express restriction in the amendment power that would prohibit such a change. Extensions to the protection could include introducing a power to pay insurance premiums out of the fund – see *Bogg v Rapier*[13] (1999) and *Dollar Academy*[14] (1995).

Implied power to buy insurance?

Even where there is no express power to purchase insurance using fund assets, such a power may be implied if there is a power to pay trustees in the trust deed (because the insurance premiums can simply be part of trustee remuneration).

There are, however, special rules that may apply where a scheme is winding-up (which we will not cover here).

Protection following transfer to the Pension Protection Fund

If a pension scheme is transferred to the Pension Protection Fund, *schedule 6* of the *Pensions Act 2004* provides that trustees continue to be protected to the

---

13 *Bogg v Raper* (1998) 1 ITELR 267.
14 *Governors of Dollar Academy Trust v Lord Advocate* [1995] SLT 596.

same extent as under the exoneration clause and indemnity from the scheme. However, trustees in those circumstances may still be vulnerable to the costs of defending a claim.

Directors of corporate trustees have more protection

11.6.13 As we mentioned above, our view is that directors of corporate trustees have more protection than individual trustees. This is because it is the trustee company that owes duties directly to the beneficiaries (not the directors) and therefore it is the trustee company that is liable for any loss suffered by the scheme as a result of the breach of those duties rather than individual trustee directors.

In relation to third parties (eg under contracts), these duties will be owed by the trustee company and not the directors. This means the directors will, as usual under company law, only be liable in unusual circumstances.

There are some limits to the protection afforded by having a trustee company because some obligations apply directly to corporate trustee directors (eg civil penalties – see above). Directors may also still be liable to the trustee company for any breach of the duties which they owe to the company. However, it is difficult for the beneficiaries to enforce these duties directly by bringing a derivative claim: *HR v JAPT*[15] (1997); *Gregson*[16] (2011), except when the trustees have acted dishonestly, in which case accessory liability may arise.

Time can run out for claims

Where a claimant has delayed in commencing proceedings against a pension trustee for breach of duty, the trustee may be able to rely on the *Limitation Act 1980* to defend any claim. These are complex rules but can be worth investigating.

---

15   *HR v JAPT* [1997] OPLR 123.
16   *Gregson v HAE Trustees Ltd* [2008] EWHC 1006 (Ch), [2008] 2 BCLC 542.

11.7 Trustee directors: exonerations, indemnities and insurance

Summary

The trustees of pension schemes are exposed to potential personal liability, by virtue of their fiduciary duties as well as statutory obligations and those under contract and tort law. Without adequate protection, it would be difficult to attract individuals to take on the role. The position of directors of a trustee company is usually more protected.

This briefing looks at the various protections available to the directors of a corporate trustee of a pension scheme, including:

- the shield of the separate corporate personality of the trustee company;

- exoneration clauses;

- indemnities out of the assets of the pension scheme and from the company; and

- insurance policies paid for out of the assets of the scheme or by the company.

These protections operate in different ways, and are subject to different limits imposed by common law and pensions and company legislation.

Trustee director liabilities

11.7.1   Trustee directors are exposed to potentially liability under various heads:[17]

- *breach of statutory duty*: if the trustee company becomes liable to a civil penalty or civil offence, liability can extend personally to a director;

- *assist in a breach of trust*: directors can be personally liable if they knowingly assist in a breach of trust by the trustee of a pension scheme;

- *maladministration*: directors may perhaps be liable for maladministration causing injustice in relation to the pension scheme (under the jurisdiction given to the Pensions Ombudsman);

---

17   *Company directors – potential liability for pension benefits?*, **1.2** above and *Things you may not know about trustee liability*, **11.6** above.

- *moral hazard liability*: if the director is 'connected' or 'associated' with an employer company (eg as a director or employee) then potentially a contribution notice could be made against him or her by the Pensions Regulator;[18]

- *tort eg negligence*: it is possible that directors could incur a personal liability in tort, for example by participating in fraud or deceit or making a negligent misstatement (on which a scheme member or employee may rely) or (less likely) by incurring a direct duty of care in negligence;

- *knowing help in discrimination*: directors can be personally liable if they knowingly help unlawful discrimination by the employer, the trustee company or the pension scheme.

Separate corporate personality

11.7.2   Large occupational pension schemes often have corporate trustees.[19] As such, the company itself is the trustee, with individuals being directors of the company. It is therefore the trustee company that is in a fiduciary relationship with the scheme members, and a claim brought against the trustee will be a claim against the trust company, and not the directors. This 'corporate veil' also usually protects directors from claims brought by third parties, such as parties to contracts with the trustee company.

The court will not usually lift the corporate veil unless a director has dishonestly assisted in a breach of trust.[20] While this structure will therefore not prevent the trustee from being liable, it gives the individual directors comfort in respect of their personal liability.

Exoneration clauses

11.7.3   Exoneration clauses are often included in the trust deed and rules and operate to exclude the trustee (and its directors) from the relevant liability. They are often expressly extended to cover trustee directors as well as the trustee company. They usually offer broad protection in the following respects:

- they may exempt trustees (and directors) from liability for all forms of conduct except dishonesty;

- former trustees (and directors) can still rely on exoneration clauses; and

- trustees (and directors) can continue to rely on exoneration clauses even in winding up.

---

18   See *Procedure for issue of a contribution notice or financial support direction*, **4.9** above.
19   See *Advantages and disadvantages of a separate trustee company*, **11.2** above.
20   *Royal Brunei Airlines v Tan* [1995] 2 AC 378.

However, exoneration clauses do not prevent trustees (or directors) having to spend money defending claims brought against them.

Exoneration clauses only apply to 'internal' claims (ie by trust beneficiaries). They do not apply to external claims by third parties (eg under contract, tort or statute) unless express limits are agreed and not overridden by legislation (eg statutory discrimination claims).

Indemnity clauses

11.7.4   Rather than exclude the liability, indemnities operate to reimburse the trustee when liability is incurred. They are often expressly extended to cover trustee directors as well as the trustee company.

An indemnity allowing trustees to be reimbursed from the trust assets for 'expenses properly incurred' is implied by *section 31* of the *Trustee Act 2000*. However it is usual to include an express indemnity in the trust deed and rules because:

- the implied statutory duty only applies to expenses 'properly incurred'; and
- it is prudent to extend the indemnity to cover directors and former trustees (and directors).

The limit on the statutory indemnity to a liability 'properly incurred' is quite restrictive, and creates uncertainty as to what is covered. Say, for example, a trustee employs an individual and then dismisses them. The individual brings a claim for unfair dismissal and wins. The trustee is clearly liable. However, it is not clear whether the liability was properly incurred, and so whether it is possible to rely on the implied indemnity. It is therefore preferable to include an express indemnity which covers a wider range of circumstances.

Exonerations and indemnities – limits

11.7.5   There is significant flexibility as to the liability which can be covered by indemnities and exonerations, subject to certain limits under pensions legislation, common law and company law.

Pensions legislation limits

There are two express limitations under pensions legislation:

- criminal/civil fines: *section 256* of the *Pensions Act 2004* prohibits an indemnity out of the assets of the scheme in relation to criminal fines or civil penalties (under *section 168(4)* of the *Pension Schemes Act 1993* or section 10 of the *Pensions Act 1995* or *sections 40* or *41* of the *Pensions Act 2008*);

- investment: *section 33* of the *Pensions Act 1995* provides that any liability of a trustee for breach of an obligation under any rule of law to take care or exercise skill in the performance of any investment function cannot be excluded or restricted by any instrument or agreement.

Common law limits

Following the Court of Appeal decision in *Armitage v Nurse*[21], indemnities or exonerations relating to the party's own dishonesty or fraud will not be upheld. Millett LJ held that there was an 'irreducible core of obligations' comprising honesty and good faith which are fundamental to the concept of a trust. Therefore to uphold an indemnity or exoneration which covered the trustee's dishonesty would be to undermine the essence of a trust. Indemnities against the deliberate commission of a crime are also probably unenforceable for public policy reasons.[22]

However, following the principle in *Armitage*, an indemnity can extend to cover gross negligence where dishonesty is absent (provided that it is drafted widely enough).[23]

Companies Act limits

As well as indemnities from the assets of the scheme, indemnities can be given by the sponsoring employer. This protection is often sought in addition to an indemnity from the assets of the scheme as it can be wider (because it is not subject to the *Pensions Acts* limits). However, *section 232* of the *Companies Act 2006* generally prohibits indemnities from a company to its directors, which will be an issue if (as is not unusual) the director of the trustee company is also a director of the employer.

This prohibition can be avoided provided that the indemnity is in a particular form, as the *Companies Act* permits the provision of indemnities to directors to the extent that it is 'qualifying pension scheme indemnity provision' (**QPSIP**s).

For example QPSIPs must not cover:

- liability to pay a fine imposed in criminal proceedings;

- any sum payable to a regulatory authority as a penalty for non-compliance with a regulatory requirement; or

- any liability of a director in defending criminal proceedings in which he is convicted.

---

21   *Armitage v Nurse* [1998] Ch 241.
22   Eg *Hardy v Motor Insurers Bureau* [1964] 2 QB 745.
23   *Spread Trustee v Hutcheson* [2011] UKPC 13.

11.7.5   *Trustees*

QPSIPs may, however, cover costs in defending civil proceedings brought against the director by the company or an associated company in which judgment is given against them.

There is an argument that the *section 232* restriction does not apply to employer indemnities to directors of the trustee company, as it only invalidates indemnities given to directors in relation to breaches of duty 'in relation to the company'. Therefore, if the indemnity is in respect of the director's duties as a director of the trustee company (as distinct from his duties to the employer company) the indemnity may not be caught. However, if it is possible to achieve the intended cover within the framework of the QPSIP this would be preferable from a certainty perspective.

Insurance

11.7.6   In addition to indemnity and exoneration clauses, it is common for trustees to also be protected by insurance. This has the advantage of covering the costs of defending directors against claims up front, and also reduces the strain on resources. The power of the scheme to pay for insurance needs to be checked.

What should be covered?

Most insurance policies exclude cover for:

- fraudulent, dishonest or criminal conduct; and

- liability incurred by failing to properly fund a scheme, particularly where the director has failed to monitor the employer's contribution to the fund properly, or agreed unreasonable actuarial assumptions.

In addition, the following should be considered:

- whether the policy should cover liability for which an exoneration or indemnity already exists;

- whether the policy should cover legal costs for defending all (successful and otherwise) claims;

- the time period and duration of the policy coverage;

- whether fraud or non-disclosure or breach by one party will invalidate the coverage for all trustee directors; and

- whether the policy covers the employer as well as the trustees.

Section 256 of the *Pensions Act 2004* prohibits payments out of scheme assets to pay premiums for insurance against fines or civil penalties. (There is no such restriction if the employer pays the premiums.)

Chapter 12

Conflicts of interest

12.1 Conflicts of interest – TPR's Guidance

Summary

This section provides an overview of the key messages contained in the conflicts of interest guidance issued by the Pensions Regulator.

Introduction

12.1.1 The Pensions Regulator (TPR) issued guidance in October 2008 on conflicts of interest.[1]

The conflicts guidance is structured as follows:

- understanding the importance of conflicts of interest;
- identifying conflicts of interest;
- evaluation, management or avoidance of conflicts;
- managing adviser conflicts; and
- conflicts of interest policy.

The main messages in the conflicts guidance are set out below.

---

1   http://www.thepensionsregulator.gov.uk/guidance/guidance-conflicts-of-interest.aspx

12.1.2 *Conflicts of interest*

The conflicts guidance is intended to provide 'educational support'

12.1.2 TPR explains that the conflicts guidance 'aims to provide educational support, particularly to smaller schemes, with a view to both sharing good practice and raising standards' (para 2). The guidance may well be updated in due course by TPR as practice in this area develops.

TPR emphasises throughout the conflicts guidance that it is not a substitute for pension schemes seeking legal advice (where appropriate) both in relation to setting, monitoring and reviewing their conflicts policies and procedures and if a conflict arises (eg para 3).

Trustees should avoid the perception of conflicts, as well as actual conflicts

12.1.3 In addition to 'actual' or 'real' conflicts, the conflicts guidance suggests that trustees should be alert to decisions and actions which could be *perceived* as having been influenced, or as open to influence by, a trustee's conflict (paras 42 and 43).

Managing conflicts

12.1.4 Disclosure of a conflict is not enough. The guidance suggests that trustees should consider the consequences and how to manage them. The existence of a conflict does not necessarily require action by the trustees. TPR recognises this in para 52 of the conflicts guidance where it explains:

> 'When a conflict has been identified, trustees should have a process for assessing its impact and deciding whether an active form of management is needed.'

Factors on which this decision could be based include the impact the conflict may have on (a) the validity of the decision-making, and (b) the scheme beneficiaries (para 52). If the trustees decide that active management is not necessary, they should be able to *demonstrate* that the position was fully considered (and, where appropriate, legal advice was sought) and the decision should be recorded.

In its guidance, TPR refers to the following non-exhaustive list of potential methods which could be used to manage conflicts:

● withdrawal by the trustee from discussions and the decision-making process; and/or

- establishment of a sub-committee; and/or
- appointment of an independent trustee; and/or
- resignation/non-appointment of the trustee; and/or
- management by the employer of the risk of a conflict arising; and/or
- application to the courts.

Confidential information

12.1.5   The Regulator states that 'acute conflicts' can arise in relation to confidential information because there is legal uncertainty over whether a trustee's duty of disclosure to the pension scheme takes priority over their duty of confidentiality to a third party (paras 81 and 82).

However, TPR questions whether this conflict issue ceases if the trustee is excluded from the decision-making process or if the trust deed absolves the trustee from sharing the information (para 82).

It is prudent to seek to modify any implied disclosure duty by including an express provision in the scheme governing documents. However, the trustee board may in some cases be reluctant to agree to such an amendment.

In any event, given that a trustee may be in breach of his or her fiduciary duty to his or her employer or in breach of other obligations (eg where the trustee is a trade union member or negotiator), the prudent course is not to disclose the confidential information without first obtaining fact-specific legal advice.

Disclosure of information to fellow trustees may not breach a trustee's confidentiality duty to his or her employer if that employer has a wide obligation to disclose information to the trustees under a confidentiality agreement.

Whether or not there is an obligation on a trustee who has a conflict to share confidential information, or whether there is an express contractual commitment to do so, trustees who are employees or officers of the sponsoring employer should be aware that TPR may seriously consider imposing a fine for failure to disclose to the trustees the occurrence of any event relating to the employer which there is reasonable cause to believe will be of material significance in the exercise by the trustees or their professional advisers of any of their functions. It appears that TPR considers taking key steps in a process which ultimately leads to the signing or completion of a corporate transaction (such as a refinancing) could constitute an event. In other words, the event is not just the ultimate signing or completion of the transaction (see para 86).

12.1.6 *Conflicts of interest*

The ongoing process

12.1.6   A theme throughout the conflicts guidance it that pension schemes should have a 'culture' of managing conflicts of interest and conflicts should not be dealt with on an *ad hoc*, stand-alone basis.

To encourage this, TPR advocates, for example:

- trustees regularly reviewing their conflicts management policies (or procedures) (para 128);

- a conflicts policy being set up with procedures for monitoring compliance with its terms (para 125); and

- trustees considering including conflicts as a standing item at each trustee meeting (paras 45 and 49).

It is likely that TPR may ask trustees for a copy of their conflicts policy (eg if there is a clearance application).

Governing documentation/Companies Act 2006

12.1.7   Conflicts duties (and disclosure duties) may be modified by the documents governing the pension scheme (usually the trust deed and rules and, for a corporate trustee or employer, their constitutional documents – memorandum and articles of association). The Guidance acknowledges this, but cautions against relying on them in unenvisaged situations.

For company directors the new conflict provisions in the *Companies Act 2006* (which also came into force on 1 October 2008) need to be considered – see *Companies Act 2006: What do directors of trustee companies need to know*, **11.3**.

Employers and trustees should be aware of the conflicts provisions in their governing documents.

12.2 Should the finance director also be a pension trustee?

Summary

The thrust of the pension legislation has been to give greater powers to trustees of pension schemes. The Pensions Regulator (TPR) interprets this to mean guiding trustees towards taking a more independent position from the sponsoring employer and 'acting like a bank'. This is leading (and will lead further) to more negotiations between the trustees and the employer.

This section looks at the conflict of duty that can arise for the individuals concerned as a result of these changes.

It also looks at the factors that companies and individuals should take into account when deciding whether the finance director (or another senior officer) should be a pension trustee.

Overview

12.2.1   It can be difficult to strike a balance in deciding whether a senior officer of an employer company (eg a director) should also be on the trustee board of the company's pension scheme.

Clearly the senior officer's role may result in a conflict between:

- the duty owed to the scheme as a trustee; and
- the duty owed to the employer as an employee, director or officer of the company.

Conflicts can arise for more junior employees, as well, but in practice this is less likely to be an issue.

In addition, a member of a trustee board may have a conflict as a member of the scheme (although there is an express statutory provision allowing such member conflicts – *s 39* of the *Pensions Act 1995*).

Pension scheme rules often (but not always) contain an express provision allowing conflicts. The articles of association of any corporate trustee company also need to be checked for any provision allowing for conflicts.

However, a senior officer who acts in breach of any duty owed to the company and/or the scheme would remain personally liable for the breach.

12.2.1 *Conflicts of interest*

Furthermore, a senior officer may be in breach of a duty to the scheme if he does not disclose to the trustee board any material information that he knows by virtue of his position with the employer. It may not be a defence that this information is confidential to the company. Historically, this situation was often not specifically covered by the scheme rules (or the trustee company's articles of association). The articles of association of a corporate trustee can be amended by the shareholders (often the employer company) to make it clear that there is no automatic breach of duty in such a case. The scheme trust deed could also be amended to this effect, though this would usually have to be agreed with the trustees.

Even if the articles or trust deed permits the individual not to disclose, the individual concerned would still have a perception issue: how can he remain in a trustee meeting while possessing relevant information?

Against this has to be balanced the desire to have relatively senior and experienced individuals on the trustee board, particularly on issues in which there is no conflict (eg in implementing an agreed investment strategy).

One solution is for the senior officers not to take part in any decisions that the company may be making. But in many cases this may be impractical.

In our experience, many companies now arrange for senior officers (eg the finance director) not to be a trustee. This is because of the increased likelihood of a conflict issue as a result of the increased powers of trustees under the pension legislation and the views of TPR (eg in fixing contribution rates etc).

It may well be possible to have a senior officer (eg the finance director) attend trustee meetings as an observer, not a trustee, or even (if it is allowed by the scheme rules or the articles of the trustee company) sit on a separate committee in some areas (this may be more difficult in the investment area).

If a conflict arises, it should be managed – in particular, by the senior officer in question. Typically this would involve abstaining from the trustees' decision-making process and not participating in any negotiations (or being present for the relevant part of meetings). The senior officer should also formally declare the potential conflict to the rest of the trustee board.

Approaching the trustee board to discuss this issue may well lead them to consider what information flows should generally be allowed between the trustee and the company. Broadly, it would be sensible for the company to:

- agree with the trustee board a protocol for the supply of relevant information; and

- enter into a formal confidentiality agreement with each set of trustees (and the individual trustee directors), so that the company can have more

594

assurance that any information provided to a trustee on a confidential basis is kept confidential (this can also help listed companies comply with the Listing Rules – see *Listed companies: giving information to trustees or the pensions regulator*, **13.3**).

Level of skills needed by trustees

12.2.2   The employer is ultimately responsible for the funding of a defined-benefit (DB) scheme. So it helps the company to have individuals on the trustee board with a high level of commercial skills, knowledge and experience. This is particularly important in the light of:

- the powers held by pension scheme trustees (increased by the *Pensions Act 2004*);

- the company's need to negotiate and agree with the trustee board on matters such as funding, investment, benefit changes etc. If clearance from TPR is needed for some corporate action, the company may be looking for the trustee board to act speedily;

- the statutory requirement (under the *Pensions Act 2004*) that trustees have appropriate knowledge and understanding. This is intended to make trustees (and trustee directors) better equipped to take decisions on key issues;

- the TPR's statement that it expects pension scheme trustees to act more like commercial business managers and large creditors of the employer (see **9.1.3**); and

- the likelihood that, over time, these increased expectations will be reflected in the courts' approach to the duties of pension scheme trustees.

However, there will be concerns regarding occasions when a senior officer, as an officer or employee of the company:

- may be required to take actions that conflict with his role as a member of the trustee board; and

- may be aware of information that is confidential to the company but that he could be under a duty to disclose to the trustee board – for example, the financial state of the company, a proposed transaction or the company's negotiating position in discussions with the trustee board.

The nature of the senior officers' roles within the employer company will often mean that this could be an ongoing concern.

12.2.3 *Conflicts of interest*

The conflict issue

12.2.3 Broadly, a conflict of interest or conflict of duty arises when there is a conflict between the interests of the scheme and the personal interests or other duties of a trustee director. If a person:

- owes a duty in his capacity as trustee to the scheme (or as a trustee director to the trustee company, which in turn owes duties to the beneficiaries of the scheme); and

- also owes a duty to the company in his capacity as a senior employee or a director of a group company (eg a fiduciary or contractual duty to act in the interests of the company and/or not to disclose confidential information to a third party),

there is the potential for that person to have a conflict of interest or duty.

The general rule is that a trustee (or director) should not put himself in the position of having a conflict between his duty and his personal interests, or between a duty he owes to one party and a duty owed to another, without the informed consent of the parties affected.

This general rule can be modified by the relevant governing document (ie the articles of association of the employer or any trustee company and the scheme trust deed and rules). The general rule may also be modified by implication, given the circumstances of the pension scheme (this is less clear, but there are court decisions to support such an approach).

If a trustee director with such a conflict is involved in a decision made by the trustee board, the consequences could be:

- a court ruling that the decision of the trustee was taken in breach of trust and therefore is invalid;

- that the conflicted person is held to be in breach of his duty as a trustee or director of the trustee company; and/or

- that TPR may be less likely to accept the decision of the trustee board (eg on a clearance matter or scheme-specific funding).

The following questions need to be considered:

- whether the senior officer can act at all as a trustee (or director of a trustee company) given the potential for conflicts;

- how each senior officer and the trustee board should deal with an actual conflict (ie a specific transaction or matter in which the senior officer is taking an active role on behalf of the company or in relation to which the senior officer has knowledge of information confidential to the company); and

- if any senior officer becomes aware of information confidential to the company in the course of his duties as a company director or employee, and that information may affect decisions taken by the trustee board, whether the senior officer is obliged immediately to disclose that information to the other members of the trustee board.

Can a senior officer act as a trustee despite potential conflict?

12.2.4 The existence of potential conflicts of interest or duty will not always prevent a senior officer from acting as a trustee (or director of a trustee company) if the parties concerned – the company and the trustee – expressly consent to it or if the relevant governing documentation allows for it. In practice, this means that:

- the company will need to consent to the senior officer's accepting the appointment in spite of the potential conflict. It is sometimes argued that company consent will be implied if the trustee appointment is made by the company;

- if a senior officer is employed by another group entity or is an officer of any group entity, it would be prudent to ensure that that entity also gives express consent (by written agreement) and/or modifies its governing documents;

- if the senior officer is also a director of a group company, its memorandum and articles of association need to be checked to see whether they allow the potential conflict;[2] and

- it is preferable for the provisions of the scheme trust deed (and the articles of association of a corporate trustee) expressly to allow the senior officer's appointment in spite of the potential conflicts. If these documents do allow this, the decisions of the trustee board should not be rendered automatically void by the potential conflicts.

It is preferable to check the conflict provisions to clarify that a trustee director:

- can act despite a conflicting duty (as well as a conflicting interest), though there is a reasonable argument that conflicting interest wording may well already support this interpretation); and

---

2   The *Companies Act 2006* affects this – see **11.3**.

12.2.4 *Conflicts of interest*

- is not under an obligation to disclose confidential information to the trustee board where doing so would be in breach of a duty owed to the company (this point is discussed further below).

Pension schemes often include an exoneration clause providing that a trustee is not liable except for a deliberate breach of trust etc. The problem in a conflict situation will often be that the individual senior officer would be acting deliberately in the context of non-disclosure and so would probably not be able to take advantage of these provisions.

Separate consideration must be given to how a senior officer should act if his duties to the company conflict with his duty to exercise his powers for a proper purpose and in the best interests of the scheme.

How should a senior officer deal with a conflict?

12.2.5 A conflict of duty would exist if there were a specific transaction or matter affecting the relevant pension scheme in which a senior officer were taking an active role on behalf of the employer or in relation to which the senior officer had knowledge of information confidential to the employer. For example, the employer could be considering proposals to change future service pension benefits or a transaction amounting to a Type A event for TPR purposes (this is discussed below).

Trust deeds and articles of association usually allow for decisions to be taken by a majority of the trustee board (eg under *s 32* of the *Pensions Act 1995*).

A majority vote rule is helpful because it means that the agreement of a conflicted senior officer is not required for a decision to be taken by the trustee board. See eg the Deputy Pensions Ombudsman decision in 2012 in *Ecart*[3] However, there may be a risk that a majority vote in such circumstances would not be conclusive. A court may be concerned about the degree of influence that the conflicted senior officer may have had on the trustee board's deliberations.

As well as being a legal issue, this is potentially an issue of whether the trustee board's decision-making process on a particular issue would be perceived by members as fair and legitimate.

---

3   85837/1.

The Pensions Regulator's approach

12.2.6   Also relevant is TPR's approach to conflicts. Its guidance on clearance statements[4] makes recommendations on how employers should deal with so-called Type A events (events that may have a material adverse effect on the ability of an employer or its corporate group to meet its pension liabilities). TPR's examples of Type A events are changes in the priority of debt or other liabilities, returns of capital and changes in control structure that reduce the strength of the employer covenant.

TPR's guidance gives the following views on how employers and trustees should deal with conflict issues in negotiations over Type A events:

> '108. Trustees, who may include directors of the employer, will often have conflicts of interest. Other conflicted trustees may include shareholders of the employer or union representatives. Conflicts will be particularly relevant when trustees are negotiating with the employer in relation to a possible detrimental event, including a type A event.
>
> 109. We would generally expect trustees to seek legal advice in those cases where material conflict is identified to ascertain the best way to proceed.
>
> 110. The regulator expects a trustee who has a conflict or potential conflict of interest to notify other trustees at the earliest opportunity.
>
> 111. Further information and assistance on dealing with conflict of interest can be found in our free e-learning programme, the Trustee toolkit (www.trusteetoolkit.com) and in the Conflicts of interest consultation document (PDF) available on our website: Online publications/Policy documents.'[5]

The TPR guidance on conflicts issued in October 2008 is also relevant (see *Conflicts of interest: TPR's guidance*, **12.1**).

In some circumstances, if an actual conflict of duties has not arisen but there is the potential for one, it should not be necessary for a senior officer who is involved in a specific transaction or matter on behalf of the company to be excluded altogether from discussions over that matter. Indeed, it may be helpful to have the senior officer present during discussions to provide the trustee board with general information on the matter. However:

---

4   Available at www.thepensionsregulator.gov.uk/guidance/guidance-clearance.aspx
5   TPR guidance on clearance (June 2009).

12.2.6 *Conflicts of interest*

- it is prudent for the senior officer to disclose formally and in advance the existence of potential conflict in accordance with the trustee's articles and the Companies Act, so that it is clearly documented that the other directors are aware of the potential conflict; and

- the company and the senior officer should identify in advance of any discussions with the trustee whether there are any issues that are likely to lead to fundamental differences in position between the trustee and the company.

The legal position is not absolutely clear on the situation should an actual conflict arise or arm's-length negotiations with the company become necessary. However, the safest approach would be:

- to assume that the burden of proof would lie with the party seeking to rely on the trustee's decision to show that the decision was reasonable and proper, was reached in good faith and was not influenced by the conflict of any senior officer; and

- for any conflicted senior officer to be absent from the part of the meeting during which the decision is taken and to play no part (on the trustee's side) in the negotiation or decision making, on the basis that any participation by the senior officer in such circumstances runs the risk of the decision's being challenged by a claimant seeking to set it aside (it is often a lot easier for a claimant to argue that a decision is invalidated by reason of a conflict than to challenge the decision on its merits).

There are various ways in which a conflicted senior officer could be excluded from a particular trustee board decision. These are set out in the table below.

Option	*Comments*
1. Resign and replace All trustee directors who are conflicted on a specific issue (eg a particular transaction in relation to which the trustee and the company must negotiate but the trustee directors are also involved in the company's decision making) resign and are replaced by new directors not involved in company decision making on that issue.	Replacement trustee board members would be needed to comply with the minimum number imposed under the scheme rules/trustee articles of association and Member-Nominated Trustees and Directors' (MNT/MND) requirements. The trustee board would lose the benefit of the senior officers' experience and knowledge on other (non-conflicted) scheme matters.

Option	Comments
2. Abstain from relevant meetings/votes All conflicted trustee board members could absent themselves from meetings at which the issue in question is being discussed and abstain from voting on the matter.	• This is permitted if the scheme rules or articles of the trustee allow decisions by majority vote. The number of directors deciding the matter must satisfy the quorum requirements.
3. Step aside and delegate to a sub-committee A decision on the specific transaction raising the conflict may be delegated to a sub-committee of the trustee board. All conflicted persons would be excluded from the sub-committee and from the trustee's decision making or any negotiations, but would continue to participate in other trustee board/ scheme matters. This would be a more formal method of excluding conflicted persons from relevant meetings than abstaining.	• Formal delegation to a sub-committee needs to be permitted under the scheme rules or trustee articles of association. Formal delegation is better for managing perceptions of the decision-making process and for creating a paper trail showing the trustee's efforts to manage conflicts. • Conflicted trustee board members would remain potentially liable for the decision taken by the trustee. • Would not trigger any MNT/MND implications and avoids falling below the minimum number of directors imposed by articles. The trustee board would retain the benefit of the current company-appointed trustees' experience and knowledge on other scheme matters.

12.2.6 *Conflicts of interest*

Option	Comments
4. Individual delegation to fiduciary or alternative director Each conflicted senior officer could personally delegate his powers and responsibilities in relation to the matter to a fiduciary agent (ie an alternative director). The agents would act for them on the specific transaction but keep all information and the trustee's position confidential. The conflicted person would continue to participate in other trustee board matters but take no part in decisions on the transaction in question.	Would need to be permitted by scheme rules or trustee articles and terms of MNT/MND arrangements. Would avoid falling below the minimum number of directors imposed by the articles. Each delegation would need to make it clear that the fiduciary agent would not share information with or take instructions from the relevant trustee. The delegation would also need to ensure that the fiduciary agent is protected against liability to the same extent as the trustee/trustee directors under the scheme rules (eg by including a mirror indemnity/limitation of liability). The conflicted person would remain liable for the decision taken by the trustees. Fiduciary agents could be liable to the conflicted person for a decision taken that exposes the latter to liability. Confidentiality agreements would need to be considered (eg to add the new party).

Should a senior officer disclose to the trustee board information confidential to the company?

12.2.7   A related point is the likelihood that a senior officer, by reason of his or her role in the employer company, may become aware of confidential information that is materially relevant to the trustee board (eg knowledge of the employer's negotiating position on a particular matter being discussed with the trustee board or of the employer's possible future intentions).

This would put the senior officer in a very difficult position. Clearly, he or she would have a duty to the employer not to disclose the information without the employer's consent.[6] There is a potential conflict of duty because it is possible that there is also a duty to disclose the confidential information to the other members of the trustee board.

12.2.8 The court decisions in this area are not clear over whether there is in fact a duty owed by a fiduciary (such as a trustee or director) to disclose to the other trustees all relevant information that he possesses. On balance, the better view is that no such implied duty exists (at least where the trustee/director has not committed any wrongdoing). But it is certainly something that is argued by some lawyers and the best course is for the relevant trust deed (and articles of association of a corporate trustee) to clarify the extent of any information or disclosure obligation on an individual trustee or director.

As mentioned above, TPR has stated in its guidance that it expects a trustee who could be involved on both sides of the negotiation over a Type A event (eg one who is also a senior officer):

- to ensure that the trustees have the appropriate information on a timely basis;

- to draw his fellow trustees' attention to the potential conflict; and

- to absent himself from trustee meetings in which the issue is discussed and to play no part in decision making.

12.2.9 There is also a perception issue. How will it look to outsiders (eg the members) if a senior officer has remained in a trustee board meeting while possessing relevant information?

Our advice is therefore that a senior officer should generally resign or abstain from the decision-making process, using one of the methods summarised in the table above. However, if the conflict is likely to be a one-off issue, the conflicted person may consider absenting himself from meetings.

Some lawyers argue that he would still be in breach of a duty of disclosure to the trustee or scheme. We do not agree with this view. However, there is a risk that the senior officer would still be in breach of duty to the trustee.

12.2.10 Another way of managing this issue would be for the employer to give its express consent to the senior officer's disclosing any relevant information (including confidential information) to the other members of the trustee board. This would remove the conflict of duty – but obviously has the drawback, from

---

6   Some lawyers argue that, because the employer has appointed the senior officer to the trustee board, the senior officer has been impliedly released from his or her confidentiality obligation to the employer. This is untested.

the employer's point of view, that it may provide confidential information to the trustee board at a time that is not of the employer's choosing.

The employer's articles of association also need to be checked to see if they allow a director to have a conflicting duty (see the discussion above of the *Companies Act 2006* and **11.3**).

12.2.11 Conversely, there may be times when the trustee board wants the relevant senior officer to keep some information confidential from the company. In practice, senior officers have often been expressly used by trustee boards as a conduit for passing the views of the trustee back to the employers. In that case, no confidentiality issue arises. But there may be other (more extreme) cases in which confidentiality does become an issue.

It is also helpful for the relevant trust deed (and articles of association of a corporate trustee) to make it clear that the senior officers' duties as members of a trustee board do not require them to disclose to the other directors confidential information if doing so would put them in breach of a duty to the company. This could be done by amending the articles of association of a company trustee (if the trustee is a subsidiary of the company, the immediate parent company could pass the necessary shareholder resolution) and should reduce the risk for the senior officers of a claim that they were personally in breach of their duties by withholding confidential information.

To be valid, the amendment would need to be a proper decision under company law. The decision to amend would be likely to be a valid one, given that the company's motives would have been to ensure that the trustee board includes people of appropriately high calibre and experience.

12.2.12 A further issue would be the potential for a claim that the senior officer (or trustee company) is, by reason of a senior officer's possession of material confidential information, in breach of its duties to the scheme beneficiaries. Therefore, a further precaution would be to amend the scheme trust deed to the same effect. The amendment would need to be a proper decision under trust law.

A disadvantage of changing the trust deed is that the change would usually need to be agreed with the trustee. This would open up the possibility of negotiations on the entire issue of conflicts and the provision of information. For this reason, the company may prefer to rely on a change to the articles alone.

12.2.13 TPR, in the extract from the guidance on clearance set out above, states that a conflicted trustee or director should 'ensure that the [other] trustees have the appropriate information'. This suggests that TPR believes that a senior officer director should not withhold any confidential information from the other directors.

This should not be taken as a statement of the relevant law. TPR has no power to affect the duties of the trustee or its directors in this respect. As discussed above, this may be stricter than the actual position under directors' and trustees' duties and would certainly be stricter than those duties if the articles or trust deed were amended. However, these comments indicate that the conduct of any trustee directors in this position may colour TPR's views on how to proceed in any application for clearance by the company.

12.2.14 An effective way of managing this perception, and any concerns the trustee board may have about being insufficiently informed, would be to agree with the trustee a protocol for the supply of information. This should be combined with a formal confidentiality agreement between the company and the trustee (these are becoming more common). Such agreements give the company more comfort that any information provided to the trustee board on a confidential basis is kept confidential (and also helps listed companies show compliance with the Listing Rules – see **13.3** below). If possible, the individual trustees (or directors of a trustee company) and any advisers should also be asked to sign the confidentiality agreement.

Chapter 13

Obligations to provide information

13.1 Notifiable events – obligation to report certain events to the Pensions Regulator

Summary

Under the *Pensions Act 2004* trustees and employers are required automatically to notify the Pensions Regulator (TPR) of certain events.

This section looks at:

- the duty of trustees and employers to notify TPR; and
- which events need to be reported.

This section reflects changes to legislation that came into force in April 2009.

13.1.1 The *Pensions Act 2004* gives TPR the main objectives of protecting pension benefits, reducing the risk of claims on the Pension Protection Fund (PPF) and promoting good administration of pension schemes. (The *Pensions Bill 2014* will, if enacted, introduce a new objective of minimising any adverse impact on the sustainable growth of an employer, but this is only relevant in the context of scheme funding – see *Pensions Bill 2014: a new statutory obligation for the Pensions Regulator*, **2.7** above).

TPR is therefore given wide powers and, to help it gather information, *s 69* of the *Pensions Act 2004* has imposed, since 6 April 2005, various duties on trustees and employers to make reports to TPR. These duties arise even in the absence of a request from TPR.

This chapter looks at trustees' and employers' duties to report certain events under *s 69* (others do not have this duty at the moment, although this may change).

What is the duty?

13.1.2   Except where TPR otherwise directs, the trustees or the employer must give TPR notice of any 'notifiable event'. The category of persons under this duty can be (but has not yet been) extended by regulations (eg to include a former employer or an associated person of an employer).

A *'notifiable event'* is an event prescribed in regulations in respect of an eligible scheme or an employer in relation to an eligible scheme.

'Eligible schemes' are those eligible to be covered by the PPF – that is, all schemes that are not money purchase schemes, prescribed schemes (eg schemes that are not registered with HM Revenue and Customs) and schemes being wound up immediately before 6 April 2005.

Which events must be reported?

13.1.3   The *2005 Notification Regulations*[1] and the *Employer Debt Regulations 2005* set out the events that are notifiable (see the tables below).

In a formal direction, TPR has set out exceptions in which trustees and employers will not be under an obligation to report certain events that would otherwise be notifiable. The exceptions will not apply if the scheme is funded below the PPF buyout level (even if the employer and scheme have agreed a recovery plan to remedy a scheme deficit). The exceptions will also not apply if the trustees have reported a materially significant failure by the employer to make a payment to the scheme in accordance with the schedule of contributions.

TPR has also issued Code of Practice 02 ('Notifiable events').

Timing and formal requirements

13.1.4   The notice to TPR must be given as soon as reasonably practicable after the person making it becomes aware of the notifiable event (this must be before the actual action concerned for some events – eg a decision to make a transfer payment must be notified before the transfer is made).

TPR's guidance indicates that the obligation implies urgency: 'For example, where a trustee is made aware of a notifiable event on a Sunday, the Regulator should be notified on Monday.'

---

1   The *Pensions Regulator* (*Notifiable Events*) *Regulations 2005*, as amended.

13.1.4 *Obligations to provide information*

The Code of Practice suggests that a procedure for making notifications should be put in place. It envisages that there will not be a need for specialist advice or to hold a trustee or board meeting about the notification.

The notice to TPR must be in writing; e-mail and fax are acceptable. A standard form used to be available on the TPR website: www.thepensionsregulator. gov.uk.

An actuary or other person under a duty to report breaches in the law to TPR (see *Reporting breaches of the law*, **13.2**) will be obliged to make a report if it becomes aware of a failure by the trustees or employer to notify under *s 69*.

Penalties

13.1.5 *Section 10* of the *Pensions Act 1995* (civil penalties) applies for non-compliance without reasonable excuse. The maximum civil penalty is £50,000 for companies and £5,000 for individuals. Directors who cause a company to fail to comply with the obligation can also be liable to a civil penalty under *s 10(5)*.

TPR has indicated in its Code of Practice 02 ('Notifiable events') that it will seek an explanation of any failure to notify. It has a range of actions that it can take, including training or other assistance. TPR will also consider any failure to notify a relevant event when deciding whether to issue a contribution notice (under the moral hazard powers given to TPR).

Obligation on non-employers (*and non-trustees*)

13.1.6 If a financial support direction (FSD) is made, the persons subject to the direction will also be obliged to notify various matters to TPR. These include the *s 69* notifiable events.

A guarantor under a withdrawal arrangement or an approved withdrawal arrangement for the purpose of the statutory debt on employer provisions (*s 75* of the *Pensions Act 1995*) is also obliged to notify TPR of the *s 69* events. There are minor differences between the events that require notification from guarantors and events that require notifications from employers and trustees.

2009 Changes to the notifiable events regime

13.1.7 From 6 April 2009 trustees are no longer required to notify TPR if there are two or more changes in key scheme posts, and employers are no longer required to notify TPR of changes in their credit ratings or two or more changes in key employer posts (see tables below for more information on which events are notifiable).

These changes are not retrospective so there will still have been a duty to notify TPR if these 'events' happened before 6 April 2009.

In October 2008 the government said that TPR proposed to clarify and update its directions that set out exceptions to the notifiable events regime. However, it has not yet published any formal proposals on this.

Sources of information

13.1.8   Sources of further information include:

- *s 69* of the *Pensions Act 2004*;

- the *Occupational Pension Scheme (Employer Debt) Regulations 2005 (SI 2005/678)*;

- the *Pensions Regulator (Notifiable Events) Regulations 2005 (SI 2005/900)*;

- the *Pensions Regulator (Miscellaneous Amendment) Regulations 2009 (SI 2009/617)*;

- *Occupational Pension Schemes (Miscellaneous Amendments) Regulations 2005 (SI 2005/2113)*;

- paras 2.56 to 2.62 of the government's response (October 2008) to the consultation on the amendments to the anti-avoidance measures in the *Pensions Act 2004*;

- the Pension Regulator's Code of Practice 02 ('Notifiable Events');

- the Pension Regulator's Directions under *s 69(1)* of the *Pensions Act 2004*;

- the Pension Regulator's table of conditions;

- the Pension Regulator's notifiable events framework.

Trustees: scheme-related events

13.1.9

Trustees (scheme-related): *Reg 2(1), Notifiable Events Regulations 2005*[2]	*Exemption conditions*	*Comment*
Debt recovery Any decision by the trustees to take action which will, or is intended to, result in any debt which is or may become due to the scheme not being paid in full.	A, B and C.	• Debt includes a contingent debt. • Relates to any debt (not just ones from employer). • Applies at decision stage. • Wording could be fairly wide – eg apply to a release of a guarantee or change in employer?
Two changes in key scheme posts that occurred before 6 April 2009 Two or more changes in key scheme posts within the previous 12 months.	A and B.	• From 6 April 2009 this notifiable event is removed from legislation. • Key scheme posts are scheme auditor or actuary. • Is cumulative: catches one change in each.

---

2   The wording in the first column of this table is based on wording found in the *Pensions Regulator (Notifiable Events) Regulations 2005 (SI 2005/900)* and the *Occupational Pension Scheme (Employer Debt) Regulations 2005 (SI 2005/678)*.

Trustees (scheme-related): Reg 2(1), Notifiable Events Regulations 2005[2]	Exemption conditions	Comment
Transfer in or out A decision by the trustees of a scheme ('the relevant scheme') to make a transfer payment to, or accept a transfer payment from, another scheme, or where the trustees or managers are required to make or accept a transfer payment without such a decision having been taken, the making or acceptance of that payment, the value of which is more than the lower of: • 5% of the value of the scheme assets of the relevant scheme; and • £1,500,000.	A and B.	• Scheme assets are as in the most recent valuation under s 224 of the 2004 Act (ie scheme-specific) (or Minimum Funding Requirement (MFR) valuation if none under s 224). • Applies at decision stage (or, if no trustee decision, when payment is made or accepted).
Granting benefits without advice and funding A decision by the trustees to grant benefits, or a right to benefits, on more favourable terms than those provided for by the scheme rules without either seeking advice from the scheme actuary or securing additional funding if such funding was advised by the actuary.	None.	• Applies to all benefit grants – not just for new members or on redundancy or to directors. • Applies at decision stage.

13.1.9 *Obligations to provide information*

Trustees (scheme-related): Reg 2(1), Notifiable Events Regulations 2005[2]	Exemption conditions	Comment
Granting big benefits to single member A decision by the trustees to grant benefits, or a right to benefits, to a member, or where the trustees or managers are required to grant benefits or a right to benefits without such a decision having been taken, the granting of those benefits or that right, the cost of which is more than the lower of: • 5% of the scheme assets; and • £1,500,000.	A and B.	• 'Cost' is not defined. For scheme assets see 'transfer-in' above. • Applies to benefits for a single member credit, regardless of whether funding is provided. • Could apply eg if consenting to early retirement or invalidity pension (if large enough). • Applies at decision stage or when benefits are granted even if no trustee decision (eg when a member reaches Normal Retirement Age or retires?).
Schedule 1B, Employer Debt Regulations 2005		
Entering into a scheme apportionment arrangement (SAA) or flexible apportionment arrangement (FAA) Any decision by the trustees to take action which will, or is intended to, result in entering into: • a scheme apportionment arrangement on or after the applicable time; or • a flexible apportionment arrangement.		• The Pensions Regulator has confirmed that, in its view, entering into an SAA before the applicable time (ie the effective time at which the *s 75* debt arises) will not constitute a notifiable event.
Condition A is that the scheme is fully funded for the purposes of a '*section 179* valuation' (ie PPF buy-out) (MFR applied where no *s 179* valuation has yet been carried out).		

Trustees (scheme-related): Reg 2(1), Notifiable Events Regulations 2005[2]	*Exemption conditions*	*Comment*
Condition B is that the trustees or managers have not incurred a duty to make a report (to TPR) in the previous 12 months under *s 228(2)* of the *Pensions Act 2004* of a materially significant failure by the employer to make a payment to the scheme in accordance with the schedule of contributions.		
Condition C is that the debt compromise is of a debt with a full value of less than 0.5% of the scheme assets calculated under a *s 179* valuation or, pending such valuation, under MFR.		

Employers: employer-related events

13.1.10

Employers (employer-related): Reg 2(2) Notifiable Events Regulations 2005[3]	*Exemption conditions*	*Comment*
Debt recovery a. Any decision by the employer to take action which will, or is intended to, result in a debt which is or may become due to the scheme not being paid in full.	None.	• Debt includes a contingent debt. • Relates to any debt (not just ones from employer). • Applies at decision stage. • Wording is fairly wide – eg could apply to a release of a guarantee or change in employer. • TPR has commented that any decision to compromise the *s 75* debt is a notifiable event.

---

3   The wording in the first column of this table is based on wording found in *The Pensions Regulator (Notifiable Events) Regulations 2005 (SI 2005/900).*

13.1.10 *Obligations to provide information*

Employers (employer-related): Reg 2(2) Notifiable Events Regulations 2005[3]	Exemption conditions	Comment
Ceasing to carry on UK business b. A decision by the employer to cease to carry on business in the UK, or where the employer ceases to carry on business in the UK without such a decision having been taken, the cessation of business in the UK by that employer.	None.	● Applies at decision stage.
Wrongful trading advice etc c. Receipt by the employer of advice that it is trading wrongfully within the meaning of *s 214* of the *Insolvency Act 1986* (wrongful trading), or circumstances being reached in which a director or former director of the company knows that there is no reasonable prospect that the company will avoid going into insolvent liquidation within the meaning of that section.	None.	● *IA1986, s 214(4)* says: '... the facts which a director of a company ought to know or ascertain, the conclusions which he ought to reach and the steps which he ought to take are those which would be known or ascertained, or reached or taken, by a reasonably diligent person having both: (a) the general knowledge, skill and experience that may reasonably be expected of a person carrying out the same functions as are carried out by that director in relation to the company, and (b) the general knowledge, skill and experience that that director has.'

Employers (employer-related): Reg 2(2) Notifiable Events Regulations 2005[3]	Exemption conditions	Comment
Breach of banking covenant d. Any breach by the employer of a covenant in an agreement between the employer and a bank or other institution providing banking services, other than where the bank or other institution agrees with the employer not to enforce the covenant.	A and B.	• Bank waiver means no notification obligation. • TPR has confirmed that the waiver would need to have been granted before the breach occurred.
Credit rating change that occurred before 6 April 2009 e. Any change in the employer's credit rating, or the employer ceasing to have a credit rating.	A, B and D.	• From 6 April 2009 this notifiable event is removed from legislation. • Applies to any change (even an improvement). • Applies only to employer – not to (eg) the parent.
Decision to relinquish control f. A decision by a controlling company to relinquish control of an employer company, or where the controlling company relinquishes such control without a decision to do so having been taken, the relinquishing of control of the employer company by that controlling company.	A and B.	• Covers the sale of any participating employer. • Covers some group restructurings and probably decisions to place the participating employer in the insolvency process. • Applies at parent company decision stage.

13.1.10 *Obligations to provide information*

Employers (employer-related): Reg 2(2) Notifiable Events Regulations 2005[3]	*Exemption conditions*	*Comment*
Changes in key employer posts that occurred before 6 April 2009 g. Two or more changes in the holders of any key employer posts within the previous 12 months; and	A and B.	From 6 April 2009 this notifiable event is removed from legislation. Includes chief executive and any director or partner responsible in whole or part for financial affairs. Cumulative for each.
Conviction of a director h. The conviction of an individual, in any jurisdiction, for an offence involving dishonesty if the offence was committed while the individual was a director or partner of the employer.	None.	
Condition A is that the scheme is fully funded for the purposes of a *s 179* valuation (likely to be PPF buyout) (MFR applies where no *s 179* valuation has yet been carried out).		
Condition B is that the trustees or managers have not incurred a duty to make a report (to TPR) in the previous 12 months under *s 228(2)* of the *Pensions Act 2004* of a materially significant failure by the employer to make a payment to the scheme in accordance with the schedule of contributions.		
Condition D is that the change in credit rating is not from investment to sub-investment grade where the credit rating is provided by a recognised credit rating agency (Standard and Poor's, Moody's or Fitch).		

13.2   Reporting breaches of law (*s 70*)

Summary

This section looks at the provisions of the *Pensions Act 2004* providing a duty on trustees, employers, advisers and others to report breaches in the law to the Pensions Regulator (TPR) (*s 70*).

The *2004 Act* imposed from 6 April 2005 various duties on these parties to make reports to the Pensions Regulator even in the absence of a request.

13.2.1   The *Pensions Act 2004* gave TPR the demanding main objectives of (broadly) protecting pension benefits, reducing the risk of claims on the Pension Protection Fund (PPF) and promoting good administration of pension schemes. (The *Pensions Bill 2013* introduces a new objective of minimising any adverse impact on the sustainable growth of an employer, but this is only relevant in the context of scheme funding – see *Pensions Bill 2014: a new statutory obligation for the Pensions Regulator*, **2.7** above).

So TPR is given wide powers: the *Pensions Act 2004* imposed from 6 April 2005 various duties on trustees, employers and advisers to make reports to TPR. These duties arise even in the absence of a request from TPR.

This chapter looks at the duty on trustees, employers, advisers and others to report breaches in the law (*s 70*).

TPR has issued Code of Practice 01 ('Reporting breaches of the law').

This is available on the TPR website: www.thepensionsregulator.gov.uk/codes/code-reporting-breaches.aspx

Statutory list	Who does this include?
A trustee or manager of an occupational or personal pension scheme.	Trustees.
A person who is otherwise involved in the administration of such a scheme.	Perhaps: ● trustee directors; ● pensions manager; ● individual employees of third parties; and ● insurance companies.

13.2.1 *Obligations to provide information*

Statutory list	Who does this include?
The employer in relation to an occupational pension scheme (regulations can extend the meaning of the term 'employer' – see *s 318(4)* (eg to include former employers)).	Could be extended by regulations eg to include a former employer.
A professional adviser in relation to such a scheme.	<ul><li>The scheme actuary.</li><li>The scheme auditor.</li><li>Actuarial advisers (to the scheme).</li><li>Legal advisers (to the scheme).[4]</li><li>Fund managers.</li><li>Assets custodian.</li></ul>
A person who is otherwise involved in advising the trustees or managers of an occupational or personal pension scheme in relation to the scheme.	Other trustee advisers eg insurers, transition managers and analysts.

Note that the duty does not fall on advisers to the employer. However, TPR states in its guidance that it regards the duty as falling on all involved individuals (eg individual employees, as well as on the firm).

The duty

13.2.2 Each of these persons must give a written report of the matter to TPR as soon as reasonably practicable where the person has reasonable cause to believe that:

- a duty relevant to the administration of the scheme has not been or is not being complied with; and

- that duty is 'imposed by or by virtue of an enactment or rule of law'; and

- the failure to comply is likely to be of material significance to TPR in the exercise of any of its functions.

Note that this is an obligation to notify. It goes wider than the previous whistleblowing duty (*Pensions Act 1995, s 48*), which only applied to auditors

---

4   But note the exclusion for legally privileged material – *s 311*.

and actuaries (under the previous law others involved could whistleblow but were not obliged to).

Reasonable cause to believe

13.2.3   This looks like an objective test, so it may not be enough for a person under a duty to say that he or she did not realise there was a breach of duty.

Presumably building on this, the guidance issued by TPR states that it considers those under a reporting duty should set up a formal internal procedure for ensuring that potential reporting events are recognised and considered. Even if not reported initially (because the breach is minor and so not material), TPR argues that it should be recorded internally in case a pattern emerges (which then could be material and so reportable).

The TPR Code of Practice also envisages that those under a reporting duty should investigate the position (eg ask questions of the trustees) if they have doubts about something and that they should take professional advice if they have doubts about whether there has been a breach of a relevant law.

It must be a breach of a duty relevant to the administration of the scheme

13.2.4   It is not very clear what duties are relevant for this purpose. Clearly not all breaches of legislation trigger the duty to report to TPR. The breach must be 'relevant to the administration of the scheme'. It is not very clear what this is trying to specify. The Code of Practice issued by TPR states that this means 'anything which could potentially affect members' benefits or the ability of members and others to access information to which they are entitled'.

This is pretty wide and will, in practice, catch practically all breaches by the trustees in relation to the scheme (eg of pensions legislation) and other breaches that could be relevant (eg a criminal offence involving dishonesty under some other statute).

The reporting obligation is not limited to breaches of duty by the trustees of a scheme. So it will cover breaches by third parties (eg the employer, an adviser, an administrator). Here the limitation that it must relate to the administration of the scheme is more relevant. A breach of some duty not relevant to the scheme is not reportable.

It must be imposed by an enactment or rule of law

Enactment

13.2.5   This is clearly any duty laid down in Acts of Parliament and statutory instruments (eg the disclosure regulations) – see definition of 'enactment' in *s 318* of the *Pensions Act 2004*. The obligation is not limited to pensions legislation. So it includes other legislation (eg the *Data Protection Act*, the *Trustee Acts*, employment legislation, the discrimination legislation – possibly even the *Human Rights Act*).

Rule of law

13.2.6   The term 'rule of law' is more vague. Presumably it will include fiduciary duties imposed by law on trustees. It is not clear if contractual duties are to be included. This seems more unlikely (is it a rule of law that a contracting party must comply with its obligations?). General tort duties may fit in more readily. The question of whether the implied duty of mutual trust and confidence is to be included is also unclear.

The failure to comply is likely to be of material significance to TPR in the exercise of any of its functions

13.2.7   The breach of duty must be 'likely' to be material to TPR. TPR has some fairly general functions (eg to wind up schemes, make court applications, collect information relevant to the PPF, prohibit trustees if they are not 'fit and proper'). So the ambit of this duty may be pretty wide.

TPR has issued Code of Practice 01 (Reporting breaches of the law) about what it wants under this section.

The guidance note issued by TPR makes it clear that not all breaches are reportable. It states that material significance will depend on: the cause of the breach; the effect of the breach; the reaction to the breach; and the wider implications of the breach.

So, for example, TPR regards anything involving dishonesty or a breach that has a criminal penalty (eg making an employer-related loan) as always being material. However, an isolated breach of a less material duty which is promptly addressed by the trustees is probably not material.

The guidance includes examples which build on the traffic light framework previously adopted by the Occupational Pensions Regulatory Authority, where legal breaches are classified as red, amber or green depending on the risks they pose to scheme assets and members' benefits.

The codes of practice and guidance are not statements of the law; however, they will have evidential value, meaning they will be taken into account by a court or tribunal where relevant.

Breaches before 6 April 2005

13.2.8   Nothing in *s 70* limits reportable breaches to those which occurred on or after 6 April 2005 (when *s 70* came into force). It seems that past events will be reportable.

Formal requirements

13.2.9   A report to TPR must be:

- in writing (the guidance envisages that email will be acceptable); and

- given as soon as reasonably practicable after the person has reasonable cause to believe there is a reportable breach – this is a pretty tight timescale.

Conflicting duties

13.2.10   Any duty owed by a person is not breached merely by making a report under this section.

Communications between a professional legal adviser and his client in connection with giving legal advice are protected (*s 311*) – but note that, in the absence of legal proceedings being contemplated, this does not cover communications with third parties eg other advisers.

Penalties

13.2.11   *Section 10* of the *Pensions Act 1995* (civil penalties) applies for non-compliance without reasonable excuse. So TPR will be able to fine breaches of this duty.

The maximum civil penalty is £50,000 for companies and £5,000 for individuals.

If a penalty falls on a company, any director or officer who consented to or connived in the act or omission or to whose neglect the act or omission was attributable may also be liable for a civil penalty.

13.2.11 *Obligations to provide information*

Trustees will want to ensure that they do not indemnify their advisers in relation to breaches of this duty.

Sources:

- TPR Code of Practice 01: www.thepensionsregulator.gov.uk/codes/code-reporting-breaches.aspx

- TPR guidance: www.thepensionsregulator.gov.uk/codes/code-related-report-breaches.aspx

13.3   Listed companies: implications of giving information to pension trustees or the Pensions Regulator

Summary

Pension trustees have become much more involved with corporate activity. It is now common for information on the employers to be given to pension trustees.

This section considers the implications of this in the case of a listed company.

Provided information is given on a confidential basis, and reasonable steps are taken to ensure that confidentiality is maintained, listed companies are allowed to give inside information to pension trustees or the Pensions Regulator (TPR) without triggering an obligation to make a market announcement.

When does information pass?

13.3.1   It has in recent years become much more common for companies to provide information about the company to pension trustees or TPR. These bodies have a wider role in corporate transactions as a result of the powers given to them under the *Pensions Act 2004*. Information about a company or group as the sponsoring employer of a pension scheme can be given to trustees or TPR:

- as part of an application for clearance for a commercial transaction (eg new banking facilities, payment of a dividend, corporate takeover);

- as part of discussions with trustees on fixing the rates of ongoing funding (the scheme-specific funding requirements under the *Pensions Act 2004*) – see **2.1**; or

- as part of trustee monitoring of 'strength of employer covenant'. The Pensions Regulator is encouraging trustees to act in the same way as other major unsecured creditors, such as banks – see **9.1**; or

- as part of discussions where there is a take-over within the Takeover code – see **15.4**.

Regulation 6 of the *Occupational Pension Schemes* (*Scheme Administration*) *Regulations 1996* also places a duty on employers and former employers in relation to an occupational pension scheme to:

623

13.3.1 *Obligations to provide information*

- disclose on request information to the trustees or managers that is reasonably required for the performance of their duties or the duties of their professional advisors; and

- disclose to the trustees or managers the occurrence of any event relating to the employer that there is reasonable cause to believe will be of material significance in the exercise of any of their functions or their professional advisors' functions.

Disclosure and transparency rules

13.3.2 Care needs to be taken to ensure that providing information on a confidential basis to trustees does not result in a breach of the disclosure requirements in the Financial Services Authority's (FSA) Disclosure and Transparency Rules (DTRs) for listed companies (or indeed the *Market Abuse Directive*).

In summary, the DTRs require companies to announce 'inside information' as soon as possible. And if inside information is disclosed to one person DTR 2.5.6R requires it to be announced simultaneously, in the case of an intentional disclosure, and as soon as possible in the case of a non-intentional disclosure, unless a delay is permitted (see below).

A listed company will therefore need to consider whether:

- entering negotiations with pension trustees (eg about funding); or
- releasing information to the trustees,

would give rise to an announcement obligation.

Do negotiations with the trustee trigger an announcement obligation?

13.3.3 The first issue to consider is whether the fact of negotiating or otherwise communicating with the trustee board, if made public, would have a significant effect on the price of the listed company's shares.

Generally, it will be unlikely that public knowledge that a listed company is providing information to its pension trustees, in isolation to the transaction or matter to which the information relates, would lead to a substantial movement in share price. Therefore a disclosure obligation is unlikely to exist. Even if this were not the case, the delaying provision in DTR 2.5.1R may well apply (see below).

Does disclosure of information to the trustees trigger an announcement obligation?

13.3.4 The listed company may be communicating price-sensitive information to the pension trustees. Does this trigger a public disclosure obligation in relation to that information?

DTR 2.5.1R contains an exception that allows a company to delay disclosure to avoid prejudicing its legitimate interests (see box below).

DTR 2.5.1R Delaying disclosure

An issuer may, under its own responsibility, delay the public disclosure of inside information, such as not to prejudice its legitimate interests provided that:

- such omission would not be likely to mislead the public;

- any person receiving the information owes the issuer a duty of confidentiality, regardless of whether such duty is based on law, regulations, articles of association or contract; and

- the issuer is able to ensure the confidentiality of that information.

Pension trustees usually owe an implied duty of confidentiality in relation to information provided to them in confidence by the employer. But it is obviously preferable to obtain an express written confidentiality agreement with the trustee board before disclosing any confidential information.

If a listed company requires the trustees to enter into a confidentiality agreement, any negotiations with (or provision of information to) the trustees are likely to fall within the exception in DTR 2.5.1R, provided the failure to make an announcement would not be likely to mislead the public and the company is able to ensure that confidentiality is maintained.

The DTRs themselves make it clear that inside information can in some circumstances be provided to third parties (DTR 2.5.7G; see box below).

DTR 2.5.7G

1. When an issuer is permitted to delay public disclosure of inside information in accordance with DTR 2.5.1R, it may selectively disclose that information to persons owing it a duty of confidentiality.

---

2. Such selective disclosure may be made to another person if it is in the normal course of the exercise of his employment, profession or duties. However, selective disclosure cannot be made to any person simply because they owe the issuer a duty of confidentiality. For example, an issuer contemplating a major transaction which requires shareholder support or which could significantly impact its lending arrangements or credit-rating may selectively disclose details of the proposed transaction to major shareholders, its lenders and/or credit-rating agency as long as the recipients are bound by a duty of confidentiality. An issuer may, depending on the circumstances, be justified in disclosing inside information to certain categories of recipient in addition to those employees of the issuer who require the information to perform their functions. The categories of recipient include, but are not limited to, the following:

   a. the issuer's advisers and advisers of any other persons involved in the matter in question;

   b. persons with whom the issuer is negotiating, or intends to negotiate, any commercial financial or investment transaction (including prospective underwriters or placees of the financial instruments of the issuer);

   c. employee representatives or trade unions acting on their behalf;

   d. any government department, the Bank of England, the Competition Commission or any other statutory or regulatory body or authority;

   e. major shareholders of the issuer;

   f. the issuer's lenders; and

   g. credit-rating agencies.

The FSA has confirmed to us that it considers that the provision of information (on a confidential basis) to the trustees of an occupational pension scheme of the listed company (or a member of its group) (and the trustees' own advisors) falls within the selective disclosure provision in DTR 2.5.7G.

The exemption in DTR 2.5.7G(2)(c) applies to disclosures to 'employee representatives or trade unions acting on their behalf'. The FSA has confirmed that there is no difference for this purpose between the positions of trustees (and their advisors) and 'employee representatives or trade unions'.

DTR 2.5.7G(2)(d) clearly applies to TPR as a statutory regulatory body.

The DTRs do make the point (DTR 2.5.8G) that:

'Selective disclosure to any or all of the persons referred to in DTR 2.5.7G may not be justified in every circumstance where [the company] delays disclosure in accordance with DTR 2.5.1R.'

The Pensions Regulator

13.3.5   There is no need for a confidentiality agreement with TPR. It owes a statutory duty of confidentiality in relation to any restricted information that it obtains. Restricted information is information that 'relates to the business or affairs of any person' (*s 82* of the *Pensions Act 2004*). This obligation extends to anyone who receives that information (directly or indirectly) from TPR.

Breaching this obligation is a criminal offence. There are, however, a number of statutory exemptions to this statutory confidentiality obligation (eg disclosure to various other authorities or in connection with legal proceedings for breach of trust etc).

Restricted information can be disclosed with the consent of the person to whom it relates (ie the company in relation to information about the company). So it may be prudent to make it clear when giving information to TPR whether the company is consenting to its disclosure to anyone else (eg the pension trustees).

See further *Confidentiality obligations on the Pensions Regulator,* **13.5** below.

List of recipients

13.3.6   Listed companies are required to keep lists of persons working for them with access to inside information and ensure that persons acting on their behalf or on their account draw up their own insider lists (DTR 2.8.1R).

Strictly speaking, it may be that listed companies are not obliged, under DTR 2.8.1R, to ensure that pension trustees (or their advisors) maintain an insider list nor to include pension trustees (and their advisors) on the listed company's own insider list. This is because DTR 2.8.1R refers to persons acting on behalf of or on account of the company, whereas trustees are acting on their own behalf.

Nevertheless, the FSA has commented that it is arguably within the spirit of the obligation under DTR 2.8.1R to include pension trustees. Therefore it would be safest for a listed company to include the individual trustees (and their advisors) on an insider list. In practice this would help the listed company should there ever be an investigation of a leak of inside information.

13.4 Pensions: when should employers disclose a proposed transaction to trustees or the Pensions Regulator?

Summary

An employer may have good reasons to delay notifying the trustees of a defined-benefit scheme, the Pensions Regulator (TPR) or scheme members about a proposed transaction – especially if the transaction is not yet finalised. But failure to notify may be a breach of the employer's legal obligations and can have significant consequences.

This section explains the legal obligations to notify these parties and when these may be triggered.

13.4.1   An employer may, for example, be reluctant to share information if it is concerned that involving more parties in negotiations will complicate, delay or frustrate a proposed transaction.

However, sharing information with a pension scheme's trustees may help build and maintain a co-operative relationship with them – something that can be crucial in scheme funding negotiations or if the employer envisages asking TPR to provide clearance for the transaction.

Furthermore, an employer is sometimes legally obliged to disclose information about a proposed transaction to the pension scheme trustees, TPR or pension scheme members. These obligations are often triggered before the transaction is finalised and breaching them can, among other things, lead to TPR imposing civil penalties on the employer and its directors.

Does an employer have to disclose information to the trustees?

Is it contractually obliged to disclose the proposed transaction?

13.4.2   An employer may have to inform the trustees about a proposed transaction if it has, or other companies in its corporate group have, entered into a legally enforceable agreement with the trustees to notify them of its corporate activity. Such obligations may form part of a broader agreement (eg a parent company guarantee) entered into by companies seeking to improve the strength of the employer covenant in connection with a scheme's valuation or funding arrangements.

Is there a statutory duty to disclose the proposed transaction?

13.4.3 Changes were made to the Takeover Code from May 2013 requiring that trustees (or managers) of pension schemes of the target company of a takeover (or its subsidiaries) must be informed and allowed to present their view on the take-over transaction in the same way as employee representatives. See further *The Takeover Code: involvement of pension trustees*, **15.4** below.

13.4.4 *The Occupational Pension Schemes (Scheme Administration) Regulations 1996 (the Scheme Administration Regulations)* require employers:

- on the trustees' request, to disclose information to the trustees or managers that is reasonably required for the performance of their duties or their professional advisers' functions – *reg 6(1)(a)*; and

- to disclose automatically to the trustees or manager the occurrence of any 'event' relating to the employer if there is reasonable cause to believe that it will be of 'material significance' in the exercise of the trustees' functions or the functions of their professional advisers – *reg 6(1)(b)*.

If the obligation to disclose information is triggered under *reg 6(1)(b)*, the employer must make the disclosure within one month of the event's occurrence.

It will not always be clear at what stage during a transaction (which is of material significance) the obligation to disclose an event will be triggered. This is because the regulations do not elaborate on what is meant by an 'event'.

In TPR's view an 'event' includes 'events which result in a corporate transaction or any event which impacts on the benefits of scheme beneficiaries'.[5] On this interpretation, an employer should consider disclosing the occurrence of key steps that lead to the signing or completion of a corporate transaction, because TPR is taking the view that an employer may trigger this disclosure obligation before ultimate signing or completion. But, in practice, it may be difficult to apply TPR's interpretation because the employer may not know (at that time) if negotiations, for example, will in the future 'result' in a transaction completing. The transaction may still not complete.

Breach of either the 'on request' or automatic disclosure requirements can lead to the Regulator imposing a maximum civil penalty of £5,000 for individuals and £50,000 for companies. This penalty can extend to the employer's directors or officers who consented to the breach.

---

5   Paragraph 86 of TPR's guidance on conflicts of interest – see **12.1** above.

What if there is a conflict between duties owed to the employer and duties owed to the trustees?

13.4.5 An employee or officer (eg the finance director) of the participating employer who has a dual role as a pension scheme trustee may face a difficult decision over whether to disclose information about the proposed transaction to the other trustees. This difficulty arises because a trustee may owe an implied duty to disclose material information to the other trustees. If such a duty exists (and the case law is unclear), this may conflict with an opposing duty of confidentiality owed to the employer.

Unfortunately the law is unclear on how a trustee's duty of confidentiality can be reconciled with a conflicting duty of disclosure. But any conflict needs to be effectively managed because there is a real risk of breaching one of these duties. Breach may result in sanctions – for instance, if TPR becomes aware of the conflict it could seek to impeach or sanction the trustee, using its powers to remove or replace trustees and announce this publicly.

There are a number of strategies that can be used to manage this conflict and avoid making a disclosure. For example, the trustee can exclude himself from the trustee board's decision-making process. However, TPR may not believe this will necessarily excuse a trustee from a duty to share information – see *Conflicts of interest: the Pension Regulator's guidance*, **12.1**.

Alternatively, a conflicted trustee may sometimes be able to share confidential information with the other trustees without breaching a duty of confidentiality that is owed to an employer (eg if the employer expressly consents to the disclosure or if the employer and trustees have entered into a confidentiality agreement that permits such disclosures).

However, given that there is a real risk of trustees breaching a fiduciary duty to the employer by disclosing such confidential information, the prudent course is not to disclose without first obtaining legal advice.

For more information see *Should the finance director be a pension trustee?*, **12.2**.

Is it in the employer's best interest to disclose the information to the trustees?

13.4.6 The employer's directors may owe a duty to the employer to inform the scheme trustees about a proposed transaction at an early stage.

Under the *Companies Act 2006* directors have a general duty to 'promote the success of the company'. In complying with this duty they are required to consider the likely long-term consequences of their decisions.

With this in mind, it may be in the employer's best interest to inform the trustees about a proposed transaction if there is a significant risk that not informing them may lead to them taking actions that are potentially more detrimental to the employer than decisions they would otherwise have taken.

The risk of the trustees taking such adverse actions will vary and depend on the trustees' powers under legislation and the scheme's documentation (eg they may be able to switch to a more conservative investment strategy). Trustees' ability to take such adverse action is further strengthened by their ability to call on TPR for assistance or by refusing to co-operate with a clearance application (see below).

Will the Regulator be asked for clearance?

13.4.7 If the employer envisages asking TPR for clearance, it is best to share information with trustees at an early stage.

Clearance is a voluntary process and provides reassurance that TPR will not, as a result of the transaction, use its moral hazard powers to make an employer or 'connected' or 'associated' third party liable for the pension scheme deficit (for more information see *Who is 'connected' or 'associated'?*, **4.2**). The trustees' support for a proposed transaction can be crucial in getting clearance from TPR.

Furthermore, TPR in its 2010 clearance guidance states:

> '96. The regulator expects trustees to, as soon as reasonably practicable, be involved in any application relating to their scheme and as part of an application, the trustees will be asked to comment on whether or not they support the application and explain why. For an application to proceed efficiently, the regulator will expect trustees to have had the opportunity to assess the impact of a type A event, to consider appropriate mitigation, and to negotiate where appropriate, taking independent professional advice where needed. The regulator will consider the trustees' views when deciding whether to grant a clearance statement, but trustee support does not ensure it will be granted and lack of support does not ensure it will not be granted.'[6]

Clearance will usually be appropriate only if the transaction is 'materially detrimental to the ability of the scheme to meet its pensions liabilities' (this is called a 'Type A event') – for example, if the transaction weakens the

---

6   Paragraph 96 of the 2010 TPR clearance guidance. On the TPR website: http://www. thepensionsregulator.gov.uk/guidance/guidance-clearance.aspx#s1392 .

13.4.7 *Obligations to provide information*

employer's covenant to such a degree that it could be considered materially detrimental to the scheme's ability to meet its liabilities. See *Pensions and transactions: applying to TPR for clearance*, **4.13**.

Confidentiality agreement?

13.4.8 It is worth considering putting an express confidentiality agreement in place if information is shared with the trustees. Information provided also needs to be accurate and not misleading.

Does an employer have to disclose a proposed transaction to TPR?

Is the transaction a 'notifiable event'?

13.4.9 *The Pensions Regulator (Notifiable Events) Regulations 2005 (the Notifiable Events Regulations)* require employers to notify TPR of proposed transactions that involve 'employer related events' (for more information see *Notifiable events: obligation to report certain events to the Pensions Regulator*, **13.1**).

Employers must always notify TPR of the following events:

- any decision by the employer to take action (eg to compromise a debt under *s 75* of the *Pensions Act 1995*) that will, or is intended to, result in a debt that is (or may become) due to the pension scheme not being paid in full;

- a decision by the employer to cease to carry on business in the UK or cessation of business in the UK without such a decision being made;

- receipt of information by the employer that it is trading wrongfully within the meaning of *s 214* of the *Insolvency Act 1986* or if a director or former director knows that there is no reasonable prospect of avoiding insolvent liquidation; and

- a conviction, in any jurisdiction, of an individual for an offence involving dishonesty while they were a director or partner of the employer.

For some notifiable events, employers are not required to notify TPR if the scheme is fully funded (on a PPF basis) and the trustees or managers have not been required (in the past 12 months) to report to TPR a materially significant failure to pay contributions to the scheme. Otherwise, an employer will have to notify TPR if any of the following occurs:

- the employer breaches a banking covenant (unless the bank agrees not to enforce the covenant);[7] or

- a decision by the controlling company to relinquish control of an employer company or, if such a decision was not taken, the relinquishing of control.

It is important to note that some of these events can trigger a notification obligation at the decision-making stage, which can be before a transaction is completed.

TPR must be notified as soon as reasonably practicable after the person making the notification becomes aware of the notifiable event (for some events this must be before the actual action – eg a decision to make a transfer payment must be notified before the transfer is made). TPR's guidance (see paragraph 16 of its Code of Practice 02) indicates that this obligation implies urgency: 'For example, where a trustee is made aware of a notifiable event on a Sunday, TPR should be notified on Monday.'

TPR can impose a civil fine on an employer (and the directors and officers who cause a company to fail to comply with its obligations) if it fails to comply with the notifiable obligation without reasonable excuse. The maximum civil fine is £5,000 in the case of individuals and £50,000 in the case of a company.

The *Pensions Act 2004* also stipulates that failure to notify a notifiable event may, in some circumstances, make it 'reasonable' for TPR to issue a contribution notice under its moral hazard powers.

What if the employer is applying for clearance from TPR?

13.4.10 Employers need to share information about a proposed transaction with TPR if seeking clearance for a transaction (see above).

Before formally applying for clearance, parties can contact TPR on a no-names basis to enable subsequent discussion between trustees and employers to take place with a high-level understanding of TPR's views (although often TPR is reluctant to express any views before it is in possession of detailed information). At this stage, TPR would probably have to be informed about the nature of the proposed transaction. However, specifics about the transactions or the parties to the transaction will not yet need to be divulged.

---

7   TPR has indicated that if the notifiable event is a breach of a banking covenant, it expects the employer to notify it within the required timescales even if the bank later grants a retrospective waiver of the breach.

13.4.10 *Obligations to provide information*

If making a formal clearance application, parties will then need to provide a full and accurate disclosure of the circumstances surrounding the proposed transaction. Failure to provide full and accurate information may render clearance worthless because TPR can set it aside if the circumstances described in the application are not the same as those arising and this is material – see *ss 42(5)* and *46(5)* of the *Pensions Act 2004*.

Confidentiality agreement?

13.4.11 Employers will probably not need to enter into a confidentiality agreement with TPR when informing it. This is because TPR is subject to express confidentiality obligations (but there are some exceptions, such as disclosure to other government departments). TPR, usually, cannot (for example) disclose the information to the trustees, unless the employer has consented to such disclosure or it is to allow TPR to carry out its functions – see *Confidentiality obligations on the Pensions Regulator*, **13.5** below.

Does an employer have to inform its pension scheme members about a proposed transaction?

13.4.12 *Sections 259* to *261* of the *Pensions Act 2004* require employers to consult affected scheme members if the employer (or another person, such as another company with the group) is proposing to make a 'listed change' to the pension arrangement. The obligation applies to employers that have 50 or more employees (not scheme members). See further *Pensions Act 2004: employers' consultation obligations*, **15.1**.

If an employer is proposing to make a listed change, it must inform affected active and prospective scheme members (or their representatives) at least 60 days before any decision is made and then consult.

A listed change includes preventing 'the future accrual of benefits under the scheme for or in respect of members or members of a particular description'. Although this appears to be directed at proposals to freeze accrual under a scheme, it is arguable that it can apply in relatively common transaction scenarios if a company stops participating in a group pension scheme following a sale of the company out of the group or there is a transfer of its business under the *Transfer of Undertakings (Protection of Employment) Regulations 2006* (commonly referred to as *Tupe*).

The argument is that such transactions may entail a listed change because cessation of participation will mean the end of future accrual of benefits under the seller's scheme. But there are strong contrary arguments – the point needs to be considered taking into account the specific circumstances.

The Regulator has the power to impose a civil penalty if an employer has, without reasonable excuse, failed to comply with its consultation obligations. The maximum civil penalty is £50,000 (£5,000 for an individual).

13.5 Confidentiality obligations on the Pensions Regulator

Summary

This section summarises the confidentiality obligations of the Pensions Regulator (TPR).

Information given to TPR (for example as part of a clearance application) is treated as confidential. TPR is under a statutory duty not to disclose 'restricted information', ie information it obtains in the exercise of its functions that relates to the business affairs of any person. This duty also applies to any person who receives information from TPR (whether directly or indirectly).

There are limited circumstances in which TPR can disclose restricted information, but these are generally narrow exceptions. For example, TPR can disclose information to its advisers or to other supervisory/tax authorities or in order to carry out its functions.

There is no time limit on the duty of TPR to maintain the confidentiality of information, although information that comes into the public domain is no longer treated as restricted information.

13.5.1 Under *section 82* of the *Pensions Act 2004*, TPR is under a statutory obligation not to disclose restricted information. Restricted information must also not be disclosed by any person who receives the information directly or indirectly from TPR– *s 82(1)*.

'Restricted information' means any information obtained by TPR in the exercise of its functions that relates to the business or affairs of any person. It does not apply to information that at the time of the disclosure is already available to the public from other sources or cannot be identified as relating to the relevant individual – *s 82(4)*.

Disclosing information in contravention of *section 82* is a criminal offence – *s 82(5)*.

A copy of *section 82* is below.

Disclosure of information

82 Restricted information

(1)   Restricted information must not be disclosed—

    (a)   by the Regulator, or

    (b)   by any person who receives the information directly or indirectly from the Regulator.

(2)   Subsection (1) is subject to—

    (a)   subsection (3), and

    (b)   sections 71(9), 83 to 88 and 235.

(3)   Subject to section [88(5)], restricted information may be disclosed with the consent of the person to whom it relates and (if different) the person from whom the Regulator obtained it.

(4)   For the purposes of this section and sections 83 to 87, 'restricted information' means any information obtained by the Regulator in the exercise of its functions which relates to the business or other affairs of any person, except for information—

    (a)   which at the time of the disclosure is or has already been made available to the public from other sources, or

    (b)   which is in the form of a summary or collection of information so framed as not to enable information relating to any particular person to be ascertained from it.

(5)   Any person who discloses information in contravention of this section is guilty of an offence and liable—

    (a)   on summary conviction, to a fine not exceeding the statutory maximum[, or imprisonment for a term not exceeding 12 months, or both];

    (b)   on conviction on indictment, to a fine or imprisonment for a term not exceeding two years, or both.

[(6)   In relation to an offence under subsection (5) committed before the commencement of section 282 of the Criminal Justice Act 2003 (short sentences) the reference in subsection (5)(a) to 12 months has effect as if it were a reference to six months.

(7)   Subsection (6) does not extend to Scotland.]

13.5.2 *Obligations to provide information*

Exceptions

13.5.2 The various exceptions to the statutory prohibition in *section 82* (see *s 82(2)*) are set out below.

- **Disclosure with consent**: restricted information can be disclosed with the consent of the person to whom it relates and (if different) the person from whom TPR obtained it – *s 82(3)*.

- **Skilled persons report**: information can be disclosed to a person if preparing a 'skilled person' report for TPR – *s 71(9)*.

- **Overseas authority**: information supplied to TPR by a corresponding overseas authority is subject to a slightly different regime – *s 83*.

- **For Regulator to exercise functions**: TPR can disclose information if this is for enabling or assisting TPR to exercise its functions – *s 84(1)*. This is a potentially wide provision – see **13.5.7** and **13.5.8** below.

- **To Regulator's advisers**: information can be disclosed by TPR to a qualified adviser to ensure that he is properly informed on matters on which advice is sought – *s 84(3)*.

- **To help PPF**: information can be disclosed if this is for enabling or assisting the Board of the Pension Protection Fund to exercise its functions – *s 85*. *Section 199* similarly allows the Board of the Pension Protection Fund to disclose information to TPR.

- **To other supervisors**: TPR can disclose information to other supervisory authorities if TPR considers the disclosure would enable or assist them to carry out specific functions. The relevant authorities are listed in *Schedule 3* to the *2004 Act* – *s 86*.

13.5.3 Other permitted disclosures are set out in *section 87* and are summarised below.

- **Government or tax authorities**: disclosure to the government or the tax authorities if this is in the interests of members or in the public interest – *s 87(1)*.

- **Anti-Terrorism Act**: disclosure for the *Anti-Terrorism, Crime and Security Act 2001* – *s 87(2)(a)*.

- **Proceedings under pensions litigation or breach of trust**: disclosure in connection with proceedings arising out of the pensions legislation or proceedings for breach of trust – *s 87(2)(b)*.

- **Company director disqualification**: disclosure for proceedings under the *Company Directors Disqualification Act 1986* – *s 87(2)(c)*.

- **Insolvency Act**: disclosure for proceedings under the *Insolvency Act 1986* that have been instituted by TPR or in which it has a right to be heard – *s 87(2)(d)*.

- **Disciplinary proceedings**: disclosure for disciplinary proceedings of a solicitor, actuary, accountant or insolvency practitioner – *s 87(2)(e)*.

- **Public servant**: disclosure for disciplinary proceedings of a public servant – *s 87(2)(f)*.

- **Overseas authority**: disclosure to an authority outside the UK exercising functions corresponding to those of TPR – *s 87(2)(g)*.

- **EU obligations**: disclosure where required by an 'EU obligation' (previously called a Community obligation) – *s 87(2)(h)*. An EU obligation is any obligation created or arising by or under the treaties of the EU, whether enforceable or not (*European Communities Act 1972, Schedule 1, Part II*, as amended).

- **Prosecuting authorities**: disclosure is permitted to prosecuting authorities, ie the Director of Public Prosecutions, Lord Advocate or a police constable, etc – *s 87(4)*.

- **Under an enactment**: disclosure is permitted if the disclosure is 'required by or by virtue of an enactment'[8] – *s 87(5)*.

- **To trustee appointed by TPR**: disclosure is permitted to a trustee appointed by TPR in relation to an occupational pension scheme if this is for enabling or assisting him to exercise his functions – *s 87(6)*.

- **To tax authorities**: TPR is allowed to disclose information to the tax authorities (and to receive information from the tax authorities) – *s 88*.

What can people who have received information do with it?

13.5.4   People who receive information from TPR are still subject to the limitation in *section 82* on themselves disclosing it – *s 82(1)*.

However, in some cases they are allowed to disclose the information if TPR consents – *s 87(8)* to (*9*).

---

8   The Regulator has disclosure obligations under the *Data Protection Act 1998* (eg to disclose to an individual any personal data held on him) and under the *Freedom of Information Act 2000*. For details see the Regulator's website.

13.5.5 *Obligations to provide information*

Seeking confidentiality undertakings from TPR?

13.5.5 In practice, TPR may well be reluctant to give express confidentiality undertakings, given the existence of the statutory confidentiality obligations (and TPR's powers to require information to be given – *s 72* of the *PA 2004*).

Advance notice?

13.5.6 The question can arise whether TPR would agree to advance notice being given of any authorised disclosure – it may be that TPR would resist such an obligation (but we have not tested this).

Public announcements

13.5.7 We have not come across TPR making public disclosures about individual companies, save for occasional reports (under *s 89*) and for publication of decisions of the determinations panel. Even then, the main thrust of the disclosure has been the regulatory act itself (and not much underlying corporate information). For examples, see:

- TPR's report about MF Global UK Limited, issued in October 2013 (see **4.11.18** above);

- TPR's report about Great Lakes, issued in 2011 (this report was in itself pretty unusual); and

- TPR's (very brief) announcement in 2010 of settlement of a funding dispute with EMI.

The Regulator seems to be pretty sensitive about public disclosure of commercial information. For example, it generally refuses to comment on specific pending cases – an example is its 2010 press release on Visteon, when it sought '… to make clear that none of the details relating to Visteon UK's pension scheme published in Pensions Week (dated 19/4/10) were disclosed by the regulator. The regulator takes very seriously its duties to keep confidential any restricted information received by it in the course of its regulatory activities. In order for the regulator to carry out its work protecting pension scheme members and the PPF, it is vital that companies, trustees and their advisers know that commercially sensitive information supplied to the regulator will be kept confidential'.

Private disclosure

13.5.8 It is, of course, more difficult to tell if TPR has any practice of making private disclosure of information – eg to trustees it has appointed, to other regulators, etc. Obviously, it will disclose information to its own advisers.

We have not come across TPR disclosing information to other parties without donor consent – but it may in some cases be able to take a view that such a disclosure would fall within the exception of assisting it carrying out its functions (*s 84*).

The 'TPR functions' exception is potentially quite wide. For example in 2013 a decision by HMRC to discuss tax matters with journalists (on an off the record basis) was held to be within the similar 'functions' exception applying to HMRC under the legislation. The judge held that it was legitimate (and not irrational) for HMRC to disclose as part of it seeking to maintain good and co-operative relations with the press.[9]

Comment

13.5.9 Broadly commercial parties will usually rely on the statutory confidentiality obligations on TPR, rather than seek any express confidentiality undertakings.

If matters reach the determinations panel of TPR, the determination (and its reasons) are likely to be published. TPR has published guidelines on when it may agree secrecy even at the determinations panel stage (see **4.9** above).

A recent example was the determination in the *Desmonds* case (see **4.15** above), where the decision of the determinations panel in May 2010 was not published until after an appeal was heard before the Upper Tribunal and the tribunal decision itself published in March 2012.

---

9   *R* (*Ingenious Media Holdings plc and McKenna*) *v HMRC* [2013] EWHC 3258 (Admin), looking at the confidentiality obligation on HMRC under *s 18* of the *Commissioners for Revenue and Customs Act 2005.*

Chapter 14

Benefit changes

14.1   Lien and forfeiture rules – recovering from a scheme a member's debt owed to an employer

Summary

The *Pensions Act 1995* generally prohibits forfeiture, assignments, charges or liens over pension scheme benefits unless the employer is seeking compensation because of a member's criminal, negligent or fraudulent act.

The law on this is not entirely clear. But where an appropriate scheme rule is in place, employers should be able to obtain compensation for financial losses suffered because of criminal, negligent or fraudulent actions of an (often former) employee.

The general rule on reducing pension benefits following a criminal, negligent or fraudulent act

General rule: no charge or lien over benefits – Pensions Act 1995, s 91

14.1.1   The Goode Report (*Pension Law Reform*) (1993) stated that:

'The prohibition against dealings with pension entitlements during a scheme member's lifetime is designed to fulfil two objectives. First, it is intended to avoid additional administrative burdens which would arise if the scheme administrator had to recognise the title of assignees and chargees. Secondly, and more fundamentally, the purpose of a pension scheme is not to build up an assignable asset but to provide income to support members upon their retirement and to their dependants on the member's death.'

To this end, *s 91* of the *Pensions Act 1995* generally prevents a person's pensions entitlement or future pensions right under an occupational scheme from being assigned or charged or a lien exercised in respect of them.

Furthermore, any agreement to effect such an assignment, charge or lien is generally unenforceable.

Section 91 of the *Pensions Act 1995* applies to all occupational pension schemes, including those not tax registered under the *Finance Act 2004*.

However, a person's entitlements may be subject to a charge or lien to enable his employer to recover sums arising out of a member's criminal, negligent or fraudulent act or omission – *s 91(5)(d)* of the *Pensions Act 1995*.

What can be covered by the charge or lien?

14.1.2   The person must owe money to the employer (not another group company) as a result of an act or omission involving:

- a crime;
- negligence; or
- fraud.

It is not enough that the member may owe money (eg on a loan account) to the employer.

The term 'fraud' is not defined. However, it seems likely that it will have its general meaning of dishonesty (and not include extended concepts such as equitable fraud for failure to comply with a particular purpose).

Conditions

14.1.3   Where a charge or lien is exercised, *s 91(6)* of the *Pensions Act 1995* provides that:

- it must not exceed the lesser of the monetary obligation or the person's accrued rights/entitlement;
- the person must be given a certificate showing:
  - the amount of the charge or lien; and
  - the effect of this on the member's benefits; and

14.1.3 *Benefit changes*

- if the charge or lien is disputed it cannot be exercised unless the obligation has become enforceable under a court order or award of an arbitrator.

In *Haque v Bevis Trustees Ltd*[1] (1996), Vinelott J, in the High Court, endorsed the concept of maintaining a suspense account until the dispute is resolved. However this judgment was made under the preservation laws in the *Social Security Act 1973* and not the *Pensions Act 1995*.

In 2008, the Pensions Ombudsman in *Dallas (SO400040)* and the Deputy Pensions Ombudsman in *Mills (27050/2)* held that it was an unlawful lien to withhold a pension benefit if the court had not yet resolved the claim.

Dallas and *Mills* did not discuss *Haque v Bevis Trustees Ltd* and look to be inconsistent with it, so may be incorrect. Nevertheless, trustees should take care before suspending payment of a member's pension in the future.

Forfeiture of accrued pension rights (*Pensions Act 1995, ss 92 and 93*)

14.1.4 Generally, a pension entitlement or right to a pension cannot be forfeited. This includes 'any manner of deprivation or suspension' (*Pensions Act 1995, s 92(7)*). However, if a person has incurred some monetary obligation to the employer arising out of a criminal, negligent or fraudulent act or omission, forfeiture is permitted – *s 93(1)*.

Similar conditions apply as under *s 91(6)* above (eg a court order or arbitrator's award is needed for a forfeiture that is being disputed).

The trustees can determine that the amount forfeited may be paid to the employer – *Pensions Act 1995, s 93(5)*. Unless they did so, the effect would be that the employee's debt owed to the employer would not be reduced.

Trust deed

14.1.5 The trust deed will need to contain a 'lien rule' to allow a lien or forfeiture provision to apply.

It may be possible to insert a lien rule by amendment if this is allowed by the scheme's amendment power.

Amendments to include lien or forfeiture rules that comply with *ss 91* to *94* of the *Pensions Act 1995* are excluded from the limits in *s 67* of that Act (which

---

1   *Haque v Bevis Trustees Ltd* [1996] OPLR 271 (Vinelott J).

would otherwise prohibit such amendments affecting accrued rights) – see *Section 67: modification of subsisting rights*, **14.7**.

Transfer credits

14.1.6   When an employee brings a transfer from an entirely unconnected employer into the scheme (and in exchange is granted benefits, called 'transfer credits'), it may not be considered fair to the member for any lien or charge in favour of the current employer to cover these. However, it seems fairer to allow the lien to apply if the transfer is from a connected scheme (eg on a scheme merger).

Section 91 of the *Pensions Act 1995* and the *Occupational Pension Schemes (Assignment, Forfeiture, Bankruptcy etc) Regulations 1997* (*SI 1997/785*) deal with this by providing that a lien cannot generally apply to transfer credits unless:

> '... *those transfer credits* are attributable to employment with the same employer or an associated employer and the benefits of which could have been charged or a lien or set-off exercised in respect of such benefits under the occupational pension scheme from which the transfer was made'.

An associated employer is widely defined under the *Insolvency Act 1986* and will, for example, cover companies in the same group – see *Who is connected or associated?*, **4.2**

The exemption allows a lien over transfer credits to the extent that there was a lien in the transferring scheme. It is not clear if the lien in the receiving scheme can be wider than that in the transferring scheme. In practice it is safest if the lien in the receiving scheme is limited to cover the same amounts as would have been covered in the transferring scheme.

Section 93 does not include a similar restriction on forfeiture of any transfer credits.

Difficulties with interpreting ss 91 and 93

14.1.7   There are various problems with applying *ss 91* and *93* of the *Pensions Act 1995*.

However, the better view is that these difficulties stand in the way of reducing a member's pension benefit in appropriate cases.

14.1.8 *Benefit changes*

Limits on the amount

14.1.8   *Sections 91* and *93* state that where there is a charge, lien or forfeiture the amount must not exceed 'the amount of the monetary obligation in question *or (if less) the value (determined in the prescribed manner) of the ... entitlement or accrued right'*.

It has been argued that the wording in italics causes difficulties because no such manner has been prescribed. However, we interpret the wording as allowing a lien or charge to be exercised. It appears that the wording in italics can be ignored if there is no prescribed manner. In practice, the better view is that the value of the benefits is assessed by reference to the member's cash equivalent transfer value (in excess of the guaranteed minimum pension and ignoring any transfer credits). This seems to be the most appropriate method of assessment given that the member will (in most cases) have been dismissed and have become a deferred member.

Member's benefits only?

14.1.9   It has also been argued that only the member's benefits can be charged (ie the employer would not be able to recover an amount owed by the member by exercising a charge or lien (or forfeiture) over any spouse or dependant's pension payable in respect of the member).

The literal wording of the original version of *ss 91* and *93* suggested that this was not correct. The better view is that the 'accrued rights' of a member were clearly defined to include the benefits 'which have accrued to *or in respect of* him' (*Pensions Act 1995, s 124*). The words in italics indicate that pensions for spouses and dependants were covered.

However, the wording of *ss 91* and *93* was amended in December 2000. A set-off or lien now only applies to the 'entitlement or right' of the 'person in question' instead of to his 'accrued rights'. The provisions dealing with forfeiture have been similarly amended.

It is less clear whether the 'entitlement or right' of a member will include the potential benefits of the relevant spouse and dependants as secondary beneficiaries. It is not clear why the wording was changed. This seems to leave open the prospect of a member committing a criminal act and having his pension forfeited, but leaving a pension payable to his spouse and dependants. This seems rather odd.

The Law Commission states that, in its view, 'derivative benefits fall with the principal benefits to the scheme member if these are forfeited or lost for any reason' – report on *The Forfeiture Rule and the Law of Succession* (LC295) (2005). So on their analysis spouses' and dependants' pension can be forfeited.

Other legal restrictions to consider

Exercising a lien (*s 67*)

14.1.10 *Section 67* of the *Pensions Act 1995* generally prohibits exercising a power that modifies a scheme and affects any entitlement or accrued right of a member. The author considers that this prohibition does not apply to the exercise of an existing charging or forfeiture power (as this is not a modification to the scheme, or is exempted from *s 67*).

However, doubts on this point have been expressed. In practice, it would be helpful if the approval of the trustees and the written consent of the member to the exercise of the charge and the forfeiture can be obtained.

Restrictions on payments to employers (*Pensions Act 1995, s 37 and Pensions Act 2004, s 251*)

14.1.11 *Section 37* generally requires that pension scheme trustees must be satisfied that the exercise of any power to make a payment to an employer is in the interests of the members and that notice has been given to the members.

These restrictions do not apply if the payment is a compensation payment under *s 178* of the *Finance Act 2004* (ie payment made to the employer as compensation for a member's liability to a sponsoring employer in respect of a criminal, fraudulent or negligent act or omission by the member).

However, there was concern that *s 251* of the *Pensions Act 2004* will allow payments to employers only if the trustees pass a prescribed resolution before 6 April 2011. *Section 251* was probably intended to apply only when a scheme surplus is paid to the employer. But the legislation lacked clarity and may have restricted all payments to employers, including those made as a result of a lien or forfeiture rule even if within *s 178* of the *Finance Act 2004*. *Section 251* applies only to schemes that were in existence before 6 April 2006 – for these schemes the effect of the legislation may need to be considered further.

The *Pensions Act 2011* changed the *s 251* provisions and made them much clearer.

Contracted-out benefits

14.1.12 Any assignment or charge over guaranteed minimum pensions (*GMPs*) and protected rights is void – *Pension Schemes Act 1993, s 159*. Forfeiture is also only allowed in limited circumstances.

14.1.12 *Benefit changes*

There is no equivalent statutory protection for s *9(2B)* rights (ie benefits for contracted-out service on or after 6 April 1997 in a scheme that is contracted out on a salary-related basis). In practice, if there is a lien rule, actuaries are willing to give the required certificate that the benefits under the scheme comply with the statutory reference scheme test (a test that ensures the quality of the pensions provided for members). Actuaries do not tend to require any exclusion from forfeiture or lien rules. Presumably they consider that these rules would reduce the benefits of less than 10% of members, as permitted by the reference scheme test.

Tax law implications of making a payment to the employer (*Finance Act 2004, ss 175 and 178*)

14.1.13 Generally any payment out of a registered scheme to an employer is an unauthorised employer payment (*Finance Act 2004, s 160*), unless authorised under *s 175* of the *Finance Act 2004*. The employer will be liable for a 40% tax charge (*s 208*) and a possible 15% surcharge (*ss 209* and *213*). In addition, the scheme may be required to pay a scheme sanction charge of 25 to 40 per cent (*ss 239* and *240*).

A compensation payment under *s 178* is an authorised employer payment within *s 175*, so should not lead to a tax charge. A compensation payment is a payment made in respect of a member's liability to a sponsoring employer in respect of a criminal, fraudulent or negligent act or omission by the member.

Tax law issues on stopping or reducing a pension

14.1.14 *Schedule 28* of the *Finance Act 2004* generally provides that a reduction in the rate of or stopping a pension *currently* in payment will mean that the pension is not an authorised payment for tax purposes. If these provisions are breached the member may be liable for a 40% tax charge on future payments, an additional charge on lump payments and a possible surcharge of 15 per cent. In addition, the scheme may be required to pay a scheme sanction charge of 25 to 40%.

This will not be an issue if the reduction of the pension is because of an order of a court (*Finance Act 2004, Sch 28, para 2(4)(f)*). Such a court order may have been granted if the employee disputed the employer's claim against him (see above discussion).

In respect of liens, HM Revenue and Customs' (HMRC's) pension scheme manual also states that 'where the employer deducts debts due from the member from scheme pension payments then the rate of pension has not been changed'. So exercising a lien would not lead to tax charges.

However, HMRC states that forfeiture 'would effect a permanent reduction in the rate of pension payable and compliance with such an order ... unless specifically exempted through legislation' would be treated as an unauthorised member payment.

The Pension Schemes (Reduction in Pension Rates) Regulations 2006 (SI 2006/138) exempt some forfeitures from the restriction on stopping or reducing pensions benefits.

The main exemptions are under *s 92(2)* (forfeiture by reference to a transaction or purported transaction which under *s 91* is of no effect), or forfeitures within *s 93* (see above) of the *Pensions Act 1995*, provided that the member is not 'connected' with either the relevant scheme's sponsoring employer or a person who is 'connected' with the sponsoring employer.

Under the *Corporation Taxes Act 2010* the scheme member (on their own or with a person connected with them) would generally need to have some level of 'control' over how the company conducts its affairs in order to be connected to it. Equally companies are connected with each other if the same person(s) has 'control' over how they conduct their affairs.

Tax impact on employee

14.1.15 There is probably no tax charge on the employee in most cases (except in the limited circumstances of a pension in payment being stopped or reduced – see above). The employee will benefit because the payment will discharge (or reduce) the debt that the employee otherwise owes the employer. However, it seems likely that this is not treated as a taxable benefit in the hands of the employee (the position may differ if the payment is out of an unregistered scheme).

The tax charges on surrender or assignment of benefits (*Finance Act 2004, ss 172* and *173*) probably do not apply because the lien is not exercised by the member (instead it is the employer or trustees).

Tax notifications

14.1.16 There is no requirement to notify HMRC of payments under a lien rule falling outside the tax charge.

Time limits for payment of cash equivalent – s 99 of the Pension Schemes Act 1993

14.1.17 A request for the payment to another arrangement of a statutory cash equivalent of a member's benefit must normally be complied with within six months of the relevant guarantee date (*s 99(2)*). Under *s 99(3)*, this is extended to a date three months after the conclusion of any disciplinary or court proceedings where:

- such proceedings have begun against a member at any time during the 12-month period beginning with the termination date and it appears to the trustees that the proceedings may lead to the whole or part of the pension or benefit payable to the member or his widow being forfeited; and

- trustees would otherwise be required to comply with the request before the end of the three-month period after the conclusion of the disciplinary or court proceedings.

It is not clear what constitutes 'disciplinary' proceedings for the purpose of this section.

Trustee records

14.1.18 Trustees are obliged to keep records of all payments made to an employer – *reg 12(1)(b)(ix)* of the *Occupational Pension Schemes (Scheme Administration) Regulations 1996*. The records must be kept for at least six years (*reg 14*).

Data protection

14.1.19 Details of the employer's claim against the member will usually be personal data protected by the *Data Protection Act 1998* (*the 1998 Act*). In practice the data will be held by the employer and then shared with the trustees (and the relevant advisers). Is this allowed by the *1998 Act*?

Personal data is only protected by the *1998 Act* if it is held on a relevant electronic filing system or within a structured file. But in practice, the information is likely to be stored on such a file. Processing of personal data (eg that the employee has committed a negligent act) should be allowed under the relevant principles in *Sch 2* to the *1998 Act*. These include the following:

- Processing that is 'necessary for compliance with any legal obligation to which the data controller is subject, other than an obligation imposed by contract'. This could protect the trustee in complying with its legal obligation to allow the employer to exercise a lien or charge (*para 3*).

- Processing that is 'necessary for the purposes of legitimate interests pursued by the data controller or by a third party or parties to whom the data are disclosed, except where the processing is unwarranted in any particular case by reason of prejudice to the rights and freedoms or legitimate interests of the data subject'. This seems to be wide enough to cover the legitimate interest of the employer in recovering amounts due from the member (*para* 6).

If the allegations against the employee relate to a crime, that fact will be 'sensitive personal data' within *s 2* of the *1998 Act*. Sensitive personal data is subject to additional risk and must only be processed in compliance with additional restrictions (*Sch 3*). These seem to allow processing in the following instances.

- If it is 'necessary for the purposes of exercising or performing any right or obligation which is conferred or imposed by law on the data controller in connection with employment' (*para* 2). Arguably this covers the exercise of a lien in the trust deed, although this depends on being able to categorise the lien as a right 'imposed by law'.

- If it is necessary for the purposes of any legal proceedings or obtaining legal advice or otherwise for the purposes of establishing, exercising or defending legal rights. This more clearly covers an employer's lien (*para* 6).

Human rights

14.1.20 *The Human Rights Act 1998* (HRA), which is derived from the *European Convention for the Protection of Human Rights and Fundamental Freedoms* (the Convention), includes provisions for the protection of property (*Art 1, protocol 1*).

In *Adam Scott Carruthers v Dumfries & Galloway Council* (2009) an attempt was made to argue that a forfeiture violated an individual's right to 'peaceful possession of his possessions' under the Convention. The Dumfries Sheriff Court in Scotland held that the individual's right to receive a pension did not amount to 'possessions' because:

- it was conditional under the relevant scheme rules (as set out in legislation) on there being no forfeiture;

- it was not yet in payment and as a right to a future income could not amount to a possession. The court also commented that even if the pension was in payment it 'might well be argued that it is a right to each payment (whether monthly or whatever) as it falls due and that any right he has will always be to future income'; and

- even if the individual's right to a pension was a 'possession', the Convention still permitted a person to be deprived of this if it was 'in the public interest and subject to the conditions provided for and by law'. In this case, Scottish legislation permitted the forfeiture.

14.1.20 *Benefit changes*

An earlier attempt was made in the bankruptcy case *Krasner v Dennison*[2] (2001) to claim that the HRA applied in a similar situation to a lien or charge. However, the Court of Appeal (like in *Adam Scott Carruthers*) held that the vesting of the pension in the trustee in bankruptcy was appropriate because it complied with conditions provided for by law.

The analysis applied in the *Adam Scott Carruthers* and *Krasner* look applicable to an employer's forfeiture, charge or lien exercised under the *Pensions Act 1995*. In particular, the requirement for the conditions to be 'provided for by law' seems to be satisfied.

Companies Act 2006 and employer-related investments

14.1.21 *Section 136* of the *Companies Act 2006* prohibits a subsidiary from owning shares in its parent company but this prohibition does not apply if the subsidiary is only a trustee and the parent company or its subsidiaries are not 'beneficially interested' in the trust.

Section 140 makes it clear that a right of recovery (including any charge or lien that would enable the employer or former employer to discharge a monetary obligation owed by the scheme member to an employer) does not make a company beneficially interested.

Therefore a charge, lien etc will not prevent incorporated pension scheme trustees from owning shares in the employer, for example as part of their investment strategy.

---

2   *Krasner v Dennison, Lawrence v Lesser* [2001] Ch 76.

14.2 Increasing a pension scheme's normal retirement age

Summary

This section looks at some of the key issues for employers considering an increase in a pension scheme's normal retirement age.

Many employers operating defined-benefit (DB) occupational pension schemes are considering ways to reduce the costs of their schemes.

Employers are increasingly looking at raising their schemes' normal retirement age from, say, 60 to 65.

This section reviews some of the key issues employers should consider when looking to reduce pension costs by increasing the normal retirement age.

Decide on what this will mean in practice

14.2.1   It is critical to decide at the outset exactly what increasing the retirement age is meant to achieve and how it is intended to work in practice. It is also helpful to obtain actuarial advice on the savings to be achieved. For example:

- Is the change intended to apply to members' past service benefits or to future service benefits only?

- Is only one pension, with two tranches of service, intended to be provided from the scheme (with one tranche calculated by reference to the lower age and the other tranche calculated by reference to the higher age) or are two pensions envisaged (less common but permitted since April 2006)?

Review all scheme rules

14.2.2   It is also crucial to carry out a review of all scheme benefit provisions that may be (even indirectly) affected by a change to the normal retirement age. For example, simply amending the definition of the normal retirement age is unlikely to suffice. In addition, other rules may need amending, such as the rules on:

- early retirement;
- late retirement; and

- death benefits (eg where the benefit is calculated by reference to number of years before normal retirement age).

Care also needs to be taken over the actual amendments, particularly following the case of *Foster Wheeler*[3] in which the High Court looked at a scheme purporting to equalise normal retirement ages by a fairly simple amendment. The Court held that, because the rules had not been amended specifically to provide for different tranches of pension having different retirement ages, the whole pension must be calculated by reference to the lower normal retirement age. This was later overturned by the Court of Appeal, but the lesson remains.

Have good reasons for the decision

14.2.3 Employers should not propose such benefit changes without good reason. They owe an implied contractual duty of mutual trust and confidence to their employees. This means that they owe a duty of good faith (broadly a duty not to act in a way that is arbitrary or capricious, or in which no reasonable employer would act).[4]

This does not mean that an employer cannot act in its own interests, but it must carefully consider the impact of the proposed changes and be able to defend them as proportionate and reasonable. Documentation showing it has acted for valid commercial reasons and considered all available options is also helpful.

Who needs to consent – scheme trustees and/or members?

Changing past service benefits

14.2.4 If an employer is looking to change the retirement age for *past service* benefits, it must comply with the requirements of *s 67* of the *Pensions Act 1995*, which usually requires trustee and member consent. Effecting a change to past benefits is less common because it raises more difficult HR issues.

Changing future service benefits

14.2.5 There are two broad approaches open to employers wishing to implement changes in the normal retirement date for future service:

---

3   *Foster Wheeler Ltd v Hanley* [2009] EWCA Civ 651.
4   See eg *Prudential Staff Pensions Ltd v The Prudential Assurance Co Ltd* [2011] EWHC 960 (Ch).

- obtaining the pension scheme trustees' consent to a scheme amendment; or

- entering into a contractual agreement with employees outside the pension scheme (followed by a confirmatory amendment to the scheme rules).

As a change to the normal retirement age can affect a number of scheme provisions and can be seen properly as a matter of scheme benefit design, it may make most sense to implement it by the first route – by deed of amendment with trustee consent.

However, trustees may be constrained by restrictions on the scheme's amendment power and would also need to consider carefully why they should consent. They are likely to look for evidence of the employer's financial circumstances and may want to know what other changes have been considered.

The second approach outlined above can be helpful in circumstances where obtaining trustee agreement is difficult. This follows a principle established in the 1997 case of *South West Trains v Wightman*[5] (see *Avoiding pitfalls in implementing non-pensionable pay* **14.4**). However, if the amendments to be made are quite complex and affect a number of benefit provisions, it may be more difficult to obtain employee consent, and employers may prefer to pursue the first option of obtaining trustee consent to a scheme amendment.

Check contracts of employment

14.2.6   Employees may have an express contractual right to a specific normal retirement age (although this is fairly unusual in the authors' experience).

If employees do have such a right, their consent is needed to implement a change in retirement age.

Consultation process

14.2.7   Regardless of whether employee consent is being sought, the statutory 60-day consultation process under the *Pensions Act 2004* (see *Pensions Act 2004: Employers' consultation obligations* **15.1**) applies to a change increasing the normal retirement age.

The Pensions Regulator (TPR) can impose a civil penalty (up to £5,000 in the case of individuals and £50,000 in the case of a company) if an employer fails to comply with these consultation obligations.

---

5   *South West Trains Ltd v Wightman* [1997] OPLR 249.

14.3 Pensionable and non-pensionable remuneration

Summary

This section considers the possibility for employers of reducing costs for employers by providing that all or part of future pay rises will be non-pensionable.

Non-pensionable pay rises: the legal issues

14.3.1 Many employers who operate final salary pension schemes are currently looking at ways to reduce the costs relating to those schemes.

New hires

14.3.2 New employees can be provided with different benefits fairly easily. All that is needed is for the offer of employment to be clear about what will be made available. This can involve closing the final salary scheme to new entrants and replacing it with a money purchase scheme.

This does not raise any legal issues – provided the practice does not result in unlawful discrimination (eg on the basis of indirect age, sex or race discrimination).

In addition, however, an employer may need to reduce the costs of providing final salary benefits for existing employees.

Existing members: non-pensionable pay rises

14.3.3 A simple pay rise generally applies to all the final salary benefits payable under a pension scheme. Employers could expressly make all or part of future non-contractual pay rises non-pensionable, or make the pay rise pensionable only on a reduced basis. For example:

- pensionable at a reduced accrual rate;
- pensionable for future service only; or
- pensionable on a money purchase basis.

In effect, the employee would be offered the pay rise on special terms. This will usually have more limited legal implications than other changes to pension benefits. It could also have a significant cost impact for the pension scheme.

Example

Current position

An employee has 10 years' service in a 1/60th final salary pension scheme.

His salary is £15,000, so his accrued pension is:

$10 \times 1/60 \times £15,000 = £2,500$pa

Employee given a pensionable pay rise

If the employee gets a 5% pay rise (to £15,750) and works an extra year, his benefit rises to a pension of:

$11 \times 1/60 \times £15,750 = £2,887.50$pa

This is a 15.5% rise in the benefit. This is attributable to the 10 per cent rise in pensionable service (from 10 years to 11) and the 5 per cent rise in pensionable pay.

Employee given a non-pensionable pay rise

If the pay rise was made non pensionable then his accrued pension is:

$11 \times 1/60 \times £15,000 = £2,750.00$pa

The increase in pension is limited to 10% (the increase in the length of pensionable service).

This cost saving would apply to all active members, so could be significant.

The contractual position

14.3.4   Changing the pension benefits provided to existing employees is more difficult than changing the benefits offered to new employees, both from a legal and an HR perspective. Existing employees may have an express or implied contractual right to be a member of the pension scheme. Even if the employer has reserved the right to terminate or amend the pension scheme at any time, the exercise of that right will be subject to the implied duty of mutual trust and confidence. It may therefore be difficult for an employer to change the benefits under the pension scheme without risking claims for breach of contract.

14.3.4 *Benefit changes*

However, employees will rarely have a contractual right to a pay rise. There are therefore unlikely to be any contractual restrictions on an employer's awarding a pay rise on the condition that all or part of it shall be non-pensionable.

An employee will not need to agree expressly that the pay rise is non-pensionable, as long as the employer makes it clear that the pay rise offer is only made on the basis that it is wholly or partly non-pensionable.

In *The Trustees of the NUS Officials' and Employees' Superannuation Fund v The Pensions Ombudsman*[6] (2002), an employee, an official at a trade union, was sent a letter offering him a pay rise on the basis that it would be non-pensionable. He wrote back to the employer (the union) stating that he did not accept that the pay rise was non-pensionable, but he continued to work and accepted the increased pay.

In the High Court, Lightman J decided that the employee had impliedly accepted the increase in his pay on the terms set out in the employer's letter. The employee could not pick and choose. Either he took the pay rise subject to the limitation or he was not entitled to the pay rise at all.

This is supported by the 1937 decision of the House of Lords in *Tibbals v Port of London Authority*.[7]

Pay bargaining

14.3.5 Offering a non-pensionable pay rise raises the same legal issues as any pay rise (where there is no contractual right). Legally, it would only be challengeable in limited circumstances (eg if it were unlawful sex discrimination or an attempt to force union derecognition). Provided it is carried out properly (eg with due notice), it seems unlikely to be a breach of the implied duty of mutual trust and confidence.

Collective bargaining

14.3.6 Of course, the issue of whether a pay rise is pensionable or non-pensionable may be the subject of collective bargaining (in the same way as the level of pay rise may be) under the employer's arrangements with unions. An obligation to negotiate on pay will include an obligation to negotiate on

---

6   [2002] PLR 93, [2002] OPLR 17.
7   *Tibbals v Port of London Authority* [1937] 2 All ER 413.

pensions – see the decision of the Central Arbitration Committee on this in *UNIFI v Union Bank of Nigeria*[8] (2001).

Discussions about whether pay rises are pensionable may well fall within the scope of national works councils.

The position of the pension scheme

The trust deed and rules

14.3.7 If the employer makes a pay increase which is expressly stated to be non-pensionable, that will have implications for the pension scheme trustees.

The trust deed and rules of a final salary pension scheme will provide for benefits based on 'pensionable' pay or salary. This definition may be flexible and expressly allow for the employer to designate (or an employer and employee to agree) that certain elements of pay will be non-pensionable. However, the definition may not envisage this, so there may be conflict between the terms of the pay rise awarded to employees and the rules of the pension scheme.

Clearly, in such circumstances, it would be preferable to amend the trust deed (and, if necessary, the members' booklet) in advance to ensure consistency between the agreement reached with employees and the terms of the pension scheme.

However, even if this is not done, the courts have been clear that the pension trust deed will not override the pay rise terms. In *South West Trains v Wightman*[9] (1997), Neuberger J held that the trustees will be obliged in any event to administer the members' benefits and contributions in accordance with the contractual agreement reached between the employer and employees.

In *SWT v Wightman*, the unions had reached an agreement with the employer to provide (in the relevant collective bargaining agreement that formed part of the relevant employment contracts) that only part of a pay rise would be pensionable (and only then for future service). The union then sought to argue that the arrangement was not binding on the pension scheme. The court held that the employees were debarred from seeking pensions at a higher rate than had been agreed and that the trustees should execute a deed of amendment to regularise the position.

---

8   [2001] IRLR 712.
9   *South West Trains Ltd v Wightman* [1997] OPLR 249.

14.3.7 *Benefit changes*

See also *Bradbury v BBC*,[10] discussed in **14.11** below

Contracting out

14.3.8   In the case of a contracted-out scheme, actuarial advice will be needed to ensure that the scheme continues to comply with the reference scheme test. However, this is unlikely to be a problem in practice.

Record keeping

14.3.9   If non-pensionable pay rises are awarded, it will be essential for HR to maintain proper records of the pensionable and non-pensionable elements of each employee's remuneration, and make them available to the pension scheme administrators.

Summary

14.3.10 In comparison with other ways of reducing the costs relating to final salary schemes, making all or part of a future pay rise non-pensionable has the merit of being much cleaner from the perspective of the legal issues that arise. It may, of course, raise HR issues in the same way as any pay negotiation.

The amount saved may be substantial. If, say, a 3% pay rise is given but is designated not to be pensionable, the saving (if the non-pensionable nature is maintained into the future) will be 3% of the total past service reserve that was otherwise held for active members – for both past and future service.

---

10   [2012] EWHC 1369 (Ch).

14.4   Avoiding pitfalls in implementing non-pensionable pay

Summary

This section considers the approach employers may wish to take when considering making non-pensionable pay rises and suggests how some common pitfalls may be avoided.

14.4.1   Many employers that operate defined benefit (DB) occupational pension schemes are considering ways to reduce costs relating to those schemes.

Employers often wish to make all or part of future non-contractual pay rises non-pensionable, or make the pay rise pensionable only on a restricted basis. For example:

- only part of the increase is pensionable;

- it is pensionable for future service only; or

- it is pensionable at a reduced accrual rate.

Do the pension scheme trustees need to consent to the change?

14.4.2   There are two broad approaches open to employers wishing to implement changes in relation to the pensionability of pay rises:

- amending the scheme rules (which most commonly requires obtaining the pension scheme trustees' consent); or

- entering into a contractual agreement with employees outside the pension scheme (followed by a confirmatory amendment to the scheme rules).

Pension scheme trustees may be reluctant to become involved in changes relating to pay, viewing it as part of the employee's benefits package that is more appropriately negotiated directly between the employer and its workforce. They may also be constrained by restrictions in the scheme's amendment power.

The second approach outlined above is helpful in these circumstances. This follows a principle established in the case of *South West Trains v Wightman*

14.4.2 *Benefit changes*

(1997).[11] The union had agreed with the employer as part of a collective bargaining process that only part of a pay rise would be pensionable and that it would be pensionable for future service only. An employee argued this was not binding on the pension scheme (because the definition of pensionable pay in the scheme rules included pay rises). Neuberger J in the High Court decided that the employees could not seek pensions at a higher rate than agreed and that the trustees were obliged to amend the scheme to reflect the 'binding pensions agreement' between the employer and employees.

Avoiding pitfalls

Check contracts of employment

14.4.3 Employees may have an express or implied contractual right to be members of the pension scheme or even for pay rises to be pensionable.

Whether a benefit is contractual will depend on the wording of the particular contract of employment. The general rule is that benefits promised to employees will be contractual, unless the employer clearly states that they are discretionary, ex gratia or merely a statement of intent.

Even if employees do not have an express right to a pay rise, it could be argued that there is an implied contractual obligation on the employer to provide a particular level of pension benefit as a result of custom and practice. But this may be a difficult claim for an employee to succeed with – see eg the decision in the *Prudential* case (2011).[12]

Ideally, obtain express employee agreement

14.4.4 In terms of legal challenge, the safest option is to obtain express employee consent to the change proposed. Express agreement will be required if the employee has a contractual right to a pensionable pay increase.

The issue of whether a pay rise is pensionable may be the subject of collective bargaining. If so, it is important to ensure that there is clear evidence of agreement. The agreement does not have to be documented but it is usual and good practice to do so (and, of course, helps to avoid dispute later over the terms of any agreement). For such agreements to be binding on individuals, the individuals' contracts of employment must incorporate the terms of the collective agreement.

---

11   *South West Trains Ltd v Wightman* [1997] OPLR 249.
12   *Prudential Staff Pensions Ltd v The Prudential Assurance Co Ltd* [2011] EWHC 960 (Ch).

If express agreement is not possible, ensure there is effective implied agreement

14.4.5   Generally, member consent is unlikely to be implied just because employees continue to work after a pension change has been announced. However, if a pay rise is given to which the employee does not have a current contractual entitlement on the specific (and express) basis that it is non-pensionable, the employee is not able to take the rise and claim that it is pensionable. There has been a decision on this point – *NUS Superannuation v Pensions Ombudsman*[13] (2002), which is supported by the decision of the House of Lords in *Tibbals v Port of London Authority*[14] (1937). See also *Bradbury v BBC*,[15] discussed at **14.11** below.

It may be helpful to allow employees an opt-out option or offer a default position if they do not agree to the change.

Ensure all communication is clear

14.4.6   Any communications with employees should make clear the pensionable (or otherwise) basis of future pay increases. Care should also be taken to ensure that no later communications contradict this approach.

Have good reasons for the decision (and document them)

14.4.7   Employers should not propose changes over pensionable pay without good reason. They owe an implied contractual duty of mutual trust and confidence to their employees. This means that they owe a duty of good faith (ie broadly a duty not to act in a way that is arbitrary or capricious or in which no reasonable employer would act).

This does not mean that an employer cannot act in its own interests but it will need to consider carefully the impact of the proposed changes and aim to be able to defend them as proportionate and reasonable. Documentation showing it has acted for valid commercial reasons and considered all available options will be helpful. Employers should also avoid giving a blanket refusal to offer future pay rises.

---

13   [2002] PLR 93; [2002] OPLR 17.
14   *Tibbals v Port of London Authority* [1937] 2 All ER 413.
15   [2012] EWHC 1369 (Ch).

14.4.8 *Benefit changes*

Involve trustees from an early stage

14.4.8   Even if the trustees are not to be asked for their formal agreement to the changes, it is sensible to involve them from an early stage in the process. This will help avoid difficulties later – for example, if they are unconvinced of the existence of the contractual agreement between the employer and employees.

Trustees are likely to seek assurances from the employer over the contractual nature of the agreement, including seeking explicit confirmations, presentations from the employer or documentary evidence.

Operate a thorough consultation process

14.4.9   Under the original consultation regulations it was not entirely clear whether the statutory 60-day consultation process under the *Pensions Act 2004* (see *Pensions Act 2004: Employers' consultation obligations,* **15.1**) applied to proposals to make future pay rises non-pensionable. In practice, employers were likely to want to consult as a matter of good practice.

The Occupational and Personal Pension Schemes (*Consultation by Employers and Miscellaneous Amendment*) *Regulations 2006*[16] (the *Consultation Regulations*) specify that the consultation obligations apply if an employer makes a 'listed change'. With effect from 6 April 2010, the *Consultation Regulations* were amended to include a specific 'listed event' covering any proposal:

> 'to change what elements of pay constitute pensionable earnings, or to change the proportion of or limit the amount of any element of pay that forms part of pensionable earnings, for or in respect of members or members of a particular description.'

This means that there should be consultation about changes in non-pensionable pay (although the limits of this obligation are still unclear – what if the rate changes each year or is from otherwise discretionary pay, such as bonuses?)

TPR can impose a civil penalty (up to £5,000 in the case of individuals and £50,000 in the case of a company) if an employer fails to comply with the obligations under the *Consultation Regulations, reg 18A*. However, the 2004 Act expressly confirms that the change will still be effective, even if the consultation process is not followed – *s 259(3)* of the *PA 2004*.

---

16   *SI 2006/349*, as amended by the *Occupational and Personal Pension Schemes* (*Miscellaneous Amendments*) *Regulations 2010* (*SI 2010/499*) and the *Pensions* (*Institute and Faculty of Actuaries and Consultation by Employers – Amendment*) *Regulations 2012* (*SI 2012/692*).

The pension scheme trustees may be reluctant to operate the pension scheme on the basis of the agreement between the employer and employee if they are not satisfied that a proper consultation process has been followed.

Obviously, the safest course is to consult. This may also draw out any potential concerns or even legal challenges (eg based on contractual terms or past practice).

Ensure adequate record keeping

14.4.10 If non-pensionable pay rises are awarded, it is essential for human resources to maintain proper records of the pensionable and non-pensionable aspects of employees' remuneration and make them available to pension scheme administrators.

14.5 What is within 'remuneration' or basic earnings: *Redrow v Pedley* and *Singapore Airlines v Buck Consultants*

Summary

This section looks at a 2002 case, *Redrow v Pedley*, where the High Court found that benefits in kind were not included within the definition of 'total remuneration'.

By contrast in *Singapore Airlines* (2011) it was held that 'earnings' and 'fluctuating emoluments' included some cash payments and also taxed benefits in kind.

The decision in any particular case about whether or not particular payments or benefits in kind are within the pensionable pay definition within a scheme will depend on the proper interpretation of the deed and rules governing the scheme.

14.5.1 Terms such as 'remuneration' and 'total remuneration' are often used in pension documents. However, unless these terms are defined clearly, it may not be evident whether benefits in kind are included. The answer will depend on their context and usage in the trust deed.

In *Redrow v Pedley*[17] (2002), the High Court found that the correct construction of 'total remuneration', as used in a trust deed for the purpose of calculating pension benefits and contributions, did not include benefits in kind.

A question had arisen regarding the first and second definitive trust deeds, that used various descriptions such as 'total pay', 'total salary', 'total remuneration' and 'total earnings' to determine members' contributions and benefits. Redrow claimed that none of the descriptions included benefits in kind (such as motor vehicles, permanent health insurance, private medical insurance, share options, and so on).

Successive deeds of the pension scheme provided that members' benefits should be calculated with reference to 'total remuneration from the Employers' and 'total earnings ... as taken into account for schedule E income tax purposes'. No reference was made to benefits in kind. In contrast, the definitions of 'remuneration' used for the purpose of determining Inland

---

17 *Redrow plc v Pedley* [2002] EWHC 983 (Ch), [2003] OPLR 29.

Revenue limits expressly referred to fluctuating emoluments, which included benefits in kind.

Sir Andrew Morritt, Vice-chancellor of the High Court, gave three main reasons for finding that the descriptions 'total pay', 'total remuneration' and 'total earnings' did not include benefits in kind:

- The reference to 'total pay' in the original interim deed and members' booklet did not include benefits in kind. Interpreted in context, these descriptions denoted cash payments only and so excluded benefits in kind. If later deeds were intended to change this situation, then some clear indication of this was to be expected, whether by recital, in the relevant rules or otherwise. Further, the word 'as' in the phrase 'as taken into account for Schedule E income tax purposes' showed that mention of Schedule E was illustrative only and did not include all benefits included within that schedule.

- The definitions of other terms in the trust deeds used for the purpose of Inland Revenue limits expressly included benefits in kind by mentioning 'fluctuating emoluments'. Therefore, the lack of reference to benefits in kind in the definitions of 'total pay', 'total remuneration' and 'total earnings' indicated that the draftsman intended that they should not be included.

- The deeds did not refer to any method of valuing benefits in kind.

Actual practice?

14.5.2   In practice, benefits and contributions had been calculated for some time on the basis that benefits in kind were not included. If the decision on interpretation had been different, could this practice override the deed – by operation of 'estoppel'?

Although, as a result of the court's finding, it was not necessary to determine whether an estoppel by convention arose, Morritt V-C expressed his views on the matter. He said that the principle should be applied with caution when seeking to establish an estoppel between the trustees and the general body of members of a pension scheme so as to bind them all to an interpretation of the trust deed that it does not bear.

In his view, a pension scheme embodies not only the terms of a contract between members and the trustees, but also a trust applicable to the fund comprising the contributions of members and surpluses derived from the past in which present and future members may be interested. Such trusts cannot be altered by estoppel because no estoppel can be binding on future members.

14.5.2 *Benefit changes*

Morritt V-C also noted that it would be necessary to show that the principle was applicable to all existing members. He agreed with Laddie J in *ITN v Ward* (1997) that it would not be necessary to produce evidence relating to every member's intention, but a claimant would need to show that the principle applied to the general body of members as such.

In addition, for estoppel to apply, it would have to be proved that each and every member has, by his course of dealing, put a particular interpretation on the terms of the rules, or acted upon the agreed assumption that a given state of facts is accepted between them as true. This would involve more than merely passive acceptance by members.

Check deeds

14.5.3   In practice, it is worth reviewing schemes' governing documentation to ensure that terms used to calculate benefits and contributions are accurate and unambiguous. They should be as specific as possible and if benefits in kind are to be taken into account, this should be expressly dealt with.

The judge's remarks about past practice or estoppel are difficult to follow but he is clearly indicating that an estoppel would not be easily found. It is likely that it will be difficult to try to rely on passive acceptance arguments as overriding trust deeds.

Singapore Airlines

14.5.4   In a later case, *Singapore Airlines v Buck Consultants*[18] (2011), the Court of Appeal considered a deed that made 'earnings' pensionable.

The term 'earnings' had been defined in the original deed to include a London weighting allowance (LWA), but the latest deed defined the term as meaning 'the annual rate of basic remuneration for the employers' and went on the include 'fluctuating emoluments' on a three-year averaged basis.

The Court of Appeal considered *Redrow v Pedley*, but held that, as a matter of construction:

* the cash payments (the LWA and a '13th month payment') were within basic pay (and hence 'earnings'. This was on the basis that:

---

18   *Singapore Airlines Ltd v Buck Consultants Ltd* [2011] EWCA Civ 1542.

- the LWA had been expressly included within the earlier deed and it would be unlikely that the new deed was intended to exclude it retrospectively; and

- following the conclusion on the LWA, it would be illogical to exclude the 13th month payment; and

- benefits in kind fell within 'fluctuating emoluments' (and hence, although needing to be averaged, within 'earnings'.

Conclusion

14.5.5   It is clear that the decision in any particular case about whether or not particular payments or benefits in kind are within the pensionable pay definition within a scheme will depend on the proper interpretation of the deed and rules governing the scheme.

It may be difficult to predict where a court (or the Pensions Ombudsman) ends up if the matter goes to litigation.

14.6 Pensions: salary and bonus sacrifices

Summary

At a time when many employers are seeking ways of reducing pension costs, some are cutting benefits and/or increasing member contributions.

However, one means of reducing costs which has a lesser effect on employees is salary sacrifice. This works by converting member's contributions to a scheme into employer contributions, which do not attract national insurance contributions.

The potential savings have been greater since 6 April 2003, when total NICs (employer and employee) on earnings above £89 per week rose by 2%.

14.6.1 Salary sacrifices have always been an attractive way to:

- reduce National Insurance Contributions (NICs);

- to allow employees to effectively contribute more than 15% of their remuneration (the maximum allowed under the pre-April 2006 tax rules); and

- to increase the maximum tax-free lump sum available from additional voluntary contributions (AVCs).

Since April 2003 with additional employer and employee NICs of 2% on earnings above £89 per week (effective since 6 April 2003), salary sacrifices can be even more attractive.

What is a salary sacrifice?

14.6.2 A salary sacrifice arrangement is one that involves an employee agreeing to take a reduced salary in exchange for:

- the provision of other benefits (eg childcare vouchers); and/or

- pension benefits (eg salary is reduced and so are employee contributions, but employer contributions are correspondingly increased).

Under the first bullet above, a benefit sacrifice, the effect may be that pensionable salary or earnings (as defined in the pension scheme) would be reduced. Often this is not intended, in which case, all that is needed is for the scheme to be amended so that member's earnings or pensionable earnings are increased by the sacrifice amount. This is achieved by the increase of pensionable earnings to reflect the salary-sacrifice reduction. Pension contributions remain based on the notional increased salary.

Under the second bullet, where there is a pension contribution salary sacrifice, the intention is that (as under a benefit sacrifice) there should also be no effect on pensionable salary (ie through the definition of 'earnings' or 'pensionable earnings'), but members' contributions are also to be reduced (generally to be compensated for by a corresponding increase in the employer contributions).

Sacrifices need be documented in the terms of the relevant pension scheme.

If a salary-sacrifice arrangement is operated, the employers' increased contribution obligations need to be included in the funding documentation (Schedule of Contributions).

Benefits based on member contributions

14.6.3 If a salary sacrifice is operated that reduces member contributions, the effect is that the employers contribute more. This should not affect the underlying benefits, save in the case where benefits are tied to a return of member contributions.

Refund of contributions

14.6.4 Most commonly this will be if a member leaves with less than two years' qualifying service, where commonly schemes give members a right to take a refund of their own contributions (less a tax charge). But even here, this may now be less common as members with over three months' qualifying service now have a statutory right to request a transfer to another arrangement of the full value of their benefits.

In practice in a scheme closed to future entrants, it will often be the case that all relevant members now have more than two years' pensionable service and so are not eligible for refunds.

Higher-paid employees (2009 to 2011)

14.6.5 From 2008 to April 2011, *paras 3(3)(b)*, *15* and *18* of *Sch 35* to the *Finance Act 2009* together allowed refunds to a 'high income individual' (broadly those with a relevant income of £130,000 in the relevant tax years). These provisions were intended to allow members to get a refund of employee contributions (but not employer contributions) if they have made contributions that took them over the special annual allowance. However, this was only possible for contributions which would be classed as Additional Voluntary Contributions (AVCs) (not regular contributions) and was only available if permitted by the scheme's rules.

Lump-sum death benefits

14.6.6   In some schemes, lump-sum death benefits are also related to members' contributions (eg as an addition to the lump sum).

In practice it is often envisaged that no (or minimal) change to benefits is envisaged by the salary sacrifice arrangements. If this is the case, these provisions would need to be amended to provide for an amount equal to what would have been the members' contributions to be added back in.

Table 1: Salary sacrifice

	Salary sacrifice for non-pension benefits (eg childcare)		Salary sacrifice for pension contributions	
Adjustment needed to:	Sacrifice affects pensionable/ contribution pay	Sacrifice does not affect pensionable/ contribution pay (eg out of non pensionable bonuses)	Sacrifice affects pensionable/ contribution pay	Sacrifice does not affect pensionable/ contribution pay
Pensionable pay	Yes	No	Yes	No
Contribution pay	Yes	No	Yes	No
Rate of member contributions	No	No	Yes	Yes

Pension contribution sacrifice

14.6.7   In a pension context, a contribution salary (or bonus) sacrifice is a binding variation to an employment contract where the employee agrees to give up a specified amount of salary or bonus (this would need to be above the minimum wage). In exchange, the employer agrees to procure that agreed additional pension contributions are paid by it.

If the sacrifice is effective in relation to a tax-registered scheme (occupational or personal), the contributions will be treated as employer contributions and will not be subject to income tax or NICs (subject to being under the relevant annual allowance). The employer will get tax relief on any additional contributions to the pension scheme as usual.

A sacrifice may be made in place of AVCs or to reduce (or eliminate) ordinary compulsory employee contributions. Sacrifices across the workforce which effectively turn contributory schemes into non-contributory schemes (or reduce compulsory contributions) could bring significant savings to both employees and employers. At a time when many final salary schemes need to find additional resources, it is an attractive option to do this by reducing NIC liabilities.

Why would an employee be interested in a salary sacrifice?

14.6.8

- *No NICs*: there are no employees' (or employer's) NICs on employer contributions to tax-registered schemes.

  Before 2003, because employee NICs were capped at the Upper Earnings Limit and in practice sacrifices often would not bring remuneration below this level, there was less financial incentive for employees. From 2003, a sacrifice achieved a 13.8% saving (for employer and employee) on earnings above £89 pw.

Pre-April 2006 benefits

14.6.9

- *More potential annual pension saving*: before April 2006 while the limit of 15% of remuneration remained (this was removed by the *Finance Act 2004*).

- *Benefits are not subject to restrictions on AVCs*: before April 2006 there was a restriction against taking benefits from AVCs as a tax-free lump sum (for those who started paying AVCs on or after 8 April 1987). However, if an employee made a sacrifice instead of paying AVCs, the restriction would not apply. The maximum lump sum was therefore increased provided final remuneration (for Revenue purposes) was not affected (eg if the sacrifice takes place well before retirement so the reduced salary is not ultimately relevant to the calculation of final remuneration for Revenue limits). The advantage given to AVCs on a winding-up would be lost as would the ability (under the then law) to have AVCs refunded if benefits exceeded Revenue limits.

Why would an employer agree to a salary sacrifice?

14.6.10 Funding pension benefits by way of salary sacrifice enables the provision of greater benefits at less cost because of the saving in NICs. NICs are payable on the member's salary, including the part the member contributes to the pension scheme. NICs are not payable on employer contributions to a tax-registered pension arrangement.

Timing

14.6.11 It is safest if salary (or bonus) is sacrificed (ie the contractual change agreed) before the salary is earned (ie before the employee has performed the services for which the remuneration is payable):

- Contractual payments generally accrue on a daily basis (this will be implied under the *Apportionment Act 1870* if not expressly stated in the contract).

- Discretionary bonuses can be sacrificed before the decision to award them has been taken, unless they have become contractual (eg through custom and practice).

- Termination payments are generally earned when employment is terminated. Sacrifice may be able to be documented in a compromise agreement if the salary (or bonus) has not already been earned.

Type of remuneration	Safest sacrifice time
Wages/salary	Before start of period of employment for which wages are paid.
Discretionary bonus	Before actual payment (or decision to award if it may then become contractual).
Contractual bonus	Before the bonus has been earned. If the bonus is calculated by reference to a period, before the reference period starts

HMRC, in its guidance on salary sacrifice (in the Employment Income Manual), states that a sacrifice can be agreed before the relevant income is treated as 'received' for income tax purposes (for non-directors, this will usually be the date of payment of the relevant pay – see EIM42765 and EIM42260). This is often a later date than the 'safest' date mentioned above (eg in the case of a bonus it may be after the relevant bonus year, but before the bonus is actually paid). This is a helpful policy, but a cautious approach would be to rely on the 'safest' approach above (or obtain express HMRC clearance).

HMRC's approach in its guidance has been upheld in a 2012 upper tribunal case, *UBS AG v Revenue and Customs Comrs*[19] despite HMRC appearing to have argued that their own guidance should not be followed.

Effect on other employment benefits

14.6.12 Similarly, the effect on other benefits, including life insurance, long-term incentive plans and maternity pay, needs to be addressed.

Other effects

14.6.13 The sacrifice could have effects outside the employment contract (eg on state benefits and mortgage borrowing limits). In practice these cannot be managed except by trying to minimise the effect with strategic timing or provision of alternative benefits.

HMRC gives details of the potential effects on some other state benefits in its guidance on salary sacrifice in its Employment Income Manual (see EIM42774). Contributions-based benefits (eg state pension, incapacity benefit, jobseekers' allowance) could be affected. So could earnings-based benefits (eg maternity pay, state second pension, statutory sick pay etc).

Documentation

14.6.14 HMRC has published guidance on salary sacrifice on in the Employment Income Manual (EIM). This is on HMRC's website at: www.hmrc.gov.uk/manuals/eimanual/EIM42750.htm

---

19 [2012] UKUT 320 (Tax and Chancery Chamber) (Henderson J and Judge Charles Hellier).

14.6.14 *Benefit changes*

The Guidance states

EIM42753 – Salary sacrifice: how the changes to the employment contract are made

ITEPA 2003 s 62

The terms of an employment are set out in the contract between the employer and employee. The contract or agreement will usually specify among other things:

- The obligations and responsibilities of the employee (eg hours of attendance at the workplace; standards of work; dress code, etc).

- The remuneration package to be paid and provided (this may include cash wages/salary, non-cash benefits, pension rights, etc).

In a salary-sacrifice arrangement the contract is changed or varied. The employee may agree to a smaller cash salary in return for a non-cash benefit.

The change in the entitlement should be reflected in the contract. If the contract is not effectively varied, the employee remains entitled to the elements of the remuneration package previously specified.

Varying the contract can be achieved in a number of ways:

- Rewriting the document in part or whole.

- Setting out agreed changes in a separate document that is attached to the main contract. This may be a letter or a pro-forma.

- Employees may be informed of proposals to make changes by the employer. The employer may specify that if an employee has not indicated his/her wish not to participate in the changes by a certain date, the absence of an 'opt out' will be regarded as an 'opt in'. This approach is often used when wholesale changes to all employees' terms and conditions are proposed. For example, changes to the employer's occupational pension scheme.

The first two points on the bulleted list are easily recognised as effective changes as the employee will usually signify his/her agreement by signing the document. The third arrangement is also effective if the employees:

- have been fully informed of the proposals;

- are given a specified date by which time the 'opt out' must be made

---

- continue working after the opt out date;

- continue working after the first pay-day when the changes have been implemented without protest.

When these conditions have been satisfied, the employees have indicated their agreement to the variation by their conduct and the revised agreement is legally binding on both parties.

Source: HMRC Employment Income Manual
See www.hmrc.gov.uk/manuals/eimanual/EIM42753.htm

Some points to note:

- The salary sacrifice and the employer's commitment to contribute additional amounts to the pension scheme/provide extra benefits can be documented in the same letter.

- It is safest to have an express signed agreement between the employee and the employer. Cost constraints may drive a notification and opt-out approach instead, but the legal issues on this should be considered carefully (the HMRC approach set out in its manual is helpful here, but could raise legal issues).

- The documentation should set out the details of the reduction to the employee's remuneration and the benefits to be granted. It should preferably highlight potential risks (see above) and address how the effect on other benefits will be dealt with (if at all).

- It is preferable that the employee does not have a unilateral right to terminate the sacrifice. A relatively old House of Lords case, *Heaton v Bell*[20] (1969), indicates that this may mean that the sacrifice is ineffective (see EIM42755). In practice HMRC seems to allow a reversal right after a year (see EIM42767, but this is untested before the courts). A reversal provision, but only with employer agreement should be outside the *Heaton v Bell* principle. This may be a cautious approach, at least where a pension sacrifice is involved – HMRC issued revised guidance in June 2012 on 'Workplace Pension Schemes and Auto-enrolment,'[21] just before the start of the new auto-enrolment requirements – see **19.1** below. This confirmed that HMRC's view is that:

  'A workplace pension scheme into which an employee has been automatically enrolled on the basis bulleted above will be a

---

20   *Heaton (Inspector of Taxes) v Bell* [1970] AC 278.
21   http://www.hmrc.gov.uk/specialist/sal-sac-question-and-answers.htm.

registered pension scheme for tax purposes. Special legislation exists to prevent a charge to tax as employment income arising in relation to contributions that the employer pays to a registered pension scheme in respect of an employee. Even if a salary sacrifice arrangement relating to a workplace pension scheme provides for the remuneration to revert to a higher cash salary on request, the tax exemption on the employer's contributions will not be affected. Consequently, it is not necessary to stipulate a period for which the arrangement must be entered into or to set out "lifestyle changes" in relation to salary sacrifice for the workplace pension scheme.'

This only seems to cover income tax and it is not clear if a similar approach would cover national insurance too.

- Cash pay should not be reduced to below the national minimum wage (see EIM42769).

Trustees

14.6.15 Pension enhancements or variations will usually need to be agreed by the trustees of the pension scheme.

Unless the benefits to be provided are money purchase, additional contributions beyond those envisaged by the company may be required.

The trustees should be consulted in advance to avoid surprises. Amendments may be needed to document the extra benefits to be provided and to avoid potential temporary reductions in benefits resulting from reduced pensionable salary.

If the scheme is contracted out on a salary related basis, the relevant changes will need to be certified by the scheme actuary as maintaining compliance with the reference scheme test (*Pension Schemes Act 1993, s 37*).

Member consultation

14.6.16 In practice salary sacrifice involves an agreement with the member affected. So it might be thought that the consultation obligations under the *Pensions Act 2004* are not really relevant (as any change requires member consent anyway). See generally on the consultation regulations, *Pensions Act 2004: employer consultation obligations*, **15.1.**

Introducing a salary-sacrifice arrangement does not increase member contributions and so does not trigger the consultation requirements under the *Consultation Regulations*.

But ending an existing salary-sacrifice arrangement could be a listed change if the members' contributions increase. However it can be argued that a salary-sacrifice arrangement does not affect the member contribution rate at all – instead, a member is able to choose not to pay pension contributions and to have the employer pay the contributions on their behalf.

In March 2010 the government confirmed that, in its view, there is no requirement to consult in relation to salary-sacrifice arrangements because there is no lasting effect on members' benefits (so the exemption under *reg 10(1)(c)* of the *Consultation Regulations* applies).

Notifications

14.6.17 There is a general obligation to tell HMRC about tax-avoidance schemes that have been entered into. But salary sacrifice is so common (and discussed in the HMRC Tax Manual), that notification would be unusual.

Subject to this, there is no requirement to notify HMRC of a salary sacrifice. HMRC can be asked (after the event) to confirm that what has happened is effective as a sacrifice (see EIM42773).

Before the tax rules changed in April 2006, pension contribution sacrifices of more than £5,000 p a should have been notified to the appropriate Schedule E tax district. It would then decide if the sacrifice is effective and notify the rest of HMRC accordingly.

2009 to 2011: Special annual allowance tax charge

14.6.18 For the tax years 2002/10 and 2010/11 a special annual allowance tax charge was introduced by the *Finance Act 2010*. This applied in some cases where employees had income of over £130,000. Special provisions added back amounts sacrificed under salary-sacrifice arrangements (if made after 9 December 2009).

14.7 Section 67: modification of subsisting rights

Summary

Section 67 of the *Pensions Act 1995* limits amendment powers in pension schemes if they operate to affect 'accrued rights'.

The Pensions Regulator has issued a code of practice on the *s 67* regime.

The current *s 67* (which came into force on 6 April 2006) is more flexible than the old in terms of what is allowed (eg the actuarial equivalence test). However, extensive procedural requirements (information to members etc) have been added.

14.7.1 *Section 67* of the *Pensions Act 1995* introduced restrictions, from 6 April 1997, on the power to make amendments to schemes which would or might affect members' accrued rights.

From 6 April 2006, *s 262* of the *Pensions Act 2004* substituted new *ss 67* to *67I*. The current provisions are much longer and more detailed but are intended to be more flexible. The concept of 'accrued rights and entitlements' has been replaced by that of 'subsisting rights', though the two expressions cover much the same ground (see **14.7.2** below).

Code of Practice 10 ('Modification of subsisting rights') was issued by TPR in June 2007 (available on TPR's website).[22] This added another layer of detail to the 2006 regime, on top of the *Occupational Pension Schemes* (*Modification of Schemes*) *Regulations 2006*.

There used to be an actuarial guidance note GN51 ('Retirement Benefits Schemes Modification of Subsisting Rights without Consent'), but this was withdrawn by the Board for Actuarial Standards (BAS) from 1 December 2008.

As before, the new *s 67* does not deal with changes to future service benefits, which are subject to a different regime (see *Pensions Act 2004: consultation obligations*, **15.1**).

The new section 67

14.7.2 Under the old *s 67* it was not permitted to amend a scheme in a way which 'would or might affect any entitlement or accrued right of any member',

---

22 See http://www.thepensionsregulator.gov.uk/codes/code-modification.aspx.

unless either the consent of the affected members/beneficiaries was obtained or the scheme actuary certified that the change would not adversely affect any member.

The current *s 67* allows rule changes which modify members' subsisting rights provided certain conditions are met. If the conditions are not met, the changes are voidable. TPR can declare an amendment void or require trustees to take specified steps to satisfy the requirements. It can also impose fines (civil penalties).

The definition of 'subsisting rights' is very similar to that of 'accrued rights and entitlements' under the old *s 67*:

- any right to future benefits which, at the time of the modification, has accrued to, or in respect of, a member under the scheme rules determined as if the member had opted immediately before that time to terminate his pensionable service (therefore excluding, for example, death-in-service benefits); or

- an entitlement to present payment of pension or other benefit – pensions or benefits in payment.

These rights include pension credit rights (but not pension debits) under the pension sharing on divorce legislation.

Examples of exclusions from s 67

Excluded schemes:

- public service schemes;

- schemes with fewer than two members;

- schemes not registered with HMRC (unapproved schemes were previously within *s 67*).

Exempt modifications include:

- certain *Finance Act 2004* implementation (eg scheme benefit limits/earnings cap);

- *Civil Partnership Act* changes;

- changes made for a purpose connected with pension debits (pension sharing on divorce).

14.7.3 *Benefit changes*

Protected modifications and detrimental modifications

14.7.3   Modifications are now divided into two categories:

- protected modifications; and
- detrimental modifications.

The procedure to be followed will depend on which type of modification is being made.

Protected modifications

Protected modifications are those which would or might either:

- convert defined benefit (DB) subsisting rights to defined contribution (DC) rights; or
- reduce a pension in payment.

These changes are so major that member consent to them is necessary. To effect a protected modification, it is necessary to obtain the written consent of all affected members.

Detrimental modifications

14.7.4   Detrimental modifications are those which are not protected modifications and which would or might adversely affect any subsisting right of an affected member (including affected survivors).

'Adverse effect' here means altering the nature or extent of the entitlements or rights in a way that would or might result in less generous benefits for the affected member.

To effect a detrimental modification, the trustees must:

- obtain the consent of affected members (see below); or
- obtain a certificate of actuarial equivalence (see below); or
- opt for the consent route for one or more classes of member and the actuarial equivalence route for another or others.

Obtaining member consent

14.7.5   The trustees must do the following before the change is made:

682

- Give written information to every affected member that is adequate to explain the nature of the change and its effect (see below); if any affected member cannot be contacted, his or her subsisting rights cannot be amended via the consent route.

- Notify the member that he or she may make representations.

- Give the member a reasonable opportunity to make those representations.

  TPR states in its code of practice that it would normally expect a period of at least four weeks to be allowed for this, though it accepts that this will vary with the complexity of the amendments proposed and the number and location of the members. Furthermore, affected members should not be made to feel under pressure to come to a decision without adequate time and opportunity to make their views known to the trustees and to ask questions about the proposal.

- Once consent has been obtained, the trustees must satisfy themselves that consent was freely given and no undue influence was exercised on members.

  TPR gives no examples of what might constitute undue influence, but note that if there has been any such undue influence, members or trustees should make a breach of law report (under *Pensions Act 2004, s 70*) to TPR (see *Reporting breaches of law*, **13.2**).

The information requirement

TPR's code suggests that the trustees should:

- notify the affected member that either his written consent is needed or, as the case may be, the actuarial equivalence requirement applies to him – if the latter, brief explanation should be given of the actuarial equivalence requirement and how it has been achieved;

- in the case of a *detrimental* modification, if the requirements are intended to apply to affected members who do not consent by a stated deadline, give a clear explanation of this – where a member does not give consent to a protected modification, his subsisting rights must remain unchanged unless the actuarial equivalence route is also available and the member has been notified of this;

- where possible provide individual illustrations of the effect of the proposed modification;

- include a statement that affected members should consider whether they need to take their own independent financial advice;

14.7.5   *Benefit changes*

- arrange for any questions from affected members about the proposals to be answered in a timely manner; and

- consider whether it would be practicable and cost-effective to provide affected members with one or more named contacts with whom they could discuss the proposed modification.

Actuarial equivalence requirement

14.7.6   A detrimental modification can be made either by obtaining member consent (as above) or by satisfying the actuarial equivalence requirement. This consists of:

- the information requirement (see box above); the actuarial value requirement – trustees must make arrangements to secure that 'actuarial value' of the members' subsisting rights will be maintained; and

- the actuarial equivalence statement requirement – trustees must obtain an actuarial equivalence statement from the actuary.

In the case of the information requirement, there is a significant difference from the consent route: when going down the actuarial equivalence route, the trustees need only 'take reasonable steps' to ensure the required information is provided to all affected members.

TPR states that what is reasonable will depend on particular circumstances. For example, use of internal post or e-mail may be appropriate for communication with affected members who are still employed by the scheme's sponsoring employer, but the post will usually be appropriate for other members. Advertisements in the local press may be necessary where contact has been lost with deferred members for whom the changes are potentially material.

The actuarial value and the actuarial equivalence statement requirements

14.7.7   Before making the decision to effect or give approval to a modification, the trustees must have made adequate arrangements or taken adequate steps to secure that actuarial value will be maintained. In addition, they must, after the change has been made, obtain from an actuary (usually the scheme actuary) a statement that the actuarial value of the members' subsisting rights has been maintained (ie that the actuarial value, immediately after the change, of the member's subsisting rights is equal to or greater than the actuarial value immediately before change).

In calculating the value of subsisting rights, the actuary must use methods and assumptions which have been notified to the trustees and are consistent with those used in cash equivalent transfer value calculations (ignoring any reduction policy).

TPR says it would normally expect the certificate to be obtained within one month of the effective date of the change.

This represents a change from the old regime, where in practice the actuarial certificate had to be obtained immediately before execution of the deed of amendment.

The concept of actuarial equivalence could prove useful (eg if it is proposed to change a survivor benefit). Before 6 April 2006 this would have been difficult without member consent because it would have adversely affected the member's accrued rights. Now, however, it is possible to look at the member's subsisting rights as a whole and provide different, but actuarially equivalent, benefits.

Revising a modification which is subject to the actuarial equivalence requirement

14.7.8   Where a proposed modification is revised after the information requirement has been fulfilled but before the trustees have determined it should be made (or have given their approval to its being made by someone else) the trustees must consider (if necessary, taking legal and actuarial advice) whether the revised modification differs from the original in any material way. Where the differences are decided not to be material to the members concerned, the information requirement is taken as having been satisfied and the revised modification need not be treated as a new modification in respect of the information requirement.

However, if the difference is material, the trustees will have to re-commence the procedure as if the revised modification were a new modification.

Trustee approval

14.7.9   Before approving a modification of members' subsisting rights, the trustees should give due consideration to any representations received. They should allow sufficient time to obtain advice where necessary in relation to issues raised and to hold discussions with employers where it may be appropriate to amend a proposed modification in the light of representations received.

As under the old *s 67* (pre April 2006), the trustees are required to formally approve the modification, no matter who has power to make amendments under

14.7.9 *Benefit changes*

the scheme rules. Before giving approval, they need to ensure that all the requirements of *s 67* have been satisfied.

Where the consent route has been used, trustee approval must normally take place within six months after the first member has consented and implementation of the change should normally be within seven months of that first consent, though TPR recognises that these periods could vary according to the period stipulated for representations, obtaining consent and any legal or other issues around implementation.

Reporting requirement

14.7.10 The trustees must within a reasonable time and before the modification takes effect notify affected members that the trustees have determined to make the change (or agreed to it if it is the employer, for example, who has the power of amendment under the scheme rules).

Members to whom the consent requirements apply must be notified and all reasonable steps must be taken to notify members to whom the actuarial equivalence requirements apply. Similar considerations apply in deciding what steps are reasonable for the trustees to take as when satisfying the information requirement.

TPR's view is that affected members should be notified as soon as is reasonably practicable – normally within one month of the decision.

Conclusion

14.7.11 The new *s 67* is more flexible than the old in terms of what is allowed (eg the actuarial equivalence test). However, extensive procedural requirements (information to members etc) have been added.

14.8   Indexation

Summary

Pensions legislation requires pension schemes to provide minimum levels of indexation to pensions in payment and as revaluation to deferred benefits.

This section summarises the current rules on the statutory minimum level of indexation. It also comments on the government's index switch from the retail price index (RPI) to the consumer price index (CPI).

Scheme administrators and employers needed to check their rules to confirm the impact of the change.

What is LPI?

14.8.1   Indexation is generally imposed based on a form of limited price indexation (LPI) (ie the change in a price index, subject to a maximum cap). So 5% LPI means looking at the changes in the relevant price index over a previous reference period and then paying the increased rate, subject to the relevant annual cap – in this case 5%.

The price index used in the legislation is chosen by the Secretary of State (see the section on switching from the retail price index (RPI) to the consumer price index (CPI) at **14.8.5** below).

Defined benefit schemes

Pensions in payment

14.8.2   Occupational pension schemes that include a defined benefit (DB) element are required by overriding legislation in the *Pensions Act 1995* to provide LPI indexation for pensions in payment attributable to DB pensionable service after 5 April 1997 – *Pensions Act 1995, s 51*. The requirements do not apply to:

- benefits attributable to voluntary contributions – *s 51(6)*;
- benefits payable before age 55 (unless on ill-health) – *s 52*; or
- benefits under investment-linked annuities – *s 51A*.

687

14.8.2 *Benefit changes*

Before 1997, there was no statutory requirement to provide for any indexation (although many schemes did as a matter of benefit design), except that:

- guaranteed minimum pensions (GMPs) for contracted-out service (on a salary-related basis) on and after 6 April 1988 have been required (by the *Social Security Act 1986*) to have 3% LPI; and

- LPI indexation of 5% was required by the *Social Security Act 1990* on all pensions (other than GMP or money purchase benefits) if there was a refund of surplus to the employer. This ceased to apply for surplus payments after 5 April 2006.

The LPI cap was 5% pa (for pensions based on service between 6 April 1997 and 5 April 2005). This was reduced by the *Pensions Act 2004* to 2.5% for increases to pensions derived from benefits accrued on or after 6 April 2005 (the date the change came into force under *s 278* of the *Pensions Act 2004*).

The increases need to be applied each year. If the relevant index becomes negative, there is no provision allowing the annual rate of pension to be reduced.

There is a limited provision allowing an increase made in one year of more than the relevant LPI minimum to be offset against the indexation required in the next year (*Pensions Act 1995, s 53*).

Pensions in deferment

14.8.3 Revaluation of pensions in deferment (in excess of the GMP) has been required by legislation since 1986. Originally, revaluation only applied to pensionable service on or after 1 January 1985 (so any early leaver before that date has no statutory right to revaluation). For leavers on or after 1 January 1991, statutory revaluation was applied retrospectively to cover all pensionable service.

The statutory minimum rate of revaluation was originally 5% LPI. For pensions relating to service on and after 6 April 2009 it was reduced to 2.5% LPI (*Pensions Act 2008, s 101*). LPI remains capped at 5% pa for benefits relating to service before that date.

Money purchase benefits

14.8.4 Contracted-out benefits on a money purchase defined contribution (DC) basis (protected rights) were required to provide indexation when in payment at:

- LPI at 3% (for service from 6 April 1988 to 5 April 1997); and

- LPI at 5% (for service from 6 April 1997 to 5 April 2005).

The *Pensions Act 1995* extended this 5% LPI obligation to all money purchase benefits for service from 6 April 1997 provided by an occupational pension scheme (but not a personal pension scheme).

The *Pensions Act 2004* removed the requirement to apply LPI to pensions paid from money purchase schemes that come into payment on or after 6 April 2005. This change applies to all such pensions, even those for service before that date.

Schemes can still provide an option for an annuity that provides LPI but members now usually have the choice. A flat-rate annuity means a member can have a higher starting pension than would otherwise be the case.

The table at the end of this chapter summarises the minimum indexation percentages applying to different types of benefit for different periods.

Switch from the RPI to the CPI

14.8.5   The government announced in July 2010 in parliament that it will from 2011 switch from using the RPI to using the CPI when setting minimum requirements for uprating occupational pension benefits to reflect price inflation. A statement in July 2010 from the Pensions Minister at the Department for Work and Pensions (DWP) provided more information on the change.[23]

The government now uses the CPI for calculating:

- from 2011, the minimum requirements for revaluation (for deferred pensions) and indexation (for pensions in payment) in DB schemes;

- from 2011, increases in GMP payments by contracted-out DB schemes for pensionable service between 1988 and 1997; and

- compensation payable by the Pension Protection Fund (PPF) and Financial Assistance Scheme.

The Pensions Regulator issued a statement[24] in July 2010 on the 'Consumer Price Index (CPI)' seeking to help employers and trustees manage the proposed changes. The statement also explained the impact of the switch to CPI on its regulatory regime.

---

23   http://www.dwp.gov.uk/newsroom/press-releases/2010/july-2010/dwp088–10–120710.shtml.
24   http://www.thepensionsregulator.gov.uk/docs/consumer-prices-index-statement-july-2010. pdf.

14.8.5   *Benefit changes*

In December 2010, the DWP issued a consultation document on the changes and confirmed in June 2011[25] that it would *not* be introducing overriding legislation to allow private sector schemes to move to CPI (instead of RPI) where the current scheme rules (and *s 67*) prevented this.

From 6 April 2012, changes to scheme rules on revaluation and indexation were made a 'listed change', requiring consultation with members (see *Pensions Act 2004: Employers' consultation obligations,* **15.1**).

A legal challenge by trade unions to the change was rejected by the Court of Appeal in 2012 – *R (FDA and others) v Secretary of State for Work and Pensions.*[26]

Comments on the switch

14.8.6   The switch from the RPI to the CPI may affect the valuation of pension scheme liabilities. For example, if the CPI increases at a lower rate than the RPI, the liabilities may increase at this lower rate. But the impact of the switch on each scheme will mostly depend on how the scheme's rules are drafted and how the new legislation is enacted. We discuss below some issues to consider.

Schemes that refer to RPI

14.8.7   If the scheme rules expressly refer to the RPI, it is likely that it will be required to continue to use the RPI as the benchmark when revaluing deferred benefits and increasing pensions in payment. However, schemes may have to adopt a CPI underpin (ie use the CPI if it increases above the RPI) because the minimum revaluation and indexation requirements override scheme rules.

The *Pensions Act 2011* includes some changes designed to reduce this underpin risk.

A change in the scheme rules may be needed to switch to the CPI. Current legislation may already be broad enough to allow trustees to use a statutory power to make these changes for future service (see below).

Schemes that cross-refer to the legislation and not to the RPI

14.8.8   Some schemes may automatically switch from the RPI to the CPI for revaluing deferred benefits and increasing pensions in payment. The scheme

---

25   http://www.dwp.gov.uk/docs/cpi-private-pensions-consultation-response.pdf
26   [2012] EWCA Civ 332.

rules may not need amending if they refer to the minimum legislative requirements and not to the RPI. In practice, this is more common for deferred revaluation rules, rather than rules dealing with indexation of pensions in payment.

Should trustees write to scheme members?

14.8.9   TPR says that trustees should plan to communicate to members the impact of the switch to the CPI 'as soon as possible, once known, even if the impact is likely to be negligible'. They should also give 'serious consideration to interim communication, to assist members who may be faced with a decision on transfers or retirement planning, or may be concerned about press coverage'. Trustees will need to take a view if, and when, such a communication is appropriate.

Scheme funding

14.8.10 If a scheme switches from the RPI to the CPI benchmark for revaluation and indexation, this is likely to affect the size of its deficit. However, TPR has said that current payment schedules should remain in force for the time being. If the legislation results in lower estimated liabilities for the scheme, TPR has said that it expects this would generally lead to shorter recovery plans. TPR's July 2010 statement is less clear on how it expects trustees and employers to approach current funding negotiations.

How will the change affect de-risking measures?

14.8.11 Many pension schemes have made investments that are intended to hedge inflation risk through financial instruments based on the RPI, not the CPI. Trustees and employers may therefore wish to review whether there is now a gap between a scheme's future risk and the de-risking solution it has in place. Concern has in the past been expressed that there may be a lack of financial instruments that trustees can use to hedge against the CPI inflation risk.

Member options

14.8.12 Trustees and employers may also need to consider if actuarial assumptions should be revised for member options. For example, if members opt to take a transfer representing their benefits to another scheme.

Changing indexation rates

14.8.13 The statutory minimum indexation rates are overriding. They apply regardless of any contrary provision in the scheme (*Pensions Act 1995, s 117* and *Pension Schemes Act 1993, s 129*). However, it is possible for schemes to give higher rates of benefit (whether as discretionary augmentations or if required under a provision of the scheme).

Schemes can amend their rules to reduce indexation, always subject to:

- the statutory minimum indexation levels; and

- not reducing 'accrued rights' for service up to the date of the change, unless each affected member consents – *Pensions Act 1995, s 67*; and

- complying with any restrictions or limitations in the relevant scheme amendment power (or the change being authorised by a statutory provision or there being an express contract with the member).

If the relevant index is not 'hard wired' into the scheme rules (eg the index is stated to be RPI or such other index the trustees choose) a change may not be contrary to the restrictions in *s 67* – see the *Qinetiq*[27] decision in 2012.

A change to future indexation levels was in April 2012 made a 'listed change' requiring consultation with members under the *Pensions Act 2004* (see *Pensions Act 2004: employers' consultation obligations,* **15.1**).

A statutory power for trustees to reduce indexation rates (both for pensions in payment and revaluation in deferment) for future service benefits is given under *s 68* of the *Pensions Act 1995*.[28] A similar statutory power may apply if trustees and employers cannot agree on funding provisions – *Pensions Act 2004, s 229*. Neither statutory power allows changes that adversely affect accrued rights.

The government is aware that its proposed changes from the RPI to the CPI as the price index used under the statutory minimum provisions may cause practical issues for schemes. It therefore considered whether to legislate to help schemes but the DWP's response in June 2011 to its December 2010 consultation stated that the government does not intend to legislate to give an overriding power to change the CPI for past service.

---

27 *Danks v Qinetiq Holdings Ltd* [2012] EWHC 570 (Ch) (Vos J).
28 See *reg 13A* of the *Occupational Pension Schemes (Revaluation) Regulations 1991* (*SI 1991/168*, as amended by *SI 2009/615*).

Tax effect of indexation

14.8.14   Granting an increase in indexation can be a crystallisation event under the *Finance Act 2004*, resulting in a further check against the lifetime allowance for tax purposes – *Finance Act 2004, s 216(v)(b) event 3*. There are complex provisions as to when this will apply – see *Finance Act 2004, Sch 32, paras 9A to 13*. Increases of more than 5% LPI can trigger the charge.

The changes in the *Finance Act 2011* to the annual allowance tax charges from 6 April 2011 provide that granting extra indexation to a deferred member (in excess of the CPI) can mean that he is no longer excluded from the accrual test for the annual allowance.

Statutory minimum indexation percentages

14.8.15   Pensions in payment

Type of benefit	Service before 6 April 1988	Service 6 April 1988 to 5 April 1997	Service 6 April 1997 to 5 April 2005	Service on and after 6 April 2005
OPS: Defined benefit (DB)	Nil	3% LPI on guaranteed minimum pensions (GMPs) Nil on excess	5% LPI	2.5% LPI
OPS: Defined contribution (DC)	Nil	3% LPI on protected rights (unless benefits start after 5 April 2005, in which case nil) Nil on excess	5% LPI (unless benefits start after 5 April 2005, in which case nil)	Nil

14.8.15 *Benefit changes*

Type of benefit	Service before 6 April 1988	Service 6 April 1988 to 5 April 1997	Service 6 April 1997 to 5 April 2005	Service on and after 6 April 2005
Personal pension	Nil	3% LPI on protected rights (unless benefits start after 5 April 2005, in which case nil) Nil on excess	5% LPI on protected rights (unless benefits start after 5 April 2005, in which case nil) Nil on excess	Nil

OPS = occupational pension scheme.

DB Pensions in deferment

Type of benefit	Service before 1 January 1985	Service 1 January 1985 to 31 December 1990	Service 1 January 1991 to 5 April 2009	Service on and after 6 April 2009
OPS: Defined benefit (DB) Left pensionable service *before* 1 January 1991	GMP revaluation (COSR service from 6 April 1978) Nil on excess	5% LPI on post 1985 service (excess over GMP) GMP revaluation (COSR service)	N/A	N/A

694

Type of benefit	*Service before 1 January 1985*	*Service 1 January 1985 to 31 December 1990*	*Service 1 January 1991 to 5 April 2009*	*Service on and after 6 April 2009*
OPS: Defined Benefit (DB) Left pensionable service *on or after* 1 January 1991	5% LPI on excess over GMP GMP revaluation (COSR service)	5% LPI on excess over GMP GMP revaluation (COSR service)	5% LPI on excess over GMP GMP revaluation (COSR service pre 6 April 1997 – no GMP accrual after that date)	2.5% LPI

695

14.9   Member agreement to benefit changes needs to be clear: The *IMG case*

Summary

In 2009 the High Court ruled in a case involving the IMG pension scheme that its conversion to money purchase in 1992 was ineffective (clear member consent had not been obtained).

It also ruled that later compromise agreements signed with individual members were ineffective as infringing the statutory prohibitions in *s 91* of the *Pensions Act 1995*, but the Court of Appeal later overturned this.

14.9.1   In November 2009 in the IMG case, *HR Trustees Limited v German*,[29] Mr Justice Arnold, in the High Court, held that changes made in 1992 to the IMG pension plan (a defined-benefit (DB) pension scheme) had been ineffective to convert members' benefits from DB to defined-contribution (DC).

The judge also held that compromise agreements later entered into with members under which they waived DB entitlements, were ineffective as contrary to *s 91* of the *Pensions Act 1995* (but this aspect was later reversed on appeal).

The facts

14.9.2   In this case, the amendment power in the IMG pension plan's 1977 deed (the 1977 Deed) stated that: 'no amendment shall have the effect of reducing the value of benefits secured by contributions already made'. However, rules of the scheme that were introduced in 1981 (the 1981 Rules) contained a different amendment power with a less restrictive fetter.

The trustees and employer executed a deed on 3 March 1992 (the 1992 Amendment Deed) to convert the DB scheme into a DC scheme and backdated the deed to have effect from 1 January 1992.

Prior to the purported conversion, the employees were given: memorandums and a scheme booklet explaining the changes to the scheme; a presentation on

---

29   *HR Trustees Ltd v German* [2009] EWHC 2785 (Ch).

the changes; and membership application forms to join the new DC scheme. The members returned the application forms after having signed and ticked the 'yes box'.

Amendment power

14.9.3   Arnold J held that it was contrary to the restriction in the 1977 Deed to convert DB benefits that accrued before the 1992 Amendment Deed into DC benefits. He gave the following reasons:

- The fetter in the 1977 Deed was the relevant restriction that needed to be satisfied before the conversion could be ruled valid. The 1977 Deed amendment power did not give trustees the power to introduce a less restrictive amendment power in the 1981 Rules. In coming to this decision Arnold J relied on *UEB Industries Ltd v W S Brabant*[30] *(1992)* and *Air Jamaica Ltd v Charlton*[31] *(1999)*.

- The effect of the fetter in the 1977 Deed was to 'render ineffective the amendments made by the 1992 [Amendment] Deed in so far as they reduced the value of benefits, and in particular the future final salary benefits, which had accrued to members by virtue of their Service'. Arnold J interpreted the fetter as having that meaning by relying on a number of cases, including *Re Courage Group's Pension Schemes*[32] *(1987)* and *BHLSPF*[33] *(2001)*.

- 'An amendment to convert such benefits from a final salary entitlement to a money purchase entitlement is permissible, but only subject to an underpin which preserves the future monetary value of the proportion of Final Pensionable Pay which the member has accrued in respect of pre-amendment Service.'

- The 1992 Amendment Deed only converted the scheme from the date it was executed in March 1992, instead of the earlier January date. To backdate the deed to January was to treat some DB benefits as though they had always accrued on a DC basis (instead of accrued on a DB basis and then been converted into DC benefits) so was an unlawful 'attempt to re-write history'. This was also restricted by the 1977 Deed fetter.

---

30 *UEB Industries Ltd v W S Brabant* [1992] 1 NZLR 294.
31 *Air Jamaica Ltd v Charlton* [1999] 1 WLR 1399.
32 *Re Courage Group's Pension Schemes* [1987] 1 WLR 495.
33 *BHLSPF Pty Ltd v Brashs Pty Ltd* [2001] VSC 512.

14.9.4 *Benefit changes*

Member agreement?

14.9.4 Arnold J also rejected the employer's alternative argument that even if the conversion was unlawful under the trust deed and rules the employees had contractually agreed to changes outside the scheme. The employers relied on *South West Trains Ltd v Wightman*[34] (1997) in support of their argument. Arnold J held that:

- Unlike the ordinary position with commercial contracts, the position in this case is 'analogous to an allegation that a contract should be inferred from conduct, and accordingly the burden of proof of intent to create legal relations is upon the proponent of the contract [the employer]'.

- The employer could not prove that there was an intention to create contractual relations because the:

  - memorandum and application forms directed attention to the booklet for the full details of the proposals;

  - the presentation could not create contractual relations because it was not a comprehensive statement of the proposed changes. So the employees would still be left with the understanding that the booklet explained the proposed changes;

  - the memorandums and the booklet presented the changes as already having been made (instead of being presented as proposals);

  - the booklet stated that it was not comprehensive and was subject to the trust deed and rules; and

  - the application form was not comprehensive, for example it did not indicate that members were being asked to give up rights they were entitled to and were protected by the 1977 Deed fetter.

- The position was fundamentally different from *South West Trains* because in the present case the agreement was contrary to restrictions contained in the scheme's trust deed and rules. Furthermore, there had been no informed consent from the members that would preclude them from asserting a breach, because the members had been: unaware of the fetter in the 1977 Deed; they received no advice; the effects of the proposals were not 'clearly explained' to them; they were 'not given any real choice as to whether or not to consent'; and they 'received the impression that they would not be adversely affected by the changes'.

- Unlike the facts of the present case, *South West Trains* only involved making future pay rises non-pensionable.

---

34 *South West Trains Ltd v Wightman* [1997] OPLR 248; [1998] PLR 113.

For similar reasons to those mentioned above (eg no consent), Arnold J rejected a further alternative argument that that the employees had represented themselves as having accepted the changes (eg by signing the forms) and it would be unconscionable for them to act otherwise.

Compromise agreements

14.9.5   In December 2010, the Court of Appeal issued its full judgment[35] overturning Arnold J in relation to one of his findings: that in relation to compromise agreements. The Court of Appeal confirmed that *s 91* of the *Pensions Act 1995* (which limits the surrender and assignment of pension benefits) is not a bar to compromising *bona fide* disputes over pension rights.

Section 91 states that rights to a future pension are not permitted to be assigned, commuted or surrendered. In the High Court proceedings, Arnold J had interpreted *s 91* in such a way that any attempt to allow a member to give up their pensions entitlements would be invalid. As such, a compromise agreement between employers and employees that would affect these rights would accordingly be unenforceable.

However, the Court of Appeal, adopting a purposive approach, held that the where the compromise relates to a bona fide pensions dispute, its enforceability will not be restricted by *s 91*.

Comments

14.9.6   This case and the High Court judgment in *Walker Morris Trustees Ltd v Masterson*[36] *(2009)* and the Supreme Court of New South Wales's decision in *ING Funds Management v ANZ Nominees*[37] *(2009)* highlight the importance of carefully examining the effect of any restrictions in the amendment powers when making changes to benefits.

Where an employer is seeking to rely on member agreement (under the principle in *South West Trains*) to directly agree a change with employees outside the scheme, this case suggests that, among other things, it is prudent to provide comprehensive information about the proposed changes to members.

However, there are elements of Arnold J's decision which are difficult to reconcile with established legal principles. For example, it is unclear why a

---

35   *HR Trustees Ltd v German* [2010] EWCA Civ 1349, [2011] ICR 329.
36   *Walker Morris Trustees Ltd v Masterson* [2009] EWHC 1955 (Ch).
37   *ING Funds Management Ltd v ANZ Nominees Ltd* [2009] NSWSC 243.

14.9.6 *Benefit changes*

contract in these circumstances is not governed by the same rules as an ordinary commercial contract or why it is important for the members to be given a 'choice' before they can consent (see further comments in the later *BBC* case[38] – **14.11** below). Furthermore, it can be prudent to ensure that members receive advice to minimise the risk of claims for mis-selling but in this case the judge suggested that not obtaining advice could also vitiate consent.

Employers should take care with any compromise agreements with members. *Section 91* remains a difficult section. The Court of Appeal was helpful in overturning the judge so that it will not be an unlawful 'surrender' of a pensions right if there is a 'bona fide dispute as the existence of those rights at the time of the agreement'.

---

38   *Bradbury v BBC* [2012] EWHC 1369 (Ch) (Warren J) – see **14.11**.

14.10 Barber windows: Sex equalisation and changing retirement dates: *Foster Wheeler v Hanley*

Summary

In 2009 the Court of Appeal in *Foster Wheeler v Hanley* gave helpful guidance on how pension schemes should provide benefits for scheme members who have accrued benefits by reference to two separate normal retirement dates.

This section examines the implications of the case. There is also a checklist to help trustees and employers decide whether their scheme rules need to be amended in light of the Court of Appeal's decision.

The issue

14.10.1 Employers and trustees should now, if they have not already, be reviewing their pension scheme rules to agree what action should be taken in light of the Court of Appeal decision in *Foster Wheeler v Hanley*[39] in 2009.

The Court of Appeal decision provides welcome guidance to employers and trustees on how to provide benefits for scheme members who have accrued by reference to two separate normal retirement dates (NRD) – so-called 'mixed NRD members'. This is a common phenomenon in UK final salary schemes.

The concept of a mixed NRD member arises most frequently because of the European Court of Justice (ECJ) decision in *Barber v GRE*[40] (17 May 1990). Men and women's NRDs under scheme rules were typically 65 and 60 respectively before 17 May 1990. *Barber* held that EU sex equality law overrode the scheme rules so that men, in respect of pensionable service after 17 May 1990, accrued benefits on the more favourable basis of NRD 60 (like the women). Men therefore had benefits on two NRDs. Many schemes then altered their rules in the mid-1990s for future service, raising the NRD to 65 for men and women (closing the 'Barber window', as it is known).

In the *Foster Wheeler* pension scheme the Barber window was closed in August 1993. The mixed NRD member position can be summarised as shown below.

The issue (or conundrum) raised by the mixed NRD member is how trustees should deliver benefits where (i) a member has accrued benefits with two

---

39 *Foster Wheeler Ltd v Hanley* [2009] EWCA Civ 651.
40 *Barber v Guardian Royal Exchange Assurance Group* (C-262/88), [1990] ECR I-1889.

14.10.1 *Benefit changes*

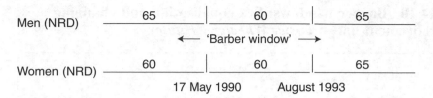

different NRDs; (ii) he or she chooses to retire before the later date; and (iii) there is no specific provision in the pension scheme to address this situation.

At first instance, Patten J was offered three possible solutions:

- *Option A*: payment in full of all benefits from age 60 with no reduction for early payments;

- *Option B*: the NRD 60 benefits and the NRD 65 benefits become payable at age 60 but with a reduction for those NRD 65 benefits being paid early; and

- *Option C*: payment of two separate (or split) pensions – ie the member takes his NRD 60 benefits at age 60 and the NRD 65 benefits at 65.

Mr Justice Patten, the High Court judge held in favour of Option A.

Patten J reasoned that as a matter of law a member must be entitled to his or her pension accrued on NRD 60 at age 60. This is correct. He then went on to reason that to deliver the NRD 65 benefits early with the NRD 60 benefits, it was necessary to look at the rule dealing with early retirement from active service (rule 8 of the Foster Wheeler pension scheme). That rule contained a company discretion to refuse early payment but Patten J held this had to be overridden by EU law for a mixed NRD member. The controversy in his reasoning (which led to the appeal) was that rule 8 did not provide for a cost-neutral reduction for early payment.

The early retirement rule (rule 8 of the Foster Wheeler pension scheme) provided that a benefit could be paid early with company consent after age 50 but, in respect of pensionable service before April 2003, the trustees' discretion to reduce for early receipt was limited to taking account of early receipt between commencement and age 60, not 65. This meant that when the rule was applied to mixed NRD members by the judge he held that if a member asked for his NRD 60 pension at 60 then he was entitled to his NRD 65 benefits as well but there could be no reduction for early receipt in respect of his pre-April 2003 service. This result was thought to increase liabilities in the Foster Wheeler scheme by at least £30 million.

In the past, the matter had not been an issue because of a surplus in the scheme. The company had recently ceased to consent to early payment of the NRD 65 benefits because of the non-cost-neutral reduction aspect. The employer and trustees had sought Court guidance on what to do under *Part 8* of the *Civil Procedure Rules* with representative beneficiaries.

The result

14.10.2   The Court of Appeal overturned the High Court decision for Option A. There was no appeal to the Supreme Court.

The Court of Appeal held that either Option B or C was acceptable but all three judges preferred Option B (ie payment as of right of the NRD 65 benefits early alongside the NRD 60 benefits when they became payable, but with a reduction for those NRD 65 benefits being paid earlier than 65). Arden LJ discussed Option C but said:

> 'The payment of a single pension in this case more closely tracks the rules of the pension scheme than a split pension. There has been no evidence as to the wishes of members or the trustees but, as I have explained, the fact that split pensions might be more convenient to trustees, or more financially attractive to members, is not a determinative consideration' (para 38).

How did the Court of Appeal reach its decision?

14.10.3   The Court of Appeal reached its decision by finding a rule to route the early payment of NRD 65 benefits. Arden LJ reasoned:

> 'In my judgment, the approach in *Bestrustees* represents in general the principled approach … the court should, where possible, give effect to *Barber* rights by adhering to the provisions of the relevant scheme where it is possible to do so in preference to some other approach. If some departure is required, it should in general, so far as practicable, represent the minimum interference with the scheme provisions. This approach is not limited to the situation where members have been led to believe that a provision will be used in a certain way or a stated aim of a provision has been only imperfectly achieved (as in *Bestrustees* itself). As the judge in this case recognised, it is a principle of more general application' (para 33).

The issue is then what constitutes minimum interference to the existing rules to deliver the NRD 65 benefit early? The Court of Appeal held that the High Court judge had gone wrong because he had interpreted minimum interference to mean simply finding a rule in the scheme that could be applied with the least modification to its wording. The Court of Appeal held that this was putting form over substance.

14.10.3   *Benefit changes*

The correct approach in determining what constitutes minimum interference requires ensuring that the solution is not *unfair* to the company and other members by delivering a *windfall* (ie if a member had accrued on the basis of NRD 65 he would not have a legitimate expectation of automatic right to early payment unreduced). Arden LJ said:

> 'By conferring a windfall on members with mixed NRDs, the judge's solution did not satisfy the principles which I have identified. It is unfair to the company and potentially unfair to other members of the scheme' (para 36).

The Court of Appeal preferred to route the early payment of the NRD 65 benefits through the deferred pensioners early payment rule (rule 17) rather than the early retirement rule (rule 8). Rule 17, unlike rule 8, allowed for full reduction (at the trustee's discretion) before age 65. Although rule 17, like rule 8, required company consent the Court of Appeal held this was overridden by EU law for a mixed NRD member's NRD 65 benefits where the NRD 60 pension had become payable. Rule 17 did not provide an automatic reduction for early receipt but instead had a trustee discretion. Lloyd LJ did not see this as an issue for the following reasons:

> 'Mr Simmonds QC for the trustees made the point that rule 17(5)(a) does not require an actuarial reduction, but rather permits one at the discretion of the trustees. He submitted that, from the trustees' point of view, it would be preferable, in one sense at least, if the modified scheme did not leave such a discretion to the trustees, but rather made it either mandatory or something which the company could require if it wished. In practice *it seems highly likely that, if the fund is actuarially insufficient* (*as most final salary schemes are at present*), *the trustees would not, and indeed could not properly, fail to require a reduction to the extent advised by the actuary, since otherwise the member in question would be getting better treatment than he or she is entitled to expect, and would be doing so at the expense of other members*, unless the company were prepared to fund the added benefit. However, if the trustees prefer not to have a discretion in the matter, in the modified scheme, then it may be fair for the modification to eliminate this element as well' (para 67).

This is an important point. The Court was directing the trustees not to use a discretion to create additional cost to a scheme in deficit.

The Court's comments that providing windfall benefits to mixed NRD members in excess of their *Barber* rights 'is unfair to the company and potentially unfair to other members' suggests that courts construing scheme rules and trustees exercising their powers in the future should consider the interests of the employer as well as those of scheme members. This is a clear move away from the notion that trustees should be mainly concerned with looking after the interests of the scheme members and should ignore the interests of employers, unless this potentially has an adverse effect on members.

Does a pension scheme need amending following this decision?

14.10.4 It is clear from Lloyd LJ's judgment that although EU law could override a scheme's rules to deliver the right result it is preferable now to amend the rules to spell out the position so the trustees, employers and members are clear on what should happen. Lloyd LJ directed Foster Wheeler and the trustees to amend their rules as follows:

> '... to fulfil the obligation of equalisation imposed on them by European law, the parties (*principally the trustees*) *need to formulate amendments to the scheme which provide properly for delivery of the mixed NRD rights which resulted from the Barber decision* and from the upward equalisation in 1993. That equalisation does not have to allow male members with mixed NRDs to take a pension in respect of their NRD 65 service before the age of 65 without a reduction for early payment. The task of devising the appropriate modifications to the scheme is one in the course of which a number of choices will need to be made, as regards the best and most sensible and practical way of achieving the necessary equalisation. The guiding approach should be that of making the least substantive alteration to the provisions of the scheme that is compatible with the required equalisation. Apart from that principle, the parties must exercise their judgment in choosing between different options in terms of how to equalise and what incidental provisions to adopt. Of the particular provisions which have been debated before us, it seems to me that rule 17(5)(a) provides a better means towards the provision of equalised benefits than rule 8(1) does, but *I would regard it as proper for the trustees, if they wish, to subject the modified rule to a requirement of reduction for early payment if so advised by the actuary, or (if the company prefers) a provision whereby such a reduction is to be imposed if the company requires it to be, rather than leaving it to their own discretion as the rule does as it stands*'(paras 75 and 76).

What should employers do?

14.10.5 Employers should consider the following.

- Does the pension scheme have mixed NRD members?

14.10.5 *Benefit changes*

- Do the rules provide clearly for how the NRD 60 and NRD 65 benefits should be paid? What if the rules confer prospective service (eg for incapacity) or have non-uniform accrual?

- If the answer to the above bullet is 'no', which rule can be relied on (if any) with *minimum interference* to deliver the benefits? What is *minimum interference* in the rules? What if there is no obvious rule to be modified?

- Should the NRD 65 benefit be paid early with reduction or should there be split pensions (ie payment of the NRD 60 and 65 benefits at different times)?

- Discuss with the trustees what amendments should be made.

- What is the position if mixed NRDs arise as a result of raising retirement ages recently rather than as a result of *Barber* sex-equalisation? Can the *Foster Wheeler* decision apply to assist in that context? What issues arise if it cannot?

- If members have been receiving unreduced pensions (Option A) because that was what was thought to be required under law, is there any scope now to reduce those pensions for future service (eg relying on the law of mistake)?

14.11 Non-pensionable pay rises upheld: Bradbury

Bradbury v British Broadcasting Corporation [2012] EWHC 1369 (Ch), Warren J

Summary

This section looks at Mr Justice Warren's decision in *Bradbury v BBC* to uphold the effectiveness of both express and implied agreements between the employer (BBC) and a member (Mr Bradbury) that part of Mr Bradbury's future pay would not be pensionable under the BBC pension scheme.

This section looks at the implications this could have for employers and trustees.

Introduction

14.11.1 Employers have become concerned about funding costs for defined benefit (DB) pension arrangements.

One way to reduce costs is to reduce the element of pay that is treated as pensionable for DB purposes. This can reduce the accrued funding estimate immediately (most funding is based on an assumption of pensionable pay continuing to rise). It can be a less drastic solution than completely closing a defined benefit scheme to future accrual. So:

- can the employer and the employee agree that future pay will not be pensionable in the future? and

- what happens if there is not an express agreement by the employee but instead pay rises are offered by the employer on the express basis that the pay rise will not be pensionable?

14.11.2 Generally the courts have found in favour of these arrangements being effective – the *South West Trains* case[41] and the *NUS* case.[42] See *Pensionable*

---

41 *South West Trains v Wightman* [1997] OPLR 249; [1997] PLR 113 (Neuberger J).
42 *Trustees of the NUS Officials and Employees Superannuation Fund v Pension Ombudsman* [2002] OPLR 17 (Lightman J).

14.11.2 *Benefit changes*

and non-Pensionable remuneration, **14.3** above. But the later *IMG* case[43] could cast doubts on this approach (although the decision in that case was based primarily on the lack of express clear agreement with the member) – see **14.9**.

14.11.3 Mr Justice Warren has now upheld the effectiveness of both an express agreement for an element of future pay not to be pensionable and an implied agreement (by way of a non-pensionable pay rise) in his decision in *Bradbury v British Broadcasting Corporation.*

Facts

14.11.4 In this case Mr Bradbury, a musician with the BBC philharmonic orchestra, complained about a BBC decision to offer a non-pensionable pay rise. This followed consultations with trade unions and members (and the trustee during 2010).[44] DB members were offered three options:

- pay rises with the DB pensionable pay element limited to 1%;[45]

- to join a career average (CARE) section that was not subject to the 1% cap; or

- to opt out of DB altogether and join a defined contribution arrangement.

Mr Bradbury chose the career average section, but later brought a complaint to the Pensions Ombudsman that there had been a change in the definition of pensionable salary without consulting the trustees, which had adversely affected his rights under the scheme.

In October 2011, the Pensions Ombudsman found against Mr Bradbury and he appealed to the High Court.

Warren J rejects Mr Bradbury's claim

14.11.5 Mr Justice Warren rejected Mr Bradbury's claim in his judgment of 23 May 2012.

Mr Bradbury had raised, on appeal, various arguments about why the BBC's conduct in imposing the 1% cap on DB pension increases could be challenged. These were:

---

43 *Re IMG Pension Plan: HR Trustees Ltd v German* [2009] EWHC 2785 (Arnold J).

44 Since April 2010, a proposal to limit the amount of pay that forms part of pensionable earnings has been a 'listed change' usually requiring prior consultation with employees under the *Pensions Act 2004*.

45 Presumably (although this is not stated in the judgment) this was the default option if the member did not respond or did not choose the other options.

- that imposing the cap was contrary to the trust deed and rules of the scheme;

- that imposing the cap was, even if the employee agreed, contrary to no assignment or surrender provisions in the *Pensions Act 1995* (*section 91*);

- that it was a breach of the implied duty of trust and confidence or the implied duty of good faith in the contract of employment; and

- that imposing the cap amounted to maladministration for the purposes of the *Pension Schemes Act 1993*.

14.11.6 Warren J rejected all Mr Bradbury's claims, but his judgment requires careful reading. He clearly held that:

- non-pensionable pay rises can be given; and

- this can be achieved by express agreement with the employee or by offering a pay rise on the express basis that it is non-pensionable.

14.11.7 But Warren J also gave a wide meaning to the protective provisions in *section 91* of the *Pensions Act 1995*, which could cause problems in future cases.

14.11.8 He did not decide the question of whether the employer could be in breach of the implied duty of trust and confidence (as this had not been raised before the Pensions Ombudsman). But conversely, he cast no doubt on the decision in 2011 in the *Prudential Staff Pensions* case[46] that employers can consider their own interests and that showing a breach of the implied term is a severe test.

Warren J refused to make a finding on the implied duty of trust and confidence on the basis this had not been argued by Mr Bradbury before the Pensions Ombudsman (this leaves Mr Bradbury free to bring another claim should he want to).

Following the High Court decision, Mr Bradbury brought a further claim against the BBC before the Pensions Ombudsman for breach of the implied duty of trust and confidence. In December 2013, the PO ruled against this further complaint. He concluded that, in light of the scheme deficit, its potential future liability, its resources and overall obligations, the steps taken by the BBC in seeking to impose the cap did not breach the implied 'Imperial' duties (*Bradbury* PO-636, 23 December 2013).

---

46 *Prudential Staff Pensions Ltd v The Prudential Assurance Co Ltd* [2011] EWHC (Ch) (Newey J).

14.11.9 *Benefit changes*

Was the BBC acting contrary to the trust deed and rules of the scheme?

14.11.9 The rules of the scheme provided that all 'basic salary' counted as pensionable. The scheme had been amended in 2006 so that 'basic salary' was the amount 'determined by the BBC'. The BBC had argued that this meant it could determine that an element of pay is not in fact basic salary.

Warren J rejected this and said that clear words would be needed in a provision that achieved such a result. He thought that such a provision would only be sensible if it only applied in cases of doubt – paragraph [44]. If it was to apply generally to give a wide discretion then clear words would be needed – paragraph [64].

Such a clause would also be subject to a concern that it could in effect be exercised retrospectively (so that basic pay in one year could be recategorised as not basic pay in a later year). Very clear words would be needed for this, particularly given the terms of the BBC scheme's amendment power as used to make the amendment in 2006 – paragraphs [65] to [67].

14.11.10 On the main point, Warren J considered that a contract between an employer and a member would be effective to accept a pay rise on the basis that any part of it is pensionable. This would apply even if there was no such provision in the trust deed and rules – paragraph [63].

Warren J thought that the comments of Arnold J in the *IMG* case were dealing with a very different situation, in which it was not clear when the individual members had in fact consented to the changes – paragraph [59].

Is the agreement to limit pay rises contrary to section 91 of the Pensions Act 1995?

14.11.11 *Section 91* invalidates surrenders or assignments of pension rights, save in limited circumstances. Unlike the limits on amendments in *section 67*, it is not limited to tax registered schemes, nor does it have a general exception for changes agreed with the member.

Warren J considered previous authorities on *section 91* and noted that it is a wide section providing that an entitlement or 'right to a future pension' cannot be assigned, committed or surrendered etc.

Having considered the cases, Warren J considered that the rights covered by *section 91* do not mean just past service 'accrued' rights at the date of the change or agreement, but instead cover future service benefits as well – paragraph [76].

14.11.12 Having said that, Warren J considered that agreeing to a reduced rate of future salary increase was not surrendering a right. Warren J considered – paragraph [84] – that: 'his right to a future pension based on the full amount of an anticipated pay rise was no right at all; and by agreeing to a pay increase only part of which would be treated as pensionable, he did not alienate anything to which he was even prospectively entitled'.

14.11.13 Warren J agreed with the BBC's submission – paragraph [85] – that: '... members have no right to a salary increase. Accepting a salary increase on terms that part only is pensionable does not, he submits, involve a surrender of anything; the member becomes entitled to a greater future pension, albeit one that is smaller than if the whole increase were pensionable. I agree.'

14.11.14 This is clearly helpful for future pay rises. However, Warren J's statement that future service benefits are also protected by *section 91* looks quite dangerous. Would, for example, members be able to agree to opt out of a pension scheme? Why does that not amount to a surrender of benefits and so be caught by *section 91*?

14.11.15 In a subsidiary argument, the BBC also argued that the purpose of the agreement was to allow a member to accrue benefits in another section of the scheme. This, the BBC argued, meant that an exception to *section 91* would apply – where the agreement was for a surrender 'for the purpose of' acquiring for the member 'entitlement to further benefits under the scheme' – *section 91(5)(b)*. However, Warren J considered that in this case the purpose of the surrender would not be the acquisition of further benefits under the scheme; instead the 'real purpose' was to achieve a larger than 1% pay rise – paragraphs [86] and [87].

14.11.16 In practice, in Mr Bradbury's case he had rejected the offer of a limited pay rise and instead chosen to join the CARE section. But Warren J held that even if he had accepted the reduced pay rise offer, it would be binding and not contrary to *section 91*.

Was the conduct contrary to the implied duty of trust and confidence?

14.11.17 Warren J briefly considered the leading cases on the implied duty of trust and confidence in a pensions context: *Imperial Tobacco*[47] and the recent *Prudential Staff Pensions* case. He commented that: 'It is important to note, however, that the Implied Duties are not fiduciary duties. Nor are they duties whose scope is to be assessed by reference to concepts of reasonableness, for

---

47   [1991] 1 WLR 589 (Browne-Wilkinson V-C).

14.11.17 *Benefit changes*

what seems reasonable to an employer may seem unreasonable to an employee and vice versa. Instead, an employer must not exercise its powers under a pension scheme so as seriously to damage the relationship of confidence between the employer and the employees and ex-employees; in other words there is a duty not to undermine the relationship of trust and confidence which exists between an employer and the members of a pension scheme similar to the duties arising in employment law between an employer and his employees. Indeed, the whole concept of the Implied Duties was borrowed from the concepts of employment law.'

He considered that working out whether the BBC had acted in accordance with the relevant implied duties would involve a detailed factual analysis of how the BBC had reached its decision.

14.11.18 Warren J noted that the relevant principles 'although easy to state' are 'sometimes very difficult to apply in practice to the facts of a particular case' – paragraph [91]. And: '... although the Vice-Chancellor in *Imperial Tobacco* went on to give some practical guidance about how the principles would work out on the ground, I do not think I am alone in finding some of the examples he gave as hard to fit within the principles.' – paragraph [91].

These issues had not been raised before the Pensions Ombudsman and Warren J therefore decided it would be wrong for him to deal with the issue only for the first time on appeal without the employer having been given the opportunity to bring evidence.

14.11.19 Warren J also commented that the position in *Prudential* shows that the scope for challenge of an employer's decision is not as wide as one reading of *Imperial Tobacco* might suggest. He repeated the comment that the circumstances in which a decision could be said to be irrational or perverse are severely limited – see paragraph [103].

Warren J commented that many employers have simply closed their schemes to any future accrual on a defined benefit basis and that 'it would be entirely unsurprising to find that the evidence gave considerable support' to submissions that this was not irrational or perverse – see paragraph [104].

Was the action maladministration within the Pension Schemes Act 1993?

14.11.20 The Pensions Ombudsman has power to make a determination if he finds a case of maladministration causing injustice. Warren J considered this point did not arise at all.

If Mr Bradbury is unsuccessful on the implied duties argument it was not easy to see how he could succeed on a maladministration argument. Conversely, if he had succeeded on breach of the implied duty then it would be a logical consequence that he would also show maladministration.

Comment

Implied consent

14.11.21 This is a helpful decision. It is clear that the binding nature of offers of non-pensionable pay rises has again been upheld (as outlined in sections **14.3** and **14.4** above). Perhaps surprisingly there was no reference to the 1937 House of Lords decision in *Tibbals*,[48] which had the effect of supporting the *NUS* decision on non-pensionable pay rises. Perhaps the parties considered that the *NUS* case was enough?

The decision helps in pointing out the difficulties with obiter comments on Arnold J in the *IMG* case (echoing our concerns set out in **14.9** above).

Trust and confidence

14.11.22 Mr Bradbury had another go based on trust and confidence arguments, but these are always difficult to win (and in December 2013 he lost before the Pensions Ombudsman – see **14.11.8** above). It is clear that employers can act in their own interests. As pointed out in **14.4** above (Avoiding pitfalls in non-pensionable pay):

> 'Have good reasons for the decision (and document them)
>
> Employers should not propose changes over pensionable pay without good reason. They owe an implied contractual duty of mutual trust and confidence to their employees. This means that they owe a duty of good faith (ie broadly a duty not to act in a way that is arbitrary or capricious or in which no reasonable employer would act).
>
> This does not mean that an employer cannot act in its own interests but it will need to consider carefully the impact of the proposed changes and aim to be able to defend them as proportionate and reasonable. Documentation showing it has acted for valid commercial reasons and considered all available options will be helpful. Employers should also avoid giving a blanket refusal to offer future pay rises.'

It may be particularly difficult for a trust and confidence argument to succeed when, as here, there seems to have been consultation with the members, trade unions and trustee – see paragraph [6] of the judgment.

---

48 *Tibbals v Port of London Authority* [1937] 2 All ER 413 (House of Lords).

14.11.23   *Benefit changes*

Section 91 of the Pensions Act 1995

14.11.23   Again this is a helpful decision in the narrow sense that benefits deriving from future pay rises are not within the protections in *section 91* (a section that seems to invalidate even express employee agreements).

However, Warren J's more general findings on *section 91* are more of a concern. He held that:

- an extended meaning should be given to *section 91* so that it covers future service benefits generally (but not pay rises); and

- a restricted meaning should be given to the exclusion in *section 91* for an agreement 'for the purpose of providing other benefits'.

Section 91 is proving a difficult section. It is clear that Parliament intended some protections to be given to benefits so that they could not be assigned or surrendered, but extending this to cover all future service benefits (ie those not yet earned in any sense) seems very strange. *Section 91* looks likely to lead to even more litigation.

14.12   Commutation and member options: trustee duties and the role of the actuary

Summary

Pension schemes often include options for members – in particular for commutation of part of the pension to a (tax free) lump sum on retirement.

This section considers trustee duties and the role of the actuary in this area, and the factors they each need to consider in order to make reasonable decisions that will withstand scrutiny from members.

Employers and Trustees should consider reminding members that they need to consider the implications of their decisions carefully (and consider if they should take financial advice).

Introduction

14.12.1 The 2012 Pensions Ombudsman determination in *Squibbs* (discussed in an annex to this section) has illustrated the pitfalls for trustees involved in setting actuarial factors in respect of member options such as:

- cash commutation;

- pension restructuring (eg an enhanced bridging pension or surrender of member pension for an enhanced spouse pension);

- exchange of a member's deferred pension and other attaching benefits for a transfer value to another scheme (in most cases, members with more than a year to normal retirement age have a legal right to a transfer value); and

- in-scheme purchase of pension using member additional voluntary contributions (AVCs).[49]

Cash commutation – an option to exchange accrued pension payable from retirement for an immediate (tax free) cash lump sum – is a common feature of

---

49 Cash commutation factors and factors applied to the conversion of AVCs into pension were also considered in the *Prudential* case on the '*Imperial*' duty – the implied duty of trust and confidence: *Prudential Staff Pensions Limited v The Prudential Assurance Company Limited* [2011] EWHC 960 (Ch).

14.12.1 *Benefit changes*

many occupational pension schemes. It is perhaps less common to see other options such as an opportunity to 'shape' pension, for example by providing a bridging pension up to State pension age in return for a reduced pension thereafter.

Member decision

14.12.2 In both of these cases, members face a financial decision. The right questions for them to ask themselves are:

- Should I take an up-front lump sum or increase in my benefits now?

- Or should I look more long-term and hope to gain better value from regular pension payments in the future?

The answers to these questions are likely to depend on an individual's personal circumstances and would be best talked through with an independent financial adviser.

14.12.3 Members need to make their own decisions on this at the relevant time (here retirement). They may later come to the view that, in retrospect, they made the wrong choice. When members choose an option which eventually results in a negative outcome, it is perhaps inevitable that some will look to blame or at least question:

- the information provided, or alternatively;

- the party (the trustees, employer or actuary) involved in setting (or advising on) the relevant actuarial factors.

It is important in such cases for the employer and trustees to feel comfortable that the option has been properly exercised.

This section considers trustee duties and the role of the actuary in this area, and the factors they each need to consider in order to make reasonable decisions that will withstand scrutiny from members. As the most common, this section focuses principally on cash commutation by members at retirement.

Incentive Exercises for Pensions: Code of Good Practice (*June 2012*)

14.12.4 The Code of Good Practice for Incentive Exercises was published in June 2012 (www.incentiveexercises.org.uk).

It provides voluntary objectives for employers, trustees and others to follow to help ensure that members make informed decisions about Incentive Exercises that seek to change the form of a member's accrued defined benefit rights in UK registered pension schemes.

The Code is clear that it does <u>not</u> apply to:

> 'Member options ordinarily available on certain events, such as retirement or leaver processes, including early retirement and options to commute pension for a tax-free lump sum.'[50]

However the Code does go on to say:

> 'However, employers, trustees and advisers should be mindful of the principles of the Code and seek to ensure that changes to benefit options offered by the scheme will maintain suitable protection of members' interests. In some cases it may be appropriate to apply some aspects of the Code to exercises that fall outside the scope of the Code. For example changes to defined benefits for current employees such as introducing restrictions on pensionable pay may impact accrued rights over time. Employers, trustees and advisers are encouraged to consider the extent to which it would be appropriate and helpful to members to apply some or all of the Code in such situations.'

Reasonableness

14.12.5 In the context of member options such as cash commutation, it is difficult to advise on how the reasonableness (or at least absence of unreasonableness) of the relevant factors should be determined. This is because (somewhat surprisingly) there is no clear guidance or case law on the issues to be taken into account.

What is clear is that fixed rates or rates based on (say) 9 to 1 commutation are seen increasingly as being inconsistent with annuity rates[51] and commutation or capitalisation rates in other areas (eg for the lifetime allowance (20 to 1), annual allowance (16 to 1), commutation of money purchase assets to pension etc). Although note that some rates deal with the whole pension (eg including spouse), while others only deal with the member pension.

---

50 Supporting Information section.
51 See the article in Investors Chronicle: 'Up to 3.6m retirees in line for "rip off" lump sums', available at http://www.investorschronicle.co.uk/2013/05/28/your-money/pensions-and-sipps/retirement-income/up-to-m-retirees-in-line-for-rip-off-lump-sums-8H6NveJcVyPZ21 ZJW5PdSK/article.html.

14.12.6 *Benefit changes*

What do the trust deed and rules say?

14.12.6 This is the first question that needs to be asked.

A fairly common sort of commutation provision might provide:

> 'The trustees shall convert pension into lump sum at a rate determined by the trustees and confirmed by the actuary to be reasonable.'

Usually the commutation reduces the member's pension only (any spouse or dependant pension payable after the member's death usually remains unaffected by the commutation).

The reference to the actuary's involvement is a clear indication that the starting point for determining commutation factors should be the actuarial value of the pension being commuted (although this would likely be implicit in any event). In this type of provision there is no requirement for employer consent (but in some schemes consultation may be necessary and increasingly the issue is likely to fall for discussion in any event in connection with funding, since commutation terms less favourable to the member can represent a saving to the scheme).

The valuation basis is not specified and the trustees are likely to wish to consult the actuary from the outset. A reasonable basis may perhaps be the scheme specific funding basis, but perhaps after removing the margins for prudence required in calculating the technical provisions (but this is untested).

What are the general principles on trustees exercising discretion?

14.12.7 A trustee discretion or power must be exercised in a fiduciary manner. This means that it must be exercised:

- for a proper purpose (with respect to pension schemes, usually described as being in the best interests of the scheme – but see further below); and

- having taken advice where appropriate and considered all relevant factors (and ignored irrelevant ones). Note that in light of the 2013 Supreme Court decision in the jointly heard cases of *Futter v HMRC* and *Pitt v HMRC*[52] the scope of this duty (or ground of challenge) is more limited than previously thought.

---

52 [2013] UKSC 26.

These are in practice two sides of the same coin – ie to exercise a power for a proper purpose, it is necessary to consider all relevant factors and ignore irrelevant ones.

Where trustees have a discretion, usually a fairly wide margin of appreciation is given by the courts.[53] Subject to the points above, the Courts or Pensions Ombudsman will often only intervene if it can be shown that the trustees acted in a way that no reasonable trustee would act.[54] In the context of commutation or transfer, more recent judgments have emphasised that in some cases an approach for no more than 'a share of fund' is required.[55]

Proper purpose

14.12.8 Acting in the best interests of the scheme does not necessarily mean that trustees must use their powers to maximise payments to some/all members. As a general principle, pension scheme trustees are obliged to act impartially:

- in a manner that they believe to be fair and equitable, having regard to the different classes of beneficiary and to the interest and expectation of the employer; and

- between individuals within the different classes of beneficiary.

This involves maintaining:

> 'a balance between assets and liabilities … so that, as far as can be foreseen, they will be in a position to provide pensions and other benefits in accordance with the rules throughout the life of the scheme.'[56]

14.12.9 Case law indicates that the courts will require trustees to take account of a pension scheme's funding position when exercising administrative powers such as powers to buy-out benefits and effect transfers:

- In *Stannard v Fisons Pension Trust Ltd*[57] the court held that the trustees' determination of an amount to be transferred out of the relevant pension scheme following the sale of Fisons' fertilizer division was flawed

---

53 Eg *Wrightson Ltd v Fletcher Challenge Nominees Ltd* [2001] UKPC 23 (a case looking at a bulk transfer value).

54 Eg *Harris v Lord Shuttleworth* [1994] ICR 991 (a case looking at a discretion on an ill health pension). In the *Squibbs* case (78488/2), 7 September 2012 (King PO), the Ombudsman emphasised that the test for unreasonableness is a high one. Similarly the deputy PO in *Baker* (PO-281) in November 2013.

55 *Independent Trustee Services Ltd v Hope* [2009] EWHC 2810 (Ch) (a case on bulk transfers out of a scheme about to wind up); *Dalriada Trustees Ltd v Faulds* [2011] EWHC 3391 (Ch).

56 *Edge v Pensions Ombudsman* [2000] Ch 602.

57 [1992] IRLR 27, Court of Appeal.

14.12.9 *Benefit changes*

because the trustees had not considered the current (increased) value of the pension fund at the transfer date and its implications in determining the amount that it would be just and equitable to appropriate in respect of the transferring members.

The trustees' duty to give properly informed consideration to the funding position was owed to the transferring members and the remaining members alike since they had both contributed to the fund. Moreover, it was the duty of the actuaries to put the trustees in a position to make a properly informed decision – by giving them information on the relevance of the value of the pension scheme to the problem in hand in relation to actuarial principles, and the implications of their decision on future contributions.

- In *ITS v Hope*[58] the scheme was in deficit and the court considered a proposal to use a buy-out power to purchase annuities which would maximise certain members' benefits in anticipation of entry into the Pension Protection Fund (PPF). It was held that there was a limitation, implicit in the relevant scheme rules, that the amount which may properly be applied in purchasing annuities would be no more than a fair share of scheme assets, considered in the light of actuarial advice.[59]

Relevant and irrelevant factors

14.12.10 There is relatively little guidance in the case law on how to determine whether a particular consideration should be taken into account by a trustee or not. In a leading text book[60] on the law of trusts, the question is said to be 'largely a matter of impression and common sense'. Some trustees (and their advisers) take a restrictive view of the limits on their discretions and consider that they must be exercised in the best interests of the members only (ie ignoring the interest of the sponsoring employer unless that impacts on the interests of the members).

In general this is too narrow a perspective and trustees should also consider a sponsoring employer in its role as the funder of the scheme. A strong corporate sponsor tends to be in the interests of the scheme, because the security of the scheme (and whether it will continue to pay benefits) will depend greatly on the continued strength of the employer that is obliged to fund the scheme. It will not usually be in the interest of the scheme to drive the employer into insolvency – this is supported by statements made by the Pensions Regulator in its funding guidance.

---

58 [2009] EWHC 2810 (Ch).
59 *Ibid.* Henderson J at paragraphs [96] and [99].
60 Underhill and Hayton, 'Law Relating to Trusts and Trustees' (17th edition), para 61.19, cited in submissions made by Mr Nigel Giffin QC on behalf of the PPF in *ITS v Hope*.

Can the tax impact be a factor?

14.12.11   Where the pension scheme is registered under the *Finance Act 2004*, pensions paid are usually subject to income tax. A cash lump sum paid on retirement is usually not taxable (subject to the lifetime allowance) if it is within the relevant limit laid down by HMRC (usually no more than 25% of the fund).

Is it proper for the trustees or actuary to take the tax effect into account when agreeing a commutation rate? In other words, to reflect that a lump sum is tax free, whereas a pension is taxable? This is untested, but it seems reasonable that the trustees should consider all the circumstances and that the tax implications are relevant.

What is the actuary's role?

14.12.12   Going back to the example rule above, the actuary is not required to determine the commutation factors; this power resides with the trustees. However, the actuary must confirm that the factors are 'reasonable'. Guidance does not tend to be given in the trust deed and rules as to how 'reasonable' should be construed, but the actuary is likely to have regard to all his knowledge and experience and usual professional standards.

The actuary's role is an important one, and may render him 'concerned with the administration of the scheme' and thus a 'scheme administrator' for the purposes of bringing a complaint of maladministration before the Pensions Ombudsman.[61]

However, as a general principle it is difficult to challenge an actuary's decision, unless it is demonstrably not one that a competent actuary could have reached, or there is evidence of a mistake or improper motive: *Re Imperial Foods Ltd's Pension Scheme*.[62] In that case, Walton J also accepted the principle spelt out by Buckley J in *Re George Newnes Group Pension Fund*[63] that:

> 'the function of an actuary in any situation which is not governed precisely by the provisions of the trust deed is to achieve the greatest possible degree of fairness between the various persons interested under the scheme.'

Whilst the starting point should typically be the actuarial value of the pension being commuted, in our view it is not inappropriate for both the trustees and the

---

61   *Government Actuaries Department v Pensions Ombudsman* [2012] EWHC 1796 (Admin).
62   [1986] 2 All ER 802 (Walton J).
63   (1969) 98 J Inst of Actuaries 251.

14.12.12 *Benefit changes*

actuary to take account of factors which are not purely 'actuarial' in nature, such as scheme funding.

Pensions Board of the Actuarial Profession: Member Options Working Party Report (2006)

14.12.13 The report of the Member Options Working Party of the Institute of Actuaries[64] was issued in December 2006. In relation to cash commutation, it notes that:

- most scheme members elect to commute pension for a cash sum at retirement. This is likely to be partly because the lump sum is tax-free, but also owing to an assumption that the financial terms relate closely to the cost of replacing the benefit foregone. However, for many schemes this is not likely to be the case in practice;

- in recent years the cost of pension benefits has increased materially, as evidenced by the costs of purchasing annuities on the open market. For many schemes, the terms for cash commutation have generally not increased by the same proportion, if at all;

- a comparison between HMRC's standard 'capitalisation' factor of 20 to compare the value of a member's benefits with the lifetime allowance and the not uncommon cash commutation multiple of 9 is stark (and remains so, even after adjustment is made for the assumed attaching dependant's benefit included in the HMRC factor);

- the advent of the PPF makes pensions more secure. Accordingly, members may now be giving up a more valuable right compared to the situation before the PPF; and

- some schemes limit the amount of AVCs that may be taken as cash on retirement by reference to the amount of main scheme pension taken as cash. In many such schemes, the terms for purchasing annuities with AVCs will be inconsistent with the terms for surrendering pension from the scheme.

The 2006 Actuary Report includes a statement on the legal issues and indicates the view that 'it is appropriate that the financial terms for member options take account of other factors than actuarial equivalence' (such as scheme funding).

14.12.14 The 2006 Actuary Report also sets out a useful summary of some of the financial issues that are relevant to valuing member options, as follows:

---

64 http://www.actuaries.org.uk/research-and-resources/documents/member-options-working-party-report.

722

Extract from the 2006 Actuary Report

'3.2 Financial issues

Financial issues that are relevant to valuing member options include the following.

(a) Discounting payments. There are different views amongst UK actuaries on how to place a value on pension scheme liabilities. These can be summarised as follows:

- discount expected payments at the expected rate of return on scheme assets, or

- discount payments at market rates (with or without allowance for credit risk).

In practice, many actuaries adopt pragmatic approaches that fall between these two philosophies.

(b) Expected frequency of exercise. Some options are exercised only rarely, eg the option to surrender pension in return for higher contingent dependants' pensions. This may be relied on in setting terms on the basis that the risks of setting terms on too generous a basis will still be immaterial in the context of the scheme as a whole. Equally, some options are widely expected to be exercised, eg commuting pension for cash sum at retirement. This may be relied on in financing the scheme – some actuarial funding valuations assume that pension will be commuted for cash at rates that are less favourable than are otherwise implied by the actuarial funding basis.

(c) Risk of adverse selection. If a scheme provides terms that are inconsistent internally or inconsistent with market terms then there is a risk that members will select against the scheme by choosing the option most favourable to them but which is consequently least favourable to the financial position of the scheme. The risk of adverse selection also exists in relation to member life expectancy if the benefit is not underwritten.

(d) Rating factors. Allowing for some of the factors that are potentially relevant for valuation such as the member's sex, the size of the pension or marital status is potentially controversial. For instance, providing higher commutation factors to members with larger pensions could result in the accusation of favouring the better paid, even though experience suggests that individuals with higher pensions live longer and therefore the pension surrendered has a higher value.

(e) Administration expenses. Providing pension benefits entails expenses. Given the general focus on scheme funding, actuaries have tended not to consider the allocation of expenses to different member benefits. Doing so could prove controversial as small benefits are not much, if at all, cheaper to administer compared with large benefits.

14.12.14 *Benefit changes*

Extract from the 2006 Actuary Report

(f) Tax effects. The favourable tax treatment of cash commutation means that members are incentivised to take the cash sum even though the terms are not cost neutral when seen from the scheme's point of view.

(g) The sponsor covenant and the PPF. It is currently unusual to take explicit account of the strength of the sponsor covenant or the existence of the PPF in setting terms for member options (other than in the case of a scheme in winding up – see appendix D). These are, however, potentially material factors in valuing a member's benefit.

(h) Asymmetry in changing terms. Changing the terms for a member option will tend to meet resistance when the members perceive that the terms are being worsened. This tends to be more an issue where the options are reviewed infrequently and not linked explicitly and objectively to market conditions. This asymmetry means that trustee and sponsors may hold back from making changes that may only be temporary to avoid the potential pain of having to reverse them.

Examples are

- low long-dated interest rates – the concern is that there is a material risk that these are a short term phenomenon, and longevity – instead of adopting the latest expectations (as would be the case in market annuity rates), the tendency is to require substantial evidence of improvement before allowing for it in member options (where this works against the scheme).'

14.12.15 Additional issues to consider (some of which were touched upon in the 2006 Actuary Report) might be as follows, but the extent to which weight can safely be placed on them (and the financial issues listed above) is untested:

- the fact that it is up to members to decide whether or not to take a cash lump sum (but members may not be relied upon to make a reasoned decision without independent financial advice);

- any funding deficit in the scheme – as actuarial equivalence depends on the discount rate, that links in with funding, as does a need to consider the impact on other members;

- whether the trustee's current investment strategy is resulting in a more valuable benefit and whether that is justified;

- a desire for consistency; and

- the argument that members should share with the sponsoring employer some of the increased cost arising from economic and demographic changes.

The trustees and actuary will each need to feel comfortable that the weight accorded by them to all or any of these factors is appropriate.

History

14.12.16 In the absence of clear guidance on the factors to be taken into account in determining the 'reasonableness' of commutation rates, it may be necessary to consider how those rates have historically been determined.

Just because there has not been a history of taking into account a certain factor, this does not necessarily mean that it would be unreasonable to take it into account now.

If the trustees and the actuary wish to take particular matters into account when certifying the reasonableness of the commutation factors applicable in respect of the scheme, it would be helpful clearly to set out that this had been done and also the reasons for it.

This would assist if the issue ever came to court (or before the Pensions Ombudsman) as it would illustrate that the matter had been carefully considered and give weight to the argument that the trustees (and the actuary) had acted reasonably.

What are other schemes doing?

14.12.17 The Member Options Working Party Report from 2006 provided some indication of what schemes were doing in this area, but a recent (2013) update[65] shows that practice has moved on since 2006.

If a practice was noticeable of schemes taking account of certain factors such as funding, this may be helpful in assessing the reasonableness test.

The PPF currently operates using factors of 17.43 for pension relating to pre-1997 service and 24.14 for pension relating to post-1997 service (in each case based on pension becoming payable at age 65 to a member in respect of whom 50% survivor's compensation is payable).

Dealing with uncertainty

14.12.18 There are several possible ways of dealing with any uncertainty as to the setting of commutation rates:

---

65 http://www.actuaries.org.uk/research-and-resources/documents/member-options-getting-it-right

14.12.18 *Benefit changes*

- Amend the trust deed? Depending on the amendment power, this could be done so as to specify the bases for setting the rate or the actuary's certification. This would allow the factors to be taken into account in deciding whether the commutation rates were 'reasonable' to clearly be set out for the avoidance of doubt. Such a change would not be within the limits on amendment in *section 67* of the *Pensions At 1995* as no 'subsisting right' would be affected. However, the trustees would need to be satisfied that any amendment was being entered into for a proper purpose and consistent with their fiduciary duties (eg to avoid uncertainty?) and to that extent this does not resolve the pre-existing question as to the relevant factors to consider.

- Set a policy for reviewing factors. Having a clear policy on when factors will be reviewed and carefully documenting the decisions reached following such reviews will help enable trustees to mount a robust defence in the event of a legal claim – as evidenced by the Pensions Ombudsman's decision in *Squibbs*.

- Issue a warning to members? Trustees may wish to consider including some risk warnings when communicating with members about their various options. Ultimately, the prospect of a legal claim is much reduced if the member has given informed consent to a particular step, fully understanding the rate available. The Member Options Working Party Report highlights this point by recommending that the actuarial profession:

  '… should support either a requirement for a risk warning and suggestion for members to take financial advice if they are considering commuting a large amount of pension to cash, or a meaningful disclosure of cash commutation terms to members consistent with its stance on member disclosure for transfer values (ie an indication of the cost to the member of securing an equivalent pension.'

- Refuse commutation requests? Finally, in some schemes, whilst members have a choice as to whether or not to take cash commutation, they are unable to insist upon it and employer consent is needed (though in practice, it is rarely refused). If agreement could not be reached on appropriate rates of commutation, one option for the employer would be simply to stop allowing members to commute. But this would be a draconian step.

- Different tranches. Schemes should also consider the impact of commutation on different tranches of pension. If a scheme (say) has no (or discretionary) pension increases on pre-1997 service, but statutory increases on post-1997 service, it is helpful for any commutation to be clear as to which periods of service the pension being commuted relates.

Annex: Squibbs

14.12.19   In the case of Captain P Squibbs,[66] the 76-year old pensioner brought a complaint against the Airways Pension Scheme in respect of the 'variable pension option' (VPO) he had chosen prior to his compulsory retirement at age 55.

The aim of the VPO was to give a more even pension throughout retirement and the relevant provision in the scheme rules stated that a pension under the VPO:

> 'shall be increased before such pensionable age and reduced thereafter in accordance with arrangements approved by the Actuary with a view to providing [the member] with a more stable aggregate pension from the Scheme and from the general social security scheme.'

In Captain Squibbs' case it resulted in an additional £1,170.72 on his pension each year up to age 65 (State pension age), followed by a deduction of £2,734.44 from his (normal) pension each year thereafter for the rest of his life. By the time of his complaint to the Ombudsman, Captain Squibbs had already 'repaid' the scheme a larger sum in yearly deductions since age 65 (£30,078.84) than he had previously received in additional payments (£11,707.20).

The terms of the VPO were explained clearly in a number of letters sent to Captain Squibbs in the year leading up to his retirement and a pamphlet was provided which stated that once begun, the VPO *'cannot be altered or cancelled under any circumstances'*. Notwithstanding this, he complained to the Ombudsman that the management trustees of the Airways Pension Scheme had breached their fiduciary duty by failing to operate the VPO in a fair and reasonable way, on the grounds that:

- he had not been given sufficient information to make a fully-informed decision on whether to take up the VPO, based on his personal circumstances – the VPO was wrongly presented to him as being cost-neutral to members and the scheme; and

- the management trustees had failed to ensure that, within the parameter of cost-neutrality for the scheme, the actuarial factors used for benefit calculations were fair and reasonable. Although the management trustees had considered the scheme factors and the VPO on a number of occasions, Captain Squibbs complained that they had failed to monitor them between 1984 (when new factors were adopted) and his retirement in 1991, or take account of improved life expectancy that had distorted the VPO over time. In addition, he contended that the terms of VPO

---

66   (78488/2), 7 September 2012.

pensions should have been reviewed by the management trustees after retirement to ensure the assumptions adopted reflected cost neutrality in light of members' actual longevity.

On 7 September 2012, the Pensions Ombudsman dismissed the complaint. It was found that the terms of the VPO were made clear to Captain Squibbs and sufficient information was provided to enable him to select the option appropriate to his personal circumstances at the time he needed to make a choice.

Moreover, the management trustees had not breached their duties. It had not been shown that between 1989 and 1991, only an unreasonable body of trustees would have left the factors unaltered. The Ombudsman emphasised that the test for unreasonableness is a high one.

It is instructive to note some of the reasons based on which the management trustees had decided (both before and after Captain Squibbs' retirement) not to change the actuarial factors/terms of the VPO. These included:

- the need to minimise anomalies in the benefits receivable by members;

- the need to maintain the conditions of the VPO as consistent between existing and future pensioners; and

- the fact that to end repayments for existing VPO pensioners after ten years (as had been suggested by the scheme actuary in relation to a disposable surplus) would cost around £15m and there were many thousands of other pensioners who had taken up other actuarially neutral options, commutation being the main example, who might consider that they should be treated in the same way (ie if actuarial assumptions were not borne out in practice some adjustment should be made).

Baker

In a later case, *Baker* (PO-281, 19 November 2013), the deputy pensions ombudsman rejected a claim that the BT Pension Scheme using a 17 to 1 commutation rate (pension to lump sum at age 60) was maladministration. The relevant rule provided that the commutation factor was to be 'determined by the Trustee after consultation with BT and certified as reasonable by the actuary to BTPS'. The deputy PO held:

'53. Dr Baker claims that because there is an element of actuarial profit then the commutation of a pension for a lump sum under BTPS is a sale under the Financial Services Act and therefore subject to the mis-selling laws. Complaints under the Financial Services Act are not matters I can consider. There will always be gains and losses under a pension scheme and these could be the result of a number of different

728

factors. Whether or not the application of a particular factor will result in a gain to the scheme is not a matter for me to decide. What I can consider is whether the factor used is reasonable and fair. It would not be unreasonable for the trustees of a pension scheme to use factors that are approved by an adviser. The actuary to BTPS had certified the commutation factor of 17 as reasonable.

54. Apart from his claims, I can see no evidence to support Dr Baker's assertion that the factor used by the Trustee is unreasonable. The test for unreasonableness is a high one and I have seen nothing to support a conclusion that no reasonable body of trustees would not have used this factor. I therefore do not uphold this part of his complaint.'

14.13   Maternity and paternity rights: overview

Summary

This section summarises the current law and practice in this area by reference to eight key issues. It covers the basic legal entitlements and also looks at those areas that are more 'grey' in terms of employee rights and employer obligations.

1. Rights before maternity leave starts

14.13.1 Female employees are given additional protection and rights under law from the moment they notify their employer of their pregnancy.

Many maternity rights are calculated by reference to the 'expected week of childbirth' (the EWC). As the name suggests, this is the week (Sunday to Sunday) in which the employee is due to give birth.

Notification

14.13.2 An employee must notify her employer that she is pregnant no later than the end of the 15th week before the EWC (ie if the EWC is week 40 then the employee must notify the employer that she is pregnant by no later than the end of week 25).

She must also tell the employer her EWC and the date she intends her maternity leave to start, which must be no earlier than the beginning of the 11th week before the EWC.

Many employees will notify their employer prior to this date so as to benefit from paid time off for antenatal classes, to ensure that appropriate health and safety adjustments can be made if required or to trigger protection from discrimination on the grounds of pregnancy.

If an employee does not notify the employer within the prescribed timeframes then she will have no right to maternity leave nor some of the rights during that leave. She will, however, retain protection against discrimination on grounds of pregnancy or maternity and the right to other benefits such as statutory maternity pay.

Discrimination

14.13.3 Pregnancy and maternity is a 'protected characteristic' for the purposes of discrimination law. There is no limit on the compensation that an employment tribunal can award for unlawful discrimination.

In particular, if an employee is treated unfavourably because of a pregnancy-related illness then this will constitute discrimination and, if the treatment involves dismissal, that dismissal will be automatically unfair.

Health and safety

14.13.4 Employers are under a general obligation to assess the health and safety risks to which all of their employees are exposed at work. For women of child-bearing age, who do work that could involve risk to the health and safety of a new or expectant mother or her baby, a risk assessment should include an assessment of those risks.

The Health and Safety Executive considers that specific risks for women of child-bearing age include working hours, stress, working alone, noise, movements/postures and temperature extremes.

Importantly, there is no obligation to do anything about identified risks until the employer has been notified that the employee is pregnant. Once so notified, the employer must take reasonable steps to remove or prevent exposure to any significant risk and tell the employee what it has done. If the risk cannot be avoided then the employer will need to consider amending the employee's working conditions or hours, offer suitable alternative work or even permit the employee to remain away from work on full pay if a suitable adjustment cannot be made.

The employer is also unlikely to be able to reduce or amend the employee's pay or benefits during a period in which her working arrangements are changed. If she is offered suitable alternative work then the employer may be able to pay her at a level commensurate with the new role, but this is not without risk of challenge if the new terms are less favourable than before.

Importantly the employee cannot be required to take sick leave if there is a health and safety issue that cannot be remedied by the employer.

Antenatal care

14.13.5 Expectant mothers may take reasonable paid time off during their working day for antenatal care. This includes medical appointments and antenatal and parenting classes, provided they are recommended by a health professional. There is no corollary right for male employees to take time off for such appointments, though some employers do agree to this as a matter of internal policy.

2. Maternity and paternity leave

14.13.6 Statutory maternity leave lasts for up to 52 weeks and the employer must tell the employee of the date on which her maternity leave will end.

The 52 weeks is broken down into two equal periods of 26 weeks, the first being 'ordinary maternity leave' (OML) and the second 'additional maternity leave' (AML). Within OML, the employee must take a minimum of two weeks' compulsory maternity leave and it is a criminal offence for an employer to allow an employee to work during this two-week period.

Ordinary statutory paternity leave, in comparison, lasts only for up to two consecutive weeks. Fathers may take up to 26 weeks' additional paternity leave (APL). However, if APL is taken:

- APL must be exhausted within a period of time starting 20 weeks after, and ending 12 months after, the baby's date of birth; and

- the individual's spouse, civil partner or partner must have returned to work from their own statutory maternity leave.

3. Maternity and paternity pay

Maternity pay

14.13.7 Pregnant employees may be eligible to receive statutory maternity pay (SMP). They may also receive enhanced contractual maternity pay if the employer so chooses. The employer can recover almost all SMP through HMRC by deduction from other payments due to the tax man.

To be eligible for SMP an employee must:

- have been continuously employed for at least 26 weeks by the end of the 15th week before her EWC;

- have normal weekly earnings that are not less than the lower earnings limit for national insurance purposes (this is a fairly complicated calculation but will normally be met for anyone other than the very low paid. The government provides a useful SMP calculator on its website);

- still be pregnant or have given birth 11 weeks before the EWC; and
- have stopped working.

The employee must also have notified the employer in advance of the date on which she intends SMP to start and have confirmed her EWC.

It is an intentional quirk of the legislation that employees who meet the eligibility criteria but subsequently resign – or are dismissed – remain entitled to receive SMP. The requirement to have stopped working captures termination of employment and it does not matter if the employee was sacked for misconduct.

Agency workers are also eligible to receive SMP if they meet the qualifying criteria, but do not necessarily have a right to take maternity leave. The obligation to provide SMP falls on the agency, rather than the end user. This means that to receive SMP agency workers will have to turn down placements so as to satisfy the criterion of having stopped work.

SMP is paid at two rates: (i) for the first six weeks at 90% of the employee's normal weekly earnings; and (ii) for the next 33 weeks at the lower of a prescribed rate set by the government and the employee's normal weekly earnings. The prescribed rate is currently £135.45 per week. The payments are all subject to deductions for tax and national insurance.

Women who are not eligible to receive SMP (because, for example, they do not have sufficient service or are self-employed) may be eligible to receive maternity allowance from Jobcentre Plus and it is good practice to notify the relevant employees of this at the time.

Enhanced maternity pay

14.13.8 Employers can choose to give maternity pay that exceeds SMP. The most common enhancement is to pay full or part-time salary for some or all of the maternity leave.

Enhanced maternity pay can be paid 'with strings attached'. Employers generally want to encourage employees to return to work and many have come up with different approaches to achieving that aim. Some are common, others less so and include:

- requiring the employee to repay some or all of her enhanced maternity pay if she does not return to work for a set length of time, say, six months; and/or

14.13.8 *Benefit changes*

- offering an ex gratia payment or additional bonus to an employee who comes back to work from maternity leave early (but not of course during the compulsory maternity leave period); and/or

- not paying enhanced maternity pay if the employee falls pregnant again within a set period of time; and/or

- setting a longer qualifying period to be eligible for the enhanced pay, ie longer than the 26 weeks for SMP.

Whilst these schemes may discourage consecutive maternity leaves, they can also be the subject of criticism on the grounds that they may have the effect of discouraging women from having their children over a short period of time so as not to interrupt their career development. This is a policy decision for the employer.

Paternity pay

14.13.9 Statutory paternity pay (SPP) operates slightly differently from SMP. It is paid at the lesser of 90% of normal weekly earnings and the government's prescribed rate. The prescribed rate is identical to that for SMP (£135.45) but is payable only for up to two weeks.

The father may be eligible for additional statutory paternity pay to cover any period of time spent on APL.

4. Rights that continue and rights that do not

14.13.10 Under the legislation, an employee on maternity leave (whether OML or AML) is entitled to all her usual benefits except her remuneration. Remuneration for that period is replaced by SMP and, if relevant, contractual maternity pay. The definition of 'remuneration' is 'wages or salary' and it remains unclear whether this captures particular payments. Our views on four 'tricky' areas – pensions, bonuses share schemes and childcare vouchers – are set out in brief below.

Pensions

14.13.11 The *Equality Act 2010* (the 2010 Act) provides that during:

- periods of OML (whether paid or unpaid); and

- paid periods of AML,

employees on maternity leave must continue to accrue rights in an occupational pension scheme. The impact of the *2010 Act* for employers depends on the type of occupational pension scheme that is operated.

14.13.12 For employers operating defined benefit schemes, the employee must continue to accrue pensionable service as if she were at work. If the scheme requires member contributions to be made, the contributions can only be calculated by reference to pay actually received by the employee (ie her statutory/contractual maternity pay), and not her usual salary. For the employer of a defined benefit scheme, therefore, while there may be no immediate impact on funding obligations (as employer contributions will continue as scheduled under the latest schedule of contributions) if there is a reduction in member contributions received during the period of maternity leave, any resulting shortfall in funding the corresponding pension benefit will ultimately fall on the employer.

14.13.13 For employers operating defined contribution schemes, employer contributions will continue as usual during this time (ie based on the employee's usual salary level). Employee contributions will again be based on the actual rate of pay during the period of leave. Employees should be reminded that they may wish to 'top up' their contributions, as their accounts will receive less contributions during that period so they do not suffer a shortfall.

During unpaid periods of AML the *2010 Act* does not require employers to continue to provide for the accrual of pension rights in an occupational pension scheme, so the above will not apply.

It is interesting to note that while the intention of the *2010 Act* was to consolidate the existing legislation in this area, the legislation no longer covers personal pension schemes. The reason for the omission is unclear, although as a matter of practice it is likely that most employers will have retained their existing pension arrangements for those on maternity leave (ie not distinguishing between occupational and personal pension schemes). Strictly speaking however, personal pension schemes are exempt from the *2010 Act's* regime.

Bonuses

14.13.14 This is a grey area. Pro-rata bonuses, whether contractual or discretionary, are payable in respect of the period before maternity leave started, in respect of the two-week compulsory maternity leave period and for any period after returning to work.

Discretionary bonuses are – oddly – less likely to fall within the definition of 'remuneration' and so there are prospects of arguing they are payable during OML and AML. In view of the lack of clarity as to the legal requirements in respect of discretionary bonus, employers often develop a policy that applies a discount to reflect time not spent at work during the relevant bonus year, so that employees do not receive a full bonus payment for the entire period of leave.

14.13.14   *Benefit changes*

Often employees will not document this approach, but rather it will exist as an unwritten policy or practice, so that it can be flexed to adapt to specific circumstances.

A pure contractual bonus should rightly be classed as 'remuneration' and as such is not payable during maternity leave.

Share schemes

14.13.15   Rights to share and option awards that form terms and conditions of employment should continue throughout OML and AML. This is because benefits under share schemes are unlikely to fall within the definition of 'remuneration'.

Deductions should still be made from employees' net salaries to fund HMRC approved savings-related schemes (such as Sharesave) and from gross salaries to buy partnership shares under an approved share incentive plan, unless in either case there are insufficient funds or the employee chooses to stop those contributions.

Childcare vouchers

14.13.16   Employers may provide childcare vouchers to employees, which is a tax-efficient way to pay for childcare. Very often the vouchers are paid for by the employee out of pre-tax gross salary by way of salary sacrifice.

HMRC has issued guidance that childcare vouchers do not constitute 'remuneration' and so should continue to be provided during OML or AML. Although there has been no case law on this point and HMRC's guidance is non-binding, given childcare vouchers are not provided in cash and cannot be converted into cash, they do not necessarily fit a 'common sense' understanding of remuneration. Employers could take the view that they do not need to continue to provide childcare vouchers during maternity leave, but this approach is vulnerable to legal challenge.

The most technical aspect of childcare vouchers is the interaction with salary sacrifice arrangements. Because salary sacrifice amounts to a contractual reduction in an employee's gross salary, employers may find that they have to continue to fund childcare vouchers even when the employee is receiving only SMP (or no maternity pay at all). This is a complicated area and will depend in part on the terms of the salary sacrifice.

The government has announced plans to introduce a new government-funded tax-free childcare system from 2015, which is expected to replace childcare vouchers over time.

5. KIT days

14.13.17 A mother may work for up to ten 'keeping in touch' days (KIT days) during her maternity leave without bringing her OML or AML to an end. This is in addition to the reasonable contact that an employer can make with an employee on maternity leave (for example, to discuss her return to work). An employer cannot compel an employee to work a KIT day, although employees should see them as a useful way of remaining in contact with the employer and feeling part of a team.

Payment for KIT days is something to be agreed between the employer and the employee and should be documented in writing. KIT day payments may be offset against the relevant week's total SMP (and not just the amount of SMP for that day). In practice, most employees are unlikely to attend a KIT day unless they are paid their normal contractual daily rate of pay, although this potentially misses the point of KIT days.

6. Redundancies during maternity or paternity leave

14.13.18 Employees can be made redundant while on maternity or paternity leave. However, particular care should be taken. The relevant employee should be included as normal in the selection process and invited to relevant consultation meetings. The employer should take steps to be flexible as to the timing and location of the consultation meetings, particularly if the employee is heavily pregnant or has only just given birth.

Employers have an obligation to look for suitable alternative employment for all employees as part of a redundancy exercise. However, employees on maternity leave take priority over other 'at risk' employees if a position comes up, including at associated companies. If the employee is not prioritised and is subsequently dismissed then she will have a claim for automatic unfair dismissal.

If an employee is dismissed because of her pregnancy, birth or maternity leave, the dismissal will be automatically unfair. There will also be a strong claim for unlawful discrimination.

Statutory redundancy pay should be calculated by reference to the employee's normal salary and not their maternity or paternity pay.

Note that the employee must continue to be paid her SMP even once the dismissal takes effect.

Fathers who take just the standard two weeks' paternity leave are likely to be back in the workplace before redundancy consultation is completed. They should be able to be included in the process as normal.

7. Return to work

14.13.19   Unless there has been a redundancy exercise, a female employee who takes only OML is entitled to return to the same job that she had before going on leave. There is some, albeit limited, scope for flexibility here. The question is whether the job is within the normal 'range of variability' that the employee could reasonably have expected under the terms of her employment contract.

If the employee has taken a period of AML then she is also entitled to return to the same job, unless it is not reasonably practicable to do so. This typically arises when there has been some form of reorganisation or restructuring with no resultant redundancies. In this situation, the employee still has a right not to be treated less favourably and any alternative job must be suitable for her and appropriate in the circumstances.

Often employers can assume that there is more flexibility on a return from AML than is in fact the case. In practice the flexibility to offer an alternative role is limited and employers need to tread carefully to ensure that business decisions not to permit a maternity returner back to her old role are challenged and defensible. The onus is on the employer to demonstrate that it is not reasonably practicable for the employee to return from AML to the same job.

8. Flexible working and parental leave

14.13.20   Once an employee has children, they may wish to avail themselves of two particular rights:

Flexible working

14.13.21   All employees with children, who meet certain eligibility criteria, have a right to request to work flexibly. An employee returning from maternity or paternity leave may, for example, request a change to the hours they work, a change to the times they are required to work or to work from a different location. Both the employee and the employer must follow a statutory procedure for making and dealing with a formal request for flexible working. Broadly speaking, this requires the employer to deal with a flexible working request within a prescribed time period.

The employer does not have to accept a request for flexible working, but may only refuse such a request for prescribed reasons. Valid reasons for refusing such a request include the burden of additional costs to accommodate the request, a detrimental effect on the ability of the employer to meet customer demand and a detrimental impact on the employee's performance. The employer must give sufficient explanation as to why the chosen grounds for refusal apply. An employee may have a claim for unlawful sex discrimination or constructive dismissal if a request for flexible working is turned down without proper consideration.

Parental leave

14.13.22 Each employee with responsibility for a child may take up to a total of 18 weeks' unpaid parental leave per child, up to a maximum of four weeks per year. This leave is 'attached' to the employee and so the 18-week per child maximum is not refreshed if they change employer.

Chapter 15

Employer consultation obligations/ communicating with members

15.1 *Pensions Act 2004*: employers' consultation obligations

Summary

The *Pensions Act 2004* requires employers to carry out consultation where they are proposing 'listed' changes to active or prospective members' pension arrangements. The list of relevant changes was extended in April 2010 and April 2012.

Before any decision is made, employers must give notice of the changes (with background information) to all affected members or their representatives and consult for at least 60 days.

This section looks at the provisions of the *Pensions Act 2004* and the accompanying regulations.

15.1.1 Increased pension deficits have forced many employers to review and implement strategies for managing their pension costs. However, it is important for employers to remember that making such changes can, in some circumstances, trigger an obligation to inform affected pension scheme members (and their representatives) before making any decision and then consult for at least 60 days. Failure to do this can now lead to the Pensions Regulator (TPR) imposing a civil penalty on the employer.

The legislation is:

- *sections 259* to *261* of the *Pensions Act 2004*; and

- the 2006 *Consultation Regulations.*[1]

These require employers to consult where employers, trustees or any other person with the power to make the listed change (relevant for multi-employer schemes) are proposing a 'listed' change to affected members' future pension arrangements. *Section 67* of the *Pensions Act 1995* deals with changes to accrued rights – see *Section 67: Modification of subsisting rights*, **14.7**.

This obligation applies only to changes that affect active members or prospective members. In relation to an occupational pension scheme, a prospective member is any person who, under their service contract:

- is able to choose to become a member;

- will become a member if they continue in the same employment for a sufficiently long period;

- will be admitted to the scheme automatically unless they opt out (potentially this may create a consultation obligation in respect of a larger portion of an employer's workforce as employers reach their staging dates for the purposes of automatic enrolment because of the *Pensions Act 2008* obligation for employers to have to enrol jobholders automatically into a qualifying scheme – see **19.1**); or

- may be admitted subject to the employer's consent.

For personal pension schemes, prospective members only include persons who, under their service contract, would be eligible, on becoming a member of the scheme, to have employer contributions paid in respect of them.

Changes affecting deferred members or pensioners do not fall under the *Consultation Regulations* (although *s 67* of the *Pensions Act 1995* restricts changes that affect accrued rights – see *Section 67: Modification of subsisting rights*, **14.7**).

This information and consultation obligation is in addition to any other consultation requirements (eg the requirements under *Tupe* on transfers of businesses – see **6.3**).

The information and consultation obligation applies only to employers that have 50 or more employees (note that the test refers to the number of employees, not the number of employees who are affected or who are scheme

---

1   The *Occupational and Personal Pension Schemes (Consultation by Employers and Miscellaneous Amendment) Regulations 2006 (SI 2006/349).*

members). It applies regardless of whether there is a recognised trade union or works council.

Excluded employers
Occupational pension schemes
Any employer:
• in relation to a public service scheme;
• in relation to a small scheme (fewer than 12 members and each is a trustee);
• in relation to a scheme with only one member;
• in relation to an employer-financed retirement benefits scheme; or
• in relation to an unregistered overseas scheme (main administration outside the EU).
Personal pension schemes
Any employer in relation to a personal pension scheme where direct payment arrangements exist but no employer contributions fall to be paid towards the scheme.

Listed changes

15.1.2 The following changes give rise to a consultation obligation.

Occupational pension schemes

15.1.3 Changes requiring consultation are:

- an increase in the normal pension age for active or prospective members;
- the closure of the scheme to new members (or a class) or for future accrual;
- the removal of the employer's liability to contribute or, in the case of money purchase schemes only, any reduction in employer contributions;
- an increase in or the introduction of member contributions by or on behalf of the member;
- a change to some or all benefits from defined benefit (DB) to defined contribution (DC);
- a change in the basis for determining the future accrual rate (eg a change from final salary to career-average salary);

- a reduction of the future accrual rate; and

- (from 6 April 2010) changes to elements of pay that constitute pensionable earnings (including changes made outside the trust deed and rules).

- (from 6 April 2012) changes to scheme rules on revaluation and indexation.

Personal pension schemes

15.1.4   Changes requiring consultation are:

- a reduction in or cessation of employer contributions; or

- an increase in member contributions.

Exclusions

15.1.5   No consultation is required where:

- the active and prospective members of the scheme to whom the listed change relates ('affected members') were notified of the proposal before 6 April 2006;

- (for occupational and personal pension schemes) as a result of a consultation on a proposal for cessation of employer contributions there is a further proposal to reduce employer contributions or (for occupational schemes only), as a result of a consultation to prevent future accrual, there is a further proposal to reduce the future accrual rate (instead of ceasing altogether); or

- the changes are made for the purpose of complying with a statutory provision or a determination of TPR; or

- the changes have no lasting effect on eligibility or benefits (eg administrative changes); or

- the changes are to accrued rights covered by the provisions of *s 67* of the *Pensions Act 1995* (as amended by the *Pensions Act 2004*) – see **14.7**.

Consultation procedure

15.1.6   Consultation must take place before any decision (or series of decisions) to make the changes is made. If the proposal to make a listed change is made by a person other than the employer (ie the trustees or managers or, in relation to a multi-employer scheme, a non-employer with power to make a listed change), that person may not make the decision without first notifying each employer and being satisfied that the employer has undertaken the necessary consultation.

Specified written information must be given to all affected members or their representatives before the consultation process can commence.

The specified information is:

- details of the listed change and its likely effects on the scheme and its members (to be accompanied by 'any relevant background information');
- the timescale for implementation; and
- the closing date for responses.

There must then be a 60-day consultation 'in a spirit of co-operation, taking into account the interests of both sides' with at least one of the following employee representatives:

- recognised trade union representatives;
- information and consultation representatives under the *Information and Consultation of Employees Regulations 2004* (*SI 2004/3426*) (*ICE Regulations*) (who have rights to paid time off, protection from unfair dismissal etc for the purpose of their functions in the consultation process); or
- representatives elected for the purpose of and in accordance with the *Consultation Regulations*.

The *ICE Regulations* have been amended so that employers will not be obliged to consult about the same issues twice (ie under both the *ICE Regulations* and the *Consultation Regulations*).

The information must be clear and comprehensive enough to enable members' representatives to consider and conduct a study of the proposed change's effects and give views to the employer.

The employer must then consider the responses received and, if the listed changes were proposed by a third party (eg the trustees or the principal employer), give them written notification of the responses as soon as reasonably practicable. The third party must then satisfy itself that consultation was carried out in compliance with the *Consultation Regulations*. If no responses are received, the consultation is deemed complete at the end of the consultation period.

The Department for Work and Pensions issued guidance in April 2010 on the consultation procedure – see www.dwp.gov.uk/docs/occ-personal-pens-schemes-regs06.pdf.

Penalty for failure to consult

15.1.7 A complaint may be made to TPR for failure to comply with the consultation obligations.

Failure to consult will not affect the validity of a change. But TPR can (from 6 April 2009) impose a civil penalty of up to £50,000 on an employer (or £5,000 if the employer is not a company) that fails, without reasonable excuse, to consult.

This civil penalty does not apply to persons other than employers who breach their consultation obligations (eg a civil penalty cannot be imposed on trustees who make a listed change and fail to notify the employer). But *s 70* of the *Pensions Act 2004* requires trustees and scheme managers, among others, to notify TPR of any material breach of law. Failure to notify may lead to TPR issuing a civil penalty if the person does not have a reasonable excuse.

TPR can also issue an improvement notice (under *s 13* of the *Pensions Act 2004*) directing the person in default to take steps to remedy the contravention.

Civil penalties can be imposed on the defaulter (or on a director responsible) for failure to comply with such a notice. If any breach of the requirements is material, trustees and employers etc will be under an obligation to notify TPR of the breach (*s 70* of the *Pensions Act 2004*) – see *Reporting breaches of the law (section 70)*, **13.2**.

TPR has power to waive or relax any of the *Consultation Regulations'* requirements, but can do so only if it is satisfied that this would be 'necessary in order to protect the generality of the interests of the members'. This may well be restrictively construed.

See also *Pensions consultation obligations – watch out for the pitfalls*, **15.2**.

15.2 Pensions consultation obligations – watch out for the pitfalls

---

Summary

The *Pensions Act 2004* requires employers to notify affected members and then consult for 60 days where they are proposing 'listed' changes to active or prospective members' pension arrangements.

Unfortunately, the legislation contains a number of gaps that make it difficult sometimes to decide whether the obligation to consult applies.

This section discusses some of the pitfalls arising in practice.

15.2.1 *Sections 259* to *261* of the *Pensions Act 2004* and the 2006 *Consultation Regulations*[2] require employers with 50 or more employees to inform affected active and prospective members or their representatives and then consult for 60 days if making a 'listed' change to these members' future pension arrangements. The legislation prescribes the different listed changes.

Unfortunately the legislation contains a number of uncertainties that make it difficult to determine whether there is an obligation to consult in some instances.

The lack of clarity has become more problematic for a number of reasons:

- First, the pressure of increased pension deficits has forced more employers to consider reducing future pension costs, therefore making a listed change more likely.

- Second, since April 2009 the Pensions Regulator (TPR) has had a new power to issue civil penalties where there is failure to consult.

- Third, the government in April 2010 expanded the scope of the legislation by introducing a new listed change, triggering an obligation to consult where there is a change to pensionable pay.

This section discusses the various pitfalls to be aware of.

For more information on the consultation obligations see *Pensions Act 2004: Employers' consultation obligations*, **15.1**.

---

2 *The Occupational and Personal Pension Schemes* (*Consultation by Employers and Miscellaneous Amendment*) *Regulations 2006* (*SI 2006/349*), as amended.

Background – what are the listed changes?

15.2.2 Changes requiring consultation are:

- an increase in the normal pension age for active or prospective members;

- the closure of the scheme to new members (or a class) or for future accrual;

- the removal of the employer's liability to contribute or, in the case of money purchase schemes only, any reduction in employer contributions;

- an increase in, or the introduction of, member contributions by or on behalf of the member;

- a change of some or all benefits from defined benefits (DB) to defined contributions (DC);

- a change in the basis for determining the future accrual rate;

- a reduction of the future accrual rate;

- changes to elements of pay that constitute pensionable earnings; and

- changes to scheme rules on revaluation and indexation.

Pitfalls and uncertainties

Changes that affect overseas and prospective members

15.2.3 The obligation to consult applies to changes that affect active or prospective members.

However, the legislation is unclear on whether this consultation obligation applies where a change is made to an affected member working abroad.

The meaning of 'prospective member' is also unclear in some instances. For example, it is unclear if a member is a prospective member where the employer has the unilateral power to allow new entrants into a closed scheme.

50-employee threshold

15.2.4 The consultation obligation applies only to employers that have 50 or more employees. This test applies to each employer, regardless of how many employers participate in a multi-employer scheme (either occupational or personal).

It is important to note that this 50-person threshold refers to employees and not scheme members. So this may, for example, still catch a medium-sized employer even if it has a scheme closed to future entry and only a handful of active members remaining.

Changes in pensionable pay

15.2.5 From 6 April 2010, changes to the elements of pay that constitute pensionable earnings for DB benefits are listed changes. This is likely only to affect agreements with employees that are or were put into place on or after this date.

'Pensionable earnings' is defined as 'the earnings by reference to which pension benefits are calculated, and an 'element of pay' includes basic salary, a pay rise, an overtime payment, and a bonus payment'.

So the consultation obligation can be triggered if (say) an employer makes future pay rises or a bonus non-pensionable.

This listed change is broad enough to catch changes made outside the scheme rules (eg a pay change or a side agreement between the member and the employer). However, the consultation obligation is probably triggered only if the change reflects a shift in the employer's policy. For example, an employer may not need to consult when making a future pay rise non-pensionable if this is in line with its previous practice.

In such cases these elements of pay have in the past never 'constituted pensionable earnings', so there is no change. But consultation may be required if all previous pay rises were pensionable. Clearly, it will be a factual question whether there has been a change in policy and there will be uncertainty only if, for instance, only 50% of previous pay rises were pensionable.

Curiously, this new listed change also appears broad enough to catch a 'change' that is an increase in the amount of a member's pay that is pensionable. However, it is not clear why any employee needs protection in these circumstances.

Interestingly, this listed change will apply only to changes to non-money purchase benefits. Perhaps this is because it is already a listed change to 'increase ... member contributions by or on behalf of members or members of a particular description' in respect of money purchase benefits. But the new listed change on changing pensionable earnings can apply in a broader range of circumstances than increasing member contributions.

From an employment law perspective, complying with the statutory consultation procedure can actually be helpful to an employer wanting to prove that it satisfied its duty of mutual trust and confidence (the *Imperial* duty) or that a change that otherwise might be age discriminatory (see Chapter **16** below) was a proportionate means of achieving a legitimate aim.

Transactions

15.2.6   It is arguable that the obligation can apply in relatively common transactions where:

- a company ceases to participate in a group pension scheme following a sale of the company out of the group; or

- a company transfers its business under the *Transfer of Undertakings* (*Protection of Employment*) *Regulations 2006* (*Tupe*).

The argument is that these transactions may entail a listed change because cessation of participation will mean the end of future accrual of benefits under the seller's scheme. The Regulator takes the view that there is nothing in the *Consultation Regulations* that excludes consultation in these circumstances.

However, there are also strong contrary arguments.

Overlap with Tupe consultation

15.2.7   There is no express exemption under the *Consultation Regulations* from the requirement to consult where parties have already complied with consultation requirements under *Tupe*.

It is not clear why employers should have to consult under each set of Regulations.

Scheme mergers

15.2.8   A scheme merger (or demerger) that results in cessation of accrual in one scheme seems on a literal approach to trigger a consultation obligation (because the active members will cease accrual in the transferring scheme) even if the active members accrue identical benefits going forward in the receiving scheme. Consultation seems rather pointless in these circumstances. There is already a requirement to inform all members one month before the transfer under the *1991 Preservation Regulations* – see further Chapter **7**, *Scheme Mergers*.

15.2.9 *Employer consultation obligations/communicating with members*

Individual agreements

15.2.9 If the employer and employee individually agree a change in remuneration and pension benefits or contributions it is unclear if consultation will still be needed.

Here consultation appears to have no purpose.

Moving members to a new section

15.2.10 Closing the scheme to new members is a listed change. However, an odd anomaly appears where a section (eg a DB section) is closed but a new section is created (eg a DC section) that a future member can join. In these circumstances there does not appear to be a consultation obligation because the employer is not preventing the prospective member from being admitted to the scheme. But, if the employer had closed the DB scheme and opened a separate new DC scheme this would trigger consultation because the member is no longer being admitted to the DB scheme.

Employers that rely on this anomaly may still want to engage in some sort of consultation to preserve good employee relations.

Salary-sacrifice arrangements

15.2.11 Introducing a salary-sacrifice arrangement does not increase member contributions and so does not trigger the consultation requirements under the *Consultation Regulations*.

But ending an existing salary-sacrifice arrangement could be a listed change if the members' contributions increase. On the other hand, it can be argued that a salary-sacrifice arrangement does not affect the member contribution rate at all – instead, a member is able to choose not to pay pension contributions and to have the employer pay the contributions on their behalf.

In March 2010 the government confirmed that, in its view, there is no requirement to consult in relation to salary-sacrifice arrangements because there is no lasting effect on members' benefits (so the exemption under *reg 10(1)(c)* of the *Consultation Regulations* applies).

Reducing the rate of revaluation

15.2.12 The legislation was unclear on whether consultation is required if lowering the rate of revaluation of deferred pension benefits to, for example, take advantage of the lower 2.5% rate introduced by the *Pensions Act 2008*.

Where scheme rules need to be amended to take advantage of this lower 2.5% cap, this change could be argued to be a listed change under the *Consultation Regulations* because it could be considered as 'any other reduction in the rate of future accrual of benefit under the scheme for or in respect of members or members of a particular description'. TPR (ultimately the body that would enforce the consultation obligations) confirmed to us that, in its view, changing the rate to the statutory revaluation rate falls under the exemption 'made for the purpose of complying with statutory provisions'.

In April 2012 the consultation regulations were amended so that 'listed changes' now include a change to the rate of revaluation for deferred members' benefits or indexation of pensions in payment.

Changes to ancillary benefits

15.2.13 It is unclear whether changing ancillary benefits (eg death benefits) is a change in the rate of future accrual and triggers a consultation obligation. Arguably this may affect the rate of future accrual if the actuarial value of the benefits is being considered.

Practical issues to be aware of and new joiners

- Do not forget to include in the consultation members on maternity leave and new joiners.

- Make sure letters to members come from the correct employer or, if they come from the principal company on behalf of all employers in a group, make this clear.

15.3 National works councils and pensions

Summary

The *Information and Consultation Employees Regulations 2004* have required employers to put in place information and consultation arrangements (national works councils) with employees from 6 April 2005. This section looks at how occupational pensions should feature.

Employers should take care, when formulating works councils proposals, to consider whether consultation about pensions matters should fall within the ambit of the works council's jurisdiction.

15.3.1 The *Information and Consultation of Employees Regulations 2004* (the *'ICE Regulations'*) were made on 21 December 2004. They came into force on 6 April 2005 and applied to undertakings with 150 or more employees from 6 April 2005, 100 or more from 6 April 2007 and 50 or more from 6 April 2008.

The government (DTI) published guidance in January 2005 on the *ICE Regulations* (guidance is also available on the ACAS website). For more information see the book *Informing and Consulting Employees: The New Law* by Nicholas Squire, Kathleen Healy and others (Oxford University Press).

Broadly, the *ICE Regulations* envisage giving employees, or a relevant number, the right to require employers to set up an information and consultation arrangement. They envisage that there will then be negotiation and discussion, either about existing arrangements or about new arrangements to be established. Only if agreement cannot be reached does a set of default arrangements come into place under the *ICE Regulations*.

Once the arrangements are in place, employers will be required to provide information and to consult as envisaged in those arrangements. Failure to do so can result in the Central Arbitration Committee (CAC) imposing a penalty of up to £75,000.

Are pensions matters included?

15.3.2 There is no reason why pensions matters could not be included by agreement within the range of matters on which information and consultation must be provided. This can either be through an existing arrangement or through a new arrangement established under the consultation structure.

Clearly it will be helpful to ensure that the terms of the arrangements are clear as to whether pensions matters are included within the matters on which information and consultation is required.

The default obligations under the *ICE Regulations* are worded in very general terms. In this they follow the provisions of the underlying EU information and consultation directive. Broadly, employers must (*reg 20*):

(a)   provide information on recent and probable development of the employer's activities and economic situation;

(b)   provide information on, and consult about, probable development of employment and relevant measures etc; and

(c)   provide information on, and consult about, decisions likely to lead to substantial changes in work organisation or contractual relations.

Pensions issues look as though they could fall within category (c). The DTI guidance on category (c) indicates that it thinks that changes to an occupational pension scheme would be within this category where there was a contractual right to participate in the scheme.

However the DTI guidance states that its view is that this category would 'not cover changes in pay or benefits that have a monetary value'. This is because the underlying directive was enacted under *Art 137* of the *EU treaty*, which states that it does not cover matters such as pay.

Our view is that pensions would normally be considered to have a monetary value. Accordingly there appear to be strong arguments that pensions are not actually covered by the default arrangements under category (c).

The lack of clarity here is a good reason to clarify the points through a clear provision, in a pre-existing or other agreement, instead of falling back on the default rules.

Other consultation obligations

Major changes to benefits: Pensions Act 2004, s 259

15.3.3   Separately from the general works council provisions, a separate obligation to consult arises under *ss 259* to *261* of the *Pensions Act 2004* – see *Pensions Act 2004: Employers' consultation obligations*, **15.1**.

Changes to accrued rights: Pensions Act 1995, s 67

15.3.4 *Section 262* of the *Pensions Act 2004* came into force on 6 April 2006 and enacted a revised version of *s 67* of the *Pensions Act 1995*. *Section 67* contains limits on amendments to occupational pension schemes that affect accrued rights.

See generally *Section 67: Modification of subsisting rights,* **14.7**.

In particular, *s 67* includes a requirement for trustees to inform affected scheme members in advance about any changes to accrued rights, whether or not accrued rights are adversely affected. The trustees must also give the member a reasonable opportunity to make representations about the proposed modification.

Consultation with a national works council is not sufficient for this purpose (given that the section is based on informing each individual member).

Other statutes

15.3.5 There are various obligations to consult on pensions. Again in practice it may well be that consultation through a national works council would be appropriate (but not mandatory). Examples are consultation:

- about the method of electing member-nominated trustees (MNTs) (see **11.1**);

- on changes to contracting-out status (currently by notice to trade unions and employees); and

- on measures applying as a result of a transfer of a business under *Tupe* (see **6.3**).

Consultation generally a good thing

15.3.6 Case law indicates that in a number of areas consultation about changes can be regarded as helpful. For example consultation may well help an employer to comply with the implied '*Imperial*' duty ie not to act in a manner that would breach the mutual duty of trust and confidence owed between employer and employees.

15.4 The Takeover Code: involvement of pension trustees

Summary

Changes to the Takeover Code took effect on 20 May 2013.

The changes to the Takeover Code provide that trustees (or managers) of defined benefit (DB) pension schemes of the target company of a takeover (or its subsidiaries, even if not wholly owned) must be:

- informed; and

- allowed to present their view on the transaction (in the same way as employee representatives).

This information requirement is not limited to UK pension schemes and consideration will need to be given to subsidiaries in other jurisdictions (eg Ireland, the Netherlands, the US or Canada) that potentially have DB schemes.

Introduction

15.4.1 From 20 May 2013, the Takeover Panel has extended various provisions of the Takeover Code, which relate to notification of, and consultation with, employee representatives of the offeree company, to the trustees of the offeree company's pension scheme(s).

The Code now includes a:

> 'framework within which the effects of an offer on the offeree company's pension scheme(s)… could become a debating point during the course of the offer and a point on which each of the offeror, the board of the offeree company and the trustees of the pension scheme(s) could have an opportunity to express their views.'

This framework is not intended to (nor does it) require agreement to be reached on the future funding of the scheme in order for an offer to become or be declared unconditional. It is merely hoped that the new provisions will ensure that the effects of the offer on any pension scheme are taken into account.

Takeover Code

15.4.2 The Takeover Code applies to listed companies who have:

- their registered offices in the UK, the Channel Islands or the Isle of Man; and

- securities listed on a regulated market in the UK or on any stock exchange on the Channel Islands or the Isle of Man.

It also applies to unlisted public companies and certain private companies registered in the UK, the Channel Islands or the Isle of Man.

The 2013 amendments to the Takeover Code are explained in full in RS 2012/2 and Instrument 2013/2.

Documents to be provided to pension trustees

15.4.3   The target company's pension scheme trustees will be entitled to receive the same documents that the bidder and target are required to make available to employee representatives – in particular:

- the announcement of a potential offer;

- the announcement of firm intention to make an offer;

- the offer document and any revised offer document;

- where an offer is not recommended, the target board's circular in response to any revised offer; and

- if required by the Panel, a document setting out relevant information on material changes or material new information.

There is no obligation under the Takeover Code for these documents to be sent to the Pensions Regulator.

Additional information the bidder must provide

15.4.4   Under the Code, the bidder will be required to provide the pension trustees of any funded DB pension scheme sponsored by the target company or any of its subsidiaries (including overseas schemes that have trustees or managers) with:

- financial information about itself;

- details of how the offer is being financed; and

- appropriate disclosure about the bidder's intentions regarding employer contributions to the scheme(s) (including in respect of any deficit), benefit accruals for current members, and the admission of new members (if there are no changes intended this must also be disclosed).

The bidder will be held to any statement it makes for a period of 12 months (unless specified otherwise or there is a material change in circumstances).

The bidder is not required (under the Code):

- to state its view regarding the impact of the offer on the employer covenant (ie an assessment by the bidder of the future ability of the target to meet its funding obligations to the pension scheme will not be necessary); or

- to reach agreement with the pension scheme trustees regarding the funding of the target company's pension schemes by a specific date.

Pensions Regulator

15.4.5   There is no requirement under the Code to involve the Pensions Regulator at any point. Any decision to seek clearance from the Pensions Regulator will remain a matter for the bidder or target.

Rights of the trustees

15.4.6   Under the Code, trustees of any of the target company's pension schemes have the right:

- to provide the target company's board of directors with their opinion on the effects of the offer on the pension scheme; and

- to have their opinion appended to the target company's circular (or published on a website if the circular has already been published).

This is a right that the trustees can choose to exercise: it is not an obligation. The content of the trustees' opinion is not regulated, but it could cover matters such as the impact on employer covenant, impact on investment policy, or describe any mitigation that is being offered by the bidder.

The effect is that trustees have the right to comment on the bid – they do not have a power under the Takeover Code to block a bid if they do not support it.

Agreement between the bidder and the trustees

15.4.7   Any agreement between the bidder and the trustees of a target company's pension scheme will be treated under the Takeover Code in the same way as other agreements entered into by the bidder in connection with the offer.

15.4.7 *Employer consultation obligations/communicating with members*

This means if the agreement between the bidder and the trustees of a target company's pension scheme is a material contract of the bidder, it will be an 'offer-related arrangement' and will need to be disclosed and published on a website. However, under the Code, the term 'offer-related arrangement' is defined to exclude agreements between the bidder and the trustees of a target company pension scheme in relation to future funding of those schemes.

Costs

15.4.8 To adequately assess the impact of a takeover bid the trustee may need to engage its various advisers (eg. lawyers, covenant adviser, and actuary). These costs will be the trustees' responsibility – no obligation to pay them is placed by the Takeover Code on either the bidder or target company.

In any event, in practice, for UK pension schemes a sponsoring employer company will normally be responsible for paying costs reasonably incurred by the trustees of the scheme(s), whether:

- directly (though an indemnity or expenses provision); or
- indirectly through the requirement to meet scheme funding.

Conditional on clearance/trustee agreement

15.4.9 It may be possible to seek Panel agreement to some pensions conditions (eg that no material *s 75* debt is triggered during the offer period on any company in the target group). However, it remains to be seen whether such conditions will be sufficient in order to block a takeover from completing.

The previous practice that offers cannot be made conditional on agreement with pension scheme trustees or clearance from the Pensions Regulator, looks likely to continue.

15.4.10 In its response to the prior consultation on the 2013 changes, the Code Committee declined to impose a requirement that, by a specified date in the offer timetable (say, Day 43), an offeror should be required to have reached a definitive position on its funding commitments regarding the offeree company's pension scheme(s), which has been agreed to by the trustees of the scheme(s), failing which the Panel should be required to refer the matter to the Pensions Regulator.

Any decision as to whether clearance from the Pensions Regulator should be sought in relation to a particular takeover will therefore remain a matter for the offeror and offeree.

Comment

15.4.11   The proposals have been reported in the press as being designed to protect pension scheme members from the unexpected closure of schemes after a takeover is completed. However, the initial consultation paper emphasised that in the Code Committee's view, the most the proposals do is to create a 'framework ... for the benefit of the trustees' which goes 'no further than the framework currently provided ... for the benefit of the company's employee representatives'. The final changes to the Code are consistent with this view.

In practice, aside from ensuring compliance with the procedural requirements, the new rules may not make a great amount of difference in cases where the pension scheme raises significant issues, as the parties are likely already to have been considering the impact of the deal on the scheme and involving the trustees early on, with a view to dealing with any funding implications and avoiding any future 'moral hazard' action by the Pensions Regulator.

However, for those cases where the offeror and offeree take an initial view that there is unlikely to be any material detriment for the pension scheme, the proposals will undoubtedly give pension scheme trustees greater leverage for a 'seat at the table' during the early days of the bid and potential issues will be flushed out much more quickly. To that end, the Panel's objective of creating a 'framework' for debate is likely to be successful.

Chapter 16

Age discrimination and pensions

16.1 Age discrimination and pensions

Summary

The decision of the EU and the UK that age discrimination in employment matters is unlawful was a giant step. The ramifications for pensions are complicated, but the legislation has enacted vague 'objective justification' defences, leaving the courts and tribunals to pick up the pieces.

This uncertainty means that the legislation's scope and impact will develop over time. Given the potential for unlimited damages claims and the relative ease in bringing cases before tribunals, with potentially no costs sanction for failure, the volume of age discrimination-related cases may continue to rise, although the new employment tribunal fees may mitigate their growth.

This section looks at the problem areas. It focuses on the impact on pension schemes, but other employment areas are covered.

Backdrop

16.1.1 In 2000, loosely in parallel with the adoption of the EU Charter of Fundamental Rights, the EU legislated to provide that age discrimination in employment relationships should be prohibited. The relevant directive[1] was passed by agreement of all Member States in 2000 and the age discrimination

---

1 *Council Directive 2000/78/EC* establishing a general framework for equal treatment in employment and occupation.

aspects were required to be transposed into the national laws of Member States by 2 December 2006.

The *Employment Equality (Age) Regulations 2006*[2] implemented the EU directive in the UK. These regulations came into force generally on 1 October 2006 (but only on 1 December 2006 for pensions matters).

The *Age Regulations 2006* were replaced from 1 October 2010 by the *Equality Act 2010*, and various secondary legislation, in particular (for pensions) the *Equality Act (Age Exceptions for Pension Schemes) Order 2010*.[3] On pensions, these broadly re-enacted the previous *Age Regulations 2006* with little change.

A further life assurance exemption has applied since 1 April 2011 under the changes to the default retirement age provisions – see *Pension schemes and changes to the default retirement age*, **16.5**.

The legislation currently outlaws age discrimination in an employment context only, but outlaws not just discrimination against older people (as in the US) but also any discrimination on the grounds of age (eg against younger people, as well).

As a social and policy aim, outlawing age discrimination is laudable. The actual implementation as a legal concept is fraught with difficulties and the route of an EU directive has meant that many legal questions remain outstanding and unresolved.

Despite having the six-year lead time, the UK managed to enact the relevant regulations required to meet the requirements of the directive only just before the deadline. The original legislation, the *Age Regulations 2006*, was massively rushed (probably because of political disputes, centring on having a mandatory retirement age at 65).

Impact on pensions

16.1.2   Age discrimination legislation obviously has the potential to have a massive impact on pension schemes.

It has been said that pension schemes are 'inherently age discriminatory', given that they aim to provide benefits on and from a particular age. Is this age discrimination because benefits (or lower benefits) are not available to an employee who has not reached that age?

---

2   *SI 2006/1031.*
3   *SI 2010/2133.*

16.1.2   *Age discrimination and pensions*

Presumably the intention of the legislation was not to outlaw pension schemes. But the EU has a structural problem in enacting detailed legislation (given that it is attempting to cover a wide range of Member States and different legal and economic systems).

More work for the courts and lawyers

16.1.3   So the directive followed past practice in tending to ignore such complications and dealt only in generalities. Obvious problem areas (pension schemes, retirement ages) were fudged. This left the Member States (which of course agreed with the directive in the first place) to try to cope with the detail and the domestic and EU courts to arbitrate on whether they have got it right.

Even more good news for lawyers (but not, obviously, anyone else) is that the courts (and tribunals) are also mandated (as for other discrimination legislation) to decide on vital business and social issues:

- *Indirect discrimination?* When will an act or practice be unlawful as indirect discrimination, even though it does not directly discriminate based on age? Indirect discrimination is often not obvious and tends to involve courts looking at competing statistics or pools of persons affected to see if the practice has a disproportionate effect. Examples here are questions such as:

  - Are benefits based on length of service indirectly discriminatory (because longer serving employees will tend to be older)?

  - Does providing benefits for infant children of an employee amount to age discrimination (on the basis that younger or older employees may be less likely to have such children)?

- *Objective justification?* Even if discriminatory, a particular act or practice will not be unlawful if it can be shown to be objectively justified. This involves convincing a court or tribunal that the potential discrimination is properly offset by some other need such that it should not be ruled unlawful. The key here is that such justification must be 'objective' – ie it is not enough that the employer has agreed the issue with the employee or does not think that the act is discriminatory. It is a matter for the court to decide on an objective basis. The courts are, in effect, required to review and oversee such employment decisions.[4]

---

4   Contrast the UK unfair dismissal legislation, under which a dismissal will not be unfair if it falls within a range of reasonable responses – in unfair dismissal cases, the employer is given a wide range of discretion.

- *Unclear legislation:* The UK legislation is badly drafted and unclear in a number of key areas. In practice this will need to be resolved by court decisions.

- *Conflict with the EU directive?* As mentioned above, the UK legislation needs to comply with the requirements of the EU directive. The directive is a broad statement of policy and so inevitably is unclear in a number of areas. One UK case has already been referred to the European Court of Justice (ECJ) (on the mandatory retirement age of 65 – see the *Heyday case* mentioned below).

Equality Act 2010 and pensions

16.1.4   The first drafts of the *Age Regulations 2006* started by including a blanket exemption for pensions. But this was dropped (without any warning or public consultation) in the final regulations issued and enacted in March 2006.

Instead, a more limited list of specific exemptions was included. It rapidly emerged (unsurprisingly, given the lack of consultation) that these did not cover a wide range of common pension scheme benefits and practices. So the pensions provisions in the UK regulations were withdrawn and did not come into force on 1 October 2006. Amending regulations were issued and finally brought into force a few weeks before the deadline date of 1 December 2006.

Perhaps unsurprisingly, the exemptions in the *Age Regulations 2006* (now in the *Age Exceptions Order 2010*) cause their own difficulties and concerns in relation to pension schemes.

More claims in future?

16.1.5   Perhaps more surprisingly, there has not, as yet, been a flood of claims either in the employment sphere or the pension sphere.

This may just be a brief interlude. Claims for age discrimination are unlimited and can be made before an employment tribunal (or perhaps the Pensions Ombudsman).[5] Even with the recent introduction of fees for bringing tribunal claims, the prospect of unlimited damages and the minimal risk of costs liability could promote an uptick in claims in the near future.

This section discusses some of the issues and problems that have arisen so far.

---

5   It seems arguable that the 2010 legislation has repealed a member's ability (previously clearly in the *Age Regulations 2006*) to bring a case before the Pensions Ombudsman on age discrimination issues.

16.1.6   *Age discrimination and pensions*

UK age 65 retirement exemption

16.1.6   The *Age Exceptions Order 2010* includes various specific exemptions. Most attention to date has been focused on the employment sphere, in particular the 'default retirement age' (DRA) provisions. These used to allow (before April 2011) an employer to require an employee to retire at age 65 without infringing the *Age Regulations 2006* (or effecting an unfair dismissal etc). There were provisions requiring the employer to give notice and to consider in good faith any employee request to be retained.

This age 65 mandatory retirement provision was the subject of a challenge by a charity – in the *Heyday case*.[6] The issue was referred to the ECJ, which in 2009 gave guidance on when exclusions from age discrimination are allowed (under the directive) where there is an objective justification. It is a matter for the national courts to decide whether that test has been met in any particular case. Subsequently, in 2009, the High Court in London gave judgment[7] upholding the age 65 provision.

In spite of the positive decision in the *Heyday* case, the age 65 DRA exception was repealed from April 2011 – see further *Pension Schemes and changes to the default retirement age*, **16.5**.

UK exemptions in the Age Regulations – how far can they go?

16.1.7   The ultimate decision in *Heyday* could have had wider effects. If the age 65 mandatory retirement provision in the *Age Regulations 2006* had been struck down, this would have caused some doubt as to the other specific exemptions in the *Age Regulations 2006* and now the *Age Exceptions Order 2010* (eg redundancy plans, requirements of national law, tax requirements). In particular, the general pensions exemptions in the *Age Regulations 2006* and now the *Age Exceptions Order 2010* could have been at risk. There may still be some prospect of them also being struck down in a future case.

This is of most relevance to those employers that are 'emanations of the state' because they are bound by the directive and cannot rely on conflicting

---

6   *R (on the application of the Incorporated Trustees of the National Council of Ageing (Age Concern England)) v Secretary of State for Business, Enterprise and Regulatory Reform* (C-388/07).

7   *R (on the application of Age UK) v Secretary of State for Business, Innovation & Skills* [2009] EWHC 2336 (Admin), [2010] ICR 260.

exemptions in UK national laws if they are inconsistent. Private sector employers are entitled to rely on UK legal provisions until they are actually amended.

Objective justification – what is the test?

16.1.8 The UK *Age Exceptions Order 2010* follows the EU directive in providing that age discrimination is allowed where there is an objective justification (see *Age discrimination: using objective justification*, **16.3**). Unlike sex and race discrimination laws, this applies in the case of age discrimination for both direct and indirect age discrimination.

Generally, the onus is on the employer to show that a particular provision or practice etc that otherwise would be age discriminatory is allowed by an objective justification. This can be a difficult test. Although the ECJ, in the *Heyday* case, suggested that the justification needs to be by reference to social policy objectives (rather than to the individual circumstances of an employer or business), this is more nuanced than it may appear. A body of ECJ jurisprudence has not only produced a list of possible 'social policy' justifications, but also developed a recognition that cost factors (for example) can coexist alongside other justifications (ie without themselves being an objective justification but not necessarily precluding a finding of objective justification based on other factors).[8] It is yet to become clear whether this 'costs plus' model will be generally accepted.

There have been various cases already in the UK dealing with when such an objective justification can be established. In a series of cases involving redundancy arrangements (which did not fit within a specific exemption in the *Age Regulations 2006*) the employment tribunal found that arrangements were objectively justified, only for the decision to be overturned by a later decision of the employment appeal tribunal (EAT), which held that insufficient weight had been given to various factors.

Although the employment tribunal correctly identified the aims cited by the employers (eg encouraging rewarding loyalty, older workers being more vulnerable in the job market, agreement with trade unions etc), it gave insufficient weight to whether the defence was proportionate in the circumstances. The relevant scheme could be looked at as a whole (rather than on an individual case-by-case basis for each employee) – see *MacCulloch v ICI*[9] and *Loxley v BAE Systems*.[10] But, conversely, a redundancy arrangement

---

8   *Fuchs and Köhler v Land Hessen* (joined cases C-159/10 and C-160/10).
9   *MacCulloch v Imperial Chemical Industries Plc* [2008] *ICR* 1334 (2008).

16.1.8 *Age discrimination and pensions*

agreed with trade unions was upheld – *Unite v Rolls Royce*.[11] More recently, the Court of Appeal in *Lockwood v Department for Work and Pensions*[12] held that a redundancy scheme was objectively justifiable as while older employees benefited more than their younger colleagues, banding was reasonable as it was statistically shown to be harder for older people to find new employment.

Indirect discrimination

16.1.9 The *Equality Act 2010* prohibits indirect age discrimination (unless an objective justification can be shown or, in the case of occupational pensions, a specific exemption is available in the *Age Exceptions Order 2010*).

An example of this is whether provisions that increase notice periods as employees get older or have increased service are indirectly discriminatory.

There is an express exemption in the *Equality Act 2010* for benefits based on length of service (subject to a reasonableness test). The ECJ decided in one case in 2010 – *Küçükdeveçi v Swedex*[13] – that a rule excluding service before a particular age (here 25) was contrary to the age discrimination laws.

'Golden number' provisions (ie those that allow more favourable benefits on the basis of an age-related factor or combination of factors – for example, age of the employee, retirement or length of service) may perhaps be discriminatory. These could apply in pension schemes and (say) share plans. A case involving a share plan was brought before the employment tribunal, but settled before hearing – see *Hung v Kellogg Brown & Root (UK) Ltd*. A case on a golden number was decided in 2006, before the age discrimination legislation came into force (but concerned the public-sector Local Government Pension Scheme and consequently was directly affected by the EU Council directive): *R (on the application of Unison) v First Secretary of State*.[14]

A specific exception for insurance benefits after age 65 (or if later the state pension age) was introduced in April 2011 – see *Pension Schemes and changes to the default retirement age*. **16.5**.

Scheme closure

16.1.10 There is an express exemption in the *Age Exceptions Order 2010* dealing with closure of a pension scheme to new entrants. Arguably, this could

---

10 *Loxley v BAE Systems Land Systems (Munitions & Ordnance) Ltd* [2008] ICR 1348 (2008).
11 *Rolls-Royce Plc v Unite* [2009] EWCA Civ 387, [2010] 1 WLR 318.
12 *Lockwood v Department for Work and Pensions* [2013] EWCA Civ 1195.
13 *Seda Küçükdeveçi v Swedex GmbH & Co KG* (C-555/07) [2010] ECR I-365.
14 [2006] EWHC 2373 (Admin).

otherwise constitute indirect age discrimination because, over time, it is likely that the new entrants will be younger as a group than the existing employees who are allowed to continue with the old-style benefits. The existence of the express exemption is useful, but care needs to be taken.

There may be arguments (which we think should fail) that the exemption is lost if any new employee is allowed to join on the old basis (other than as a result of a block transfer or a transfer under the *Transfer of Undertakings (Protection of Employment) Regulations – Tupe*). This could mean the exemption is lost even if another new hire cannot compare themselves properly to the employee being allowed to join the old arrangements.

Flexible benefits

16.1.11 There is no express exemption in the *Age Exceptions Order 2010* for the practice of providing flexible benefits. If the cost of the relevant benefit is itself age dependent (eg the cost of increased life cover), can that be reflected in the flexible benefits package? Similar issues arise where employee contributions to an occupational pension scheme are themselves age-related in some way because of a flexible benefits package.

There has been one case in the employment tribunal, *Swann v GHL Insurance Services*, where a flexible benefits package was upheld as not being age discriminatory. However, this was a split decision with one member of the tribunal dissenting.

There is no express exemption for salary sacrifice arrangements.

Any retrospective effect before 2006?

16.1.12 One key exemption in the age regulations and now the *Age Exceptions Order 2010* in relation to pensions is that discrimination cannot apply to benefits relating to service before 1 December 2006 (when the pension aspect of the regulations took effect).

This has been upheld in a Scottish case, *Standard Life Bank v Wilson*.[15] But even here there is some doubt about whether (say) a decision made after 1 December 2006 can be subject to age discrimination complaints even though it relates to service before that date.

---

15 *Standard Life Bank Ltd v Wilson* [2008] ICR 947 (2008).

16.1.12 *Age discrimination and pensions*

Two cases in the ECJ have raised doubts on the UK time limits. In 2008, in a sexual orientation case, *Maruko*,[16] a civil partner was awarded a full pension (where such full pension would have been awarded to a spouse). Any attempt to limit the civil partner's rights to those accrued after a particular date was rejected.

Later in 2008, in *Bartsch*,[17] a widow claimed a pension even though she was more than 15 years younger than her husband and the scheme rules did not allow for a pension where there was such a large age gap. This claim was unsuccessful because the member died before the relevant German law came into force in relation to age discrimination. However, the advocate general's opinion had indicated that he would have considered that such a limitation was not allowed.

Justification of dismissal

16.1.13 The partnership case of *Seldon v Clarkson Wright & Jakes*[18] is relevant here. A partner in a firm of solicitors brought a claim for age discrimination when the firm refused to allow him to continue in office beyond age 65 (the exemption for an age 65 mandatory retirement provision then in force applied only to employees, not office holders or partners).

The employment tribunal held that the firm could objectively justify this. On appeal, in 2012, the Supreme Court held that the objective justification provisions need to be considered in the light of the underlying EU directive and the ECJ case law. This meant that direct discrimination needed to be justified by legitimate social policy objectives and not the individual objectives of the firm. In this case the firm had identified three legitimate objectives, namely staff retention, workforce planning and dignity, and these could potentially justify its compulsory retirement of a partner at the age of 65.

However, the employment tribunal had not considered whether the legitimate aims identified were still proportionate, so the case was remitted to the employment tribunal to consider again. Ultimately, following the Supreme Court decision, the Tribunal decided that, while other ages apart from the specified age of 65 would be appropriate, this age was within the range in which the aims would best be achieved, and this was sufficient.[19]

---

16   *Maruko v Versorgungsanstalt der deutschen Bühnen* (C-267/06) [2008] ECR I-1757.
17   *Bartsch v Bosch and Siemens Hausgeräte (BSH) Altersfürsorge GmbH* (C-427/06) [2008] ECR I-7245.
18   *Seldon v Clarkson Wright and Jakes (a partnership)* [2012] UKSC 16.
19   ET/1100275/07.

In *Chief Constable of West Yorkshire Police v Homer*,[20] a requirement for employees to have a degree in order to be promoted was held by the CA not to be age discriminatory, but this was reversed by the Supreme Court on appeal. The SC held that, when considering whether a measure is proportionate, a court must consider whether there are other, less discriminatory, measures which could achieve the same aim.

Who is liable?

16.1.14 The primary rule is that an employer is the person who will be liable for age discrimination. However, any person who knowingly helps the employer in relation to that discrimination can also be liable (see *Equality Act 2010, s 112*). This could mean (say) other companies within a group or, say, directors and officers.

Trustees are also liable if there is unlawful discrimination by an occupational pension scheme (*Equality Act 2010, s 61*). This is potentially onerous, as often the trustees will not know and have no practical means of finding out if a particular practice or benefit is unlawfully discriminatory. The rules of the pension scheme will be subject to the general non-discrimination rule, and the trustees are given a special statutory power to amend the rules (by resolution) if necessary (*Equality Act 2010, ss 61* and *62*).

Detriment for bringing a claim

16.1.15 Note that any detriment suffered by an individual as a result of bringing a claim is itself also unlawful.

For example, in the *Seldon* case, the solicitors offered an *ex gratia* payment to the partner who had been forced to retire. The employment tribunal held that it was unlawful for the solicitors to withdraw that offer merely because the partner had brought an age discrimination claim. The offer had not been linked expressly into the partner retiring or not bringing a claim. This meant that the partner was able to claim the *ex gratia* amount even though he had brought a claim.

---

20   *Chief Constable of West Yorkshire Police v Homer* [2012] UKSC 15.

The Age Discrimination Regulations and pensions made easier

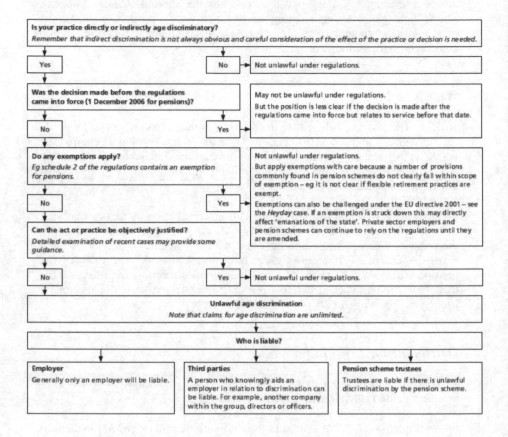

Is your practice directly or indirectly age discriminatory?
Remember that indirect discrimination is not always obvious and careful consideration of the effect of the practice or decision is needed.

Yes

No → Not unlawful under regulations.

Was the decision made before the regulations came into force (1 December 2006 for pensions)?

No

Yes → May not be unlawful under regulations.
But the position is less clear if the decision is made after the regulations came into force but relates to service before that date.

Do any exemptions apply?
Eg schedule 2 of the regulations contains an exemption for pensions.

No

Yes → Not unlawful under regulations.
But apply exemptions with care because a number of provisions commonly found in pension schemes do not clearly fall within scope of exemption – eg it is not clear if flexible retirement practices are exempt.
Exemptions can also be challenged under the EU directive 2001 – see the *Heyday* case. If an exemption is struck down this may directly affect 'emanations of the state'. Private sector employers and pension schemes can continue to rely on the regulations until they are amended.

Can the act or practice be objectively justified?
Detailed examination of recent cases may provide some guidance.

No

Yes → Not unlawful under regulations.

Unlawful age discrimination
Note that claims for age discrimination are unlimited.

Who is liable?

Employer
Generally only an employer will be liable.

Third parties
A person who knowingly aids an employer in relation to discrimination can be liable. For example, another company within the group, directors or officers.

Pension scheme trustees
Trustees are liable if there is unlawful discrimination by the pension scheme.

16.2 Age discrimination and pensions: money purchase arrangements

16.2.1

Summary

The age discrimination laws relating to pensions came into force on 1 December 2006. Originally in *the Employment Equality (Age) Regulations 2006*, the legislation is now in the *Equality Act 2010* and secondary legislation made under that Act.

This section looks at the issues that arise in relation to contributions by employers to defined contribution (money purchase) arrangements. There are some specific exemptions in the regulations, but it is unclear how wide they are.

The legislation broadly prohibits discrimination in employment (including pensions) on the basis of age, whether direct or indirect. There are, however, a number of specific exemptions in the secondary legislation. The current exemptions for pensions are mainly in the *Equality Act (Age Exceptions for Pension Schemes) Order 2010*.[21] On pensions, these broadly re-enacted the exemptions in the previous 2006 regulations with little change.

Many employers now contribute on a money purchase or defined contribution (DC) basis to pension arrangements for their employees, including stakeholder plans. These contributions are paid either to a personal pension scheme (contract based) or to an occupational pension scheme (trust based). The contributions are then credited to an account held by the provider or trustees and, on retirement or crystallisation, the value of the account is used to provide a lump sum and pension benefits.

Historically, there has been a regulatory divide between:

- a DC occupational pension scheme (which is subject to pensions legislation); and

- a DC personal pension (which is subject instead to the financial services regime). Most (all?) stakeholder arrangements are personal pensions.

---

21 *SI 2010/2133.*

16.2.1 *Age discrimination and pensions*

There also used to be different tax rules for occupational schemes and personal pensions, but the pensions tax reforms under the *Finance Act 2004*, which took effect from 6 April 2006, have (broadly) ended this distinction.

But the regulatory distinction remains. Broadly:

- personal pension providers are not specifically within the age discrimination laws – this is because the benefits are provided by a third-party provider (eg an insurance company); but the amount of contributions paid by the employer to such arrangements can raise issues of age discrimination; and

- trustees of occupational pension schemes are expressly made subject to the age discrimination laws by the legislation. This is not expressly envisaged by the underlying EU Council directive of 2000, but this approach is supported by some decisions of the European Court of Justice (eg *Coloroll*[22] in 1994).

Equal input or equal output?

16.2.2 For DC benefits, there are two potential issues. Does the discrimination legislation require equal treatment of:

- contributions (ie input); or
- ultimate benefits (ie output)?

For example, could an older employee claim that even equal contributions for all employees is unlawful age discrimination because he has less time than a younger employee for his account to grow before retirement age and so he is more likely to receive a smaller ultimate pension benefit?

The regulations aim to deal with uncertainties like these by including various specific exemptions relating to DC arrangements, both personal pensions and occupational pension schemes. But the pensions exemptions within the *Age Exceptions Order 2010* are not as wide as was anticipated in the draft regulations circulated in 2005. Some doubts remain about whether particular DC practices are allowed by the regulations.

Of course, the Claimant must be able to demonstrate that he has been treated unfairly as compared to an actual, comparable employee. In *Dumbreck v*

---

22 *Coloroll Pension Trustees Limited v Russell* (C-200/91).

Ofcom[23] the Claimant had had the right to participate in a DB scheme, when his employer decided to transfer all employees to a DC scheme. The Claimant's claim for age discrimination was based on the grounds that he had been terminated for failing to agree new terms and conditions incorporating the DC scheme. As he had been treated in the same way as comparable employees, his claim failed.

Flat-rate contributions

16.2.3   Flat-rate contributions to an occupational pension scheme or a personal pension scheme are expressly exempted by the *Schedule 1, paragraph 4* of the *Age Exceptions Order 2010*. This exempts 'equal rates of member or employer contributions irrespective of the age of the members'. The exemption applies to both employers and trustees and therefore there is no requirement for it to be objectively justified.

Age-related contributions

16.2.4   Many employers contribute to schemes on the basis of increasing contributions for older employees. This can be by reference to various age bands. Employers often established these schemes with the aim of achieving a more equal output benefit, particularly where the DC arrangement replaced an existing final salary scheme.

In 2013, in *HK Danmark v Experian*,[24] the ECJ found that an employer could provide a pension scheme under which employer contributions increased with the age of the employee, however the question of whether this treatment was necessary to achieve a legitimate aim was remitted to the national court.

There are some specific exemptions in the *Age Exceptions Order 2010* which deal with age-related contributions.[25]

One allows 'actuarial calculations' in relation to member contributions, but it is unclear whether this would apply here. More relevant is another, which exempts different rates of member or employer contributions under a money purchase arrangement according to the age of the members where the aim is:

- to equalise the amount of benefit; or
- to make the amount more nearly equal.

---

23   *Dumbreck v Ofcom* ET/2375284/11.
24   *HK Danmark v Experian AS* (C-476/11) [2013] All ER (D) 01 (Oct).
25   *Articles 3* and *4* of, and *Schedules 1* and *2* to, the *Age Exceptions Order 2010*.

16.2.4 *Age discrimination and pensions*

Clearly, this is not a blanket exemption. There must be an aim (it is unclear whose) of equalising benefits or making them 'more nearly equal'.

The government's (DTI's) original guidance on the impact of the *Age Regulations 2006* on pensions (March 2006) took a restrictive view of this exemption, considering that it required a significant number of age bands (so that two bands (ie a one-step contribution increase) may well not qualify). The December 2006 version of the guidance[26] is more flexible, noting that there are no restrictions on the number of bands allowed within a scheme.

The previous guidance seemed to us to be taking an unduly restrictive view of the exemption. The *Age Regulations 2006* (and the current equivalent provisions) do not require benefits to be precisely equal, merely that there be an aim of making benefits more nearly equal. If the two extremes – flat-rate contributions and contributions that vary, for example, every month based on age – are allowed, it is difficult to see why all the intermediate stepped approaches (including perhaps just one step) would not be exempt too (having said that, the larger the number of bands, the easier it may be to show that the exemption applies).

In practice, employers (and trustees) will want to arrange for evidence to be produced that the age-related contributions have the relevant aim in order to fall within the exemption. This will usually involve obtaining an opinion from the relevant actuary on the issue.

There is a similar exemption for contributions to personal pensions.

If contributions are age-related, care should be taken in occupational pension schemes to comply with the exemption from uniform accrual under the preservation legislation (see box).

Preservation legislation – uniform accrual risk

Where contributions to an occupational pension scheme increase after a particular length of service or particular age, the uniform accrual provisions in the preservation legislation may apply.

● This is a rather complex area but is designed for occupational schemes – it does not apply to personal pensions – to avoid attempts to get round the rules on preservation of benefits for early leavers by back-end loading benefits near normal pension age (NPA).

● If uniform accrual applies, the legislation requires the total benefit

---

26 See http://webarchive.nationalarchives.gov.uk/+/http://www.berr.gov.uk/files/file35877.pdf.

> at NPA to be treated as accruing uniformly over all relevant service. This could mean that members at a younger age could claim to be entitled to a proportion of the higher benefit payable for older members.
>
> - There is an exemption from uniform accrual in cases of increasing contributions to a money purchase scheme in some cases under *reg 14A* of the *Occupational Pension Schemes (Preservation of Benefits) Regulations 1991.*[27] A complex actuarial calculation is involved and actuarial advice should be sought to confirm that the relevant test is met.

Service-related contributions

16.2.5 Some employers have set up schemes under which contributions increase as length of service increases. This could be indirectly age discriminatory: older employees may be more likely to qualify for increased contributions.

There is no specific exemption for this in the legislation. There are exemptions for different benefits based on length of service (employers: *para 10, Sch 9, Equality Act 2010*; trustees: *art 6, Age Exceptions Order 2010*). These (broadly):

- exempt a benefit for which there is a qualifying period of less than five years; and

- allow a benefit for which there is a qualifying period of over five years, if the employer reasonably thinks there is a 'legitimate business need'. An example given in the legislation itself is 'by encouraging ... loyalty or motivation or rewarding experience'.

The original 2006 regulations did not apply this exemption expressly to trustees, but this was changed and the current exemptions apply to both employers and trustees (the trustees must ask the employer for confirmation of the position).

The issue on uniform accrual under the preservation legislation also applies here (see box above).

---

27 *SI 1991/*167.

What if the contributions are not set out in the rules?

16.2.6   Some schemes merely provide in the rules that contributions will be paid by employers as specified by them from time to time or as agreed with the individual members. If all the trustees do is accept the contributions paid, do they still run a risk of an age discrimination claim against them (as opposed to just against the employer)?

The trustees will still need to keep a watchful eye on such arrangements to ensure that they are not knowingly aiding discrimination by the employer (under the legislation the trustees can be liable for 'knowingly aiding unlawful acts'). Trustees are already obliged to monitor payment of contributions and to keep a payment schedule – *Pensions Act 1995, s 87.*

Contributions related to the amount of pay

16.2.7   Some schemes include provisions for contributions to be capped or not to apply below a certain salary level. This could potentially constitute indirect discrimination.

However, for occupational schemes there is an express exemption which permits differences in the rates of member or employer contributions to the extent they are attributable to any difference in the 'pensionable pay' of members. 'Pensionable pay' means 'that part of the member's pay which counts as pensionable pay under the scheme rules'. So a limit written into the scheme rules is exempted. It is unclear whether a limit outside the rules (eg set by the employer or agreed in the employment contract) is exempted.

This exemption would seem to allow different definitions of 'pensionable pay' to be included in the scheme rules for different members (eg limiting pay to the former earnings cap for post-1989 joiners).

There is a similar exemption for contributions to personal pensions, but this exemption allows differences only by reference to differences in 'remuneration', so it would not exempt a difference by reference, say, to the date of joining the scheme or joining the employer.

Money purchase for new joiners

16.2.8   Another potentially discriminatory practice would be if new joiners (likely on average to be younger) were eligible only to join a money purchase arrangement but the existing employees (likely on average to be older) could stay in a final salary scheme.

However, in relation to an occupational scheme, the regulations exempt 'the closure of a scheme, from a particular date, to workers who have not already joined it'.

For the purpose of these provisions, each separate section of a scheme is to be treated as a separate scheme. 'Section' is not defined, so it seems that (say) closing a defined benefit (DB) section of a scheme but allowing the DC section to remain open to new joiners is allowed, even if the separate sections do not have completely segregated assets.

Care needs to be taken with this exemption. It is unclear whether it will continue to apply if, say, one new member or one category of new members were allowed into the DB arrangement. For example, if it remained open to senior executives, could a junior employee claim that this meant the exemption did not apply?

The exemption does not apply to personal pensions. So having different rates of contribution to a personal pension (depending on when an employee started or reflecting previous membership of another scheme) could potentially be age discriminatory. The objective justification defence would need to be shown.

Vesting periods

16.2.9   Having a waiting period before joining a scheme, or a vesting period before benefits are preserved within a scheme, could be indirectly discriminatory: older employees may tend to get benefits whereas younger ones will not because they have less service.

In practice these vesting periods look to be mainly service-related (so the exemption for employers will apply – see above).

Occupational pension schemes have often included vesting periods of up to two years (the maximum allowed under the preservation legislation). No vesting period generally applies in relation to personal pensions.

There is an exemption for the vesting of benefits where there is a minimum period of service of not more than two years. It is unclear whether this would allow a waiting period which, when added to the vesting period, could exceed the two-year period (the preservation rules allowing a two-year vesting period apply from the date of joining the scheme, not from the date of starting service).

This will, of course, be an issue only for schemes open (or only recently closed) to new members. The *Pensions Act 2004* rules, which (from 6 April 2006) required occupational schemes to offer a full transfer value after three months' pensionable service, will also reduce any impact of the regulations in this area.

16.2.10 *Age discrimination and pensions*

Minimum age for joining a scheme

16.2.10 A minimum age for admission to an occupational scheme or a personal pension is allowed under specific exemptions. There is also an exemption for a maximum age for joining occupational pension schemes (but this exemption does not apply for personal pensions).

However, this exemption for occupational schemes does not apply if the scheme (or section) provides any benefits that are not a retirement-benefit activity (within *Pensions Act 2004, s 255*). The Department for Work and Pensions and TPR issued guidance (in February and June 2006, respectively) to the effect that provision of lump sum death benefits for non-pensionable members could be outside *s 255* in some circumstances. If this applies, there may be a risk that the exemption will not apply.

Maximum age for accrual

16.2.11 Currently many employers and schemes envisage either that there will be no further accrual of benefits after normal retirement age (NRA) or that employees will switch from a DB to a DC arrangement for service after NRA.

Compulsory retirement ages were completely abolished with effect from 2011 (see *Pension Schemes and changes to the default retirement age*, **16.5**).

In relation to benefits for service after age 65 (or any NRA), the normal age discrimination rules will apply. If the employee was (say) previously accruing benefits within DB plan and is continuing in precisely the same job, then requiring him or her to exit the DB arrangement and join the DC arrangement does not have an express exemption under the regulations.

A maximum number of years of accrual is also exempted for occupational schemes (not personal pensions).

Any other change in benefits would require to be objectively justified.

The 2011 changes to the DRA provisions introduced a new exemption for benefits under an insured arrangement for those aged over 65 (or if greater the state pension age). This could well apply to insured personal pensions and to insured benefits under occupational pension schemes – see further *Pension Schemes and changes to the default retirement age*, **16.5**.

16.3 Age discrimination: using objective justification

Summary

The concept of objective justification came into prominence from 1 October 2006, when the age discrimination legislation came into force. Under the age discrimination legislation it is possible to justify direct as well as indirect discrimination.

Employers and trustees must understand the standards they need to meet if they are to avoid successful age discrimination claims.

16.3.1 The concept of objective justification is familiar from the existing strands of anti-discrimination legislation. However, it came into more prominence after October 2006, when the *Employment Equality (Age) Regulations 2006* came into force. The current legislation is now the *Equality Act 2010* (and underlying secondary legislation), but in relation to pensions they have not significantly changed the law from that under the previous *Age Regulations 2006*.

Unlike other forms of discrimination, it is possible to justify direct (as well as indirect) age discrimination. It is important for employers and trustees to understand the standard they need to meet if they are to avoid successful age discrimination claims.

The test

16.3.2 The legislation says that, to justify discrimination, the employer or trustee must be able to show that the treatment (for direct discrimination) or provision, criterion or practice (for indirect discrimination) is a 'proportionate means of achieving a legitimate aim'.

This reflects the approach towards objective justification taken by the European Court of Justice (ECJ) in cases such as *Bilka Kaufhaus v Weber von Hartz*.[28] In that case the ECJ said that, to show objective justification, the employer had to demonstrate that the requirement he had adopted:

- corresponded to a real need;

- was appropriate with a view to achieving that need; and

---

28 *Bilka-Kaufhaus GmbH v Weber von Hartz* (C-170/84) [1986] ECR 1607.

• was necessary to achieve that need.

The UK approach

16.3.3   The ECJ has made it clear that the decision about whether a particular practice is justified is a decision for national courts rather than the ECJ. Various principles indicate the approach that tribunals or courts should take when assessing whether an employer/trustee has shown that a potentially discriminatory practice is justified.

The tribunal must balance the discriminatory effect of the practice on the individual(s) concerned (including how many people are affected and the severity of the damage caused) against the reasonable needs of the party imposing the requirement. The greater the detriment caused, the more cogent the justification needs to be.

In *Dansk Jurist* (2013)[29] the Danish civil service wanted to prevent employees over 65 years old from receiving redundancy pay. It was argued that, otherwise, employees over 65 years old would recover twice, as they could claim their pension from this age. The ECJ found that, while this was a legitimate aim, the means were not proportionate, as the Danish authorities could have implemented less restrictive measures.

• The employer/trustee does not have to show that the business need is essential or that the proposal was the only course open to him, provided that it was at least 'reasonably necessary'. It is not, however, sufficient for the employer to show that it *believed* that its reasons were adequate or fell within a 'range of reasonable responses'.

• Tribunals must take an objective approach to assessing whether an employer's defence meets the relevant standard. This should include an analysis of the employer's economic position and needs, which should be thorough and critical.

In *Allonby v Accrington and Rossendale College*[30] (2004), as a cost-saving measure, the college dismissed all part-time employees (predominantly women) and re-engaged them on a self-employed basis.

---

29   *Dansk Jurist- og Økonomforbund v Indenrigs- og Sundhedsministeriet* (C-546/11).
30   *Allonby v Accrington & Rossendale College* [2004] EWCA Civ 1630.

The tribunal accepted the employer's arguments uncritically and did not explore the extent to which costs savings could have been achieved through another, less discriminatory, approach.

As a result, the employee's appeal (against the finding of no discrimination) was upheld.

- It is possible to put forward justifications for a particular practice that were not considered when a decision was initially taken. However, in practice, it may obviously be difficult to persuade a tribunal that a factor reflected 'a real need' if it did not feature at all in an employer's reasoning.

- Appeal courts will be reluctant to interfere with tribunal decisions by substituting their own views. If the tribunal has reviewed the evidence presented by an employer properly and answered the questions it is required to have regard to (outlined above), its decision will not be overturned on appeal. This makes it particularly important for employers and trustees to consider the issue of objective justification at an early stage and make sure the factors relied upon are fully documented.

What does this mean in practice?

16.3.4 Employers and pension schemes should now be finalising a review of their pensions (and, in the case of an employer, other) policies to assess whether there is a risk of an age discrimination claim. Figure 1 illustrates the thought process that employers and trustees should be adopting to assess whether there is in fact a risk.

If the review identifies the possibility of a direct or indirect discrimination claim, careful thought needs to be given to whether objective justification is likely to provide a defence.

Figure 2 is taken from the Department for Trade and Industry (DTI) guidance[31] 'The impact of Age Regulations on pension schemes'. It provides a useful snapshot of the questions an employer or trustee needs to ask when conducting that assessment.

As demonstrated in the *Dansk Jurist* case (box at **16.3.3**), the existence of alternative, less discriminatory, options to achieve the same legitimate aim makes it difficult to show that the adoption of a particular measure is proportionate.

---

31 See http://webarchive.nationalarchives.gov.uk/+/http://www.berr.gov.uk/files/file35877.pdf.

16.3.4   *Age discrimination and pensions*

In practice, an employer or trustee may seek to rely on a number of potentially legitimate aims to justify an otherwise discriminatory practice. The extent to which these will be successful will obviously depend on the particular circumstances of each case. Three factors are likely to be particularly relevant in the pensions context.

Rewarding loyalty

16.3.5   The reason for treating one person differently from another may be related to length of service. To the extent that it is, it may be possible to bring a particular benefit within the relevant exemptions, in which case the benefit simply has to 'fulfil a business need' of the undertaking (arguably a less onerous test than objective justification).

There are exemptions for different benefits based on length of service (employers: *Equality Act 2010, Sch 9, para 10*; trustees: *Age Exceptions Order 2010, art 6*). These (broadly):

- exempt a benefit for which there is a qualifying period of less than five years; and

- allow a benefit for which there is a qualifying period of over five years, if the employer reasonably thinks there is a 'legitimate business need'. An example given in the legislation itself is 'by encouraging ... loyalty or motivation or rewarding experience'.

The original 2006 regulations did not apply this exemption expressly to trustees, but this was changed and the current exemptions apply to both employers and trustees (the trustees must ask the employer for confirmation of the position).

Even if the express length-of-service exemptions do not apply, rewarding loyalty may well be a legitimate aim if an employer or trustee can show that it reflects a business need and is proportionate.

In *Barry v Midland Bank*[32] (1999), a redundancy scheme that used length of service and final salary to calculate severance payments was challenged as indirectly discriminatory against part-time employees. Although the claim failed on different grounds, two members of the House of Lords considered that the policy would have been objectively justified. The redundancy payment scheme was to compensate for the

---

32   *Barry v Midland Bank plc* [1999] 3 All ER 974.

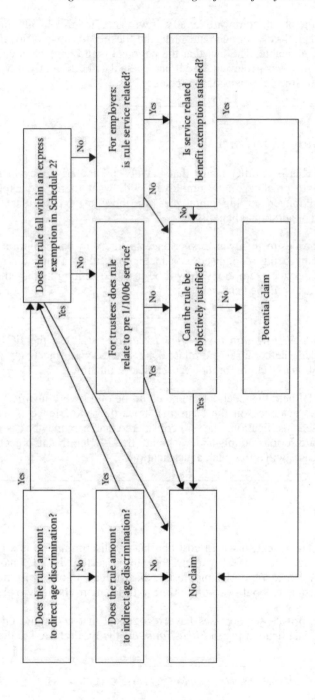

> loss of a job and to reward loyalty. It was accepted that loyalty increased with length of service and that the desire to reward loyalty was unexceptionable. The fact that the payment could have been calculated differently was irrelevant; had it been calculated differently it would not have met the objectives of the scheme.

Rewarding experience

16.3.6   This is another factor that may be particularly relevant to pension schemes. In practice, many employers will want to reward experience by providing longer serving employees, or those of a particular level, with enhanced or additional benefits.

Again, the desire to reward experience is likely to be a legitimate aim, as indicated by being recognised as a factor that fulfils a business need in the length of service exemptions. It will be justified as long as the employer can meet the tests outlined above.

> In *Cadman v Health and Safety Executive*[33] (2006), the ECJ had to consider whether a service-related pay scheme was objectively justified in relation to a claim for indirect sex discrimination.
>
> The ECJ held that such a scheme could be objectively justified without specific evidence on the basis that rewarding experience is usually a sufficient justification. The ECJ considered that there may be cases where there are serious doubts about whether this is a legitimate objective, but most cases will allow such a justification.

Cost

16.3.7   The extent to which cost can justify discrimination is a particularly difficult area. In a case involving the public sector, the ECJ has held that budgetary considerations cannot justify discrimination; otherwise fundamental rights of equality would vary from time to time and from place to place.

However, private sector cases have recognised that economic grounds may provide a justification (eg in *Bilka-Kaufhaus* the ECJ referred to the employer

---

33   *Cadman v Health and Safety Executive* (C-17/05) [2006] ECR I-9583.

needing to put forward economic or administrative reasons for the apparent discrimination). In practice, cost as a sole factor is unlikely to provide objective justification for direct or indirect discrimination.

In *British Airways v Starmer*[34] (2005), the airline had refused a pilot's application to reduce her hours by 50 per cent following her return from maternity leave. The airline argued (among other factors) that the cost of training a pilot to cover the additional hours would be £53,000 and this figure was broadly accepted by the employee.

The employment tribunal accepted that cost could amount to a legitimate aim but nonetheless found that the requirement was not reasonably necessary, so the objective justification argument failed. The decision was upheld by the Employment Appeal Tribunal.

16.3.8   The 2012 Supreme Court decision in *Seldon v Clarkson Wright & Jakes*[35] is relevant here. A partner in a firm of solicitors brought a claim for age discrimination when the firm refused to allow him to continue in office beyond age 65 (the exemption for an age 65 mandatory retirement provision then in force applied only to employees, not office holders or partners).

The employment tribunal held that the firm could objectively justify this. On appeal, in 2012, the Supreme Court held that the objective justification provisions need to be considered in the light of the underlying EU directive and the ECJ case law. This meant that direct discrimination needed to be justified by legitimate social policy objectives and not the individual objectives of the firm. In this case the firm had identified three legitimate objectives, namely staff retention, workforce planning and dignity, and these could potentially justify a compulsory retirement age. The former two objectives were found to justify compulsory retirement of a partner at the age of 65, though the appropriate age for a 'dignity' justification would depend on the particular circumstances of the job (and, in this case, on remittal to the employment tribunal, it was held that the 'dignity' justification would not on its own have justified retirement at age 65).

This may mean that cost cannot be a legitimate aim.

---

34   *Starmer v British Airways plc* [2005] IRLR 862.
35   *Seldon v Clarkson Wright and Jakes (a partnership)* [2012] UKSC 16.

16.3.8   Age discrimination and pensions

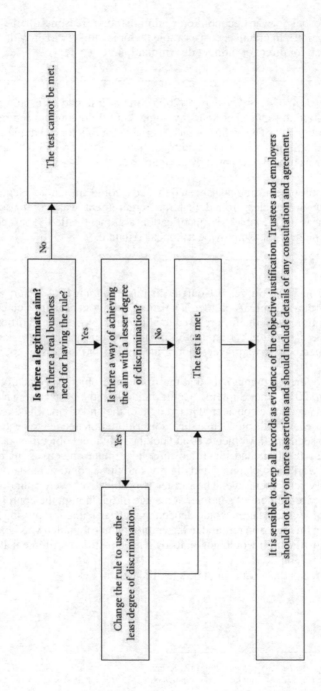

786

Conclusion

16.3.9 The ability of employers and trustees objectively to justify what would otherwise be direct or indirect age discrimination under the legislation throws the issue into sharp relief.

It seems likely that employers and trustees will seek to justify many common practices in relation to pensions.

As shown in some of the cases outlined above, tribunals are likely to apply a 'tough test' (in the words of the DTI) to an employer's assertions about justification.

These arguments seem most likely to succeed if employers and trustees have applied their minds to issues well in advance and conducted (and recorded) a careful assessment of the areas where problems are most likely to arise.

16.4 Age discrimination: flexible benefit issues

Summary

The age discrimination came into force generally on 1 October 2006 and for pensions on 1 December 2006.

This section looks at the issues that arise if employees stay in service and continue to accrue benefits after the normal retirement date that otherwise applies under an occupational pension scheme. It also looks at the issues if an employee asks to start drawing benefits while still in service (whether before or after normal retirement date).

16.4.1 The *Employment Equality (Age) Regulations 2006*,[36] from 1 December 2006, broadly prohibited discrimination in occupational pensions on the basis of age, whether direct or indirect. There are, however, a number of pension-specific exemptions in the legislation regulations. Even if the specific exemptions do not apply, it may be possible for an employer or trustee to show a defence of objective justification. Unlike other forms of age discrimination this applies to both direct and indirect age discrimination.

The current legislation is now the *Equality Act 2010* (and underlying rules, in particular for pensions the *Equality Act (Age Exceptions for Pension Schemes) Order 2010*).[37] In relation to pensions the *Equality Act 2010* and regulations have not significantly changed the law from that under the previous 2006 regulations.

The legislation clearly envisages that the obligation to comply with the non-discrimination provisions applies to both employers and trustees of occupational pension schemes.

Old tax rules: stopping benefit accrual at NRD

16.4.2 Many occupational pension schemes contain an age-based limitation. Even if a member continues to be in employment after the normal retirement date (NRD), many schemes do not envisage a continued accrual of benefits (they may well prohibit a member from drawing his or her pension while in service but instead give an actuarial enhancement to reflect the delay in drawing benefits after NRD).

---

36 *SI 2006/1031.*
37 *SI 2010/2133.*

The old Inland Revenue requirements (before the new rules under the *Finance Act 2004* came into force on 6 April 2006) were generally taken to mean that members should not be able to draw benefits from an occupational pension scheme while still in service with the employer. There was an exception to this where members had joined the scheme before June 1989 and so had continued rights (generally meaning that the earnings cap did not apply to them). Such members were also able, within the Revenue rules, to draw benefits at NRD even though they stayed in service.

The new tax rules introduced by the *Finance Act 2004* do not contain these limitations. With effect on and from 6 April 2006, there is no tax restriction on individuals drawing benefits while they are still in service. It becomes a matter of scheme design whether this is allowed.

New rules: accruing benefits while over NRD

16.4.3   The age discrimination legislation means that, since 2011, compulsory retirement ages for employment purposes are generally invalidated.

If employment does continue beyond age 65, the normal rules apply during that continued employment. In particular, there is no express exemption for any scheme provision that refuses to give further accrual of pension benefits for this period. Thus employers were faced with the choice:

- refuse a request to work beyond 65; or

- allow work beyond age 65, but with no discrimination on benefit accrual.

A third choice (allow work beyond age 65 but with different benefit/pension accrual) is not expressly exempted.

There is an exemption where an occupational pension scheme includes a provision for a maximum number of years for accrual. This applies to both age-related benefits and death benefits and to both defined benefit (DB) and defined contribution (DC) schemes. Such maximum periods are relatively common in DB schemes (eg maximum 40 years of service in a 1/60th scheme).

If this is not available, the employer/trustees would need to be able objectively to justify not giving a benefit (or giving a different benefit) for those over age 65. For example, a practice of removing life cover or moving individuals to DC benefits would need to be objectively justified.

See further *Pension schemes and changes to the default retirement age*, **16.5**.

Generally, care needs to be taken when seeking to rely on the objective justification defence. This is because it depends on what the court/tribunal considers is appropriate and proportionate, not what the individual employer or employee or trustees agree or think. It is possible that vastly increased cost could be a factor in showing an objective justification, but this is by no means clear. For further detail on objective justification, see *Age discrimination: using objective justification*, **16.3**.

Minimum age

16.4.4   The *Finance Act 2004* also generally prohibited benefits from being drawn before age 50 (unless there is ill-health shown with a relevant doctor's certificate). This minimum age rose to 55 from 2010 (but there is some transitional protection for members who already have this right).

It is generally not contrary to the age legislation for a registered pension scheme to follow a practice if this is required by the *Finance Act 2004* and there could otherwise be a tax charge.

Drawing benefits while still in service

16.4.5   A blanket rule within an occupational pension scheme, that a member cannot draw benefits until he or she has left service, could either be not age discriminatory or be objectively justified.

In some cases members who have left service (and become deferred members) will be able to draw benefits at a particular age. This may still mean it is difficult for an active member (still in service) to compare himself or herself with such a deferred member and so to claim that failure to allow the active member to draw the benefit while in service is age discriminatory. The active member and the deferred member are not in identical positions, so it may be possible to say that there is no discrimination on the grounds of age at all.

But care needs to be taken with this, in particular if drawing benefits early is allowed with consent (of, say, the trustees or the employer). The act of giving or refusing consent could also be attacked as directly or indirectly age discriminatory depending on the circumstances.

There is more of an issue in relation to age discrimination if some members have the right to take benefits even while they are in service (eg members with continued rights drawing benefits from NRD). This may well lead other active members to claim age discrimination – pointing to the members who have the right to take benefits from NRD and saying that the only reason they are not allowed to take benefits in a similar situation (while remaining in service) is because of a difference in age.

In practice, it may well be difficult to take away an existing right of members to take benefits at a particular age while remaining in service.

If trustee consent was a requirement before members could take benefit while remaining in service, it seems that any age discrimination claim could relate only to benefits accrued in respect of service from 1 December 2006 onwards.[38] The issue of how to apportion benefits before and after that date would remain.

It may still be possible for an employer or trustee to seek to rely on objective justification. Here the reasons could be said to be not merely cost but also issues of scheme design (the scheme is not intended to give benefits to members who are still in service) or complexity. However, it is difficult to anticipate if this would succeed.

Technical issues

16.4.6   Generally, if members are allowed to draw benefits while remaining in service, various technical pensions law issues remain to be considered.

Schemes are generally allowed to carry out only 'retirement benefit activities' – *Pensions Act 2004, s 255*. Arguably allowing a member to draw benefits before he has in fact left service (ie retired) could perhaps be seen as not qualifying within this limitation.

The pension legislation dealing with issues such as preservation of benefits, revaluation and cash-equivalent transfer values (CETVs) is clearly generally framed on the basis that a member takes all of his or her benefits at one time and does not have separate accrual. The legislation may well need to be clarified by changes, but at present does not deal with the situation of separate benefits terribly well (eg does a member have a CETV right and how does preservation apply to the second chunk of accrual?).

In the case of a member who continues to work after NRD, the issue arises of how his or her accrued benefit (for service accrued up to NRD) is to be treated. Does he or she become entitled to revaluation based on an actuarial factor for the period of any delay in drawing benefit? Conversely, should his or her benefit remain linked to the ultimate final salary while in employment after age 65/NRD?

---

38   *Age Exceptions Order 2010, art 3(a).*

16.4.7 *Age discrimination and pensions*

Liability

16.4.7   Trustees and employers need to take care about incurring liabilities under the rules. If a practice is discovered to be age discriminatory, the relevant affected member can claim unlimited damages as a result. Under the *Equality Act 2010*, liability can fall on either trustees or employers or on any third party who 'knowingly helps' the trustees or employer.

If a practice or activity is discovered to be discriminatory, generally the obligation is on the trustees or employer to 'level up' benefits to the new non-discriminatory level (at least pending any amendment, which would presumably be effective only for future service).

In *Haq v Audit Commission*[39] the notion of 'red circling' was discussed. Red circling is the converse of levelling up, as the benefits of certain employees are frozen to allow those on a discriminatory (worse) level of pay to catch up. The EAT held that this method of removing discrimination over time should not be used without careful consideration, as there is still a period during which the discrimination continues before the pay levels even out.

---

39   *Haq v Audit Commission* [2012] EWCA Civ 1621.

16.5 Pension schemes and changes to the default retirement age

Summary

Since 6 April 2011, compulsory retirement is discriminatory unless it can be objectively justified (and a dismissal could give rise to an unfair dismissal claim). This is likely to mean more employees will stay in employment beyond their pension scheme normal retirement age.

This section looks at the pension implications of this for employers:

- How is life cover affected?

- What pension options are possible?

This section discusses the likely implications.

How the changes affect employees working beyond normal retirement age

16.5.1   Before 6 April 2011, employers could rely on an express statutory exemption to retire employees aged 65 or over without breaching the age equality laws – which are now in the *Equality Act 2010* – provided a set procedure was followed. This procedure included giving the employee six months' notice (the employer also had to consider any request the employee made to continue employment).

However, in January 2011, the Department for Business, Innovation and Skills (BIS) published the response to the government's July 2010 consultation paper on removing both the default retirement age (DRA) of 65 and the linked statutory procedures. The outcome of this consultation was that, with effect from 6 April 2011, compulsory retirement at DRA is no longer exempted from age discrimination laws. Therefore, imposition of a DRA will now constitute age discrimination, unless the employer can objectively justify this.

The conciliation service ACAS issued guidance at the same time as the BIS response, with advice for employers on how they should look to retire employees (at any age) now that the express exemption has been removed.

16.5.1 *Age discrimination and pensions*

The relevant regulations are the *Employment Equality (Repeal of Retirement Age Provisions) Regulations 2011*.[40] These implemented the removal of the DRA exemption and contained transitional provisions from 6 April 2011; they also contain a carve-out for 'insured benefits' (see below).

Abolition of the DRA: timing

16.5.2 After 6 April 2011, no new notices of retirement could be given by an employer under the old DRA exemption.

The regulations contained transitional provisions to phase out the pre-6 April regime. In effect, the last date on which an employer could have given notice (of between 6 and 12 months) to an employee to retire at age 65 or over was 5 April 2011. This is provided that the employee reaches (or already is) age 65 before 1 October 2011. Until 5 January 2012, the employee could request the right to remain employed beyond age 65, but not beyond 5 October 2012. After that date no more retirements under the pre-6 April 2011 regime were permitted.

Employers can still choose to retain a set retirement age, but – in order for this to be lawful – it must be capable of being objectively justified by the employer. The ACAS guidance, which refers to this as an 'Employer Justified Retirement Age', confirms it is possible, but also states that 'the test of objective justification is not an easy one to pass'.

Implications for pension schemes

16.5.3 The removal of the DRA does not mean that occupational pension schemes can no longer have a normal retirement age (NRA). The regulations make no changes to the list of pension exemptions contained in the *Equality Act (Age Exceptions for Pension Schemes) Order 2010*.[41] A scheme NRA is permitted by the exemptions for early and late 'retirement pivot ages'.

The main implication for employers (and trustees) in a pensions context is to decide what benefits should be provided to the employees who remain in employment beyond the pension scheme's NRA and to build this new cost into the funding assumptions.

A pension scheme's NRA may, of course, already be lower than the DRA, so this issue may already arise,

The age discrimination issue arises because the legislation does not contain an express exemption for ceasing to provide pension benefits beyond the NRA. If

---

40 *SI 2011/1069.*
41 *SI 2010/2133.*

794

an employer (or trustee) does not provide benefits for employees over the NRA or the DRA, this looks like age discrimination, unless it can be objectively justified.

Life cover through a pension scheme after 65?

16.5.4   The BIS response said that there would be a carve-out for 'group risk insured benefits' (eg so that employers would not have to provide life cover to an employee over the age of 65).

The regulations contain exemption wording as follows; 'it is not an age contravention for an employer to make arrangements for, or afford access to, the provision of insurance or a related financial service to or in respect of an employee' for a period ending when the employee attains whichever is the greater of 65 or state pension age,

The exemption only applies 'where the insurance or related financial service is, or is to be, provided to the employer's employees or a class of those employees (a) in pursuance of an arrangement between the employer and another person or (b) where the employer's business includes the provision of insurance or financial services …'.

It is not clear from this wording whether the exemption would apply to carve-out life cover benefits provided through an occupational pension scheme (whether insured by trustees or not). Although we cannot see any policy reason for not extending the exemption to life cover benefits provided in this way, unless the government (or subsequent case law) provides some clarification, employers (and trustees) will be faced with having to take a view that the wording is wide enough to cover such benefits, or rely on objective justification.

Implications for DC schemes?

16.5.5   While the issue for DC schemes will be less acute (and less costly), they should review their rules to check whether:

- employer and employee contributions continue after 65; and

- the target retirement age should change.

Any investment strategy and other changes should be communicated to members.

16.5.6 Age discrimination and pensions

Objective justification

16.5.6 To justify discrimination, an employer or trustee must show that the treatment (for direct discrimination) or provision, criterion or practice (for indirect discrimination) is a 'proportionate means of achieving a legitimate aim'. This reflects the approach of the European Court of Justice (ECJ) in cases such as *Bilka Kaufhaus v Weber von Hartz*.[42] In that case, the ECJ said that to show objective justification the employer had to demonstrate that the requirement he had adopted:

- corresponded to a real need;

- was appropriate with a view to achieving that need; and

- was necessary to achieve that need.

There have been a number of recent court and tribunal decisions relating to this issue and there is a noticeable contrast in the decisions reached by the UK employment tribunals[43] (which have found that a set retirement age should not be classed as a proportionate response to a legitimate aim) and those reached by the ECJ and European courts[44] (which have tended to find that a default retirement age is capable of objective justification). Even so, the majority of EU member states appear not have decided not to impose a blanket mandatory retirement age.[45]

16.5.7 The 2012 Supreme Court decision in *Seldon v Clarkson Wright & Jakes*[46] is now the leading UK case in this area. A partner in a firm of solicitors brought a claim for age discrimination when the firm refused to allow him to continue in office beyond age 65 (the exemption for an age 65 mandatory retirement provision then in force applied only to employees, not office holders or partners).

The employment tribunal held that the firm could objectively justify this. On appeal, in 2012, the Supreme Court held that the objective justification provisions need to be considered in the light of the underlying EU directive and

---

42 *Bilka-Kaufhaus GmbH v Weber von Hartz* (C-170/84) [1986] ECR 1607 (1986).
43 See eg *Marlin v Professional Game Match Officials* (2010/ET/2802438/09) and *Baker v National Air Traffic Services Ltd* (HT/2203501/2007).
44 See *Wolf v Stadt Frankfurt am Main* (C-229/08), *Petersen v Berufungsausschuss für Zahnärzte für den Bezirk Westfalen-Lippe* (C-341/08) and *Rosenbladt v Oellerking Gebäudereinigungsges mbH* (C-45/09). More recently see *Prigge v Deutsche Lufthansa AG* (C-447/09) *Fuchs and Köhler v Land Hessen* (joined cases C-159/10 and C-160/10), *Tyrolean Airways* (C-132/11), *Hörnfeldt v Posten Meddelande AB* (C-141/11), *Hennigs v Eisenbahn-Bundesamt* (C-297/10), *Commission v Hungary* (C-286/12) and *Odar v Baxter Deutschland GmbH* (C-152/11).
45 EU Commission (DG Justice), 'Age and Employment' (July 2011).
46 *Seldon v Clarkson Wright and Jakes (a partnership)* [2012] UKSC 16.

the ECJ case law. This meant that direct discrimination needed to be justified by legitimate social policy objectives and not the individual objectives of the firm. In this case the firm had identified three legitimate objectives, namely staff retention, workforce planning and dignity and these could potentially justify a compulsory retirement age. The former two objectives were found to justify compulsory retirement of a partner at the age of 65, though the appropriate age for a 'dignity' justification would depend on the particular circumstances of the job (and, in this case, on remittal to the employment tribunal, it was held that the 'dignity' justification would not on its own have justified retirement at age 65).

For more information, see *Age discrimination: using objective justification*, **16.3**.

What benefits must be provided if an employee keeps working after NRA?

16.5.8   In practice, the NRA will usually be the same as the normal pension age for preservation purposes. That is, deferral of benefit starting beyond NRA will often, under a scheme's rules, result in an actuarial revaluation factor being applied. The member:

- would not accrue any additional pensionable service;

- would cease paying contributions; and

- may lose lump sum life cover.

The benefit position needs to be split in two: pre-NRA accrual and post-NRA accrual. Death benefits (and member contributions) also need to be considered.

The most natural combinations are:

- salary linkage (or best of) (pre-NRA), plus continued DB accrual (post-NRA); and

- actuarial revaluation (pre-NRA), plus new joiner benefits (post-NRA).

Taking account of the issues above and that the number of members in the scheme is likely to increase, administering the scheme may become more complicated.

For the government's consultation, see www.bis.gov.uk/retirement-age.

Pre-NRA accrual

16.5.9

Choice	Comment
Revaluation factor Apply the late retirement revaluation factor (based on service to the NRA and final pensionable pay at the NRA).	This may be the current method. It could be that, in practice, pay rises are limited and end up as less than the revaluation factor. The aim is to be actuarially cost-neutral, so it may already be allowed for in the valuation. Will fit more easily if there is no continued accrual on the same basis after the NRA (egswitch to no accrual or defined contribution etc).
Salary linkage Allow continued salary linkage – ie based on pensionable service to the NRA, but with the benefit based on ultimate final pensionable pay at the date of leaving pensionable service (after the NRA).	Likely to be the easiest for the member to understand. Fits in best if the continued benefit accrual on current defined benefits (DB) basis (or 'best of') is allowed for post-NRA service.
Member choice Give the member the right to choose between revaluation factor and salary linkage.	Member choice and 'best of' are the safest. It is difficult to see how they could be challenged later. Member choice may be a more difficult choice for the member. He has to decide whether any increase in pensionable pay is likely to be more than the extra accrual/actuarial revaluation factor. There is a risk of later claims by a member that he did not fully understand the choice.
Best of Give whichever works out best for the member, between revaluation factor and salary linkage.	Member choice and 'best of' are the safest. It is difficult to see how they could be challenged later. 'Best of' may be the most expensive option.

Post-NRA service

16.5.10   There are perhaps three choices.

Choice	Comment
No benefit No benefit in relation to service after the NRA.	Likely to be directly age discriminatory – unless linked to a maximum number of years/accrual or the member choosing to draw benefits. No express general exemption in the age legislation. The Department for Work and Pensions' guidance (December 2006) includes a case study that shows failure to provide continued accrual would need objective justification.
Continued DB accrual Allow continued accrual based on current salary.	Likely to be the easiest for the member to understand. Fits in best if salary linkage (or 'best of' or member choice) is allowed for pre-NRA service.
Treat as new entrant Give the same benefit accrual as for a new entrant into employment.	Would need objective justification (egon basis of the current open scheme/section if old DB section is closed).

Chapter 17

Investment issues

17.1 Pension fund investment: an overview of legal issues

Summary

Pension funds together hold a large proportion of the wealth and savings of the country. One of the most important duties of the trustees of a pension plan is to invest and look after the assets.

This section looks at the legal issues for pension scheme trustees (and so indirectly employers as funders of schemes) when considering investment of the pension fund. It looks at the following questions:

- What does the trust deed say?

- What does the legislation say?

- What are the trustees' fiduciary duties?

- What about money purchase assets?

This section looks at the legal issues when considering investment of a pension fund.

It considers:

- requirements imposed by the trust deed and by legislation;

- trustees' fiduciary duties;

- investment of money purchase assets; and

- the legal issues relating to investment management agreements.

This section focuses mainly on the issues for trustees. Employers will also be interested as the main funders of an occupational scheme.

What does the trust deed say?

17.1.1   Trustees need to consider their investment powers under the trust deed and rules. Trust deeds generally give a wide power of investment – this is reinforced by a general power to make investments which is implied under *s 34* of the *Pensions Act 1995* (see below).

- Trust deeds can also contain express limitations (eg on all investment in an employer or on loans to members).

- The decision-making powers under the trust deed must also be checked.

- Is delegation of investment decisions (eg to a fund manager) allowed? There is now a statutory delegation power in *s 34(2)* of the *Pensions Act 1995*.

- How can the trustees act (eg by a majority)?

- Does the investment power allow investment in general products (eg including options, partnerships, land, derivatives etc)?

What does the legislation say?

17.1.2   Investment issues are obviously important, so there has been a fair amount of legislation specifically on this for pension trustees. Unfortunately, it is messy and almost nonsensical in a number of areas, but the government shows no sign of seeking to make it any more intelligible.

Unauthorised investments

If restrictions in a trust deed are present they must be complied with (or the provision suitably amended).

If not, any investment contrary to the restriction will be a breach of trust and the trustees will be liable for any losses that result (but will not be able to keep any gains – even offsetting any gains against losses is difficult).

This liability will apply even if the investment looked to be a suitable one otherwise.

It will also apply even if the scheme includes an exoneration clause (see *s 33* of the *Pensions Act 1995* – discussed below).

17.1.3 *Investment issues*

Financial Services and Markets Act 2000 (FSMA)

17.1.3 The financial services regime would often not apply to pension trustees (because they would be able to say that they are not acting in the course of a business and there are a number of exemptions for trustees in any event).

In view of this, the legislation contains a specific provision for pension trustees: an authorised person must make 'day-to-day or routine' investment management decisions. This means that either the trustees must be authorised or they must delegate these decisions to an authorised person (eg an authorised fund manager), retaining only strategic decisions (eg broad asset allocation).

This requirement was previously in the *Financial Services Act 1986* – see *Occupational pensions and the financial services regime,* **17.4**. Breach of this provision will often mean that the trustees should obtain authorisation under FSMA. Failure to do this is a criminal offence.

Pensions Act 1995

17.1.4 This Act also contains a number of provisions dealing with investment issues.

Fund manager – *Pensions Act 1995, s 47(2)*

17.1.5 Trustees must appoint a fund manager in relation to investments (as defined in the FSMA). Arguably this applies (bizarrely) even if the investment is in a pooled product (such as an insurance policy or a unit trust) run by an authorised person under the FSMA. This is one of the more unintelligible provisions.

Appointment issues – *Pensions Act 1995, s 47(3)*

17.1.6 Trustees cannot rely on fund managers or asset custodians unless they have appointed them properly. Regulations set out the manner of appointment (eg must be in writing, must include provisions on dealing with conflicts etc).

Exonerations not effective – *Pensions Act 1995, s 33*

17.1.7 Trustees cannot exclude or restrict any liability for breach of an obligation under any rule of law to take care or exercise skill in the performance of any investment functions.

This is an important issue for trustees. It is one reason why trustee insurance can be valuable. It is arguable that it operates to cancel even indemnities from an employer (on the basis that the employer is owed duties by the trustees in relation to investment matters – see below). Note that some assistance is given to trustees by the later provisions in *s 34* (see below).

Trustees not liable if act reasonably – *Pensions Act 1995, ss 34(4)* and *34(6)*

17.1.8 Trustees are not liable if they take reasonable steps to check that the fund manager is suitable and monitor that he is carrying out his work competently.

Limits on employer-related investment – *Pensions Act 1995, s 40*

17.1.9 This section sets out the limits on 'employer-related investments':

- not more than 5% of the fund in shares of employer (or associate); and
- no employer-related loans (includes not recovering a debt when due).

Note that there is a wide definition of 'associate' – it includes other companies which have a common director with an employer.

For further detail see *Employer-related investment limits,* **17.5** below.

Cash to be in a bank – *Pensions Act 1995, s 49*

17.1.10 Cash must be held in a bank (or in an account, with proper records kept).

Implied general investment power – *Pensions Act 1995, s 34(1)*

17.1.11 This subsection contains a wide implied investment power for trustees, subject to any restriction imposed by the scheme. Trustees have power to 'make an investment of any kind as if they were absolutely entitled to the assets of the scheme'. However, there are some residual doubts whether the term 'investment' includes non-income producing assets.

Provision for employer consent is ineffective – *Pensions Act 1995, s 35(5)*

17.1.12 Neither the scheme nor the statement of investment principles (SIP) can limit investment powers by reference to the consent of the employer.

17.1.13 *Investment issues*

Implied power to delegate to fund managers – *Pensions Act 1995, s 34(2)*

17.1.13 Power is given to trustees to delegate investment discretions to fund managers (authorised under the financial services legislation under *FSMA*) or a committee of trustees etc, but not otherwise.

Statement of investment principles (*SIP*)

17.1.14 Trustees must prepare (and periodically revise) a SIP – *Pensions Act 1995, s 35(1)*. The review must be at least every three years, but also without delay after any significant change in investment policy. Further details about the SIP are in the *2005 Investment Regulations* (*SI 2005/3378*).

The SIP must (*reg 2(3)*) cover the trustees' policy on:

- securing compliance with the obligations under *s 36* (ie including the way diversification and suitability of investments);

- the kinds of investments to be held;

- the balance between different kinds of investment;

- risks, including ways in which risks are to be managed and measured;

- the expected return on investments;

- the realisation of investments;

- the extent (if at all) to which social, environmental or ethical considerations are taken into account in the selection, retention and realisation of investments; and

- the exercise of the rights (including voting rights) attaching to investments.

Trustees must consult with the employers before preparing or revising the SIP – *reg 2(2)(b)*. The decision in *Pitmans*[1] (2004) says consultation must:

- be genuine;

- allow enough time for the employers to consider the SIP or revised SIP and respond; and

- include sending sufficient information for the employers to understand the position.

---

1   *Pitmans Trustees Ltd v The Telecommunications Group plc* [2004] EWHC 181 (Ch).

Consultation must be with all participating employers (unless one has been nominated by them to act as representative for them all).

See further: *Consultation with Employer*, **17.7** below.

The trustees must obtain written advice from a suitable person (with practical experience of financial matters etc) before preparing or revising the SIP – *reg 2(2)(a)*.

There are further detailed obligations in the 2005 Investment Regulations – see *Pensions: changes in investment laws from 2005*, **17.2** below.

Trustees (and fund managers) must seek to comply with the SIP so far as reasonably practicable – *Pensions Act 1995, s 36(5)*.

Trustees must obtain and consider proper written advice on whether investments are suitable. The advice must generally be from an authorised person under the FSMA (if it relates to FSMA investments) – *Pensions Act 1995, ss 36(3) and (4)*.

Myners report (2001)

17.1.15 The findings in this report can be summarised as follows:

- Trustees lack necessary resources and expertise.
- There is too much blind reliance on investment consultants.
- There is insufficient attention to asset allocation.
- Objectives are not linked to the pension fund.

Actions

17.1.16 Myners recommended that trustees:

- reassess expert advice;
- set out objectives;
- focus more on asset allocation;
- beef up investment agreements;
- focus more on transaction costs;
- encourage greater shareholder activism (eg vote the shares held by them);
- provide greater transparency for members; and

- be more effective at decision-making.

Pensions Act 2004

17.1.17 The *Pensions Act 2004* included various provisions dealing with investment issues. Some of these derive from Myners' recommendations. Others come from the *European Directive on Institutions for Occupational Retirement Provision* (the *Iorp Directive*).

Briefly, the *Pensions Act 2004* (and the underlying regulations) provide for:

- a duty on trustees to be 'conversant with' trust documents (including the SIP);
- a duty for trustees to have 'knowledge and understanding' of:
  - pensions and trusts law; and
  - funding; and
  - investment.
- regulations to lay down investment limits; these:
  - require investment 'predominantly' on regulated markets;
  - limit the use of derivatives; and
  - allow borrowing only in limited cases.

See further *Pensions: changes in investment laws from 2005*, **17.2**.

What are the trustees' fiduciary duties?

17.1.18 For non-professional trustees the prudence standard was laid down by the courts in *Learoyd v Whiteley*[2] (1887):

'to take such care as an ordinary prudent man would take if he were minded to make an investment for other people for whom he felt morally obliged to provide.'

A professional trustee has an even higher duty – commensurate with the level of service he purports to provide – *Bartlett v Barclays Bank Trust (No 1)*[3] (1980).

---

2   *Learoyd v Whiteley* (1887) 12 App Cas 727.
3   *Bartlett v Barclays Bank Trust (No 1)* [1980] Ch 515.

Factors for the trustees to consider

17.1.19

- The courts have moved away from the rigid approach of considering the 'riskiness' of each investment in isolation. Hoffmann J (as he then was) in *Nestlé v National Westminster Bank Plc*[4] (1984), considered that trustees should be judged by modern portfolio theory. The risk level of the whole portfolio is, therefore, considered rather than individual investments.

- Trustees should seek to act impartially among the various classes of beneficiaries: *Cowan v Scargill*[5] (1984).

- Trustees should take advice. Although not bound by that advice, a trustee is not entitled to reject it unless this complies with the reasonableness and prudence test: *Cowan v Scargill*.

- Trustees should take investment decisions in the best interests of members and beneficiaries – *reg 4, 2005 Scheme Investment Regulations*. Generally this will mean their best financial interests – *Cowan v Scargill*.

- Trustees should consider the impact on the employer – *Edge v Pensions Ombudsman*[6] (2000) and *Alexander Forbes Trustee Services v Halliwell*[7] (2003). Depending on the scheme rules, the employer may be a residuary beneficiary on a winding-up. It may also be considered a quasi beneficiary under the scheme because it is the ultimate funder of any defined benefits. In addition, the trustees need to consult the employer on the SIP.

For DB schemes, trustees should take account of the employer's investment recommendations on the following grounds.

- It retains the employer's goodwill, which is often in the best interests of the scheme members (eg because funding may be improved, future service benefit provision is more likely to continue).

- Arguably the employer is a quasi beneficiary in any event. It may not directly benefit in the form of cash being paid out of the scheme (at least before a winding-up), but it has a financial interest in the plan in that its contribution rate is affected by the investment decisions. If there is an adverse experience, the trustees will look to it to increase contributions.

---

4   *Nestlé v National Westminster Bank Plc* [2000] WTLR 795.
5   *Cowan v Scargill* [1985] Ch 270.
6   *Edge v Pensions Ombudsman* [2000] Ch 602.
7   *Alexander Forbes Trustee Services Ltd v Halliwell* [2003] EWHC 1685 (Ch).

17.1.19 *Investment issues*

The employers will be obliged to fund the scheme – see *Scheme-specific funding requirements*, **2.1** above.

Schemes often require the consent of the employer for various matters. Each scheme deed should be checked, but employer consent is often required:

- to augment benefits;

- to increase pensions in payment (over the statutory or deed minimum);

- to amend the scheme;

- to accept transfers in;

- to make transfers out (if not statutory);

- as to the level of contributions (subject to the statutory obligations);

- to terminate participation;

- to wind up the scheme;

- to allow a member to be admitted late; and

- to allow a member to commute pension to a lump sum.

Money purchase assets

17.1.20 Pension schemes often include money purchase (DC) benefits. Even DB (final salary) schemes will usually have some DC benefits (eg additional voluntary contributions (AVCs) or credited on individual transfers in).

Here, obviously, the member's benefit is tied to the underlying investment performance. The employer may well be less concerned, unless there is a DB underpin as well (eg a GMP underpin is sometimes found).

The issues concerning the investment of assets representing money purchase benefits include the following:

- The money purchase assets must be covered by the SIP and by fund management agreements.

- It is usual for trustees to specify a range of funds available to members, but for members then to have the choice about where to invest within that range.

- Trustees often retain responsibility to review and monitor the range. Allowing the member to choose within the range is allowed by the FSMA. Trustees should make this clear to the member (it also helps to include provisions on this in the trust deed).

808

- Generally there is no duty to advise the member, but trustees should pass information from fund managers/AVC providers to the member. There may well be an obligation to ensure that the member is aware of details that he or she could not otherwise find out (eg changes in interest rates paid or that there is a guaranteed annuity rate option in an insurance contract – see the Pensions Ombudsman determination in *Wood v Royal Mail Pension Plan* (November 2003)).

- If trustees (or employers) do in fact give investment advice (as opposed to mere information) they may well be liable if they are negligent – eg the Court of Appeal in *Lennon v Metropolitan Police Commissioner*[8] (2004).

The Pensions Regulator has published extensive guidance on investment in DC schemes (both occupational and personal). This is available on the TPR website[9]. Trustees and employers may also want to refer to the principles published by The Investment Governance Group.[10]

Investment management agreements

17.1.21 In practice, only the largest schemes are likely to be authorised under the FSMA and to have their own internal fund managers. Most schemes will need to appoint a fund manager. Legal issues to be considered include the following:

- Is there a segregated fund (ie with assets identified as belonging to the scheme) or will a pooled vehicle (unit trust, open-ended investment company, insurance policy etc) be used?

- For a pooled arrangement, there is likely to be little scope to negotiate the standard terms of business used by the provider. However, larger schemes may have their own standard terms and require managers to negotiate based on their template. Trustees should be aware of any issues that could arise (eg the agreement may well include tax indemnities from the trustees, and there are likely to be various discretions given to the provider – on dilution charges, exit charges etc).

- For a segregated arrangement the fund manager is likely to have a standard form that it will look to apply. This is likely to make it clear that the fund manager does not owe any absolute duty to guarantee a particular return – only to act competently (and without negligence). Trustees need to consider from the outset of negotiations with a fund manager what level of expertise they are looking for. Any targets or risk

---

8   *Lennon v Metropolitan Police Comr* [2004] EWCA Civ 130, [2004] 2 All ER 266.
9   www.pensionsregulator.gov.uk.
10 http://www.thepensionsregulator.gov.uk/about-us/investment-governance-group.aspx.

profiles will need to be expressly built in to the IMA. The fund manager is also likely to look for indemnities from the trustees.

- Trustees should seek assurances that any fund manager to whom it has delegated any discretion will exercise the discretion and carry out its functions as a fund manager in accordance with *section 36* of the *Pensions Act 1995* and the *Investment Regulations* and that the fund manager has the appropriate knowledge and experience for managing the investments of the scheme. If trustees do not satisfy themselves that the fund manager will comply with these requirements, they will not be able to take advantage of the statutory exclusion of liability in respect of the delegate's actions under *section 34* of the *Pensions Act 1995*.

- Offering a default option is mandatory for scheme used for auto-enrolment purposes – see *Auto-enrolment – issues for employers*, **19.1**.

17.2 Pensions: changes in investment laws from 2005

Summary

Summary

The *Pensions Act 2004* amended the investment provisions of the *Pensions Act 1995* to implement changes required by the *EU Occupational Pensions Directive (Iorp)*:

- Trustees' and fund managers' duties are codified to a degree.

- Specific restrictions will apply on borrowings, use of derivatives etc.

This section looks at the requirements which came into force on 30 December 2005.

Introduction

17.2.1   The *Pensions Act 2004* amends the investment provisions of the *Pensions Act 1995* to implement changes required by the EU Occupational Pensions Directive (Iorp).

The *Occupational Pension Schemes (Investment) Regulations 2005*[11] (the *Investment Regulations*) and the changes to the *Pensions Act 1995* came into force on 30 December 2005 (at the same time as the provisions on scheme specific funding).

The major changes included:

- an obligation for trustees and fund managers to exercise their powers of investment or discretions in a manner calculated to ensure the 'security, quality, liquidity and profitability' of the portfolio;

- a requirement that assets must be invested 'predominantly' on regulated markets;

- sanctioning of investment in derivatives to the extent they 'contribute to a reduction of investment risks' or 'facilitate efficient portfolio management'; and

- a prohibition on borrowing money (save for temporary liquidity).

---

11   *SI 2005/3378.*

17.2.1 *Investment issues*

There are exemptions from some of the requirements in the *Investment Regulations*, for example for schemes with fewer than 100 members. However, there is no express exemption in relation to assets in money purchase schemes or sections. This should not be a concern if the trust deed allows members to make a binding choice as to the form of investment, but there may be issues in applying the rules where the trustees retain the investment discretion.

Statement of investment principles

17.2.2 The primary requirement in *s 35* of the *Pensions Act 1995* to maintain and revise a statement of investment principles (SIP) remained but was amended.

New provisions in the *Investment Regulations* included a requirement for a triennial review of the SIP, as well as 'immediately after a significant change in policy'.

Wholly insured schemes (ie whose only investment is an insurance policy) are subject to simplified requirements and must state the reasons why the scheme is wholly insured.

Choosing investments

17.2.3 Trustees, and fund managers to whom trustees' discretion is delegated, continue to be required to exercise their powers of investment to comply with the SIP. A new requirement is that investment must be in accordance with regulations.

The requirement in the *Investment Regulations* that trustees and fund managers must exercise their investment powers or discretion in a manner calculated to ensure the security, quality, liquidity and profitability of the portfolio as a whole aroused concerns at the time that this would require trustees to meet potentially conflicting aims.

The Department for Work and Pensions (DWP) responded that the government's intention was not to impose on trustees a higher duty of care than that which already exists.

The regulations now provide that assets must also be invested 'in a manner appropriate to the nature and duration of the expected future retirement benefits payable under the scheme'.

The DWP hoped that this means that 'the focus of the regulations will be on matters which trustees should consider when making their investment decisions, not on judging trustees against the outcomes of the overall investment strategy'.

Investment of assets

17.2.4   Assets must be invested in the best interests of members and beneficiaries – *reg 4(2)*.

The assets of a scheme must consist 'predominantly' of investments admitted to trading on regulated markets – *reg 4(5)*. Collective investment schemes (CISs) are deemed to be regulated markets to the extent that the underlying investments held by the CIS are so invested. Insurance policies are also to be treated as investments on regulated markets.

Concerns had been expressed about the use of the undefined term 'predominantly'. The DWP's response was that the government does not want to preclude investment in any particular class of assets or set an arbitrary limit on the proportion of assets that must be invested in regulated markets, although if all of the scheme assets were invested outside regulated markets, the trustees would risk being in breach unless unusual circumstances applied.

Assets which are not admitted to trading on a regulated market must be kept to a 'prudent level'. Trustees must ensure diversification to avoid 'excessive reliance' on a particular asset, issuer or group of undertakings and to avoid 'accumulations of risk in the portfolio as a whole' – *reg 4(7)*. Investment in assets issued by the same issuer must not expose the scheme to 'excessive' risk concentration.

Investment in derivatives

17.2.5   The regulations provide that investments in derivative instruments may be made only insofar as they 'contribute to a reduction of investment risks' or 'facilitate efficient portfolio management', and in making such an investment trustees must avoid 'excessive risk exposure to a single counterparty and to other derivative operations' – *reg 4(8)*.

At the time of releasing the first draft of the regulations, the DWP's position was that the terms 'derivative instruments' and 'efficient portfolio management' did not need to be defined in the regulations, as these terms are familiar in the financial services sector. However, during the consultation period the industry expressed concern at the lack of clarity as to these terms' meaning in this specific context.

17.2.5 *Investment issues*

The term 'derivative instruments' is now defined in the regulations in terms of the arrangements listed in the *EU Directive on Markets in Financial Instruments*. The reference to 'efficient portfolio management' is expanded to provide that transactions entered into for this purpose will include ones where the intention is to reduce risk or costs or generate additional capital or income with an acceptable level of risk.

Restriction on borrowing by trustees

17.2.6 The new *s 36A* of the *Pensions Act 1995* and *reg 5* of the *Investment Regulations* contain a prohibition on trustees (and fund managers to whom any discretion has been delegated):

- borrowing money; or

- acting as guarantor where the borrowing is likely to be repaid, or the liability under the guarantee is likely to be satisfied, out of the assets of the scheme.

The fact that the restriction on borrowing is limited to 'money' suggests that borrowing of other assets (such as shares or bonds) could be permitted. This intention was confirmed in the DWP's response to the consultation.

Sanctions

17.2.7 Trustees who fail to comply with the new requirements can be liable to a civil penalty imposed by the Pensions Regulator (TPR) (eg failure to comply with a SIP or to take proper advice).

However, there is no express sanction for breach of the new requirements (eg limits on borrowing). It is unclear if breach of the investment provisions also could give rise to civil actions by affected parties (eg beneficiaries) in the same way as a breach of trust.

Transition

17.2.8 There are no express transitional provisions. It seems that the new provisions apply to any arrangements in existence on 30 December 2005. It is possible that the courts could hold that older arrangements can remain in place with a reasonable time for the trustees to unwind them – see *Wright v Ginn*[12] (1994) (but note that this case was based on a provision in the *Trustee Act 1925* which has now been repealed).

Employer-related investments

17.2.9 The existing restrictions on self-investment are largely reproduced under the revisions to *s 40* of the *Pensions Act 1995* and the *Investment Regulations* – see *Employer-related investment limits: section 40, Pensions Act 1995,* **17.5** below.

Long term investment

17.2.10 Since 2011 there have been a number of consultations, both in Europe and the UK, which have considered the role of pension funds in providing long term investment for the UK and European economies.

The UK government appointed Professor John Kay to carry out an independent review into investment in UK equity markets and its impact on the long-term performance and governance of UK quoted companies in June 2011. Professor Kay published his report (the Kay Review) in July 2012, concluding that 'short-termism is a problem in UK equity markets, and that the principal causes are the decline of trust and the misalignment of incentives throughout the equity investment chain'.[13] The report noted the decline in investment by pension funds in equities, and the increased role of asset managers, as contributing factors. The report included a number of recommendations which could affect pension funds and their trustees. In particular, it recommended that:

- the Stewardship Code should be developed to incorporate a more expansive form of stewardship, focussing on strategic issues as well as questions of corporate governance; and

- the Law Commission should be asked to review the legal concept of fiduciary duty as applied to investment to address uncertainties and misunderstandings on the part of trustees and their advisers.

The Law Commission has since published a consultation paper on fiduciary duties of investment intermediaries in October 2013.[14] The Law Commission's 'tentative view' is that the legal duties placed on trustees to act in the best

---

12 [1994] OPLR 83.

13 http://www.bis.gov.uk/assets/biscore/business-law/docs/k/12–917-kay-review-of-equity-markets-final-report.pdf.

14 http://lawcommission.justice.gov.uk/docs/cp215_fiduciary_duties.pdf.

interests of beneficiaries are satisfactory, but considered that duties placed on providers of workplace contract-based pensions are 'unduly uncertain'. The paper also noted a number of pressures on trustees which discourage long-term investment strategies (such as the statutory funding objective and the need to show any deficit in an employer's accounts). The Law Commission suggested that one method for encouraging long-term investment strategies would be to move towards greater consolidation within trust-based pension funds, both DB and DC funds.

The European Commission also consulted on whether legislative change, or other measures, are required to support long-term financing in the European economy, after publishing a Green Paper on 25 March 2013.[15] The Commission indicated that certain of the proposals being considered as part of its review of the IORP Directive (in particular, the capital requirements based on the Solvency II insurance regime) should be adjusted to ensure there are no obstacles to long-term financing by pension funds – see European Proposals to reform pension scheme regulation, **17.8** below.

---

15   http://eur-lex.europa.eu/LexUriServ/LexUriServ.do?uri=COM:2013:0150:FIN:EN:PDF.

17.3 Ethical investment: practical guidance for trustees

Summary

Trustees are generally under fiduciary duties in relation to the investment of scheme assets. Often this will mean that they should balance risk and anticipated return.

An open issue is how far ethical or socially responsible investment issues should play a role in the investment decisions made by pension trustees.

From July 2000, trustees of occupational pension schemes needed to include in their statement of investment principles (the SIP) a statement about their ethical investment policy and voting practices.

The Law Commission published a consultation paper[16] on fiduciary duties of investment intermediaries in October 2013. The Law Commission's paper considers the role of ethical or socially responsible investment.

17.3.1 The statement in the SIP on ethical investment policy should include details on the extent to which the trustees take social, environmental or ethical considerations into account when they are selecting, retaining and realising investments.

The statement on voting practices should set out the trustees' policy (if any) on exercising voting and other rights attaching to investments.

Trustees have been considering the issue of socially responsible investment (or SRI) and how best (if at all) to formulate an SRI policy. They also need to allow time to consult with the employer and investment managers before making any changes to their SIP.

For most occupational pension schemes, the law is clear. Trustees should act in the 'best interests' of all beneficiaries, which generally means for a proper purpose and in their best financial interests. Trustees cannot therefore draw up an SRI policy without considering the financial consequences and the beneficiaries' best financial interests.

---

16   http://lawcommission.justice.gov.uk/docs/cp215_fiduciary_duties.pdf

17.3.2 *Investment issues*

Law Commission paper (*October 2013*)

17.3.2   The Law Commission's consultation paper[17] on fiduciary duties of investment intermediaries (October 2013) looked at ethical investment issues.

It commented that this is a difficult area, not least because in relation to pension schemes it is not possible to know with any certainty what the prevailing views are. The Law Commission's paper considers the role of ethical or socially responsible investment (Chapter 10). It comments:

Extract from Law Commission consultation paper (*October 2013*)

'10.110 We think that there are only three circumstances when trustees should be swayed by general ethical issues, unrelated to risks, returns or the interests of beneficiaries.

Affinity groups

10.111 The first is where the pension fund is set up by a religious group, other charity or political organisation. As was stated in *Harries*[18], trustees should not be required to make investments which conflict with the aims of the charity. Nor should they be required to make investments which would reduce support for the group by alienating the organisation's donors or recipients. This is in line with the guidance of the Charity Commission.

10.112 However, this exception is likely to be construed narrowly. As was remarked wryly in *Harries,* not all members of the Church of England eschew gambling, alcohol or tobacco. Similarly, other organisations may employ staff who take a relaxed view of their employer's moral stance. Ideally, the limitations imposed on trustees in these specialists schemes should be written into the trust deed and made explicit to all concerned.

Consent

10.113 In DC schemes it is common to allow members a choice of fund. For example, in Chapter 3 we gave a case history of a large trust-based hybrid scheme. The DC "offering" consisted of 12 funds, including ethical and Shariah options. We think it is acceptable to offer

---

17 http://lawcommission.justice.gov.uk/docs/cp215_fiduciary_duties.pdf
18 *Harries v Church Commissioners* [1992] 1 WLR 1241.

members an ethical pension which will or may produce a lower return, provided that that the scheme has been explained fully and each member has given informed consent.[19]

A tie-breaker

10.114 Finally, where trustees think that scheme members would hold a particular moral view, they may use this as a tie breaker. They may avoid investments which they consider scheme members would regard as objectionable, so long as they make equally advantageous investments elsewhere.'

The Law Commission went on to seek views:

Extract from conclusions and questions section of the Law Commission consultation paper (October 2013)

'*Allow investments in line with generally prevailing ethical standards?*

14.25 As we have seen, trustees should consider ethical issues in only very limited circumstances. Trustees should not invest in activities which are illegal. Nor do we think that trustees should invest in activities which contravene international conventions. For example, trustees should not invest in firms manufacturing cluster bombs, banned by the Convention on Cluster Munitions.

14.26 Outside these narrow areas, however, ethical issues are highly contested. To take a recently debated example, some people think that payday lending at high interest rates is wrong, while others think that the ability to borrow money quickly for short periods provides a useful service. Moral condemnation of payday lending is not necessarily "generally prevailing".

14.27 As explained in Chapter 10, the current law permits trustees to disinvest from payday lending if they think that public condemnation of the practice will lead to a risk that the business model is unsustainable. But trustees should only disinvest for purely ethical reasons if two conditions are satisfied. Firstly, the trustees must have good reason to think that scheme members would share their outlook.

---

19   This 'informed consent' requirement looks too high a threshold to us.

Secondly, they should anticipate that the decision will not result in financial detriment to the scheme. In practice it is unlikely that trustees will be aware of members' views or that members will have common views unless the scheme is small and has members from a common source, such as a religious group.

14.28 The law requires trustees to focus on providing pensions to their members, setting aside their own political, moral or religious views. As Lord Murray observed in *Martin v City of Edinburgh District Council*,[20] it is not reasonable or practicable for fiduciaries to divest themselves "of all personal preferences, of all political beliefs, of all moral, religious or other conscientiously held principles".

Nevertheless, they must do their "best to exercise fair and impartial judgment" on the merits of the issue before them. We see advantages to legal rules which remind trustees that their duty is to provide pensions and not to improve the world in some general sense, possibly at the expense of their beneficiaries. We ask consultees whether they agree.

Q8: Do consultees agree that the law is right to allow trustees to consider ethical issues only in limited circumstances?'

Policy options

17.3.3 Many trustees already have a policy on the exercise of voting rights. However, they have three main options regarding ethical investment policies:

- do not formulate a policy at all;
- liaise with the investment managers in formulating a policy; or
- invest part of the scheme's assets in an ethical pooled fund.

Trustees do not have to formulate an SRI policy. Instead, they can merely state in their SIP that they do not take social, ethical and environmental considerations into account when making investment decisions. However, many trustees will feel uncomfortable with this approach (not least because it might bring them under pressure from members) and in practice, it seems that many private sector funds have chosen to adopt some kind of policy.

The trustees can lay some groundwork before getting into the detail of formulating an ethical investment policy.

---

20   1988 SLT 329.

First, they should start discussing with their current (and possibly other) investment managers how far they already take account of ethical considerations. The investment managers will be able to advise on their own experience with ethical investment and what ethical products and approaches are available to the trustees.

A possible compromise between having no ethical investment policy and developing a policy with the investment manager would be to allocate part of the scheme's assets to an ethical pooled fund. This way, the trustees are effectively buying into an ethical policy which has already been formulated.

Possible SRI strategies

17.3.4 Having laid the groundwork, various strategies are becoming recognised as possible approaches to formulating an SRI policy. Some examples include:

- *screening* – using ethical criteria to 'screen' companies and so create a list of acceptable ethical investments;

- *preference* – choosing the 'best' from a portfolio with similar size and sector characteristics to the market but which also reflects the ethical criteria selected by the trustees; and

- *engagement* – approaching companies to encourage them to improve their policies and practices.

Alternatively, the trustees could decide to use an investment manager who already has a policy on ethical investment which is acceptable to them.

Screening

17.3.5 Screening involves drawing up a 'checklist' of ethical criteria which will either eliminate from the portfolio companies involved in negative activities (negative screening) or include companies with a good record on ethical issues (positive screening).

Both negative and positive screening will have implications for the risk profile of the resulting portfolio. This is because applying ethical criteria to a portfolio will alter the weighting of certain sectors and the range of companies included in it. Also, ethical screening may mean that the portfolio will include a greater proportion of smaller companies (larger companies are more likely to be excluded by negative screening as they will generally have a greater range of activities).

17.3.5 *Investment issues*

If they wish to adopt this strategy, trustees would need to ensure that their ethical criteria are not so restrictive that the investments are insufficiently diversified.

The trustees would also need to consider which ethical criteria to use. Though there are no hard-and-fast rules as to what makes an investment 'ethical', a consensus appears to have developed among ethical investment providers. For example ethical providers commonly avoid investments connected with alcohol, tobacco or the defence industry; companies which use child labour or invest in oppressive regimes; nuclear power; the fur trade; and intensive farming. Those regarded as ethically positive include investments connected with conserving energy or promoting alternative energy (eg hydroelectricity); recycling; or manufacturing industries using environmentally friendly and sustainable resources. Even investments in companies with a good employment record or which promote worker participation have been classified as ethically sound.

Preference

17.3.6 The 'preference' approach involves the investment manager putting together a portfolio which has similar size and sector characteristics to the market but at the same time reflects the ethical criteria selected by the trustees.

Companies are ranked according to how well they meet certain ethical policy criteria and trustees can then invest in the higher ranking companies wherever this does not adversely affect investment performance.

The main attraction of this approach is that the portfolio will have a similar risk profile to the market. However, it may not be seen presentationally as an 'ethical' portfolio.

Engagement

17.3.7 The 'engagement' approach involves:

- identifying areas of improvement (in ethical, environmental or other socially responsible issues) for individual companies and then seeking to persuade the companies to commit to change; and

- monitoring the implementation of any commitments and changes made.

The 'engagement' approach allows the investment manager to adopt the same risk characteristics as he would for a portfolio with no ethical constraints. However, the resulting portfolio may include companies which fall short of the chosen ethical criteria, perhaps because the fund will generally not have the flexibility (eg to stop investing in a company if it does not improve its record on ethical issues).

This approach might be constructive in the context of a large chemical manufacturer seeking to improve pollution control measures, but less effective for investment in a tobacco company (which cannot be expected to give up its main business of tobacco production).

Using an investment manager with an acceptable SRI policy

17.3.8   The trustees may decide that, instead of formulating their own policy on ethical investment, they will use one or more investment managers who already have an SRI policy which is acceptable to them.

For the trustees, this approach effectively transfers the responsibility for formulating an ethical investment policy onto the investment manager, so that the trustees will not need to identify their own preferred ethical approach. Instead, the investment manager will construct a general, non-client-specific policy on their approach to ethical investment issues and produce a written policy statement for the trustees to consider. Provided that the policy is acceptable to the trustees, they should be reasonably comfortable with proceeding with that investment manager and reflecting their approach in the SIP.

Concerns about investment performance

17.3.9   Many trustees are concerned that pursuing an ethical investment policy means that investment performance will be compromised.

Though there is a perception that ethical investment may not perform as well as other investments, analysis does not always bear this out. Ethical considerations may well lead trustees to the same conclusion as financial ones. There may be grounds for maintaining that investors tend to desert companies with a poor record on ethical or environmental issues in the medium to long term.

However, an ethical investment policy is, by definition, subject to certain investment restrictions, meaning that the fund cannot take advantage of the full range of investment opportunities in the market.

The trustees can go some way to assuaging these concerns by considering the range and nature of the ethical investment policy which they implement. For example, it seems reasonable to expect that implementing an ethical investment policy by way of the 'engagement' approach outlined above (and to a lesser extent the 'preference' approach) has more chance of producing a result close to that which would be achieved if the only investment policy were to maximise financial returns. The 'screening' approach, on the other hand, probably has more potential to lead to underperformance by comparison with the market, though this will depend on the criteria used for screening and how far they are applied.

The way forward

17.3.10 First, the trustees will need to decide whether they are prepared to say that they have no ethical investment policy.

If not, and they decide to implement an SRI policy, they may be tempted to 'pass the buck' to investment managers. Unless the trustees adopt the alternative strategy (outlined above) of using investment managers with an SRI policy acceptable to them, the investment managers will need the trustees to set some ethical criteria before they can apply an ethical investment policy, meaning that the trustees and the investment managers will need to co-operate in formulating and implementing an ethical investment policy.

Understandably in this increasingly litigious culture, trustees will be concerned to do the right thing and not leave themselves open to criticism as a result of their ethical policy. However, if trustees take the following steps, it will be difficult to challenge their ethical investment policy:

- give due consideration to the range of investments in which the scheme assets are invested;

- satisfy themselves that the scheme's investments (including any ethical choices) are suitably diversified;

- take care in selecting and monitoring investment managers;

- consider the interests of beneficiaries and the particular ethical policy (if any) which they wish to employ;

- if they propose to use an investment manager with a suitable SRI policy, consider the manager's SRI policy and ensure that it is acceptable to the trustees; and

- where members can choose investments (eg for an AVC fund) ensure that they are given sufficient information about any ethical choices to enable them to make an informed investment choice.

Trustees will probably want to retain some flexibility and not be too specific in the ethical policy statement which must be included in their SIP. Any such statement should be carefully tailored to reflect the approach which the trustees have taken to ethical investment.

17.4   Occupational pensions and the financial services regime

Summary

Occupational pension schemes are generally excluded from the obligations imposed by the financial services legislation – rights under a scheme are excluded from being 'investments' and they are excluded from being collective investment schemes.

However, there is an obligation on trustees to ensure that day-to-day investment decisions are taken by an authorised person (subject to some exceptions). Trustees who take a day-to-day decision run the risk of falling within a requirement to become authorised under the legislation (failure to become authorised is a criminal offence).

Conversely personal pension schemes are investments under the financial services legislation and so regulated.

The *Financial Services and Markets Act 2000* came into force in December 2001. The FSMA replaced the *Financial Services Act 1986*, the *Insurance Companies Act 1982* and the *Banking Act 1987*. It provides the framework for the modernisation of the financial services industry with the detail provided by secondary legislation.

This section considers how the FSMA 2000 regime affects pension funds.

Authorisation

17.4.1   Under the *FSMA*, no firm may carry on a regulated activity in the UK, or purport to do so, unless it is an 'authorised' or 'exempt person'.

Contravention of the general prohibition is a criminal offence and resulting agreements are unenforceable.

An authorised or exempt person must not carry on or purport to carry on a regulated activity unless it does so in accordance with permission given by the Financial Conduct Authority (FCA) under *Part IV* of the *FSMA*.

Under the *FSMA* regime, an authorised firm's *Part IV* permission will comprise:

- the regulated activities for which the firm has permission;

17.4.1 *Investment issues*

- limitations incorporated in the description of the regulated activities; and
- any requirements imposed on the firm.

All authorised firms will have received their Scope of Permission Notice setting out both the scope and the limitations of their authorisation.

Definition of investments

17.4.2 A person carrying on, or purporting to carry on, investment business in the UK had to be authorised. However, interests under the trusts of an occupational pension scheme are specifically excluded from the definition of investments – *reg 89(2)* of the *Regulated Activities Order 2001*.[21]

However the establishing, operating or winding-up of a non-trust based stakeholder pension scheme is a regulated activity, even if it is an occupational pension scheme. Interests in personal pensions are investments.

Definition of collective investment scheme

17.4.3 A collective investment scheme (CIS) is an investment for the purposes of FSMA, but occupational pension schemes are excluded from being a CIS – see *para 20* in the schedule to the *Collective Investment Schemes Order 2001*.[22]

Under the *Collective Investment Schemes Order* individual pension accounts and personal pension schemes do not amount to collective investment schemes (CISs). However, personal pension unit trusts which are constituted as feeder funds or which comprise feeder funds do fall within the definition of CISs.

The net effect of these exemptions is that occupational pension schemes, unlike personal pensions, are largely exempt from financial services regulation.

---

21 *Financial Services and Markets Act 2000 (Regulated Activities) Order 2001 (SI 2001/544)*. This replicates an exclusion in *Sch 1* to the *1986 Act*.
22 *Financial Services and Markets Act 2000 (Collective Investment Schemes) Order 2001 (SI 2001/1062)*.

Day-to-day investment decisions

17.4.4 *Art 4* of the *Regulated Activities by way of Business Order*[23] makes specific provision for trustees of an occupational pension scheme to need to become authorised person if they carry on day to day investment activity. From 1 December 2001 (the date FSMA came into force) this replaced a similar provision in *FSA 1986, s 191*. *Art 4* went further than *s 191*, in making routine decisions could also require authorisation. In effect an authorised, or exempt, person needed to take all routine or day-to-day investment management decisions.

It was not clear whether the addition of the word 'routine' changed the position so that the category of decision which an authorised person needed to make was:

- those 'day-to-day' decisions which in their nature are 'routine';

- either those decisions which are 'day to day' or those which are 'routine'; or

- all 'routine' decisions and all 'day-to-day' decisions.

The *Regulated Activities by way of Business Order* was amended in April 2005 to delete the 'routine' limb.

Private equity

17.4.5 In the 2001 Budget, the then Chancellor confirmed that the government would reduce regulatory obstacles to pension funds investing in private equity limited partnerships by removing the requirement to invest through an authorised person.

The result was a new exemption in *art 4* of the *Regulated Activities by way of Business Order* for decisions by the trustees of an occupational pension scheme to buy, sell or subscribe for:

- units in a CIS; or

- contracts of insurance; or

- shares or debentures of a body corporate (which would include a limited partnership)

as long as the criteria below are met.

---

23 *Financial Services and Markets Act 2000 (Carrying on Regulated Activities by Way of Business) Order 2001 (SI 2001/1177).*

17.4.5 *Investment issues*

The exemption was further relaxed in April 2005.

- The decision to invest must follow the obtaining and considering of advice given by an exempt, authorised or overseas person.

- In the case of a body corporate (ie not a CIS or contract of insurance), its primary purpose must be the spreading of investment risk and giving members the benefit of the results. An example is likely to be an investment trust.

- The property of the CIS or body corporate no longer needs to be managed by an authorised, exempt or overseas person.

Information provision/ Financial promotion

17.4.6 The FSMA included an entirely new regime on financial promotion (*s 21*). In general such a financial promotion is only allowed if it is issued or approved by an authorised person, unless an exemption applies. This replaced the *1986 Act* provisions requiring an authorised person to approve 'investment advertisements'.

This regime does not apply to information about occupational schemes because interests under an occupational pension scheme do not fall within the definition of 'investments'.

However it clearly does apply to personal pensions. This can impact on employers regarding promotional material for any personal pensions they had set up. Under the 1986 regime, the government clarified that it would be prudent to ensure that such material was approved by the relevant provider – as an authorised person. The government also issued a Department of Social Security leaflet confirming that generic advice contrasting the merits of an occupational scheme against personal pensions generally was not caught by the investment advertisement regime. However, specific advice or information on specific personal pensions could well be.

A financial promotion will usually only be caught by *s 21* if it is made 'in the course of business'. There may well be arguments that neither an employer nor pension scheme trustees are acting in the course of business, particularly if they are not separately remunerated as a result. However, the cautious view is not to rely on this.

The financial promotion regime in and under *FSMA 2000, s 21* is wider than that formerly applicable in the *1986 Act* to investment advertisements. In particular it is not limited to advertisements, nor is it only related to matters that concern investments.

Broadly *s 21* applies to persons who 'communicate an invitation or inducement to engage in investment activity'. The term 'engaging in an investment activity' is widely defined to include entering into an agreement to carry out what is defined as a 'controlled activity', or dealing with a 'controlled investment'.

Rights under occupational pension schemes are not an investment for this purpose – see *reg 89(2), Regulated Activities Order*[24] – and so the second part will not apply. However some of the activities of trustees and employers could involve engaging in a 'controlled activity'. For example, effecting and carrying out contracts of insurance, as principal, is a controlled activity.

There is no general exemption for financial promotions by employers or trustees of occupational pension schemes. However there is a fairly wide exemption for communications between a 'settlor or grantor' of a trust, which would probably include an employer, or a trustee with any beneficiary of the trust. The communication must relate to the management or distribution of that trust fund. This exemption should cover most communications by trustees or employers with existing members of a scheme.

The exemption does not apply to communications with prospective future members. Trustees and employers should seek advice on such promotional material to determine whether it amounts to a 'controlled activity'. If there is any doubt whether a communication is a financial promotion, an authorised person should approve it before it is issued.

The FSMA financial promotion regime will apply to other pension products which are not occupational pension schemes (eg personal pensions and trust-based stakeholders and non-trust based stakeholder arrangements).

Limited exemption for employers promoting personal pensions

There has, since 1 July 2005 been an exemption allowing employers to promote pension schemes to their employees if the relevant conditions are met.

Article 72 to *72E* of the *Financial Promotions Order*[25] exempts any solicited or unsolicited real time or non-real time financial promotion made by an employer to an employee in relation to a group personal pension scheme or a stakeholder pension scheme provided that all of the following requirements are satisfied:

- The communication informs the employee that the employer will make a contribution to the pension that the employee will receive from the pension scheme to which the communication relates in the event of the employee becoming a member.

---

24 *Financial Services and Markets Act 2000 (Regulated Activities) Order 2001 (SI 2001/544).*
25 The *Financial Services and Markets Act 2000 (Financial Promotion) Order 2005 (SI 2005/1529, as amended).*

17.4.6 *Investment issues*

- The employer has not received and will not receive any direct financial benefit as a result of making the communication[26] (such as commission from, or a reduction in the amount of the premium payable by the employer in respect of any insurance policy issued to the employer by, the provider of the scheme).

- The employer notifies the employee in writing, prior to the employee becoming a member, of the amount of the contribution that the employer will make to the scheme in respect of that employee.

- Where the communication is a non-real time financial promotion, it contains, or is accompanied by, a statement informing the employee of his right to seek independent advice from an authorised person or an appointed representative.

The Treasury provided guidance on the *article 72* exemption on its website.[27]

Consultation on changes to article 72

The exemption was amended from 13 April 2010[28] to dis-apply the financial promotion restriction to communications made by a person (A) contracted by an employer to employees in relation to group personal pension schemes and stakeholder pension schemes – new *article 72A*.

The new exemptions only apply if specified requirements for the employees' protection are met. These are:

(1) the employer and A must have entered into a written contract specifying the terms on which the communication may be made;

(2) in the case of a communication made by a person ('B') on behalf of A, A and B must also have entered into a written contract specifying the terms on which the communication may be made;

(3) the employer must not receive or have received, any direct financial benefit (including any commission, discount, remuneration or reduction in premium) as a result of the communication being made;

(4) the employer must make a contribution to the scheme in the event of the employee becoming a member of the scheme and the communication must contain a statement informing the employee of this;

---

26 This reflects changes to the exemption made in 2010.
27 http://collections.europarchive.org/tna/20080821090815/http:/www.hm-treasury.gov.uk/ documents/financial_services/pensions/finance_promoting_pensions.cfm.
28 The *Financial Services and Markets Act 2000* (*Financial Promotion*) (*Amendment*) *Order 2010* (*SI 2010/905*).

(5)   where the communication is a non-real time financial promotion, it must contain, or be accompanied by, a statement informing the employee of his right to seek advice from an authorised person or an appointed representative; and

(6)   the employer or A must notify the employee in writing prior to the employee becoming a member of the scheme of:

(a)   the amount of the contribution that the employer will make to the scheme in respect of that employee, or the basis on which the contribution will be calculated; and

(b)   any remuneration A or B has received, or will receive, as a consequence of the employee becoming a member of the scheme, or the basis on which any such remuneration will be calculated.

The FCA's guidance[29] comments that:

'Communications which are intended to educate or give employees information with no element of persuasion or incitement will not be invitations or inducements under section 21. Employers may wish to give their employees investment material prepared and approved by an authorised person. This material may be given under cover of a communication from the employer. If so, the covering communication will not itself be an inducement if all it does is to refer employees to the material and explain what they should do if they wish to act on it, without seeking to persuade or incite them to act. Where the covering communication is itself a financial promotion it will need to be approved by an authorised person provided it is a non-real time financial promotion unless an exemption applies. If it is a real time financial promotion it cannot be approved (see, for example, COBS 4.10.4 R). In such cases, an exemption would need to apply.'

The FSA (the predecessor to the FCA) has published a guide: '*Promoting pensions to employees*'[30] and the FSA and TPR have jointly published '*A guide on the regulation of work place contract-based pensions*'.[31]

---

29   http://fshandbook.info/FS/print/FCA/PERG/8/4 (at para 8.4.34).
30   http://www.fca.org.uk/static/documents/fsa-promoting-pensions-employees.pdf
31   http://www.fsa.gov.uk/pubs/pensions/regulation_workplace.pdf

17.5   Employer-related investment limits: *Pensions Act 1995* *s 40*

Summary

This section provides an overview of the issues raised by the limitation on employer-related investment imposed by *s 40* of the *Pensions Act 1995*.

These provisions can be technically difficult, but potentially severe civil and criminal penalties apply for trustees and managers who breach them. There may also be secondary criminal liability for employers who persuade trustees to invest in employer-related investments.

17.5.1   Segregation of a pension scheme's funds from the employer's assets, so that they will not be available to the employer's creditors, is a key control mechanism in safeguarding the security of benefit provision by private sector funded pension schemes. If trustees invest part of the pension fund in the sponsoring employer, the invested assets become part of the employer's general assets and the scheme's dependence on the ability of the employer to pay is increased.

To protect against this, the legislation imposes limits on such investments.

However, the legislative provisions are complex and lead to a number of unexpected pitfalls. It is important that trustees, fund managers and employers understand these issues because they arise surprisingly often and have the potential to lead to severe civil and criminal consequences. In addition, the legislation changed on 23 September 2010, so trustees needed to ensure that their arrangements were still permitted following those changes.

An overview of the law

17.5.2   *Section 40* of the *Pensions Act 1995*, together with the *Occupational Pension Schemes* (*Investment*) *Regulations 2005* (*SI 2005/3378*) (*the Investment Regulations*), restrict 'employer-related investments' by occupational pension schemes (including both defined benefit and money purchase schemes).

The restrictions reflect and expand upon the obligations under the EU Directive on the activities and supervision of institutions for occupational retirement provision (the *Iorp Directive*), but take advantage of provisions that allow the application of the *Iorp Directive* requirements to be postponed until

23 September 2010. However, since that date the legislation has changed to bring the restrictions fully in line with the *Iorp Directive*.

Broadly, *s 40* and the *Investment Regulations*:

- limit the proportion of a scheme's assets that may be invested in employer-related investments to a maximum of 5% of the current market value of the scheme's resources;

- prohibit 'employer-related loans' altogether; and

- prohibit any employer-related investment that involves the trustees entering into a transaction at an undervalue.

There are civil and criminal penalties for breach. TPR has no power to validate arrangements that would otherwise contravene the restrictions on employer-related investment, regardless of the merits of any particular proposal and the interests of scheme members.

Employer-related investments and loans

17.5.3   The definition of employer-related investment is quite technical and it is important to consider whether a particular transaction or investment will fall within its scope. It includes the categories of investments set out in the box below.

Having established that an investment falls within the categories of employer-related investments, it is crucial to establish whether it is also an employer-related loan. There is a total prohibition on employer-related loans (rather than the 5% limit for other employer-related investments).

An employer-related loan includes the categories of employer-related investments highlighted in italics in the box below (categories 4, 6 and 7). It would also include:

- debentures, loan stock, bonds, certificates of deposit or similar instruments (unless such securities are listed on a recognised stock exchange) of an employer (or connected or associated person); and

- leaving amounts outstanding that are due and payable to the scheme by an employer (or a connected or associated person).

What are employer-related investments?

1   Shares or other securities issued by the employer or by any person who is connected with, or an associate of, the employer.

---

2   Land occupied or used by or leased to the employer (or any connected or associated person).

3   Property other than land used for the purposes of any business carried on by the employer (or any connected or associated person).

4   *Loans to an employer (or any connected or associated person).*

5   Investments made through a collective investment scheme, which would have been prohibited had they been made directly.

6   *Any guarantee of, or security given to secure, obligations of the employer (or of any person who is connected with, or an associate of the employer).*

7   *Any loan arrangements entered into with any person where repayment depends on the employer's actions or situation.*

8   Investment in some insurance policies to the extent that the investments held under the policy would be employer-related investments if held directly by the scheme.

Employer-related loans in italics

Transactions at an undervalue

17.5.4   Transactions in which the trustees make a gift to the employer (or a connected or associated person), or receive significantly less than market value in a transaction with such a person, are also prohibited. This could, for example, occur if a trustee leases property to the employer at significantly less than market rent.

Penalties for non-compliance

Civil liabilities

17.5.5   The Pensions Regulator can issue a civil penalty (of up to £5,000 for an individual or £50,000 for a company – *PA 1995, s 10*) on trustees or managers who fail to take all reasonable steps to secure compliance with *s 40*.

Trustees will have the burden of proving they took all reasonable steps and so should carefully minute decisions. Reasonable steps could include having restrictions in their agreements with investment managers (and monitoring compliance) in addition to undertaking due diligence to try to ensure that the requirements of *s 40* are met.

Further, contravention of *s 40* might (this is not clear) result in the investment being unauthorised for trust purposes, meaning the trustees would be personally liable for any resulting losses.

Criminal penalty

17.5.6   A trustee or manager who agrees in the determination to make an investment that is in contravention of *s 40* is guilty of a criminal offence, which can result in an unlimited fine, a maximum period of imprisonment of two years or both.

There should be no criminal liability on a trustee if, for example, a fund manager made the investment decision or if that particular trustee was outvoted.

Both the criminal and civil penalties can extend to directors and other officers of a corporate trustee if the breach is due to his 'consent, connivance or neglect'. Further, there can be no indemnity (or insurance cover) paid from scheme assets against a criminal or civil liability.

Employer concerns

17.5.7   No civil penalty can be issued against an employer. However, because there is also a criminal offence there could be secondary criminal liability for an employer (eg if the employer persuaded the trustees to invest in employer-related investments contrary to *s 40* and so 'aided, abetted, counselled or procured' their offence).

The employer may also be concerned about employer-related investments because of the knock-on effects for scheme funding:

- assets invested in breach of *s 40* do not count for the purposes of scheme-specific funding valuations under the *Pensions Act 2004*; and

- such assets also do not count for the purposes of calculating a debt under *s 75* of the *Pensions Act 1995*.

Therefore, prohibited employer-related investments can increase an employer's liability to fund the scheme on an ongoing basis or if a statutory debt is triggered.

Identifying employer-related investments: how wide is the net?

17.5.8   Given the severity and scope of penalties, it can be disconcerting to trustees to find that identifying employer-related investments can be difficult because of the broad 'net' of persons that the restrictions will apply to for any particular scheme.

The term 'employer' is very wide and may include companies that the trustees would not normally consider to be an employer for the purposes of the scheme.

- Following *Cemex*[32] (2009) and *Pilots*[33] (2010), it appears that an employer can include a company that has ceased to employ any active members but has employees who are eligible to join the scheme or employs deferred or pensioner members of the scheme (see **3.2.3**)

- In a multi-employer scheme, an employer will also include a former employer following an employment-cessation event, until the *s 75* debt has been paid.

- In a frozen scheme, the last set of employers before the freezing event are treated as employers (unless and until they trigger and pay their *s 75* debt).

See *Who is the employer?*, **2.4.1**.

The restrictions also extend to investments with a person who is 'connected or associated' with the employer (as defined in the *Insolvency Act 1986*).

This definition is also very broad. It includes holding companies and subsidiary companies of the employers but may extend beyond the employers' accounting groups. For example, it will include a company in which the employer has a shareholding of one-third or more (see *Who is 'connected' or 'associated?'*, **4.2**).

There is a specific exclusion for employer-related investment purposes if the only reason for the connection is that another company and the employer have a common director. However, the exclusion may not apply if there is any other connection (eg if the director is also an employee).

Due diligence will be important for trustees to establish the extent of the net for employer-related investment purposes.

Holding an interest in a pooled investment?

17.5.9 In some cases there can be a 'look through' to treat pension schemes as owning underlying employer-related investments. This can apply if a scheme holds an interest in a pooled investment (eg an insurance policy, a unit trust or a

---

32 *Cemex UK Marine Ltd v MNOPF Trustees Ltd* [2009] EWHC 3258 (Ch), [2010] ICR 732.
33 *PNPF Trust Co Ltd v Taylor* [2010] EWHC 1573 (Ch).

collective investment scheme) and that pooled vehicle holds employer-related investments.

What if a permitted employer-related investment subsequently exceeds the limit?

17.5.10 There is no periodic testing of whether a scheme's investments breach the 5% limit on employer-related investments: the test is applicable at all times. If the trustees have invested in employer-related investments below this limit, the limit could be broken as a result of investment performance (ie either the value of the employer-related investment going up or the value of the rest of the fund going down).

This may make trustees extremely cautious about having any significant employer-related investment (unless well below the 5% limit) because it will be extremely difficult to ensure that on a day-to-day basis the limit is not breached.

What if an investment unexpectedly becomes employer-related?

17.5.11 Because the restrictions apply to persons who are connected and associated with the employer, investments or loans that were not employer-related when made could become so subsequently (eg following a change in the ownership of the employer). In these circumstances, a loan would not immediately become prohibited. There is an exemption, which enables it to be held for a limited period (normally two years). However, from 23 September 2010, the value of such a loan counts towards the overall 5% limit. There is no similar exemption for an investment that is not a loan. Therefore, if the 5% limit is breached, the trustees will need to take reasonable steps to disinvest.

What about contingent asset arrangements?

17.5.12 *Section 40* provides that to the extent that 'sums due and payable by a person to the trustees or managers of an occupational pension scheme remain unpaid', this shall be treated as a loan and the resources of the scheme shall be treated as invested accordingly. This means any arrangement with an employer (or person associated or connected with an employer) that might result in a payment being due to the scheme from such a person would, if there were a default on the obligation, become a prohibited employer-related loan. This could include parent company guarantees and other contingent assets.

Guidance from TPR in 2010 on '*Monitoring Employer Support*' comments on contingent assets saying:

17.5.12 *Investment issues*

'The regulator's view is that certain investment arrangements that may be agreed by trustees and employers, including some Special Purpose Vehicles such as limited partnership structures could be ERI. Employers and trustees should take legal advice as to whether any proposed asset could be considered as an ERI breach.'

In practice, the key concern for trustees will be to ensure that, if the obligation is defaulted on, or the circumstances change to make the investment potentially employer-related, they take all reasonable steps to recover the amounts due.

What is excluded and what changed in September 2010?

17.5.13 There are a number of investments that do not count as employer-related investments and do not need to be taken into account for the purposes of the 5 per cent market value test or the prohibition on employer-related loans.

The exemptions for some of these investments changed from 23 September 2010 – see the table below.

Trustees had to consider the implications of the changes to these exemptions. Unhelpfully, the position in relation to excluded collective investment schemes and the transitional protection afforded to pre-6 April 1997 investments was unclear. In April 2009, the Department for Work and Pensions (DWP) decided not to implement proposals to remove these exemptions, but indicated that this 'should not be taken as an indication that the exemptions are to remain indefinitely'. In fact the exemptions were removed in September 2010.

Changes to exemptions from 23 September 2010

Exemption before 23 September 2010	*Position following 23 September 2010*
Small schemes (less than 12 members).	No change: exemption continues
Amounts due under the statutory schedule of contributions or *s 75*.	No change: exemption continues
Additional Voluntary Contributions (AVCs) invested with member written agreement	Now count towards 5% limit
Authorised bank and building society accounts	• Still do not count as a prohibited loan. • Now count towards the 5% limit.
Excluded collective investment schemes	Exclusion removed.

Exemption before 23 September 2010	Position following 23 September 2010
Excluded insurance policies.	Now count towards the 5% limit.
Investments held prior to 6 April 1997.	Exclusion removed.

One practical concern about these changes is the difficulty in keeping track of potential employer-related investment with a pooled fund. Even if the 5% limit on shareholdings is not an issue, there are still concerns that:

- this 5% exemption does not apply for loans – eg potentially bonds etc (although debentures listed on a stock exchange should be outside this absolute prohibition on loans); and

- schemes are obliged to inform members of any employer-related investment as part of the scheme's annual report.

17.6 Loans from employers to pension schemes

Summary

A loan from a sponsoring employer to a defined-benefit (DB) pension scheme can sometimes be an attractive way to provide short-term funding for the scheme.

This section discusses the UK pension and tax law implications of funding the scheme in this way.

Introduction

17.6.1 A DB pension scheme will sometimes need short-term liquidity (eg to fund a lump-sum payment). A loan from a sponsoring employer can be an attractive way of providing this funding.

Trustees and employers may prefer funding the scheme through a loan because the scheme may otherwise need to raise the finance by selling some of its investments (something they may wish to avoid in a weak financial market).

Employers may be using a loan so that their money is not trapped in a pension scheme that may be in surplus in the near future. This is important because *s 37* of the *Pensions Act 1995* restricts the circumstances in which a pension scheme can return a surplus to a sponsoring employer. However, if the scheme is paying the employer interest on a loan or repaying the capital this should not be caught by the *s 37* restrictions.

This section discusses the pensions and tax law issues for trustees and employers to consider before a loan is agreed to be made to the pension scheme's trustees.

When can the trustees accept the loan?

17.6.2 The scheme's trustees must have the power to borrow under the scheme's trust deeds and rules before they can accept the loan.

The trustees will also need to be satisfied that borrowing the money is in the scheme's best interests and that they are not acting in breach of their fiduciary duties.

What type of loans can a pension scheme accept?

17.6.3   Under   the   *Occupational   Pension   Schemes   (Investment)*
Regulations 2005 a pension scheme can borrow from a sponsoring employer (or
anyone else) only if the loan is:

- 'for the purpose of providing liquidity' for the scheme; and

- on a 'temporary basis'.

No further guidance is given in the legislation as to what is meant by this
provision. In relation to the 'temporary basis' requirement, we think it would be
difficult to justify a loan lasting more than one year.

Will the scheme's statement of investment principles need to be revised?

17.6.4   *Section 35* of the *Pensions Act 1995* requires schemes to put in place a
statement of investment principles (SIP) that governs decisions about the
scheme's investments.

The trustees may need to revise this statement to reflect the loan.

Trustees are required to review the principles every three years and, without
delay, after any significant change in investment policy.

The loan itself is not an investment, but any changes in other assets will involve
investment so the trustees will need to consider this issue.

Are the trustees personally liable to repay the loan?

17.6.5   The trustees will be individually liable to repay the loan to the
employer unless the loan agreement expressly sets out otherwise by limiting
their liability.

Under *s 31* of the *Trustee Act 2000* the trustees will benefit from an indemnity
from the scheme's assets if the loan was for a proper purpose and there is no
other breach of trust.

The scheme rules may also expressly provide for the trustees to be indemnified
out of the scheme's assets.

Trustee liability is less of an issue if there is a trustee company because the
company will be the contracting party, not the trustee directors. Unless the

trustee directors give a personal guarantee, it is the trustee company that will be liable to repay the loan.

Can the pension scheme pay interest on the loan or repay the loan?

17.6.6   Payments of interest and repayment of the loan would be payments to a sponsoring employer. This raises tax and pensions law implications.

Under the *Finance Act 2004* a registered occupational pension scheme will need to ensure that payments made to the sponsoring employer are 'authorised payments', otherwise they risk incurring substantial tax charges.

If the interest rate on the loan is at an 'arm's-length' rate (or less), interest payments or repayment of the loan by the pension scheme are likely to be considered a 'scheme administration payment' and will be authorised under *s 175* of the *Finance Act 2004*.

However, if the interest payments exceed the amount that might be expected to be paid to a person who was at arm's length, the excess amount is likely to be an unauthorised payment. The company may therefore want to consider charging interest below the market rate to ensure that the scheme does not incur tax charges.

Section 37 of the *Pensions Act 1995* contains restrictions on when a scheme can make payments to a participating employer. From 6 April 2009 a 'scheme administration payment' is excluded from the requirements of *s 37* of the *Pensions Act 1995*. Therefore trustees will not generally need to consider *s 37* restrictions if they are repaying the loan or capital after 6 April 2009.

17.7 Pension scheme investments – consultation with employer

Summary

One of the main responsibilities of trustees of occupational pension schemes is managing the relevant fund. Pensions legislation provides a framework for trustees to follow – framing a statement of investment principles (SIP), delegating to fund managers, etc.

Although the employer is the ultimate funder of a scheme (and so is primarily economically affected if investments don't go well), pensions legislation severely limits the control that the employer is allowed to have on investment matters.

Pension trustees are, however, obliged to consult with the employers on the SIP.

This section looks at the legal issues on employer involvement with pension scheme investment and the consultation obligation on trustees.

Requirement for employer consent is invalid – s 35(5)

17.7.1   A restriction in a tax-registered occupational pension scheme (or SIP) on any power to make investments by reference to a need for the consent of the employer is invalid – *Pensions Act 1995, s 35(5)*. This restriction does not apply to a scheme with fewer than 100 members (*reg 6, 2005 Investment Regulations*).[34]

Section 35 means that it is common for schemes to give a general investment power to trustees, without any requirement for employer consent. There are, in addition, various statutory restrictions on how the trustees may exercise an investment power. See: *Pension fund investment: an overview of legal issues,* **17.1**; *Pensions: changes in investment laws from 2005*; **17.2**; and *Employer-related investment limits*, **17.5**.

The limitation in *s 35(5)* only applies to a restriction requiring the consent of the 'employer'. It is possible (but untested) that a restriction requiring the consent of a non-employer (eg the employer's parent company, which is itself not an employer) is not invalidated by the section.

---

34   *The Occupational Pension Schemes (Investment) Regulations 2005 (SI 2005/3378).*

Consultation with the employer

17.7.2   The trustees (and the relevant fund manager) must exercise powers of investment with a view to giving effect to the principles contained in the SIP, so far as reasonably practical – *s 36(5)*.

The *2005 Investment Regulations* also state that the trustees must review the SIP at least every three years and without delay after any significant delay in investment policy – *reg 2(1)*. Trustees must also obtain written advice (from a person reasonably believed by the trustee to be qualified) about the SIP, before preparing or revising it – *reg 2(2)(a)*.

In addition, the *2005 Investment Regulations* stipulate that the trustees must consult the employer – *reg 2(2)(b)*.

Multi-employer schemes

17.7.3   Where there is a multi-employer scheme, consultation by the trustees must be with all the employers, unless someone has been nominated by all the employers to act as their representative or all the employers have notified the trustees that they need not be consulted – *reg 3(1)*. See *Multi-employer pension schemes: giving authority to the principal company*, **10.3**.

Where all the employers need to be consulted (because no person has been nominated) the trustees can specify a reasonable period (at least 28 days) within which they must receive representations from the employers (otherwise they aren't required to consider them) – *reg 3(2)*.

This express reasonable period limitation seems only to apply where consultation needs to be with all the employers. It doesn't expressly apply where consultation has to be with a nominated person (but a reasonable period obligation is probably implied anyway – see 'What is consultation?' below).

Frozen schemes and former employers

17.7.4   The term 'employer' for this purpose (and *s 35*) includes:

- where a scheme has frozen so it has no active members, the employers who were in place immediately before the scheme became frozen – *reg 1(4);* and

- any former employers, unless they have paid any relevant *section 75* debt or it has been reduced by a legally enforceable agreement – *reg 1(5)*.

See Who is the employer?, **2.4**.

What is consultation?

17.7.5 The consultation requirement in the *2005 Investment Regulations* is not amplified in the legislation.

It is clear that consultation in this context doesn't mean that the employer has a veto – its agreement or consent isn't required. Indeed any consent requirement is invalid – see *s 35(5)*.

However, it seems clear that proper consultation will involve the trustees:

- providing enough information to the employers (or the person nominated) to allow them to understand what is being envisaged;

- allowing enough time for the employers to consider the materials and make representations; and

- considering any representations and entering a dialogue with the employers about them.

All of this means that consultation may not be a short process.

In practice, consultation may well happen relatively informally – employers and trustees may act together in considering the SIP and any changes to it. It's quite common for employers to help trustees in investment matters (this was encouraged by the 2001 Myners report).

Although there is no express provision for this in the legislation, it seems likely that a court would hold that consultation has been properly carried out if the employer (or the relevant person nominated) has agreed the SIP or agreed that consultation can end.

Failure to consult properly

17.7.6 In *Pitmans Trustees v The Telecommunications Group*[35] the Vice Chancellor (Sir Andrew Morritt) held that trustees had not properly carried out a consultation on a proposed change to their SIP. They had sent some documents to the employer by fax just before a bank holiday and allowed only two working days after for comments.

The Vice Chancellor considered that there was no proper consultation – 'there was no genuine invitation to give advice nor a receptive mind to receive it'. The

---

35 [2004] EWHC 181 (Ch).

17.7.6 *Investment issues*

Vice Chancellor referred to other cases[36] (on other legislation) where a requirement for consultation was considered. He agreed with statements that:

- 'the essence of consultation is the communication of a genuine invitation extended with a receptive mind to give advice'; and

- 'to achieve consultation sufficient information must be supplied by the consulting to the consulted party to enable it to tender helpful advice'.

It is noticeable that the obligation under the pensions legislation is only to consult – for example, it is not an obligation to consult 'with a view to reaching agreement' (as is required with collective redundancies under the *Trade Union and Labour Relations (Consolidation) Act 1992*).

In practice, in most cases, there's likely to be a full exchange of dialogue between the trustees and the employer, perhaps even with employer representatives sitting in at relevant trustee investment committee meetings (or indeed serving on relevant investment committees).

Comment

17.7.7   Care needs to be taken. The Vice Chancellor in the *Pitmans* case went on to hold that consultation is a pre-condition to the existence and exercise of the relevant investment power and production of the SIP. Accordingly, he held that the failure to consult meant that the purported new SIP was invalid (in that case this meant that the trustees could not adopt a gilts matching policy that would, under the then legislation, have had the effect of increasing the relevant *s 75* debt).

This seems an extreme sanction for failure to consult and it may be that this would not be followed by future courts. It looks to be inconsistent with other decisions dealing with *s 75* debts – for example *Gleave v Board of the PPF*.[37]

---

36   The other consultation cases followed were *Agricultural, Horticultural and Forestry Industry Training Board v Aylesbury Mushrooms* [1972] 1 All ER 280 and *R v Secretary of State for Social Services ex parte Association of Metropolitan Authorities* [1986] 1 All ER 164.
37   [2008] EWHC 1099 (Ch).

Chapter 18

Pensions tax

18.1 Annual allowance (AA) and lifetime allowance (LTA): changes from 2011

Summary

The *Finance Act 2011* significantly changed the rules on the taxation of pension accrual from tax year 2011/12.

The annual allowance was reduced to £50,000. Accrual over that figure in a registered pension scheme (personal pension or occupational pension) will count as income and be subject to income tax at the individual's marginal tax rate.

The *Finance Act 2013* provides for further reductions to apply from tax year 2014/15.

This section gives a summary of the tax charges.

AA and LTA

Since 2010, the annual allowance (AA) and lifetime allowance (LTA) have been fixed as follows:

Tax year	AA	LTA
2009/10	£245,000	£1,750,000
2010/11	£255,000	£1,800,000
2011/12	£50,000	£1,800,000

18.1.1 *Pensions tax*

Tax year	AA	LTA
2012/13	£50,000	£1,500,000
2013/14	£50,000	£1,500,000
2014/15	£40,000	£1,250,000

Tax changes

18.1.1   The main 2011 changes at a glance are:

- For the tax year 2011/12 the amount of the annual allowance reduced from £255,000 to £50,000.

- The lifetime allowance reduced from £1.8m to £1.5 million in tax year 2012/13.

- The method of calculating the amount of pension saving (pension input amounts) for a defined benefits or a cash balance arrangement changed. For DB, Pension accrual over a year above CPI[1] inflation for that year will be multiplied by a factor of 16 to give a lump sum. There is no change in how to calculate the pension input amount for a money purchase (DC) arrangement.

- There is a three year carry-forward rule. Unused annual allowance from the last three tax years can be carried forward if the tax payer made pension savings in those years. This means if pension saving is more than £50,000 he or she may still may not have to pay the annual allowance charge.

- The legislation has removed the pre-2011 blanket exemption from the annual allowance in the year benefits are taken. There is, however, an exemption in the case of death or serious ill-health. No exemption for enhanced benefits on redundancy applies.

- From 6 April 2011 the exemption from the annual allowance for those with enhanced protection no longer applies.

- The special annual allowance rules (anti-forestalling) introduced in the *Finance Act 2009* were repealed from 2011.

---

1   Consumer price index.

18.1.2

The Government announced in December 2012 that it intended to change these figures again with effect from tax year 2014/15. The *Finance Act 2013* provides for the reduction in the annual allowance from £50,000 to £40,000 and the lifetime allowance from £1.5m to £1.25m.

18.1.3

Example: 1/60th accrual rate, no lump sum entitlement

Tina is a management consultant. She is a member of a final salary scheme giving her a pension of 1/60th pensionable pay for each year of service. At the start of the pension input period (PIP) Tina's pensionable pay is £80,000 and she has 31 years' pensionable service. At the end of the PIP, Tina's pensionable pay has risen by 5% to £84,000 with 32 years' pensionable service.

Tina's pension input amount is the increase in the value of her pension saving over the year. This is the difference between the opening value and the closing value of her promised benefits.

Working out the opening value

Tina's opening value is calculated as:

1   find amount of annual pension

$31/60 \times £80,000 = £41,333.33$

2   multiply annual rate of pension by flat factor of 16

$£41,333.33 \times 16 = £661,333.28$

3   increase by CPI (Consumer Price Index) (in this case 3%)

$£661,333.28 \times 1.03 = £681,173.27$

Tina's opening value is £681,173.27.

Working out the closing value

Tina's closing value is calculated as:

1   find amount of annual pension

$32/60 \times £84,000 = £44,800$

2   multiply annual rate of pension by flat factor of 16

$£44,800 \times 16 = £716,800$

18.1.3 *Pensions tax*

> Tina's closing value is £716,800.
>
> The difference between the closing value and the opening value is £35,626.73. This is less than the annual allowance of £50,000, so Tina does not have to pay the annual allowance charge.
>
> Although Tina is a high earner and receives an above average pay rise (in the current economic climate) she has not exceeded the annual allowance.
>
> *Source*: Example 4 on examples given on HMRC website
> http://www.hmrc.gov.uk/pensionschemes/annual-allowance/
> examples.htm manuals/rpsmmanual/RPSM06107170.htm

Points to note

18.1.4

- Death benefits do not count.

- A flat × 16 multiplier applies. This does not vary with age/normal pension date etc.

- Deferred members will not incur any tax charge, but only if benefits do not increase by more than the CPI (or a greater index if this was required by the scheme rules in force on 14 October 2010). Members with (say) continued salary linkage will not count as deferred. The Finance Bill 2103 (published in December 2012) envisages some changes here).

- Enhancements by reason of redundancy can count. But based on the formula envisaged, enhancements by reason of allowing pension to be paid early with no (or reduced) reduction for early payment will not be treated as an accrual (and so not trigger a tax charge). Added years will trigger a charge.

- The tax charge is on the individual. Schemes and employers can anticipate increased calls for information.

- A 'scheme pays' option is given to members so that individuals can require any tax to be paid out of the benefits.

- Tax charges depend on the pension input periods (PIPs) chosen by schemes (and members).

- The *Finance Act 2011* also added new complex 'disguised remuneration' rules applicable when non-tax registered vehicles are used. These provisions can catch employee benefit trusts (EBTs), and funded employer-financed retirement benefit schemes (EFRBS). The aim is to make them no more attractive than other forms of remuneration. This can still leave unfunded simple promises as more tax efficient.

- NIC charges are not payable on taxable accrual over the AA.

Fixed Protections for LTA

18.1.5   Both the *Finance Act 2011* and the *Finance Act 2013* allow members to elect (before the relevant change date) for a form of fixed protection against the reduction in the LTA from the relevant change date, 6 April 2012 or 6 April 2014 as appropriate.

In effect if an election is made to HMRC and there is no relevant benefit accrual after the relevant change date, the member can retain the old LTA applicable before the change date.

The protection is called 'fixed protection' for the 2012 change and 'fixed protection 2014' for the 2014 change.

Chapter 19

Auto-enrolment

19.1 Auto-enrolment: issues for employers

Summary

New laws came into force on 30 June 2012 that will eventually require all UK employers to automatically enrol eligible workers into the central National Employment Savings Trust (NEST) or another 'qualifying scheme'.

This section provides an overview of an employer's obligation to automatically enrol its employees into NEST or another 'qualifying scheme'.

This section summarises the key employer obligations and examines the implementation of the reforms. It also reviews which workers are eligible for auto-enrolment, the right to opt out of a scheme and inducements, along with how employers can utilise existing schemes.

The prohibition against inducements to opt-out is discussed in more detail in section **19.2**.

Background

19.1.1 The *Pensions Act 2008* put in place the main structure governing auto-enrolment and compulsory employer contributions. The *2008 Act* followed significant consideration by the UK government of how to lift the burden of providing for retirees through a state-funded pension.

The then government identified a behavioural tendency of people to fail to act when faced with difficult financial concerns – eg financial planning. It has ultimately settled on mandatory enrolment of certain workers into a 'qualifying scheme' and endorsed the National Employment Savings Trust (*NEST*) to provide a large-scale, low-cost scheme granting access to pensions saving for the growing number of employees who do not belong to a current scheme.

19.1.2 Following the general election in 2010 the Department for Work and Pensions (DWP) appointed an independent commission to re-examine the approach to auto enrolment contained in the *Pensions Act 2008*. Their report entitled, 'Making automatic-enrolment work' (the Report) was published on 27 October 2010 and suggested various changes to the *Pensions Act 2008*, which have since been implemented by the *Pensions Act 2011*.

19.1.3 Many of the detailed provisions relating to the new regime are contained within the following sets of regulations, as amended (all came into effect by 1 July 2012):

- *Employers Duties (Implementation) Regulations 2010 (SI 2010/4) (Implementation Regulations)*.

- *Occupational and Personal Pension Schemes (Automatic Enrolment) Regulations 2010 (SI 2010/772) (Automatic Enrolment Regulations)*.

- *Employers' Duties (Registration and Compliance) Regulations 2010 (SI 2010/5) (Compliance Regulations)*.

The DWP has also published detailed guidance for both employers and actuaries on certifying DB and hybrid schemes (updated in September 2013).

The Pensions Regulator (TPR) has also issued detailed guidance on the key aspects of auto-enrolment and workplace pension reform.

Auto enrolment began in October 2012 and is being phased in over six years depending on the size of the employer's PAYE scheme on 1 April 2012. The transition phase ends in 2018 and after that time all employers will have automatic enrolment obligations.

There is an optional transitional period for defined benefit and hybrid schemes as these schemes will be able to defer auto-enrolment up to October 2016 for eligible workers who are employed as at the employer's staging date and are entitled to scheme membership (but have not opted to join). This exception does not cover new joiners. For these schemes, the employer needs to notify members if it wants to take advantage of this transitional period, otherwise the auto-enrolment obligation will apply immediately.

Employers who close their scheme during the transitional period must automatically enrol employees into an alternative qualifying scheme. Where that alternative is a defined contribution scheme they will need to pay employer contributions with effect from the jobholder's original automatic enrolment date (which could amount to five years' worth of contributions).

19.1.3 *Auto-enrolment*

Employers will need to check if their existing pension schemes allow employees to join within the automatic enrolment timeframe.

Jobholders

19.1.4 An employer must comply with its new pension duties by automatically enrolling its eligible jobholders into an automatic enrolment scheme, unless they are already active members of the employer's qualifying scheme.

Jobholders are 'workers' or employees who ordinarily work in Great Britain, aged between 16 and 75, who have 'qualifying earnings' – that is, gross earnings (including bonus and overtime) between £5,668 and £41,450 for the 2013/14 tax year (reviewed annually by the DWP).

However, employers are required automatically to enrol and pay contributions only if the jobholder is an 'eligible jobholder', namely someone who:

- is between 22 years of age and the state pension age (SPA); currently 65 for most people; and

- has earnings greater than the 'earnings trigger' (£9,440 a year for the 2013/14 tax year, corresponding to the PAYE threshold).

Certain jobholders are not eligible to be enrolled automatically if they are aged under 22 or over SPA and/or their earnings are below the earnings trigger, but above the lower end of the qualifying earnings band. Such 'non-eligible jobholders' are able to opt in and are to be treated in the same way as someone who has been automatically enrolled in the scheme (ie entitled to employer contributions).

Entitled workers

19.1.5 Likewise, certain jobholders called 'entitled workers' whose earnings are below the lower end of the qualifying earnings band may also opt in, but the employer is not required to contribute and the scheme does not need to be a qualifying scheme, but must be registered (and for a personal pension scheme have 'direct payment arrangements' set up). If within 12 months they then opt out, the employer is not required to offer them an opportunity to opt back in until the following year.

Who is a worker?

19.1.6 The application of auto-enrolment to 'workers' is intended to be in broad alignment with employment legislation, where the concept of a worker is frequently used (eg in discrimination and national minimum wage legislation). Broadly, a 'worker' is anyone who has entered into or works under either a contract of employment or any other contract by which they undertake to do work or perform services for another party (but not if the status of the other party is a client or customer of a profession or business undertaking).

This definition should not capture the genuinely self-employed, but is likely to capture any individual who works as a subordinate to another as part of that other person's business. The contract can be oral or in writing. Typically, the difficulty in practice with this definition is where to draw the line between a genuinely self-employed contractor (who is not a worker) and someone who has contracted to perform the work or services personally (who is a worker). This will be an important issue in practice since incorrectly identifying individuals as self-employed, and thereby excluding them from automatic-enrolment, risks enforcement action by the Pensions Regulator, including fines.

Where a jobholder is an agency worker the automatic enrolment obligations are placed on whichever of the agent or principal (ie the employer) is responsible for paying (or actually pays) the agency worker in respect of the work.

Employer preparations

19.1.7

- Employers need to identify their jobholders; and
- Employers should put in place processes to monitor and identify when non-eligible jobholder employees turn 22 or when they reach the earnings trigger and must be auto-enrolled.

Qualifying earnings

19.1.8 A jobholder's qualifying earnings for that employment in any 12-month period are the gross earnings payable between £5,668 and £41,450 (as at 2013/14 and indexed annually). Qualifying earnings include the following types of payments:

- salary, wages, commission, bonuses, overtime;
- statutory sick pay and statutory maternity pay;
- ordinary or additional statutory paternity pay;
- statutory adoption pay; and
- other prescribed sums.

19.1.8 *Auto-enrolment*

If the jobholder has a pay reference period that is less or more than 12 months, then the above bands apply as if proportionately less or more (eg the automatic enrolment obligations will be triggered by a temporary employee who works for only one month and earns at least £787 in that month).

Systems

19.1.9 Employers will need to have systems capable of recording all these types of pay and re-adjusting correct contributions throughout the year so the right contributions are paid into the scheme.

Automatic enrolment date

19.1.10 This is the primary concept of the new regime. It is an employer's obligation to automatically enrol all eligible jobholders (ie those jobholders who work mainly in the UK aged between 22 and SPA and reaching qualifying earnings) into a qualifying scheme.

Employers' automatic enrolment obligations are triggered on the day a jobholder becomes eligible (ie once the jobholder is over 22 and has qualifying earnings) (the 'automatic enrolment date'). However, there is an optional three month waiting period that an employer can elect to use before a jobholder must be automatically enrolled (ie the automatic enrolment date may be postponed for up to three months). A jobholder may however, opt in during the three month waiting period.

19.1.11 The Regulations set time limits for a jobholder to be enrolled into a 'qualifying scheme':

- Employers sponsoring occupational schemes must make arrangements with the trustees or managers for the jobholder to become an active member within one month (to change to six weeks as of 1 April 2014) from and including the automatic enrolment date (taking into account any postponement period).

- Employers providing access to personal pensions must make arrangements with the pension provider so that, again, within one month (six weeks as of 1 April 2014), from and including the automatic enrolment date (taking into account any postponement period), the jobholder is enrolled in the scheme and given information about the terms and conditions of the agreement.

Where a jobholder has more than one employer, or a succession of employers, the automatic enrolment obligations apply separately in relation to each employment.

19.1.12 If, after an automatic enrolment date has passed, the jobholder ceases to be an active member of a scheme (or the scheme ceases to be qualifying) and in either case it is not because of any action by the jobholder, the employer must make arrangements by which the jobholder becomes an active member of an automatic enrolment scheme with effect from the day following that date.

Opting out

19.1.13 The Regulations at present provide that a jobholder who has become an active member of an occupational pension scheme or a personal pension scheme[1] may opt-out by giving their employer a valid opt-out notice obtained and given in accordance with the Regulations. A jobholder will have one month to do this, which runs from the later of the date the jobholder became an active member and the date he was given the enrolment information.

Jobholders may opt out of the arrangement once enrolled, but if they choose to do so, then they will be automatically re-enrolled once within every three years and will be required to opt out again if they so choose on each occasion. There is flexibility for employers around the date of re-enrolment, allowing a three month window either side of the re-enrolment date for employers to affect this re-enrolment.

An opt-out notice must include the language set out in *Schedule 1* to the Regulations.

Opting out has the effect of treating the employee as if they had never become an active member of a qualifying scheme and any contributions made by or on behalf of the employee must be refunded (see below).

19.1.14 Opt-out notices cannot be provided by the employer but only by the trustee or scheme provider (the aim is to avoid the risk of pressuring by the employer). If the decision is made to opt out, the form is expected to be sent from the jobholder to the employer and then forwarded to the qualifying scheme provider, to give the employer the best chance to halt payroll deductions as soon as possible. The opt-out period must be open for at least 30 days from the date the employee becomes an active member.

19.1.15 Tailored opt-out letters (rather than the standard form) were initially not acceptable, however, the Regulations were clarified in November 2013 to clarify that schemes can customise notices. There is a duty on the employer to vet each form and notify the employee why the notice is invalid. In these circumstances, the one-month opt-out period is extended to six weeks.

---

1   Which includes group personal pensions, stakeholders and group self-invested personal pensions (all contract based).

19.1.15 *Auto-enrolment*

At present, the opt-out provisions also apply in respect of jobholders who opt in (ie those who are younger than 22, older than SPA or do not make qualifying earnings). This is probably an unintended obligation.

19.1.16 Once an opt-out form is received, the employer has no legal basis for continuing to deduct contributions. Once deducted, the employer must pass contributions to the trustees within 19 days of the end of the month in which the contributions have been deducted. Under the Regulations, refunds to the jobholder must be made within one month from the date on which the employer is given a valid opt out notice (or the following payroll period if the opt out notice is submitted after payroll arrangements have closed).

Opting in

19.1.17 Jobholders will be permitted to change their minds later and opt in after they have opted out, at least once every 12 months. The regulations are silent on how quickly an employer must respond – ie if employers can nominate one 'opt-in day' per year or if, say, they have to allow opt-ins within two weeks of an employee request.

19.1.18 An employer will be required to provide certain information to those jobholders who are not auto enrolled about the opportunity to enrol if they so wish. Employers are required to enrol those jobholders who submit a formal opt-in notice. The notice must be in writing and signed by the jobholder, or if the notice is in electronic format, it must include a statement confirming that the jobholder personally submitted the notice.

Employer actions

19.1.19

- The employer should have communication systems set up with the trustee or scheme provider to ensure they are provided with the correct information.

- The employer should have a process in place to prevent continued deduction after an opt-out form has been received.

- The employer should consider the implications of using salary-sacrifice for members who subsequently opt out.

Information requirements

19.1.20 Employers are required to provide certain enrolment information to jobholders within one month (six weeks as of 1 April 2014) of the automatic enrolment date including personal details, contribution details and details regarding opt-out provisions amongst others. In addition employers are required to give certain personal details of jobholders to scheme administrators.

Employers, and relevant third parties, may also be required to provide information to the Pensions Regulator (TPR), so that TPR can police compliance with the regime.

19.1.21 Employers, trustees, managers and pension providers will be required to keep records for up to six years. These records include information about jobholders (eg automatic enrolment dates, gross earnings, contributions and opt-out notices, where relevant) and about the pension scheme (eg employer pension scheme reference). Failure to comply with this obligation could lead to a penalty of up to £50,000 in the case of the company.

Employer actions

19.1.22

- The employer should check if it has adequate systems in place to collate this information and send it out within one month.

- The employer should put fact-checking procedures in place.

- The employer should arrange effective training for its pension and payroll administrators.

- The employer should consider what it will do if it has to auto-enrol and the jobholder is failing to provide the necessary information.

- The employer should check it has adequate record-keeping systems to meet the requirements and respond to TPR's requests.

Existing qualifying schemes

19.1.23 To be a qualifying scheme the benefit structure provided by a defined benefit (DB), defined contribution (DC) or hybrid scheme must satisfy minimum prescribed quality requirements and must not levy charges on its members that exceed a prescribed amount – *s 16(3), PA 2008.*[2] The scheme's trust deed and rules must not contain provisions that are specific barriers to entry in the form of restrictions that:

---

2   The prescribed amount is to be fixed in regulations. No limit on administration charges has yet been announced.

- prevent an employer using the scheme to meet its auto-enrolment, opting-in and re-enrolment duties – *s 17(2)(a), PA 2008*; or

- require a new joiner to make a choice or provide information in order to become an active member – *s 17(2)(b), PA 2008*.

Contracted-out DB schemes

19.1.24 An employer wanting to use an existing DB scheme for auto-enrolment must ensure the scheme satisfies the 'test scheme standard' – *s 22, PA 2008*. This requires the pensions to be provided from the employer's scheme to be broadly equivalent to, or better than, the pensions that would be provided under a test scheme.

A contracted-out DB scheme can satisfy the qualifying scheme test based on the rate of benefit accrual rather than on contribution levels. It uses the existing reference scheme test – ie the test currently used for satisfying requirements for a contracted-out DB scheme. If the scheme is contracted-out, it can continue to be used for existing members. If the employer wants to use it for the automatic enrolment of future eligible jobholders, it will also need to have some additional features.

Contracted-in DB schemes

19.1.25 A second test has been included for contracted-in schemes. They will qualify if they have an accrual rate of 1/120th of average qualifying earnings over the last three tax years preceding the end of pensionable service, providing a pension for life from age 65 based on a maximum term of service up to 40 years. This test will need to be considered carefully. The employer will need to arrange for an actuary to certify that this standard is met, although in some circumstances, the employer may be able to certify themselves. The DWP has issued guidance notes for employers and actuaries on the certification of qualifying schemes and the comparison of the qualifying scheme test. If the scheme does meet the standard, it can continue to be used for existing members. If the employer wants to use it for the automatic enrolment of future eligible jobholders, it will also need to have some additional features.

DC schemes

19.1.26 For an existing occupational DC scheme wishing to satisfy the qualifying scheme test, a contributions-based test is currently used. The DC scheme basic test is that it must have a minimum contribution of 8 per cent for each employee with a minimum 3% from the employer, based on qualifying earnings. Alternatively, employers will be able to certify that their scheme meets 'alternative requirements' based on pensionable pay (provided that this is not less than basic pay). See **19.1.31**.

There are also transitional contribution provisions that apply until October 2018. See **19.1.28**.

Hybrid schemes

19.1.27 Broadly, hybrid schemes (ie schemes which pay out both DC and DB benefits) must meet only one of either the DB or DC scheme quality tests (*s 24* of the *PA 2008*). However, in some cases hybrid schemes can be required to meet both. This depends on the structure of the hybrid scheme.

Transitional period

19.1.28 The transition will begin when the employer's duties start to apply (the 'staging date'). For existing employers, the staging dates range from 1 October 2012 (for employers with over 120,000 employees) to 1 April 2017 (for employers with fewer than 30 employees).

The requirements for minimum contributions to DC schemes are being phased in over two transitional periods spanning six years as follows:

Year	Employer contribution	Total employer and jobholder contribution (including tax relief)
First transitional period: from employer's staging date to 30 September 2017	1%	2%
Second transitional period: from 1 October 2017 to 30 September 2018	2%	5%
Steady state: from 1 October 2018	3%	8%

For an employer operating a DB or hybrid scheme, an optional five-year transitional period applies, running from the employer's staging date. Employers will be able to postpone automatic enrolment for existing jobholders who were allowed to become active members qualifying DB and hybrid schemes before the staging date, and continue to be allowed to join. Employers will need to give notice to jobholders if it intends to postpone (see above).

Certification

19.1.29 An employer's scheme will be deemed to satisfy the relevant quality requirements upon certification of the same at least every 18 months. Where DC schemes are concerned, certification would be based on whether the employer is 'confident' that workers are on course to receive the required minimum level of contributions. Self-certification is mandatory for employers who intend to rely on one of the three alternative quality requirements for DC schemes. If the employer's contributions fall short during the certified period the employer will be required to reconcile only once certain detriment thresholds are breached and the minimum levels for reconciliation will be set to protect individuals from significant detriment. Where DB schemes are concerned, an actuary will usually need to give a certificate in relation to whether the scheme meets qualifying scheme test.

Details of the self-certification process are set out in a combination of regulations and accompanying guidance published by the DWP.

19.1.30 As set out above, for a defined contribution (DC) scheme to satisfy the quality requirements, the employer must contribute at least 3% and the total amount of contributions must be at least 8% of the band earnings over a 12 month period (subject to the transition provisions).

However, there may be a tension between the usual calculation of contributions payable in an occupational DC scheme, which is typically by reference to 'basic pay', and the calculation required under the definition of qualifying earnings. To address this tension 'alternative requirements' based on pensionable pay have been added.

19.1.31 Employers will also be able to certify that their defined contribution schemes meet the required contribution levels when they meet one of the following 'alternative requirements':

Tier 1	• total contributions of at least 9% of pensionable earnings, • including at least 4% employer contributions.
Tier 2	• contributions of at least 8% of pensionable earnings, • including at least 3% employer contributions, • provided that total pensionable earnings of relevant employees are at least 85% of the total earnings of 'those jobholders'.
Tier 3	• contributions of at least 7% of total earnings, • including at least 3% employer contributions.

For these purposes:

- 'Pensionable earnings' are the jobholder's earnings on which contributions are payable to the pension scheme in question by the employer and the jobholder and must be equal to or more than basic pay;

- 'Total earnings' are sums payable to the jobholder in connection with their employment (including salary, wages, commission, bonuses and overtime, and various statutory payments).

- 'Basic pay' means the jobholder's earnings, disregarding any commission, bonuses, overtime or similar payments.

If the scheme does not pass any of these tests then the employer would need to improve scheme quality going forward or carry out individualised checking.

Practical considerations for employers

19.1.32

- Employers should review their existing pension schemes and decide whether all jobholders will be enrolled in the same scheme or whether more than one scheme will be used.

- If an existing scheme is to be used for some or all jobholders, employers should review whether it counts as a qualifying scheme and an automatic enrolment scheme under the legislation and consider whether any rule amendments are required (for example, rules in relation to eligibility provisions, joining formalities, re-joining and re-enrolment, maximum pension age, opting-out, investment options, expenses and pensionable salary and contributions will need to be carefully reviewed for compatibility with auto-enrolment requirements).

- If an existing DB scheme is to be used for existing jobholders, employers need to decide whether to take advantage of the five-year transitional period.

- If changes to the schemes trust deed and rules are required, employers may be obliged to consult with affected members.

Issues for trustees

19.1.33

- Trustees may be asked by the employer to advise members of an existing scheme as to how automatic enrolment will affect them.

- The overall responsibility for scheme administration, management and investment will continue to lie with the trustees. Trustees should ensure that the efficient administration of the scheme will not be jeopardised by an increase in scheme membership and must choose a default investment option that is best suited to the needs of the members. The DWP has produced guidance on choosing the default investment option. Trustees will also need to consider whether any changes will be needed to the range of investment options in light of the post automatic enrolment membership profile.

- Trustees must make sure they receive new membership details from the employer in the format prescribed by the auto-enrolment legislation.

- Crucially, trustees must confirm with the employer whether they have any role in the opt-out process.

NEST

19.1.34 Employers who do not have their own qualifying scheme will be able to use NEST – a central DC scheme established by the Government aimed at workers who earn low to moderate wages.

Interestingly, a deliberate decision was made to avoid having NEST compete with private sector qualifying schemes. This has been achieved by a limitation on annual contributions to NEST of £4,500 in the 2013/14 year (indexed). Members cannot generally transfer their pensions in or out of NEST. This limit and the restriction on transfers are under review. The ban on transfers is due to be reviewed in 2017.

Compliance

19.1.35 The compliance regime was intended to be 'light-touch and designed to support employers in their new obligations'.

19.1.36 TPR will be responsible for enforcing employers' automatic enrolment, re-enrolment and opt-in obligations. It has powers to issue compliance notices. In more serious instances the Regulator can issue fixed-penalty notices (up to £50,000) and escalating-penalty notices (with an escalating daily penalty rate of up to £10,000). Criminal offences have been introduced where an employer wilfully fails to automatically enrol, automaticity re-enrol or permit opt-ins. Conviction carries a maximum sentence of two years' imprisonment.

Prohibited conduct

19.1.37 The *Pensions Act 2008* also prohibits conduct that will encourage employees to opt out – for example:

- suggesting to proposed candidates that opting out will be considered favourably;

- offering inducements to opt out; or

- proposing to take or taking detrimental action against an employee who seeks to take advantage of automatic enrolment generally (the employee can enforce this right against the employer in the employment tribunal).

Employers could face penalties of up to £50,000, or an escalating daily penalty rate of up to £10,000, if they breach this prohibition.

19.1.38 TPR guidance gives examples of 'clear cut' inducements (eg one-off payments, or promotions for employees who opt out, and withholding pay rises or dismissing employees who do not opt out). TPR also cites flexible benefits packages and giving advice to employees on the benefits of opting out as 'less clear cut' examples. In the latter case, TPR will look to the employer's intention (ie whether their 'sole or main purpose' was inducing employees to opt out). See *Auto-Enrolment: Inducements,* **19.2** below.

19.2 Auto-enrolment: inducements

Summary

A new regime prohibiting all employers (regardless of their staging date) from inducing jobholders to opt out from pension saving under the auto-enrolment regime came into force from 1 July 2012. This prohibition is one of a range of measures intended to prevent employers from taking action to avoid their duties under the auto-enrolment regime. It aims to ensure that an individual's decision to opt out is 'taken freely and without influence by the employer'.[3]

Employers that breach this rule could face compliance notices from the Pensions Regulator (TPR), penalties of up to £50,000, plus escalating penalty notices with a daily rate of up to £10,000.

What is an 'inducement'?

19.2.1   An inducement is an action taken by the employer for the sole or main purpose of:

- inducing a worker to give up active membership of a relevant scheme (ie a scheme which meets the auto-enrolment quality requirements) without becoming an active member of another relevant scheme; or

- inducing a jobholder to give an opt out notice.[4]

19.2.2   Both the concept of inducement in the *Pensions Act 2008*, and guidance from the Pensions Regulator (TPR) regarding the meaning of 'inducing', are vague. However, it seems less likely that a claim will be made with respect to actions where there is no particular benefit or incentive for the employer (as without such benefit it would be difficult to show that inducement was the 'sole or main purpose' for such action). Where there is a benefit to the employer, a claim for breach of this rule appears more likely.

---

3   TPR guidance: 'Safeguarding Individuals' (August 2012), p. 4 (http://www.thepensions regulator.gov.uk/docs/pensions-reform-safeguarding-individuals-v4.pdf).
4   *Section 54* (Inducements), *Pensions Act 2008*.

TPR Guidance

19.2.3 TPR has a duty to maximise compliance with the employer duties under the auto-enrolment regime, including the prohibition on inducement.[5] TPR has provided non-statutory guidance for employers on how it will exercise its enforcement powers to this end.

TPR provides the following 'clear cut' examples of inducements:

- offering the following benefits to employees who opt out of their pension scheme: extension or renewal of a short term contract, a one-off payment, a higher salary level, a promotion; and

- threatening the following penalties to those who fail to opt out: withholding a promotion or pay increase, redundancy, and dismissal.[6]

19.2.4 TPR also cites the following 'less clear-cut' cases, where a particular action may amount to an inducement:

- flexible benefit packages where membership of a pension scheme is one of a range of benefits on offer;

- employment agencies that charge a higher rate for individuals who are pension scheme members (although TPR acknowledges that charges will be determined by a range of factors); and

- advice to employees that there may be benefits to opting-out (eg for those with enhanced or fixed protection).

19.2.5 In relation to flexible benefits packages, TPR advises that they will look to the intention of the employers in offering a range of pensionable benefits when considering whether this amounts to an inducement:

'The intention of the legislation is to encourage pension saving at a minimum level, not to restrict flexible benefit packages that employers wish to offer their workers. The individual retains the right to choose the makeup of their flexible benefits.

However, employers must be confident that, in offering such a package, their sole or main purpose is not to induce individuals to opt out of a qualifying scheme. Although the jobholder may choose not to complete an opt-out notice if they move to a non-qualifying scheme or section of an otherwise qualifying scheme, they are still giving up membership of a qualifying scheme. The employer must therefore still

---

5   *Section 5(1)(ca), Pensions Act 2004.*
6   TPR guidance: 'Safeguarding Individuals' (August 2012).

be confident that they can demonstrate that, in offering membership of non-qualifying schemes or sections of an otherwise qualifying scheme as part of the overall package, their sole or main purpose is not to induce individuals to leave the qualifying scheme or section of the scheme.'[7]

19.2.6 TPR has confirmed that it does not matter if the inducement is unsuccessful, and that the employer will be assessed on the action taken and the intention behind it.

Meaning of 'sole or main purpose'

19.2.7 Whilst the concept of 'sole or main purpose' is not defined in the *Pensions Act 2008*, there are other statutes which use a similar test. These relate to TPR's moral hazard powers, inducements to give up collectively agreed terms and anti-avoidance tests in tax legislation.

19.2.8 TPR is permitted to issue a contribution notice where 'the main purpose or one of the main purposes' of an act or omission was to avoid or reduce a *s 75* debt.[8] In the *Bonas case*,[9] Warren J considered that this would involve both an objective element (the act must be capable of achieving the purpose identified) and a subjective element (what the party intended) [para 90].

19.2.9 Prohibitions in employment legislation on inducements relating to union membership and collective bargaining also refer to the 'employer's sole or main purpose'.[10] The legislation sets out specific factors which may be taken into account in determining whether the 'sole or main purpose' test is met, including:

- the timing when the employer's offer was made and whether this coincided with arrangements for collective bargaining being proposed or agreed with a union; and

- whether the offers were made to particular employees and 'were made with the sole or main purpose of rewarding those particular workers for their high level or performance or of retaining them because of their special value to the employer'.

---

7   TPR guidance: 'Safeguarding Individuals' (August 2012).
8   *Section 38* of the *Pensions Act 2004*.
9   In the matter of the Bonas Group Pension Scheme; *Michel Van de Wiele NV v the Pensions Regulator (FS/2010/0007)*. See the *Bonas* case, **4.8** above.
10 *Sections 145A* and *145B* of the *Trade Union and Labour Relations (Consolidation) Act 1992*.

Interestingly, a wider view of the concept of inducement can be found in the case of *Commission for Racial Equality v Imperial Society of Dancing*[11] which considered the meaning of the word 'induce' in *s 31* of the *Race Relations Act*. In that case the EAT held that the word 'induce' covers a mere request to discriminate. It does not necessarily imply an offer of some benefit or the threat of some detriment. The EAT held that the ordinary meaning of the word 'induce' is 'to persuade or to prevail upon or bring about' and there is no reason to construe the word narrowly or in a restricted sense.

It remains to be seen whether the courts will take a more pragmatic approach by requiring there to be some benefit to the employer before upholding a claim for breach of this rule.

Enforcement

19.2.10 TPR is responsible for enforcing employers' automatic enrolment, re-enrolment and opt-in obligations. It has powers to issue compliance notices requiring the recipient to refrain from taking the steps specified in the notice if it believes an inducement has occurred.[12] The time limits for compliance notices are:

- six months before the time when a complaint was made to TPR about the alleged inducement; or

- four years before the time when TPR informed the employer of an investigation of the alleged contravention, if no complaint was made before that time.[13]

TPR may also issue a fixed penalty notice of up to £50,000 where it believes a person has failed to comply with a compliance notice and escalating penalty notices with a daily rate of £10,000.[14]

19.2.11 Unlike the main enrolment duties there is no express provision in the *Pensions Act 2008* stating that individual employees do not have a claim for breach of statutory duty if the inducement prohibition is breached.[15] But in practice a civil action by an employee (or ex-employee) against an employer for breach of statutory duty may not be provable (courts usually construe statutory

---

11 [1983] IRLR 315, EAT.
12 *Sections 35* and *54(2)* of the *Pensions Act 2008*.
13 *Section 54(3)* of the *Pensions Act 2008*; *reg 16* of *the Employers' Duties (Registration and Compliance) Regulations 2010* (*SI 2010/5*).
14 *Sections 40* and *41* of the *Pensions Act 2008*.
15 *Section 34(1)* of the *Pensions Act 2008*.

duties in this way where a specific enforcement mechanic is enacted – see, for example, the *Scally* case).[16]

Communication with employees

19.2.12 Employers have raised concerns previously that providing information to higher paid workers on the relative merits of staying in or opting out of pension scheme membership could also constitute an inducement.

The Department for Work and Pensions (DWP) has provided guidance that:

- 'an employer giving their workers information about the implications of the higher rate tax relief changes' should not be at risk of being considered an inducement;

- but that 'employers should avoid giving their workforce advice on whether or not it would be worthwhile saving in a pension as such advice should only be provided by an authorised professional'. [17]

19.2.13 TPR and the Financial Services Authority have also provided guidance that employers 'cannot tell [their] employees whether or not it's a good idea' for them to join the pension scheme.[18] (in context, this is probably referring to a particular personal pension and not an occupational pension scheme).

Accordingly, when communicating with employees, an employer may provide information about the implications of the higher rate tax relief changes but should avoid advising on whether or not the contributions should be paid into a pension.

Flexible benefit packages

19.2.14 Employers could be accused of inducing employees to opt out where they offer alternative benefits to employees who opt out through flexible benefit packages. For example offering to pay:

- contributions into an Individual Savings Account;

---

16 *Scally v Southern Health and Social Services Board* [1992] AC 294.
17 Para 445, DWP consultation response dated January 2010 http://www.dwp.gov.uk/docs/wpr-comp-pict-govt-res.pdf.
18 Page 9, TPR, Talking to your employees about pensions – A guide for employers (October 2012) http://www.thepensionsregulator.gov.uk/docs/guide-talking-to-your-employees-about-pensions.pdf.

- pension contributions which do not meet the auto-enrolment requirements (eg where the employee is unwilling to make contributions themselves); or

- cash alternatives directly to employees.

19.2.15 Employers with flexible benefits schemes who annually invite workers to reconsider their arrangements would not normally have this as their 'sole or main purpose', but care should be taken by employers to ensure that matters cannot be construed in that way. Employers will need to ensure that they document the reasons for these options appropriately, so that they can show that inducing opt outs is not their 'sole or main purpose' in making such an offer. In particular, employers should document other reasons for these options such as:

- recruitment and retention of employees by offering a wider range of benefits;

- minimisation of tax where employees are close to the lifetime allowance; or

- ensuring a minimum level of pension savings for employees who choose not to make contributions themselves.

Index

Index

Index

Index

Index

Index

Index

900

Index

913

Index

Index